T0328721

Cases in European Competition Policy

Competition between firms is usually the most effective way of delivering economic efficiency and what consumers want. However, there is a balance to be struck. Firms must not be over regulated and so hampered in their development of innovative products and new strategies to compete for customers. Nor must they be completely free to satisfy a natural preference for monopoly, which would give them higher profits and a quieter life. The economic role of competition policy (control of anti-competitive agreements, mergers and abusive practices) is to maintain this balance, and an effective policy requires a nuanced understanding of the economics of industrial organisation. *Cases in European Competition Policy* demonstrates how economics is used (and sometimes abused) in competition cases in practical competition policy across Europe. Each chapter summarises a real case investigated by the European Commission or a national authority and provides a critique of key aspects of the economic analysis.

BRUCE LYONS is Professor of Economics and Deputy Director of the ESRC Centre for Competition Policy at the University of East Anglia, Norwich.

Cases in European Competition Policy: The Economic Analysis

Edited by

Bruce Lyons

CAMBRIDGE
UNIVERSITY PRESS

CAMBRIDGE UNIVERSITY PRESS
Cambridge, New York, Melbourne, Madrid, Cape Town,
Singapore, São Paulo, Delhi, Mexico City

Cambridge University Press
The Edinburgh Building, Cambridge CB2 8RU, UK

Published in the United States of America by Cambridge University Press, New York

www.cambridge.org
Information on this title: www.cambridge.org/9780521886048

© Cambridge University Press 2009

First published 2009

A catalogue record for this publication is available from the British Library

ISBN 978-0-521-88604-8 Hardback
ISBN 978-0-521-71350-4 Paperback

Contents

Contents by potentially anticompetitive business practices

Contents by markets

List of figures

List of tables

List of contributors

Mark Armstrong
Professor of Economics
University College London

Paul Dobson
Professor of Competition Economics
The Business School
Loughborough University

Eliana Garces-Tolon
European Commission

Christian Gollier
Professor of Economics
IDEI, University of Toulouse

Morten Hviid
Professor of Competition Law
Norwich Law School
University of East Anglia, and ESRC
Centre for Competition Policy

Marc Ivaldi
Professor of Economics
IDEI, University of Toulouse

Kai-Uwe Kühn
Associate Professor
Department of Economics
University of Michigan

Bruce Lyons
Professor of Economics
School of Economics
University of East Anglia, and Deputy
Director of ESRC Centre for
Competition Policy

Peter Møllgaard
Head of Department of Economics
Copenhagen Business School

Massimo Motta
Professor of Economics
European University Institute
Florence, and University of Bologna

Damien Neven
Chief Economist
DG COMP, European Commission
and Professor of Economics (on leave)
at HEI Geneva

Patrick Rey
Professor of Economics
University of Toulouse

Jean-Charles Rochet
Professor of Economics
IDEI, University of Toulouse

Paul Seabright
Professor of Economics
School of Economics
University of Toulouse

Margaret Slade
Professor of Economics
Department of Economics
University of Warwick

Gianandrea Staffiero
IESE Business School
Barcelona

Rune Stenbacka
Professor of Economics
Swedish School of Economics
Helsinki, and Göteborg University

Andreas Stephan
Lecturer in Law
Norwich Law School
University of East Anglia, and ESRC
Centre for Competition Policy

John Van Reenen
Professor of Economics
Department of Economics
London School of Economics and
Director of Centre for Economic
Performance

James Venit
Partner
Skadden, Arps, Slate, Meagher & Flom
LLP, Brussels office

Frank Verboven
Professor of Economics
Katholieke Universiteit Leuven and
CEPR

Xavier Vives
Professor of Economics and
Finance Director of the
Public–Private Sector
Research Center
IESE Business School
Barcelona

Michael Waterson
Professor of Economics
Department of Economics
University of Warwick

Julian Wright
Associate Professor of Economics
National University of Singapore

Preface

Competition between firms is usually the most effective way of delivering economic efficiency and what consumers want. However, there is a balance to be struck. Firms must not be over-regulated and so hampered in their development of innovative products and new strategies to compete for customers; but nor must they be completely free to satisfy a natural preference for monopoly, which would give them higher profits and a quieter life. The economic role of competition policy is to maintain this balance, and an effective policy requires a nuanced understanding of the economics of industrial organisation.

The seed of an idea for this book was first sown in 1989 after an editorial board meeting of the *Journal of Industrial Economics* when Larry White kindly gave me a copy of his new book, co-edited with John Kwoka: *The Antitrust Revolution*. That book, now entering its fifth edition, was to become a classic publication in the field because it showed how economics was being used very practically by leading American academics in US antitrust (i.e. competition policy) cases. While this may have been revolutionary at the time, as the reader will see, the application of well-argued and finely tuned economic analysis in competition cases has long since crossed the Atlantic. Competition policy has come out of the legal closet.

This book demonstrates how economics is used (and sometimes abused) in competition cases across Europe. It also aims to show how the use of economics in case analysis can be improved. Each chapter summarises a real case investigated by either the European Commission or a national authority in Europe, and provides a critique of key aspects of the economic analysis. The style is largely non-technical so as to be accessible to lawyers, practitioners and economics undergraduates and advanced undergraduates (for whom it provides a supplementary text for a course in industrial organisation). The book is arranged in three parts that reflect the main elements of competition policy familiar to lawyers. A supplementary table of contents provides a guide for those who wish to use the book to illustrate economic concepts, business practices or the operation of particular markets. I have also written an introduction which provides a wider context for understanding the role of competition policy in twenty-first-century Europe.

The book is written by an outstanding team of Europe's leading industrial economists. Each lead author has been a senior adviser for either a competition agency or firms being challenged under competition laws, or both. However, each is first and foremost an independent academic economist, teaching and researching in a highly rated university. Most advised on the case they analyse in this book, and where this is the case it is made clear in the first footnote. Of course, where payment has been taken, the reader may think that the author's analysis is compromised. However, despite a little understandable advocacy here and there, I do not believe there is any bias in the essential analysis presented here. Apart from inherent academic integrity, this is because their economics is laid bare by publication and the authors are putting their substantial economic reputations on the line by contributing to this book.

I would like to thank all the authors, some of whom have shown amazing patience in waiting for the project to be completed, Steve Davies for editing Chapter 5, and Larry White and John Kwoka for their blessing for this European complement (and indeed compliment) to their American project. Cheryl Whittaker provided her usual excellent editorial assistance in CCP and thanks also to the CUP team of Chris Harrison and Philip Good. The support of the Economic and Social Research Council in funding time for editing this book is gratefully acknowledged.

Finally, I dedicate this book to the memory of my father, Philip, who would have relished both the content and the pan-European collaboration embodied in this project.

BRL
ESRC Centre for Competition Policy, University of
East Anglia, Norwich
July 2008

Introduction: the transformation of competition policy in Europe[1]

Bruce Lyons

Competition arises when firms fight for customers by offering them a better deal in terms of price, quality, range, reliability or associated services. It is messy. Some firms lose market share and others exit. Successful firms can make substantial profits. The reward for consumers is that it gives them products they want and at a price that reflects the resource cost of providing them. This book is about how competition policy is used to maintain competition in European markets. Such policies are effective when they stimulate competition but counterproductive if they stifle it. This is a tricky balance to achieve. It requires a subtle understanding of competition economics.

The first three sections of this chapter start from a satellite picture of the economic system and progressively zoom in on the detail of individual markets and business practices. Section 1 introduces the merits of competition as the fundamental force driving the economy in the right direction. It also notes the temptation for businesses to suppress competition, though this is not always easy to do. How can we identify when business practices are likely to be harmful? And how can we balance such dangers against heavy-handed suppression of efficient and innovative strategies? The branch of economics that has developed this understanding is known as industrial organisation. It focuses on individual market outcomes and provides the intellectual foundation for what has become known as the economic (or effects-based) approach to competition policy. Section 2 provides a glimpse of this research into the implications of various business practices under alternative market structures. Section 3 identifies the channels through which a particular business practice may or may not harm competition. This is a helpful step in formulating the economic analysis in a way suitable for legal screening.

---

[1] I thank Steve Davies for his typically insightful comments. Neither he nor the authors of the case studies bear any responsibility for the views contained in this chapter.

The economic approach to competition policy has not always been favoured in Europe (or in North America). Different countries have had different motivations for laws relating to competition. Some interventions have been more anticompetitive than pro-competitive. In recent years, however, there has been a fundamental shift towards the economic approach. There has also been a unifying focus provided by the European Commission – the world's only supranational competition agency. Section 4 gives a flavour of these early differences and the evolving convergence.

Each of the seventeen case studies in this book illustrates both the economic approach and how far it has (and sometimes has not) developed in Europe. Section 5 completes this introductory chapter by explaining the organisation of the book into three parts. It is left to separate introductions for each part to outline each case study and sketch the relevant legal background.

1. The benefits of competition

It is a marvel of the market economy that the apparent chaos of competition results in such significant benefits. The system works because market prices summarise a vast amount of information on supply and demand conditions in a way that is most relevant for commercial and private buyers. If these prices are set competitively, the outcome has a strong claim to be the most efficient that can be achieved.

The essential economic benefits were articulated with enduring clarity by Adam Smith in *The Wealth of Nations*, first published in 1776. Competition not only keeps prices low and close to cost,[2] it also reduces costs as firms fight for market share and survival.[3] Individual producers may be driven by a selfish profit motive and have no direct interest in the welfare of unrelated

---

[2] '… the price of free competition … is the lowest which the sellers can commonly afford to take, and at the same time continue their business'. 'The price of monopoly is upon every occasion the highest which can be got' (Book I, Chapter VII).

[3] This applies both aggressively – 'in order to undersell one another, have recourse to new divisions of labour, and new improvements of the art, which might never otherwise have been thought of' – and defensively – 'Monopoly … is the great enemy of good management, which can never be universally established but in consequence of the free and universal competition which forces every body to have recourse to it [i.e. good management] for the sake of self-defence.' As quoted in Vickers (1995). Sir John Hicks (1935) summarised this in his famously pithy phrase: 'The best of all monopoly profits is a quiet life.'

customers, but as long as the process is competitive it is as if an 'invisible hand' guides the outcome so that it is indeed beneficial for consumers.[4,5]

Modern economics has honed and formalised Adam Smith's insight in a number of ways that enable a deeper understanding of competition and its benefits. One approach, known as general equilibrium theory, derives a sufficient set of conditions such that apparently anarchic, decentralised decision making across many different markets results in a Pareto efficient economy, which is to say an outcome in which no one could be made better off without making someone else worse off. Competitive pricing is the first of these essential conditions. In contrast, textbook monopoly pricing is Pareto inefficient because output is restricted, driving a wedge between consumer valuation and marginal cost. Other conditions necessary for an efficient economy are the absence of uncompensated externalities and no distortions due to asymmetric information. This particular formalisation of the efficiency of a competitive economy is known as the first fundamental theorem of welfare economics.[6] Other approaches highlight more dynamic aspects of the competitive process and identify further benefits for technical progress.[7]

Economic history provides much macroeconomic evidence on the economic benefits of a broadly competitive market economy. For example, Douglass North (1991) contrasts how the early colonists of North America took British institutions with them, and these enabled competitive markets to develop based on secure property rights and decentralised decision making. In contrast colonisation of South America took place at a time of bureaucratic, centralised monarchy in Spain and set in place institutions such that 'wealth-maximizing behaviour by organizations and entrepreneurs (political and

---

[4] 'It is not from the benevolence of the butcher, the brewer, or the baker, that we expect our dinner, but from their regard to their own interest. We address ourselves, not to their humanity but to their self-love, and never talk to them of our necessities but of their advantages' (Book I, Chapter II); '... by directing that industry in such a manner as its produce may be of the greatest value, he intends only his own gain, and he is in this, as in many other cases, led by an invisible hand to promote an end which was no part of his intention' (Book IV, Chapter II).

[5] Competition also has a more controversial claim to political benefits, in particular the promotion of freedom. On this view, it does more than deliver the best opportunity to satisfy consumer wants – it is also desirable because it allows individuals to make their own choices (even if those choices may be against their own best interests). Hayek (1960) makes the classic case and Sen (1993) provides a recent critique. The political benefits are also stressed in German ordo-liberalism where the benefits are expected not through individual choice but through the avoidance of a political process dominated by monopolies hand in hand with government (see Gerber, 1998).

[6] A second fundamental theorem proves that concerns about social inequality should not undermine the attractions of efficient competitive markets as long as there are suitable tax and social insurance schemes.

[7] For example, see Schumpeter (1943) on competition as 'creative destruction'; also Kirzner (1978) on entrepreneurship and competition. See also section 2.

economic) entailed getting control of, or influence over, the bureaucratic machinery' (i.e. competition was diverted away from satisfying customers and into gaining political influence). The consequent, contrasting economic development of America north and south of the Rio Grande is clear to all.

Back in Europe, the former command economies of central and eastern Europe provided a natural experiment lasting over forty years in the second half of the twentieth century. Contrast the fortunes of Poland and Spain.[8] Both countries were Catholic and had populations of around 25 million in the 1950s (and 40 million by the end of the century!). They had similar geographic areas and agricultural economies. In 1950, Poland had a per capita gross domestic product (GDP) of around $750 and Spain only $500. Over the next forty years, Poland was a highly centralised economy with little room for competitive markets. Spain's economic system was market based.[9] By 1990, when Polish communism formally ended, Spanish per capita GDP was four times higher than in Poland. The comparative evolution of the communist command economy of East Germany and the social market economy of West Germany over the same period provides an even sharper contrast of fortunes.

This is not to say that competitive markets solve all economic problems. They do not. As we shall see in the next section, there are occasions when some apparent restrictions of competition can be justified. Furthermore, competition appears to create some problems when inefficient firms lay off workers and successful firms pay huge bonuses to senior managers while their activities deplete resources and contribute to climate change. Complementary economic and social policies are essential to create a pleasant and sustainable society. This is not the place to develop the economics of unemployment, environmental pollution and social equity, though these are important issues. The point to note is that they are best addressed by complementary policies of education, environmental regulation, taxation and social insurance, but not by abandoning competitive markets.

These broad-sweep ideas and observations establish the firm presumption that a broadly competitive market economy has very much more to recommend it than one dominated by central planning or monopoly. However, there are numerous possible variants of a market system and many were tried across Europe in the second half of the twentieth century (and not just eastern communism versus western markets). Within western Europe there were

---

[8] See Sachs (1993).

[9] Though economic and political freedom were severely compromised by Franco's dictatorship until his
    death in 1975.

national differences in degrees of state ownership and state subsidies to private business, price, entry and trade regulation, and policies in relation to cartels. The evidence mounted that state ownership was less efficient than private ownership and from the 1980s privatisation began to roll across Europe, reaching the East in the 1990s following the collapse of communism.

Another influence around this time was the single European market programme, which aimed to eliminate non-tariff barriers to trade within the European Community. Further reforms liberalised entry into previously regulated markets. One high-profile example was the deregulation of airline competition and consequent appearance of low-cost airlines using a very different business model to the very uniform product previously offered by national flag carriers. There are continuing moves to deregulate in other areas such as energy. Further EU initiatives have attempted to reduce the impact of state subsidies, at least inasmuch as they distort competition between firms located in different Member States.[10]

While many national differences remain, there is an increasing European consensus that a prosperous economy responsive to consumer needs is best achieved by private ownership, deregulation of entry and a limit on state subsidies (at least when given by other countries!).[11] Of course, this is a multifariously interpreted consensus that is characteristic of the cultural cassoulet that is Europe.

The issue then becomes: should firms be left completely free to compete as and how they wish, or would complete laissez-faire result in firms themselves subverting the competitive process? The pressure on firms to maximise profits provides an alert to the dangers. Business life is much easier if competition is suppressed, even if it is also less productive and less creative. This observation is not new. Adam Smith recognised it back in 1776 when he wrote about the enduring temptation to fix prices.[12] Although it can be hard for firms to act on

---

[10] See Davies et al. (2004) for some interesting, accessible case studies of the benefits of deregulating markets.
[11] See Megginson and Netter (2001) for a review of the empirical literature on the ownership effects of privatisation. Nickell (1996) provides an example of evidence that competition enhances productivity, and Aghion et al. (2004) of evidence showing how foreign entry raises domestic productivity.
[12] 'People of the same trade seldom meet together, even for merriment and diversion, but the conversation ends in a conspiracy against the public, or in some contrivance to raise prices' (Smith, 1776, Book I, Chapter X). He was less optimistic about the ability to legislate against such conspiracies. His next sentence reads: 'It is impossible indeed to prevent such meetings, by any law which either could be executed, or would be consistent with liberty and justice. But though the law cannot hinder people of the same trade from sometimes assembling together, it ought to do nothing to facilitate such assemblies; much less to render them necessary.' Modern advocates of competition policy are less pessimistic. Although the law in a free society indeed cannot prevent meetings, it can try to stop competitors discussing price when they meet.

these temptations, especially if the number of rivals is high or entry is easy, some form of referee is necessary to stop the invisible hand turning into a fist. To understand the referee's role, we need to dig deeper into the operation of individual markets.

2. Understanding business practices and market competition

The economics of industrial organisation (IO) provides a detailed theoretical and empirical understanding of how firms compete, whether it be in natural resource, manufacturing, utility, retailing or other service markets. The theory develops how rational profit-maximising firms must be expected to behave in markets with a limited number of firms (i.e. oligopolies). Since senior managers are under a fiduciary duty to their shareholders to maximise shareholder value, it is reasonable to assume that this is the way that experienced managers will indeed behave. But if they are tempted to relax or pursue non-profit objectives, there are other pressures that encourage them back to profit: supervision and performance monitoring within the firm, incentive schemes (e.g. bonuses, share options), internal promotion and external job offers for the most successful managers, threat of takeover by a more profit-oriented management team and natural selection in a competitive product market.

The most familiar issue investigated in IO is how the power to set price above cost is related to the number and relative size of firms in the market.[13] Price is always a core element of competition but it is rarely the only element. The literature has been developed to understand a very wide range of strategies used by firms. It investigates how firms compete when they choose prices, including price discrimination, quantity and bundling discounts and price restraints and guarantees, product design, quality and range, investments in capacity, distribution, marketing and research and development (R&D), the range of production and distribution activities undertaken within the firm, and the nature and content of contracts entered into with customers, other firms as suppliers, or joint ventures. IO investigates the optimal choice by each firm, the ramifications and responses of its rivals, and how these can be anticipated. Thus, even when each firm makes its decisions unilaterally, the whole market is affected and we

---

[13] The core modelling technique originates from Cournot (1838), but Adam Smith already had the nub of the idea: 'If this capital [i.e. relevant assets sufficient to trade in a town] is divided between two different grocers, their competition will tend to make both of them sell cheaper, than if it were in the hands of one only; and if it were divided among twenty, their competition would be just so much the greater, and the chance of their combining together, in order to raise the price, just so much the less.' As quoted in Stigler (1987).

are interested in working out the implications for all firms and consumers once everyone has adjusted their pricing and other relevant decisions.[14]

Each market has different characteristics which influence the strategies firms choose and the competitiveness of outcomes. Such characteristics include the degree of production and distribution economies of scale and scope, availability of risk capital, technology, scarce skills and management expertise, market size, other entry barriers and the number of firms, scale, stability and lumpiness of demand, knowledge, sensitivity and rationality of consumer behaviour, consumer network benefits or switching costs, potential for technological improvement, scope and security of intellectual property rights, technological lock-in, transaction costs of doing business with other firms, contract, competition, trade and other laws, and market history. IO theory now provides a large and expanding toolkit for the analysis of markets with different blends of such characteristics.[15]

One preliminary insight is that some apparently quite different business practices can be equivalent in their effects. As a very simple example, suppose a supplier wants a retailer to charge no more than a certain maximum price when selling its product. If the demand curve is known, then the supplier could achieve exactly the same effect by requiring the retailer to sell an equivalent minimum quantity. A maximum price or a minimum quantity are alternatives that are equivalent in their effects.[16] The importance of this is that a poorly designed competition policy may both prohibit resale price restrictions and allow quantity incentives. Even without considering whether intervention against such strategies is desirable, we can say that it is inconsistent to outlaw one and permit the other.

Other insights relate to pricing and investment incentives. For example, the time and effort needed to develop a new product may not be forthcoming if

---

[14] An outcome such that no firm has an incentive to deviate from its current strategy is known as a Nash equilibrium. A companion concept of subgame perfect Nash equilibrium is appropriate when firms make long-term investment or product design decisions in anticipation of the consequences for future pricing behaviour.

[15] An introduction to IO theory can be found in a number of textbooks and handbooks. Tirole (1989) is old, but it remains as a classic on the modern foundations of industrial organisation theory. Church and Ware (2000) is more recent and more applied. Motta (2004) is most recent and most direct in applying the approach of IO to competition policy issues. Three volumes of *Handbook of Industrial Organization* (Schmalensee and Willig, 1989, and Armstrong and Porter, 2007) include some excellent review articles. Less demanding textbooks that still provide good introductions to industrial economics at a level similar to the exposition in this book include Cabral (2000), which has a more European perspective than others such as Carlton and Perloff (2000) or Pepall *et al.* (2008). Klein and Lerner (2008) provide a useful compilation of classic journal articles.

[16] Quantity discounts can also have an equivalent effect, though none of these strategies is exactly equivalent if the demand curve is uncertain.

non-inventors can immediately copy someone else's invention. This is familiar as the justification of patents (i.e. time-limited monopoly rights). Similarly, expert advice, samples and other services provided 'free' by some retailers would not be sustainable if low-service retailers can undercut price and free-ride. This loss of marketing support might be solved by certain types of exclusionary behaviour: refusing to sell through low-service retailers ensures that high-quality retailers capture the benefit of their investment in premises and training. Economic analysis can help distinguish such cases from others where refusal to deal is just a means of preserving or enhancing market power.

Empirical substance to IO theories is provided by a large body of econometric studies that tests theoretical predictions and identifies other patterns to explain. A general finding is that, just as the theory suggests, market outcomes are highly sensitive to the specific characteristics of the market. This means that there are no simple rules like 'four firms are necessary (or sufficient) for effective competition' or '50 per cent market share is necessary (or sufficient) for a firm to be able to raise price substantially above the competitive level'. Nevertheless, there is much empirical knowledge relating to competition and productivity growth,[17] pricing,[18] entry, exit and market concentration,[19] contracts and investment,[20] and experimental markets.[21]

There is space to provide only one illustrative example of this rich econometric literature. Bresnahan and Reiss (1991) investigate five retail and professional service markets in around 150 isolated American towns of varying sizes. Entry barriers are low in these markets but each firm must incur some fixed costs. As expected, the authors find that larger towns can support more firms in each product market, but how many more? If price did not fall with entry, the number of firms should be proportional to market size, but if each extra firm introduces more competition such that price and margins fall, then greater sales for each firm will be needed to cover fixed costs. Consequently, the greater the competitive effect of entry, the larger must be the incremental size of market in order to support that entry. Using this insight, they find that reasonably competitive outcomes can be established by a market structure of between two and four firms. Thus, we learn that, even for reasonably similar types of market, different numbers of firms may be necessary to establish

[17] See Ahn (2002) for a review.
[18] See Berry and Reiss (2007) and Hendricks and Porter (2007) for partial reviews. There is also much econometric work on collusion and cartel behaviour, as well as numerous case studies (e.g. on airline pricing).
[19] See Berry and Reiss (2007) and Sutton (2007) for reviews.
[20] See Lafontaine and Slade (2007) for a review.
[21] See Holt (1995) and selective reviews in Plott and Smith (2008).

competition and this number *may* be as small as two. However, it would be unwise to project this finding on firm numbers into a wider generalisation for more complex markets; for example, these small-scale trades were chosen because they operate in the shadow of a fairly immediate threat of entry. Furthermore, more differentiated product markets may require more firms to establish a competitive outcome.

The IO approach also provides a guide to defining a meaningful market. This is important because market definition is not usually as clear-cut as well-defined trades in isolated towns. There are always two dimensions to be assessed: the range of products that compete and the geographic extent of the market. How can we determine, for example, whether apples and bananas are in the same market? Some people will find them close substitutes as healthy snack fruits but others will have a strong personal preference (e.g. it takes good teeth to bite into a crisp apple). Economic meaning can be put into the issue by asking whether a hypothetical monopolist of bananas would be able to raise price without so many consumers switching to other fruit such that this price rise would be unprofitable. If the answer is yes, then bananas can be considered to be a separate market, but if the answer is no, then the banana market is too narrowly defined for competition purposes so we need to consider a wider definition (e.g. bananas and apples). Starting from a narrow product market, potential substitutes can be added until the hypothetical monopolist could profitably raise price. This approach to market definition gets to the heart of its use to understand competition. A similar approach can be applied to geographic market definition by asking: would a hypothetical monopolist in Germany be able to raise price without losing customers to French or Dutch firms?

This summary of IO analysis has so far focused on understanding the world that we observe. It can also help in passing judgement: would a feasible intervention in the market improve social welfare? This gets to the core of the economic analysis necessary for good competition policy. Consumer welfare is measured by consumer surplus (i.e. the excess of consumer willingness-to-pay over what they actually have to pay) and producer welfare is measured by profits (which may be distributed to shareholders or shared with employees). Total welfare refers to the sum of the two. It is a virtue of the approach that the welfare of consumers and firms can be analysed separately and then an evaluation can be made using an appropriate weighting.[22]

---

[22] See Farrell and Katz (2006) for a discussion of appropriate welfare objectives in the context of competition policy.

As an example of this welfare approach, consider a horizontal agreement between firms to share a market according to regions. This conveys monopoly power in each region and raises prices and profits for all firms. However, consumer surplus falls and the standard monopoly analysis shows that consumers lose more than the firms gain. Next, consider a vertical agreement between a manufacturer and a supplier. This might take many forms, but as a freely negotiated deal it must be expected to raise profits for both. However, unlike a cartel, this need not come at the expense of the manufacturer's customers. In fact, they may benefit if some of the efficiency is passed through as a price cut. This suggests a very different welfare analysis and consequent policy stance towards horizontal and vertical restraints. Similar considerations apply to horizontal compared with vertical mergers. Nevertheless, there are specifiable circumstances where a vertical restraint or vertical merger may foreclose rivals and harm consumers. By the 1970s, the Chicago School had highlighted the benign features of vertical restraints but had used restrictive assumptions to get the message across. More nuanced game theoretic analysis began to pick away at the potential for foreclosure and it is only from the 1990s that a significant post-Chicago consensus has begun to develop.[23]

The next step is to formulate the economic analysis in a way suitable for legal scrutiny.

3. Harm and redemption in competition analysis

Modern competition policy is about refereeing free markets to ensure there is no foul play. The idea is to let those offering the best deal win customers. To pursue the sporting analogy, competition economics appraises tackles so that the competition is robust and exciting without breaking down into lethargy, match fixing or kicking the other side off the field.[24] If there is an offence, the referee has to decide how serious it is and how to deal with it most effectively. It is not the referee's job to protect weak competitors from losing. The best referees blow their whistles infrequently but are firm and clear in their decisions when they do. They gain the respect of the players, foul play is deterred and there should be little for them to do except to observe the game very closely. I start with markets where it is not possible to create a sufficiently level playing field for a competitive game to begin.

---

[23] See Kovacic and Shapiro (2000) for a history of economic ideas in relation to US antitrust policy.

[24] Competition economics can also advise on best rules for the game (e.g. guidelines for implementing competition policy). This book focuses on the role as referee.

Markets where competition is not feasible. Some markets are natural monopolies in the sense that economies of scale are so large relative to the size of the market that only one firm can supply at reasonable cost efficiency. This can arise particularly with major distributional infrastructures like electricity, gas or water networks. Conventional competition cannot be created in such markets, so it is necessary to regulate price and other aspects of their investment programme and service quality.[25] Sometimes the domain of natural monopoly can be reduced by vertical separation. For example, ownership of electricity generation can be separated from the distribution network as a first step to creating a competitive market in generation. A deep-rooted problem with price regulation is that a regulator knows less than the regulated firm about its costs, demand and technological and market opportunities. This makes it extremely difficult to set the right price without eroding efficiency and innovation incentives – price regulation should be applied only when strictly necessary. The economics of the pricing game between regulator and regulated is quite different to that between firms and it lies outside the scope of this book.[26]

This leaves us with the field of play for competition policy. Our agenda lies between the levels of control implied by full economic regulation and complete laissez faire. It is relevant for that preponderant part of the economy where markets work pretty well, but where it may be possible for firms to subvert competition by creating or abusing market power.[27] It is possible to categorise a number of ways in which competition may be harmed.

Unilateral effects. A firm may act alone to raise price. When it does, this is likely to have a knock-on effect for other firms which find it profitable to raise price probably by a little less. Consumer harm may also come through non-price elements of the product offer (e.g. reduced service support or product development). It is sometimes also argued that price discrimination can be abusive, but the circumstances always require very careful analysis.[28]

Cartels and coordinated effects. A group of firms may coordinate to raise price. This is known as a cartel if they coordinate explicitly (e.g. by exchanging information about price intentions or coming to a verbal agreement to share the market). It is known as tacit collusion or 'coordinated effects' if they do so

---

[25] It may be possible to create competition *for* the market by an appropriate auction of monopoly rights, but this still requires a regulatory apparatus of the sort discussed in this paragraph.

[26] See Armstrong and Sappington (2007) and Laffont and Tirole (1993) for the economics of regulation. Price regulation is not entirely missing from this book because it can be used to remedy a specific problem in an otherwise competitive market (e.g. see Chapters 3 and 7).

[27] See Geroski (2004).

[28] See Chapters 1, 4, 9 and most explicitly 11 for a discussion of those circumstances.

without explicit contact (e.g. by observing each other's behaviour and with-holding from competitive pricing). The latter is far harder to achieve than explicit collusion, but both result in higher prices than if each firm acts unilaterally.[29]

Horizontal mergers that eliminate an actual or potential competitor.[30] The reduction of competition depends on the extent to which product ranges are viewed by customers as substitutes and the effectiveness of remaining rivals at filling the competitive gap. The merger may enhance unilateral effects (e.g. by reducing the loss of sales following a price rise) or coordinated effects (e.g. by eliminating a 'maverick' price cutter). It may also have a positive side if it facilitates synergies and so enables the merged firm to compete more effectively.

Strategies that reduce competition by excluding rivals (known as foreclosure). The unilateral market power of an incumbent is indirectly enhanced by strategies that deter entry, force exit or raise a rival's costs. These are known as exclusionary abuses. For example, exclusive contracts may be signed to reduce a rival's purchasing options or customer opportunities or to raise their supply prices; rebates and quantity discounts or product bundling may also be used to squeeze market opportunities for rivals; or a vertically integrated firm may refuse to deal with an upstream or downstream rival. A vertical merger may similarly enhance the prospect of foreclosure. Alternatively, a firm may make its core product incompatible with a rival's complementary range or a few firms may agree an industry standard that disadvantages a rival. The problem is that it is also quite possible for these forms of behaviour to be beneficial for consumers, even if competitors are harmed (see Section 2). This makes the analysis of such strategies highly contentious in competition analysis and they require particularly careful economic analysis.[31]

Strategies that soften competition between existing rivals. A firm may take actions or invest to reduce the incentive for firms in the market to compete for customers. For example, it may differentiate its products so as to make them less close substitutes to those offered by others. Alternatively, it may build limited capacity so it has no great incentive to capture customers from rivals.

[29] In terms of IO theory, a unilateral effect is a Nash equilibrium in the one-shot game and a coordinated effect is a higher-price equilibrium in the repeated game.

[30] We use the term 'merger' to include acquisitions of individual businesses from another firm or a joint venture that could have been an independent business.

[31] It is also possible that a firm may set prices below-cost for sufficient time to force exit, or invest in excess capacity to threaten a predatory response to entry. However, closer economic scrutiny of predatory pricing suggests this type of behaviour is rarely rational unless reputation effects carry over to other markets.

Another example is a commitment to match a rival's price, which undermines the rival's incentive to cut price in the first place. However, it is extremely difficult to distinguish competition suppression of this type from active competition, natural caution or customer service.[32]

Customers can soften or stiffen competition. The behaviour of customers plays a crucial role in incentivising firms to compete. Competition relies on them responding to price differences and switching between the offerings of rival firms. However, particularly if the customers are final consumers, they do not always have the time, ability or inclination to search for the best offer. Even if aware of a better offer, they may be deterred by the risk and cost of switching brand or supplier. While firms cannot be held responsible for consumer ignorance or sloth, they can exploit it if they act to obfuscate choices or make switching difficult. This is an area of increasing research and relevance to competition policy. Yet customers can stiffen competition by negotiating discounts or by creating the conditions for fierce competition (e.g. putting a large contract to tender). Thus, buyer power can reduce or eliminate failings in upstream competition.[33]

Having identified channels of harm, we can turn to redemption. If the economic analysis reveals that a business practice is harmful to competition, what should be done about it? For some practices, most notably price-fixing cartels, there is no saving grace and they should clearly be prohibited. However, for other practices (e.g. restrictive contracts and mergers), there may be parts that are problematic and other parts that cause no competitive harm. In such cases, it is often possible to eliminate the harm while allowing the unproblematic part to proceed. This might be achieved by requiring the parties to a horizontal merger to divest overlaps in their product ranges while allowing other parts of the merger to proceed. In vertical mergers, or where a vertically integrated dominant firm is excluding competitors by refusing access to an essential asset, the concerns may be alleviated by requiring the firm to grant access to competitors on appropriate terms. In the case of restrictive contracts, it may be possible to limit duration or change particular terms in order to retain beneficial incentives while eliminating the damage to competition.

While it is crucial that a remedy should be effective in eliminating the competitive harm, success should not be penalised and wise policy follows a principle of minimum necessary intervention. It is the essence of competition

---

[32] But see Chapter 3 for an example where such behaviour was at least discussed.
[33] Chapter 4 discusses whether buyer power can be abused.

that firms should seek to produce more efficiently, to entice customers to buy from them and to experiment with novel strategies. An important way in which the law brings some balance between the general incentive to compete and the specific strategy under scrutiny is to take account of how market power has been achieved.

This is best illustrated by thinking about high prices associated with high market shares. A similar market structure and market power might be achieved by a single large firm with a 50 per cent market share, or a tight cartel with the same share and product range, or a horizontal merger creating the same share and range. The first of these may have achieved market share over time by controlling costs, providing a product consumers want and being an effective competitor. We still need to be alert to potential abuses of this market position, but investigation can await a serious complaint. The merger must come under routine scrutiny because it is not the result of customer choice. Nevertheless, they may provide a quick way to achieve synergies which ultimately do benefit customers. A classic cartel, however, can have no such justification as it does not have the possibility of creating efficiencies and is in place only to make life easy for firms and to exploit consumers. This underpins *per se* illegality and tough enforcement including active policies to encourage cartel discovery.

Having set out the economic approach to competition policy, we can now see how this fits in with the law and practice that have evolved in Europe.

4. Competition policy in Europe[34]

Competition policy is the set of laws, institutions, precedent, analysis, guidelines and evolving regulatory practice that aims to prevent firms from subverting competition. Americans refer to this as 'antitrust policy'. Few of the original laws were motivated by the single purpose of protecting competition. There have also been many national differences across Europe. A brief diversion into US competition policy provides some perspective.

In the US, the Sherman Act of 1890 prohibited cartels and 'monopolisation' strategies (roughly equivalent to 'abuse of dominance' in Europe). It provided for criminal sanctions, including imprisonment, and gave powers to break up

---

[34] Some of the histories in this section rely on the OECD Reviews of Competition Policy Frameworks, including EU (2005), France (2003), Germany (2004) and UK (2005). Motta (2004) Chapter 1 provides an extended introduction to the US and EU.

dominant firms. In 1914, the Clayton Act provided for merger control and treble damages for private actions (i.e. actions not instigated by a government agency). It also introduced the control of price discrimination. The interpretation of this powerful set of laws has evolved substantially over the last century. Until the 1970s, the laws were used to protect small competitors and restrain large corporations, as well as to control cartels. There was sometimes an aversion to efficiency-creating practices, including mergers, even for firms with negligible market power because these might harm rivals. A substantial number of business practices became *per se* illegal, so could not be used even when they enhanced efficiency. Since then, however, there has been a fundamental, though incomplete, shift towards a 'rule of reason' or 'economic effects' approach. The struggle for the ascendancy of the economic approach can be seen in the cases in Kwoka and White (1989 and later editions).

Competition policy in Europe is more recent, as is the economic effects-based approach to its implementation. Also, the absence of treble damages has left enforcement in the hands of competition authorities, while many actions in the US are taken privately. The following review does not cover differences in institutions, legal traditions or the relationship between agencies and courts. It focuses on the evolution of the role of competition policy and the place of economic analysis. It aims to show how the latter is achieving an increasingly important role across Europe.

The most influential competition policy has developed at the EU level, which has also proved the model for reform in current and aspirant Member States. It started with the original EU Treaty in 1957. This included key Articles 81 and 82 prohibiting anticompetitive agreements and the abuse of a dominant position.[35] The Treaty also had provisions for liberalisation of markets, equal application to state-owned and private firms, and control of state aid. A major theme has been the use of competition provisions to pursue the objective of an integrated European market.[36] In 1957, there were only six Member States, but three waves of expansion during 1973–95 brought in most west European countries and most of the former communist central Europe was embraced during 2004–7.

---

[35] These Articles were originally numbered 85 and 86. Key elements of the competition policy were already established in relation to coal and steel under the Treaty of Paris (1951). To avoid confusion, I refer in this chapter to the political and economic entity of the European Community since its inception as the European Union (EU), even though that name dates only from 1993. The Treaty is more usually referred to as the EC Treaty. However, I reserve 'EC' for the executive and administrative institutions of the European Commission, particularly DG Competition (previously DG IV) located in Brussels.

[36] See Chapter 11 for an example of the conflict between integration and economic effects as objectives.

The provisions of the EU Treaty on restrictive agreements and abuse of dominance were activated in 1962 in a way that centralised enforcement in the European Commission (EC).[37] Implementation was initially slow and rule based, and there was little activity on cartels. Fines for violating prohibitions could theoretically be as much as 10 per cent of turnover, but high fines were rare until very recently. Even comparing the 2000s (up to mid-2008) with the 1990s, the number of prosecuted cartels has trebled and the value of fines has risen fifteen-fold. Explicit merger regulation was not passed until 1989 but it soon became established as an active area with the ability to meet tight deadlines. It also proved a seedbed for new ideas.[38] The economic approach to mergers, agreements and abuse of dominance has pervaded a growing set of official guidelines on how competition analysis should be done. Important examples include market definition (1997), vertical restraints (2000), horizontal cooperation agreements (2001), horizontal mergers (2004), non-horizontal mergers (2007) and exclusionary abuses by dominant firms (2008).[39] Note the important economic distinction between horizontal and vertical (non-horizontal) issues, which is not apparent in the original law. Last but not least, the economic approach has also received important support and impetus from some appeal decisions by the Court of First Instance (CFI) and the European Court of Justice (ECJ).[40]

The year 2004 saw the implementation of a series of major reforms that reinforced the economic approach and pushed it out to Member States. Member States were enabled to enforce the full treaty provisions on agreements between firms and required to appraise agreements in the same way as the EC. The European Competition Network of National Competition Authorities was created to share best practice. Reform of the merger regime included a symbolic change in wording of the substantive test from 'dominance' to a 'significant impediment to effective competition'; although

---

[37] The first Commissioner for DG Competition (then known as DG IV) was German and the next four were Dutch or Luxembourgeois. Part of the competition culture they brought was influenced by that in their home countries; see the following paragraphs. The sixth was an Irishman who, as a member of the reforming Delors Commission in the late 1980s, introduced merger regulation at the European level.

[38] See Lyons (2007) for a review of EC merger control.

[39] These are all available on the DG Competition website.

[40] For the role of the courts and the evolution of precedent, see Furse (2006), Jones and Sufrin (2007) or Whish (2008). Essentially, the EC makes decisions which can be appealed by interested parties to the CFI. The CFI conducts a judicial review of the decision to ensure that it is well argued and takes proper account of the evidence. If it thinks this has not been done, it uses language like 'this part of the decision is vitiated with manifest error' and refers it back to the EC for proper consideration. The CFI does not replace the EC's economic judgement but it does clarify appropriate principles for analysis. A further appeal over the CFI decision can be made to the ECJ.

the practical impact is likely to be modest, it signals a clearer emphasis on economic effects. The new post of Chief Competition Economist was created, with fixed three-year terms for a leading academic IO economist to advise the Commissioner on policy and the Commission on cases. The chief economist was also given a permanent team of around twenty PhD trained economists to advise case teams.[41] Thus, the economic approach has become embedded.[42]

The Treaty's competition law applies only to activities that may affect trade between Member States. Although this has been interpreted quite widely, it still leaves much room for national policies. The main elements of modern German competition law were established in the same year as the original EU Treaty but the motivation was different. Historically, German law permitted registered cartels, which were legally enforceable until forbidden by the occupying forces after World War II. The disasters of the first half of the twentieth century had culminated in an unholy alliance between Nazism, big business and cartels. In response, an intellectual movement known as ordo-liberalism saw strong competition policy as essential to protect individual freedom and to act as a bulwark against political and corporate repression. In order not to be corruptible, ordo-liberals argued that policy should be implemented formulaically and without discretion. The Act against Restraints of Competition (ARC) was passed in 1957, since when the independent Bundeskartellamt enforces a ban on cartels, controls the abuse of a dominant position and since 1973 controls mergers. This history has resulted in strong policy implementation that has been market share and form based, leaving little room for more nuanced economic analysis. A 1999 ARC amendment brought the law into line with Articles 81 and 82.[43]

---

[41] There is also an advisory group of academic IO economists, Economic Advisory Group on Competition Policy (EAGCP), with a mandate to support DG Competition in its economic reasoning and to provide advice to the Commissioner on topics of special interest. Written advice is published on the DG Competition website. Eight of the thirteen members of the current EAGCP are authors of chapters in this book, as is the current Chief Competition Economist.

[42] Neven (2006) provides a fascinating analysis of this process, including the evolving case law. One illustrative statistic he compiled relates to the rise of specialist consultancies providing economic advice on competition issues in Europe. Prior to 1994, their turnover was less than £1 million p.a. Turnover grew to £7 million in 1999, after which it more than trebled by 2004. It has almost certainly grown significantly since then. Part of this was driven by an increase in cases, but not all of it. Over the same period, the economics advice share of professional fees (including legal advice) rose from around 5 per cent to 15 per cent, which was similar to the share in US cases. See also Vives (2009) for a series of reviews of and reflections on the first half century of EC competition policy.

[43] The Dutch preference for cartels lasted much longer than in Germany. Dutch competition law for most of the twentieth century was honoured only in its breach. Numerous cartels riddled the economy and private and public regulation often controlled entry. Significant reform in the 1990s culminated in the establishment of a new enforcement agency, the NMa, in 1998.

Meanwhile, the UK, which did not join the European Community until 1973, was developing its own traditions. War and recession in the first half of the twentieth century saw the previous century's liberalism descend into restrictive practices and cartels, often with state collaboration. In 1948, an Act established a commission to investigate monopolies and restrictive practices, with the apparent aim to reduce unemployment.[44] The Commission was to have little effect until given powers of merger control. The lack of genuine concern for competition was demonstrated by the associated nationalisation programme that was creating public monopolies. A restrictive practices court was set up in 1956 and was a considerable success in eliminating explicit cartels.[45] Merger control was introduced in 1965, the Office of Fair Trading was established in 1973 and there was other piecemeal legislation up to 1980 which created a rather unfocused set of laws. Policy was based on a 'public interest' test which was primarily interpreted on competition grounds but could include other issues such as employment or regional matters. Price controls and government-sponsored industrial restructuring prevailed until the late 1970s. From the mid-1980s, a radical programme of privatisation put highly concentrated markets and monopolies in private hands, supervised by a set of specialist regulators. Other potentially competitive markets were deregulated. A ministerial declaration stated that the public interest was to be interpreted in terms of competition alone (i.e. economic effects). Two major reforms brought much-needed consolidation of this tangle of legislation and replaced the 'public interest' with explicit competition tests: the Competition Act (1998) introduced the EU prohibitions and fines for anti-competitive practices and abuse of dominance and the Enterprise Act (2002) greatly stiffened penalties for cartels (e.g. gaol sentences and disqualification from directorships) and introduced formal competition tests for mergers and market investigations. The latter have been a long-standing and distinctive feature of UK competition policy.

France can lay claim to one of the earliest competition laws when the Revolution listened to Adam Smith and prohibited cartels in 1791. This was incorporated into the Napoleonic Code but fell into disuse during the nineteenth century. Post-World War II legislation included the principle of abuse of dominance and merger control, but implementation was weak and secondary to bureaucratic direction of the economy, state ownership and the creation

---

[44] See Wilks (1999).
[45] Covert cartels were another matter. The punishment for cartel membership was that you had to promise not to do it again – and you could be punished for contempt of court only if you did.

of national champions. A marked change in the consensus was manifested in the 1986 *ordonnance* on competition and freedom, which set out to raise competition above administrative intervention, incorporated the competition provisions of the EU Treaty and established a more powerful Conseil de la Concurrence. More recent reforms have made merger control more independent and the economic approach is gaining ground. Nevertheless, there remains a political distrust of competition and approval for common pricing as an expression of equality and social solidarity. Substantial state ownership also remains with full or controlling interests in leading firms ranging from utilities to manufacturing and transport.

Italy, like France, has a long tradition of pervasive state intervention and ownership in large-scale industries. The economy is also riddled with regulations on pricing, entry and product quality. The complexity is greatly increased by the devolved powers of the regional governments. There was no tradition of competition policy until the 1990 Competition Act establishing a new Antitrust Authority. Although the new law's objectives are formally very broad public interest, the new authority has established early credentials for a competition focus.

Most other European countries also came late to national competition legislation but now have it in place and, with many national quirks, attempt to emulate methods of analysis similar to those of the EC. The same applies to both east and west. The collapse of the former communist regimes of east and central Europe brought new competition laws echoing those in the EU Treaty as a way to consolidate and protect the new economic freedoms (e.g. Hungary and Poland both introduced new laws in 1990).

Over the last ten years, the rhetoric of the economic approach has arrived. The implementation still has a long way to go. This is demonstrated by a number of the case studies in this book. Each European country also has its own idiosyncrasies and there is much progress still to be made. However, there is a clear direction of travel and the pace is picking up.

What has driven this? As the above accounts of different regimes show, the EC has had a powerful demonstration role. Adoption of an EC-style policy has also become a necessary condition for accession to the EU. But that does not explain why the EC practice evolved this way or why many Member States have supported this evolution and others have not fought too hard against it. Globalisation has been another force. Merging firms now need to get anti-competition clearance from several countries and this is much easier if a similar approach is used in each jurisdiction. Given the trend in US implementation since the 1980s, there is much corporate support for a similar trend in Europe.

However, the common force operating for convergence of competition appraisal across Europe and America has been the convergence of economic ideas since the 1970s. The academic ideas of IO economists have converged with the unifying application of game theory as a tool for understanding how firms interact in markets, and the use of econometrics to test and measure the impact of such theories. The research and textbooks mentioned in section 2 of this chapter are used internationally, students attend universities internationally and professional competition economists in agencies, consultancies and universities increasingly work internationally. This is a very powerful community of ideas that is illustrated further by the international authorship of this book and the shared mode of analysis with Kwoka and White's American authors. It does not mean that all economists agree in each case, but it does mean that most disagreement is over the facts more than the mode of analysis. This consistent message has proved persuasive in getting more economists appointed to competition agencies and in lawyers wanting to listen to and comprehend their analysis.[46] Economists still have to work harder to explain the economic approach in a way that is compelling in a legal process.[47] I hope this book demonstrates that we are improving in this task.

5. Organisation of this book

There are several ways in which a book of case studies might be organised. A very traditional book on industrial economics might have arranged them by industry classification (e.g. manufacturing, services). This would focus on the particular circumstances of individual industries. However, competition issues cut right across industrial classification, so this would provide little help to the reader interested in the economic analysis. Nevertheless, we have provided a table of contents by market to guide the reader who is interested in particular sectors of the economy.

A more attractive organisation might be according to the form of potentially anticompetitive business practice at issue (e.g. pricing practices, product strategies). This would have the virtue of collecting together similar types of economic analysis and it would map more closely into a modern IO textbook.

---

[46] The UK has been particularly enlightened in appointing leading IO economists to head its agencies, including four of the last five heads of the Office of Fair Trading (OFT) and the Competition Commission.

[47] See Vickers (2006), who succinctly discusses this and a number of other themes in this chapter.

However, the real world is rarely that neat and most cases touch on a range of strategies, so the cases are not that easily pigeonholed. The table of contents by business practices provides the student of industrial organisation with a guide to the main strategies discussed in each case.

The chosen organisation of this book reflects the main elements of the law under which the cases were investigated. The law categorises by form of behaviour (e.g. independent action by one firm, agreements between firms, acquisition of ownership). Economic analysis shows how these legal categories are sometimes sensible but can also be misleading. For example, similar economic effects can result from different forms of strategy (e.g. vertical agreements and vertical mergers), but similar legal forms can also have very different economic effects (e.g. horizontal mergers and vertical mergers). Nevertheless, the legal categories will be helpful to lawyers and they also reflect the important context of how market power was acquired (as discussed at the end of section 3).

Thus, the book is arranged in three parts. Part A covers anticompetitive behaviour by firms with market power. This includes two different types of market structure. The first is where there is a single dominant firm which is under investigation for abusing its dominant position. This provides two classic examples of potentially exclusionary behaviour: quantity discounts and incompatibility. Two UK investigations are also included in this part of the book. In both cases, there are several firms apparently competing but with some identifiable concern that the competition is not as effective as it might be. These cases have wider interest because they relate to markets that are more heavily regulated in other countries and which are in the front line of the economic life of most consumers: supermarkets and mobile phones.

Part B considers three types of agreement between firms. The first is cartels, where the offence is clear so the main economic interest is on deterrence, discovery and damages. The second type of agreement is also horizontal (i.e. between firms at the same level of economic activity), but in these cases there are identifiable externalities and benefits from coordination. These cases examine how the balance can be appraised. The third type of agreement is vertical between buyer and seller, in particular, manufacturer and wholesaler or retailer. Such agreements can often be justified as having beneficial effects, but they can also be anticompetitive.

Part C contains case studies of merger appraisal and is also arranged in three subsections. The first applies recent econometric techniques designed to estimate the unilateral effects of horizontal mergers when firms have differentiated products. The second section considers how to form an expectation of whether a merger will enhance coordinated behaviour. The third looks at cases where the main dimensions of the merger are vertical or conglomerate.

This organisation of cases inevitably leads to some overlap of similar types of economic analysis (e.g. coordinated effects arise in both market investigations and mergers; vertical effects arise in agreements and mergers; two-sided markets arise in agreements and market investigations).[48] Each part of the book is prefaced by a little more legal background and introduces the individual case studies.

The selection of cases for inclusion in this book was not systematic. As editor, I left it largely to the authors to choose cases they knew well and which interested them for the economic analysis. It turns out that this has provided remarkable balance across each part of the book. However, it may be that this selection method creates a bias towards more controversial interventions and away from cases which have been cleared. In particular, economic expert witnesses and academic advisers are appointed only for difficult cases where the competition authority is at loggerheads with the firms. In the language of statistics, the book may include more Type 1 errors (too much intervention) and fewer Type 2 errors (too little intervention) by European competition authorities. It certainly under-represents clear-cut cases where the authorities got the decision right. This should be borne in mind when reading a case which is critical of a decision for being over-interventionist.

Finally, the real value of a good competition policy is in not just the restoration of competition in a particular case but also the incentive for good behaviour by other firms.[49] It is far better to encourage firms to act competitively in the first place. Firms and their advisers must understand the rules and how they will be applied. Cases must be argued properly and the economic analysis must be clear. Only then will the appropriate level of deterrence be attained. Effective deterrence means both that anticompetitive practices do not develop and that vigorous competition is not deterred by fear of inappropriate intervention. The payoff to good economic analysis in one case has a multiplier effect in guiding behaviour in many more markets.[50] We hope that this book will contribute to that end.

---

[48] The reader is reminded to use the table of contents by business practice to find these links to similar concepts.

[49] Fans of contact sports will be aware of the importance of the first few decisions made by a referee to establish the mood and vigour of the competition.

[50] One recent study suggests that the deterrence effect is an order of magnitude greater than the number of actual cases; see Deloitte (2007).

A

Anticompetitive behaviour by firms with market power

Introduction

The first two chapters consider cases where there is a single firm that can be identified as dominant in the market. Each was engaging in identifiable business practices that rivals considered to be an abuse of economic power. The two dominant firms in question could claim that they achieved their dominance by success in the competitive process of giving customers what they wanted. The core economic issue was whether the practices in question went beyond consumer satisfaction. Did they entrench dominance and stifle the competition that would be necessary for consumers to continue to be given what they wanted at a reasonable price?

Both cases were investigated by the European Commission under Article 82 of the EU Treaty which prohibits the abuse of a dominant position. Both cases were also appealed unsuccessfully to the CFI. Article 82 is not specific as to what is an abuse but it provides a number of examples, including 'unfair purchase or selling prices' and price discrimination that leaves trading parties at a 'competitive disadvantage'. If a firm is found to have broken the prohibition, it can be fined up to 10 per cent of its turnover and be required to comply with remedies that eliminate the identified problem. Article 82 has almost exclusively been applied to business practices that exclude rivals and not to directly exploitative high prices. This can be justified up to a point in the context of dominant firms that have achieved their position by virtue of offering consumers what they want. However, it is less persuasive if dominance has been achieved by virtue of government regulation or structural barriers to entry.[1]

In the 2001 case known as *Michelin II*, the tyre manufacturer was found to have abused its dominance by using a complex system of rebates in the French

---

[1] See Lyons (2007).

market for heavy-vehicle tyres. Michelin, which had a market share of 55–60 per cent, was fined €20 million and required to change the scheme. Motta takes issue with the lack of economic analysis used by both the EC and the CFI to reach this verdict. The Commission did not provide a coherent theory of exclusionary effects and made no serious attempt to identify consumer harm – it merely considered the scheme capable of harm. Motta acknowledges that some elements of the rebate schemes might have had an equivalent effect to tying or exclusivity contracts, but there were also identifiable incentives for service support. Furthermore, quantity discounts can be pro-competitive by encouraging dealers to fight for marginal customers. Motta outlines the theoretical framework necessary to formulate a theory of foreclosure due to various types of rebate and so points the way to a better economic analysis. He notes that Michelin's market share and prices were falling at the time of the case and concludes that it was fairly implausible to expect the rebate schemes to exclude multinational rivals such as Continental, Goodyear, Pirelli, Bridgestone and Sumitomo/Dunlop.

Microsoft has been involved in a number of competition cases on both sides of the Atlantic. In 2004, the EC found that Microsoft had abused its dominant position by deliberately restricting the interoperability between Windows PCs and non-Microsoft workgroup servers and bundling Windows Media Player with its Windows operating system. It had a market share exceeding 90 per cent in PC operating systems and its share of server operating systems rapidly rose from 20 per cent in the late 1990s to over 60 per cent in 2001. It was fined €497 million and a further €280 million for delaying compliance with a required remedy, which was to provide technical information on the Windows interface that would facilitate interoperability.[2] Kühn and Van Reenen concentrate on the interoperability issue. Their analysis supports the Commission's case, though the EC's economic argument could have been improved. The authors demonstrate how Microsoft had both the ability (through restricting interoperability) and the incentive to foreclose rivals in server operating systems. The incentive came both in extracting surplus from consumers and in preserving its PC operating system monopoly. This could be achieved in the long term by preventing users from being able to switch to server-based operating systems and so bypassing the need for a sophisticated PC operating system. An important issue was the extent to which these competition issues should outweigh Microsoft's intellectual property rights. The authors argue that

---

[2] This is a large sum of money that would build several new hospitals, but from another perspective it is less than a half a per cent of Microsoft's market capitalisation.

even if Microsoft's incentive to invest in developing better software may be compromised by the remedy, the incentive for rivals will be much enhanced. Finally, they briefly review the Windows Media Player part of the case and criticise the Commission's chosen remedy.

The next two chapters address rather different issues under different legislation. A common feature is that both have four leading firms with broadly similar market shares. In each case, these firms appeared to be competing reasonably vigorously with each other, but there were concerns expressed about some of their practices. These raised a Goldilocks problem: were these practices leading to prices that were too high, too low or about right?[3] The first case investigates the boundary between full regulation and competition policy. The case followed an appeal by lightly regulated firms over a price cap on mobile phone termination charges. The second is based on a distinctively UK element of competition policy which allows for the investigation and remedy of markets which do not have a single dominant firm yet are apparently not working well.[4]

Mobile networks charge the originating network for providing the service of delivering a call from a fixed line to their subscribers. This is known as a termination charge. Since most customers have only one mobile phone, each network holds a monopoly on call delivery to its customers. It must therefore be expected to set inefficiently high termination charges, which will be passed on to fixed-line customers. This makes it very attractive to sign up mobile subscribers and leads to strong competition for them, so creating some off-setting benefits (e.g. in the form of 'free' handsets). The monopoly delivery is sometimes called a bottleneck and the competition for customers makes it a 'competitive bottleneck'. Mobile-to-mobile calls are different in that mobile networks negotiate reciprocal charges. With similar-sized networks, these charges will more or less cancel out and the parties argued that this changes the economics. It may even become more profitable to set inefficiently low termination charges in order to soften competition for subscribers. The Competition Commission was unconvinced by this argument and determined that negotiated termination charges were too high and would have to be

---

[3] Goldilocks is a fairy-tale character who stumbled across the house of the three bears (Daddy, Mummy and Baby) while they were out and found that the three bowls of porridge they had left on the table were either too hot, too cold or just right.

[4] Since 2003, the European Commission also has powers to investigate markets, though it does not have the powers of remedy that are available to the UK Competition Commission. UK powers under the Fair Trading Act (1973) have since been revised in part 4 of the Enterprise Act (2002). This major revision included a move from a public-interest test to an explicit competition test. EC powers derive from Article 17 of Regulation 1/2003 EC.

reduced. Armstrong and Wright show how a simple model which takes account of the essential characteristics of the market can help to reveal where the truth lies. They conclude that the Competition Commission's findings and the implications of their own modelling are broadly consistent, though the model does point out some inconsistencies in the reasoning.

The top four UK grocery chains in 1999 commanded 84 per cent of the sales of large supermarkets and nearly two-thirds of all grocery sales. The sector accounted for 40 per cent of all retail spending, so it had a very high profile and the leading firms were investigated in 2000 as a 'complex monopoly' (i.e. an oligopoly).[5] Concerns related to both pricing practices and buyer power. The former included below-cost selling and price flexing (geographic price discrimination). One finding was that price flexing was against the public interest because consumers paid more when their local supermarket faced weaker competition. However, Dobson draws on economic theory to observe that this is unlikely to harm consumers on average because, if there is national pricing, consumers will be charged a price that reflects average market power, so some consumers will get lower prices just as others pay more. Furthermore, national pricing may facilitate coordinated effects. The case also raises issues relating to the effect of buyer power on the dynamics of retail competition, the possibly predatory effect of below-cost selling and the difficulty of designing effective remedies even when a problem is identified. For example, drawing on evidence from elsewhere in Europe, remedies to make prices more cost reflective might soften competition and so do more harm than good.

[5] Since this chapter was written, the Competition Commission has published another report into the wider groceries market.

A.1

Abuse of a dominant position

Michelin II – The treatment of rebates

Massimo Motta[1]

1. Introduction

In 2001, the European Commission found that the French firm Michelin had – via its various types of rebates – abused its dominant position in the French markets for new replacement tyres and retreaded tyres for heavy vehicles, and imposed a fine of €19.76 million to Michelin.[2] Two years later, the Court of First Instance upheld the Commission's Decision in its entirety.[3]

In many respects, this case is exemplary of the strict formalistic approach followed in abuse of dominance cases by the European Commission and the Community Courts, which severely limits the possibility of dominant firms to resort to certain business practices, such as exclusive dealing, rebates and tying. Indeed, the EU case law has so far disregarded the actual effects of the allegedly abusive practices (the Commission does not need to prove that exclusionary effects have indeed taken place, nor does it need to show that consumers have been hurt), the mere possibility that they could distort competition being enough for a finding of infringement of Article 82 of the Treaty. As a matter of fact, *Michelin II* is even stricter than previous decisions and judgments because for the first time it is found that a dominant firm cannot even resort to pure (non-individualised) quantity discounts,[4] a practice until then accepted by the Courts.

Perhaps, though, the very fact that it pushed a formalistic interpretation of Article 82 to its limit will paradoxically and unintentionally make *Michelin II* a

---

[1] The author has not been involved in this case and his information about the case was only and exclusively drawn from public sources, such as the Commission Decision and the Court of First Instance's judgment. I am very grateful to Chiara Fumagalli for her comments on a previous draft.

[2] Decision 2002/405 of 20 June 2001, published in the Official Journal of the European Communities on 31 May 2002.

[3] Case T-203/01, *Manufacture française des pneumatiques Michelin* v *Commission*, Judgment of the Court of First Instance of 30 September 2003.

[4] Unless it can show that such discounts can be justified by per-transaction savings; see below for a discussion.

judgment which will contribute in a positive way to European competition law. The judgment made it apparent that economic, effects-based considerations were completely absent in abuse cases and so contributed to open a debate on how to reform Article 82 enforcement policy.[5]

This chapter is organised as follows. In section 2 I briefly describe the markets at hand and summarise the commercial policies followed by Michelin. In section 3 I report the main arguments followed by the European Commission and the Court of First Instance. Section 4, which is the main section, contains my own assessment of the case:[6] in particular, I criticise the fact that rebates may be found *per se* abusive, without any need to formulate a coherent theory of foreclosure, without looking at any evidence of the actual effects of the practices at issue and without considering possible pro-competitive effects. Section 5 concludes.

2. A short description of the case

In this section I first briefly describe the relevant markets and then summarise the commercial policies that were the object of the investigation.

The markets

The discussion of the product and geographic markets is important to understand the case, but will be kept short here because it is not particularly controversial.

There exist several different types of tyres and there is consensus among the parties that tyres for trucks and buses are not substitutable with tyres for cars, vans, tractors and so on. There is also a difference between *new tyres which are sold in the original equipment market* (directly to truck and bus producers) and *new tyres sold in the replacement market* (buyers are final consumers, who mainly purchase at specialised outlets). This case concerns the latter market only.

A customer who needs to replace his truck or bus tyres may either buy *new tyres* or *retreaded tyres*:[7] this is because the tread of a worn tyre casing can be renewed. There exist two different processes for retreading tyres: mould-cure,

---

[5] In the 2008 *Guidelines on the Commission's enforcement priorities in applying Article 82*, the European Commission claims that it intends to undertake a more economics-based approach. It is not yet clear to what extent this objective will be followed in practice.

[6] *Michelin II*, and the EU policy on rebates, are also discussed in two excellent articles, Spector (2005) and Waelbroeck (2005).

[7] The replacement market for truck tyres is composed of 53 per cent of new replacement tyres and 47 per cent of retreaded tyres.

the prerogative of tyre manufacturers, and pre-cure (by middle-size firms). Mould-cure and pre-cure retreading are considered close substitutes.

The markets for new replacement tyres and for retreaded tyres are the two relevant product markets of this case. They are considered distinct because apparently the quality of new tyres is perceived as superior (more reliable) to that of retreaded tyres, which are cheaper, being sold at less than 50 per cent of the price of new 'brand' tyres, but new 'white brand' or 'third-line' tyres are also more expensive than retreaded tyres.[8] The Commission Decision does not put it in these terms,[9] but we know that in order to define relevant markets we should use the available information to answer the SSNIP test question: could a hypothetical monopolist of new replacement tyres profitably raise prices by 5–10 per cent? Only in this way could we appreciate the competitive constraint that the products exert on each other. From what is reported in the Decision, we do not have data to answer this question, but it is possible that the answer would be positive because of the higher reliability of new tyres.

Finally, the geographic scope of these product markets is considered to be France, given that the French market appears to have sufficiently distinct features from other markets which are considered not to exercise a competitive constraint on the French market.

The industry

The industry for new tyres is quite concentrated both in the world and in the EU, with the first six producers accounting for around 75–85 per cent of the markets. There are different leaders in different markets: at the world level (according to 1997 data referring to all types of tyres) Michelin and Bridgestone share the leadership each with 18–20 per cent of the market, followed by Goodyear (15 per cent), Continental (8 per cent), Sumitomo/Dunlop (6 per cent) and Pirelli (5 per cent).[10] In Europe, however (1995 data for all tyres) the leader is Michelin, with 31 per cent of the market, followed by Continental (17 per cent), Goodyear (13 per cent), Pirelli (9 per cent), Bridgestone (8 per cent) and Sumitomo (8 per cent). The relative competitive positions of the firms change further when different EU countries are considered, Michelin being stronger in France, Pirelli in Italy and so on.

---

[8] 'Third-line brands' are low-quality tyres – often 'white brands' – produced in low-cost countries but sometimes also by major manufacturers. They still had a limited penetration at the time of the Decision.

[9] The Commission still defines the relevant markets by looking at price similarities, physical features of the products and so on. For a critique to this approach, see e.g. Motta (2004: Chapter 3).

[10] Goodyear and Sumitomo merged in 1999, but the period of the infringement considered here was 1991–8 inclusive.

Public sources put Michelin's market share for new tyres in 1995 at 55–60 per cent (no data are reported for the retreaded tyres market). Its leadership during the period 1991–8 is stable even though the market share is decreasing (see also below).

As for production capacities, Michelin has eleven of the nineteen production plants in France, the others being owned by Kléber (controlled by Michelin), Continental and Sumitomo/Dunlop with two plants each, and Bridgestone/Firestone and Goodyear with one each.

Specialised distributors have 75–85 per cent of the truck segment for tyres, their position of strength being due to the fact that the choice, fitting and management of truck tyres require technical knowledge. Probably because of this, there is a growing tendency for manufacturers to control distribution and vertically integrate.

Michelin owns the largest network among the 2,225 specialised sales outlets (data refer to all tyres) with the chain Euromaster, which is composed of 330 outlets,[11] while Sumitomo/Dunlop has 120 specialised outlets and Bridgestone/Firestone only 26.

As for the retreading market, Michelin does mainly mould-cure retreading, while its main rival, Bandag, which operates through a network of franchisees, does pre-cured retreading. Shares for this market are not reported, although the judgment indicates that the pre-cure retreading segment is growing (75 per cent in 2002).[12]

Michelin's commercial policy

Michelin's commercial policy, central to this case, was composed of three elements:

1. The *general price conditions* for professional dealers, consisting of a list price ('invoicing scale') plus a system of rebates (quantity rebates, service bonus, progress bonus, individual agreements).
2. The so-called *'PRO agreement'*.
3. The *'Club des amis Michelin'*, an agreement on business cooperation and assistance.

In what follows, I briefly describe each of these elements.

---

[11] Interestingly, Euromaster sells not only Michelin tyres but also competing brands. We shall come back to this point, which raises some doubts about Michelin's alleged intention to exclude rivals (why sell competing brands if Michelin intended to foreclose them?).

[12] The most common practice in France is 'custom retreading' (where the old tyres are retreaded), while in the EU 'standard-exchange retreading' is more common.

Table 1.1 Scale of quantity rebates, 1995: discount rate offered for a turnover of up to a certain amount

T/O 95	Rate	T/O 95	Rate	T/O 95	Rate	T/O 95	Rate
<9000	7.50	172000	10.65	5855000	11.85	10660000	12.45
15000	8.50	241000	10.75	6242000	11.90	11170000	12.50
25000	9.00	492000	10.85	6604000	11.95	11730000	12.55
30000	9.25	757000	10.95	6934000	12.00	12520000	12.60
35000	9.50	1030000	11.05	7280000	12.05	13380000	12.65
45000	9.85	1306000	11.15	7640000	12.10	14314000	12.70
60000	10.00	1656000	11.25	8020000	12.15	15314000	12.75
80000	10.10	2100000	11.35	8415000	12.20	16385000	12.80
100000	10.20	2663000	11.45	8830000	12.25	17532000	12.85
118000	10.35	3376000	11.55	9260000	12.30	18792000	12.90
142000	10.50	4280000	11.65	9710000	12.35	20145000	12.95
		5136000	11.75	10180000	12.40	22000000	13.00

Source: CFI Judgment, para. 69.

1 General price conditions (1980–1996)[13]

A dealer buys (new or retreaded) tyres according to the official 'invoicing scale' and pays within thirty days of the end of the accounting month. It then receives the total rebates as a lump-sum only at the end of February of the following year.

Let us analyse the various types of rebates.

i. Quantity discounts

Two grids – one for new tyres, the other for retreaded tyres – showing the percentages deductible from the list price for the entire turnover achieved represent the main quantity discount scheme. As one can see from Tables 1.1 and 1.2, the larger the volume of purchases of a customer, the higher the rebate it can enjoy. For example, a buyer purchasing 10,000 FF of new tyres in 1995 will receive a yearly rebate of 8.5 per cent, i.e. 850 FF. Seen from a one-year window, this effectively amounts to a reduction in the unit price paid by the buyer: if a tyre's list price is, say, 100, the fact of having bought 100 tyres through the year reduces the unit price of a tyre from 100 to 91.5. In other words, although it takes the form of a lump-sum payment once a year, this rebate amounts to a reduction of the unit price to be paid. If a buyer was able to

---

[13] Michelin changed its policy in 1997, after the entry into force of the French law prohibiting selling at a loss. Since the policy followed in 1997 and 1998 contains similar features to the previous one, for brevity I do not describe it.

Table 1.2 Scale of quantity rebates for retreaded tyres (1995)

Retreading turnover excluding VAT	Discount rate
< 7 000	0
7 000	2
7 400	3
8 000	3.5
10 800	4
14 700	4.5
19 600	4.75
29 400	5
49 000	5.1
88 200	5.2
166 600	5.3
323 400	5.4
637 000	5.5
1 127 000	5.6
1 813 000	5.7
2 499 000	5.8
3 185 000	5.9
3 920 000	6

Source: CFI, para. 70.

anticipate correctly the exact number of tyres he would buy, and apart from the possible cash-flow effects (the rebate is obtained with a delay of some months), this scheme amounts to assigning a certain unit price to any intended total volume purchase.

However, it should also be noted that in case of some additional unexpected purchases, i.e. changes relative to the expected purchase volume, the effect at the margin is larger than it may appear at first sight. Consider for instance a buyer who decides to order an extra 10,000 FF of tyres. This will bring the total amount purchased to 20,000 FF, a threshold subject to a 9 per cent discount. However, the effective discount is larger, since due to the new threshold met the buyer will also receive an extra 0.5 per cent on the first 10,000 FF worth of tyres bought. Overall, therefore, the marginal purchase has a unit cost of 90.5 rather than 91. But the cost of an additional purchase may be even much smaller when a very small number of additional units allow the firm to reach a higher quantity threshold. For instance, if 9,000 units command a discount of 7.5 per cent, buying one additional unit would bring the discount on *all* units to 8.5 per cent: if the list price of one unit is 100 FF, the effective marginal cost of buying this extra unit would be 1.5 FF, which brings the actual discount on this extra unit to 98.5 per cent![14]

ii.   *Service bonus*

The main objective of this type of rebate is to provide an incentive to the specialised dealer 'to improve his equipment and after-sales service'. To qualify, a minimum turnover with Michelin was necessary (the threshold was reduced from 160,000 FF in 1980 to 45,000 FF in 1996). The size of the bonus depends on the dealers' compliance with commitments they have taken in a number of areas; each commitment gives a number of points – the more points a dealer scores the higher the bonus, which was up to 1.5 per cent until 1991 and up to 2.25 per cent in 1992–6.

The criteria used to assign points include features related to the quality of the services provided by the dealers, such as carrying out *staff training*, having *certain machinery and know-how*, and the level of *quality of the facilities*; features related to the dealer's behaviour with clients, such as supplying customers with *new Michelin products*, promoting and advertising them; and providing Michelin with detailed *information* (mileage of tyres, performance, statistics on sales, also comparing Michelin and competitors) to help it plan its production. As for retreading, points are achieved by providing roadside assistance for trucks, by showing knowledge about how to sort casings and by having Michelin tyres systematically retreaded by Michelin.

iii.   *Progress bonus*

This bonus rewards dealers who agree to commit in writing at the beginning of the year to exceed a certain minimum base of purchases (which is fixed by common agreement between the dealer and Michelin and which depends on various factors) and manage to do so.

The system changed over the years. In 1995–6, it specified for sales of 30–999 tyres: 12 per cent of the amount by which the base was exceeded if the progress was lower than 20 per cent and 2 per cent of the *aggregate* turnover if the progress was higher than 20 per cent. For sales above 1,000 tyres: 15 per cent of the amount by which the base was exceeded if progress was lower than 20 per cent, and 2.5 per cent of the aggregate turnover if progress was higher than 20 per cent. If the base was reached but not exceeded, a bonus of 0.5 per cent of the turnover was granted.

---

[14] $100 - (100 \times 8.5 \text{ per cent}) - (9000 \times 1 \text{ per cent}) = 1.5$, where 100 is the unit price for the extra unit, 8.5 per cent is the discount applied to this extra unit and 1 per cent is the additional rebate granted on all the 9,000 units previously bought.

iv. Individual agreements

This scheme was applicable to dealers who reached the maximum amount in the quantity discounts table (Table 1.1) (amounting to a turnover of FF 22 million in 1995), who could then sign a cooperation agreement with Michelin. The scheme required dealers to commit to provide technical information and after-sales service, help launch Michelin products, submit forecasts and get regular supplies from Michelin. The benefits foreseen were an extension of the discount tables (up to 2 per cent additional rebate), a favourable system to calculate the progress bonus and an extension of the payment deadline (e.g. sixty rather than thirty days).

2 The 'PRO agreement'

This scheme offers a dealer a rebate for each tyre given to Michelin for retreading. In exchange, the dealer commits to a truck progress bonus and will have Michelin retread all the Michelin truck tyres which have reached the legal limit for the tread wear.

This scheme contains an element of tying, in that the maximum number of bonuses a dealer can achieve is limited by the number of new Michelin tyres bought during the previous year (and the bonus is conceived not as a cash payment but as a credit towards buying new Michelin tyres).

3 The Michelin Friends Club

The 'Club des amis Michelin' is an agreement that Michelin signed (bilaterally) with a large number of sales outlets (375 in 1997, accounting for some 20 per cent of the truck tyres market). According to the agreement, Michelin helps the club members to improve their performance and professionalism; in return, members guarantee a certain level of 'Michelin temperature' (i.e. large enough volumes and market share).

More specifically, Michelin contributes to investment and training of the dealers. This includes a financial contribution if a specific target is attained, but also the transfer of know-how in many areas, priority access to training courses (50 per cent of courses at Michelin's training centre are reserved for members), transmission of data on market trends and exclusive distribution of BFGoodrich car tyres.

Members commit to communicate balance sheets and provide Michelin with disaggregate sales statistics (but Michelin also carries out individual financial analyses and helps members to find solutions to their financial problems). They also permit Michelin to carry out analyses of the outlets in areas such as staff qualification and competence, quality of services and sales promotions, and sales facilities. They promote Michelin products by displaying advertising material, carrying product information and taking part in advertising campaigns. They commit 'not to divert customer demand away from Michelin', carry enough stock of Michelin products to meet customer demand immediately, have their first retreading made by Michelin and play an active role in truck tyre sales and services.

4 The Commission's findings and the CFI review

To prove that a firm has abused a dominant position, i.e. that it has infringed Article 82 of the Treaty, the Commission first has to find that the firm is dominant in a given relevant market and then has to show the abusive nature of the firm's practice.

Michelin's dominance

In this case, the relevant markets are defined (see above) as the (i) new replacement truck tyres in France and the (ii) retreaded truck tyres in France. The Commission finds that Michelin has a stable leadership in these markets, with market share above 50 per cent (however, we know from the CFI judgment that Michelin's share is decreasing over time). Moreover, its strength is also due to its technological lead and expertise, its strong reputation, the wide range of its products and its strength in commercial and technical services, demonstrated by its leading position in the French distribution channel (where it owns directly sales outlets and has strong links with a large number of other outlets thanks to the Club des amis Michelin).

These points of strength should therefore support the idea that Michelin is dominant, i.e. it has considerable market power. In other words, it can keep prices well above cost because little demand would switch to rivals and importers that according to the Commission are not competitive enough. Further, the Commission argues that buyers do not have much power, as specialised dealers 'must deal' with Michelin, else they would lose credibility (since clients would ask for Michelin's products).

The issue of dominance may deserve some further analysis (Michelin's market share appears to decrease over time, even if we do not have precise data on this;[15] further, the Commission itself indicates at para. 212 that in the last

---

[15] At para. 176 of the Decision, the Commission reports some publicly available estimates which put Michelin's share in the new replacement tyres for trucks in France at 55 per cent in 1995 and 51 per cent in 1996. The strongest competitors appear to be Dunlop (9 per cent in both years) and

few decades, new firms have entered the French market and have become more competitive), but the absence of data in the Decision suggests that we should focus on other issues.

One element that I would like to point out for further discussion below is that the Commission stresses strong competition among dealers and indicates it as an element which compels dealers to accept Michelin's rebate schemes:

> Competition between dealers [is] very keen and margins small (in 1995, for example, the average operating margin of French specialised dealers was 3.7 per cent of their turnover). Under this pressure, independent dealers are constrained to obtain the best terms possible when purchasing Michelin products, especially as regards truck tyres. In order to preserve the competitive edge on which their survival probably depends, dealers do not hesitate to take part in the majority of 'programmes' and 'agreements' that they are offered, if as a result they can benefit from rebates or other additional economic advantages. Very slight variations in the rebate rates can prove to be essential to the dealers, who will do their best to make the most of them. (Commission Decision, para. 206)

The abusive nature of Michelin's commercial policy

According to the Commission, when faced by new entrants and stronger rivals Michelin has adopted a complex system of rebates and discounts to maintain dominance, thus leading to the finding of Michelin's infringement of Article 82 and the imposition of a large fine. In what follows, I review the Commission's arguments, delaying my own considerations to the next section.

General price conditions

Quantity discounts are criticised by the Commission because the purchase of some additional units may determine reaching a higher quantity threshold and thus entitle the buyer to a larger rebate on *all* units (additional and previously bought). Such rebates (which indeed may determine a very low price associated with marginal purchases, as discussed above) would therefore

---

Bridgestone/Firestone (whose share drops from 12.5 per cent in 1995 to 9 per cent in 1996); Goodyear (6.5 per cent in 1995 and 7 per cent in 1996) and Continental/Uniroyal (5 per cent in 1995 and 6.5 per cent in 1996) and Pirelli (3 per cent in both years) follow, while minor suppliers (including third-line) grow from 9 per cent to 14.5 per cent.

create a strong incentive to buy additional units from Michelin, determining a *loyalty-inducing effect*.

The Commission also criticises, following an established case law, the fact that the discounts would not reflect economies of scale. This is because the case law of the Community Courts allows only discounts which are justified by *transaction-specific savings*: if a firm can show that the unit cost of supplying in one particular transaction a particular buyer with 100 units is lower than the cost of supplying the same buyer with, say, 50 units, then a discount to that buyer would be justified. But claiming that a rebate scheme would induce one or more buyers to purchase more over several transactions, which in turn allows the firm to reduce unit costs of production, would be considered a generic claim which does not qualify as efficiency gain.

The Commission also judges the scheme *unfair* because rebates are not paid until February of the following year, which would determine cash-flow problems for buyers and even oblige them to operate at a loss until the rebate was paid; dealers have to negotiate the progress bonus with Michelin before they have received the quantity rebates for the previous year, which would put them 'in a weak psychological position during negotiations' (para. 223); buyers would suffer from uncertainty, as until the end of the year they do not know the actual cost of inputs.

I always find it difficult to evaluate fairness arguments in connection with competition policy issues, but I would nonetheless like to stress the paternalistic approach of the Commission, which seems to view buyers (which in this case are firms, not final consumers) as being unable to make forecasts and organise their business.

Finally, according to the Commission this system would have market-partitioning effects because rebates are applied only to purchases from Michelin France, thereby making parallel imports difficult, as tyres bought outside France do not qualify for the thresholds established by the rebate schemes. (Recall that preventing parallel imports, that is, arbitrage between different EU Member States, is a very serious violation of EU competition law.)

Curiously, it is in this section devoted to parallel imports that the Commission gets the closest to formulating a theory of foreclosure in the Decision:

… thanks to its market shares, Michelin was able to absorb the cost of these rebates, while its competitors were unable to do likewise and therefore had to either accept a lower level of profitability or give up the idea of increasing their sales volume. (Commission Decision, para. 241)

The *service bonus* scheme shows, according to the Commission, similar abusive features as quantity discounts. In particular, it is *unfair* because a) it is subjective (Michelin has a wide margin of discretion in assigning 'points' to buyers), b) it asks dealers to provide market information, which would not be in their interest and for which they would have no return (e.g. in the form of market studies), and c) subjectivity is inevitably a source of discrimination (recall that a dominant firm may not discriminate among customers, discrimination being abusive). It is also *loyalty-inducing*, in that reaching a minimum turnover is necessary for a dealer to qualify and strengthen links with Michelin, and because it assigns points if Michelin tyres are systematically given to Michelin for retreading, which effectively amounts to a tying practice.

As to the *progress bonus* (as well as the 'achieved target bonus' which replaced it in 1997), it is particularly abusive because it is *loyalty-inducing* by pushing dealers to buy more than previous years (or meet the target), thus denying sales to rivals, and *unfair* because a) it is discriminatory (two dealers who buy the same quantity but have different bases get different rebates) and b) it 'creates insecurity' in dealers (they do not know whether they will get the bonus).

Individual agreements are equally abusive because they give extra incentives to large dealers and put pressure on them to buy only from Michelin, so that they can reach the highest rebates.

The other rebate schemes

Similar arguments to those made above are also used by the Commission to explain why the remaining rebate programmes are abusive. The 'PRO agreement' contains a 'double-tying' component, since Michelin casings have to be sent exclusively to Michelin for retreading. The effect of this practice is abusive – according to the Commission – because Michelin would use dominance in the new tyres market to strengthen it in the retreading market and vice versa. Further, the fact that the bonus is limited to the number of new Michelin tyres sold during the previous year (no matter how many tyres are sent for retreading) would imply that dealers are discouraged from buying rivals' new tyres, for the following year the bonus would be lower.

As for the Michelin Friends Club, it would also contain abusive obligations in that dealers a) need to achieve a certain 'temperature' (i.e. proportion of sales from Michelin), b) cannot divert spontaneous customer demand away from Michelin and c) need to carry sufficient stock of Michelin products to meet demand immediately. These obligations would aim at eliminating competition and maintaining dominance, with an effect similar to a 'fidelity clause', further aggravated by the fact that Michelin also has an integrated network which ensures it a large market share. Finally, the Commission also objects to the 'excessive' monitoring of dealers' business, which Michelin would use to control dealers and make sure they do not buy from its competitors.

There is no doubt that Michelin's rebate programme contains some elements of aggressive competition, as we shall discuss below. For the time being, it is important to underline that the Commission's arguments are either non-economic in nature (the alleged unfairness of the practices followed by Michelin) or insufficiently motivated. As we shall discuss below, it is conceivable that rebates (as with tying and exclusivity provisions) may exclude rivals, but here there is neither an attempt to explain why foreclosure should occur, nor a presentation of evidence which indicates that foreclosure was indeed taking place, not to mention the complete absence of possible pro-competitive justifications for the rebates or of an assessment of the effect of such practices upon consumers.

The Commission's Decision is appealed by Michelin, but the Court of First Instance upholds the Decision and accepts all the Commission's arguments (which in many cases just followed an established case law).

The main element of novelty in the Judgment is the fact that for the first time the Court rejects the use of pure quantity discounts. According to the Court, they induce loyalty because the rebates were calculated on the overall turnover, and are abusive because they are not justified by cost savings:

… a rebate system in which the rate of the discount increases according to the volume purchased will not infringe Article 82 EC unless the criteria and rules for granting the rebate reveal that the system is not based on an *economically justified countervailing advantage* but tends, following the example of loyalty and target rebate, to prevent customers from obtaining their supplies from competitors … (para. 59 of the Judgment, italics added)

A quantity rebate system has no loyalty-inducing effect if discounts are granted on invoice according to the size of the order. If a discount is granted for purchases made during a reference period, the loyalty-inducing effect is less significant where the additional discount applies only to the quantities exceeding a certain threshold than where the discount applies to total turnover achieved during the reference period. (para. 85 of the Judgment)

But perhaps the most striking, and potentially important, element in the Judgment is the way in which the CFI dismisses Michelin's argument that the rebate system did not have any effect on competition, as Michelin's market shares and prices were falling:

… In any event, it is very probable that the falling in the applicant's market shares (recital 336 of the contested decision) and in its sales prices (recital 337 of the contested decision) would have been greater if the practices criticised in the contested decision had not been applied. (para. 245 of the Judgment)

As one can immediately see, the Court's arguments may completely undermine an effects-based approach: for any evidence that a firm may produce in support of its claim that rivals have not been hurt, and/or that consumers have benefited from the practice, the Court could always counter such evidence with an argument (which does not need to be supported by evidence) that rivals and consumers would have benefited even more had the dominant firm not engaged in the (abusive) business practices at hand.

5 An economist's assessment of *Michelin II*

Most business practices which are potentially exclusionary – and this holds not only for rebates but also for tying, exclusive dealing, refusal to supply – may also have pro-competitive effects. Since the objective of competition policy is not to protect competitors but to protect competition and increase welfare, economic analysis suggests to undertake the following four-step approach in order to find whether a firm has engaged in abusive practices: first, find whether the firm is dominant, that is whether it has considerable market power; second, identify whether the practice does indeed have possible anticompetitive effects, including the formulation of a coherent hypothesis about the strategy of the firm; third, analyse the possible pro-competitive (efficiency) effects of the practice at hand; fourth, balance the anti- and pro-competitive effects, that is, carry out an assessment of the net effects on consumer (or total) welfare.[16]

The Commission and the Community Courts instead basically adopt a *per se* rule of prohibition of rebates (but also exclusive dealing and tying) by a dominant firm. They do not present a theory of why the dominant firm may use rebates so as to foreclose rivals, do not consider necessary to show any

---

[16] See for instance Motta, 2004. The particular way in which the test is proposed does not matter much. The important thing is that an explicit analysis of both the anticompetitive and the pro-competitive effects, and an estimation of their net effect on welfare, is carried out. Gual *et al.* (2006) suggest that there is no need to separately show that the alleged violator has market power, but this is in my opinion a useful screening device, which has the further advantage of bringing the test in line with EU competition law.

actual foreclosure, do not analyse the possible efficiency rationale behind the practices and do not try to assess whether ultimately the practices would have harmed or benefited consumers.[17]

In what follows, I try to assess the *Michelin II* case from the perspective of the economic approach delineated above. However, I do not discuss the issue of dominance (which is simply assumed to be proved) and focus instead on anticompetitive effects and the possible pro-competitive ones.

Do rebates have anticompetitive effects?

Rebates can be defined as discounts applicable where a customer exceeds a specified target for sales in a defined period. There are different types of rebates, according to the sales 'target' given to the customer. Rebates can be conditional on increasing purchases, on buying only (or in a sufficiently high percentage) from the given supplier or on buying over a given number of units (quantity discounts). They can also be individualised or standardised.

Interestingly, Michelin's commercial policy included more or less the whole range of possible rebates. The progress bonus belongs to type (i), as it established a minimum turnover, which represented the base to measure 'progress', that is the extent to which the target was met or exceeded, in turn determining the discount. The Michelin's Friends Club was of type (ii), since it required a 'certain temperature', i.e. a sufficiently high volume and share of purchases from Michelin to qualify; the service bonus and the individual agreements also contained elements of type (ii) by requiring a certain minimum turnover to qualify (the scheme does not apply if rebates are below the threshold). As for the quantity discounts, they belong to type (iii), since the different discount rates were conditional on the purchase of different numbers of units (for any given amount bought during one year, one could easily compute the unit cost associated with it). Further, the rebates offered by Michelin can be either individualised (indeed, the Commission and the Court criticise the fact that both the service bonus and the progress bonus are discretionary and discriminatory, since two identical buyers can be offered different rebates) or standardised (quantity discounts are in principle identical to any consumer).

---

[17] In the US, there is a very different approach, which considers rebates as 'competition on the merit' and puts the burden to prove anticompetitive behaviour on the plaintiff. However, recent decisions such as *LePage* and *Dentsply* may signal a change. See Kobayashi (2005) for a discussion of the US policy on rebates.

Conceptually, the first two types of rebates are similar to exclusive dealing provisions, in that they try to induce a buyer to purchase all (or most of) its inputs from the same supplier, either directly (specifying that a certain percentage or volume is purchased) or indirectly (by conditioning the discount to buying the same or increased number of units than in the previous year).[18] It is therefore appropriate to consider separately the economics literature on exclusive dealing before looking at pure quantity discounts.

The literature on exclusive dealing explains precisely how rebates may foreclose rivals.[19] In particular, Rasmusen *et al.* (1991) and Segal and Whinston (2000a) have shown that if buyers cannot coordinate their purchase decisions and a new firm needs to secure a certain minimum number of buyers to operate efficiently, exclusive dealing allows an incumbent monopolist to exclude the rival.[20] Indeed, the incumbent monopolist just needs to induce a certain number of buyers to purchase exclusively from it, thereby preventing the entrant from achieving the minimum number of orders necessary to operate profitably, and effectively obliging all remaining buyers to buy from the incumbent as well.

Although there are some differences between rebates and exclusive provisions (unlike the latter, the former practice does not include any ex ante commitment on the side of the buyer), one could presumably formalise a story whereby an incumbent could use discounts conditional on buying more than in the past, or on buying at least a certain percentage of input needs, to prevent rivals from reaching a minimum size of its business.

Next consider pure quantity discounts (i.e. unrelated to the share of purchase). It is not straightforward to see at first sight their exclusionary potential: how can an incumbent use non-individualised quantity discounts to exclude a more efficient firm? Note that – unlike exclusive dealing – under rebates there is no contractual commitment for the buyer to buy only from the incumbent: here the incumbent can offer only a price-quantity menu which can in principle be matched by the rival.

Karlinger and Motta (2006) take seriously the argument of the Commission and the Court of First Instance and show that it is indeed possible for an incumbent to exclude a more efficient rival, even if the latter can use the same

---

[18] Indeed, such types of rebates have always been considered 'abusive' in the EU because they are said to amount to exclusive dealing, a practice which dominant firms are not allowed to engage in.

[19] See Motta (2004: section 6.4) for a presentation of the literature.

[20] See also Bernheim and Whinston (1998). In their model, in which markets appear sequentially, an incumbent is able to use either explicit exclusive dealing provisions or a sort of quantity discount to exclude an entrant from the first market; since the entrant needs to sell in both the first and the second market to operate profitably, foreclosure will arise.

rebate scheme. However, they also question whether consumers are harmed by the practice.

In their model with buyers of differing sizes, the incumbent has an advantage given by an established customer base that the (more efficient) rival firm does not have. In order to be profitable, the rival needs to attract a certain minimum turnover, while the incumbent has already reached it.[21] In this model exclusion may arise even under linear pricing (because of miscoordination of buyers – if a buyer expects that all other buyers would buy from the incumbent, s/he would have no incentive to buy from the entrant, since its orders would not be sufficient to trigger entry). However, the authors show that quantity discounts have a higher exclusionary potential. To understand why, consider first the benchmark situation where the incumbent could make *explicit price discrimination*, and suppose that the entrant is not able to reach the minimum threshold size if it does not sell to the large buyers. In this case, the incumbent could break an equilibrium where the rival sells to all buyers by making a below-cost price offer to the large buyers, while recovering profits by imposing the monopoly price to the small buyers (who, given the failure of the rival, would have no other possibility than to buy from the incumbent). Karlinger and Motta (2006) show that – unless the incumbent is considerably less efficient than the entrant – under price discrimination the only type of equilibrium arising in the game is the exclusionary one, where only the incumbent serves.

Next, observe that the incumbent can use this 'divide and rule' strategy through *quantity discounts*, which are nothing other than a form of *implicit price discrimination*. Indeed, the only difference between a scheme which explicitly offers different prices to a small and a large buyer and a quantity discount scheme is that under the latter buyers have to self-select, i.e. can choose freely which offer to accept. However, provided that the price offers are not 'too imbalanced', so that a small buyer does not want to behave as if s/he were a large buyer, some price discrimination can still be attained, thus achieving exclusion, at least under some conditions.

The power of the exclusionary effect depends on the aggressiveness of the pricing scheme: linear pricing is the least aggressive, since the firm cannot discriminate, followed by quantity discounts where in order to discriminate successfully the self-selection constraint of buyers must be satisfied, and finally by explicit price discrimination. Karlinger and Motta show that the more

---

[21] The main model in Karlinger and Motta (2006) considers an industry with network externalities and assumes that the entrant needs to achieve a sufficiently large number of buyers for them to derive utility from the consumption of the network product. Here, I am describing the mechanism of the paper assuming economies of scale in production rather than in demand, but the two are equivalent.

exclusionary potential it has, the more likely that at equilibrium the incumbent operates in monopolistic conditions.

However, they also show that when comparing equilibria where exclusion cannot be achieved (for instance, if the incumbent is much more inefficient than the rival, or if the minimum threshold size needed by the entrant is small), the welfare ranking is exactly the opposite: the more aggressive the pricing scheme, the lower the prices at equilibrium and therefore the higher the welfare outcome.

These results demonstrate the fundamental dilemma that one faces when establishing the policy towards rebates (and pricing schemes in general): by prohibiting dominant firms from using aggressive pricing policies (such as rebates), one lowers the risk that exclusion will occur; however, a prohibition would at the same time prevent competition from taking place, which would promote entry but also higher prices.

Facing such a trade-off, different policy options are possible: (i) always allowing rebates (or other 'aggressive' pricing policies), for instance by putting the burden of proving anticompetitive behaviour on the plaintiff and imposing a very high standard of proof (which, by and large, has been the US case law so far, at least until the *LePage* and *Dentsply*'s District Court decisions); (ii) imposing a *per se* prohibition of rebates by dominant firms, which by and large corresponds to the current EU policy; and (iii) using a *rule of reason* approach, which admits that rebates may be exclusionary, but also recognises that they can be an instrument of market competition and create important welfare gains for consumers. The third approach is certainly more difficult to implement because it calls for detailed investigations, but it is the only one which is consistent with economic analysis. If one decides to follow this route, one needs to carry out a detailed analysis of the case and understand to which extent in the case at hand it is sufficiently likely (rather than simply conceivable) that rebates might achieve exclusion of rivals.

Let us now come back to our case. We know that theory admits the possibility that the various types of rebates used by Michelin could be used for exclusionary purposes.[22] But how likely is it that in the facts of this particular case, rebates would have the effects of foreclosing rivals?

In all the models mentioned above, rebates (and exclusive dealing) are anticompetitive if they exclude competitors. But is it credible that Michelin's

---

[22] Apart from the similarities with exclusive dealing, we should also mention that the PRO agreement contained some features which make it similar to tying and that tying may be used to exclude (see e.g. Whinston, 1990).

competitors would exit the market, or at least be relegated to small niche markets? From the description of the industry, we know that Michelin is certainly the leader of the French market, but its rivals are no minnows and even in France have strong positions (also in distribution). Further, it does not seem that Michelin's policies – even though they span a long period of years[23] – have had such strong effects on its rivals, whose collective market share – as we are told in the CFI Judgment – is increasing over the years.

Perhaps we could be more convinced of Michelin's anticompetitive strategies if it had been shown that it was selling below-cost to some groups of customers (as we have seen above, discriminatory strategies might help a dominant firm to exclude by denying key buyers to the rivals), but there is no information about this point in the case.

Furthermore, we know from the literature on exclusive dealing that when there is strong competition among buyers (a fact that is emphasised by the Commission), it is *less likely*, rather than more likely as the Commission claims, that the incumbent will manage to exclude an efficient firm. Indeed, Fumagalli and Motta (2006) show that if buyers compete fiercely in the downstream retailer market, each of them will have a strong incentive to deviate from the incumbent and buy from a more efficient supplier, in order to guarantee itself a competitive advantage over the other retailer-buyers (and if they steal business from the latter, they manage to (endogenously) increase the size of their orders, allowing the entrant to reach its minimum threshold size).

Finally, a natural question which arises from the reading of the proceedings is the following: if Michelin really intended to exclude rivals from independent outlets, why did it sell rivals' products in its own Euromaster outlets?

Possible efficiency effects of rebates

Neither the Commission nor the Court of First Instance consider the possible pro-competitive effects that Michelin's rebate schemes may have (with the exception, as indicated above, of transaction-specific cost savings), whereas economics does suggest that rebates may have efficiency effects.

Let us continue for convenience to divide rebates into two categories: those that 'resemble' exclusive dealing provisions and those which consist of quantity discounts. For the first category, one should note that exclusive dealing

---

[23] Para. 359 of the Commission Decision recites: 'The infringement extended over a period of 19 years or more, since the commercial policy at issue was in operation at least from 1980 onward, and … Michelin agreed to amend its agreements with effect from 1 January 1999.'

may promote investments by preventing freeriding by rivals and so capturing more of the return for the investor.[24] In particular, Segal and Whinston (2000b) and Motta and Rønde (2006) show that exclusive dealing is welfare beneficial if it helps protect investments made by the supplier which have the effect of improving the retailer's productivity in selling both the supplier's products and the other suppliers' products. In the case at hand, rebates may serve the purpose of trying to mimic exclusivity provisions (recall that exclusive dealing by a dominant firm is not allowed in the EU) and reduce the risk that an investment made by Michelin into a retailer's premises or human capital is then used by the retailer to sell products produced by Michelin's rivals. Although we do not have an explicit discussion of such efficiency effects in either the Decision or the Judgment, there are some indicia that rebates may have served the purpose of protecting Michelin's investments. Several clauses in the rebates schemes (for instance in the Service bonus and in the Club des amis Michelin programmes) explicitly aimed at improving promotion, advertising and services provided by dealers, and in some of these schemes, Michelin committed to provide training, investments and funds. It seems logical that it does not want to invest in a dealer which sells mostly rivals' products. And in turn, by requiring a retailer to buy mostly from it, Michelin would invest more into this relationship, which would be welfare-beneficial.

As for the other category of rebates, quantity discounts, we have already seen above that they represent an instrument of price competition and therefore – to the extent that they do not exclude rivals – are inherently beneficial to consumers.

A slightly different way to look at quantity discounts is that they can be seen as a form of two-part tariff: the more a buyer purchases, the lower the unit price paid. And we know that this is going to reduce inefficiencies due to double marginalisation: when dealers' variable cost decreases, so will final consumers' prices, causing an increase in welfare.

Furthermore, quantity discounts may indeed be justified by scale economies (even if not for any single client and transaction in isolation, as the CFI requires): the more a supplier produces and sells, the lower its production costs.

Although we do not have enough information in the published case material to quantify the importance of such efficiency effects, there seems to be enough ground to conclude that the efficiency effects of rebates might have been substantial.

---

[24] See Segal and Whinston (2000b) and references cited therein.

6 Conclusions

The European Commission and the Community Courts de facto consider rebates by a dominant firm *per se* abusive, as *Michelin II* demonstrates. But economics teaches us that rebates may serve as a way to foster investments into the relationship between a seller and its retailers. Furthermore, like any reduction in prices and to the extent that they do not exclude more efficient rivals, they have beneficial welfare effects. This should call for a completely different approach in dealing with rebates, where first the exclusionary potential of rebates is analysed and then possible pro-competitive explanations are considered, and if appropriate weighed against the anticompetitive ones.

In this case, the Commission and the Court have made no effort in trying to formulate a coherent theory of why Michelin's rebate programmes had anti-competitive effects. Likewise, they have not considered possible efficiency effects arising from such programmes, while it is conceivable that by reducing prices in the market and by giving incentives to invest more, considerable pro-competitive effects may have arisen from them.

From the information available, it does not seem particularly likely that Michelin's rebates could exclude (efficient) rivals. In fact, Michelin's market position has worsened over time despite its use of such rebate schemes. Nor can one exclude that these schemes could achieve important efficiency gains which also benefited final consumers. Had the Commission and the Court followed an economic approach rather than a form-based one, they would have probably concluded that Michelin's commercial policy was not abusive.

2 Interoperability and market foreclosure in the European Microsoft case

Kai-Uwe Kühn and John Van Reenen

1. Introduction

The cases in the US and Europe against Microsoft have been perhaps the most high-profile antitrust cases in the last twenty years. In the various Microsoft cases, antitrust authorities in the US and Europe took on what was at some points the most valuable company in the world and its CEO Bill Gates, the world's richest man. After five years of investigation, on 24 March 2004,[1] the European Commission held Microsoft guilty of an abuse of a dominant position under Article 82 and imposed the largest fine ever for such an antitrust violation in Europe – €497 million. The Commission also demanded major forward-looking behavioural remedies including compulsory licensing of intellectual property and forced unbundling. This degree of behavioural intervention is highly unusual and led to continued conflict about the implementation of the remedies.

The Decision found that Microsoft had abused its dominant position in the PC operating system market in two ways:[2]

- 'deliberately restricting interoperability between Windows PCs and non-Microsoft workgroup servers, and
- by tying its Windows Media Player (WMP), a product where it faced competition, with its ubiquitous Windows operating system.'

As remedies for these violations the European Commission ordered Microsoft:

- 'within 120 days, to disclose complete and accurate interface documentation which would allow non-Microsoft workgroup servers to achieve full interoperability with Windows PCs and servers';
- 'within 90 days, to offer to PC manufacturers a version of its Windows client PC operating system without Windows Media Player'.

---

[1] ec.europa.eu/comm/competition/antitrust/cases/microsoft/investigation.html (downloaded 30.1.07).
[2] europa.eu/rapid/pressReleasesAction.do?reference=IP/04/382&format=HTML&aged=1&language=EN&guiLanguage=en (downloaded 30.1.07).

The case is fascinating as it touches on one of the key issues concerning the conduct of modern competition policy': how should we think about the role of antitrust in high-tech industries dominated by rapid innovation?

In this chapter we give an overview of the economic issues in the Microsoft case. Space constraints mean that we focus on the part of the case relating to the workgroup server market. But we also touch on the media player case (see Kühn *et al.*, 2005, for a more detailed analysis). We also briefly contrast the European and US Microsoft cases. Many of the economic issues and fore-closure mechanisms in the server case are closely related to those in the 'browser wars' around which the US case was centred (see Rubinfeld, 2004, for a more detailed discussion of the 2001 US case).

The structure of the chapter is as follows: in section 2 we look at the 'Big Picture' and give a case overview. In section 3 we sketch the timeline of the legal evolution of the case. Section 4 describes the products and section 5 briefly looks at two topics that were extensively discussed in the case – interoperability and market definition. The next two sections are the economic meat of our discussion – the incentives to foreclose (section 6) and the impact of remedies on innovation incentives (section 7). We make some concluding remarks on lessons learned in section 8.

2. The big picture

Before plunging into the details, it is worthwhile to have an overview of the case. The Commission's essential argument was that Microsoft leveraged its market power from its primary market for PC operating systems[3] into the secondary, complementary market for workgroup server operating systems. In the terms of Article 82, it abused its dominance of PC operating systems to gain market power through the refusal to supply interoperability information.[4] According to the Commission, Microsoft had the *ability* to do this because it controlled over 90 per cent of the market for PC operating systems (hence-forth 'OS') and this monopoly was protected by a powerful 'applications' barrier to entry (see section 5).

---

[3] The Commission also pointed to Microsoft's dominant position in the supply of personal productivity applications such as spreadsheets, word processing, etc. (i.e. the Office Suite). Although this aided their ability to limit interoperability, all of the economic arguments would carry through if these applications were controlled by a third party, so we focus on PC operating systems.

[4] The parallel case on the Windows Media Player alleged that Microsoft leveraged the market power derived from the PC operating system into the market for encoding software for media content. It did so by bundling decoding software (the core of the Windows Media Player) with the Windows operating system.

Workgroup servers are low-end servers that link with PC clients (see section 3 for more on this). For the OS of workgroup servers to be effective they have to work well with the PC OS, which is dominated by Windows. Microsoft has the ability to reduce the *interoperability* of rival vendors of workgroup server OS because it controls the interfaces (protocols and Application Programmer Interfaces known as APIs[5]) of the PC OS. This control of access to the functionality of the PC OS gives Microsoft the power to exclude potential rivals that produce complementary products to the PC OS by denying them access to the PC OS functionality.

Naturally, the ability to monopolise a secondary market does not mean a dominant firm has *incentives* to monopolise this market. The Chicago School tradition (e.g. Bork, 1978) emphasises that there are many efficiency reasons why the monopolist of market A will want to enter and monopolise market B (e.g. to solve the double-marginalisation problem arising in markets with complements), but there is no leverage of market power beyond what can be achieved in market A alone. The Commission argued that Microsoft's incentives were not so benign and that there were anticompetitive reasons for degrading interoperability and monopolising the workgroup server OS market.

The Commission argued that there are both static and dynamic incentives to foreclose rivals from the workgroup server market. The dynamic reasons are probably most important as Microsoft was clearly concerned that a strong presence of rivals in the server OS market could threaten the profits it enjoyed from its Windows monopoly of the PC market in the future. For example, by running future applications mostly on servers, customers could reduce their reliance on the PC OS functionality by effectively substituting server functionality for PC functionality. By extending the Windows platform dominance from the PC OS market to the server OS market, Microsoft could reduce the probability of such competition in the future (see section 6 for more details).

Various internal e-mails by Microsoft senior executives suggest that this strategy was not conjured from thin air by the Commission. For example, in 1997 Bill Gates wrote:

What we're trying to do is use our server control to do new protocols and lock out Sun and Oracle specifically ... the symmetry that we have between the client operating system and the server operating system is a huge advantage for us.

---

[5] Application Programmer Interfaces (APIs) are interfaces that an application programmer can use to have his application call up specific underlying functions of the operating system. They thus provide the link between the functionalities of the underlying operating system and the application that is written to the operating system. APIs are typically proprietary, so that an application has to be written to a specific operating system and cannot be used for a different operating system without substantial modification.

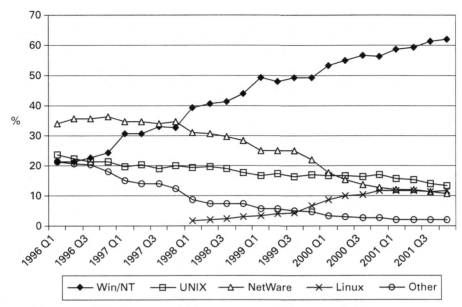

Figure 2.1 The growth of Microsoft's share in the workgroup server market 1996–2001
Source: IDC Quarterly Server Tracker.
Notes: Initial server shipment units of all servers under $100, 000.

This may have just been cheap talk, of course, but Microsoft's share of the workgroup server market did rise dramatically in the late 1990s from about 20 per cent at the start of 1996 to over 60 per cent in 2001, as shown in Figure 2.1. By this point Novell, the combined UNIX platforms (e.g. IBM and Sun) and Linux could muster only about 10 per cent market shares each. The Commission argued that at least some of the forty percentage point increase was due to anticompetitive actions.

3. The legal timeline

The case began with a complaint by Sun Microsystems in December 1998 lodged against beta versions of Windows 2000. The complaint revolved around the limited interoperability of Windows with the OS of other server vendors due to a switch to proprietary communications protocols. These protocols were software interfaces which made it very difficult for non-Microsoft server OS to communicate with the Windows OS. Many of these protocols had been non-proprietary open standards when initially adopted by Microsoft (e.g. the Kerberos security protocol developed at MIT), but gradually, through often secretive extensions, became closed to rivals.

These problems had been around for several years (since 1996, the arrival of NT 4.0 and Windows 95). But the number of proprietary protocols had greatly increased with the new version: Windows 2000.

The Commission issued a Statement of Objections against Microsoft on 1 August 2000 taking up the complaints over the interoperability issues in the workgroup server market. It then issued a second Statement of Objections on 31 August 2001 adding the media player issues, which the Commission had started to investigate on its own initiative. An (unprecedented) third Statement of Objections was sent out on 6 August 2003 refining some of the issues. The Oral Hearing took place between 12 and 14 November 2003 and in March 2004 the Commission issued its Decision finding Microsoft in violation of Article 82 and imposed the remedies.

Microsoft appealed against the Decision in front of the Court of First Instance. It also sought interim relief, which would have suspended the implementation of remedies until a judgment on the appeal. However, this application was rejected by the Court of First Instance in December 2004. The appeals case was heard by the Court in 2006. On 17 September 2007 the Court upheld the Commission's decision in just about every part,[6] although it did annul the role of the Monitoring Trustee (see below). Microsoft chose not to appeal.

The remedies on the server side have been a point of contention between Microsoft and the Commission ever since the Court denied interim relief. Microsoft was required to make available a full technical description of the protocols and interfaces that would enable rival server OS to fully interoperate with Windows. This raised complicated issues of the existence of intellectual property rights and compensation for Microsoft in the form of 'reasonable' licensing fees, as well as the required scope of disclosures.

To oversee the implementation of the remedy, the Commission appointed an independent Monitoring Trustee acceptable to both the Commission and Microsoft, Professor Neil Barrett. But both the Trustee and Commission came to the conclusion that Microsoft delayed the process and did not supply complete and accurate interoperability information. As a result, another Statement of Objections was issued on 21 December 2005. When the response to this Statement of Objections remained unsatisfactory for the Commission, Microsoft was fined another €280.5 million for failing to comply with the Commission's decision on 12 July 2006.[7] Since the Decision prospectively also applies to future versions of Windows, there have been ongoing discussions between the Commission and

---

[6] www.microsoft.com/presspass/presskits/eucase/docs/T-201-04EN.pdf
[7] ec.europa.eu/comm/competition/antitrust/cases/microsoft/implementation.html (downloaded 31.1.07).

Microsoft about compliance with the Decision in the new Vista OS. On 27 February 2008 the Commission fined Microsoft a further €899 million for failure to comply with the 2004 Decision, an amount that is, at the time of writing, under appeal.

4. The role of servers in modern computers and the definition of markets for server operating systems

In the late 1980s and at the beginning of the 1990s computing architecture went through a paradigm shift. The mainframe-orientated system was overthrown by the 'PC client/server' computer architecture that is familiar today.[8] Instead of computer intelligence being centralised and users interacting via 'dumb' terminals, processing power was more decentralised, distributed between PCs with their own operating systems and increasingly powerful servers linking together these PCs in networks.

Computing can be performed locally on stand-alone appliances such as using a laptop computer away from the office. Most computing, however, is performed on multi-user networks in which users communicate through 'clients' and in which much of the computing activity takes place behind the scenes on 'servers'. The clients in a client-server network take many forms. Some are 'intelligent', such as a desktop computer; others are 'non-intelligent', such as a dumb terminal (e.g. an ATM machine). Servers vary in size and in the nature of the tasks they are asked to perform. The mixture of servers in a client-server network depends on the kinds of computing that the network is designed to support. The server requirements of a small office, for example, are considerably different from the server requirements of a large international bank.

Like all computers, servers consist of both hardware (e.g. the processors and storage facilities/memory) and software (e.g. the operating system and server applications). Server hardware is manufactured using various types of processors. Intel processors are used in many servers and Microsoft's Windows operating system is compatible only with hardware that uses Intel processors. Novell's NetWare and SCO's UNIX variants are also designed to run on Intel processors. The leading hardware manufacturers for Intel-based servers include Compaq/HP, Dell and Gateway.

Server vendors mostly sell Intel-based systems on a non-integrated basis. An organisation usually purchases server hardware from one vendor with the

---

[8] See Bresnahan and Greenstein (1996) for an economic analysis of this transition.

server operating system installed from another vendor. Sometimes the organisation will install the server operating system itself. Server systems are also sold on an integrated basis in which the vendor supplies both the server hardware and a proprietary operating system that has been specially designed for the vendor's hardware (e.g. Sun Microsystems).

Servers differ in the tasks they perform in a computer network. To understand how the requirements for servers differ depending on the different tasks involved we now discuss the most important functions performed by servers. These are needed to generate the benefits of using computer networks.

One of the principal benefits of a computer network is that it allows an organisation to share computer resources among multiple users. Clients connected to a network can share printers and files. Application programs can be maintained on central servers and then 'served' to clients on an as-needed basis. In addition, computers connected to a network can run distributed applications. Distributed applications are computer programs in which different blocks of the program are executed on different computers within the network. Servers will facilitate these networking tasks.

So-called 'workgroup servers' are used to perform a number of the basic infrastructure services needed for the computers in a network to *share resources*. Workgroup servers most commonly handle security (authorisation and authentication of users when they connect their clients to the network), file services (accessing or managing files or disk storage space), print services (sending print jobs to a printer managed by the server), directory services (keeping track of the location and use of network resources), messaging and e-mail, and key administrative functions in the management of the workgroup network. In addition to infrastructure services, workgroup servers execute certain kinds of server-side applications.

But servers also perform very different tasks. In many organisations, there is a pressing need to manage enormous (and growing) amounts of data that are critical to the mission of the organisation. Inventory control, airline reservations and banking transactions are just a few examples. The 'mission-critical' data used for these purposes need to be stored, updated, quality controlled and protected. They also need to be readily available to authorised users. The servers that perform these mission-critical data functions are frequently referred to as 'enterprise servers'.

Enterprise servers tend to be larger and significantly more expensive than workgroup servers. Around 2001 a workgroup server usually had one microprocessor, modest memory (around four gigabytes) and typically provided services for between twenty-five and thirty-five clients. Enterprise servers, in contrast, tended to have at least eight processors, usually cost more than $100,000 and in some circumstances cost more than $1 million. The uses to which mission-critical data are put, and the methods by which they are stored, accessed and used, vary widely across organisations. Thus, in contrast to the standardised applications that run on workgroup servers, application programs for enterprise servers tend to be custom written and specific to a particular organisation.

The case focused on workgroup servers for several reasons. First, the protocols involved in the interoperability issues all focused on protocols used for the execution of workgroup server functions. These are protocols that are not necessarily used for the functions executed by enterprise servers. Second, since enterprise servers rely largely on customised software, whole solutions tend to be customised, which requires less reliance on standardised interfaces than standardised applications programs do.

5. Some technical issues in the case

Interoperability

The Commission gave many examples of where it believed Microsoft had limited interoperability. For example, the critical area of security services (e.g. authentication and authorisation) in Windows 2000 is based on a protocol called Kerberos. Kerberos was developed in the 1980s at MIT and has been used since then on a number of open standard networks, mostly UNIX-based.[9] Kerberos is a public protocol. However, in implementing Kerberos for Windows 2000, Microsoft added proprietary extensions that create interoperability problems. When presented with a Kerberos 'ticket' (basically, a computer passport), the Windows 2000 server will permit access to the services requested only if the authorisation information appears in the Windows format. Conversely, if a non-Windows 2000 server is presented with a Kerberos ticket in the Windows 2000 format, it cannot process the request

---

[9] Simplifying, in a network that uses the Kerberos protocol there is a server (the 'Kerberos server') that acts as a 'trusted intermediary'. When a user logs on to the network, the Kerberos server verifies the user's identity and issues a ticket that, in effect, vouches for the user's identity and specifies the network resources (e.g. files, printers, application programs, databases, distributed objects) to which the user is allowed access. Once issued, these Kerberos tickets can be used for authentication and authorisation around the network, as long as the user remains online. One of the advantages of the Kerberos system is that authentication and authorisation can take place without the need to send passwords back and forth across the network – a process that runs the risk of password theft.

for authorisation. This means that, if a network wanted to use Windows 2000 on any machine, it needs to run Windows on *all* of the servers or encounter significant burdens. Similar problems were alleged with other basic work-group server tasks such as file and print (the CIFS protocol) and Directory services (Active Directory).

A great deal of discussion in the case centred on the factual question of whether or not interoperability between Microsoft and non-Microsoft oper-ating systems was really limited. Microsoft argued that interoperability was 'good enough' – much information was disclosed and there were many ways to get around any compatibility problems through installing other 'bridge' software (either on the PC client or server), reverse engineering, etc. In the end, talking to customers, survey evidence and expert testimony convinced the Commission that there were genuine serious compatibility issues. The key evidence was that bridge solutions were extremely rare and essentially never worked satisfactorily. The greatest barrier to such solutions is that they require considerable reverse engineering. However, such reverse engineering is slow and any success can be made obsolete through the next version of the Microsoft PC OS. Given the short product cycle in software products it appeared unlikely that satisfactory bridge products could work around the ever increasing interoperability problems.

In the end this issue was not central to the economic analysis of the case. As long as the interoperability problems created can significantly increase the costs of achieving interoperability with the PC OS, foreclosure effects can be generated in the economic theories underlying the Commission's case. Interoperability restrictions by a dominant firm like Microsoft can then only be justified by efficiency benefits that are gained from restricting the access to protocol information.

Market definition

As is usual in these cases, there was a huge amount of discussion concerning the existence or not of a market for workgroup servers OS. Although rather arcane to academic economists, market definition is usually a major issue in antitrust cases.

The really key issue in this case was not the workgroup server OS market, however, but rather the market for PC operating systems. The Commission's theory asserted that Microsoft had monopoly power in PC OS and used this to leverage into other markets. So the critical issue was whether or not there was a well-defined marker for PC OS. If this was not the case, attempts by

Microsoft to use its power here would be swiftly undermined as many consumers could easily switch to rival PC OS vendors if they were unhappy with the reduced interoperability of Windows with their servers.

For PC OS it appears clear that there is little substitutability between Windows and other operating systems. If a UNIX-based PC operating system or even Apple's OS would lower their prices by, say, 5 per cent, this can be expected to have a minute effect on the sale of Microsoft OS. Part of the reason comes from an application network effect. There are a large number of software applications (e.g. Office-type word processing, spreadsheets, etc.) that are written specifically to the Windows APIs. This means that these programs cannot easily be made to run on an alternative operating system, creating for users an enormous cost of switching the operating system. The failed attempt of IBM's OS/2 in the first half of the 1990s is an example of how OS switching can be undermined because of compatibility problems with application software. On the basis of such evidence, it is highly unlikely that there is significant substitution in the period in question between Microsoft's PC OS and that of other companies.

Microsoft pointed to the possibility of a disruptive entrant that could change the whole face of computing. They argued that the risk of such potential entry disciplined their behaviour. Theoretically, it is questionable whether this should be the case. Microsoft should lower prices only once competitive entry occurs. But Microsoft insisted that Linux was an example of price-constraining competition. However, the example seemed to show the opposite. Linux achieves low penetration rates on PCs despite being priced very competitively: at zero price. This suggests that Microsoft's dominance was unlikely to end soon. Finally there was some consensus over Microsoft's dominance of a well-defined market for PC OS among most commentators (even Microsoft did not contest this very strongly).[10]

There was much more disagreement, however, over the workgroup server OS market. As discussed above in section 3 there were clearly demand-side characteristics that distinguished workgroup servers from more powerful enterprise servers. Prima facie these types of servers appeared to be at best very imperfect substitutes (or could even be considered complements in multi-tiered corporate computing networks). Recent econometric work seems to have confirmed this intuition.[11]

Microsoft argued that software running on enterprise and workgroup servers had to be considered perfect substitutes in terms of physical

---

[10] Although see the debate between Evans *et al.* (2001) and Werden (2001) for some issues.
[11] See Ivaldi and Szcolin (2004) or Van Reenen (2004, 2006).

characteristics. They pointed to their own software that they used indistinguishably on any type of server. This argument is irrelevant for market definition if firms can discriminate in their pricing policies between different uses of a server operating system. Indeed, evidence was presented that Microsoft in fact price discriminated between workgroup, web and enterprise server OS by offering different licences at very different terms. In addition there was strong evidence that market shares differed strongly across these different server types. For example, the advance of Linux in server markets (see Figure 2.1) was somewhat limited to 'edge' tasks like that of web serving rather than the core infrastructure tasks of workgroup servers like file, print, security and directory services. These pieces of evidence suggest that Microsoft had sufficient market power to price discriminate and that substitution in the workgroup server market was limited.

The evidence on Linux finding a niche primarily on web servers also supported another important point on market definition. Web servers are not subject to the interoperability problems with Microsoft's PC OS that workgroup servers are. The reason is that web serving is done using exclusively public (open) protocols. However, an operating system that can be sold for web serving or even as an OS for enterprise servers would find it difficult to prosper as a workgroup server because of the low interoperability between non-Microsoft enterprise OS and the PC OS. In a world of limited compatibility (and if this was not the case then the Commission had no argument at all) the markets could be effectively separated[12] – even without reference to the price-discrimination evidence.

From an economic point of view, however, the existence or otherwise of a workgroup server market was largely a sideshow. Although Figure 2.1 and the arguments above suggest that Microsoft did have de facto market power in the workgroup server market, the Commission's case did not really hinge upon this, as we will explain as we proceed to develop the theory of the case.

6. Key economic issues I: economic incentives to foreclose

As stressed in section 2, a theory of incentives is critical for economists seeking to understand the case. Not all of these incentive-based theories are clear from the decision.

---

[12] The economic logic of this is compelling even though it may be troubling for lawyers as it mixes the abuse accusation with the market definition, two stages of the case that are usually considered independently.

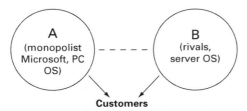

Figure 2.2 Leveraging incentives

The one monopoly profit theory

To see the issues at stake consider Figure 2.2. Firm A the monopolist (PC OS) faces firm B in a complementary market (server OS). When will firm A exclude firm B from the adjacent market? Microsoft's essential argument rested on the Chicago view that a monopolist in one market will never have anticompetitive incentives to leverage. The basic reason is the 'one monopoly profit theory'. Degrading interoperability would cost Microsoft lost revenues as consumers would not be willing to pay as much for a Windows OS for their PC due to its lower performance with non-Microsoft servers. Instead of going to the expense of attempted monopolisation of servers through interoperability degradation, Microsoft could simply charge a higher price for its PC OS and extract all the rents from the server market in this way. Consequently, the entry of Microsoft into the server market must have benign reasons, such as its desire to end double marginalisation (the excessive profits earned by oligopolistic server vendors) or the superior efficiency of Windows technology.

There are many reasons why the Chicago critique of the leveraging theory breaks down that are addressed by modern foreclosure theory (see Rey and Tirole, 2007, for a survey). For this case it is useful to distinguish between long-run (dynamic) and short-run (static) incentives in understanding why the standard Chicago argument will break down.

Dynamic incentives to foreclose

The lack of any long-run incentive to foreclose in the one monopoly profit theory arises primarily from the assumption that the monopolist has a permanent unchallenged position with no threat of future entry in his primary market. This assumption is unlikely to hold for Microsoft's position in the PC OS market. Although in the short run it is protected by the applications barrier to entry, in the longer run a variety of threats exist to its stream of profits. Consumers desire a computer operating system for the applications it provides and Windows has the advantage that it has a wide range of applications written to its interfaces (APIs) due to its ubiquity. But major platform threats emerged in the late 1990s associated with the growth of the internet. One version of the threat was that increasing numbers of applications could be delivered through servers and the need for a sophisticated and expensive OS on the PC client would erode. Server OS typically run on open standards (variants of UNIX) and APIs. Developers could increasingly write to these standards and APIs rather than Windows. Since they are operating systems that have to support a similar range of applications as PC OS, server operating systems can credibly be expected to offer a rich set of APIs to programmers. This would mean that the server OS became a potential alternative applications platform. This could then introduce effective competition into the PC OS market. If applications needed only a slimmed-down version of the PC client, OS users would not necessarily need PC OS upgrades to buy into new OS functionality supporting their applications (this is why it was called the 'thin client model'). Effectively, a server platform based on a server OS could have become a potential competitor for the PC platform running a Windows OS. One way to prevent this danger was for Microsoft to monopolise the server market through degraded interoperability – even if this meant in the short run sacrificing profits.

This dynamic argument is closely related to the US 'browser wars' case. There, Microsoft monopolised the market for web browsers by giving away Internet Explorer. The Department of Justice's argument was that the web browser of the new entrant Netscape posed a threat to Microsoft not because it cared about profits of browsers *per se* but rather because software developers were increasingly writing applications for Netscape interfaces (in conjunction with Java) rather than Windows interfaces. As the number of applications written to these non-Microsoft APIs increased, the applications barrier to entry in PC OS would weaken, allowing new entrants into Microsoft's primary monopoly. This argument is even more credible in the European workgroup server case, since a server operating system could even more credibly expose a rich set of APIs to application program developers than Netscape in conjunction with Java.

There are other related dynamic incentives to monopolise the workgroup servers market because there are many other software markets that are complementary to servers and for which interoperability with servers is of great importance. These include web-enabled phones and PDAs. What is key about dynamic foreclosure theories is that an action that shifts short-run market share can have long-run benefits to the monopolist through depressing rivals' investment and innovation incentives (for example, see Bernheim and Whinston, 1998; Carlton and Waldman, 2002).[13] In many cases these arguments may be suspect as there is no obvious mechanism whereby this could take place. In the Microsoft case the mechanism is well established due to the applications network effect. Shifts in share towards Microsoft in the server market (current and expected) will mean that developers will start switching away from writing to non-Microsoft interfaces. Customers will shift away from rivals because there are fewer applications and this will further reduce developers' incentives to write software. This applications network effect makes foreclosure arguments much more plausible than in other industries. Note that developers' incentives are reinforced by the incentives to invest in innovation. Falling share will, in general, mean that rival server vendors have lower incentives to invest in improving their software which again will lower their attractiveness to customers in a 'vicious circle' of decline.

Static incentives to foreclose

The dynamic arguments work even though, in the short run, the monopolist may suffer some losses. However, foreclosure arguments are even more compelling when there are short-run incentives to foreclose. One short-run incentive effect is the desire to more effectively use second-degree price discrimination in the primary market (in this case the PC's OS) through monopolising the secondary market. Such imperfect price-discrimination possibilities are assumed away in the one monopoly profit theory as it relies on the monopolist's ability to fully extract all the rents from the primary market. This assumption is generally not satisfied because monopolists cannot perfectly price discriminate due to arbitrage. Large businesses with less elastic product demand, for example, can pretend to be small businesses when they buy their computers.

In the context of the Microsoft case, consider the idea that there are two types of customers, large firms (which are less sensitive to the price of the PC OS) and small firms (which are very sensitive to the price of the PC OS). A price-discriminating monopolist would like to charge a high price to the large firms and a low price to the small firms. Arbitrage will limit the ability to do this however, so that systematic differential pricing of PC OSs is typically not possible among different businesses. But consider the case that large firms also place a high valuation on a complementary product – servers – whereas small

---

[13] See also Whinston (1990, 2001).

firms do not because the gains from sharing computing resources are smaller. In this case, by monopolising the server market and charging a higher price for the PC and server OS bundle, the PC OS monopolist effectively 'restores' second-degree price discrimination in the primary market.[14]

From a welfare perspective price discrimination has ambiguous effects because output may rise. But in this case the welfare effects are likely to be negative as reducing interoperability immediately degrades the quality of rival products and causes a welfare loss to consumers who purchase those goods.

Both long-run and short-run incentives are part of modern foreclosure theory. Although often expressed legally in the language of 'acquiring profits' in the secondary market, foreclosure is really about extracting rents more effectively from the monopolist's primary market both today and in future periods.

7. Key economic issues II: remedies and innovation

Software markets are fast moving and highly innovative and some advocates have suggested that existing European competition law is inadequate in such markets. In particular, Microsoft argued that the proposed remedy of forced disclosure of interoperability information would have a severely negative effect on innovation as it would lead to the wholesale 'cloning' of Microsoft's valuable intellectual property. Whatever the supposed short-run gains, it argued that the long-run costs in terms of lower innovation by Microsoft would swamp these purported benefits.

These are legally difficult areas as the Commission was under no legal obligation to consider the effects on innovation, despite the economic importance. It chose to do so, however, and claimed:

… a detailed examination of the scope of the disclosure at stake leads to the conclusion that, on balance, the possible negative impact on Microsoft's incentives to innovate is outweighed by its positive impact on the level of innovation of the whole industry. (Commission, 2004, 783)

In order to consider these claims we must investigate the Commission's remedies and their likely impact on innovation incentives on Microsoft, on its rivals and therefore on the market as a whole. It is worth bearing in mind that there is no theoretically unambiguous answer to these inherently difficult – but important – questions.

---

[14] These ideas are formalised and tested for the PC and server markets in Genakos, Kühn and Van Reenen (2006). There does appear to be evidence that this incentive matters for Microsoft's behaviour.

What did the Commission ask for in its remedies?

The Commission asked Microsoft to reveal interoperability information (interfaces, protocols, etc.) necessary to allow rivals to interoperate with Microsoft's Windows platform. This amounts to a compulsory licensing remedy. The Commission conceded that Microsoft could charge a reasonable fee for such licences, reflecting the intellectual property embedded in the information. An independent Monitoring Trustee was chosen to arbitrate on the appropriate degree of information and Microsoft was left with the choice of how best to allow this to occur subject to the reasonableness of the licensing conditions (we discuss what 'reasonableness' might mean below).

It is worth noting an important analytical distinction between demanding information to enable *interoperability* compared with *imitation*. The Commission wants the former to enable firms to connect to Microsoft's PC OS monopoly in the same way that telecom regulators force fixed-line incumbents to share their network with firms selling complementary services even if the incumbent also offers these services (such as mobile telephony where the fixed-line incumbent often also operates in the mobile market). Another analogy would be that a monopolist of cars was required to disclose how rival tyre manufacturers would be able to be compatible with the wheels of the car. If the remedy allowed *imitation* – of the key security features of the PC OS – there would be a stronger concern over innovation. Consequently, the remedy *did not* require release of Windows' source code – the 'crown jewels'.

Interestingly, Windows' source code is not what the rival server vendors wanted in any case. Instead they were after a detailed technical description of the interfaces to enable them to design their own code to interoperate with Windows. The description of the remedy as allowing 'cloning' is therefore inaccurate. There was no desire to obtain what software engineers describe as the 'implementation'.[15] Indeed, use of the information beyond that necessary for interoperability would be a violation of intellectual property rights by the rival server OS producers.

Effects of the remedy on the incentives of server OS rivals to invest in innovation (R&D)

The remedy effectively reduces the price for some interoperability features from infinity (refusal to supply) to a price that would lead to rivals being able

---

[15] An issue arises over whether providing interoperability information would of necessity reveal so much that rivals could imitate. This can be protected by technical and legal provisions. Part of the 'necessity' reflects Microsoft's own design decisions of its software, however.

to offer interoperable solutions. The main effect of giving interoperability information to rivals is that the level of interoperability with Microsoft products increases, making rival products more valuable and increasing their sales. This will increase their return to R&D (relative to the world without interoperability information) as any innovation will be spread over a larger number of units sold. The remedy essentially reduces the cost of rival innovation and should, therefore, increase innovation incentives.

Second under the remedy, rivals would no longer have to incur costs to overcome barriers to client-server interoperability created by Microsoft's disclosure policy. This includes creating bridge software, etc. This is an innovation of a sort, but it is duplicative and socially wasteful.

Both of these effects should increase rivals' R&D incentives to improve quantity and quality of their productive innovations.

Effects of the remedy on Microsoft's incentives to invest in innovation

Again there are several considerations. First, with better disclosure, rivals will be able to compete on a level playing field. To the extent that this reduces the expected market share and increases price competition from now higher-quality rival products, the remedy may lead to some reduction in Microsoft's incentive to invest. However, unlike its rivals, Microsoft will still obtain substantial profits from general operating system innovation in the PC OS market, where it will continue to enjoy a monopoly position. There is therefore little reason to expect that Microsoft's incentives to innovate on OS solutions would fall substantially.

A further effect may also contribute strongly to increased innovation incentives: through innovation a firm can escape harsh competition with rivals and secure rents for a transitory period. This effect will tend to increase the investment incentives of all firms, including Microsoft. The theoretical and empirical literature is somewhat ambiguous on the net impact of all of these effects, but on balance it is believed that intensifying competition will usually lead to increased innovation (e.g. Vives, 2005).[16]

Finally, Microsoft may change the quality as well as the quantity of its R&D. There could be positive effects on quality because Microsoft will no longer have incentives to block innovations that raise quality but have high

---

[16] There is some support for the notion that in high-innovation industries like OS software the intensity of innovation is enhanced by more competition. An example comes from the computer industry: Macieira (2006) estimates that in the supercomputer industry an increase in competition would increase not only the rate of innovation of the industry as a whole but also the rate of innovation of the industry leader.

interoperability with non-Microsoft servers. There is some evidence that Microsoft has sacrificed its own innovative potential (especially in areas where the innovations would be cross-platform) in order to protect the Windows desktop monopoly. This was known internally to Microsoft as the Windows 'strategy tax' – the need to close down research lines that, although leading to innovative products, could potentially weaken the lock-in of Windows.[17]

In summary, there are likely to be positive effects on rivals' innovation from the remedy and ambiguous effects on Microsoft's incentives. While no one can sign the eventual outcome, the discussion highlights that it is far from clear that the remedy will chill industry-wide innovation. There are as many reasons for believing that it could have a positive effect on aggregate innovation.

Interoperability at what price?

The most contentious issue after the Commission Decision has been the conditions under which the interoperability information should be licensed and what information was necessary to achieve full interoperability. The Commission left the exact conditions out of its initial decision because it involved intricate review of technical information which was beyond the scope of the investigation and which was delegated to the Monitoring Trustee.

Microsoft's initial suggestions were far from acceptable to industry rivals, the Commission and the Trustee. Microsoft proposed that the protocol and interface information could be purchased only as one bundle and specified a licence fee for each rival software copy shipped in the order of magnitude of the Microsoft software itself. This would have clearly continued the exclusive effect simply through high prices. Indeed, the position of rivals was far removed from this. Many industry insiders doubted that any innovation of significance was embedded in the interfaces themselves. Just changing the language of the protocol would not be a substantive innovation that had material value and therefore should not be compensated. Indeed, to the extent that Microsoft has innovation embedded in processes that use the protocols, such innovations should not matter for the assessment of the licence fee because the protocols themselves do not constitute the innovation. Typically interface and protocol information in other software sectors are licensed at only nominal fees so that the demands of Microsoft appeared by far exaggerated.

---

[17] See Banks (2001). For example, 'Many of Microsoft's best innovations were killed before they ever came to market. Inside Microsoft such sacrifices were known as paying the "strategy tax"' (p. 71).

A second contentious issue is the amount and type of information that Microsoft has to provide. To interconnect with Microsoft's software rivals do not need code, which no one could interpret, but information about how exactly the interface works. When the Trustee strongly stated that Microsoft was not forthcoming with sufficient information to make this possible, the Commission stepped in with a Statement of Objection and eventually the large fine for non-compliance. However, this tug of war has red to considerable delay in the effective implementation of the remedy.

8. The media player part of the case

While among the general public the case against bundling the Windows Media Player with the PC OS has been perceived as another case analogous to the US browser wars case, this is in fact not the case. The rival Real Player, unlike the combination of the browser and Java, was unlikely to ever expose a rich enough set of APIs to programmers to credibly develop into an alternative operating system platform. The theory of the case is therefore quite different from that of the workgroup server part of the case.

The Media Player case is really about competition for clients that produce media content. To such clients Microsoft and Real sell at considerable prices software solutions that encode media content into proprietary digital media formats that make files transferable over the internet and may allow media streaming. Media content providers themselves sell the media content to the desktops of individuals. There are large benefits to content providers to specialise in one format, not the least because of the technical support involved. Besides quality characteristics like transmission speed that is influenced by the format and the encoding software, media content providers also care about how many desktops they can easily reach. This depends on whether or not the desktop already has a decoder for the particular format installed. By bundling Windows Media Player with the PC OS, Microsoft assured ubiquity on the desktop, a property that rivals have to struggle with. This gives Microsoft a competitive advantage and market power in the market for encoding software that has nothing to do with the actual quality of its product.[18]

---

[18] A more detailed discussion of this part of the case can be found in Kühn, Stillman and Caffarra (2005).

A remedy for this case could have come from ordering total unbundling and prohibitions on exclusivity contracts with OEM manufacturers of PCs. This would have then allowed PC users to decide on the set of media players they wanted loaded on their desktop at the time of purchasing the computer. Alternatively, Microsoft could have been forced to allow the loading of all three decoders, i.e. Media Player, Real Player and Quicktime, when the machine was shipped.[19]

Unfortunately, the Commission chose a remedy that did not address the basic issues. Instead of an unbundling measure the Commission forced Microsoft to sell a version without Media Player but also allowed selling a version with Media Player. Microsoft then has incentives to sell both at the same price. A customer can then only gain by buying a version with Media Player and the ubiquity advantage of Microsoft in the market for encoding software is preserved. The basic anticompetitive issue in this part of the case was therefore not resolved by the remedy.

9. Conclusions

In this chapter we have focused on the workgroup server part of the *European Commission* v *Microsoft* (2004) case, which is perhaps the most high-profile European antitrust case of all time. Microsoft was found to be in violation of Article 82 of the Treaty of Rome through abusing its dominant position. It was fined and instructed to meet several behavioural remedies, including compulsory licensing of information to enable rivals to interoperate with its operating system.

We end with some remarks on the case and suggest that there may be more general lessons to be learned about antitrust enforcement in high-tech markets and elsewhere.

First, it is worth remembering that at the time of writing the case has gone on for nine years with three Statements of Objections issued and still no final resolution. This is partly a reflection of the complexity of the technical issues, legal necessity of due process and the financial strength of the Microsoft Corporation. Many of the server rivals have long since died. An obvious

[19] Although there are many other media players there are only these three that have decoders for their own, proprietary, format. When they play files they actually use the decoders of the other programs in the background. For example, Real Player does not 'play' Windows Media files. It simply calls up the Windows Media Player to decode the file and then displays the video in the Real Player frame. In contrast to proprietary interfaces there are large gains from making media formats proprietary because on those there is considerable innovation.

problem is that the legal timescale is so long compared with the rapid evolution of these markets. By the time a remedy is in place, the marketplace has moved quickly beyond the problems over which the case was fought. Even if the judgment and remedy are appropriate, is it 'too little, too late'? We would like to argue that even if the impact on Windows 2000 turns out to have been limited, some impact may have been retained because the Commission's decision is prospective so that it gives the Commission leverage over all future Windows versions.

Furthermore, we believe that, although caution is always warranted before intervention, antitrust authorities cannot take a completely laissez-faire approach to innovation markets. Much of the positive impact of competition policy is through deterring anticompetitive behaviour without the need for ever taking legal action. In fact, software markets are replete with examples of similar complementarity issues and the case may have contributed to higher deterrence effect against anticompetitive exclusionary behaviour.

A second observation concerns the status of foreclosure theory. Part of the Commission's case was an explicit consideration of economic incentives and an analysis of the effects of the remedy on innovation. These are clearly important from an economic perspective, even though European legal practice is often ambivalent about getting into these issues. Despite the difficulty of bringing empirical evidence to bear compared to, say, a standard share calculation in a market-definition exercise,[20] consideration of innovation and foreclosure was unavoidable in making a credible economic case. One of the challenges facing modern economics is to develop guidelines for the type of empirical evidence that could be used to test the likelihood of foreclosure being a problem in different markets.

The European Commission has come in for much criticism in its use of foreclosure theories in merger cases. For example, the Commission blocked the proposed merger of General Electric and Honeywell after it had been cleared by the US authorities only to see its judgment (although upheld) severely criticised by the Court of First Instance in 2005 (see Vives and Staffiero, this book, Chapter 17). In 2002 the Court actually overturned the Commission's blocking of the Tetra/Sidel merger in 2001 which was based on over-speculative theories. In a sense, foreclosure theories in a merger case are inherently highly speculative. Opponents of the merger must produce arguments that a particular type of foreclosure behaviour is more likely to occur as

---

[20] Or more sophisticated attempts at market definition and merger analysis using econometrics such as Hausman *et al* (1994).

a result of the merger, although there are no exclusionary practices in the pre-merger situation. The evidential position is better in an abuse of dominance case because the exclusionary behaviour is already alleged to have happened, so there can be an empirical discussion over whether the behaviour has in fact occurred, whether it could have pro-efficiency justification and whether there was any material effect on the marketplace as a result of this behaviour. This was the case in Microsoft where an ex-post evaluation was possible. Furthermore, the exclusionary mechanisms of Microsoft were lent credibility by internal e-mails from senior executives. This is the type of evidence that is rarely seen but is legally persuasive.

Unfortunately, although foreclosure may be easier to detect in an Article 82 case compared with a merger case, remedying the problem is much harder. In a merger there is always the clear choice of simply blocking the proposed transaction. Remedies under Article 82 are harder to frame and even harder to enforce. The Commission and Microsoft have been in long-standing dispute over the terms of the disclosure remedy and it is still not perceived to be effective.[21] Microsoft's main rivals have reached out-of-court settlements, so one concern may be that smaller firms and potential new entrants could be the main parties to suffer. Most importantly, this type of settlement does not necessarily help consumers of computer software.

We are unlikely to have heard the end of this case.

---

[21] news.bbc.co.uk/1/hi/business/5153570.stm (downloaded 30.1.07).

A.2

Market investigations

3 Mobile call termination in the UK: a competitive bottleneck?

Mark Armstrong[†] and Julian Wright[‡]

1. Background

We discuss policy towards call termination on mobile telephone networks, illustrated by the 2002 Competition Commission inquiry into the UK mobile market.[1] This was an unusually complicated inquiry (the report was printed in three volumes). The case demonstrates the utility of employing stripped-down economic models to cast light on complex interactions between firms and consumers. Doing so reveals that, by and large, the findings of the Competition Commission and existing economic models are consistent, although we also highlight some points of divergence. In some cases these differences reflect inadequacies in the theory, which we will try to address, while in other cases they reflect statements by the Competition Commission – and especially by some of the mobile networks during the inquiry – which are difficult to reconcile with reasonable economic analysis.

The investigation concerned the call-termination charges levied by four mobile networks in the UK: O_2, Orange, T-Mobile and Vodafone.[2] Call termination refers to the wholesale service whereby a network completes (or 'terminates') a call made to one of its subscribers by a subscriber on another telephone network. Typically, the originating network pays the terminating network for completing calls. The wholesale price it pays is known as the termination charge. There are two broad kinds of call termination on mobile networks: termination of calls made from other mobile networks (termed mobile-to-mobile, or MTM, termination in the following discussion)

[†] University College London, e-mail mark.armstrong@ucl.ac.uk. Armstrong acted in a very limited way as advisor to Oftel, then the telecommunications regulator, during the course of the inquiry discussed in this paper.

[‡] National University of Singapore, e-mail jwright@nus.edu.sg.

[1] See Competition Commission (2003b).

[2] At the time of the inquiry, a fifth network, H3G, had just entered the market. However, this firm used a newer 'third-generation' technology which was specifically excluded from the inquiry.

and termination of calls made by callers on the fixed telecoms network (fixed-to-mobile, or FTM, termination).[3]

The existing economics literature raises two concerns regarding the level of these call-termination charges.[4] Broadly speaking, FTM call termination is likely to involve unilateral monopoly pricing if left unchecked. The vast majority of mobile subscribers join just one mobile network, so callers on the fixed telephone network must route calls through a subscriber's chosen network. A mobile network therefore holds a monopoly over delivering calls to its subscribers and has an incentive to set high (in fact, monopoly) charges for granting access to these subscribers. Since mobile networks compete to attract mobile subscribers, but hold a bottleneck over terminating calls to these subscribers, this type of situation is sometimes known as a 'competitive bottleneck'.[5]

A distinct literature has analysed the setting of MTM termination charges, assuming these are set through negotiation.[6] In this case, the central issue is whether mobile networks can use negotiated termination charges in order to relax competition for subscribers. For instance, MTM termination charges directly affect each network's cost of making an MTM 'off-net' call (that is, a call to a subscriber on a rival mobile network) but do not affect a network's cost of making an 'on-net' call (that is, a call between two subscribers on the same network). As such, MTM termination charges have an impact on the balance between off-net and on-net call charges and this in turn can affect competitive conditions in the market for subscribers. As we will see in a formal model, when networks can coordinate on the MTM termination charge, they will often have an incentive to choose too *low* a charge in order to soften retail competition.

The Competition Commission argued in favour of the competitive bottleneck story. However, a key point of difference between the existing theory and the Commission discussion was that the Commission did not take seriously

---

[3] Two of the mobile networks, Cellnet (the precursor to O_2) and Vodafone, faced an earlier inquiry into their FTM termination charges in 1998 – see MMC (1999b). This earlier inquiry did not investigate MTM termination charges, nor did it investigate FTM termination charges levied by the two more recent entrants to the market (Orange and T-Mobile). The inquiry concluded that the two networks' FTM termination charges were too high in relation to cost, and based on its recommendations Oftel (then the telecommunications sector regulator) regulated FTM termination by means of a price cap. It was the imminent expiry of this price cap which led to the inquiry discussed in this chapter.

[4] Surveys of the economic literature relating to mobile call termination include Armstrong (2002, sections 3 and 4) and Gans, King and Wright (2005).

[5] See Armstrong (2002, section 3.1) and Wright (2002) for an analysis of this competitive bottleneck in the context of mobile telephony, and Armstrong (2006) and Armstrong and Wright (2007b) for a more general analysis which applies to other industries.

[6] See, in particular, Laffont, Rey and Tirole (1998) and Gans and King (2001), who extended the literature on two-way interconnection to handle the situation in which networks set different on-net and off-net call charges (which is relevant for the UK market).

the prediction that MTM termination charges may be set too low to soften competition. On the contrary, the Commission treated MTM termination charges in the same way as FTM termination charges.

Borrowing from Armstrong and Wright (2009), here we discuss how this puzzle can be resolved by developing a model which integrates the two strands of literature, analysing both FTM and MTM mobile termination in a single model. Doing so raises the issue of wholesale arbitrage and retail substitution. Wholesale arbitrage arises if, facing high termination charges for FTM calls but low termination charges for MTM calls, the fixed network 'transits' its calls via another mobile operator so that it pays only the low MTM rate plus a small transit charge. Such arbitrage will constrain a network's FTM termination charge from being too far above its MTM termination charge.

Taking into account this arbitrage constraint, a mobile operator which is forced to set a uniform termination charge for FTM and MTM traffic will have more incentive to extract termination profits through a high (common) mobile termination charge than to set a low termination charge in order to soften retail competition. This therefore provides some justification for the Competition Commission's focus on bottleneck issues, even for MTM termination charges. Nevertheless, we find that the incentive to set a high termination charge is reduced, since high charges will induce high on-net/off-net call charge differentials, which act to intensify competition for subscribers.

In addition, we discuss the implications of the substitutability of FTM and MTM calls. In this setting firms will set prices so that a mobile subscriber will prefer to call another subscriber on the same network with her mobile phone, even when she is at home and has access to her fixed line. This amplifies the impact of on-net/off-net call charge differentials and makes firms place greater weight on the danger of stimulating competition with high termination charges. The result is that firms will choose a termination charge which is closer still to the efficient level. This potential softening effect was not taken into account by the Commission at the time of the inquiry (nor was it present in the economics literature at the time).

Before developing these arguments further, though, we provide some background on the market in the UK at the time of the inquiry (see Table 3.1). At the start of 2002, the performance of the four mobile operators is summarised as follows.[7] Thus, at the time of the inquiry, the four networks were reasonably

---

[7] See Competition Commission (2003b, Table 2.1). At the time of the inquiry there were also a number of mobile virtual network operators (MVNOs), which provided some extra competition at the retail level. However, they were not permitted to set different call-termination charges from those levied by the 'host'

Table 3.1 Industry statistics (2002)

	Vodafone	O$_2$	Orange	T-Mobile
Annual turnover (£m)	3,596	2,759	3,397	2,062
Average subscriber numbers (m)	12.8	10.8	11.1	9.4
Average revenue per year per subscriber (excluding call termination)	£276	£231	£246	£202
Outgoing call minutes per year per subscriber (including on-net calls)	1,070	787	1,161	925
Incoming call minutes per year per subscriber (excluding on-net calls)	531	454	568	500

symmetrically placed. In contrast to the situation in many other countries, all four mobile networks are separately owned from the significant fixed networks.[8] In the years leading up to the inquiry, the mobile market was characterised by explosive growth. The total number of subscribers in 1997 was 7 million, whereas there were 45 million subscribers by the end of 2001. The inquiry stated, though, that 'it seems likely that there will be at best only modest further growth in customer numbers'.[9]

Prior to the Competition Commission's case, MTM call termination was not regulated by Oftel. Possibly this reflected the fact that the dominant source of termination revenue was from FTM calls. MTM termination was certainly less significant in terms of volumes. In 2000/1 72 per cent of the mobile industry's termination traffic originated on the fixed network, while the remaining 28 per cent came from rival mobile networks.[10]

Table 3.2 Average call charges

	Off-net MTM	On-net MTM	FTM	Mobile to fixed
Pence per minute	24.9	5.9	14.6	7.1

The Competition Commission (2003b, Table 6.10) reports that average retail revenue per minute for all four networks in the period 2000/1 was as in Table 3.2. This shows a striking degree of differential pricing between

network and so did not play a major role in the determination of termination charges – see Competition Commission (2003b, paras. 2.32–2.33).

[8] O$_2$ was previously owned by the dominant fixed operator, BT. However, the two companies demerged in November 2001. See Competition Commission (2003b, Chapter 5) for more details on the history and ownership structure of the four networks.

[9] See Competition Commission (2003b, paras. 2.24 and 2.28).

[10] This excluded traffic originating outside the UK. See Competition Commission (2003b, Table 6.8).

Table 3.3 Shares of types of mobile calls

	Off-net MTM	On-net MTM	Mobile to fixed
%	14.6	30.3	55.1

off-net and on-net calls.[11] As we will show, the difference between on-net and off-net prices observed at the time is difficult to reconcile with the theory. Due in part to this price differential, the volumes of off-net and on-net calls were very unbalanced and the Competition Commission (2003b, Table 6.5) reports that the share of outgoing call minutes from mobile networks in 2001/2 was as in Table 3.3. With equal off-net and on-net charges and four roughly symmetric networks, one might perhaps expect that off-net traffic would be approximately three times greater than on-net traffic, rather than only half as much as was in fact the case. As well as the price differential between on-net and off-net MTM calls, additional explanations for the high level of observed on-net calls include the presence of calling groups who call each other on the same network (for example, a company which makes its employees join the same network)[12] and the possibility of substitution between on-net MTM calls and FTM calls to take advantage of the price differentials between the different types of calls. From the prices given in Table 3.2, a mobile subscriber who calls from home should often make an on-net MTM call if the recipient is on the same mobile network and a FTM call if the recipient is on another mobile network, thereby increasing the share of MTM calls that are on-net.

The Commission distinguished between the (wholesale) market for call termination on mobile networks and the (retail) market for mobile subscribers and their outbound calls. In the former case, they concluded (para. 1.4) that each mobile network 'has a monopoly of call termination on its own network. This is because there are currently no practical technological means of terminating a call other than on the network of the [mobile network] to which the called party subscribes and none that seems likely to become commercially viable in the near future. There are also no ready substitutes for calling a mobile phone at the retail level, such as calling a fixed line instead.'

---

[11] One reason for why on-net charges appear to be so much lower than off-net charges is that, in the period before the inquiry at least, networks did not typically allow off-net calls within their bundles of inclusive calls. Competition Commission (2003b, Figure 6.8) shows how the differential between on-net and off-net MTM calls rose steeply in the period 1999 to 2002. The differential has reduced somewhat since 2002, presumably due to the reduction in termination charges since that time, although it is still substantial.

[12] See Competition Commission (2003b, paras. 2.113–2.121).

However, there was some debate in the inquiry about the competitiveness of the mobile retail market. Oftel, then the industry regulator, suggested that the retail market was not yet 'effectively competitive' and this was because 'of the room for improvement in consumer awareness of different prices and tariffs, evidence of the existence of some barriers to customers switching networks and poor levels of consumer information. Prices were above the level that would be found in an effectively competitive market; and Vodafone's return on capital employed (ROCE) had consistently, and substantially, exceeded the cost of capital.' Nevertheless, Oftel believed that the mobile sector was 'prospectively competitive'.[13] The four mobile networks argued vigorously that the retail market was competitive and that any profits from high termination charges would be competed away and passed on to their subscribers. The Competition Commission concluded (2003b, para. 2.211) that 'while there is intense competition among the [mobile networks] to attract and sign up subscribers to their networks ... there is less effective competition in call origination ... as evidenced by high margins for off-net calls, a substantial level of unused free minutes in mobile packages, and the bundling and complexity of call tariffs. All of this indicates, in our view, less than effective competition at the retail level.'

Finally, we provide data about the costs and charges for mobile call termination at the time of the inquiry. A good deal of effort by the Commission and the inquiry participants was put into estimating the costs of providing call termination, and of course much depends on the details of the accounting procedure employed – for instance, the relevant time horizon, the treatment of common and joint costs, the depreciation procedure, the cost of capital and so on. (See Competition Commission, 2003b, Chapter 7.) To cut a long story short, the Commission estimated that the long-run average incremental cost of call termination, in 2000/1 prices, was about 7.1 pence per minute in 2002 and was expected to fall to 4.1 pence per minute by 2006.[14]

The networks' termination charges varied by the time of day and week, and the Competition Commission (2003b, Table 6.13) reports the charges at the time of the inquiry to be as in Table 3.4. Note that the networks did not set

---

[13] Competition Commission (2003b, para. 2.155). However, in 2003 Oftel determined that the mobile retail market was effectively competitive – see Oftel, *Mobile Access and Call Origination Market: Identification and Analysis of Market and Determination of Market Power*, 3 October 2003.

[14] See Competition Commission (2003b, Table 2.8). These figures are for a combined 900/1800 MHz spectrum network (that is, the older networks operated by Vodafone and O_2) and include a 'market share adjustment' which was not part of Oftel's own calculations. (The Commission otherwise broadly followed Oftel's model for calculating costs.) Oftel's corresponding figures were 5 pence per minute in 2002 and 3.4 pence in 2006.

different termination charges for FTM and MTM calls. Since MTM termination charges were not regulated before the inquiry, the existing literature predicts they should have agreed to MTM termination charges that were below-cost. We will replicate this result in the benchmark model below, where in the absence of regulation networks will wish to set very different charges for the two kinds of traffic. However, we also establish, consistent with the Commission's treatment, that in many cases the welfare-maximising charges will be the same for the two kinds of calls.

Recall that the two older networks, O_2 and Vodafone, had had their FTM termination charges explicitly regulated since 1998. Both networks were required to set their average weighted termination charges no higher than 11.7 pence per minute in 1999/2000 and then to implement real cuts in these charges of 9 per cent per year for the following two years. In particular, in comparison with the estimated cost of termination in 2000/1 of 7 pence per minute, the permitted termination charge was substantially in excess of the estimated cost. Thus, the issue for the 2002 inquiry was not just that the previous control regime was expiring but also that it may have been too lax.

The newer networks, Orange and T-Mobile, were not explicitly regulated before the 2002 inquiry. However, they were informally controlled, in that Oftel indicated that if it were asked to make a determination on their FTM termination charges, it would set these to be roughly equal to those prevailing on the two regulated networks.[15] (The newer networks were allowed to charge slightly more since they used a different part of the spectrum with different cost characteristics.) As such, all networks set termination charges which were broadly similar, even though only two were formally regulated. In particular, the figures in Table 3.4 should not be regarded as an indication of what *unregulated* networks would charge. (Table 3.5 in section 2.3, however, gives some indication of this.)

Table 3.4 Termination charges in March 2001 (pence per minute)

	Daytime	Evening	Weekends
O_2	12.4	12.4	1.1
Orange	15.2	11.0	4.5
T-Mobile	16.8	10.8	2.5
Vodafone	13.2	9.8	4.7

[15] See Competition Commission (2003b, para. 2.10).

2. A benchmark model

Here we present a basic formal model of the mobile telephony industry (taken from Armstrong and Wright, 2009). We present this 'stripped-down' benchmark model to establish the basic forces in pricing and welfare. The framework contrasts the pricing of MTM termination with the pricing of FTM termination in a setting where there are no constraints (such as wholesale arbitrage and retail substitution) that force a network's two termination charges to be equal. We will compare the unregulated outcome our model predicts with the optimally regulated termination charge for each type of call.[16]

In this benchmark model we abstract away from call and network externalities. In this case, provided there is no retail margin on FTM calls, we find that welfare is maximised when both the FTM and MTM termination charges are equal to cost. Without regulation, we will see that mobile networks in this model will each wish to set an excessive FTM termination charge, while they will jointly set MTM termination charges which are too low.

To model MTM calls, a standard model of two-way interconnection between symmetric networks is adopted. In section 3 we show how the model can be extended by introducing some realistic features that help explain some empirical regularities that are inconsistent with the predictions of the benchmark model (in particular, the large observed difference between off-net and on-net call charges.) Readers who are not interested in the modelling details can skip to the discussion of the results starting in section 2.3. Two mobile networks, denoted $i = 1, 2$, are assumed to offer differentiated services. Each network charges the other a termination charge for completing its calls. Given symmetry and that the firms negotiate over these termination charges, we assume the MTM termination charge, denoted by a, is set to be the same in both directions.

For simplicity, we ignore any heterogeneity in the demand for calls.[17] Facing a per-minute charge p for calling, each subscriber will choose to make $q(p)$ minutes of calls to each other subscriber. In particular, each

---

[16]   The terms of reference for the 2002 inquiry explicitly required the Commission to consider the outcome in the absence of regulation – see Competition Commission (2003b, Appendix 1.1).

[17]   Clearly, this is a significant simplification. Indeed, the complexity of the tariffs used by mobile networks is intended in part to sort subscribers into groups with different calling patterns. The simplification is most restrictive when market expansion is considered: in the real world we expect that marginal

subscriber is equally likely to wish to call each other subscriber. Let $v(p)$ be consumer surplus associated with the demand function $q(p)$.

In addition, there is a fixed-line network, from which a demand for FTM calls is generated. As is the case with the UK industry, we assume this fixed sector is separately owned from the mobile sector. Each mobile network i chooses a termination charge A_i for completing FTM calls. In the first stage firms negotiate a reciprocal MTM interconnection price a and subsequently, in stage two, they set their FTM termination charges A_i together with their retail tariffs to mobile customers. If the retail price for FTM calls to mobile network i is P_i per minute, suppose that there are $Q(P_i)$ FTM minutes of calls to each subscriber on network i.[18] Let $V(P)$ be the consumer surplus function associated with the demand function $Q(P)$. Note in our framework, mobile-to-fixed calls and fixed-to-fixed calls play no role in the analysis, which is why we ignore them.

In general, we expect the price P_i to be an increasing function of the FTM termination charge A_i, and write $P_i = P(A_i)$. For instance, it may be that

$$P(A_i) = C + A_i, \tag{1}$$

where C is the fixed network's marginal cost of originating a call. Here, the FTM call charge is equal to the fixed network's total cost of making such calls. Such pricing could arise as a result of regulation of the fixed network or vigorous competition between fixed networks. An earlier inquiry focused on BT's FTM call charges and recommended that BT's 'retention' – its FTM call charge less the FTM termination charge payable – be directly regulated.[19] This regime expired in 2002 and after that BT's retention continued to be regulated, but within its overall retail price cap. As such, 'any reduction in termination charges by the [mobile networks] will be fully passed through one way or the other into retail prices to the [fixed network] customers, although such pass-through would not necessarily be into charges for fixed-to-mobile calls specifically' (Competition Commission, 2003b, para. 2.42).

---

subscribers are likely to have a reduced demand for calls compared with the average subscriber (although it is less clear that marginal subscribers will *receive* fewer calls than others).

[18] Notice that we assume the fixed network can set different call charges to different mobile networks to reflect the networks' different termination charges. A different modelling assumption is that the fixed network cannot set discriminatory prices, perhaps because callers do not always know which mobile network they are calling. If so, the market failures identified in the following analysis are likely to be amplified. See Gans and King (2000), Wright (2002) and Competition Commission (2003b, paras. 2.48 and 2.136) for further details.

[19] See MMC (1999a) for further details.

Each mobile firm is assumed to incur a marginal cost c_O of originating a call and a marginal cost c_T of terminating a call, so the actual marginal cost of an MTM call is $c_O + c_T$ while the actual cost of an FTM call is $C + c_T$. In addition, there is a fixed cost f of serving each mobile subscriber, which includes the subscriber's handset, billing costs and so on. For now, assume that FTM and MTM calls are independent markets and that the call charge for one call type does not affect the demand for the other call type.

In this basic model, we assume there is an exogenously fixed number of mobile subscribers, which we normalise to 1. Denote firm i's on-net MTM call charge by $\hat{p}_i$ and its off-net MTM call charge by p_i. In addition, the firm charges a fixed (rental) charge r_i for subscribing. If firm i's market share of subscribers is s_i, its subscribers make a fraction s_i of their calls on-net and the remaining $1 - s_i$ calls off-net. Therefore, a subscriber's utility if she joins network i is[20]

$$u_i = s_i v(\hat{p}_i) + (1 - s_i)v(p_i) - r_i. \tag{2}$$

If we assume a Hotelling specification for subscriber choice, the market share of network i given the pair of utilities u_i and u_j is

$$s_i = \frac{1}{2} + \frac{u_i - u_j}{2t}, \tag{3}$$

where t is the 'transport cost' parameter which represents the degree of product differentiation in the market for mobile subscribers.[21]

Network i's profit is then

$$\pi_i = s_i \times \left[\underbrace{r_i - f + s_i(\hat{p}_i - c_O - c_T)q(\hat{p}_i) + (1 - s_i)(p_i - c_O - a)q(p_i)}_{\text{retail services}} \right.$$

$$\left. + \underbrace{(1 - s_i)(a - c_T)q(p)}_{\text{MTM termination}} + \underbrace{F(A_i)}_{\text{FTM termination}} \right], \tag{4}$$

---

[20] In this analysis, as with the assumption of differential FTM pricing, we are probably being over-optimistic about the extent to which subscribers are aware of price differences in off-net and on-net calls. For instance, see Competition Commission (2003b, para. 2.136) for evidence that only a small fraction of subscribers were likely to know whether they were calling a mobile phone on the same network as themselves or not. On the other hand, Table 3.3 suggests that subscribers do respond to these price differentials.

[21] We assume networks are sufficiently differentiated so that problems of equilibrium inexistence do not arise.

where

$$F(A) \equiv (A - c_T)Q(P(A)) \tag{5}$$

is the per-subscriber profit from providing FTM call termination. The overall profit π_i consists of the retail profit from supplying service to its subscribers, the profit from providing termination for the rival mobile network and the profit from providing termination for the fixed network.

2.1 Fixed-to-mobile call termination

From expression (4), it is clear each mobile network will set its FTM termination charge A_i to maximise its profits from FTM call termination, $F(\cdot)$. This is a dominant strategy for each network, regardless of the choices for retail tariffs and the MTM termination charge. It is clear from (4) that $F(\cdot)$ acts as a per-subscriber subsidy to a mobile network and a network will always want to maximise this subsidy (just as it would like to reduce its cost per subscriber, f). This situation, in which the equilibrium termination charge is equal to the monopoly charge even though there is competition for subscribers, is an example of the competitive bottleneck referred to in the introduction. The result does not depend on the competitiveness of the market for subscribers (as measured by t). Even if the market for mobile subscribers is highly competitive, each operator maintains a monopoly position with respect to FTM call termination.

How does this unregulated level of A compare with the efficient level? Suppose social welfare is measured as the unweighted sum of consumer surplus and profit.[22] When there are no call or network externalities, welfare (as measured by the sum of consumer surplus and profit) in the FTM segment when the termination charge is A is

$$\underbrace{V(P(A))}_{\text{consumer surplus}} + \underbrace{F(A)}_{\text{FTM termination profit}} + \underbrace{[P(A) - C - A]Q(P(A))}_{\text{retail profit by fixed network}}. \tag{6}$$

This is maximised by choosing A to equate the retail price of FTM calls $P(A)$ to their actual cost $C + c_T$. In the particular case in which the FTM call charge is

---

[22] However, some of the mobile operators appeared to view the objective of policy to be to maximise mobile subscriber numbers or the number of calls involving mobiles – see Competition Commission (2003b, para. 2.404), for instance.

equal to the fixed network's call cost, so that (1) holds, welfare is maximised with an FTM termination charge equal to cost, so that $A = c_T$. On the other hand, if $P(A) > C + c_T$ then welfare would be maximised by setting $A < c_T$ to counteract the markup present in the FTM call charge.

2.2 Mobile-to-mobile call termination

Suppose that the FTM termination charge is set at some level A (which could be at the monopoly level, the efficient level or any other level) and the MTM termination charge is set at a. Using standard arguments detailed in Armstrong and Wright (2009) one can show in equilibrium each network will set its on-net call charge $\hat{p}$ and its off-net call charge p equal to perceived marginal cost, so that

$$\hat{p} = c_O + c_T; \quad p = c_O + a \tag{7}$$

and call charges are not distorted.[23] Each network offers subscribers the greatest surplus by pricing calls at its perceived marginal cost, then competes through the fixed rental charge, r.

Analogously to $F(A)$ in (5), write

$$M(a) \equiv (a - c_T)q(c_O + a) \tag{8}$$

for the profit from providing MTM termination. From (4) and the call charges in (7), network i's profit is

$$\pi_i = s_i \times [r_i - f + (1 - s_i)M(a) + F(A)]. \tag{9}$$

Expression (3) implies that firm i's market share s_i satisfies

$$s_i = \frac{1}{2} + \frac{r_j - r_i + (2s_i - 1)(\hat{v} - v)}{2t},$$

where $\hat{v} = v(c_O + c_T)$ and $v = (c_O + a)$. Solving this explicitly in terms of s_i implies that

$$s_i = \frac{1}{2} - \frac{r_i - r_j}{2t - 2(\hat{v} - v)}. \tag{10}$$

---

[23] Expression (7) is at odds with a strange statement made by the Commission (Competition Commission, 2003b, para. 2.50): 'Changes in mobile-to-mobile termination charges do not affect the aggregate finances of the industry as a whole, and for this reason may prima facie be expected to have no effect on [the mobile networks'] retail prices.'

Substituting (10) into (9), maximising with respect to r_i and setting $r_i = r_j$ shows that the equilibrium rental charge is given by

$$r = f + t - F(A) - (\hat{v} - v).$$ (11)

Substituting (11) into (9) shows that industry profit in the mobile sector, denoted Π, is

$$\Pi = t + \frac{M(a)}{2} - (\hat{v} - v).$$ (12)

In particular, in this benchmark model the FTM termination profit $F(A)$ has no impact on equilibrium profits in the mobile sector and collectively firms should not object to regulatory policy that lowers A to cost for all operators. This is because, although a lower A may result in a lower profit from FTM termination, it is exactly balanced by a reduced ability to raise the rental charge (see expression (11)).

   In contrast, the mobile networks do care about the level of the MTM termination charge and they are jointly better off with a low MTM termination charge. Recall that the off-net call charge p in (7) depends on a. Without regulation, and given the collective negotiation of the mutual termination charge, the industry will choose a to maximise (12). This is achieved when

$$a = c_T + \frac{q(p)}{q'(p)} < c_T,$$ (13)

which is below the cost of termination, c_T. Note that if the difference between on-net and off-net surplus $(\hat{v} - v)$ increases, this tends to reduce equilibrium rental charges and industry profits (expressions (11) and (12)). The reason is found in the fight for market share. The intuition for this is subtle and provided in section 2.3. In contrast, the efficient termination charge is $a = c_T$, just as with FTM termination. Through (7) this delivers the socially optimal MTM retail prices, for both on-net and off-net calls, which are equal to cost $c_O + c_T$. In summary, in this benchmark model the optimal regulatory policy treats the two termination charges symmetrically, but absent regulation the firms will choose an MTM termination charge which is too low and an FTM termination charge which is too high.

2.3 Discussion

Given that mobile firms choose their FTM termination charges unilaterally, it is a dominant strategy for them to set their charges equal to the monopoly level (that is, the termination charge that would be chosen by a monopoly mobile network). This maximises the subsidy a firm receives from each subscriber it attracts to join its network. Indeed, a firm would be at a competitive disadvantage if it chose a lower FTM termination charge while its rival set the monopoly charge, since its rival would then have greater ability to attract subscribers. However, we find this monopoly pricing at the whole-sale level need not lead to any excessive overall profit for mobile operators. Essentially, this subsidy is competed away through the competition for sub-scribers at the retail level.

The high levels of the FTM termination charge predicted by this model were quantified in the 2002 inquiry. For instance, Oftel stated that 'it was quite possible that the profit-maximising [FTM termination charge] would be substantially above the current level, possibly exceeding 20 ppm'. Vodafone stated that the unregulated level was in the range 17 ppm to 20 ppm. At the time these estimates were given, the cap on O_2 and Vodafone's termination charge was 9.3 ppm, so Vodafone was suggesting that the FTM termination charge would roughly double without the charge control.[24]

That high FTM termination charges do not ultimately increase the profits of mobile networks also implies that if regulation squeezes out excess FTM call-termination profit, this will lead to price rises (here, in terms of higher rentals) for mobile subscribers.[25] (From expression (11), the rental charge increases by an amount equal to the fall in FTM termination revenue, F.) This result is sometimes termed the 'waterbed' effect: if one source of a network's per-subscriber profit is reduced (for example, by regulation), that will cause the networks to compete less hard for subscribers and the overall impact of the profit reduction is mitigated or eliminated altogether. In this basic model, there is a '100 per cent' waterbed effect, in that reduced profits from one

---

[24] See Competition Commission (2003b, paras. 2.440–2.445). Somewhat implausibly, the other three mobile networks claimed that they would not raise their termination charges if the charge control was lifted.

[25] The Competition Commission (2003b, para. 1.13(b)) did not expect retail prices to rise if call termination charges were reduced by regulation: 'The [mobile networks] need not increase their retail prices to restore revenue lost through the capping of termination charges, as their business plans project a continued downward trend in retail prices and they could recoup these revenues by reducing the rate of retail price reductions for a period.' Nevertheless, the main point, that reducing the profits from call termination is likely to lead to higher retail prices than would otherwise be the case, remains.

source are completely clawed back from subscribers so that the overall profit impact is zero.[26]

Nevertheless, the four mobile networks *did*, in broad terms, object to the proposed reduction in the FTM termination charge, which suggests that this basic model with a 100 per cent waterbed effect fails to capture important aspects of the real-world market. Alternative ways of modelling competition for subscribers might lead to a smaller waterbed effect.[27] For instance, allowing for market expansion possibilities when there is incomplete mobile penetration implies that mobile firms may collectively prefer a higher rather than a lower FTM termination charge. This issue is taken up in the appendix of Armstrong and Wright (2009), which extends the model above to allow for network externalities and market expansion. Although this does not mitigate a mobile network's incentive to choose the monopoly FTM termination charge (when this is set separately from MTM termination charges), it does explain why mobile operators would collectively oppose lowering the FTM termination charge from the monopoly level given the waterbed effect is no longer 100 per cent. It also implies that the efficient FTM termination charge is above cost, although still below the monopoly level. A high FTM termination charge leads to low rental charges (through the waterbed effect), which in turn leads to more people to subscribe to mobile networks. These additional mobile subscribers benefit all users (fixed and mobile) who wish to call them.

A feature of the waterbed effect is that unregulated monopoly profits from FTM call termination are passed on to mobile subscribers in the form of low rental charges (for example, free handsets and the like). To the extent this occurs, the market failure associated with FTM termination does not lead to excessive profits by mobile networks, but rather to a sub-optimal balance of prices. Of course, this observation should not affect the welfare analysis: if high margins on FTM call termination lead to negative margins on services to mobile subscribers, there is allocative inefficiency regardless of whether overall profits in the mobile sector are excessive or not.[28] Relatedly, mobile firms 'advanced the argument that, because most people had a mobile phone, what

---

[26] In a panel data study, Genakos and Valletti (2007) uncover a strong long-run waterbed effect resulting from regulated changes in termination charges.

[27] See the discussion in Competition Commission (2003b, pages 292–294).

[28] Competition Commission (2003b, para. 1.8(d)) noted that 'the excess charges for termination have the further effect that they serve to encourage or facilitate significant distortions in competition because [mobile networks] are not obliged to charge and subscribers are not obliged to pay the economic cost of handsets. This leads to the undervaluation of mobile phone handsets by the … customers combined with a greater turnover ('churn') than would take place if customers paid charges which reflected the proper valuation of such handsets.'

they lost in high termination charges they gained in low access and outbound call charges'.[29] However, even if *all* fixed-line subscribers also had a mobile phone, this argument is flawed: since high termination charges lead to allocative inefficiency, the total 'size of the cake' is shrunk and the gain to subscribers from handset subsidies and the like is *smaller* than the harm to them caused by high FTM call charges.[30]

A somewhat related point was made by several mobile networks, which is that their tariffs would approximate 'Ramsey' prices in the absence of regulation.[31] The argument is that networks offer subscribers a bundle of services, including inbound and outbound calls, in return for a specified tariff. Competition between networks forces them to offer subscribers the best deal consistent with the networks earning a reasonable profit. (Prices which maximise aggregate consumer surplus subject to the firm earning a reasonable profit are termed Ramsey prices.) One half of this argument is perfectly valid: if the retail market is reasonably competitive, then we expect firms to compete by offering a tariff package which tends to maximise their subscribers' surplus subject to achieving reasonable profit. However, the argument completely ignores the fact that mobile subscribers do not pay for their incoming calls (or choose the volume of such calls); that is to say, competition may well ensure that networks maximise their subscribers' surplus, but it ignores the consumer surplus of callers from the fixed network to mobile subscribers. Indeed, without regulation, competition *forces* the mobile networks to exploit fixed callers in order to be able to attract mobile subscribers. There is no reason at all to expect that, in the absence of regulation, the structure of outbound and inbound call charges will approximate Ramsey prices.[32]

The logic for why symmetric mobile networks set excessive FTM termination charges also applies to asymmetric mobile networks. A small network will set a monopoly FTM termination charge in exactly the same way as a network with many subscribers.[33] Any asymmetric regulation of firms is therefore likely to handicap larger (and possibly more efficient) networks. An illustration of what can happen if one firm receives favourable regulatory treatment is

---

[29] See Competition Commission (2003b, paras. 2.390–2.400).

[30] The Competition Commission (2003b, paras. 2.550–2.558) suggests that the impact on overall welfare (that is, consumer surplus plus profit) of the proposed reduction in termination charges is of the order of £325–700 million over the period of the proposed regulation.

[31] See Competition Commission (2003b, paras. 2.429–2.446).

[32] This basic market failure was understood and acknowledged by at least Vodafone. (See Competition Commission, 2003b, paras. 2.80 and 2.107.)

[33] To the extent that FTM callers do not know the identity of the network they are calling, a small network may have an even greater incentive to set excessive FTM termination charges.

given in Table 3.5, where the figures (in pence per minute) state the (now) five mobile networks' termination charges in March 2006.[34]

Table 3.5 The impact of regulation on termination charges

	Daytime	Evening	Weekends
O$_2$	6.4	6.3	3.1
Orange	7.6	5.4	4.3
T-Mobile	8.1	4.0	4.0
Vodafone	8.5	3.4	2.8
H3G	**15.6**	**10.8**	**2.5**

At around the time of the 2002 inquiry there was a fifth entrant, H3G, whose termination charges in 2006 were controlled less stringently. As is clear, on weekdays at least, this firm took advantage of its less regulated position to set charges which were roughly double those levied by its regulated rivals. This higher termination revenue meant H3G received a greater subsidy from each of its subscribers than its rivals. In addition, high profits from completing calls gave the network a strong incentive to encourage its subscribers to receive calls. For instance, in January 2006 H3G announced that it would *pay* its subscribers 5 pence per minute for receiving calls.

In contrast to the incentives for mobile operators to set high FTM termination charges, we saw in (13) that their incentive for a negotiated MTM termination charge was to set it below-cost. For instance, networks may coordinate on a 'bill-and-keep' solution, in which they agree to terminate each other's calls for no charge. (Gans and King, 2001, were the first to establish that this might be optimal behaviour.) In contrast, the efficient MTM termination charge is equal to the marginal cost of terminating calls, at which point both on-net and off-net prices will equal cost.[35]

Unlike the bottleneck result obtained for FTM termination, where monopoly pricing was a dominant strategy, the reason for setting low prices for MTM termination is subtle. Unless firms set a termination charge below-cost, call charges (see (7) above) will mean it is more expensive to make an off-net call than an on-net call. This makes subscribers prefer to join a larger network

---

[34] Taken from Figure 1 in Ofcom (2006).

[35] Allowing for network externalities and market expansion, in Armstrong and Wright (2009) we show above-cost MTM termination charges are efficient. High MTM termination charges act to intensify competition between mobile operators due to stronger network effects. High MTM termination charges are therefore a means by which to transfer surplus from mobile networks to their subscribers, which expands the number of mobile subscribers, creating positive externalities for other fixed and mobile users.

so they can then make a larger fraction of their calls at the cheaper rate. In other words, the market will exhibit (positive) network effects. In such markets, retail competition is particularly fierce and profits are low, as the gain to attracting subscribers from one's rival is greater than normal. By setting a termination charge below-cost, so that off-net call charges are below on-net charges, firms can reverse this effect, leading to negative network effects. In this case, subscribers will, all else equal, prefer to join the smaller network, which acts to relax retail competition.

While policymakers have taken seriously the market failure to do with high FTM termination charges, they do not seem to have been concerned about the possibility of MTM termination charges being set too low.[36] This is despite there being some historical examples, such as in France and New Zealand, where mobile operators did use the bill-and-keep system. However, in both France and New Zealand, the low MTM termination charges were short lived. For whatever reason (and we will discuss some possible reasons in the next section), each mobile operator decided instead to set their FTM and MTM termination charges at a uniform level. Thus, there are some aspects of reality that the benchmark model is not able to adequately explain.

3. Extensions

In this section we explore the extent to which various extensions to the base model above can help better explain some of the puzzles highlighted in the previous discussion, thereby bridging the gap between the Competition Commission's view of the main market failures and the benchmark theory model.

Externalities arising from benefits of receiving calls you do not pay for. One puzzle discussed above is the relatively high off-net prices compared with on-net prices for MTM calls. One way to explain this is to allow for the fact mobile subscribers benefit from receiving calls. Allowing for such receiver benefits also allows us to address a claim made by the mobile networks in the 2002 inquiry – that the existence of these receiver benefits will help solve the bottleneck problem arising from FTM calls.

---

[36] Indeed, the Competition Commission (2003b, para. 2.51) states that if call traffic between mobile networks is balanced (as it is in our model), 'the finances of the individual [mobile networks] would be unaffected whatever the level of mobile-to-mobile termination charges, except perhaps at extremes far beyond any level discussed in this report'. This conclusion would be correct in our model only if on-net and off-net price discrimination was absent (but Table 3.2 shows very clearly that it is present).

Specifically, assume a mobile subscriber obtains a linear benefit $BQ + bq$ if she receives Q calls from the fixed network and q calls from the mobile networks. Here B and b measure the strength of the respective call externalities. The impact of call externalities on the choice of the FTM termination charge is relatively straightforward to explain. Without call externalities, unregulated firms would like to choose an FTM termination charge A to maximise $F(A)$, but with the externality B, firms would like to choose A to maximise $BQ(P(A)) + F(A)$. As a result, the unregulated FTM termination charge will be lower than without call externalities. If a network sets a high FTM termination charge, this will reduce the volume of calls received by its subscribers from the fixed network and hence reduce the attractiveness of its network to subscribers. Taking this into account, each operator's profit-maximising FTM termination charge will be lower. So, as emphasised by the networks in the 2002 inquiry, call externalities do mitigate a network's incentive to set high FTM termination charges.[37]

On the other hand, welfare in the FTM segment is as in (6), plus the additional externality term $BQ(P(A))$. This is maximised by setting a termination charge so that fixed-line callers face an FTM price equal to the true marginal cost of their calls, adjusted to take account of the impact of their calls on mobile recipients. That is, the socially optimal FTM termination charge solves $P(A) = C + c_T - B$. When (1) holds, welfare is maximised with an FTM termination charge below marginal cost: $A = c_T - B$. In summary, when mobile subscribers obtain benefits from receiving calls from the fixed network, this causes both the unregulated termination charge and the welfare-maximising termination charge to fall. As such, the presence of such externalities does not diminish the potential need to regulate these termination charges.

Turning next to the MTM termination charge, in the specific model analysed one can show that when this charge is set equal to a, each network sets its on-net price $\hat{p}$ and off-net price p in the following manner:

$$\hat{p} = c_O + c_T - b; \quad p = c_O + a + \frac{1}{K-1}\,b, \tag{14}$$

where K is the number of competing mobile networks. (See Armstrong and Wright (2007a) for the full analysis using a K-firm generalisation of the Hotelling duopoly demand framework.) The on-net retail call charge is set efficiently, equal to a network's cost for the call, adjusted downwards to reflect the call externality its subscribers enjoy from being called more often by others

---

[37] For instance, see Competition Commission (2003b, para. 2.109).

on the same network. In contrast, the off-net call charge p is equal to a network's cost for the call adjusted *upwards* to reflect the fact that when its subscribers make fewer calls to subscribers on rival networks, call externalities imply that its rivals' abilities to compete are harmed and this benefits the original network. This represents an anticompetitive motive to set high off-net retail call charges.[38]

Expression (14) helps to explain why off-net MTM retail prices are higher than on-net prices. In fact, such a differential arises even if MTM termination charges are set at cost. Nevertheless, it is still not easy to reconcile the predicted prices in (14) with the actual, rather extreme, differences reported in Table 3.2. Even if termination charges exceed cost c_T by 5 pence per minute, which is roughly what the Competition Commission concluded at the time of the inquiry, to obtain a difference between p and $\hat{p}$ of nearly 20 pence per minute with four firms would require a call externality of an implausible size (around 11 pence per minute), a size which would probably make $\hat{p}$ in (14) negative. In the inquiry, the mobile networks themselves did not provide compelling reasons for why they set such different prices[39] and so it remains something of a puzzle why such an extreme pattern of prices was observed at the time.[40]

What about the industry's profit-maximising choice of MTM termination charge in the presence of call externalities? One can show that networks will choose a to make off-net call charges equal to

$$p = c_O + c_T - \frac{K}{K-1}b + \frac{1}{K-1}\frac{q(p)}{q'(p)}. \tag{15}$$

As in the benchmark model, this call charge is below the welfare-maximising off-net call charge, which (like the on-net call charge) is here equal to $c_O + c_T - b$. In particular, if mobile operators set their termination charges in this way, then the predicted off-net retail call charge p is still below the corresponding on-net charge ($\hat{p} = c_O + c_T - b$), which is again at odds with real-world observation (as in Table 3.2 above).

Another possible reason why existing operators prefer high MTM termination charges is that high charges may deter entry or induce exit of a smaller

---

[38] In fact, the inquiry barely discussed call externalities at all – see Competition Commission (2003b, paras. 8.257–8.260). But it is beyond doubt that call externalities are significant, since why else would anyone leave their mobile phone turned on to receive calls?

[39] See Competition Commission (2003, paras. 2.124–2.125).

[40] Using more recent data from 2005, Armstrong and Wright (2007a) find that observed price differentials are consistent with the theory presented above provided receiver benefits are between 0.75 pence and 4.5 pence per minute, which is more plausible.

rival. By setting above-cost MTM termination charges, the incumbent networks can induce network effects which make entry less attractive for the newcomer. With high MTM termination charges, off-net calls will be more expensive, which particularly hurts a small network since the bulk of its subscribers' calls will be off-net.[41] An additional effect of high off-net call prices will be to reduce the number of calls subscribers receive from the small network's subscribers, thereby further reducing its ability to compete when call externalities are important.[42]

Uniform termination charges. One way to alter the model to resolve this remaining puzzle (that unregulated MTM termination charges are chosen to be below the efficient level) is to take into account the strong possibility that firms are forced to set the same charge for terminating both FTM and MTM traffic. For instance, a mobile operator may not be able to maintain a high FTM termination charge together with a low MTM termination charge, since the fixed network could then 'transit' its calls via another mobile operator and so end up paying the lower MTM rate (plus a small transit charge). As a result, a mobile operator may be forced to set (approximately) a uniform termination charge for FTM and MTM traffic. For instance, this seems to be the reason why mobile operators abandoned bill-and-keep in the examples of France and New Zealand, where they switched to uniform FTM and MTM termination charges. An alternative explanation is that, fearing their FTM termination charges would be regulated to the same low level that they had chosen for their MTM termination charges, they adopted MTM charges that were the same as their higher FTM termination charges.

Regardless of the reason, here we consider the implications of mobile networks having to set uniform termination charges. In this case it is also natural to model the mobile networks setting these uniform charges unilaterally in the absence of regulation. The analysis of such a model is more complex than the benchmark model, and details are given in Armstrong and Wright (2009). There we find that when network i raises its uniform termination charge it benefits from the usual increase in termination revenue (which is now generated both from FTM callers and off-net MTM callers). This alone would lead network i to choose the monopoly termination charge (that is, the same uniform charge that a monopoly mobile network would set). However,

---

[41] Calzada and Valletti (2008) formally demonstrate that incumbent networks will sometimes use high MTM termination charges to deter entry.

[42] Hoernig (2007) analyses the impact of on-net and off-net price differentials on the profitability of small networks in the presence of call externalities. He shows that larger firms will choose greater differentials than smaller firms.

network i also benefits by raising its rival's off-net call charge, which places its rival at a competitive disadvantage compared with firm i. Together, this suggests network i would like to set its uniform termination charge above the monopoly level. However, setting a high termination charge amplifies the differential pricing between on-net and off-net calls in the market which, as we argued in section 2, tends to intensify competition for subscribers through the creation of positive network effects. Thus, mobile operators will avoid setting termination charges too high. In Armstrong and Wright (2009) we find this last effect dominates the 'raising rivals' cost' effect, so that the net incentive is to set termination charges that are below the monopoly level, although still above the efficient level.

In contrast to the case where mobile networks were able to jointly choose an MTM termination charge separately from their unilaterally set FTM termination charges (where the danger was that firms would choose too low a charge), this result suggests the more intuitive danger is that the charge will be too high. Despite this, the result implies the competitive bottleneck result found in section 2 for FTM calls is softened to some extent. This, together with the result that the efficient termination charge will be above cost due to network externalities, casts some doubt on our conclusion from the basic model that the unregulated termination charge will necessarily be set too high.

This is likely to be particularly the case if mobile networks could be forced to collectively agree on a uniform FTM and MTM termination charge. With the termination charge set collectively, the incentive to raise the rival's off-net call charge to put it at a competitive disadvantage is absent and this lowers the level of the termination charge which will be chosen. In Armstrong and Wright (2009) we give an example where negotiations can result in the networks choosing an inefficiently low termination charge. Thus, forcing the networks to collectively negotiate a uniform FTM and MTM termination charge may be a way, as an alternative to regulating the level of termination charges directly, to bring these charges down.[43]

Substitution between fixed and mobile calls. These insights are strengthened further when we consider the case in which subscribers who have both a mobile phone and a fixed line can substitute an MTM call for an FTM call. Where MTM calls are cheaper than FTM calls (for instance, Table 3.2 suggests this was likely to be the case for on-net calls), then

---

[43] Interestingly, in the 2002 Competition Commission inquiry Vodafone suggested that MTM termination should not be explicitly regulated but rather that firms should be required to enter into bilateral negotiations over this termination charge (implying that this was not already happening). See Competition Commission (2003b, para. 2.473).

mobile subscribers who are considering making an FTM call (for example, because they are at home) to someone on the same network may wish to make the call with their mobile phone instead. In Armstrong and Wright (2009) we consider how the previous analysis is modified in the presence of such demand-side arbitrage. There we find that FTM to MTM substitution helps to further reduce the incentive mobile networks have to set inflated termination charges. Given FTM and MTM termination charges are set at a uniform level, the only plausible substitution is between FTM calls and on-net calls.[44] By increasing the importance of on-net calls, this substitution raises the relative importance of positive network effects when operators set high termination charges. To avoid these (and the resulting strengthening of retail competition), operators will set lower termination charges. This possibility does not seem to have been recognised in the 2002 inquiry (or in the wider economics literature from that time).

4. Conclusion

After its detailed investigation, the Competition Commission concluded that the four mobile networks should each be subject to two termination charge caps, set at the same level: one to control FTM termination charges and one to control MTM termination charges.[45] The cap on average termination charges (separate for the two kinds of termination) for the combined 900/1800 MHz spectrum networks (that is, Vodafone and O_2) was set at 9 pence per minute for 2002/3 and falling (sharply) to 4.7 pence per minute in 2005/6, all measured in 2002/3 prices. In particular, networks were permitted to set different termination charges for FTM and MTM traffic, but these would each be controlled.

The Commission's decision to regulate both termination charges seems consistent with the economic models we have presented. While there is a coherent economic rationale for setting the FTM termination charge above cost in order to boost mobile penetration rates, it is probably also true that the benefits of subsidising mobile subscribers with inflated FTM call

---

[44] Where the actual cost of FTM calls is less than on-net MTM calls, this substitution can give rise to its own inefficiency. For instance, with the call charges in Table 3.2, it is plausible that mobile subscribers make too many on-net calls relative to FTM calls. In the inquiry (Competition Commission, 2003b, paras. 2.408 and 2.424), BT raised the issue that high FTM termination charges acted to distort competition between FTM and (probably more costly) on-net MTM calls.

[45] See Competition Commission (2003b, para. 2.578 and Table 2.12). The four networks were treated roughly symmetrically, with some small differences to reflect differences in spectrum allocation.

charges decline as mobile penetration levels off. The downward path of termination charges prescribed by the Commission is consistent with this view.

While the benchmark theoretical model we presented indicates a danger of mobile networks agreeing to set MTM termination charges which are inefficiently low, such models assumed that mobile firms could negotiate agreements with each other to set these low termination charges and maintain them at much lower levels than their FTM charges. In other, more realistic situations (such as when the FTM and MTM termination charges must be set at a uniform level), there is a plausible danger of inefficiently high MTM termination charges. It appears that the Commission put more weight on the latter possibility, and it placed a ceiling, not a floor, on MTM charges. After the event, it appears its judgment was correct: since the report the mobile networks have set a uniform termination charge for both FTM and MTM traffic and there is no evidence that they have attempted to negotiate low MTM charges.

After the Commission's decision (in January 2003), several of the mobile networks appealed against the ruling. However, the High Court rejected the appeals in June 2003 and the Commission's judgment was implemented. Soon afterwards, European policy required Ofcom (the new UK combined telecommunications and broadcasting regulator set up in 2003) to revisit policy towards mobile call termination. Ofcom conducted a review of the voice call-termination market and concluded in June 2004 that regulation of the form suggested by the Commission was still required.

The sector continues to be highly controversial. The fifth mobile operator, H3G, had entered the market well before the June 2004 statement by Ofcom, but Ofcom did not choose to regulate its termination charges (although Ofcom did determine that H3G had significant market power in call termination). H3G has since claimed in appeal that it does not have significant market power, arguing that BT has 'countervailing buyer power'. (Nevertheless, Table 3.5 above suggests that H3G is nevertheless able to set high termination charges.) This issue is legally complex and still unresolved.[46] In addition, regulation currently applies only to voice services and termination charges for text (SMS) services are not controlled. Most of the MTM issues discussed here also apply to text messages, which are an increasingly important and profitable part of the mobile market, and it may be necessary in the future to examine the efficiency of termination charges for these newer services.[47]

---

[46] See Ofcom (2006) for more detail.

[47] SMS termination charges are already controlled in France and Israel, for instance. Ofcom announced that it planned to review the market for SMS termination in 2007/8 – see Ofcom, *Wholesale SMS Termination Market Review*, 13 September 2006.

Acknowledgements

We are grateful to David Harbord, Bruce Lyons, Paul Muysert, David Sappington, John Vickers and Helen Weeds for helpful comments. Armstrong gratefully acknowledges the support of the Economic and Social Research Council (UK) and Wright gratefully acknowledges the support of the Singapore Ministry of Education AcRF Tier 1 fund under Grant No. R122000080-101/112/133.

4 Relationship between buyer and seller power in retailing: UK supermarkets (2000)

Paul W. Dobson

1. Introduction

In October 2000, the UK Competition Commission (CC) reported on its fifteen-month 'supermarkets' market investigation.[1] This monopoly inquiry examined the supply of groceries from multiple stores (specifically supermarkets in chains of ten or more outlets with store sales areas greater than 600 sq. metres), looking at both the procurement side and retailing side of the sector.[2]

While by no means the first investigation of this sector,[3] the 2000 report issued by the CC turned out to be a watershed in respect of the depth and type of analysis for a sector-wide inquiry in the UK. This included detailed analysis of the geographic and product/service dimensions of the relevant economic markets and examining in considerable detail the structure, behaviour and performance of these markets using relatively sophisticated empirical methods.

A notable feature of the inquiry was the examination of circumstances when oligopolistic firms hold both buyer and seller power but no single firm holds a dominant position. Thus, the inquiry allowed for consideration of how the two forms of power can interact and how they may individually and in combination affect competition at successive stages of a supply chain. It is this relationship between retailer buyer and seller power that is the main theme of

---

[1] All case references are to Competition Commission (2000a).

[2] The author provided independent evidence to the inquiry and attended a hearing and his research is cited as background to the inquiry – see Competition Commission (2000b, paras. 15.550–15.552 and 3.13).

[3] For instance, an earlier inquiry looked at the general issue of discounts to retailers (Monopolies and Mergers Commission, 1981). In addition, prior to the CC investigation, the Office of Fair Trading commissioned a number of reports to examine specific competition aspects relevant to grocery retailing – see Dobson and Waterson (1996), Dobson, Waterson and Chu (1998) and London Economics (1997). In addition, the European Commission had commissioned research on buyer power in grocery retailing across the EU – see Dobson Consulting (1999) and summaries of this work in Clarke *et al.* (2002) and Dobson *et al.* (2001).

this review of the CC's findings and policy recommendations, which centres on the leading retailers' pricing practices and relations with suppliers and their consequences for market outcomes.[4]

This case review is organised as follows. The next section sets out the background to the inquiry and the key economic issues for consideration. Section 3 looks at market definition and concentration levels, examining the CC's determination of the geographic and product/service scope of markets and the resulting evidence on market concentration levels. Section 4 examines retailers' pricing behaviour, considering their general pricing policies and the use of specific practices that may adversely affect competition. Section 5 reviews the evidence on retailer buyer power, looking at the extent to which the major supermarket chains enjoy superior terms (in respect of larger discounts) from suppliers than smaller retailers as well as the terms and conditions that retailers place on suppliers that may have competition-distorting effects. Section 6 considers whether, in the absence of intervention, the interaction of retailer buyer and seller power puts in train a process by which the sector will inevitably become more concentrated over time, with large retailers gaining at the expense of small retailers, and what implications such a process would have for consumers. Section 7 provides a brief summary and conclusion.

2. Case background and key economic issues

Grocery purchases through supermarkets represent a sizeable proportion of consumers' total expenditure on retail goods. Indeed, in the UK, supermarkets account for around two-fifths of all retail spending by consumers. Accordingly, for consumers, the levels of prices, choice, quality and innovation they face, in respect of the goods and service provided by supermarkets, take on considerable importance. Weak or ineffective competition in the sector has the potential for causing significant consumer welfare loss in absolute terms. Not surprisingly, then, this is a sector constantly in the public eye and in which any developments that might lessen competition are subject to close scrutiny.

---

[4] This focus comes at the necessary expense of this case review not covering all of the key issues addressed in the CC's report. In particular, the review omits to discuss the CC's detailed analysis of international price comparisons, store costs and firms' financial performance, along with the range of social and environmental issues covered, all of which significantly added to the CC's report in providing a suitably rounded and comprehensive picture of the sector.

In the late 1990s, the broad concern about the sector was the extent to which it had become concentrated. While no single firm could be construed as holding a dominant or monopoly position, the leading retailers appeared to be gaining ever-stronger market positions at the expense of smaller retailers. Thus, while by 1998 there were still some twenty-four multiple grocery retailers operating in the UK, the top five controlled around three-quarters of UK sales through supermarkets, with consequent concerns about whether growing retailer market power might be working (or expected to work) against the public interest.

At the time, there were specific concerns that suggested competition might not be especially effective. In particular, public and media interest focused on three aspects:

- alleged high grocery prices in the UK compared with other countries;
- accusations of grocery multiples profiteering (based on apparent disparity between farm-gate and retail prices);
- concerns about large out-of-town supermarkets contributing to the decay of the high street in many towns.

The Office of Fair Trading in investigating these concerns also identified further competition concerns of its own related to barriers to entry (arising from the nature of the business, the strategic behaviour of firms and institutional restrictions), land prices for supermarket developments (driven up as a consequence of the restrictive UK planning regime limiting available land), focused competition (whereby not all products sold were found to be subject to the same level and intensity of competition) and retailer buyer power over suppliers. On the basis of these concerns, in April 1999, the Director General of Fair Trading used the monopoly provisions of the Fair Trading Act 1973 to make a referral to the CC for a full-scale monopoly investigation of the sector.

The terms of the referral provided the CC with a sufficiently broad remit to examine a very wide set of competition and public interest issues relating to the operation and performance of multiple-store retailers selling grocery products.[5] For the purpose of this case study, though, we focus on the relationship between buyer and seller power and consider the following key economic issues addressed directly or indirectly by the CC's investigation:

---

[5] See Competition Commission (2000a, Chapter 3). The Fair Trading Act's requirements were for investigations based on assessing the implications for the 'public interest', a somewhat broader test than current UK competition law, notably the Enterprise Act 2002, focused simply on consumer welfare.

- What levels of market share are required for firms to be in a position where they can exercise strong buyer and seller power? Are these levels different for seller and buyer power?
- How might pricing behaviour extend and exploit seller power to the detriment of consumers?
- How is buyer power exercised? Does this result in any economic harm?
- How can seller and buyer power interact to reinforce one another?
- How is the market likely to progress in the longer term in the absence of intervention/regulation?
- Are there available remedies that could *suitably* correct or counter anti-competitive effects to the benefit of consumers?

3. Market definition and concentration levels

In some situations, defining relevant economic markets can be a straightforward activity. However, market definition in grocery retailing is complicated by the multiple contexts in which retailers operate – dealing with both procurement and retailing while often being national operators but with individual stores selling to local consumers – and the continuous spectrum of market positions that can be taken in respect of differentiation through a plethora of variables including service characteristics, general pricing policy, product range, store sizes and location, amongst others.

After due consideration, the CC sought to distinguish between retail markets in the product/service dimension in respect of how the retailers catered for the grocery shopping needs of consumers. This resulted in a separation between what the CC perceived as retailers serving primary as opposed to secondary shopping needs according to store size. Thus, the CC designated the market for 'one-stop grocery shopping' as relating to those stores with sales areas of at least 1,400 sq. metres, where the store size allowed for sufficient breadth and depth of products to be stocked to allow consumers to undertake their main weekly shopping in one store. In contrast, smaller stores were seen as predominantly serving different secondary shopping needs, such as for 'top-up' and 'convenience' shopping, sufficient to put them in a separate economic market.[6]

---

[6] Competition Commission (2000a, paras. 2.18–2.40).

While many of the main retail chains operated nationally, using the same fascias and retail brands and generally common pricing/marketing policies and store configurations across their networks of outlets, the CC nonetheless took primarily into account consumer shopping behaviour when considering the geographic extent of retail markets. In this regard, the CC deemed retail markets to be local, with markets delineated by consumer travel times by car as ten minutes or less in urban areas and fifteen minutes or less in rural areas.[7] Thus, for example, a local monopoly market in an urban area amounted to a situation in which, on drawing a ten-minute drive-time isochrone around a store, there were no other comparable stores belonging to rival retailers within that area. The CC recognised that local markets would in practice overlap but argued that it would not be to the extent of leading to a 'chain of substitution' serving to integrate local markets into broader regional or even national markets.[8]

Also, while supermarkets had moved into selling a wide range of non-food items (including clothing, books, toys, electrical appliances, DIY products, over-the-counter (OTC) pharmacy products as well as petrol), the CC limited its inquiry to the sale of 'groceries', taken as food, drinks (both alcoholic and non-alcoholic), cleaning products, toiletries and household goods.[9]

In contrast to retail markets seen as having a generally broad product dimension (one-stop shops selling grocery products) but narrow geographic scope (within ten- or fifteen-minute drive times), on the buying side, the CC saw procurement markets as being product/category specific and mainly national. Thus, it could be quite conceivable for retailers to be designated as operating in different retail markets but in the same procurement markets.

With these comments in mind, Table 4.1 provides some summary evidence in regard to the composition of the sector, the positions of the main parties and the extent of concentration in relevant markets.

Table 4.1 shows that five retailers – Tesco, Sainsbury, Asda, Safeway and Morrison – had primarily positioned themselves as one-stop shop operators using relatively large store formats, but being somewhat differentiated by their pricing policy, target markets and product ranges. The other retailers mainly operated with smaller stores, again differing by their pricing/marketing positions. Concentration at the national level is seen to be high. Taking the sector as a whole, the top five retailers (which include Somerfield/Kwik Save) have in

---

[7] Competition Commission (2000a, para. 2.53).
[8] Competition Commission (2000a, paras. 2.41–2.53).   [9] Competition Commission (2000a, para. 3.2).

Table 4.1 Market characteristics in UK grocery retailing, 1998/9

Main UK grocery retailers	General character and pricing policy	Number of grocery stores	National market shares (by sales)		Regional market shares (by sales)		Local concentration	
			All grocery stores (%)	Grocery stores > 1,400 sq m (%)	Highest regional share (12 broad UK regions) (%)	Highest broad postcode share (120 narrow regions) (%)	% stores in local monopoly (10/15-minute drive time)	% stores in local duopoly (10/15-minute drive time)
One-stop shops								
Tesco	Value-led Hi-Lo	642	23.0	28.5	46.5	53.6	6.0	10.3
Sainsbury	Hi-Lo	424	18.7	24.8	35.9	56.7	0.5	4.1
Asda	EDLP	227	12.2	16.8	24.8	46.8	0.0	3.1
Safeway	Hi-Lo	498	11.5	13.8	28.4	51.0	9.2	9.8
Morrison	EDLP + deals	95	3.9	5.4	21.9	45.0	0.0	4.2
Other chains								
Somerfield/Kwik Save	Hi-Lo soft discount	1,442	9.8	3.1	17.2	30.0	NA	NA
M&S	Premium	294	4.9	2.2	12.1	NA	NA	NA
Waitrose	Premium	119	3.0	2.5	9.0	NA	NA	NA
Aldi	Hard discount	219	1.4	0.0	3.1	NA	NA	NA
Lidl	Hard discount	173	0.9	0.0	2.6	NA	NA	NA
Netto	Hard discount	120	0.7	0.0	2.1	NA	NA	NA
Budgens	Hi-Lo	177	0.7	0.0	0.9	NA	NA	NA
Iceland	Specialised/deals	770	3.0	0.0	0.3	NA	NA	NA
Booth	Premium	24	0.2	0.1	1.3	NA	NA	NA
Co-Operatives	Hi-Lo	1,920	6.4	2.8	7.7	NA	NA	NA

Source: Dobson and Waterson (2006) as adapted and interpreted from Competition Commission (2000a, Tables 5.2, 5.3 and 8.30, Appendices 5.2 and 7.1).

excess of 75 per cent of sales through grocery stores.[10] Yet, when looked at in respect of sales through one-stop shops (i.e. with sales areas greater than 1,400 sq metres), we can see that the top five (which include Morrison) account for nearly 90 per cent of sales.[11] Also, because there are differences in regional positions across the chains, regional concentration levels are higher than national levels.[12] Furthermore, at the local level, the CC identified a significant number of local monopolies and duopolies, mainly occurring in more remote rural areas (notably in Scotland and Wales) and certain urban areas where a proliferation of stores from the same chain existed. Over 10 per cent of stores surveyed by the CC were found to have a 'monopoly' or 'duopoly' status (or 37 per cent between one-stop-shopping stores and ten-minute drive times), with two retailers, Safeway and Tesco, found to have the largest proportion of their stores (respectively, 19 per cent and 16 per cent) operating in local monopoly or duopoly areas.[13]

4. Pricing practices

Retailers in the sector had adopted a range of pricing policies that broadly characterised each retailer's proposition to consumers. Table 4.1 (second column) summarises these pricing positions as the author's interpretation of the information provided by the retailers to the CC (though the CC does not itself assign these terms to particular retailers). These essentially fall into five types:

- 'Hi-Lo' promotional pricing (with fluctuating prices over time);
- 'EDLP' (i.e. 'every day low prices' indicating consistent pricing over time);

[10] For 1998/9, total grocery sales through all 7,144 identified grocery stores amounted to £56.6 million. The Herfindahl-Hirschman index (HHI) of concentration, measured as the squared sum of market shares, at the national level was calculated to be 1,324 (out of a possible maximum of 10,000 under complete monopoly).

[11] Grocery sales through one-stop shops amounted to £41 million and the national HHI was 1,995 (i.e. equivalent to five equally sized retailers controlling all sales). Furthermore, for superstore/hypermarket-sized stores, with sales areas of at least 2,300 sq metres, the top five retailers were found to control in excess of 95 per cent of the £32 million grocery sales, with the national HHI at 2,223. To put these HHI levels into some perspective, US Department of Justice's *Horizontal Merger Guidelines* (1997) suggest that when HHI is over 1,800 then a merger that further increases concentration can give rise to 'significant competitive concerns'.

[12] To measure the significance of regional variations in the positions of the retailers, the CC calculated sales weighted averages of HHIs across the twelve broad regions of the UK. The regionally weighted HHI was calculated as 1,572 for all grocery stores, 2,314 for all one-stop shops and 2,672 for all superstores/hypermarkets.

[13] Competition Commission (2000a, Appendix 6.3).

- hybrid EDLP/Hi-Lo pricing (combining general pricing consistency interspersed with temporary promotional deals);
- discount pricing (with low prices on a limited product range, with 'hard discount' focusing extensively on budget/own-label goods and 'soft discount' on branded goods);
- 'premium' pricing (reflecting a more upmarket position allowing for higher pricing).

The wide array of positions indicated that consumers were generally well served in respect of the extent of choice they faced through competing retail offers.[14] However, the CC was concerned about particular pricing practices that may have an adverse effect on competition and consumer welfare. The CC considered five practices:

1. Persistent below-cost selling.
2. Price flexing – varying prices across stores according to local competitive conditions.
3. Focused competition on frequently purchased 'known value items' (KVIs).
4. Pricing own labels with reference to branded goods rather than costs (also known as 'umbrella pricing').
5. Retail price changes slow to respond to wholesale price changes (especially in regard to passing on lower costs to consumers).

However, the CC's attention focused on the first two of these practices in view of limited evidence on the other three practices having any significant anticompetitive effects.

4.1 Persistent below-cost selling

All but two multiple retailers (M&S and Lidl) acknowledged that they sold a limited number of goods at below-cost on a persistent basis (i.e. over a long period of time rather than the usual 2–4 weeks on which short-term price promotions might usually apply). Typically this was applied to staple products (like bread, butter, milk, sugar and meat) and other KVIs (i.e. regularly purchased goods that consistently form a core part of the consumer's typical shopping basket, including well-known branded items and budget own-label items). However, the CC provided only limited detail on the extent of the practice, finding some 370 common product lines sold with gross margins of less than 5 per cent, collectively representing 6 per cent of supermarket sales but 10.8 per cent of convenience store sales.

---

[14] For further details on the competitive implications of the presence of a mix of such retail pricing strategies, see Bolton and Shankar (2003), Ellickson and Misra (2006) and Lal and Rao (1997).

While the practice clearly entails the retailer making a loss on sales of the product, there might be a number of reasons explaining its use:

- promotional pricing – to build store traffic (but normally carried out through short-term loss leaders);
- competitive price discrimination – discounting KVIs to build or maintain a value reputation to influence consumers' store-choice decision;
- predatory pricing – constant cross-subsidisation to undermine small/specialist retailers;
- bargaining leverage over suppliers – undermining product/brand image to intensify supplier competition and obtain better terms of trade.

Yet, whether deliberately or unintentionally made, the practice can have detrimental effects on both retailer and supplier competition. In particular, on the retailing side, the practice can result in dampened competition in respect of non-KVIs (i.e. products infrequently purchased or with limited appeal) when the retail emphasis is placed solely on KVIs to attract store custom. It can also increase retail concentration if its predatory effects result in the exit or weakening of small/specialist stores. On the supplier side, the effects of the practice may be to reduce demand if product image is cheapened and/or supplier brand investments are undermined. It may also result in a reduction in secondary/tertiary brands in favour of an emphasis on below-cost selling of own-label goods and leading brands.

The net result for consumers may potentially be a number of adverse effects:

- distorted category pricing architectures with high prices for non-KVIs;
- reduced consumption value if product image is cheapened;
- reduced store accessibility and choice with the exit of small/specialist retailers;
- reduced product choice and variety of higher quality/branded goods with the exit of secondary/tertiary brands and reduced brand investment;
- reduced product quality if producers are pushed into saving costs by 'cutting corners' in order to remain in business.

4.2 Local price flexing

Price flexing represents a form of geographic third-degree price discrimination, offering different prices to different groups of consumers based on their location – so that some consumers are disadvantaged in facing higher prices than other consumers depending on which of the retailer's stores they visit.

The competition concerns with local price flexing are that it can distort retail competition and be a means of exploiting local market power. For instance, large, out-of-town stores protected by planning restrictions may represent

'islands of monopoly' from which retailers can set high prices to local consumers, but set lower prices where competition is present. More generally, the
unevenness of competition at the local level may mean higher prices for
shoppers in certain localities compared with others based on the presence or
absence of certain competitors (say, aggressive discounters) and the degree
to which shoppers are constrained (e.g. by drive times) in their local choice of
different retailers. Furthermore, there is the worry that when used jointly with
persistent below-cost selling, the combination of the two practices may serve as
a very effective predatory tool for targeting (smaller) rivals at the local level, thus
driving higher retail concentration and reducing consumers' store choice.[15]

Table 4.2 summarises the CC's evidence on the extent and character of the
practice. The CC found that all but eight multiple retailers used the practice, with
Budgens, Tesco, Safeway, Co-op and Somerfield/Kwik Save using it most extensively. As shown in Table 4.2, individual product prices were found in some
retailers to vary considerably (by as much as 100 per cent), but average prices
differed across each chain by less than 3 per cent.[16] The CC investigated the basis
on which local pricing operated, identifying the critical factors influencing store-
level pricing (as shown in the final column of Table 4.2). Broadly speaking, it was
the retailers that employed Hi-Lo promotional pricing that predominantly used
price flexing, while the EDLP, hard discount and premium positioned retailers
tended to adopt national pricing. For the seven retail groups that did vary prices
across their stores, both differences in local demand (in respect of income or
regional effects) and local competition (in respect of local market power or
facing particular price-focused competitors) were found to be important in
determining the price band applied to individual stores and the variation in
prices across the chain of stores (with prices generally higher in those areas
where incomes were higher and competition was less). Cost elements (like
differences in store size) were also found to play a role, but not so significantly
as to explain the full extent of store-to-store price variation, suggesting that
retailers sought to use the practice to raise profits at consumers' expense.[17]

[15] See Dobson (2007) for a detailed discussion about how these practices can be used in conjunction for this
purpose.
[16] While the percentage variations might appear fairly small, the monetary sums involved can be quite
significant given the size of the sector. For example, the Competition Commission (2000b, para. 7.124)
found that for the largest retailer, Tesco, customers in its lower-price stores saved between £10.5 million
and £25.9 million a year over the prices charged in higher-price stores.
[17] For instance, the CC undertook detailed analysis on the relative profitability of stores operated on
different price tiers by Tesco and Sainsbury. In both cases, the CC found that the higher prices in their
higher-price tier stores were more than was required to meeting higher operating costs, or indeed higher
asset costs. See Competition Commission (2000a, Tables 8.31 and 8.32, paras. 8.109 and 8.114).

Table 4.2 Local price flexing by UK grocery retailers, 1998/9

Store fascia	Price-flexed products[18] (%)	Widest price range on any price-flexed product	Average price range for price-flexed products (%)	Basket price range across stores (sales weighted) (%)	Identifiable store-level price bands (1=uniform)	Factors influencing store-level pricing[19]
Tesco	8.5	43.4	19.2	1.69	5	R/Y/E/D
Sainsbury[20]	NA	NA	NA	NA	2+	S/R/E
Asda	0	0	0	0	1	–
Safeway	59.5	31.0	4.3	1.09	3	M/E/D/S/R
Morrison	0	0	0	0	1	–
Somerfield	23.7	100.0	6.3	0.20	10	E/S/M
Kwik Save	2.3	16.1	9.8	0.79	3	D/M
M&S	0	0	0	0	1	–
Waitrose	0	0	0	0	1	–
Aldi	0	0	0	0	1	–
Lidl	0	0	0	0	1	–
Netto	9.9	23.5	13.7	0.001	2	R
Budgens	64.5	62.0	9.8	3.04	5	Y/D/M
Iceland	0	0	0	0	1	–
Booth	0	0	0	0	1	–
Co-Operatives	33.7	57.0	6.7	0.54	4	R/S/M

Source: Dobson and Waterson (2006) adapted from Competition Commission (2000a, Tables 7.2 and 7.3, Appendices 7.5 and 7.8).

4.3 CC's views on pricing practices

In its assessment of pricing practices, the CC concluded that both persistent below-cost selling and local price flexing were anticompetitive and could be expected to operate against the public interest when employed by the leading one-stop chains possessing market power. Both practices were viewed as contributing to a situation where the parties' products were not fully exposed

---

[18] This is based on a basket of up to 200 common products with prices collected from up to sixty stores for each party on 28 January 1999. As shown in the final three columns of the table, an average basket price was then determined, along with how it varied across stores in the retail chain according to the number of distinct price bands used (from one group of stores to another), and then the CC undertook empirical analysis to see which competition, demand and cost factors appeared to affect the store-level basket price.

[19] Store-level pricing factors identified by CC empirical analysis: R = regional effect (e.g. lower in North, higher in South); Y = local average income; E = local presence of EDLP retailer (Asda or Morrison); D = local presence of hard discount retailer (Aldi, Lidl or Netto); S = store size; M = local market share.

[20] Sainsbury did not provide the CC with the requested price data, but instead provided a complete list of stores that might selectively offer lower prices (with 111 of its 422 stores on a lower price tier).

to competitive pressure and distorted competition in the supply of groceries. Persistent below-cost selling was viewed as damaging smaller grocery retailers and operated against consumer interests (particularly the elderly and less mobile who tended to rely on such small retailers) when practised by Asda, Morrison, Safeway, Sainsbury and Tesco.[21] Price flexing, when carried on by Safeway, Sainsbury and Tesco, was viewed as operating against the public interest because their customers tended to pay more at stores that did not face particular competitors than they would have if those competitors were present in the area.[22]

In regard to the other three pricing practices investigated by the CC, only 'focused competition' was found to be evident. Yet, while this practice was deemed to distort competition (because not all retailers' products were fully exposed to competitive pressure), it was considered not to be operating against the public interest (because it appeared neither to raise overall prices nor to restrict choice for consumers).[23]

The CC considered a number of possible remedies for both practices. In the case of persistent below-cost selling, it considered banning the practice but based on experience in France and Ireland considered that this might result in generally higher prices (as such a ban may serve to reduce competitive intensity and possibly facilitate collusion). Other possibilities were considered but rejected on the basis that they would have distorting effects of their own, be impractical (because of monitoring or compliance costs) and/or not be proportionate (i.e. relative to adverse effects arising). With no suitable remedy identified and no subsequent action taken, the retailers were free to continue using the practice. Similarly with price flexing, the CC ruled out the imposition of national pricing (on grounds that this would not allow for differential pricing based on legitimate factors such as regional cost differences) or requiring that any price differences between stores should be broadly related to costs (on the grounds that this would be impractical to implement and regulate).[24] Again, other possibilities were considered, but all were rejected on the basis that they would be ineffective, distorting, impractical and/or not proportionate. So, again, the parties were allowed to continue using the practice with no suitable remedy identified.

---

[21] Competition Commission (2000a, para. 1.6(a)).
[22] Competition Commission (2000a, para. 1.6(b)).
[23] Competition Commission (2000a, para. 1.6(c)).
[24] See also discussion of Dobson and Waterson (2005, 2006) below.

However, questions remain over whether the CC did reach the right conclusions and about the lack of suitable remedies. First, in regard to persistent below-cost selling on certain (but far from all) items, it is clear that this can have a pernicious if not necessarily intended effect on small/specialist retailers. This can be viewed as somewhat akin to a slow poisoning rather than outright shooting to kill off rivals; with the implication that there is little chance of finding a 'smoking gun' if a case were brought under existing laws against predatory pricing (especially given that the practice can be conducted without making the whole operation run at a loss). Indeed, this is a problem that has been widely recognised across Europe, and many states, not just Ireland and France, operate bans on below-cost selling (see Dobson, 2002). Nevertheless, *blanket* bans are likely to encounter the problem that they may simply result in a softening or even avoidance of price competition, particularly if they can serve as a facilitating device for tacit collusion with producers' compliance.[25] Even so, *targeted* bans, akin to that applying in Germany, that focus only on retailers possessing market power and using below-cost selling on a persistent rather than a temporary basis, may be more effective in avoiding dampened competition (perhaps as evidenced by the continued intense price competition witnessed in Germany's retail markets). Yet, determining a suitably clear legal wording for such a targeted ban would be no easy matter, given powerful retailers' incentives not to comply with such a restriction on their pricing behaviour and instead devise ways around the ban.[26] Accordingly, other than for very blatant cases, monitoring and enforcement costs for the relevant competition authority may be high.

Second, on price flexing, it is not clear from the CC's analysis that it did come to the right decision about whether the practice is anticompetitive. The fact that price flexing led to shoppers in some locations paying more at stores that did not face particular competitors compared with what they would have paid if those competitors were present in the area is not the

---

[25] For instance, producers could set high invoice prices that serve as a high floor for retail prices and then they could compensate retailers through high lump-sum or retrospective discount payments which cannot be passed through to reduce retail prices – with such vertical collusion serving to raise the profits of both producers and retailers.

[26] For example, retailers might seek to avoid restrictions by rotating temporary promotions, providing bundled offers like free home delivery, or having multi-product suppliers structure their invoice terms differently across the products supplied to allow the retailer to offer discounts that are then not technically sales below-cost.

relevant test. The empirical finding of differential prices related to the intensity of local competition simply shows that competition across local markets varies and that retailers can judiciously exploit this with geographic price discrimination. However, even if the retailers did not practise price flexing and instead adopted uniform pricing across their store network, the problem of variable local competition would still be present. As Dobson and Waterson (2005, 2006) show, the reason for this is that the adoption of uniform national pricing (whether by retailers' own volition or from imposition by a competition authority) would lead retailers to set prices according to the (weighted) average of their market power across the local markets they serve (i.e. they would not simply lower their prices to match those in their most competitive market). With this averaging process amounting to a balancing effect, the result would be one group of consumers gaining from lower prices (where under price flexing they faced high local prices) while the other group (which previously faced lower local prices) would lose out from higher prices. Thus, in comparing price flexing with no price flexing, there is a balance of interests to consider, which could go one way or the other and may depend delicately on the composition and nature of the local markets.[27] Thus the critical point, overlooked by the CC, is that without changing the underlying structure of local markets, uniform pricing will be based on an average of local market power across the local markets served and would not necessarily lead to lower prices *on average*. Accordingly, the key requirement for lowering prices to consumers is not over which pricing policy choice is made *per se*, but rather reducing the local market power that would allow average prices to be lower either way. Specifically, price flexing is essentially a *manifestation* of variable local market power existing, not necessarily the *source* of it, and thereby not likely the *reason* for higher average prices than would be the case if this power were absent.

This suggests that a more appropriate test of whether price flexing is or is not anticompetitive is to consider its effect on a retailer's *average prices* across the markets served compared with uniform pricing or local prices varying merely in line with local cost differences.[28] This is not necessarily an easy test to execute as it relies on comparing actual outcomes with those from the

---

[27] Again, see Dobson and Waterson (2005, 2006). They show that while the respective trade-offs are quite complicated, retailers' and consumers' interests may not necessarily be at odds with each other. Indeed, it is possible for both retailers and consumers in aggregate to prefer pricing flexing in some circumstances and uniform pricing in other circumstances.

[28] A more sophisticated test would be to consider the number of consumers who would gain as opposed to lose out by the balancing effect of having uniform pricing instead of local price flexing and then weigh their respective gains and losses to make a judgement about the aggregate effect on consumers' welfare.

counterfactual hypothetical situations. However, any judgement should also consider two other possible effects – one negative and the other positive – arising from the use of price flexing.

First, on the negative side and as alluded to above, there is a concern that price flexing may be used jointly with below-cost selling (e.g. deeply discounted local prices or unusually generous vouchers) as a predatory tool for targeting smaller/specialist rivals at the local level. This may then drive higher retail concentration and reduce consumers' store choice (i.e. the practice can become a source of differential local market power). Moreover, selective targeting in this way may be an attractive option as it is considerably less expensive and a potentially much more potent means of predatory pricing than selling below-cost in all markets (as would be required with uniform pricing). Here, any lost income can be quickly recovered by simply accruing market share once rivals are driven out of the market or forced to serve a more limited segment of the market.

Second, though, on the positive side, price flexing involving retailers setting a wide array of different prices is likely to make tacit collusion difficult. In contrast, national pricing with each retailer setting a single uniform price for each product may facilitate tacit collusion since monitoring prices is much more straightforward (making it easier to identify and adopt common focal prices and then allow for tacitly collusive parallel pricing because any deviations can be quickly spotted and punished). The more retailers that adopt uniform pricing (e.g. a simultaneous mass switch away from local pricing), the more competition authorities should be concerned by this possibility (as there is less likelihood of local pricing disrupting tacit collusion through surreptitious local price cutting).

Nevertheless, it should be apparent that, even though the CC chose to focus exclusively on pricing practices, retailers have a range of variables at their disposal to alter the retail offer and thus ultimate value that consumers receive beyond price. For example, even if retailers do not blatantly tailor local prices, they have other means available to alter the local retail offer, such as by adjusting local advertising, in-store promotions, product range, category depth and quality emphasis. Retailers can also adjust their service levels and investment decisions (rather than merely tactical marketing decisions) on a local basis, such as regarding decisions over store format, size, specific location and even fascia, as well as amenities and service levels to suit local competitive conditions. All of this suggests that rather than merely focusing on prices, the CC should have been looking for broader evidence on whether the major supermarket chains adapted their local offer in a manner to exploit local market power. For example, in areas where retailers faced less competition (in respect of either competing stores or competing fascias), did they restrict (beyond what can be justified by local costs and local market size and demand differences) the number, range and quality of products, store amenities/ services and special promotions compared with their stores in areas where they faced greater competition?

The point here is that the problems that the CC identifies are really down to the existence of market power at the local level, and not simply how retailers choose to determine and adapt their retail propositions. If competition were effective across *all* local markets then promotional pricing entailing some below-cost selling and local price flexing would likely not raise anticompetitive concerns. Accordingly, any remedies should be primarily directed at tackling local market power – to ensure that consumers have both a wide store choice and fascia choice at the local level. To this end, and in addition to considering the entry-restricting effects of the UK planning regime, the CC could have looked beyond behavioural measures to consider possible structural measures. In this regard, enforced store divestments have been widely utilised in retail merger decisions to allow for partial rather than full merger clearances (e.g. the Safeway/Morrison merger in 2004), but not something as yet to come out of a market investigation. Yet Smith (2004) provides empirical evidence on the competition benefits of supermarket demergers. Moreover, this does not have to be undertaken in a way that would unduly discriminate against particular retailers and undermine their efficiency by simply taking stores away from successful retailers and letting less successful retailers purchase them (i.e. a policy that might be viewed as akin to punishing success and rewarding failure). Instead, a more effective means of reducing the extent of local market power would be to spread the intensity of local competition by having a divestment programme mostly operated through 'store swaps' along with certain 'land bank' disposals. In principle, these could be designed in such a fashion that they would result in a broadly neutral effect on retailers' existing relative positions (by leaving existing national market shares largely unchanged overall but significantly enhancing consumers' choice at the local level).

5. Retailer buyer power

Retailer buyer power can take many forms but essentially boils down to two aspects: obtaining the lowest possible prices from suppliers for supply of their goods and controlling the terms and conditions of trade (e.g.

Table 4.3 Buying effectiveness of the main grocery retailers, 1998/9

	Number of product lines (max = 130)	Relative buying performance % (average = 100)	% of lines for which prices paid are less than average	% of average paid relative to Tesco's price (average = 100)	Market share in grocery retailing
Tesco	126	96.2	80	100.0	23.0
Sainsbury	125	97.7	74	101.6	18.7
Asda	127	97.8	66	102.3	12.2
Somerfield	130	98.4	65	103.0	9.8
Safeway	123	98.8	65	103.1	11.5
Morrison	122	99.8	46	104.6	3.9
Co-op	NA	100.5	NA	NA	6.4
Iceland	66	101.0	38	105.3	3.0
Budgens	85	103.6	24	109.4	0.7
Netto	24	104.2	21	109.5	0.7
Waitrose	103	104.4	23	110.1	3.0
Booth	74	104.4	26	111.1	0.2

Source: Dobson (2005) adapted from Competition Commission (2000b, Tables 5.6, 11.9 and 11.10).

imposing requirements and/or restrictions on suppliers) in such a manner as to benefit the buyer at the expense of suppliers and possibly rival retailers as well.

On buying effectiveness, measured in respect of the extent to which major retailers are better positioned to extract discounts on suppliers' prices, the CC provided empirical evidence showing that the major retailers enjoyed significantly better buying terms than their smaller rivals. Table 4.3 summarises the CC's findings.[29] This shows that the market leader, Tesco with a 23 per cent market share of all grocery store sales, generally secured the lowest prices, followed by the other major supermarket chains (respectively Sainsbury, Asda, Somerfield, Safeway and Morrison). All other retailers paid above-average prices. Indeed, some of the price discrepancies among retailers were seen to be particularly wide. For example, expressed in terms of comparisons with the price paid by Tesco, a number of smaller chains (notably Budgens, Netto,

---

[29] The following points regarding this table should be noted. The analysis is based on top five branded product lines for twenty-six suppliers. The price is averaged over all parties and is not weighted by turnover. Aldi, Lidl and M&S do not (generally) stock manufacturers' brands, so are excluded from the table. The figure for the Co-op's average price is averaged over different Co-op groupings, where 100.5% was the average with an actual range of 99.6–101.5%.

Waitrose and Booth) paid around 10 per cent more, a level which potentially placed them at a serious competitive disadvantage compared with Tesco and other major multiple operators. More generally, as the table indicates, the CC's findings suggest a close relationship between market share and buying effectiveness, in terms of obtaining relatively low prices.

Perhaps the observed price differentials across the retailers were cost-justified. However, the CC concluded that the lower prices for the major retailers were attributable to the exercise of buyer power rather than to operating cost differences.[30] Even so, the CC did not go on to consider whether such asymmetry in buying terms was having an adverse effect on competition, say, by exacerbating small retailers' competitive disadvantage and setting in place the prospect of reduced retail competition leading to higher prices.

Yet retailing bargaining strength is not limited to securing direct price concessions. It can also be directed at obtaining other favourable terms of dealing. These terms can take the form of direct financial benefits at the expense of suppliers (such as payments for promotional support or shelf-space allocation) or less direct benefits that affect trade with other parties (e.g. exclusive supply obligations that limit suppliers' freedom to supply rival retailers). The CC found that both types were common and used extensively by the major retailers. Moreover, the terms and conditions of trade dictated by the major retailers were found to arise in numerous forms and typically applied as a combination of requirements. They were also applied in parallel, with different retailers seeking the same or very similar terms and conditions. As such, this gave rise to the concern that it is not just individual practices by individual retailers that may have anticompetitive effects (i.e. unilateral effects in isolation), but that there may be cumulative effects arising from the multiple and parallel application of terms and conditions of trade placed on suppliers.

In total, the CC identified fifty-two practices associated with retailer buyer power that when practised by the major multiple grocery retailers could have potentially distorting effects on supplier and/or retailer competition. The CC grouped these practices into eight categories – see Table 4.4.

The CC concluded that the leading five multiples, each with a market share in excess of 8 per cent, had sufficient buyer power that thirty (of the fifty-two) identified practices 'adversely affect the competitiveness of some of their suppliers and distort competition in the supplier market – and in some

---

[30] Competition Commission (2000b, para. 2.451).

Table 4.4 UK supermarket practices concerning relations with suppliers

Category of practices	Number of practices	Number of retailers engaging in practices (min – max)	% of practices against public interest
Payments for access to shelf space	8	5–13	50
Imposing conditions on suppliers' trade with other retailers	2	1–4	0
Applying different standards to different suppliers	1	3	100
Imposing an unfair imbalance of risk	12	1–12	83
Imposing retrospective changes to contractual terms	8	1–7	75
Restricting suppliers' access to the market	1	10	100
Imposing charges and transferring costs to suppliers	8	2–13	63
Requiring suppliers to use third-party suppliers nominated by the retailer	2	2–11	50

Source: Dobson (2005) adapted from Competition Commission (2000b, paras. 2.437–2.550, Table 2.14 and Appendix 11.3).

cases in the retail market – for the supply of groceries'.[31] The result of the practices was that

suppliers are likely to invest less and spend less on new product development and innovation, leading to lower quality and less consumer choice. This is likely to result in fewer new entrants to the supplier market than otherwise. Certain of the practices give the major buyers substantial advantages over other smaller retailers, whose competitiveness is likely to suffer as a result, again leading to a reduction in consumer choice. (Competition Commission (2000b, para. 1.11))

Although the CC recognised some advantages in buyer power and offsetting benefits, it nonetheless determined that twenty-seven of the practices operated against the public interest.[32]

Rather than recommend the outright prohibition of any of the individual practices (as they might simply materialise in other, amended forms), the CC

---

[31] Competition Commission (2000b, para. 1.10).

[32] For the full list of identified practices and details of which multiples engage in each practice, an explanation and discussion of the practices, and a list of the practices found to be anticompetitive, see respectively Competition Commission (2000b, Appendix 11.3, pages 98–136 and Table 2.14).

recommended that a code of practice be established, with the intention to eliminate or at least restrict the practices determined as being anticompetitive, with compliance required by the five largest supermarket groups (each accounting for in excess of 8 per cent of the retail grocery market).[33]

Several notable issues arise from the CC's findings and conclusions on retailer buyer power and how it should be tackled. Some of these issues are discussed further in the next section, looking at how retailer buyer and seller power interacts. However, for the present, the following remarks appear pertinent on the extent and implications of buyer power. First, the finding of significant differences in prices paid by retailers according to their size should not come as too great a surprise, as there are good reasons why a retailer's bargaining power may be related to both its relative and absolute size (in the sense of increasing supplier dependency due to the size of the available contract and lack of outside options relative to the retailer's ability to switch to or sponsor alternative suppliers). Even so the magnitude of differences should be a cause for concern as a smaller retailer is likely to be very heavily handicapped if it faces a 10 per cent or more supply price differential compared with some of its larger rivals, making it harder to compete on effective terms and ensure that competition is kept keen for all players (as the larger ones will enjoy a significant margin of comfort arising from their lower supply prices). This in turn may have a dynamic effect on the market – making it easier for larger retailers to grow at the expense of smaller retailers and thus the retail sector to become more concentrated over time (which is something considered in more detail in the next section).

Second, the fact that retailers' practices concerning relations with suppliers were so extensive and being operated in combinations and in parallel with other retailers points to concerns about anticompetitive effects arising at lower levels of market control than single firm dominance. However, the figure of an 8 per cent market share appears arbitrary in determining whether a retailer has significant buyer power. No rationale or basis is offered for this specific level in its absolute or relative context.[34] Furthermore, if there were genuine

---

[33] Competition Commission (2000b, paras. 2.588–2.596). Following this recommendation, a code of practice was subsequently introduced. For details, see DTI press release, *Hewitt Backs Good Behaviour Code for Supermarkets & Suppliers*, P/2001/606, Department of Trade and Industry (31 October 2001), available at www.gnn.gov.uk/environment/dti/

[34] In contrast, the European Commission in its assessment of the Carrefour/Promodes merger determined that significant buyer power could be exercised with 22 per cent of the relevant market, as this level could be considered as sufficient to offer the retailer a credible 'threat point' to undermine the supplier's business if it switched to alternative suppliers (European Commission, Case No. COMP/M.1684, Carrefour/Promodes Article 6 and Article 9 Decisions (January 2000)).

concerns about parallel application of the practices (i.e. in a complex rather than just scale monopoly sense), then it would appear more suitable for any code of practice to apply to all identified main party retailers (and in this way it would not be discriminatory in nature) and for such practices to be restricted if not prohibited in a meaningful way (rather than merely regulated but allowed to continue essentially unchanged).

Third, in investigating buyer power, the CC failed to obtain or provide any hard evidence on these practices having an adverse effect on supplier or retail competition and appears to have reached its conclusions based on the expected or anticipated effects of these practices. Thus, for instance, in respect of distorting supplier competition, the CC did not look to see at a general level (i.e. beyond specific instances) how investment patterns may have been distorted or how small suppliers were faring compared with their larger rivals (e.g. by comparing growth patterns or insolvency levels).[35] Equally, there was no empirical assessment of whether and precisely how differential buyer power might be distorting retail markets and having an adverse effect on consumers, including markets for secondary shopping needs (like 'top-up' shopping) that may involve convenience stores and specialist food retailers. Specifically, if competition was being distorted, how was it being manifested in harm to consumers? Were consumers facing reduced product/service choice, reduced quality and/or higher retail prices than they would otherwise expect to receive in the absence of differential buyer power or the allegedly anti-competitive retailer practices? The CC provided no general empirical evidence on any of these aspects to tie in retailer buyer power with consumer harm. Instead, it relied only on arguments about expected effects, with at best anecdotal evidence of economically harmful effects.

6. Retailer buyer and seller power interaction

As is clear from the preceding discussion, the CC's concerns with retailer buyer power relate to competition being distorted at both the supplier level and the retailer level. On its impact on suppliers, retailer buyer power

---

[35] Specifically, it might have been useful for the CC to undertake empirical analysis to see whether retail buyer power effects were already evident in the sector by looking at investment levels and returns on investment, perhaps carefully distinguishing between situations where under-investment might be anticipated – such as when small or vulnerable suppliers' returns are inadequate to cover required product or process investments – as opposed to where over-investment might arise – such as when leading brand producers have to keep on adapting their brands' packaging or formulation to keep ahead of retailers' copy-cat own-label items freeriding on brand producers' investments.

(working through the terms, conditions and restraints imposed on suppliers) can serve to drive down supplier margins. This may be expected to have greatest impact on suppliers that are least able to resist such buyer power: specifically those in weak financial positions and not possessing any market power of their own (leaving them perhaps unable to cover fixed costs when buyer power pushes them towards marginal cost pricing). The result is likely to be the exit of small and otherwise vulnerable suppliers, especially given the lack of availability of other, more profitable routes to market with the demise of small/specialist retailers over recent years. Still, even for the remaining suppliers, the squeeze on their margins may adversely affect their ability to recover all their fixed costs, causing them to cut back on investments in product quality, variety and innovation, all of which may lead to future consumer detriment.

Yet it is in regard to how buyer power can distort retail competition that we perhaps might see the most profound effects on the market. This might be anticipated because of the way that retailer buyer and seller power could work together to drive retail concentration and tip in a decisive way competitive advantage in favour of a limited number of retailers. Arguably, the CC does not give sufficient consideration to this dynamic aspect of the development of the market, resulting from the interaction of buyer and seller power, and to the implications for future competition and consumer welfare.

First, we can observe that because of differences in their existing market positions, some retailers will likely have more bargaining power over suppliers than other retailers (as evident in Table 4.3 in regard to buying effectiveness). Principally, retailers that have large, loyal and/or distinct customer bases will be relatively well positioned in bargaining with suppliers keen to gain shelf space and thereby access this pool of consumers. Holding a strong 'gatekeeper' position, such retailers should be well placed to play off suppliers against each other to obtain the best possible terms; the more so if they can extend supplier competition by sponsoring new entry through operating own-label product ranges.[36] In contrast, other, particularly smaller retailers may not be so fortunate. Having fewer (and probably less loyal) shoppers and fewer supplier substitution options (especially when they rely on selling leading KVIs and

---

[36] The only notable exception would be where they individually and uniquely provide a 'pivotal role' in sponsoring entry or maintaining viability for their suppliers because of their size to the extent that without generous contracts these suppliers would not exist, allowing smaller retailers to freeride on these suppliers being kept in play by agreeing lower supply prices with them (i.e. once the suppliers' fixed costs are covered). See Raskovich (2003) and Adilov and Alexander (2006).

cannot afford investments in developing own-label ranges), suppliers will not be so desperate to offer favourable terms and conditions of trade to such retailers.

The point is that an individual retailer's buyer power may depend on its seller power. To the extent that the latter is linked to retailer size, then with different retailer sizes we should expect to observe *differential* buyer power resulting in larger retailers obtaining better terms than smaller retailers. However, this in turn is likely to affect retail competition on the selling side. With smaller retailers already at a competitive disadvantage from not having the scale economies and resources of larger retailers, differential buyer power could further tilt the already uneven playing field. As a consequence, large retailers could be better positioned to gain additional shoppers and increase market share at the expense of smaller retailers. With increased market share, large retailers would then likely be in an even stronger position to exert buyer power while smaller retailers would be in a weaker position in future negotiations with suppliers. This would widen the gap in differential buyer power and further extend the relative competitive disadvantage of smaller retailers vis-à-vis large retailers.

Accordingly, as a result of *differential* buyer power, small retailers can suffer a 'waterbed effect' where the improved terms for larger retailers ultimately lead to worse terms (in both a relative and absolute sense) for them.[37] Moreover, once initiated, this process could become self-perpetuating, with the widening gap in terms received from suppliers strengthening the market position of large retailers but weakening that of small retailers. This, in turn, may allow large retailers to gain market share at the expense of small retailers, thereby further widening their relative ability to exert buyer power, and so on. Consequently, ever-widening differential buyer power may assist large retailers to benefit from a 'virtuous circle' (or 'upward spiral') of growth while small retailers suffer a 'vicious circle' of decline.

Crucially, the trigger for benefiting from a *virtuous* circle would seem to be that once competitive advantage on the retail side is achieved this is translated into higher market share. At this point the retailer can benefit from further

---

[37] Note that this is a more involved argument than the naive perspective often attributed to a waterbed effect argument that runs along the lines that as a major retailer uses its buyer power to extract greater discounts from suppliers, these suppliers compensate for their lost income by raising prices to smaller retailers (say, to cover their fixed costs or to achieve a certain targeted profitability level). The fallacy of this argument is that if suppliers were able to raise prices to small retailers then they would have done so already and not have waited until forced to give discounts to the major retailer. For details on the underlying economic theory about the market circumstances that can more credibly allow for a waterbed effect to arise and the consequences for consumer welfare, see Dobson and Inderst (2007).

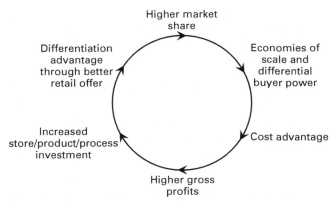

Figure 4.1 The virtuous circle of growth for large retailers
Source: Adapted from Dobson, Starkey and Richards (2004)

efficiency gains through reaping economies of scale and increased buyer power which lead to high gross profits (through superior profit margins and higher volumes). These high gross profits can then be ploughed back into the business in the form of further expansion of the store network (i.e. opening new stores), improvements to existing stores (through better store amenity and facilities) and/or investments in product and process innovation (e.g. own-label goods and improved logistical support) to provide a (further) differentiation advantage. This, in turn, can allow the firm to increase its market share, and so on. Figure 4.1 illustrates this argument diagrammatically.

The *vicious* circle facing smaller retailers is the reverse case, where reduced market share leads to a loss of economies of scale and decreased buyer power feeding through to higher unit costs and reduced profits, in turn leading to reduced investments and a weakened retail offer, resulting in reduced market share, and so on.

Of course, anything that can extend seller power may in turn feed through to increased buyer power and propel such circles. For instance, anticompetitive practices which undermine small retailers' market positions, such as large retailers combining local price flexing with below-cost selling to target small/specialist retailers, can have predatory effects both directly (by causing small retailers to lose market share) and indirectly (by the loss of market share leading to worse trading terms with suppliers). Equally, market restrictions that impose a greater burden on smaller retailers than on larger retailers seeking to grow can exacerbate relative market positions.[38]

---

[38] For instance, large incumbent retailers may be able to grow more easily when they can simply extend their existing stores or build on existing land holdings. Smaller, newer retailers may face greater barriers

The implication of virtuous and vicious circles operating is that over time the retail market will become more concentrated – large retailers will gain share while small retailers will lose share. Whether this is likely to have an adverse effect on consumers depends on a number of factors. To the extent that increased retail concentration results in increased retailer efficiency, while still allowing for intense competition between a group of evenly placed leading retailers, consumers may continue to benefit from low prices and without significant loss of choice or amenity, especially where small retailers can successfully occupy differentiated niche positions. However, if the market becomes very asymmetric, allowing one or two very large retailers to dominate the market and leaving all other retailers struggling to survive, price competition may be dampened and choice and amenity may be reduced, all to the consumer's detriment.

Nevertheless, there may be factors that restrict the possibility of a dynamic process leading inevitably towards a 'winner takes all' monopoly position emerging as a result of the operation of virtuous/vicious circles. First, there may be practical reasons why the virtuous circle runs out of steam for many if not most retailers – for example, market saturation, limits to retail brand appeal, brand fatigue in consumers' eyes, poor management decisions and/or complacency. This may then open up opportunities for other retailers to exploit with a differentiated offer (perhaps through competing with a different image, store locations, retail service and/or product range). Second, it seems reasonable to consider that suppliers can be squeezed only so far before their viability is undermined and to the extent that a major retailer then holds a pivotal buying position, determining whether suppliers stay in business or exit the market, it may be forced to support their continued existence by limiting its demands. Third, supplier competition itself may be impacted whereby the increased retailer buyer power of the growing major retailers pushes the sector to consolidate (as a result of some suppliers either being forced out of business or induced to merge in order to compete more effectively). This consolidation might restore suppliers' profitability by allowing them to set higher prices (if at different levels to different customers and thus may be a further source of a waterbed effect). However, it might also create 'must-use' supplier positions where retailers have no ready alternative (to suppliers' 'must-stock'

---

to expansion when tight planning restrictions limit new store openings. Similarly, in respect of obtaining additional grocery supplies, large established retailers may be able to rely on their extensive network of existing suppliers while smaller, newer retailers may be prevented access to key supplies due to exclusivity contracts held by the large retailers.

products) and so cannot exploit buyer power regardless of how advantageous is their retail position.

All of these arguments suggest the need for careful empirical analysis to determine whether there really is a dynamic process in operation entailing relentlessly increasing retail concentration with little prospect of significant new entry. This is especially important given that such a situation may lead on to future market ossification if a limited set of retailers were completely to dominate the sector and learn to avoid intense profit-damaging competition. As well as providing a better understanding of the dynamic competitive processes in local retail markets, such empirical analysis could be directed at considering how effective and consistent retail buyer power is exercised and whether this is solely the preserve of the very largest chains or whether it is possible for skilful smaller chains to negotiate competitive (if not sometimes better) deals. Put simply, is the gap in net supply prices across retailers increasing or stable/declining over time and how is this impacting retail competition?

7. Conclusion

The CC's investigation shows the UK grocery sector dominated by a handful of large integrated superstore retailers operating in a separate economic market for 'one-stop shopping' compared with other grocery retailers predominantly serving consumers' secondary ('top-up' and 'convenience') shopping needs. Overall, the CC finds the market to be 'broadly competitive', but with concerns about the extent of local concentration and the operation of certain pricing and buyer power practices.

In respect of pricing practices that allow the major retailers to extend and exploit their seller power, the CC argued against imposing invasive remedies that would directly prohibit or alter incentives to use such practices on the grounds that they would be (i) undesirable (e.g. giving rise to adverse competition effects), (ii) disproportionate (e.g. too restrictive or interventionist compared with economic harm caused by the practices) and/or (iii) impractical (e.g. the regulatory monitoring costs of overseeing remedies). The result was that no remedies were administered and retailers were allowed to carry on with practices deemed anticompetitive and against the public interest.

On the procurement side, the CC found that retailers with as low as 8 per cent market share possess significant buyer power. The CC produced evidence that buying effectiveness is closely related to market share. Moreover, relative differences in retail market shares appear just as important as absolute levels. Yet it is not just in respect of squeezing suppliers on supply prices where retailers exercise buyer power. The CC found that buyer-led vertical restraints are extensive, operate in parallel and have a cumulative impact that can distort supplier and/or retailer competition to the ultimate detriment of consumers. The remedy proposed by the CC was for curbing (but not prohibiting) the worst buyer power abuses through the establishment of a code of practice to be overseen by the Office of Fair Trading and to apply to the five retailers with greater than 8 per cent market share of the grocery sector.

For better or worse, the CC chose to eschew remedies that would directly tackle the identified anticompetitive effects of retailer behaviour. Yet, left unregulated, retailer power may be like an unstoppable juggernaut – with increased buyer and seller power going hand in hand to build ever stronger positions at the expense of smaller retailers and thus ultimately likely to restrict the extent of variety and range of service choice on offer to consumers. This consolidation process is likely to be exacerbated by incumbency advantages held by the major players when there are significant barriers to entry for large-format grocery retailing (due in large part to the UK's tight planning restrictions). Taken together, this would suggest that policy action – of either a behavioural or structural nature – might be required sooner rather than later to preserve effective retail competition and thereby ensure that consumers are (and will continue to be) well served in respect of the prices, product/service choice and quality on offer in such an essential market.

Postscript

Subsequent to the CC's 2000 inquiry, the UK competition authorities have undertaken further investigations relating to the grocery retailing sector. The CC conducted merger inquiries in 2003 and 2005. Most significantly, the CC's 2003 inquiry resulted in Tesco, Sainsbury and Asda being prevented from acquiring Safeway, and allowing Morrison to do so only on condition of making a number of store divestments (Competition Commission, 2003a). Following continued competition concerns about the buyer and seller power of leading grocery retailers, the Office of Fair Trading decided in May 2006 to make a broad sector-wide referral to the CC (Office of Fair Trading, 2006).

The resulting 'groceries market' inquiry was due to be completed by the CC in 2008 (see www.competition-commission.org.uk/rep_pub/reports/2008/538grocery.htm).

Acknowledgements

The author is grateful for comments received from Steve Davies, Roman Inderst, Mike Walker, Mike Waterson and participants at the conference on 'Cases in European Competition Policy: The Economic Analysis' held at the ESRC Centre for Competition Policy, UEA, 6–7 July 2006.

B

Agreements between firms

Introduction

Any contract between firms limits the freedom of the parties involved. Even a simple contract to deliver 100 widgets next month at price €1,000 restricts the buyer's ability to switch to a lower-cost provider in the meantime and, if there are capacity constraints, also the seller's ability to supply one of the buyer's rivals. This is an example of a simple vertical contract. Such contracts are the essence of everyday business practice. They enhance the efficiency of trade and encourage investment. Freedom to engage in such contracts and the institutional environment that allows them to be enforced are essential ingredients to a well-performing market. The competition problems arise when contracts are used beyond this to include clauses that more directly exclude or suppress competition. Horizontal agreements (i.e. between alternative suppliers) ring a very direct warning bell of coordination for customer exploitation. When the agreement is vertical (i.e. between buyer and supplier) competition concerns usually relate to the potential exclusion of rivals which may then indirectly harm consumers. The common theme in this part of the book is the identification and deterrence of agreements that are harmful in their effects.

All of the cases in the following chapters relate to the enforcement of Article 81 of the EU Treaty (or the equivalent national provision). Article 81 prohibits any agreements or concerted practices 'which have as their object or effect the prevention, restriction or distortion of competition within the common market'. Examples include agreements that 'directly or indirectly fix purchase or selling prices or any other trading conditions', 'share markets or sources of supply' or 'apply dissimilar conditions to equivalent transactions with other trading parties, thereby placing them at a competitive disadvantage'. If a contract breaks the Article 81 prohibition, it is illegal and cannot be enforced. However, unlike the Article 82 prohibition, it is possible to argue for exemption under Article 81(3). This allows an agreement 'which contributes to improving the production or distribution of goods or to promoting technical or economic progress, while allowing consumers a fair share of the resulting benefit'. Either an individual agreement may be exempted or, in the case where a particular type of agreement is common-place, a class of agreements satisfying certain properties may be given a block exemption (usually relating to a particular industry).[1]

The first pair of cases relates to secret price-fixing cartels, for which there is no possibility of exemption. Cartels have become a major priority for EC competition policy. The main economic harms are textbook monopoly price raising and the stifling of the wider competitive process of improving offers to fight for customers. Although econometric evidence can be used to identify suspicious pricing patterns, there is little subtle economics in identifying a cartel.[2] EC investigation of international cartels has frequently been prompted by prior discovery by authorities in the US. The evidence usually comes from a whistleblower or incriminating documents and e-mails found in a 'dawn raid' on businesses under suspicion. In order to encourage whistleblowing, the EC first introduced a leniency scheme in 1996, with the latest revision in 2006. Leniency offers a reduction of the fine if a firm comes forward with evidence of a cartel, even if it has been a participant in the recent past.

The graphite electrodes cartel was a global conspiracy involving eight suppliers in Europe. They were fined a total of around €170 million. Hviid and Stephan examine the theory of optimal deterrence to see whether this level of fines is sufficient to deter firms that are economically motivated (i.e. do not obey the law on ethical grounds). They then apply deterrence theory to the case in hand. Fines ranged from less than 1 per cent to 6 per cent of turnover. These are small percentages relative to the price-raising capability of a cartel. They are unlikely to suffice for economic deterrence, especially given the chance of not being caught. The authors work through the EC fining guidelines applied and highlight further weaknesses in the incentives they create. Many of these weaknesses survive in the 2006 revision and the authors conclude that the EC is still not creating the right incentive for firms not to participate in future cartels.

If a cartel's customers were expected to sue for damages, this would be an additional disincentive to their formation. The US system of treble damages is a potent force for litigation across the Atlantic. European legal systems allow

---

[1] The legal niceties need not concern us here, but the legality of restrictive agreements can potentially be argued either under Article 81(1) as pro-competitive or under Article 81(3) as having offsetting efficiencies such that consumers benefit. The essential economic analysis is the same for both, although the latter is clearer in focusing on the effect on consumers.

[2] See Porter (2005).

only for single damages (i.e. a victim can claim only for losses shown to have been incurred). Given the chance of losing, this gives a very much reduced incentive to litigate for damages except when law firms offer contingency fees following a successful case brought by a competition authority. Even this is rare in Europe because of problems in proving the degree of harm. However, the EC is actively trying to encourage private actions.[3] Møllgaard considers the district heating pipe cartel in Denmark, Italy and Germany. This ten-member cartel was fined €87 million. It took ten years between the first dawn raid and rejection of the final appeal in 2005. Four Danish municipalities won damages of €21 million. While the EC has only to prove that a cartel existed, a damage claim additionally requires an estimate of the actual harm incurred by the customer. This requires an estimate of how much prices were elevated and how much of this was then passed on to downstream customers. Fortunately, the latter was not an issue for the municipalities because they did not resell the pipes. The author describes the range of methods available for estimating damages and provides an economic critique of the strengths and weaknesses of each.[4]

The next two cases are not of secret price fixing but of publicly known collective pricing agreements that can claim to enhance efficiency due to the presence of externalities. Like the chapter on mobile phone calls, they both involve markets in which there are network externalities between different groups of customers. These have become known as two-sided markets.

Credit and debit cards are increasingly used as a means of paying for transactions. They benefit both customers and retailers as convenient alternatives to cash or cheques (e.g. less risk of theft), so both might be charged for their use. When the customer has a card issued by a different bank to the one used by the retailer, this opens a third possible charge known as the interchange fee. This is paid between the banks to compensate for any imbalance of their customer and retailer transactions. Associations of banks (e.g. Visa, MasterCard) operate these payment-card systems and set the interchange fee and other rules. The fee is usually levied on the retailer's bank and the EC challenged Visa as an agreement between banks that set the fee well in excess of the cost of the transaction. The fee is then passed on to retailers as a high price for Visa services. Rochet identifies the usage externality caused by consumers using a card instead of cash. They cause banks to incur a cost of administering the transaction and retailers avoid the cost of handling cash. Interchange fees can be used to internalise this externality and so reduce distortions in usage. Furthermore,

---

[3] See EC White Paper on Damages Actions for Breach of the EC antitrust rules; COM(2008) 165, 2.4.2008.
[4] Damages are also discussed in Chapter 10.

competition between banks for customers means that extra revenues gained from retailers find their way into subsidies for customers. The author argues that careful economic modelling reveals no systematic bias and very limited justification for the Commission's price-cap remedy.[5]

The commercialisation of sports creates important interactions between honest and exciting sporting competition and the economic competition which is the focus of this book. The highest-profile cases across Europe have concerned the sale of exclusive TV rights, but competition law can stretch much further. The UK OFT took the British Horseracing Board (BHB) to task over a range of its rules (i.e. agreements) relating to the organisation of fixtures and the way in which non-exclusive rights to take bets were sold to book-makers. Betting is a distinctive feature of horseracing and has been used to justify much greater state regulation in countries other than the UK, where there is a strong governing authority. Lyons analyses the externalities in this sport to understand the appropriate division between rules supporting good governance to the benefit of consumers and rules that might be an abuse. He identifies several groups of 'consumers' of the sport, including owners, punters and spectators. The author develops a simple model to understand the implications of different types of collective and individual agreement. He finds that the OFT's initial objections to certain rules could have had a seriously adverse effect on the quality of the product enjoyed by most con-sumers. The OFT was eventually persuaded to revise its position, but some ancillary court decisions on database rights have since undermined what had looked like a good economic effects-based settlement.

The third group of agreements relates to vertical restraints between man-ufacturers and wholesalers or retailers. Such agreements often have efficiency benefits, including the reduction of double marginalisation,[6] but this does not mean that they cannot also have the effect of distorting competition. Such cases require careful economic analysis and supporting evidence in order to balance the overall effect on consumer welfare.

Car manufacturers have traditionally sold their cars through independent dealerships subject to contracts that limit the commercial freedom of their dealers in a number of ways. These include exclusive territories (dealers must not sell to consumers outside a designated area), selective distribution (dealers must achieve a specified service level or sell a minimum quantity) and

---

[5] A similar case for MasterCard was settled with a similar remedy in December 2007.
[6] Double marginalisation is where successive stages of production and distribution each add markups which cumulatively may even exceed the integrated monopoly markup.

exclusive dealing (dealers must not sell cars made by other manufacturers). The first two soften intrabrand competition between retailers of the same cars and the third softens interbrand competition between manufacturers (e.g. making it more difficult for consumers to compare cars or new manufacturers to enter a market). However, each restraint can also be justified on efficiency grounds, for example encouraging dealers to invest in local marketing, preventing low-quality retailers from freeriding on the showroom services provided by others (and so undermining the incentive to provide those services) or protecting the investment of manufacturers in training and equipping their dealers. Verboven explores the EC's attitude to these restraints in the form of the evolving block exemption under Article 81(3), observing that the main preoccupation, at least until 2002, was with the common market rather than balancing competition and efficiency. He also takes us through the economic evidence for efficiencies, competition softening and foreclosure effects in relation to cars. He concludes that the EC is moving in the right direction but still has some way to go.

Brewers also have a tradition of exclusive dealing in relation to their 'on-trade' (i.e. selling to pubs as distinct from off-licences and supermarkets for home consumption). The Crehan case concerns both the anticompetitive effect of a form of such exclusivity and the pursuit of damages for the consequences. Waterson tells the tale of one publican's battle against a 'pubco' controlled at the time by the Courage brewery. Pubcos own a large number of pubs which they lease to tenant publicans. Like thousands of other tenants, Bernie Crehan signed a lease for his pub, including an exclusive agreement to buy beer only through the pubco. This is known as tying and is a variant of exclusive dealing – you cannot have one thing (e.g. a pub or photocopier) without also buying your supplies (e.g. beer or paper) from the same firm. The advantage of tying for an independent pubco is that it can use its buyer power to play off one brewery against another and so negotiate advantageous terms. Alternatively, a pubco owned by a brewery secures market share. The problem for the tenants is that their wholesale price is not part of their exclusive purchasing contract but is 'negotiated' under the constraint that the pub cannot buy beer from anyone else. Nevertheless, this apparently vulnerable position may be compensated by other benefits or a lower rent. Mr Crehan went bust in 1993 claiming that this was because his high wholesale price of beer meant he could not compete with neighbouring pubs that could secure cheaper supplies. Although the case formally relates to just one poor publican, it was expected to set a wide-ranging precedent and it reached the highest courts in both the UK and the EU. Waterson sets out the economic analysis and documents the twists and turns of the legal process. He concludes that the final outcome was a victory for arcane legal argument over economic analysis. The case provides a vivid example of the dangers of arguing competition cases before non-specialist courts – especially when it takes thirteen years to reach a conclusion!

The car-distribution block exemption touches on the EC preoccupation with unimpeded trade in a common European market, but the Glaxo case brings it into sharp focus. The case relates to a practice under which Glaxo sold its medicines to Spanish wholesalers at prices differentiated according to where the medicine would be consumed. Thus, the price for a medicine to be sold in Spain was set at the level mandated by Spanish price regulation, but the same wholesaler would have to pay more for supplies to be re-exported to countries willing to pay more, notably the UK. While not explicitly prohibiting parallel trade (i.e. trade by arbitragers in parallel to that by the original manufacturer), the practice had the same effect. The EC prohibited this dual-pricing agreement on *per se* grounds that it impeded trade in the common market. Glaxo appealed the decision. Venit and Rey argue that restraints on parallel trade should not be *per se* illegal and each case should be assessed on its economic merits. They draw on the economics of price discrimination and argue that the EC should have taken account of the fact that pharmaceuticals prices are regulated by national purchasing policies. For example, in the absence of any restraints, low-price countries might not be supplied. Also, if parallel trade was allowed and this drove price down to that of the lowest regulated price, this would undermine R&D incentives. Thus, the Glaxo agreement was in principle justifiable on the grounds of consumer benefit. In 2006, the CFI agreed that restraints on parallel trade should be judged on consumer welfare grounds (i.e. the economic approach). This case shows how the courts can be a positive force for good economic analysis, in particular in promoting consumer welfare as the ultimate focus for competition policy.[7]

---

[7] Other examples of positive influence can be found in Chapters 14 and 17. Note that while the CFI is not a truly specialised court, competition-related cases form the bulk of its work (unlike for most of the courts deciding Crehan).

B.1

Cartels

5

The graphite electrodes cartel: fines which deter?

Morten Hviid and Andreas Stephan

1. Introduction

Agreements between undertakings aimed at fixing prices, limiting output or sharing markets without any expectation of offsetting benefits to consumers are prohibited under Article 81 of the EC Treaty. Cartels are obviously included in this. A violation of this prohibition can for each violator attract a fine up to 10 per cent of its worldwide turnover. This fine will in the first instance be levied by the Directorate General for Competition following their investigation and is formally an administrative rather than a criminal fine.[1] Their decision can be appealed to the Court of First Instance (CFI) and subsequently to the European Court of Justice (ECJ). In order to overcome the information problems in detecting and prosecuting cartel agreements, the EU has introduced a leniency programme which rewards cooperation by cartel members through a reduction in the fine.

The law on cartels, like other areas of competition policy, is founded on principles of economics, but economists are rarely involved in its application against explicit hard-core collusive agreements. In part, this is due to the absence of evidentiary problems – direct evidence may be found from a whistleblower or in dawn raids (e.g. e-mails) – and thanks to leniency programmes, cartel members may either reveal details of their infringement in return for immunity from fines or start cooperating and providing evidence in return for a leniency discount once an investigation into their industry has been opened. This evidence will normally indicate the affected market, the scale of the infringement and the extent of each protagonist's involvement. Once this has occurred, it is left to lawyers to sift through the evidence to determine whether an infringement exists.

---

[1] Several EU Member States have in addition to administrative fines criminal sanctions against hard-core cartel violations.

Nevertheless, economics has a role after a breach of competition law has been established, to determine the appropriate level and form of subsequent punishments.[2] Ideally, the level of punishment should deter future infringement of competition law without leading firms to choose an excessive (costly) level of compliance. When considering cases of naked price fixing, we may be less concerned about over-deterrence, but we will provide an example where even here, excessively aggressive punishment could lead to unwanted behaviour.[3] Assuming that at least some cartels are more constrained by profit incentives than by ethical standards, the key to deterrence of price fixing is to ensure that the expected loss from being found guilty of a violation outweighs the expected benefit from collusion. To work, this requires first that firms make this type of cost–benefit analysis before joining the cartel and second that expected fines are such as to tip the scales towards non-violation. Setting the fine thus involves not just a moral/ethical judgement about breaching the law but also an economic analysis to determine the appropriate size of the fine.

The aim of this chapter is to illustrate the extent to which the economics of deterrence is used in setting the fines in the EU, basing our analysis on the *Graphite Electrodes*[4] cartel case. The price fixing in this case was global, with fines imposed in several jurisdictions including the EU and the US.[5] We will focus on the EU case in which eight firms were found to have infringed Article 81 EC. The chapter is organised as follows. Section 2 provides a brief overview of the theory of optimal deterrence. Section 3 describes the industry and section 4 the case of the Commission and the subsequent appeals. Section 5 summarises the relevant EU fining guidelines, while section 6 looks at how the fines were calculated in the *Graphite* decisions as well as the subsequent appeals to the CFI and the ECJ. Section 7 focuses on the treatment of a firm that appeared to be on the fringe of the cartel. Section 8 concludes.

---

[2] This chapter is concerned with public enforcement of competition law, relying on appropriate punishments for an infringement. The next chapter by Møllgaard considers private action aimed at extracting damages.

[3] See also Kobayashi (2001, 732).

[4] European Commission Decision of 18 July 2001 relating to a proceeding under Article 81 EC and Article 53 of the EEA Agreement (Case C.36.490 – Graphite Electrodes) (notified under document number C(2001) 1986). (2002/271/EC) OJ [2002] L 100/1.

[5] For a discussion and a presentation of the case, see e.g. Levenstein and Suslow (2003, 826–843).

2. The theory of optimal deterrence

The theory of optimal deterrence relies on firms making a rational cost–benefit analysis of whether or not to take an action which may infringe the law. At an abstract level, the theory of optimal deterrence is straightforward.[6] Rational firms will balance the expected gain from a violation against the expected punishment. The fact that the only form of punishment available in EU competition law is a monetary fine simplifies the calculations as there is no need to compute how individuals assess the loss of their personal freedom.[7] If B is the expected benefit to a cartel member arising from price fixing, F the fine imposed if price fixing is established, P^d the probability of detection and P^c the probability of conviction given detection, then price fixing is deterred if the expected benefit is less than the expected fine, or:

$$B \leq P^d \cdot P^c \cdot F$$

For example, if there is a 25 per cent chance of detection and an 80 per cent chance of conviction once detected, effective deterrence requires a fine of at least five times the benefit. Suppose the cartel can achieve a price rise of 10 per cent and demand is highly inelastic, so quantity demanded does not fall, this translates into a profit benefit equivalent to 10 per cent of sales. Consequently, if we set aside ethical considerations and investigation costs, the deterrence fine would have to be at least five times this, or 50 per cent of sales!

There are a number of subtleties behind this deterrence formula. First, authorities are unlikely to be able to impose arbitrarily high fines because of concerns over bankruptcy – see Stephan (2006). Moreover, P^d depends on leniency programmes, the effectiveness of which depends on the size of the fine, so P^d depends on F. F also affects the conditional probability if there is either scope for plea bargaining or, as in the EU, where leniency can be granted to more than the first firm to come forward with information.

---

[6] For early expositions, see Becker (1968) and Landes (1983). For recent expositions and evaluations, see Camilli (2006) and Wils (2006).

[7] Some might want to argue that there is a loss of reputation from having been found guilty. There is little evidence of this in reality. In our present case, according to a Dresdner Kleinwort Wasserstein report on SGL Carbon, one of the participants in the graphites cartel, dated 13 February 2006, 'many of the old guard are still in charge' (p. 3). Even though the association with price fixing according to the report means 'many investors are still negatively disposed towards the stock', the management team has not been replaced. In particular, Robert Kohler, who had the (to that date) largest personal fine ever imposed by the US DoJ (see Kobayashi (2001 fn. 66)), remains CEO at least as of 2008.

In practice we do not have a good estimate of either of the two probabilities[8] so that even if we could estimate B, and leaving aside the endogeneity of these probabilities, it is difficult to determine the optimal size of F. Moreover, if firms can assess neither the probabilities nor the likely size of the fine, there may be either under- or over-deterrence. Given this slightly pessimistic view of applying optimal punishment theory, we set a more limited task for this chapter. The aim is to see whether the European Commission's arguments and the fining policy are at least consistent with a policy of deterrence.

3. The graphite electrodes industry

The product in *Graphite Electrodes* is ceramic-moulded columns of graphite mainly used in the production of steel in electric arc furnaces ('mini-mills'). This is essentially a recycling process whereby scrap steel is converted into new steel: graphite electrodes form part of the roof of the furnace and electricity is passed through them, creating sufficient heat to melt the scrap metal. This process accounted for a third of all steel production in the EU during the 1990s and by 1998 was worth €420 million in the European Economic Area (EEA) alone.[9]

During the period of the cartel, there were nine firms active in the European market: SGL Carbon AG (SGL), UCAR International (UCAR), VAW Aluminium (VAW), Conradty, Carbide Graphite Group Inc. (C/G), Showa Denko K. K. (SDK), SEC Corp. (SEC), Nippon Carbon Co. Inc. (Nippon) and Tokai Carbon Co. Ltd (Tokai). Table 5.1 shows publicly available market shares, some of which are suppressed due to the Commission's policy on commercial confidentiality.

The industry has characteristics typical of those where collusion is considered likely, with a high concentration (e.g. four-firm concentration ratio of 95 per cent in the US), high entry barriers and a crisis preceding the formation of the cartel. In the 1980s graphite electrodes was characterised by a large number of national producers. A strong fall in demand caused the industry to operate at just 60 per cent capacity in 1982, leading to an intensification of competition

---

[8] The only estimate is from Bryant and Eckard (1991).
[9] European Commission Press Release 18 July 2001, 'Commission Fines Eight Companies in Graphite Electrode Cartel' (IP/01/1010).

Table 5.1 Market share in graphite electrodes (1998 turnover[10])

Firm	EU[11]	US	Worldwide
SGL	X%	23%	>10%
UCAR		36%	>10%
VAW	Y%[12]		< 5%
Conradty			?
C/G	7%	18%	5–10%
SDK	3–4%	18%	5–10%
SEC			< 5%
Nippon			< 5%
Tokai		1%	5–10%

Source: EU case; Kobayashi (2001, Table 2)

prior to the year when the cartel was allegedly formed. As Levenstein and Suslow (2003, 828) note:

There was a shakeout and consolidation in the industry in the late 1980s and early 1990s, just prior to the price-fixing conspiracy, reducing the number of major firms in the industry from eighteen to ten … [this was] precipitated in part by slumping steel production, which 'chipped 30 percent off electrode prices late in the decade, triggering a round of consolidations'.

Following the restructuring, capacity utilisation increased to 85 per cent by 1996, with SGL and UCAR emerging as the two global leaders, controlling most of the market between them (Graphite Electrodes Commission Decision, hereafter GE, recital 13). The industry's high entry barriers were mainly due to the complicated and expensive processes necessary for production. The Antitrust Division of the US Department of Justice in its civil action noted that '[t]here have been no significant entrants in the graphite electrode industry since 1950' and that '[o]pening a new facility would require approximately a $250 million investment and roughly 18 to 24 months'.[13] Levenstein and Suslow (2003, page 830) also note the importance of implicit technical and market knowledge which cannot easily be duplicated.

---

[10] The last full year in which all members participated in the cartel.

[11] Where the rows are combined, the market share is for the aggregate of the relevant firms. Thus collectively, SDK, SEC, Nippon and Tokai have 3–4% of the EU market.

[12] Where 7% < Y% < X%.

[13] Verified Complaint, United States v SGL Carbon Aktiengesellschaft, No. 03–521 (W.D. Pa. filed Apr. 15, 2003), paras. 34–37, available at http://www.usdoj.gov/atr/cases/f200900/200935.htm

4. The case and the appeals

The European Commission opened its investigation into the graphite electrode industry in June 1997 alongside parallel investigations in the US and
Canada. On 5 June 1997, Commission officials carried out simultaneous and
unannounced investigations at the premises of SGL, Conradty and VAW in
Germany and UCAR in France. Despite this, the infringement continued into
the following year and there were attempts to obstruct the investigations;
documentation was destroyed and in January 1998 SGL 'attempted to per-
suade the Japanese producers not to cooperate with the Commission' (GE
recital 124).

The investigation found that the cartel was well organised and character-
istically involved the direct participation of executives at the highest level.
The prices for graphite electrodes were to be fixed by chairmen/general
managers only (GE recital 50). Prices were set in regular 'top guy' meetings,
typically held in Switzerland, and efforts were made to conceal their purpose.
Side payments were used to counter any gains made from cheating the
agreement.

The decision of the Commission was delivered on 18 July 2001, finding
that eight of the nine firms active in the market had infringed Article 81 during
the period 1992–8.[14] The missing firm from the list was Conradty. Conradty
never admitted participating in any collusive arrangements, nor did it cooperate with the Commission. In view of the insufficiency of direct documentary
evidence against Conradty, and certain inconsistencies in the accounts of its
possible participation, the Commission did not proceed against that undertaking.[15] Another firm, C/G, behaved consistently differently from the rest in
that it did not participate in any of the group meetings, although it did get
information about the decisions in these meetings from one of the participants. From the case[16] it would appear that C/G used this information to price
slightly below the cartel and although it did not expand its capacity, it
expanded its production within the EU, more than doubling its sales between
1993 and 1996. From the CFI decision, one gets the impression that had C/G

---

[14] It is not possible to give a clear picture of the resulting overcharge in the EEA. The Commission decision
mentions only specific local price rises. While Levenstein and Suslow (2003, 838) mention that
customers suing for damages argued that overcharges over the period 1992–7 averaged 45 per cent,
this does relate to prices in general, not prices in the EEA.

[15] This was despite an admission by SGL that it had warned Conradty about the forthcoming investigation.

[16] Especially the CFI decision recitals 332 and 338.

not cooperated with the Commission, the latter might not have been able to construct a case against it.[17]

Subsequently, seven of the eight firms (SGL, UCAR, SEC, Nippon, Tokai, SDK and C/G) appealed the Commission's decision to the CFI. The CFI decision was given on 29 April 2004.[18] The nature of the appeal as regards those parts relating to the calculation of the fine as well as the CFI decision is integrated into the discussion in section 6 below.[19] The EU Commission then appealed to the ECJ with respect to the part of the CFI decision which increased the leniency award for SGL. SGL and Tokai also appealed the CFI decision to the ECJ with respect to the size of fines. The ECJ in its decision of 29 June 2006 rejected the appeals by SGL and Tokai but upheld the appeal of the Commission.

5. The Commission guidelines on fines

In imposing fines on the eight undertakings, the Commission followed the 1998 guidelines.[20] The guidelines outline principles which should 'ensure the transparency and impartiality of the Commission's decisions in the eyes of the undertakings and of the Court of Justice alike' while upholding the Commission's discretion in setting fines. 'This discretion must, however, follow a coherent and non-discriminatory policy which is consistent with the objectives pursued in penalising infringements of competition rules.'

The method of calculating fines as set out in the 1998 guidelines is summarised in Figure 5.1.[21]

---

[17] See CFI decision recitals 444–448.

[18] Judgment of the Court of First Instance (Second Chamber) 29 April 2004 (1) in Joined Cases T-236/01, T-239/01, T-244/01 to T-246/01, T-251/01 and T-252/01.

[19] In particular we will ignore the parts of the appeal dealing with *ne bis in idem*, where the firms claim that, as they had already been fined for the infringement in the US, they should not be punished again and that at least the fines imposed in other jurisdictions should have been deducted from the final EU fine. Both the CFI and the ECJ rejected these parts of the appeals. In terms of deterrence it would clearly have been problematic had they not as one would have to rely on the first jurisdiction to offer a verdict to produce a fine which would deter on a global rather than a jurisdiction level. See CFI decision recitals 119–155.

[20] The 1998 'Guidelines on the Method of Setting Fines Imposed Pursuant to Article 15 (2) of Regulation No. 17 and Article 65 (5) of the ECSC Treaty' (98/C 9/03). The fining guidelines were reformed in 2006 ('Guidelines on the method of setting fines pursuant to Article 23 (2)(a) of Regulation No. 1/2003' (2006/C 210/02)).

[21] The most significant differences between the 1998 and the 2006 guidelines relate to the calculation of the *basic amount*. Gravity is now based on the 'value of sales'. Value of sales is based on the 'value of the undertaking's sales of goods or services to which the infringement directly or indirectly relates in the relevant geographic area within the EEA' (Section 1A recital 13). Note the important change from

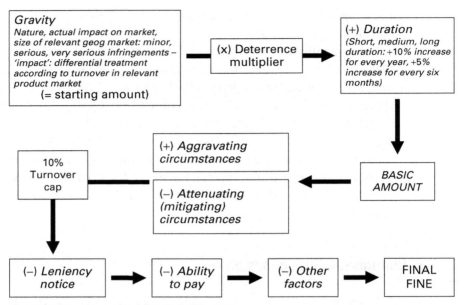

Figure 5.1 Summary of the 1998 EU fining guidelines

The 1998 guidelines are discussed in more detail in section 6 below, which is organised to fit with the flowchart in Figure 5.1. However, it is worth noting at this stage that most adjustments in the calculation of fines, including the deterrence multiplier, aggravating and attenuating circumstances, ability to pay and other factors, were not subject to any specific guidance. Their application and quantification were thus entirely discretionary. It should also be noted that the duration adjustment were regressive rather than proportionate to the length of an infringement.

6. Calculating the fines

The actual fines set by the Commission at the different stages in the calculation and the revisions following the appeals are summarised in

worldwide to EEA sales as the basis for the starting amount, which can be up to 30 per cent of value of sales (recital 21). In another radical change, duration is now determined by multiplying the gravity amount by the number of years of the infringement, rather than a fixed percentage increase for each year. For cartels of a duration of five years, the duration multiplier has increased from 1.5 to 5. Finally, a new so-called 'entry fee' with the purpose of deterring firms from even entering into cartels is imposed. For a full discussion and evaluation of the changes to the guidelines, see Veljanovski (2007).

Tables A5.1–A5.3 in the appendix. Over the duration of the cartel[22] (five and a half years), total EEA sales were in the region of €2.3 billion.[23] Thus total fines of €218.8 million are the equivalent of approximately 9.5 per cent of EEA turnover during the period of collusion. In the following, we take each component of the fines and ask whether it is consistent with the efficient deterrence of cartels.

6.1 The basic amount

6.1.1 Categories

In terms of gravity, the Commission viewed this as a deliberate and *very serious* infringement that permeated the whole industry and was encouraged at the highest levels of the undertakings, operating entirely for the benefit of producers to the detriment of consumers and ultimately the general public. The guidelines indicate that the likely fines in such a case are above €20 million. To take account of the real impact of the offending conduct of each undertaking on competition it may be necessary to apply weightings to the size of the fines. Basing this solely on the *worldwide* product turnover in the last year of the infringement (1998), the Commission identified three categories with relative weights 5–2–1 and allocated the firms as follows:

Category 1: SGL and UCAR. Starting point €40 million.
Category 2: Tokai, SDK and C/G. Starting point €16 million.
Category 3: VAW, SEC and Nippon. Starting point €8 million.

The Commission did not offer any explanation about how the starting amount in the most serious category was set at €40 million. In its appeal, SGL claimed that this size 'is incompatible with the Commission's former decision-making practice'.[24] The CFI in its decision rejected SGL's appeal and left the freedom to set the starting amount with the Commission without requiring the latter to offer an explicit justification for its size.

Several of the firms criticised the use of global market shares in defining and allocating firms to categories. The CFI recognised that using EEA market shares as a basis for the fines, as argued by e.g. the Japanese firms, would have wrongly rewarded those who stayed out of the 'local' market and that using global market shares avoids this problem (see Table 5.1). The CFI also made plain that the Commission is entitled to rely on a single criterion when differentiating between the different firms in terms of gravity so long as the

---

[22] Most firms were members of the cartel for five and a half years.
[23] Based on 1998 EEA sales of €420 million (GE recital 19).   [24] CFI decision recital 173, 189–193.

formula is applied consistently. The CFI found that it was not. While the first category was correct and the gap between the first category and SDK was likewise correct, as Tokai is about half the size of SDK, those two firms cannot be in the same category and Tokai is relegated to the third category. As C/G is close in size to Tokai, it is likewise relegated to category three. The former third category is internally consistent but firms in this group are about half the size of Tokai and C/G and hence a fourth category with a starting amount of €4 million is created.

Category 1:   SGL and UCAR. Starting point €40 million.

Category 2:   SDK. Starting point €16 million.

Category 3:   Tokai and C/G. Starting point €8 million.

Category 4:   VAW, SEC and Nippon. Starting point €4 million.

From a deterrence perspective, it is debatable whether or not fines should be related to worldwide market shares as in the 1998 guidelines or to market shares in the EEA as in the revised 2006 guidelines. A firm would accept to stay out of a particular market as part of a market-allocation agreement only if it obtained compensation elsewhere by others staying out of its core markets. As such it must generate direct harm through over-pricing in another jurisdiction and could in theory be caught and fined there. Ideally for deterrence we want the worldwide aggregate fine to be distributed to the violators in relation to their individual gains, for which their worldwide turnover might well be a good proxy. If and only if globally competition law is enforced equally effectively and uses the same method for calculating fines in all the markets in which the conspirators are active, it will not matter how the overall fine for the total harm in each jurisdiction is allocated among the conspirators. However, assume either that enforcement is weaker in some of the jurisdictions outside the EU or that they use different allocation rules, then the 2006 guidelines with its focus on the EEA could disadvantage EEA producers. Where the cartel involves some market allocation towards EEA producers, these will take on a greater share of the overall EU fine relative to foreign producers which may escape fines altogether.

6.1.2 'Means testing'

To ensure sufficient deterrent effect, the Commission took into account the overall economic capacity of the undertakings and applied a deterrence multiplier in two cases. In the case of VAW Aluminium the need for deterrence required that the starting point of its fine should increase by a factor of 1.25 to €10 million. In the case of Showa Denko K. K., by far the largest undertaking concerned by the decision, the starting point of its fine was increased by a factor of 2.5 to €40 million. In its response to SDK's appeal to the CFI, the Commission pointed out that the factor was not to do with size as such but with the need for the punishment to be proportionate to the means of the firm. Essentially the fine had to be made bigger to ensure that SDK felt it. Just as overall size may not be a good proxy for their part in the infringement, so it may not be a good proxy for financial means. While the CFI accepted that the use of a deterrence factor was lawful, it did not accept the actual size of the factor applied to SDK, believing the Commission to have made a mistake. 'According to the logic which the Commission itself followed in VAW's case, it was therefore appropriate to adjust SDK's starting amount by twice the real increase applied to VAW, in order to take account of the fact that SDK was twice as large and had twice as many global resources.'[25] Abstract for the moment from the fact that the two firms were in different fining categories. If the intention of the Commission was that SDK's fine should be twice that of VAW irrespective of the level of any other fine, then the Commission's method is correct. However, if the intention was that VAW's fine should be 25 per cent higher than standard and SDK twice that, i.e. 50 per cent higher, then the CFI's method is correct. The correction was based on differences in worldwide turnover. Since the worldwide turnover of VAW was three times that of SGL, the largest firm not to have a factor applied, and SDK six times SGL, without more information than contained in the decisions, we cannot assess whether there was an economic basis for the two decisions.

The idea of means-tested fines is not consistent with an optimal deterrence argument since it is generally accepted that deterrence is not based on ability to pay but rather on a balance between gains and losses. While speeding fines might have to be means tested to deter rich drivers who might be willing to pay €100 for the 'privilege' of driving fast, it is not clear that fixing prices means more to large diversified corporations which hence need a larger fine for deterrence.

6.1.3 Duration

According to the guidelines a distinction should be made between cartels of different duration. For infringements of more than five years, which are considered of *long duration*, the basic fine can be increased by up to 10 per cent per year of the infringement (5 per cent for each complete six months). While no explicit rule is in place for infringements of between one and five years, the Commission clearly used the same formula and used it to the maximum. For

[25] CFI judgment recital 247.

most of the firms, the duration was five and a half years, leading to an increase of the starting amount of 55 per cent. There is no basis in deterrence theory to suggest that a cartel of five years' duration should be fined only half as much again as one that has been generating illicit profits for only one fifth as long. The marginal increase in the expected fine from continuing the cartel one more year is clearly modest even if the probability of detection went up. In the absence of a leniency programme, this would provide almost no inducement to stop once the cartel is established. The increase of the fine of up to 100 per cent per year introduced in the 2006 revision to the guidelines may be aimed at providing better marginal incentives.

While one might think that with this explicit formula there was little scope for appeals, this is not the case. This is partly because a number of firms continued the infringement after the investigation was started and apart from being an aggravating circumstance, it increased the period of the infringement by nine months and consequently increased the multiplier by at least five percentage points. These appeals were rejected by the CFI. Nippon unsuccessfully claimed not to have been part of the collusion during the first ten months. As the Commission had granted Nippon a leniency discount because it was not challenging the facts of the Commission's decision, and Nippon with the appeal was challenging this, the Commission requested that the CFI increase Nippon's fine and it did so, but by two percentage points rather than the requested 10 per cent. The CFI did this by reducing Nippon's leniency discount by 2 per cent. At least this seems broadly consistent with leniency incentives.

6.2 Aggravating and attenuating circumstances

The basic amount is increased or decreased where there are aggravating and/or attenuating circumstances. The guidelines do not provide an exhaustive list of these circumstances, but do provide examples. Aggravating circumstances include 'the repeated infringement of same type; refusal to cooperate or obstruction; acting as leader or instigator; using retaliatory measures to enforce infringement; the need to increase penalty to exceed improper gains; other'. Attenuating circumstances include 'a passive or follow-my-leader role; non-implementation or termination of infringement when Commission intervenes; reasonable doubt; infringements committed as result of negligence or unintentionally; other'.

From the CFI appeal, we know that the following aggravating circumstances were allowed for:

1. Continuing the infringement after the investigation started: 10 per cent (SGL, UCAR, Tokai, SEC, Nippon).
2. Ringleader: 50 per cent (SGL and UCAR).
3. Obstructing the proceedings (warning other companies): 25 per cent (SGL).

SGL, UCAR, SEC and Nippon contested the Commission's findings in their appeals, all of which were rejected by the CFI. As regards the warning, the CFI points out that 'the warnings given by SGL sought to ensure the continuation of a cartel which is accepted as having constituted a flagrant and undisputed breach of Community competition law'.[26]

C/G received a 40 per cent fine decrease for mitigating circumstances: it took only a passive role as a 'price follower', not having attended any 'top guy' meetings or working-level meetings, and did not fully implement the offending agreements. In its rejected appeal, C/G argued that this reduction was inadequate. Two other firms (SEC and Nippon) also argued that they took a passive role. The CFI rejected their arguments as their passive role had been rather different from that of C/G. They had been represented by Tokai at some meetings and present at other meetings.[27] The claim by Nippon that it had not reduced sales was rejected as unsubstantiated.[28] While the CFI accepted that SEC had quadrupled its output between 1992 and 1997, it obtained only a minimal market share in the EEA and hence the 'non-implementation remained below the threshold of reasonable effectiveness'.[29]

On appeal three firms (C/G, SGL and UCAR) argued that the disastrous economic situation in the sector in the early 1990s was an attenuating factor and should have been allowed for. Such an argument has been accepted by the Commission before.[30] The CFI rejected these arguments: 'As the Commission properly observed, as a general rule cartels come into being when a sector encounters problems. If the applicants' reasoning were to be followed, the fine would have to be reduced as a matter of course in virtually all cases.'[31] From a deterrence perspective, the CFI decision can only be welcomed.

---

[26] CFI judgment recital 313.   [27] CFI decision recital 335.   [28] CFI decision recital 338.

[29] CFI decision recital 339. SEC's market share was below 2 per cent while C/G's was almost 8 per cent.

[30] Seamless steel tubes and pipes (OJ L 140, 06.06.2003, pp. 1–29) recital 168–169. Alloy surcharges (decision of the European Commission 21.1.1998) recital 83–84. In neither case does the Commission offer any reason for this. Given the Commission's general attitude to violations of Article 81, it is difficult to understand why a plea of 'poverty' would make it OK to overcharge consumers. This would certainly not help deterrence.

[31] CFI decision recital 345.

6.3 10 per cent annual turnover cap

As emphasised in the 1998 guidelines, the final amount imposed by the Commission may not in any case exceed 10 per cent of the worldwide turnover of the undertakings in the year preceding the year in which the decision is taken.[32] UCAR benefited from this as its annual turnover for the year 2000 was €841 million, making it necessary for the Commission to cap its fine at €84.1 million rather than €99.2 million, so as not to exceed the permissible limit (GE recital 199).

SDK and SGL tried to argue that the 10 per cent limit should apply after the leniency discount. Since this would remove the incentive to apply for leniency for any serious infringement where the fine was likely to be large relative to worldwide turnover, it is appropriate that the CFI rejected this argument. SDK argued that it was penalised because of its organisational structure which makes it a large firm, even though graphite electrodes is a relatively small part of its business, but as the Commission was following its own guidelines, the CFI rejected this part of the appeal.

6.4 Leniency notice

It is worthwhile to note that no firm got 100 per cent leniency. In graphite electrodes, SDK was the first company to provide substantial and decisive evidence of the cartel, handing over several crucial documents to the Commission in March 1998, leading to a reduction in the fine of 70 per cent. Although not the first to cooperate, UCAR contributed substantially to establishing important aspects of the case and was granted a 40 per cent reduction. SGL was granted a 30 per cent fine reduction for information received that went beyond that specified in the formal request for information, in particular information about meetings the Commission was unaware of and information about national implementation of the cartel in Europe. C/G received only a 20 per cent discount, as opposed to the 50 per cent reduction it claimed to be entitled to, because it initially gave ambiguous information as to its role in the cartel. VAW received a 20 per cent reduction for cooperation that started before the Commission adopted its Statement of Objections and continued afterwards. Tokai, SEC and Nippon did not contest the factual allegations and each received a 10 per cent discount. The Commission has a substantial degree of freedom when it comes to awarding leniency. Whether for incentive purposes only the

---

[32] If figures are not available for that accounting year, the immediately preceding year is used.

first to come forward should receive a leniency discount is still an open question: see Chen and Rey (2007). Granting a 10 per cent discount to every party simply for not contesting the facts does not seem an appropriate incentive where fines are the only sanction. Such discounts have the effect of unnecessarily reducing the aggregate of fines imposed (for no party faces the full fine) and also weaken the incentives behind leniency. These rely on the difference between immunity and the fine a revealing firm would have incurred had it not cooperated. The smaller this difference, the less likely it will be that firms will come forward.

Moreover, if part of the aim of a leniency programme was to avoid costly appeals as firms are agreeing not to contest factual allegations, this has not been met. Instead part of the focus for appeals has been on the size of the leniency discount awarded. In this case, SGL, UCAR and C/G appealed. The CFI first increased SGL's leniency discount by ten percentage points, but then reduced it by two percentage points[33] so the net gain for SGL is 8 per cent.[34] UCAR got a 10 per cent extra discount. C/G argued successfully that in reality it provided all the relevant evidence as regards the nature and the duration of its participation in the infringement and the CFI found that the Commission had not adequately allowed for this and increased the leniency discount from 20 per cent to 40 per cent.

The EU Commission appealed the part of the CFI decision which regarded the increase in the leniency award for SGL. The ECJ found for the Commission to the extent that the CFI had overestimated the voluntary help SGL had afforded the Commission. The ECJ in effect halved the additional leniency discount offered by the CFI from eight percentage points to 4 per cent and ordered SGL to pay costs. To date this is one of the few cases where a fine has been increased on appeal.[35]

The lack of clear guidelines as to what determines the level of leniency discounts together with the way in which the CFI and ECJ are prepared to make what on occasion look like fairly marginal adjustments to the awards by the Commission must be a cause of concern to those relying on the predictability of the leniency programme for cartel detection.

6.5 Ability to pay and other factors

The guidelines leave open the possibility to reduce the fine to take account of a firm's ability to pay in certain circumstances. Three firms, SGL, UCAR and C/G, argued for such a reduction. In all cases the Commission turned this

---

[33] On the grounds that SGL substantially contested before the Court the facts which it had previously admitted during the administrative procedure (CFI decision recitals 417–418).
[34] Oddly enough, they got their maths wrong, leading to an incorrect fine for SGL.
[35] For example, Veljanovski (2007) reports no instance of a reduction in his sample of thirty fully reported cartel decisions.

down, stating that 'to take account of the mere fact of an undertaking's loss-making financial situation due to general market conditions or changes in the company's corporate structure would be tantamount to conferring an unjustified competitive advantage on undertakings least well adapted to the conditions of the market'.[36] On appeal to the CFI, this decision was upheld.

Of the (rejected) arguments put forward by the firms, SGL's is noteworthy. 'SGL [argued] that the company's situation was weakened by the high fines imposed by other competition authorities and civil damage payments' (para. 184) and that further sanctions by the Commission might force the company into bankruptcy. Although mitigating arguments on the grounds of ability to pay were rejected in *Graphite Electrodes*, in two other cartel cases involving some of the same firms, including SGL, Specialty Graphites and Electrical Carbon & Graphite, the Commission did grant SGL two 33 per cent discounts on the grounds of 'financial constraints'.[37] The issue of bankruptcy considerations is discussed at length in Stephan (2006). These discounts may have been applied to prevent SGL's collective fines in the three infringements from exceeding 10 per cent of its annual turnover. Regardless of its motivation, no reasoning is given as to why the discounts were necessary despite the fact that SGL was deemed 'able to pay' the full fines, or as to how the 33 per cent figure was arrived at. If bankruptcy discounts are not applied transparently, they may be left open to abuse.

7. The odd one out – C/G

The Commission's treatment of C/G stands out and seems generally harsh. Recall that it took a passive follow-my-leader approach and more than doubled its sales during the period. On appeal C/G argued unsuccessfully that, as it had only a marginal role, its conduct could not be described as 'very serious'.

According to the Commission's findings, although C/G had not participated in the 'Top Guy' or 'Working Level' meetings of the cartel, it none the less maintained bilateral contacts with the other members of the cartel and gained from the information which it obtained from them concerning the decisions taken by the 'home producers' on price-fixing within the cartel.[38]

[36] Commission decision recital 185.
[37] European Commission Decision C (2002) 5083 final of 17 December 2002 relating to a proceeding under Article 81 EC and Article 53 of the EEA Agreement (Case COMP/E-2/37.667 – Specialty Graphite), OJ [2006] L 180/20, recitals 43–44; European Commission Decision of 3 December 2003 relating to a proceeding under Article 81 EC and Article 53 of the EEA Agreement (Case C.38.359 – Electrical and mechanical carbon and graphite products), OJ [2004] L 125/45, recital 360.
[38] CFI decision recital 332.

The argument for including it in a finding of a violation is that it had access to early information about proposed price increases, not available to other firms outside the cartel, and that it used this information in its pricing. Between 1993 and 1996 C/G actually increased production in Europe, thereby not respecting a basic principle of restricting sales in non-home markets. To an outsider, this firm did exactly what you would expect of a firm which was not part of a conspiracy. By expanding its output, the cartel members would have to cut back production even further to keep prices high, affecting the profitability of being a cartel member and hence stability of the cartel adversely. On the basis of this, C/G should be lauded, not condemned. While increasing sales helps to destabilise a cartel, one could argue that C/G could have done more as it did not increase its capacity.[39] Doing so would have had a much more severe adverse effect on the cartel, but it would also have been an action which it would be easier for the cartel to detect and respond aggressively to. A counter-argument could be that C/G should have passed on its information about the cartel to the Commission, but without attending meetings, how certain could it have been about what was going on? Given the adverse effects on firms from an investigation, one would imagine that the Commission would have to have strong evidence before initiating an investigation. If not, firms might be able to raise rivals' costs through false accusations.

Even if one accepted that C/G should have been found to have violated Article 81 EC, the fine appears to give the wrong incentives. First, worldwide market shares of the affected products were used to allocate firms to a category for gravity so that the bigger the firm, the larger the fine. Take a firm considering whether or not to join a cartel. If it does, it will produce X, if not it will double this output to 2X. Were this firm to be found in violation of Article 81 EC, then the former strategy may well see it placed in a lower category for the basic amount discussed in 6.1.1 than the latter strategy. Imagine that C/G's response to the cartel behaviour of other firms had been to double its sales worldwide and not just within the EU. Then as a counterfactual, if it had colluded and not increased its production, it would have been a category 3 with a gravity of €8 million, rather than a category 2 with a gravity of €16 million. Allowing for the duration, increasing the amount by 35 per cent, but not any alleviating circumstances since it would have been part of the cartel, colluding would have left C/G with a fine of €10.8 million before leniency, much less than the fine it was facing of €12.96 million. Without knowing exactly how C/G responded to the cartel outside the EEA, we cannot

---

[39] CFI decision recital 336.

know whether C/G by colluding would have cut market shares so much that it would have been allocated to a lower category for the basic amount, but this is clearly a possibility. In that case, to avoid giving the firm an incentive to collude to lower its fine, either its infringement should not have been classified as very serious or the 40 per cent discount for attenuating circumstances was inadequate. Notice that the C/G appeal about both was rejected.

Interestingly, while continuing the infringement after the investigation has started counts as an aggravating circumstance, ending the infringement before the investigation starts does not count as an attenuating circumstance. The CFI notes[40] that 'the fact that C/G voluntarily put an end to the infringement before the Commission had opened its investigation was sufficiently taken into account in the calculation of the duration of the infringement period found in C/G's case'. Since the internal stability of a cartel is threatened as more and more firms leave it and expand their output, incentivising firms to stop the infringement early would seem to be in the interest of the Commission. If so, this is evidently not reflected in its fining policy.

Finally, C/G was also unlucky with how the CFI decided to lower the fine. Accepting that C/G provided most of the information necessary to finding an infringement, the CFI increased its leniency discount by twenty percentage points. Note that this gives C/G first a 40 per cent discount and then another 40 per cent discount. The total value of that discount is 64 per cent. C/G would have been better off with any asymmetric application of the overall eighty percentage point discounts. One wonders whether the CFI considered this point.

If the aim is to deter or destabilise cartels, arguably C/G should not have been found in violation of Article 81 EC or at least should have been treated more leniently than it was. That it could be dragged into the investigation and fined illustrates that over-deterrence is a potential problem even when considering an infringement as egregious as price fixing. The new 2006 guidelines do not address the key issues raised in this section.

8. Conclusion

We have highlighted a number of problems with the EU's fining policy from a deterrence perspective. First, fines and leniency discounts are not calculated in a manner that is transparent. This is inconsistent with economic deterrence theory and is compounded by the fact that there is no specific

---

[40] CFI decision recital 341.

guidance to adjustments for ability to pay, aggregating and attenuating circumstances. These adjustments are purely discretionary and are sometimes made without reasoning. Second, the means-tested element of setting fines is also incompatible with an economic model of deterrence based on expected benefits and gains. Third, the harsh treatment of C/G, despite its passive role, is a missed opportunity to encourage firms to pursue cartel-destabilising strategies, such as cheating. Incentives which make such behaviour more likely will enhance deterrence by making cartels less sustainable. By treating C/G harshly, the Commission risks making it less likely that firms will cheat cartels, in the knowledge that their initial involvement will still be treated as a 'very serious' infringement.

The 2006 guidelines have failed to address these problems, although they have resolved one: the adjustment for duration is no longer regressive; the fine can now be increased by up to 100 per cent for each year of the infringement. In one respect, the 2006 guidelines may have made deterrence less likely. Basing fines on EEA market shares, rather than worldwide shares under the previous guidelines, will not be deterrence enhancing for as long as external enforcement (save a handful of jurisdictions) is weak. It may actually favour some firms with low EEA market shares which have entered international market-sharing agreements.

While this chapter has highlighted a number of shortcomings of the EU's fining policy, many of which have survived the 2006 reform, the arbitrary 10 per cent turnover cap played only a minor role in this case. The importance of the turnover cap is likely to change with the revised guideline. With the greater weight on duration, the basic fine will be much inflated and the cap will bind especially with firms which are heavily engaged in collusion so that a large part of their revenue arises from the affected products. As leniency discounts are rightly subtracted after the cap is imposed, the actual fine will typically be a lot lower than 10 per cent. Connor (2004b) estimates that the overcharge is well in excess of 10 per cent, suggesting that only very diversified firms, where the cap does not bind, might be deterred by current fine levels.

More generally from a deterrence perspective, the fine should be reasonably well correlated with the benefit to the cartel, i.e. the value of the overcharge which the cartel has enabled. There is little evidence for this either in this case study or more generally (see Veljanovski (2007)). It is an open question whether the actual fines, had they been known about at the time, would have deterred the cartel from a five-year-long infringement. In Table 5.2 we present the size of the fines before and after appeal in percentage of worldwide turnover. As is evident, these are relatively modest.

Table 5.2 Fines as a percentage of worldwide turnover (2000)

FIRM	Turnover (€ m)	Fines	After appeal
SGL	1,262	6.35%	6.00%
UCAR	841	5.99%	5.00%
Tokai	471	5.20%	2.61%
SDK	7,508	0.23%	0.14%
VAW	3,693	0.31%	0.31%
SEC	155	7.87%	3.96%
Nippon	189	6.46%	3.32%
C/G	225	4.58%	2.88%

Source: Commission decision recitals 21–29.

In the case of SGL, its EU sales in 1998 were roughly €250 million[41] so that the fine of €75 million represents approximately 30 per cent of EEA turnover. The elasticity of demand for graphite electrodes, being a derived demand for steel and only a fraction of steel production costs, is likely to be highly inelastic. In this case, even if the conspirators were certain that they would be discovered and fined after five years, SGL would have broken even if the cartel achieved a price rise of about 6 per cent. While recognising that these calculations rest on a number of assumptions, judging from the estimates of overcharges put forward in Connor (2004b), 6 per cent would be at the modest end of what cartels generally achieved.

Apart from getting firms to apply for leniency, the other way in which cartels can break down is through internal problems. In this light, the treatment of C/G is very problematic on two fronts. Marginal undercutters like C/G should be encouraged. If a sufficient number of firms increase their output, then the cartel will be destabilised and the Commission can save its resources. Second, the Commission's turnover-based formula means that the outsiders to the cartel who expand output are given a much larger starting fine than otherwise. Unless the discount for attenuating circumstances is substantial, the incentive is for the firm to collude and accept its risk of punishment. Notice that SDK's leniency discount of 70 per cent is worth much more than the two 40 per cent discounts offered to C/G, yet without being part of the cartel, how could C/G have had enough information to get the 70 per cent or more in leniency discount?

One general observation about the guidelines is that they make it difficult for the size of a fine to be foreseeable with a good degree of precision. While

---

[41] According to its 1998 Annual Report, available at http://www.sglcarbon.com/ir/public/annual/index. php4, the revenue from graphite electrodes was DM 1,034 million, which with the exchange rate used in the report is €528 million. As 48 per cent of SGL's sales were to Europe, annual sales must be approximately as given in the text.

part of the calculation of the fine has a formulaic feel to it, other parts, such as the basic amount and the level of the leniency discounts, are largely unexplained in the guidelines or the decisions. This leaves past decisions as the best guide for firms in carrying out their cost–benefit analysis. Note that a considerable part of SGL's appeal – e.g. recitals 173 and 229 – concerns how the fine is unprecedentedly high. Where the past suggests low fines, firms with only impressionistic expectations are likely to have a downwards biased estimate of the fine. Even if actual fines would be appropriate, unless they are properly anticipated they will have an inadequate deterrence effect. The 1998 guidelines did not offer much assistance to firms in terms of assessing the size of a likely fine. While the 2006 guidelines arguably are an improvement in that firms may be able to have a better estimate of the basic amount, they are still far from the ideal where the cost of collusion (the sanctions imposed on infringing firms) will be transparent and predictable. Without this, optimal deterrence is unlikely. This does not seem to be a concern for the Commissioner for Competition who stated:

I cannot see how allowing potential infringers to calculate the likely cost/benefit ratio of a cartel in advance will somehow contribute to a sustained policy of deterrence and zero tolerance (Kroes 2005).

Appendix A: Summaries of the fines imposed in the Commission decision, the CFI decision and the ECJ decision

Table A5.1 Category 1 offenders

	SGL Carbon AG			UCAR International	
	DG Comp	CFI	ECJ	DG Comp	CFI
Gravity (€ millions)	€40	€40	€40	€40	€40
Deterrence multiplier	–	–	–	–	–
Duration	55%	55%	55%	55%	55%
Basic fine (€ millions)	**€62**	**€62**	**€62**	**€62**	**€62**
Aggravating circ.	85%	85%	85%	60%	60%
Attenuating circ.	–	–	–	–	–
10% annual turnover cap	–	–	–	Binding	Binding
Fine before leniency (€ mill)	**€114.7**	**€114.7**	**€114.7**	**€84.1**	**€84.1**
Leniency discount	30%	38%	34%	40%	50%
Final fine (€ mill)	**€80.2**	**€69.114**[42]	**€75.7**	**€50.4**	**€42.05**
Share of total costs of appeal		7/8	All costs		4/5

[42] The CFI appears to have difficulties calculating 62 per cent of €114.7 which should have been €71.114.

Table A5.2 Category 2 offenders

	Tokai Carbon Co. Ltd		Showa Denko K. K.		Carbide Graphite Group Inc.	
	DG Comp	CFI	DG Comp	CFI	DG Comp	CFI
Gravity (€ mill)	€16	€8	€16	€16	€16	€8
Deterrence multiplier	–	–	2.5	1.5	–	–
Duration	55%	55%	45%	45%	35%	35%
Basic fine (€ mill)	**€24.8**	**€12.4**	**€58**	**€34.8**	**€21.6**	**€10.8**
Aggravating circ.	10%	10%	–	–	–	–
Attenuating circ.	–	–	–	–	40%	[40%][43]
10% annual turnover cap	–	–	–	–	–	–
Fine before leniency (€ mill)	**€27.28**	**€13.64**	**€58**	**€34.8**	**€12.96**	**€10.8**
Leniency discount	10%	10%	70%	70%	20%	40%
Final fine (€ mill)	**€24.5**	**€12.276**	**€17.4**	**€10.44**	**€10.3**	**€6.48**
Share of total costs of appeal		1/2		3/5		3/5

Table A5.3 Category 3 offenders

	VAW Aluminium	SEC Corp.		Nippon Carbon Co. Ltd.	
	DG Comp	DG Comp	CFI	DG Comp	CFI
Gravity (€ mill)	€8	€8	€4	€8	€4
Deterrence multiplier	1.25	–	–	–	–
Duration	45%	55%	55%	55%	55%
Basic fine (€ mill)	**€14.5**	**€12.4**	**€6.2**	**€12.4**	**€6.2**
Aggravating circ.	–	10%	10%	10%	10%
Attenuating circ.	–	–	–	–	–
10% annual turnover cap	–	–	–	–	–
Fine before leniency (€ mill)	**€14.5**	**€13.64**	**€6.82**	**€13.64**	**€6.82**
Leniency discount	20%	10%	10%	10%	8%
Final fine (€ mill)	**€11.6**	**€12.2**	**€6.138**	**€12.2**	**€6.2744**
Share of total costs of appeal			1/2		1/2

Acknowledgements

The support of the Economic and Social Research Council (ESRC) is gratefully acknowledged, as are extensive comments by Bruce Lyons and Catherine Waddams on a previous draft. Stephan also gratefully acknowledges support by the Arts and Humanities Research Council (AHRC). The usual disclaimer applies. The authors have not been directly involved in this case.

[43] Although the CFI decision appears not to have altered the Commissions decision regarding the discount for attenuating circumstances [recital 349] for the Carbide Graphite Group Inc., the subsequent calculations by the CFI appears to leave out this 40% discount.

6

Assessment of damages in the district heating pipe cartel

Peter Møllgaard

1. Introduction and motivation

Following a complaint by Swedish competitor Powerpipe, the European Commission paid a surprise visit to nine producers of pre-insulated pipes for district heating systems[1] and their trade association on 28 June 1995. The EU Commission found detailed evidence that the companies had conspired to share markets, fix prices and rig bids in various markets during the period 1990–6 and that they had attempted to eliminate Powerpipe by organising a boycott of suppliers. Powerpipe had resisted invitations to join the cartel and had won several contracts that cartel members had allocated amongst themselves. According to the decision of the EU Commission taken on 21 October 1998, the cartel continued to operate for nine months after the dawn raid.[2] The European Commission decided to impose fines totalling €92.21 million to the ten members of the cartel. In March 2002, the Court of First Instance reduced the fines by €5.1 million but upheld the decision of the EU Commission in broad terms.[3] All but one firm (viz. Sigma) appealed this decision to the European Court of Justice, which dismissed the appeals on 28 June 2005.[4]

In European competition policy fines are issued by the European Commission as a penalty for illegitimate behaviour (anticompetitive agreements or abuse

---

[1] District heating is a system for distribution of heat produced at a central cogeneration (combined heat and electricity) or a boiler station (producing heat only). Distribution to end users (residential or commercial) is done through an underground network of insulated pipes that carries hot water into houses and takes cooled water away. This case pertains to the production and sales of such district heating pipes. In Europe, district heating is found especially in the Nordic countries, Northern Germany and Eastern Europe, but is also used even in Mediterranean countries.

[2] Case IV/35.691/E-4 (OJ L24/1; 30.1.1999). See also press release IP/98/917 of 21 October 1998.

[3] CFI cases T-9/99 (Henss/Isoplus); T-15/99 (Brugg); T-17/99 (KE KELIT); T-21/99 (DRI); T-23/99 (LR); T-28/99 (Sigma); T-31/99 (ABB).

[4] ECJ joined cases C-189/02 P (DRI); C-202/02 P (Henss/Isoplus); C-205/02 P (KE KELLIT); C-206/02 P (LR); C-207/02 P (Brugg); C-208/02 P (LR); C-213/02 P (ABB).

of dominance) with the aim of discouraging such behaviour in the future. The fines contribute to the budget of the European Communities and hence do not compensate the victims of the behaviour. There is no European system that may award compensation for damages to, for example, the customers that suffer from high cartel prices. Such compensation has to be established by courts of the different Member States according to the national legislation.

More than ten years after the dawn raid, in one of the first serious suits for damages connected to an EU cartel case, four Danish municipalities succeeded in retrieving €21 million in compensation for damages. The case was litigated at the High Court of Western Denmark during 2004/5 and resulted in a settlement within court. The damages amounted to 25 per cent of the fine, which is significant compared with previous European experience. As a percentage of the damages claimed (€38 million), realised damages amounted to 57 per cent.

This chapter aims to discuss the methods used (and not used) for calculating the damages. It is organised as follows. In section 2, I summarise the decision of the EU Commission and the judgments of the European Court of Justice, emphasising the information that is particularly interesting for the calculation of damages. In section 3, I give a brief account of the modern industrial organisation of cartels. Section 4 gives an account of methods that can be used to calculate damages and section 5 describes the methods that were employed by the parties to the Danish case, namely the before and after method and a cost-plus method. Section 6 discusses why the parties did not use supplementary methods such as oligopoly models, econometrics and yardstick or benchmark methods. Finally, section 7 provides a conclusion and broader perspectives on the case.

2. The decision of the European Commission

The cartel was established in November or December 1990 in Denmark, extended to Italy and Germany during 1991 and reorganised in 1994 to cover the entire common market. Cartel members engaged in market sharing along national boundaries, price fixing, bid rigging in tenders and procurement auctions, and coordinated predation against the only independent rival, Powerpipe of Sweden. In addition, they used industry standards to delay introduction of new, cost-saving technology. The dawn raid took place in June 1995 but the Commission found evidence that cartel meetings took place until at least March 1996 – albeit more secretively than before. Thus, in Denmark the cartel period ran from late 1990 through the first quarter of 1996.

Four Danish firms, ABB I. C. Møller (ABB in the following), Løgstør Rør (LR in the following), Dansk Rørindustri (a.k.a. Starpipe; DRI in the following) and Tarco made up the core of the cartel. These four firms controlled 50 per cent of production capacity in the EU. In addition, two German firms, Henss/Isoplus and Pan-Isovit, as well as Finnish KWH were significant international cartelists, while three companies played only a smaller role in that they only served their local markets and participated in the cartel for only a short period (German Brugg Rohrsysteme, Austrian KE KELIT Kunstoffwerk and Italian Sigma Tecnologie).

Pre-insulated pipes are used to supply hot water from district heating stations to households in a certain district and to return cold water. The product consists of an inner steel carrier pipe, an outer dense plastic jacket and foam insulation (polyurethane) in between the two pipes. The standard production method around 1990 was discontinuous production of inflexible pipes of standard lengths 6, 12 and 16 metres. Discontinuous production involves filling the void between the inner pipe and the plastic jacket through injection holes in tightly fitting caps at both ends. The standards (e.g. EN243) were set by standard authorities in collaboration with producers, their trade association and customers.

Already before 1990, a more modern, cost-saving technique of continuous pipe manufacturing had been developed. Continuous pipe production first has the insulating foam moulded or sprayed on to the inner pipe, after which the outer casing pipe is extruded or wound around the pre-shaped (modified) polyurethane foam. This technique is suitable to big production runs of pipes of the same diameter and results in fast production at a relatively low variable cost: material costs are reduced due to lower foam overpack, lower filling density and reduced casing pipe thickness. However, set-up times of continuous production are longer than with discontinuous production and capital costs are higher. Thus continuous production entails less flexibility, lower variable costs and higher fixed costs than discontinuous production, making continuous production the obvious choice if the scale is sufficiently large.[5] The Commission found that cost reductions that would result from the introduction of continuous production would amount to 10–15 per cent, according to internal ABB documents.[6]

---

[5] Source: www.huntsman.com/pu/index.cfm?PageID=262

[6] See case IV/35.691/E-4 (OJ L24/1; 30.1.1999) at paras. 114–115. ABB obstructed the introduction of the new technology that its competitor, LR, possessed already in 1988 until ABB could introduce 'ABB slimline quality pipes' in 1994. (See also para. 5.)

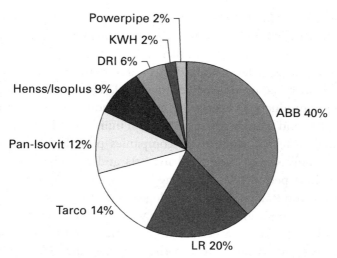

Figure 6.1 Market structure
Source: European Commission decision, para. 8–18, see footnote 2.

The markets for district heating pipes in (Western) Europe were relatively concentrated in the late 1980s and the four largest players were ABB (40 per cent), LR (20 per cent), Tarco (14 per cent) and Pan-Isovit (12 per cent), so that the four-firm concentration ratio CR4 amounted to 86. The Herfindahl-Hirschman Index, which incorporates the smaller rivals' market shares, was 2461. This is normally considered a characteristic of highly concentrated markets. Figure 6.1 illustrates the distribution of market shares.

Customers were district heating stations that could be owned by municipalities or be house-owners' cooperatives. For larger projects, they would typically buy district heating pipes through tenders or EU procurement (60 per cent); for repair or maintenance of district heating systems they would enter fixed-term supply contracts.

In the EU the turnover in the market was roughly €400 million in 1995. The Member State with the largest consumption was Germany (40 per cent), followed by Denmark (20 per cent). Both of these markets were considered mature and stable so that no growth in revenues was expected. Outside the EU markets were found in Eastern Europe and the Baltic countries. Total revenues in these markets amounted to around €100 million. Russia and China were emerging markets.

The effect of the cartel on prices is discussed inconclusively in the Commission decision at paras. 125–126. Prices in Germany were 15–20 per cent lower than in Denmark and it was the stated intention of the cartel to raise German prices by 6–8 per cent. Swedish prices were even lower than this, on occasion

Table 6.1 Fines decided by the EC (1998) and later by the Court of First Instance (2002)

Company	Commission fine (ECU)	Fine decided by CFI (EUR)
ABB Ltd	70,000,000	65,000,000
Brugg Rohrsysteme GmbH	925,000	925,000
Dansk Rørindustri A/S	1,475,000	1,475,000
Henss/Isoplus	4,950,000	4,950,000
Ke-Kelit Kunstoffwerk GmbH	360,000	360,000
Oy KWH Tech AB	700,000	No appeal
Løgstør Rør A/S	8,900,000	8,900,000
Pan-Isovit GmbH	1,500,000	No appeal
Sigma Tecnologie di Rivestimento Srl	400,000	300,000
Tarco Energi A/S	3,000,000	No appeal
Total	92,210,000	87,110,000

Note: In 2005, the ECJ upheld the ruling of the CFI.
Source: European Commission decision, see footnote 2; CFI decisions, see footnote 3.

only half of Danish prices, but according to the Commission there is evidence showing that ABB and LR carried out predatory pricing in Sweden and Finland with a view to forcing local firms to exit through bankruptcy or acquisition.[7]

When the cartel was extended to cover the entire EU in 1994, the intention of the cartel was to increase prices by 30–35 per cent in two years and according to minutes from a cartel meeting in the spring of 1995, prices did go up by 15–20 per cent during the first year of operation in those markets where the outsider, Powerpipe, was not present.

The decision by the European Commission is nowhere more precise than this when it comes to price effects of the cartel. Legally, in order for the Commission to fine the firms, it is not necessary to show that the cartel was successful in raising prices, just that there was illegal conduct. Indeed the section on restriction of competition (Decision, paras. 146–148) includes a long list of illegal agreements and other prohibited arrangements. To the contrary, victims of high prices that enter private litigation to get compensation for damages will need to demonstrate their loss and that this loss resulted from cartel overcharges. They have to carry out an economic analysis of what the prices would have been had the cartel not existed (i.e. an unobserved

---

[7] Decision at para. 125: '[A]t times Swedish prices were as little as half those in Denmark. Indeed, there is a good deal of evidence that ABB and Løgstør had a common strategy of entering the Swedish and Finnish markets with low prices so as to put pressure on the local producers with a view to acquiring them and taking them off the market: this is set out in KWH's Reply to the Statement of Objections, pp. 7, 8 and 9.'

counterfactual) and for this purpose it is not possible for the victims to rely on the Decision of the European Commission: price effects are simply not established with any precision by the Commission.

The fines issued by the European Commission and those decided by the Court of First Instance are indicated in Table 6.1.

3. Essential cartel economics

A cartel is a group of firms producing substitute goods that colludes or conspires with the aim of raising prices, lowering production and/or sharing markets or customers with the aim of achieving monopoly profits. Cartels have been illegal in the United States since 1890 but were to varying degree and extent legal in Europe until the 1950s. For customers, the cartel implies that they pay more than they would have had the firms competed head-on. For society, the cartel implies that less is sold since some customers refrain from buying at all and other customers buy less than they would have had it not been for the higher price (the deadweight loss).[8, 9]

Cartels arise in oligopolies, i.e. markets characterised by a few firms that, exactly because they are few, understand that their profitability depends on their rivals' behaviour. This interdependence means that they think strategically. By entering a collusive agreement or a coordinated practice, the oligopolists can raise prices and possibly achieve monopoly prices. However, high prices create an incentive for the cartelists to cheat on the agreement by undercutting their rivals or increasing output: the cartel price is above the cost of production so extra profits can be earned by cheating. If everybody cheats, the cartel breaks down.

The cartel's solution to this problem is to reach a common understanding that punishment will follow cheating that is thus discouraged. The harsher the punishment, the less likely it is that it will have to be carried out. In the industrial economics literature, there are a number of suggestions as to how a punishment strategy can operate. A very simple (and for that reason very popular) version is

---

[8] Good summaries of the modern industrial economics of collusion with a view to competition policy may be found in Bishop and Walker (2002, sections 5.07–5.31) and in Motta (2004, Chapter 4). Advanced treatments may be found in Tirole (1989, Chapters 5 and 6) and Martin (2001, Chapter 10).

[9] The payment of damages is related to the overcharge paid for the amounts bought by customers. In principle, customers that bought less (or nothing at all) because of the high price may also have suffered a loss. However, it is considered too difficult to assess just how much more customers would have bought had the price been competitive, so damages are not awarded that correspond with the deadweight loss. The fines imposed on the firms that engage in cartels could thus be seen as compensating society for the deadweight loss.

that cheating triggers a reversion to full competition for ever (Nash reversion, see e.g. Friedman (1971a, b)), but there are examples of even better and more complex punishment strategies that involve even lower prices during punishment but a return to cooperation when the punishment is over (see Abreu (1986)). One well-documented example is the triggering of a temporary price war by an unexpected drop in the price – see Porter (1983a, b).

Apart from detecting and punishing cheating, the cartel will have a problem if there are some producers of the good that are not members of the cartel or not taking part in the collusive agreement. They then run the risk of being undercut by non-cartel members or even by potential competitors that might enter the industry. The degree to which such outsiders to the cartel pose a real threat depends on the technology that they possess: if their marginal costs are low and 'flat' (i.e. relatively independent of the level of output – constant returns to scale) and if capacity is not an issue, then they pose a serious threat to the high price level that the cartel wishes to sustain; however, if the outsider has a small capacity and/or quickly increasing marginal costs (decreasing returns to scale), then they may be perceived as a mild nuisance that can be largely ignored.[10] The attempts made by members to first invite their independent rival, Powerpipe, to join the collusive scheme and then to eliminate it should be seen in this light.

4. Calculating damages

In 2001, while the second appeal of the European Commission's decision was pending before the ECJ,[11] four Danish municipalities sued three of the firms (ABB, DRI, LR) that were most active in setting up the cartel in Denmark in an attempt to retrieve some of the extra money that they had spent on district heating pipes due to the cartel overcharge. Tarco was not sued, a controversial act since it had been involved in the cartel and since it was owned by municipalities in Denmark. Total damages claimed amounted to DKK283 million or €38 million. Table 6.2 summarises the distribution of the claims.

---

[10] See Scherer and Ross (1990, Chapters 7 and 8) for a general exposition of factors that facilitate respectively limit oligopolistic coordination, as well as Motta (2004, Chapter 4.2).

[11] The judicial history of the cartel case was as follows. The European Commission carried out its dawn raid in June 1995 and decided the case in October 1998. The firms appealed the Commission's decision, first to the CFI (the lower court of the two-tiered judicial system of the EU) that delivered its judgment in March 2002, reducing the fines a bit, and then to the ECJ (the highest possible instance) which confirmed the CFI's ruling.

Table 6.2 Claims made by four municipalities against three cartel members

Million euro	ABB	LR	DRI	Total
Copenhagen	3.35	4.71	–	**8.06**
Aarhus	0.81	1.21	–	**2.02**
Odense	12.92	–	–	**12.92**
Aalborg	12.65	–	2.42	**15.07**
Total	**29.73**	**5.92**	**2.42**	**38.07**

Source: The various summons of the four municipalities as summarised by PricewaterhouseCoopers (2002) page 14.

Essentially the way damages are calculated involves the determination of the quantity, Q, purchased from each defendant and the price, P, paid during the cartel period. This information is relatively easily available by studying the invoices paid. The most problematic part is then to determine the price that would have obtained in the absence of the cartel, the 'but-for' price, p. The damages may then be calculated simply as:

$$\text{Damages} = (P - p)Q$$

i.e. the overcharge multiplied by the quantity traded during the cartel period. Note that the quantity traded is lower than it would have been in the absence of the cartel, but that the calculation of damages does not take this into account (see also footnote 9 above).

The calculation of the 'but-for' price, p, involves a counterfactual – what would the price have been but for the cartel? – and hence begs the use of economics. The literature[12] identifies five different ways of establishing the counterfactual 'but-for' price:

1. The before or after method.
2. The benchmark or yardstick method.
3. The cost-based method.
4. Econometric estimation of the effect of the cartel.
5. Oligopoly models.

1. *The before or after method*

   The before or after method simply alleges that the but-for price would have been the price that existed before the cartel was set up or after it was dissolved. Absent an agreement, these prices would constitute the

---

[12] See e.g. American Bar Association (1996), Connor (1997, 2001, 2004a) and Finkelstein and Levenbach (1983).

non-cooperative Nash equilibrium of the oligopoly. Arguably, any break-down of the cartel, e.g. a price war during its existence, could serve the same purpose, although a counter-argument would be that according to some theories of oligopoly, price wars could be harsher than the Nash equilibrium.[13]

2. *The benchmark or yardstick method*

   The benchmark or yardstick method suggests using the price that obtains in a comparable market unaffected by the cartel as the but-for price. The challenge is to find such a market. Typically a separate geographic market (country or region) is used.

3. *The cost-based method*

   The cost-based method takes as its starting point that the perfectly competitive price would be marginal costs and that in the long run the price would be competed down to long-run average costs that include a normal return. The but-for price is then this competitive price. Since marginal costs are not readily observable, typically some average cost concept is used as a proxy and an allowance is made for the normal return. This method typically relies on accounting data.

4. *Econometric estimation of the effect of the cartel*

   The econometric method may be used if there is a time series of prices that extends before and after the cartel period. If the cartel period is already identified, a time-series regression that includes a dummy variable that takes the value 1 in the cartel period and 0 outside may be used to estimate the price effect of the cartel. The value of the estimated coefficient to the dummy is then essentially the mean of the overcharge, $P-p$. This method allows for the neutralisation of the effect of other factors that may have affected pricing, such as changes to the cost of inputs and seasonal variations in demand.

5. *Oligopoly models*

   Setting up an oligopoly model essentially amounts to describing the market in game-theory terms: Who are the players? What are the rules of the game? And how do their payoffs reflect their actions? Underlying these questions is a hierarchy of important questions that have to be answered, e.g. how may the technologies be described? Are capacity constraints important? How are the markets designed? How do customers react to changing prices, i.e. what is the elasticity of demand? Based on information such as this a model may be constructed that fits the industry at hand and

---

[13] See the discussion of (optimal) punishment strategies in section 3 and Abreu (1986).

this model may be confronted with available data through calibration or estimation depending on the availability and quality of data. The but-for price would then be the Nash equilibrium of the static version of the model.

All five methods come in a variety of shapes and forms. In applying any of the five methods it is obviously important to control for differences or changes in underlying variables such as prices of inputs. If, for example, input prices are low before or after the cartel, this may partly explain why prices are lower in the reference period and if the but-for price is not corrected for this, the overcharge will be overestimated. These details are often subject to contention.

In a survey and meta-analysis of evidence on cartel overcharges, Connor and Bolotova (2006) show that of 512 cartel cases from all over the world, the prevalent method for calculating the overcharge is the before or after method (supplemented with a few that use within-cartel price wars) to estimate the overcharge – see Figure 6.2. Econometric modelling is also significant, followed by the yardstick and cost-based methods. The rest ('Other') signifies that in some of the cases the method for calculating the overcharge was not identified.

Surprisingly, none of the methods, except yardstick, provides systematically different estimates of the overcharge – see Connor and Bolotoya (2006, pages 1132–1133). Overcharges were on average 11 per cent higher when estimated using the yardstick method than when estimated by the other methods.

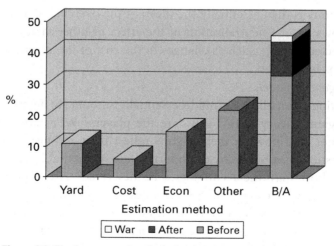

Figure 6.2 The frequency of method of estimating overcharges in a survey of cartel cases
Source: Connor and Bolotoya (2006, Table 5).

5. Damages in the district heating pipe cartel

After method

In the district heating pipe cartel, the plaintiffs used a relatively simple version of the after method to calculate the damages mentioned in Table 6.2. As a starting point they noted that after the cartel was revealed, the prices observed at the first subsequent tender were on average 35–40 per cent lower than during the cartel period and that no other significant factors seemed to be able to explain this. Thus the but-for price was essentially taken to be the lowest price obtained in the first tender in each municipality after the cartel was revealed. This was adjusted by a common price index to control for changes in other factors that would influence the price of district heating pipes in a relatively coarse correction of the but-for price for changes in the prices of iron, steel and plastic as well as wages. This was done on an annual basis for the years 1994–8.

The resulting annual overcharges were then multiplied by the quantities of the invoices for those years and their summation resulted in the damages claimed. The plaintiffs opted to include flexible pipes, although these were expressly left out of the EU Commission's decision. The reason for this was that they found the price behaviour to match that of the non-flexible pipes. Examples of the price behaviour are found in Figure 6.3.

The defendants criticised the plaintiffs' method on a number of accounts, including the range of products, the level of detail and disaggregation of the calculation, and the way the price index was calculated, emphasising for example that 'plastic' was at a level of aggregation that was far too general and that it would be more proper to replace it with 'isocyanate' (i.e. the type of plastic used for the insulation foam in the pipes). However, these imprecisions were found to matter relatively little to the size of the calculated damages. See PricewaterhouseCoopers (2002c). In addition, a defendant argued that if the after method used by the plaintiffs were extended to all customers, then the defendant would have made large losses in all of the cartel period, hence showing that the method was unrealistic.[14]

---

[14] In contrast, Harrington (2004) argues that litigation for damages would give the defendants an incentive to up the post-cartel price, since a lower after price results in higher damages. In non-cooperative post-cartel equilibrium there would be an upward bias of the price and hence a downward bias of the overcharge, if the but-for price is partly or wholly based on the post-cartel price average across firms.

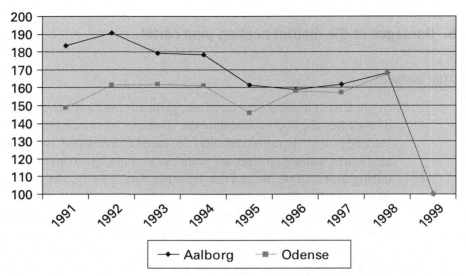

Figure 6.3 Price index for goods delivered from ABB to two plaintiffs/municipalities (1999 = 100)
Source: KPMG (2003) pages 62 and 66.

Before method

The defendants then argued that the plaintiffs had used an after method and that a before method would in principle be at least as valid, so they recalculated the damages using the price of 1990 rather than 1999. As a result, calculated damages dropped by more than 80 per cent since 1990 prices were a good deal higher than their 1999 counterparts, thus raising the but-for prices significantly. For example, ABB found that the municipalities' total claim should be €5 million rather than €30 million (see PricewaterhouseCoopers, 2002d, page 16). The defendants claimed that the after price was negatively affected by low demand in 1999 and that 1990 was much more representative for the demand and supply conditions during the cartel period, making the before price the better but-for price.

The weakness of using the before price to calculate the overcharge is that the European Commission in its decision (at paras. 29–30) mentions that Denmark was considered a high-price area already by the late 1980s and that it found that ABB initiated a series of meetings with LR, Tarco and DRI already in 1988–9. The Commission decided not to include the two years prior to November 1990 in the cartel period even though LR had acknowledged that the anticompetitive behaviour had started already in 1988–9; see the decision at para. 151. So it seems that the European Commission opted for the safe evidence and decided not to decide on the degree of competition during 1988–90. Harrington (2004, page 530) also notes that the but-for price might be overestimated if some cartel periods erroneously are included in the pre-cartel period.

Cost-based method

One of the defendants also provided an alternative calculation of the damages based on the cost-based method.[15] Normally, the starting point for the cost-based method is the calculation of unit costs (i.e. total costs divided by the number of units produced of a given good). A normal return on capital is added to the unit costs and the result is an estimate of the but-for price. Due to the large number of goods produced by the defendants and the inherent problems in distributing common costs among these, the defendants opted to use an approach – the economic profit method – that was intended to circumvent these problems.

Economic profit is the extra profit a company earns more than the normal return on capital. It can be thought of as the opportunity cost of capital: what would the capital be worth in the second most attractive use? Thus if economic profit is 0, then the company's owners earn as much investing their money in the particular industry as they would have if they moved their capital to the second-best alternative. Economic profits of zero do not imply that accounting profits are also zero: on the contrary, if economic profits are zero, then accounting profits must be positive to provide the normal return on capital. Economic profits are competed down to zero when competition is very intense, as for example in the reference model of perfect competition.

The defendant decided to estimate the overcharge as the positive economic profit earned in the cartel period taking the firm rather than the single good as the unit of analysis. The defendant calculated earnings before interest, taxes, depreciation and amortisation (EBITDA) and related that to the invested capital (operational assets, financial assets and equity). The requirement to normal return on capital was then varied between 0 per cent and 15 per cent and depending on this number, corresponding overcharges were calculated.

Using this method, the damages that were to be paid would be much reduced compared with the claims made by the plaintiffs. The precise number

---

[15] PricewaterhouseCoopers (2002e).

would obviously depend on the required normal return on capital, but roughly speaking the defendant's calculation amounted to one fifth of the claims.

The economic-profit method was criticised on a number of accounts. Most obviously, the normal return on capital is not a well-defined concept. It would, among other things, depend on the company's risk profile. Second, it is not obvious how many of the assets to include.

Furthermore, it requires that the company is run efficiently. Industrial organisation acknowledges the possibility that limited competition can have a negative impact on firms' efficiency and costs; they may have too high costs and innovate too little due to the lack of competitive pressure (Motta, 2004, page 39). The fact that costs are too high may be due to lacking incentives to cut costs but also that the 'Darwinian process' of eliminating inefficient competitors is obstructed.

Lacking incentives to cut costs was already described by Adam Smith but treated extensively by Leibenstein (1966, 1973), who coined it X-inefficiency. X-inefficiency describes the idea that the quiet life of market power leads to reduced focus on cost cutting. The idea was criticised by Stigler (1976), who argued that profit-maximising firms would minimise costs, but modern principal-agent analysis has shown that it is possible to combine profit maximisation with lack of cost minimisation due to separation of ownership of control in complex organisations: owners delegate responsibility for costs (among other things) to managers who may have their own agenda; see e.g. Hart (1983). Empirically, recent research indicates that competition increases productivity and lowers costs, see e.g. Nickell (1996) and Nickell, Nicolitsas and Dryden (1997).

The 'Darwinian selection' of efficient firms at the cost of less efficient firms is obstructed when competition is limited or absent. In a competitive situation, efficient firms will grow and inefficient firms will shrink to eventually disappear if they do not manage to become more efficient. Empirical results show that cost reductions and productivity increases in an industry are a result of closure of old, inefficient firms and the appearance of new, efficient ones – see Olley and Pakes (1996) for a study of producers of telecommunications equipment.

In sum, the cost-based method suffers from the possibility that reduced competition may have inflated the costs in three ways. First, because the owners may not have had full control over managers' incentives to cut costs, second, because a high price may have allowed inefficient firms to survive and third, because the cartel may have delayed the introduction of new, cost-cutting technologies (continuous production of pipes).

The settlement that they reached in 2005 totalled €21 million, which was 57 per cent of the damages claimed by the municipalities. The settlement was roughly half way between the damages calculated by the plaintiffs using the after method and those calculated by the defendants using the before method and the cost-based (economic profit) method. Thus it constituted a genuine compromise and reflects the legal uncertainty of the parties as to what the court would have decided, had it been called upon to do so.

From an economic point of view it is interesting that the parties abstained from using three of the five methods mentioned in section 4.

6. Methods not used

In their litigation, the parties to the suit for damages only used the before and after methods supplemented by the cost-based method in its economic-profit version. It is interesting that the plaintiffs and the defendants agreed not to employ the three remaining methods. It could have provided extra evidence and made the calculation of damages more precise. Recall that Connor and Bolotova (2007) find that the different methods normally concur, although the yardstick method has a tendency to result in higher estimates than the other methods – see section 4.

The yardstick method was not used since the cartel was not limited to the Danish market according to the decision of the European Commission. However, the cartel was extended to Germany only during the early 1990s and indeed during 1990–3 prices in Germany were 15–20 per cent lower than in Denmark. Thus it might have been possible to use the situation of Germany in, for example, 1991 as a basis for the calculation of a but-for price in Denmark.

The econometric method regresses the price paid by the plaintiffs on a number of background variables that aim at controlling for changes in input prices, changes to technology, demand variations unrelated to prices and of course the existence of the cartel. The parties decided that this method was not practical since 'the method requires data of a level of detail that it is not possible to provide in this case' (PricewaterhouseCoopers, 2002a, p. 22). However, the background material to the case included quite detailed information on prices both in terms of the level of disaggregation in the product dimension and in terms of the time-series properties. Thus it is not clear that this method could not have been used.

Finally, the parties did not build an oligopoly model to fit the industry. The reasons for not doing this build on misinterpretation of economics to a large extent. Although the parties show knowledge of other models of short-term oligopolistic competition, the defendants succeeded in arguing that the relevant model would have been a Cournot model where firms compete in quantities. They then criticised this particular oligopoly model on the following grounds:[16]

- The method does not take into account capacity utilisation among cartel members.
- It assumes a homogeneous product and high barriers to entry.
- It assumes that competitors are naïve and that they do not take into account entry and exit of competitors.
- It does not take into account parameters such as marketing and product differentiation.

The method was dismissed on the basis of this critique and the non-availability of data. This critique of the Cournot model is erroneous and shallow in that the modern view of Cournot sees it as the possible outcome of capacity choice followed by price competition; see Kreps and Scheinkman (1983). While it is true that the standard introductory textbook Cournot model assumes a homogeneous product and a fixed number of firms (and hence high barriers to entry), the model may be easily adapted to accommodate both product differentiation and entry; see e.g. Martin (2001, Chapter 3). In Cournot fully rational players find a Nash equilibrium, so the third critique is not valid either and the model can be adapted to endogenise product differentiation and advertising/marketing; see e.g. Friedman (1983).

Thus all in all, the critique of the Cournot model is erroneous – but it is quite likely that the proper model of this particular industry would not have been of the Cournot type. It is for this reason particularly regrettable that the parties did not attempt to employ an oligopoly model. The oligopoly model would quite obviously have to be adapted and calibrated to take account of the particulars of the district heating pipe industry.[17] The parties would then have had to discuss what kind of competition would be a reasonable assumption (tenders for a large part of the contracts); they would have had to discuss existing technology and the introduction of new production methods and how that would affect costs (think of the evidence on the delayed introduction of continuous pipes); they would have had to provide evidence on capacity constraints and utilisation; and they might have had to discuss the likely

---

[16] See PricewaterhouseCoopers (2002a, 16).

[17] For a discussion of how simple simulation models should be selected and modified to fit a particular competition case, see Davis and Lyons (2007).

changes to the industry structure that might have followed a competitive scenario that would have led to bankruptcies, mergers and acquisitions. Most of this information was missing, making judgements as to the proper but-for price theoretical at best.

7. Conclusion

The European Commission successfully decided to fine ten producers of district heating pipes for cartel behaviour in the first half of the 1990s. The evidence provided by the Commission to convict the cartel included proof that the cartel existed and demonstrated that it had been operating at least between 1990 and the spring of 1996. In the decision by the Commission it is strongly hinted that the cartel might have operated before 1990 and that it could still be operating at the time of the decision (1998). However, the Commission nowhere indicated, let alone quantified, the effect of the cartel on prices.

Hence the customers when deciding to sue cartel members for damages were provided with strong evidence on the existence of the cartel and the cartel period, but were left to demonstrate that they had in fact suffered damages and what the size of those were. In the process of proving damages, the plaintiffs used two out of five methods, arguably the most low-tech methods from the toolbox (the before and after method and the cost-based method). In future cases it is to be hoped and expected that the evidence is consolidated better through the use of high-tech economic evidence (especially econometrics and tailor-made oligopoly models). If employed sensibly, this would likely improve the precision of the estimate of the overcharges and damages. As private litigation becomes more prevalent in European antitrust, legal counsel and courts will hopefully experience a better use of economics.

Epilogue

The recent history of the district heating pipe industry provides further perspective on the case. In 1999, LR bought Tarco's district heating pipe production. ABB's district heating pipe production was first bought by ALSTOM and in 2005, ALSTOM and LR merged to form LOGSTOR. Measured by the market shares of Figure 6.1, the combination would control

74 per cent of production. DRI still exists as an independent competitor. However, as the four-firm concentration ratio approaches 100 per cent, the firms may not have to agree explicitly to reach a common understanding of what prices should be. In Germany, a new cartel case was recently (2005) opened by the public prosecutor in Munich for cartel behaviour on the German market.[18] Thus oligopolistic coordination of one sort or the other seems to be a permanent feature of this industry.

Acknowledgements

The author acted as one of two experts on the appraisal of damages appointed by the High Court of Western Denmark in the combined case of the four municipalities v. three cartel members during 2004–5. Thanks are due to Anette Boom, Niels Blomgren-Hansen and Bruce Lyons for comments on an earlier draft.

[18] See Staatsanwaltschaft München (2005).

B.2

Other horizontal agreements

7 Interchange fees in payment card systems: price remedies in a two-sided market

Jean-Charles Rochet

Introduction

All forms of payment cards (credit, debit, charge, etc.) are gradually becoming the most popular non-cash payment instrument all around the world. In Europe alone, there were more than 450 million cards in 2005, accounting for more than €1.5 trillion in transaction volume.[1] A payment card system provides a convenient way for consumers to pay merchants (e.g. retailers). In principle, the system could charge consumers, who gain convenience, and/or merchants, who gain customers attracted by the ability to pay conveniently. Alternatively it may subsidise one and charge more to the other. Because both consumers and merchants buy into the system as a way to trade with each other, this structure is called a 'two-sided market'. Even though the two largest payment card systems, MasterCard and Visa, have recently decided to become for-profit corporations, they were initially set up as not-for-profit associations of several thousands of banks. In many countries, domestic debit card systems are also organised as not-for-profit associations of banks.

Within a payment card system, access charges (known as interchange fees) are levied between the cardholder's bank and the merchant's bank. Interchange fees are collectively determined at the network level. This collective determination, as well as other rules (honour-all-cards, no discrimination), has been challenged by retailers' associations, antitrust authorities and regulators in several regions of the world (US, Israel, UK, EU, Australia). This chapter focuses on one of these cases: DG Comp case 29.373-Visa International.

The theoretical literature on price formation in payment card networks is very recent (Rochet-Tirole 2002, Wright 2003). It has highlighted some common patterns with other network industries: internet, media, software, video games and intermediaries (shopping malls, supermarkets, exchanges) (Caillaud-Jullien

---

[1] *Nilson Report*, Issue 857, May 2006.

2003, Rochet-Tirole 2003b, 2006c, Armstrong 2006). The literature on these 'two-sided markets' is growing rapidly (see in particular the 2006 special issue of the *Rand Journal of Economics*). This chapter has two main objectives:

- to present a simple benchmark model of the payment card industry that captures the fundamental externalities inherent to the functioning of payment card systems;
- to use this model to assess the decisions made by the DG Competition in the case against Visa International.

The rest of this chapter is organised as follows. Section 1 presents a short overview of the payment card industry. Section 2 briefly sketches DG Comp case 29.373 against Visa International. Section 3 explains the externalities that are inherent to payment systems and the role of interchange fees. Section 4 presents a formal model of the payment card industry and uses it to provide the main insights that can be obtained from the recent theoretical literature on the economics of card payment systems. Section 5 presents a welfare analysis of the payment card industry, with a particular emphasis on the consequences of the price structure in this industry. Section 6 analyses the 'must-take card' argument put forward by Vickers (2005): are retailers 'forced' to accept payment cards? Section 7 concludes and gives a short appraisal of the DG Comp decision.

1. An overview of the payment card industry

This section briefly sketches some important features of the payment card industry. For a detailed account of this industry, the reader is referred to Evans and Schmalensee (2005), where the history of this industry is presented in detail and other examples of antitrust cases are analysed. An important feature of the payment card industry is that different types of payment cards typically follow different business models: credit card networks are typically organised either as international associations of thousands of banks (like Visa or MasterCard before their decisions to demutualise) or alternatively as proprietary systems like American Express. By contrast, debit card systems are often run by the owners of ATM networks or by national bank associations.

Each bank in an association issues its own range of debit and credit cards which provide cardholders with access to, say, the Visa payments system. Bank associations have often adopted specific by-laws,[2] usually referred to as

---

[2] Another important by-law, that is not always adopted, is the 'no-surcharge' or 'no-discrimination' rule. It is discussed in section 3 of this chapter.

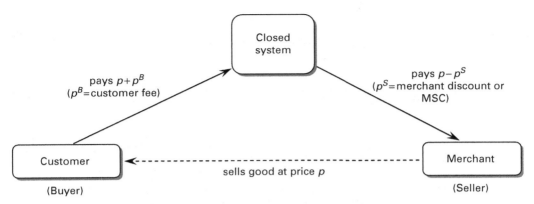

Figure 7.1 The flows of funds associated with a card payment in a closed system

'honour-all-cards' rules or 'honour-all-issuers' rules, that provide cardholders with the guarantee that their card will be accepted by a retailer (provided this retailer is affiliated with the card network), independently of the identity of the bank that has issued the card. The 'honour-all-cards' rule goes further than the 'honour-all-issuers' rule, in that it requires retailers to accept all cards, e.g. debit and credit, issued by the network members. It was abandoned by Visa and MasterCard in 2003, following a settlement in the Wal-Mart class action suit.[3] An economic analysis of the honour-all-cards rule is provided in Rochet and Tirole (2006a).

In a proprietary system, cards are issued and merchants are signed up directly by the payment system and not by member banks. Figure 7.1 represents the flows of funds associated with a card payment in a closed (or proprietary) system such as American Express or Discover.

The main feature of a closed system is that it is able to set directly the two prices faced by the final users: a fee (or subsidy) to the cardholder and a charge to the retailer (called a 'merchant service charge', MSC). Figure 7.2 represents the flows of funds associated with a card payment in an open network.[4] This time, user prices p^B and p^S are not set by the network but by individual banks and so result from competition on downstream markets. The customer and the merchant typically use different banks. The customer's bank is known as the (card) issuer and the merchant's bank is the ('paper' transaction) acquirer,

---

[3] In 2001, Wal-Mart initiated a class action against the honour-all-cards rule, on the grounds that it constituted an illegal tie-in between the credit card market and the debit card market. This class action involved more than 5 million US merchants. In 2003, Visa and MasterCard agreed to abandon this rule and to pay over $3 billion in damages to the merchants.

[4] For simplicity, this figure neglects system fees, which are much smaller than interchange fees.

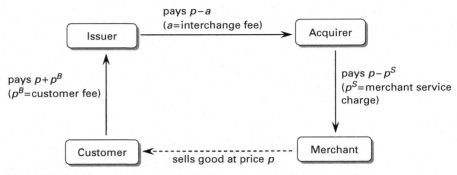

Figure 7.2 The flows of funds associated with a card payment in an open system

and they charge each other an interchange fee for each transaction. The interchange fee a, that typically (but not always)[5] flows from the acquirer to the issuer, reallocates the total cost of the card payment between the two providers (issuer and acquirer). This fee is set by the association of banks (e.g. Visa) and is known as the multilateral interchange fee (MIF). It is significant that the MIF impacts indirectly the prices paid by final users.

Note that, in practice, the transaction fee p^B paid by customers (buyers) is often zero (for debit cards) or even negative (for credit cards). A negative transaction fee means that customers receive money (cash-back bonuses) or incentives (air miles) every time they use their card. Whereas a negative price is impossible in standard one-sided industries (it would lead to arbitrages by consumers), it is a frequent feature in two-sided platforms such as media, where one side of the market (readers, viewers) is subsidised, while the other side (advertisers) pays more than the total cost of the interaction.

2. The case: DG Comp 29.373-Visa International

2.1 The facts

On 23 May 1997 EuroCommerce (an association of retailers) files a complaint against Visa about multilaterally set interchange fees (MIFs), arguing that they constitute a price-fixing agreement between competitors and as such infringe Article 81(1) of the EU Treaty, for Visa intra-regional transactions. The EC subsequently opens an investigation and issues a Statement of Objections to Visa.

---

[5] In the Australian EFTPOS system it is the reverse: Figure 7.2 is still accurate but a is then negative.

On 27 June 2001 Visa proposes to reduce the level of intra-regional MIFs by more than 20 per cent and a future cap (for the period 2002–7) based on three categories of costs: the cost of processing transactions, the cost of free funding for cardholders and the cost of providing the payment guarantee.

On 11 July 2001 the EC grants temporary exemption to Visa MIFs, under Article 81(3) of the EU Treaty.

2.2 The reasoning of DG Comp

It can be articulated along the following lines: because of the honour-all-issuers rule, the price at which acquirers accept the 'paper' issued by other banks has to be specified in advance. Therefore, interchange fees (IFs) can be viewed as agreements between issuers and acquirers that increase the economic value created by card payment associations. But MIFs can potentially restrict competition between acquirers as they increase the marginal cost of all acquirers by the same amount and therefore set an effective minimum for MSCs. However, bilaterally set IFs are in general infeasible (they would necessitate bilateral agreements between thousands of banks) and might also restrict entry of new acquirers. Some issuers might also be tempted to require very large IFs from acquirers, given that retailers are committed, by the honour-all-issuers rule, to accept all cards issued in the network, independently of the identity of the issuer. Therefore, even if MIFs violate Article 81(1), they can be exempt under Article 81(3) as necessary for efficiency and beneficial to consumers. However, there is a presumption that an issuers' controlled association may in some cases earn supercompetitive profits by setting excessively high IFs. This is why a cap on IFs might be needed.

In order to assess the reasoning of DG Comp through the filter of economic analysis, we now present the basic lessons that can be drawn from the economic theory of payment card systems.

3. Some economics of payment card systems

3.1 Two different kinds of externalities

It is important to distinguish network and usage externalities. Our main focus is on the latter, but first we say a few words about the former. Indeed, payment card networks are characterised by two-sided network (or adoption) externalities. This is because the value of a card (for a consumer) depends on how many retailers accept this card and symmetrically the value of accepting a card (for a retailer) depends on how many consumers hold this card. However, even in mature networks (where almost every consumer has a card and almost every retailer accepts cards and therefore adoption externalities become negligible), the price *structure* of card payments (how the total cost of a card payment is allocated between the two users: the cardholder and the retailer) determines the efficiency of card usage, that is how often cardholders *use* their cards. This is a different type of externality that can be called the usage externality.

3.2 Usage externality

When a cardholder decides to pay by card, instead of cheque or cash, it exerts two externalities by modifying two things beyond its own costs and benefits:
- the operating cost of the retailer, who has to pay the MSC p^S but, in compensation, benefits by avoiding the cost of the alternative payment instrument (fraud, theft, accounting) denoted b^S;
- the net cost of the banks, which incur the total marginal cost of a card payment c (shared between acquirer and issuer) but collect the revenue p^S from the merchant.

The total usage externality exerted by the cardholder on the rest of the economy is therefore equal to $(p^S - b^S) + (c - p^S) = c - b^S$. In words, consumers who choose to pay by card do not take direct account of either the card transaction costs incurred by the banks or the retailer's savings from not having to handle cash (or cheque). Note that the cost of paper transactions (cash or cheque) is often higher for banks than that of card transactions, implying a negative incremental cost c.

3.3 Efficient usage of cards

Efficient usage of cards is obtained (i.e. social welfare is maximised) when the cardholder faces the correct price signal. To achieve this, the cardholder fee must be equal to the total usage externality. The condition for efficient usage of cards is thus: $p^B = c - b^S$. Of course, the price p^S paid by sellers must also be lower than the maximum price that they are ready to pay: otherwise merchants may reject cards. But once this condition is guaranteed (we discuss it in more detail in section 4), the customer is in the driver's seat in that she alone chooses the means of payment. This is why efficiency of card usage is fundamentally governed by the cardholder fee p^B. If the cardholder fee is too low, there is excessive card usage. If it is too high, cards are insufficiently used.

The analysis is more complex when different types of cards (say, debit and credit) are taken into account. In this case the difference in fees has to equal the difference in usage externalities.

3.4 The role of interchange fees

The seminal paper of Baxter (1983) was the first to analyse the role of interchange fees. Baxter examines the case of an association of perfectly competitive banks. As already mentioned, social welfare is maximised if a card payment occurs whenever social benefits exceed social costs: $b^B + b^S \geq c = c^B + c^S$. Competition (even perfect) on downstream markets is not enough to guarantee this, since marginal cost pricing on both sides of the market ($p^B = c^B$ and $p^S = c^S$) implies that the card is used whenever $b^B \geq c^B$ and $b^S \geq c^S$. Except in the unlikely case where $b^S = c^S$, this leads to under-efficient usage. However, Baxter (1983) shows that efficiency can be restored with an appropriate interchange fee.

Indeed, suppose that the interchange fee is set by a social planner, who seeks to maximise social welfare. By choosing an interchange fee $a^0 = b^S - c^S$, the planner modifies the marginal cost of issuers to $c^B - a^0 = c^B + c^S - b^S = c - b^S$. If issuers are perfectly competitive, they then set a cardholder fee p^B equal to this new marginal cost $c - b^S$, which corresponds to the price level identified above leading to an efficient usage of cards. Baxter's interchange fee a^0 thus allows a perfect internalisation[6] of the usage externality and gives rise to an efficient usage of cards, provided that p^S does not exceed the maximum price acceptable to merchants. This last condition is satisfied if acquirers are perfectly competitive, in which case $p^S = c^S + a^0 = b^S$, but it is also true if acquirers' margin is not too high, as explained in section 4.

Note that the optimal interchange fee is merchant specific: contrarily to what a cost-based approach would give, the interchange fee that perfectly internalises the usage externality may differ across retailers depending on their relative costs of card and cash transactions.

---

[6] Carlton and Frankel (1995) give (in theory) an alternative way to internalise the externality, namely differentiated prices for cash and cards: $p^{cash} = p$, $p^{card} = p + c^S - b^S$. But surcharges are seldom used in practice: this phenomenon has been termed 'price coherence' by Frankel (1998). In countries where surcharging is possible (such as the UK or Australia), only a small number of retailers actually use this possibility.

However, Baxter's analysis is insufficient to analyse competition policy issues for two reasons:

- Banks are unlikely to charge marginal costs, even if they are competitive. This is because payment card networks are characterised by large fixed costs that have to be recovered by banks.
- IFs are not selected by a social planner but by private payment systems, whose objectives are not to maximise social welfare.

To respond to these limitations, and extend Baxter's analysis, Rochet and Tirole (2002, 2006a, b) and Wright (2003) have developed a fully fledged model of the payment card industry that is presented in the next section.

4. A model of the payment card industry

4.1 The model

The model was developed by Rochet and Tirole (2002) and extended, among others, by Wright (2003) and Rochet and Tirole (2006a, b). As assumed implicitly by Baxter, consumers/buyers have a downward-sloping demand for card payments. The net benefit b^B from a card payment is distributed according to a cumulative distribution function $H(b^B)$. The probability that a consumer wants to pay by card in a particular transaction is thus $D(p^B) = \Pr(b^B \geq p^B) = 1 - H(p^B)$, which can be called the demand for card payments by consumers. On the other side of the market, merchants/sellers enjoy transaction benefit b^S from a card payment. In the benchmark model, this net benefit is the same for all merchants (or heterogeneity, if any, is observable). Merchants set retail prices and decide whether to accept cards. First consider a unique network (monopoly situation).

Banks compete for providing payment services to the two categories of users. Issuers compete for buyers/consumers, while acquirers compete for sellers/merchants. Issuers face a (gross) cost per transaction c^B and a net cost per transaction $c^B - a$, since they receive the interchange fee a. To fix ideas, we assume that issuers charge a constant margin m over this cost. Thus the cardholder fee p^B that results from competition between issuers is just $p^B = c^B - a + m$. Note that issuer profit $mD(p^B)$ increases with interchange fee: this is because the volume of payments decreases with p^B.

Acquirers face a (gross) cost per transaction $c^S + a$ and a net cost $c^S - a$, since they pay the interchange fee a. We assume for simplicity that they are perfectly competitive and thus charge merchant discount: $p^S = c^S + a$. The analysis can

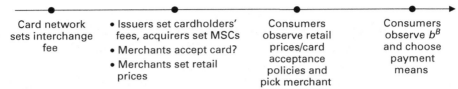

Figure 7.3 The timing of the model

easily be extended to include an acquirer margin. The timing of the model is represented in Figure 7.3.

4.2 Merchant acceptance

It can be shown that, at equilibrium, merchants accept the card if and only if the merchant discount does not exceed the sum of the merchant direct benefit b^S and consumer benefit, that is internalised by the merchants:

$$p^S = c^S + a \leq b^S + s(p^B),$$

where $s(p^B)$ equals the average surplus obtained by a consumer who pays by card:

$$s(p^B) = E(b^B - p^B | b^B \geq p^B).$$

This condition is satisfied for a wide range of different models of the retail sector (Hotelling-Salop, local monopolies, differentiated Bertrand). The intuition is simple: retailers care not only about their own convenience benefit b^S but, given they are competing for customers, also about the quality of service provided to their customers. This has an important implication: since a monopoly network selects the maximum interchange fee that is compatible with merchant acceptance, the price paid by a merchant typically exceeds his convenience benefit, which might ultimately lead to an increase in retail prices by merchants. Does this imply social inefficiency of card usage? We show in the next section that this is not necessarily the case.

The reason why a monopoly network would choose the maximum interchange that is accepted by retailers is simply that banks' profit increases with the volume of card payments and thus with the interchange fee. The monopoly interchange fee a^m is the maximum a that satisfies:

$$p^S = c^S + a \leq b^S + s(c^B - a + m).$$

Moving away from a monopoly card payments system, when two (or more) card networks compete, merchants can reject the most expensive card as long as they know that consumers can also pay with the other card(s). Wright (2003) shows that competition between systems leads to a reduction of interchange fees to $a^C = b^S - c^S$. Note that this competitive interchange fee coincides with Baxter's interchange fee:

$$a^C = a^0 = b^S - c^S.$$

5. Welfare analysis

Social welfare can be computed easily in this model, as the integral of net surplus (total benefit $b^B + b^S$ minus total cost $c^B + c^S$) for all transactions settled by card (i.e. such that $b^B \geq p^B$). This gives:

$$W = \int_{p^B}^{\infty} (b^B + b^S - c^B - c^S)dH(b^B).$$

Given the issuer margin, social welfare is maximised when:

$$p^B = c^B - a + m = c^B + c^S - b^S$$

which corresponds to the following interchange fee:

$$a = a^w = b^S - c^S + m.$$

The socially optimal interchange fee is higher than Baxter's benchmark because of the need to internalise issuers' margin m. Notice that this total welfare optimal MIF depends on the retailer's cost of taking cash, the acquirer bank's cost of processing card transactions and the issuer bank's margin. This is a complex formula for a competition authority to work out and, in particular, there is no reason for it to be closely correlated with the fraction of the issuer's cost that the competition authority declares 'eligible' for the computation of the IF.

Note that this interchange fee may be higher than the monopoly interchange fee, which is defined by:

$$a^m \equiv b^S - c^S + s(c^B - a^m + m).$$

However, when issuers' margin is large, the first-best interchange fee a^w is larger than a^m, the maximum interchange fee that merchants are ready to accept. In this case, the monopoly interchange fee is (second-best) socially optimal and any binding regulation of interchange fees would be distortionary.

The following proposition summarises our results for the monopoly case.

Proposition 1: *The monopoly interchange fee a^m is the maximum interchange fee that is compatible with merchant acceptance.*

a) *When issuers' margin is small, this monopoly interchange fee is excessive: $a^m > a^w$, where a^w denotes the level of interchange fee that maximises social welfare.*

b) *When issuers' margin is large, interchange fee a^w is incompatible with merchant acceptance. The (second-best) socially optimal interchange fee coincides with the monopoly interchange fee a^m.*

Competition law often highlights customer welfare above total welfare. In this case, the customers of the payments system are the cardholders and the retailers. This suggests an alternative criterion for competition authorities is total user surplus (TUS), computed as the integral of net user surplus (total benefit $b^B + b^S$ minus total price $p^B + p^S = c + m$) for all transactions settled by card (i.e. such that $b^B \geq p^B$). This gives:

$$TUS = \int_{p^B}^{\infty} (b^B + b^S - c - m)dH(b^B).$$

Total user (buyer + seller) surplus is maximised when the cardholder pays the net cost (usage externality) inflicted on the seller alone (which includes the profit margin m of banks).

Thus the user surplus maximising cardholder fee is equal to the usage externality inflicted on the seller:

$$p^B_{TUS} = c + m - b^S.$$

This corresponds to Baxter's interchange fee, which is also the competitive interchange fee: $a^C = a^0 = b^S - c^S$. The TUS optimal MIF still depends on the retailer's cost of taking cash and the acquirer bank's cost of processing card transactions but, unlike for total welfare, not on the issuer bank's margin. While the monopoly MIF exceeds this, competition between networks brings about the TUS optimal MIF.

Proposition 2: *If two (or more) identical networks compete, they select the interchange fee that maximises total user surplus, which also coincides with Baxter's interchange fee:*

$$a^{TUS} = a^C = a^0 = b^S - c^S.$$

In this sense, competition between payment card systems is sufficient to achieve the best outcome under the total user surplus standard. Is it appropriate that competition authorities should care only about short-term user surplus and not about social welfare? This is justified if the profit of firms (here, banks) is completely dissipated (business stealing, useless advertisement). This is not justified if part of this profit is reinvested for providing better quality of service (diversity, efficiency). Long-term user surplus is then maximised for a value of the IF that is typically above the competitive interchange fee a^C.

6. Are retailers 'forced' to accept cards?

Competition authorities often argue that retailers cannot reasonably turn down payment cards and are thus forced to accept excessively high merchant service charges. This is the 'must-take' card argument put forward by Vickers (2005).

Rochet and Tirole (2006a) give an empirical content to this argument by putting forward a test which they call the 'tourist test'. A fee satisfies the tourist test if a retailer would not prefer a customer to pay by cash rather than card. More precisely, the interchange fee a (and the associated merchant service charge $p^S = c^S + a$) passes the tourist test if and only if the merchant is not inclined to reject a card payment by a 'tourist' (i.e. a customer who will not patronise the store again in the future) who has enough cash in his pocket to settle the transaction. This condition is satisfied if and only if the merchant service charge does not exceed the convenience benefit of the seller:

$$p^S \leq b^S.$$

This is equivalent to the following condition on the interchange fee:

$$a = p^S - c^S \leq b^S - c^S = a^{TUS}.$$

Proposition 3: *If retailers are homogeneous, the merchant service charge (or the associated interchange fees) passes the tourist test if and only if it is not excessive from the point of view of total user surplus maximisation.*

Rochet and Tirole (2006a) show that when retailers are heterogeneous, the tourist test is only relevant on average. When interchange fees are set at the level that maximises total user surplus, the average retailer is just indifferent between accepting card payments from tourists or rejecting them. Because different retailers have different costs, some above and some below the average, the fact that interchange fees do not pass the tourist test for some retailers does not imply that they are too high, even from the point of view of short-term user surplus. Rochet and Tirole (2006a) also study the long-term impact of interchange fees and show that, whenever some fraction of issuers' profits is invested for improving the quality of service provided by payment card networks, the interchange fee that maximises long-term consumer surplus also fails the tourist test.

7. Conclusion: an appraisal of the DG Comp decision

Economic theory shows the MIF chosen by a monopoly association may sometimes exceed the socially optimal level, but this bias is not systematic. It is likely, however, that this monopoly MIF exceeds the level that maximises total user surplus. Interchange fees are a transfer between banks. While they importantly affect the structure of prices, they do not raise all prices. In fact, a higher MIF acts as a subsidy to the customer charge even if it tends to raise the MSC. Careful economic modelling is necessary to identify the appropriate MIF and the conditions under which it is likely to be distortionary. Nevertheless, while a cap on MIFs based on issuers' costs has no economic basis, competition authorities may consider such a cost-based cap on interchange fees as a transparent standard that allows a reduction in excessive cards usage.[7] Although there is a no evidence of a clear market failure, the EC reasoning (and the must-take argument of Vickers) could possibly be justified under Article 82 (market failure based on a competitive bottleneck situation leading to an overuse of cards), but probably not under Article 81 (infringement of competition law). Finally, some commentators have argued that a mandated regulation of IFs would lead to a decrease in retail prices (retailers passing on to consumers some fraction of the reduction in their cost), thus benefiting all consumers, including those who do not have cards and so must use cash. The Australian experiment[8] suggests that this effect is likely to be negligible.

---

[7] This argument is not grounded upon sound economic analysis but it can be viewed as a pragmatic agreement between a competition authority (which suspects that IFs might be excessive but is unable to prove it) and a card network (which prefers a reduction in its IF to a regulation setting it to zero).

[8] In 2002, the Reserve Bank of Australia mandated a substantial reduction in IFs on credit card transactions. Analysing the impact of this regulation, Evans and Schmalensee (2005) find that retail prices did not decrease in a significant way.

8 The Orders and Rules of British Horseracing: anticompetitive agreements or good governance of a multi-sided sport?

Bruce Lyons

1. Introduction

In a sport that is linked with betting and its associated problems, British horseracing is internationally renowned for its quality, diversity and integrity. It is the second most popular sport in Britain, with nearly 6 million spectators watching it live and millions more watching at home, including a TV audience of 10 million for the Grand National each year. Racehorse owners spend £275 million for the excitement of watching their horses race.[1] British horseracing also provides the punter's favourite bet, leaving bookmakers with a gross win of over £1 billion, 10 per cent of which is put back into the sport. It is a key feature of the competitive analysis that three such diverse sets of consumers (spectators, owners and punters) buy into the same British horseracing product. This is the reason for calling it a multi-sided sport in the title to this chapter.

Successful sports are built on strong governance, which is necessary to keep the competition exciting and free from corruption. Sports with weak, fragmented governance structures tend to lose public interest (e.g. boxing, wrestling). The fact that British horseracing has had a unified governance structure for over 250 years is undoubtedly one of the contributing factors to its success. As one might expect over such a long period, a fairly lengthy set of regulations has been developed to govern the rules of individual races and the control of race, fixture and commercial rights. These rules and regulations are known as the 'Orders and Rules of British Horseracing', some of which were challenged by the UK Office of Fair Trading (OFT) as anticompetitive agreements under Chapter 1 of the Competition Act 1998 (equivalent to Article 81EC).

---

[1] They recover only a third of this in prize money and sponsorship.

The competition issues under review in this chapter concern those Orders and Rules which had the effect of creating joint-selling rights in dealing with bookmakers, limiting the rights of individual racecourses to run fixtures whenever they want and restricting relative prize money across races.[2] Such issues get to the tension between ensuring good governance and creating cartel-like restrictions. This is where economic analysis is necessary to determine which rules are necessary for good governance and which are not.

A recurring theme in this chapter is that good governance in sport requires the appropriate treatment of externalities, which may be either positive (e.g. betting opportunities for bookmakers) or negative (e.g. inappropriate prize money in one race distorting incentives in another). A particularly important network externality is that the pleasure of horseracing for punters depends on the number and quality of horses in training (i.e. the number of owners and how much they spend).[3] A famous idea in economics, known as the Coase Theorem, sets out the conditions under which bilateral bargaining can eliminate the inefficiencies associated with externalities. As we shall see, these conditions are unlikely to hold in the absence of certain of the Orders and Rules because property rights would be too fragmented and uncertain and transaction costs would be high.

This case illustrates an important lesson for the practical application of competition policy. Restrictive agreements should not be considered exclusively from the perspective of their potential to create distortions, because many such agreements have a beneficial, efficiency-enhancing purpose. In such situations, it is necessary to consider the net benefit to consumers and act only against those agreements that are harmful or unnecessarily restrictive.[4] More specifically, economists have become increasingly aware that there are important cases where more than one group of consumers gains benefit from the same product. While all such groups have similar interests in being able to buy into a high-quality product (or interface or platform or sport), the structure of prices (i.e. who contributes how much to funding the British horseracing product) can directly affect not only the distribution of benefits but also the design and quality of the product itself. In the case of horseracing,

---

[2] Joint-selling of betting rights is similar to, but as we shall see importantly different from, the sale of media rights. For a short summary of competition issues in the sale of media rights in football, see Hatton *et al.* (2007).

[3] A network externality arises when the value of the product to one consumer depends on the number of others. This is a cross-group externality when the benefit to one group of consumers depends on the number of consumers in another distinct group.

[4] A similar point is emphasised by Motta in Chapter 1 and Rey and Venit in Chapter 11. See also EAGCP (2005) for the economic approach to competition policy.

a central issue is that a higher price charged to bookmakers for being able to take bets on British horseracing automatically feeds through to a lower price for owners and better quality racing for spectators. The reverse holds if bookmakers contribute less. Careful economic analysis is necessary to identify a benchmark optimum price structure and to understand the consequences of alternative structures for each group of consumers.[5]

With this last point in mind, section 2 discusses the preferences of the main groups of consumers. Section 3 introduces the roles of some key institutions of British horseracing. Section 4 summarises the statement of objections (known as a 'Rule 14 Notice') by the relevant UK competition authority – the Office of Fair Trading. My own economic analysis is set out in section 5. Section 6 summarises the outcome of the case, both in terms of the modernisation of British horseracing and what has happened in various UK and European courts. It also provides a brief conclusion.

2. The consumers of British horseracing[6]

The aim of competition policy

The principal objective of modern competition policy is to ensure that markets operate competitively in the interests of consumers. The OFT sums this up admirably in its mission as stated in successive annual reports and highlighted in its web home page headline: 'Making markets work well *for consumers*.'[7]

The obvious first question to ask is, what are consumers buying? For most sports, it is rarely a single event such as an isolated race or self-standing football match that creates the thrill. The excitement is generated by a sporting competition which links results in different events. In the case of horseracing, there is no major league or knock-out cup, but horses develop their ratings to qualify for more highly rated events. Their form in one race also matters for handicapping in later races which may be run at any racecourse. Furthermore, the integrity of races run under a common governance structure underpins consumer confidence. This suggests a product definition of British horse-racing, not an isolated race or day of racing, but an interlinked programme over the season. We return to this after considering consumers in more detail.

---

[5] See Armstrong and Wright in Chapter 3 and Rochet in Chapter 7 for other examples of competition policy applied to two-sided markets.

[6] Many of the figures used in this section can now be found in Deloitte (2006).

[7] Emphasis in original.

What is the definition of a consumer? Generally speaking, we expect consumers to be the ones who spend money in order to enjoy the product, as distinct from producers who receive income in return for providing the product. This is a fairly straightforward definition for markets with a single category of consumer, but the concept is not so straightforward in a multi-sided market. When different groups of consumers are buying into the same product or 'platform' created with a large element of fixed costs, there are many possible 'prices' that could generate the same level of funding.[8] However, this does not mean that all such sets of prices are equally good because they may affect the quality of the product itself. Put another way, the structure of prices matters. This theme is picked up in section 5.

How should the interests of different groups of consumers be weighted? Given the difficulty of making interpersonal comparisons of utility, it seems reasonable to claim that any weights attached to groups of consumers should be non-negatively related to their total spending (i.e. financial contribution to the creation of the product) – those who spend more should not be considered less worthy than those who spend less on the product. For example, it would be inappropriate to consider the effect of a particular rule on bookmakers independently of its effect on owners and spectators.

Consumers and consumer preferences

At the time of the case in 2003, there were around 9,000 racehorse *owners* with 13,000 horses in training. It cost around £17,000 p.a. to keep a horse in training and average prize money was only £6,000. The average price of a horse bought at two principal auction firms in Britain in 2005 was £28,000 (Deloitte, 2006). Although a very exceptional few horses go on to earn their owners a fortune at stud, most have a very much lower resale value.[9] Racehorses are not attached to particular racecourses but kept and trained at trainers' yards and raced at different courses across the country.

---

[8] For example, newspapers typically sell advertising space to advertisers and content to readers. For some newspapers, the spend of each group is similar, but others vary enormously in the financial contribution of advertisers and readers. At one extreme, 'free newspapers' get all their revenue from advertisers and at the other extreme readers pay for 'free ads' papers. Armstrong and Wright (see Chapter 3) refer to this as a 'waterbed effect' when a similar total revenue can be collected from different consumer groups in various alternative proportions.

[9] The vast majority of owners have horses that fall into the latter category and can have no reasonable expectation of increasing their wealth through horseracing. Consequently, it is conservative to ignore the cost of horses and focus on training costs when considering the financial contribution of owners.

There were fifty-nine racecourses in Britain, including flat and national hunt (i.e. jumping) courses, at which *spectators* could watch horseracing. The highest quality of racing is on grass, but some courses have built all-weather tracks in recent years. The amount of racing on a grass course is strictly limited in any one period because it needs to recover from being cut up by galloping horses. All-weather tracks do not have this constraint. Most courses are individually owned, but there are three significant racecourse groups: Racecourse Holdings Trust (RHT) (thirteen courses), Northern Racing (nine courses) and Arena (seven courses including three with all-weather tracks). In 2003, there were 1,220 fixtures at which just over 8,000 races were run and a total of £94 million in prize money was on offer, 80 per cent of which went to winning owners.

A very distinctive feature of horseracing is its link with the betting industry. *Punters* enjoy a bet on the races, either on-course, in off-course betting shops or increasingly on the internet. At the time of the case, in 2002/3, the gross win (i.e. revenue less payout) for bookmakers on British horseracing was £858 million, which was 42 per cent of their gross win from all betting.[10] In recognition of this, the betting industry makes a substantial financial contribution to horseracing through the Levy (see below). This is used mainly for prize money to attract racehorse ownership, but also to fund integrity services and other support for horses and courses.[11]

Based on expenditure shares in 2000, the net financial contributions of the various consumer groups into British horseracing worked out at owners (via training fees, keep, vets' fees, etc. net of prize money) 50 per cent, punters (via the Levy) 25 per cent, spectators (via racecourse attendance) 18 per cent, and sponsors and media (who are mostly interested in access to owners, punters and spectators) 7 per cent. In this context, although owners are less numerous than punters or spectators, they have a strong claim to being the most important consumer group.[12]

---

[10] Football, fixed-odds computer bets and other sources are now increasing the non-horseracing share, but British horseracing is still seen as a particularly attractive bet for punters. As recently as 1999, the British horseracing share of turnover (i.e. not quite equivalent to gross win) had been 70 per cent and latest figures for 2004/5 show it reduced to 38 per cent of gross win. However, this should be seen in the context of rapid growth in all betting so gross win on British horseracing had grown to £1.12 billion by 2004/5.

[11] This is a very much smaller proportion of betting turnover than is contributed in other countries such as France, the US or Hong Kong (data from the International Federation of Horseracing Authorities). One consequence is that prize money is a lower proportion of training costs in Britain. Highest levels of prize money are available in countries with a state-sponsored tote or betting monopoly, which contrasts with the competitive British betting industry.

[12] There are many other non-consumer interests, most of whom make their living out of horseracing, including trainers, jockeys, stable lads, transport drivers, vets, etc. These are sometimes referred to as 'the industry'. Breeders merit a particular mention because horseraces are a crucial testing ground for their breeding skills, and true-run races provide important information in the continuing search for the best possible racehorse (known as 'improvement of the breed').

While owners are very direct consumers, punters enjoy horseracing through the bookmaking intermediary. We adopt the standard convention in competition law and economics that direct customers (e.g. bookmakers) have an incentive to represent the interests of consumers who buy through them (e.g. punters), as long as they act competitively. A similar point may be made in relation to racecourses and spectators. This association between intermediate business customer and final consumer is not entirely unproblematic but it is a useful starting point.

Having identified the various consumers, it is useful to reflect on what they value from horseracing. Independent market research provides a guide to spectator utility functions. They value true-run races, competitive balance, seeing the fastest horses in the world, accurate information to help predict results, diversity of races and spectacle and glamour. Owners enjoy much the same attributes, but magnified by the vicarious pleasure of participating in a sport and added trips to the trainer's yard to plan their horse's campaign (i.e. season's races). As an indication of punter preferences, there is unpublished econometric evidence (commissioned by bookmakers) that betting increases with TV coverage, racing on a British racecourse, large fields (i.e. ten-plus runners), high prize money (i.e. higher quality of racing), turf (i.e. grass as distinct from all-weather tracks) and handicap races (i.e. more uniform spread of odds). Punters, spectators and owners all rely on racehorse form (results), built up across previous races at different racecourses, to predict results and plan campaigns.

Thus, the same essential qualities are valued by different groups of consumers, though not necessarily with the same weightings. For example, owners generally prefer smaller race fields (and so a better chance of winning) than do punters (who dislike short-odds favourites). It is central to understanding this case that the core product each group of consumers is enjoying is the programme of races which costs half a billion pounds to put on each year. This is the 'platform' into which each of the consumer groups buys. The central competition issue is the extent to which an appropriately representative governing body is necessary to design horseracing for its various consumers and whether market mechanisms can be designed to deliver a more consumer-responsive product.

3. The institutions governing British horseracing

Different aspects of horseracing and its funding were coordinated by three key institutions: the Jockey Club, the British Horseracing Board (BHB) and the Horserace Betting Levy Board (HBLB).

The Jockey Club was formed in 1752 and governed most aspects of British horseracing until 1993. At the time of the case, it still governed sporting rules relating to the conduct of individual races (e.g. licensing of individuals, horses and courses; common standards across racecourses; anti-doping and maintaining integrity on- and off-course; veterinary care). Alongside its regulatory functions, it owned a portfolio of thirteen racecourses under the name of RHT.[13] The Jockey Club was a not-for-profit organisation with all its net income going to support horseracing and the development of the thoroughbred as a breed. It had a charitable function in looking after retired and injured human and equine participants in horseracing.[14]

In 1993, BHB was formed to take over commercial activities and the sport's overall coordination and organisation (e.g. funding, the fixture list, race planning, liaison with the betting industry and HBLB, marketing, strategic planning). BHB distributed no profits to its members, but invested all its income in the interests of the sport (racing, breeding and veterinary science). An important feature of BHB decision making was that it was representative of both regulatory and consumer interests, with the exception of the betting industry with which it negotiated at the HBLB.[15]

The OFT case mainly focused on those Orders and Rules of British Horseracing which enabled BHB to negotiate funding with bookmakers and determine fixtures and race planning. Owners, racecourses and others must accept these regulations if they want to take part in the races BHB puts on. The overall effect of these rules appears to give BHB considerable power over which courses can have fixtures at what times and the prize money for races run under different conditions, as well as in negotiating with bookmakers. In practice, the power to determine the fixture list is very severely constrained by implicit 'grandfather rights' of racecourses to keep their fixtures from one year to the next and by bookmakers through negotiations at the HBLB.

Since 1961, the HBLB has been the statutory body (i.e. set up by government) which assesses and collects a monetary contribution (i.e. the Levy) from

---

[13] The Racecourse Holdings Trust courses include four which host some of the most famous races in the world: Aintree (Grand National), Cheltenham (Gold Cup), Epsom (Derby and Oaks) and Newmarket (2000 and 1000 Guineas).

[14] This was the governance structure at the time of the case but it has since changed. All remaining regulatory functions of the Jockey Club have been brought together with BHB to create the British Horseracing Authority (BHA). For the economic role set out in this chapter, the BHA has effectively the same role as BHB.

[15] BHB policy was determined by a thirteen-person board of directors, appointed by the following: Jockey Club (three), Industry Committee (two), Racecourse Association (RCA) (two), Racehorse Owners Association (two), Thoroughbred Breeders Association (one) and the board itself appointed a chairman, another independent director and the chief executive.

bookmakers in support of the attractive betting opportunity that British horseracing provides.[16] It determines the size of the Levy in conjunction with incentives to provide a fixture list that suits the bookmakers. Under the mediation of an independent HBLB chair, representatives of BHB negotiate with representatives of the Bookmakers' Committee (a committee of leading bookmakers and bookmakers' associations). Formally, the Bookmakers' Committee makes an annual proposal to the HBLB with a view to BHB agreeing to provide a fixture list that suits bookmaker interests (i.e. regular races of sufficient quality spread out across the week).[17]

The UK government's role in horseracing and the betting industry appears anomalous, so it was receptive to proposals that would allow disengagement without harming the sport.[18] What was needed was a mechanism for BHB to prevent bookmakers from freeriding on British horseracing and they came up with a creative proposal. Since bookmakers need precise information on runners, riders and associated pre-race data in order to take bets on races, BHB proposed to sell this data to bookmakers as a replacement for the Levy.[19] This new 'commercial mechanism' was phased in over a period of five years from 2001, with the amount charged for supplying pre-race data being set against the Levy. The intention was that this would allow the HBLB to be abolished in 2005 (i.e. once the robustness of this commercial mechanism had been tested). The price for the data was on exactly the same basis as the Levy (i.e. a proportion of each bookmaker's gross win on British horseracing) but this proportion rose under the commercial mechanism and stabilised at around 10 per cent of the gross win on British horseracing. The increasing importance of the Levy at the time of the case (2000–4) is shown in Figure 8.1.[20]

---

[16] In 1928, the Tote was established by Act of Parliament with a statutory monopoly in non-fixed odds pool betting and the requirement to distribute its profits for 'purposes conducive to the improvement of breeds of horses or the sport of horseracing'. HBLB was established in anticipation of the legalisation of high-street betting shops in 1962. It brought together contributions from the fixed-odds high-street bookmakers and Tote profits.

[17] If there is a failure to agree, the Secretary of State (i.e. a government minister) is required to decide and this is usually a sufficient threat for agreement to be reached.

[18] Having said this, there is far less government intervention in British horseracing than in almost any other jurisdiction. The UK government was also looking for ways to privatise the Tote without compromising the funding of British horseracing. A private sale at a discount to the Racing Trust (a consortium including BHB, the Jockey Club and RCA) was blocked by the European Commission on state-aid grounds (competition policy has a pervasive effect!) and the proposal at the time of writing is to sell the Tote on the open market.

[19] At the time of the case, BHB's property (database) rights on pre-race data, which are essential if it is to be sold at an appropriate price, had been confirmed in the High Court (2001) when challenged by William Hill (a leading bookmaker). This decision was overturned by the Court of Appeal in 2005.

[20] The increase is substantially attributable to a change in betting tax in the 2001 budget away from a 9 per cent tax on bets taken (which punters saw as directly reducing their odds, i.e. raising the price of a bet) in

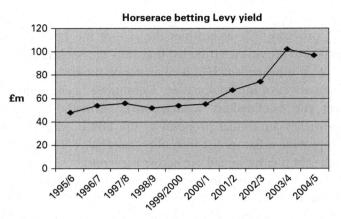

Figure 8.1 Trend in betting's contribution to British horseracing
Source: HBLB website.

Part of the Levy goes to fund integrity services and other support for horseracing and race courses, and around 60 per cent goes into the prize fund. £100 million p.a. provides ample incentive for a wide range of interests to use whatever legal means might be available (including competition law and IPR law) to increase their slice of the cake even if, as we shall see, their actions if successful would lead to a product less attractive to consumers (i.e. a smaller cake may be baked). Bookmakers lobbied hard with the OFT and divisions arose between racecourses.

4. The OFT Statement of Objections

In summer 2000, BHB and the Jockey Club notified to the OFT the Orders and Rules and other agreements which govern British horseracing in order to gain clearance that they did not infringe competition law. Eventually, in April 2003, the OFT issued what is known as a Rule 14 Notice, setting out a Statement of Objections under Chapter 1 of the Competition Act (i.e. equivalent to EC Article 81). The full Rule 14 Notice contains confidential information, but a non-confidential informal summary was issued at the same time:

favour of a less distortionary 15 per cent tax on a bookmaker's gross win (i.e. the difference between bets taken and winnings paid out). In addition to this tax-related increase in betting, the proposed price of pre-race data now came from BHB, not the Bookmakers' Committee, which improved BHB's relative bargaining power. The formal Levy adjusted to the price of pre-race data.

'In essence, the OFT has taken the preliminary view that certain Orders and Rules infringe the [Competition] Act on the grounds that they have the combined effect of:

- limiting the freedom of racecourses to organise their racing, in particular by fixing how often and at what times they stage races and the type of race they stage;
- fixing the amounts that racecourses must offer owners to enter their horses in a race; and
- monopolising the supply of race and runners data to bookmakers by foreclosing competition from alternative suppliers.'[21]

The influence of the Orders and Rules in regulating race fixtures and types, prize money and the sale of pre-race data was not in dispute. The dispute was over who were the relevant consumers and the impact on consumer welfare. The OFT accepted that the application of competition rules to a sport must be sensitive to the distinctive characteristics of that sport so that 'certain sporting rules will not infringe the Chapter 1 prohibition if they are essential to enable the sport to operate' (OFT654, 2003, para. 2.1). However, it considered that some consequences were hard-core market sharing and price fixing and were not essential to achieving the sporting objectives. It made no serious attempt to consider the implications of striking out the apparently offending Orders and Rules (i.e. the counterfactual).

The OFT did attempt to define a relevant market for each of the three bullet points above. It then proceeded by identifying the producers and customers in each of its three defined separate markets and drew the implication that there should be no rules to interfere with the freedom of action of individual producers in each market. In section 5, we argue that a fundamental problem with the OFT's original analysis is that it is inappropriate to consider horseracing as the sum of three independent markets.[22] This commits the serious mistake of applying one-sided logic to the analysis of a multi-sided product. Before developing this point, however, we set out the OFT position on the three 'markets' in a little more detail.

The 'market for fixtures and programmes'

A fixture is an event at a racecourse that contains a programme of five or six races on a particular date. The programme refers to the number of races at a

---

[21] OFT654, 2003, para. 1.5.
[22] More precisely, the OFT position was that there were many other component markets (e.g. the market for racehorse training), but these three were the ones for which it thought the Orders and Rules were anticompetitive.

fixture, the conditions for each race (e.g. handicap versus equal weight carried by horses; flat racing versus national hunt over fences) and start times. The OFT view was that racecourses are the natural producers of fixtures and so should be allowed to organise them whenever they individually perceive there to be the demand. New racecourses should also be free to enter, and a healthy market should see weaker racecourses exit. This does not happen. The number of racecourses had been stable at fifty-nine with neither entry nor exit for over half a century, which suggested that the licensing system was over-restrictive. Basically, there was no mechanism to reward efficient racecourses and penalise those that were unattractive to consumers.

The rules that were deemed anticompetitive included those preventing racecourses, without BHB approval, from introducing new fixtures even when the course could physically take more, or holding a fixture under the same code (i.e. flat versus jumps) at the same time as another racecourse if located within fifty miles. The OFT also argued that each racecourse should be allowed to determine the content of a day's racing, including running however many races its track could safely run, at whatever time and with whatever conditions on the race that it wanted.

The 'market for British racing opportunities'

The OFT saw this as a separate market in which the racecourses supply opportunities for owners (i.e. the customers) to race their horses. The price of such opportunities has two main components: the stakes owners must pay in order to enter a race and the prize money they might receive if their horse wins or is highly placed. Various Orders and Rules restrict the range of stake money and, quantitatively much more important, regulate prize money. Prize money regulation has several dimensions, including minimum prize money for a race, relative prize money across different classes of race (e.g. according to the quality rating of horses) and amount of place money relative to the winner's prize. These were seen as classic price fixing.

The 'market for pre-race data'

Before bookmakers can take money on a race, they and their punters need to know which horses are racing, the handicap weight being carried and preferably also who is riding each horse. Further important information includes each horse's 'form' (i.e. recent results) and other details that may affect judgements as to each horse's chances of winning. Such information is meticulously collated for BHB by a private company called Weatherbys.[23] This information is provided free to newspapers to publicise race fixtures. However, from 2001 it was sold to bookmakers by BHB as part of the new 'commercial mechanism' to replace the Levy.

The OFT considered that BHB had created an effective monopoly in the supply of this data because the notification requirements in the Orders and Rules mean that owners and trainers are obliged to notify Weatherbys of which horses they propose to run in which races. If a race is oversubscribed, Weatherbys follows fixed priority (based mainly on a horse's rating) and balloting rules and notifies owners whose horses are excluded from being able to run in that race. The OFT claimed that these rules effectively excluded racecourses or third parties from being able to sell their own pre-race data to bookmakers and so prevented competition in the supply of data.

Some problems with the OFT's Statement of Objections

The OFT analysis identified three apparently independent 'markets'. From this perspective, it could see no connection, for example, between owners as suppliers of racehorses for the 'market for fixtures and programmes' and owners as consumers of the 'market for British racing opportunities'! It provided no view of how the organisation and quality of British horseracing would evolve in the absence of the offending Orders and Rules (i.e. the counterfactual). There was no recognition of the pre-race data as a legitimate property right over the overall British horseracing product, its role in the commercial mechanism, or the consequences if several firms competed in the supply of pre-race data. Finally, there was no appreciation of the beneficial effects of some of the key rules under challenge. Of course, the adoption of a purely prosecutorial position might be seen as a legitimate strategy for a competition authority operating in a court system, in order to encourage the defendants to articulate and evaluate what the benefits are. However, this is not appropriate in a UK or EU-type administrative system where the authority acts as judge and jury.

---

[23] This is a family company that has a centuries-long relationship with horseracing. Since 1770 it has traced the lineage of every racehorse and so has a crucial role in horse breeding. It also performs banking functions for horseracing (e.g. related to stake and prize money) and prints racecards for the courses.

5. Economic analysis of the offending Orders and Rules

Several of the Orders and Rules challenged under the 'market for fixtures and programmes' were indeed overly restrictive, but others have essential incentive and efficiency properties. Their prohibition would have fundamentally devalued British horseracing. Economically the most important relate to the sale of pre-race data, so this is the main emphasis of this chapter, though we return to the role of other Orders challenged by the OFT at the end of this section.

The betting externality and optimal bookmaker contribution to British horseracing[24]

In this section, we provide a simple model designed to capture the essential features of the relationship between horseracing and bookmakers, in particular, the role of prize money in raising the quality of horseracing enjoyed by its various consumers. The model allows us to conceptualise the contribution from bookmakers that would maximise the benefit of all consumers. It also provides a benchmark from which to conduct a counterfactual analysis of what would happen if certain Orders and Rules were prohibited. For simplicity, we focus on racehorse owners and bookmakers, leaving racecourses/spectators and others in the background. However, a substantial proportion of the Levy goes towards providing integrity services, vet science and racecourse investment, for which very similar arguments apply.

A simple model of the betting externality[25]

Bookmakers make profits on bets taken on races and these bets increase with the number (and quality) of racehorses. Apart from providing more races on which to bet, punters bet more on higher-profile races, well-known horses and races with larger 'fields' (i.e. more horses per race).[26] To capture this, we write

---

[24] This section is more technical than others in this chapter, but the text has been written with a view to it being self-explanatory for those who prefer to avoid equations.

[25] The formal approach taken here is similar to that in the recent literature on two-sided markets. See the references given in Chapters 3 and 7. It differs in that the two-sided market literature has one or more platform owners who set out to maximise profits. The literature then examines the implications for pricing structures. In the current context, it is more appropriate to model negotiations between different groups with similar interests in developing a common product or 'platform'. Nevertheless, the key ideas of multiple groups of consumers and appropriate pricing structures in the presence of positive externalities are essentially the same, and so too are the essential insights.

[26] These assumptions reflect research by leading bookmakers.

the 'gross win' for bookmakers as $B(n)$ where n is the number of racehorses in training and available to race. The more horses in racing, the greater the benefit to bookmakers: $B'(n) = \beta(n) > 0$.[27] If bookmakers could not, for any reason, take bets on British horseracing, they could offer punters alternative betting opportunities (e.g. Italian horseracing, computer-generated horse-racing, dog racing) on which they could expect a gross win of $\bar{\pi}$. The 'betting externality' is the positive contribution that is specific to British horseracing: $B(n) - \bar{\pi}$. If bookmakers also contribute $P \geq 0$ to the prize fund for races, the net benefit to bookmakers is:[28]

$$\pi = B(n) - \bar{\pi} - P \tag{1}$$

Racehorse owners gain enjoyment out of seeing their horses race, and particularly seeing them win. We write the (inverse) demand for racehorses in training as $v(n)$ with $v'(n) < 0$. Racehorse ownership is expensive, both the original purchase of a horse and the costs of training and keep. We represent the annualised cost as c per horse. Part of the cost is mitigated, at least in expectation terms, by the opportunity to win prize money. On average, each racehorse can expect to win P/n out of the bookmakers' contribution to the prize fund, so the net benefit of owning the nth horse is $u(n) = v(n) - c + P/n$.[29] The equilibrium number of horses in training is determined by where ownership of the marginal horse brings pleasure and expected prize money just equal to the costs of ownership:

$$v(n) + P/n = c \tag{2}$$

Lower costs or higher prize money encourage new owners into racing and existing owners to keep more and better quality horses in training. In particular:[30]

$$dn/dP = 1/[(P/n) - nv'(n)] > 0 \tag{3}$$

To give an idea of the size of this prize-fund effect, the increased Levy shown in Figure 8.1 was associated with a growth (2002–5) of: total prize

---

[27] A prime denotes a partial derivative. There is diminishing marginal benefit so $\beta'(n) < 0$.

[28] In practice, the prize fund depends on the gross win, so we could write $P = t\beta(n)$ where $t = 10$ per cent is the size of the Levy. It turns out that, because a lump-sum Levy has the same economic effect as a 'profits tax', we do not need to be concerned about the precise specification of the prize fund.

[29] Owners also contribute stake money for races, but this goes to the winner, so it does not affect the average net benefit of ownership. Average prize money per horse is over £6,000 p.a., though the distribution is highly skewed, with the top ten horses winning £300,000–£800,000 each and many winning nothing. There is no doubt, however, that most owners of the latter still have a positive *expectation* of winning!

[30] This is derived by totally differentiating (2) and rearranging.

money (net of owner contributions) of 20 per cent; and horses in training, runners, races and fixtures, each of between 11 per cent and 13 per cent. The long-term effects are likely to be larger. There is also some evidence of an increase in the quality of British-trained horses.[31]

Since there are n horses, the benefit to owners as a group is:

$$U(n) = V(n) - nc + P \qquad (4)$$

where $V(n)$ is the gross utility of racehorse ownership.[32] Even without a prize fund from the bookmakers, a lower level of horseracing would exist. We define $\bar{n}$ as the number (and quality) of horses that would be in training if $P = 0$ and the consequent benefits to owners as $\bar{U} = V(\bar{n}) - \bar{n}c$.[33]

Before developing implications for negotiations between bookmakers and owners, we establish the socially optimal outcome for this two-sided market with a one-sided externality (i.e. bookmakers benefit from racehorse ownership but not directly vice versa). Consider what the optimal size (and quality) of British horseracing, and so also the optimal prize fund, would be if we were interested in *maximising the joint benefit of owners and bookmakers*. Adding (1) and (4):

$$\omega(n) = V(n) - nc + B(n) \qquad (5)$$

This implies that the socially optimal number (and quality) of racehorses is n^*, which is found by solving:

$$v(n^*) + \beta(n^*) = c \qquad (6)$$

In words, the combined marginal benefits to owners and bookmakers of an extra horse should equal the marginal cost.[34] Of course, the optimal design of horseracing is a lot more complex than a single number, n^*, and this is discussed briefly below, but for now it will serve as a simple measure of

---

[31] It is very difficult to measure quality but one international comparison casts light at least on the best racehorses. If we calculate the difference between prize money won abroad by UK-trained horses and prize money won in the UK by foreign-trained horses, and compare the 2004/6 average with the 2002/3 average, this also grew by 13 per cent. All figures in this para. are taken from the BHB annual report (2005) supplemented by the BHB (2006) report on 'Fixtures, Races and Prize Money' available on its website. As the Levy and prize money have reduced more recently, there is evidence of these effects reversing (BHA, 2007).

[32] Formally, $V(n)$ is the integral of $v(n)$ over the n horses. Non-marginal owners obtain positive consumer surplus which is measured by $U(n)$.

[33] Formally, from (2), $\bar{n}$ solves $v(\bar{n}) = c$.

[34] Note that $v(n^*) - c < 0$ for (6) to hold which explains why extra prize money is necessary to bridge the deficit for owners. Prize money has no direct effect on ω because for every £1 that owners gain, bookmakers lose the same. However, there is a crucial indirect effect because a higher prize fund means more (and better quality) racehorses, which benefits both owners and bookmakers.

the overall quality of racing and facilitate discussion of the fundamental economic issues.

The Coase Theorem does not hold for horseracing

The Coase Theorem states that *if there are clearly defined property rights* and in the *absence of transaction costs*, free negotiations should eliminate any distortions due to an externality and so result in the optimal outcome (in this case the optimal number and quality of racehorses).[35] The intuition is that it is mutually beneficial for bookmakers and owners to get round a table to agree on n^*, which maximises joint utilities, and make a payment to compensate owners for providing more races than they would otherwise do. This transfer payment would only affect the distribution of utility between the parties (and ensure that each gets at least their reservation utilities $\bar{U}$ and $\bar{\pi}$).

The first problem with this is that it is not practical to negotiate directly over n, which is determined by the decisions of thousands of owners. Even if it was possible to negotiate with so many dispersed individuals, it is simply not feasible to negotiate in a way that does not compromise the integrity of racing – it is not credible to expect true-run races when bookmakers are seen to be 'bribing' owners (even if for the best of motives). Owners have to negotiate through an intermediary with the power to act on their behalf (e.g. BHB). However, even then, the intermediary cannot force owners to keep n^* horses in training. This can only work indirectly through a prize fund attracting ownership. The consequences are developed below, particularly focusing on the fact that the quality of racing is not independent of the distribution of bargaining power between owners and bookmakers.

An additional complication is that negotiations simultaneously take place over the fixture list and timing of races with a view to maximising the positive betting externality (e.g. by having fixtures throughout the week, every week and spread out during the day, so that betting opportunities are enhanced). This means that the negotiating intermediary must be able to deliver the fixture list as well as ownership incentives. This requires an intermediary who can also represent racecourses.

In order for the intermediary to be able to represent these interests it must have a secure 'property right' to be able to exclude bookmakers from taking off-course bets on British horseraces; otherwise, it would have no bargaining power. The Levy system acted equivalently and the ownership of pre-race

---

[35] The classic references are Coase (1960) and Williamson (1985), but the basic principles are set out in any good intermediate microeconomics textbook.

database rights was intended to enable commercial rights without the necessity of government intervention through the HBLB. At the time of the case, this key property right appeared to be in place and BHB had the ultimate right to exclude bookmakers from taking bets on their races.[36]

Collective negotiations between BHB and the bookmakers

In order to understand the problems raised by the OFT's 'preliminary view' that multiple suppliers should be free to provide competing databases, I set the scene by considering the status-quo negotiations (i.e. as of 2003), with BHB selling the right to take bets and the Bookmakers' Committee buying this right. The outcome of such bargaining is hard to predict precisely, but it is instructive to consider the extremes, such as when one party can make a take-it-or-leave-it offer to the other.

If *bookmakers* had all the bargaining power, maximising (1) gives the implicit number of racehorses, n^B, that they would want to support:[37]

$$[v(n^B) + n^B v'(n^B)] + \beta(n^B) = c \tag{7}$$

Equation (7) differs from (6) in that marginal *revenue* (i.e. the term in square brackets) replaces the *benefit* of the marginal owner. The second element of the term in square brackets is negative which means that $n^B < n^*$. In other words, from the perspective of all consumers, there would be too little horseracing (of too low a quality) taking place. Thus, even with all the bargaining power, bookmakers want to contribute to a limited prize fund in order to bring more horses into racing and so generate a higher gross win on the associated bets.[38] However, there would be too little horseracing (and of a quality that is too low).

At the other extreme, if *BHB (acting on behalf of owners and spectators)* had all the bargaining power, the bookmakers would still have the option to stop taking bets on British horseracing, and they would exercise this option if BHB demanded too much. This 'quit option' is the key to considering what would happen if owners could dictate terms to bookmakers. BHB could force net benefit down to zero, so from (1) it could press for $P^{\max} = B(n^O) - \bar{\pi}$. We can find the number of racehorses this would bring into training by substituting into (2):

$$v(n^O) + \left[\frac{B(n^O) - \bar{\pi}}{n^O}\right] = c \tag{8}$$

---

[36] See footnote 19.   [37] This expression follows after the substitution of (2) and (3).
[38] The prize fund would be positive as long as $n^B > \bar{n}$, which is certainly the case for British horseracing.

The first term in square brackets is the average benefit to bookmakers, which exceeds the marginal benefit so, by comparison with (6), this tends to result in too many racehorses. However, the $\bar{\pi}$ term works in the opposite direction, so the overall effect depends on the outside opportunities of bookmakers and may result in too little prize money.[39] Combined with our result when bookmakers can dictate terms, we find:

$$\bar{n} < n^B < n^* \leq n^O \tag{9}$$

Thus, whatever the allocation of bargaining power, bookmakers will want to invest a positive amount in racing, but if their bargaining power is strong, they will invest too little. The efficiency of owners having maximum bargaining power is less clear. As long as there is collective negotiation on both sides, the bookmakers' contribution is likely to lead to between n^B and n^O. The actual outcome is then determined by relative negotiating skills and the institutional setting of the bargaining process. We cannot say that this outcome will be precisely the optimal n^*. However, this analysis does give reason to believe that the outcome is at least in the right ball park when there is collective negotiation on both sides; BHB is able to exclude bookmakers from taking bets on British horseracing and bookmakers are free to walk away.

It is helpful to illustrate issues in the following subsection with some rough orders of magnitude to set the bounds of negotiation. The cost of filling daily fixture gaps in the racing calendar (i.e. fixtures that would not happen in the absence of bookmaker funding) might be achieved for around £20 million, though this would not bring about high-quality racing. At the other extreme, while bookmakers take a gross win of over £1 billion p.a. on British horseracing, there would undoubtedly be considerable substitution to other bets if punters were prevented from betting on this. The extent of possible substitution is possibly known by bookmakers, but if it is, it is a closely guarded commercial secret. An educated guess might put the maximum bookmakers would conceivably pay at £200 million, a figure which will serve for illustrative purposes.

The central conclusion of this section is that due to the positive externality created for the betting industry by British horseracing, and the dispersed decisions by owners, an efficient market requires bookmakers to return a substantial share of their profits to invest in prize money and so enhance the size and quality of racing: $\bar{n} < n^*$.[40] This contribution should be higher than

[39] With a sufficiently strong outside option $n^O < n^*$ and $n^B \leq n^O$. Inequality (9) assumes the bookmakers' outside options are more limited.

[40] This efficiency argument is quite separate from any moral case that beneficiaries should pay for positive externalities.

what bookmakers would provide on their own initiative: $n^B < n^*$. It is against this broad background that we can evaluate the counterfactual, i.e. the consequences of the OFT proposal to require disaggregated bargaining on the part of horseracing interests, with each racecourse negotiating separately.

Implications of alternative institutional arrangements for negotiating over the betting externality

Competition policy practitioners should carefully consider the economic consequences of their actions. They need to be particularly careful when there are beneficial effects of apparently anticompetitive restrictions. Consider the following alternative negotiating structures which represent the range of possibilities that might have arisen depending on the precise outcome of the OFT's investigation.[41] The first four assume the continued existence of clear property rights that permit BHB (or, for cases 3 and 4, individual racecourses) to exclude bookmakers from taking bets unless prior agreement has been reached:

1. BHB negotiates with collective bookmakers.
2. BHB negotiates with individual bookmakers.
3. Individual courses negotiate with collective bookmakers.
4. Individual courses negotiate with individual bookmakers.
5. No property rights for BHB (or racecourses) to exclude bets on British horseracing.

1. BHB negotiates with collective bookmakers

This represents the status quo as already discussed. Both the racing side and the betting side act collectively. If negotiations between two parties are balanced, we expect that the benefits will be shared roughly equally. Equal monetary shares between the maximum and minimum contributions by bookmakers would suggest a Levy (or sale of pre-race data) of around £110 million ($= \frac{1}{2}[\text{£}20\,\text{m} + \text{£}200\,\text{m}]$).

2. BHB negotiates with individual bookmakers

Suppose the OFT had focused only on the collective bargaining of bookmakers, instead of the collective bargaining only of the racing side in its

---

[41] The OFT was silent on whether bookmakers would continue to be able to negotiate collectively. We separate out the consequences of 'competitive provision of pre-race data' because it would have distinctive economic effects.

Rule 14 Notice, and prohibited the Bookmakers' Committee. This would have allowed BHB to play off one bookmaker against another in order to extract the full surplus of £200 million. It might even go further and offer exclusive betting rights to one bookmaker, who would then be able to act as a monopolist (e.g. offering worse odds to punters). This might bring in even more money for the racing side, but it would do so by exploiting punters.[42]

3. Individual courses negotiate with collective bookmakers

This would have been the most likely outcome if the OFT had pursued its 'preliminary finding' that racecourses should independently negotiate their fixtures and funding from bookmakers. If no single racecourse group was essential to providing a full set of fixtures required by the bookmakers, the latter could play one off against the other to drive payment down to the minimum £20 million. In effect, the bookmakers would design British horseracing with no account taken of other consumer interests.[43]

4. Individual courses negotiate with individual bookmakers

Large bookmakers would continue to fund certain fixtures but only as long as they could prevent rivals from freeriding on them. Bookmaker-funded fixtures would be subject to exclusivity clauses, thus foreclosing smaller bookmakers. The effects would be to increase horizontal concentration amongst bookmakers and vertical integration with racecourses. As with case 2, punters would be faced with more expensive bets. With or without exclusivity, this set of negotiations would create enormous coordination problems in the design of the racing calendar because horses are not tied to courses in the UK. The problems created by the absence of a single governing body coordinating and creating sporting competition are vividly illustrated by the loss of consumer interest in boxing when sanctioning bodies proliferated.

5. No property rights for BHB (or racecourses) to exclude bets on British horseracing

The OFT's preliminary view was that the supply of pre-race data was being monopolised by BHB and others should be given the right to sell it. Suppose that competitive supply could be established. This would cost around £5 million p.a. for each provider. If a genuinely contestable market could be

---

[42] At present, British horseraces provide a 'low price' bet compared with other betting opportunities, i.e. an odds-weighted bet on each horse in a race would on average return a punter a higher percentage of his outlay than on alternative bets such as racing from another country, dog racing, etc. Of course, this percentage is less than 100 per cent, so the bookmakers earn a profit.

[43] In terms of our formal analysis, this would result in n^B.

created, bookmakers could purchase at cost price. If acting collectively, they would buy the data for £5 million, but none of this would contribute to the fixture programme for which they could then negotiate and fund as in case 3. If acting individually, they would pay for the data, but no doubt freeride on fixtures with an outcome no better than in case 4. Of course, the idea of a competitive market in pre-race data provision completely misses the point of a commercial mechanism designed to replace the Levy. At best (i.e. if book-makers act as a cartel) it would arrive at the unbalanced outcome of case 3, and at worst (i.e. if bookmakers act individually) it would make everybody worse off.

In practice, competitive data supply would be even worse than in cases 3 or 4. It is important that the details of pre-race data are accurate in order to maintain the distinctive qualities of betting on British horseracing (e.g. many punters get pleasure from studying information on a race before placing their bets). The current system provides an extremely high level of accuracy with very rapid internet dissemination of information which changes by the hour. It is difficult to envisage how this accuracy could be replicated by a third party (e.g. trainers might not inform all data providers of entries and withdrawals) and the loss of reputation for accuracy would be harmful all round. The problem is even deeper in that, in the absence of a body representing the collective interests of all those in racing, contributors to the database would likely claim ownership of their own bits of data (e.g. owners' racing colours or entries, racecourses on race times, Jockey Club on handicaps) and the trans-action costs of compilation would be enormous.

Conclusion on agreements that enable BHB to negotiate collectively

BHB is a not-for-profit organisation that coordinates negotiations on behalf of non-bookmaker interests. Sixty per cent of the Levy goes towards prize money, thus cutting the price of racing for owners, and the remainder goes towards integrity services, developing racecourse facilities for the benefit of spectators and improving the breed. The Levy is a betting-profits tax and its proposed replacement was a charge for data based on betting profits. Neither is significantly distortionary for punters because it remains optimal for book-makers to set the same odds that maximise their profits, whether they keep 100 per cent or only 90 per cent. For this and other reasons, British horse-racing offers punters amongst the lowest price of a bet.

The OFT proposals would have fragmented negotiations and undermined property rights, with the consequence of unbalancing the outcome. With very considerably reduced funding, the quality of British horseracing (the common product into which the various groups of consumers each buy) would be greatly diminished. Furthermore, competition in the betting industry would have been seriously undermined if individual negotiations had been required and resulted in exclusive deals.

Coordination of fixtures and race planning

Another part of the OFT's Statement of Objections (see section 4) related to 'limiting the freedom of racecourses to organise their racing, in particular by fixing how often and at what times they stage races and the type of race they stage'. There are good reasons to have an element of central planning of fixtures. Different groups of consumers have somewhat different preferences over fixtures. For example, bookmakers want racing all day every day, spectators want weekend and Bank Holiday racing and owners need to plan a campaign for their horses over the season. The matching of the needs of the horse population and a suitable set of races, plus a relatively fixed pot of funding for prize money, cannot be achieved without an element of central planning for fixtures and race conditions. However, this raises the issue of which racecourses should be able to run which fixtures and whether competition could be beneficially introduced.

Historically, fixture allocation was determined by 'grandfather rights', i.e. if you had a fixture on the first Friday in May last year, you have first rights on it this year. This had the inevitable consequence of freezing the number of courses and limiting the incentive for each course to work at developing sponsorship and facilities. Trade in fixtures between racecourses was very limited. Furthermore, there was a 'fifty-mile rule' which prevented two meetings from taking place on the same day at courses within fifty miles of each other. Some racecourses felt seriously constrained by these rules and lobbied hard for their reform, while others were disturbed at the prospect of change.

While there are strong arguments for central planning of the general pattern of fixtures to meet the requirements of bookmakers and others, this could be achieved with far less rigid rules. In particular, the fifty-mile rule had little economic justification. Fixture allocation could also be freed up by an auction system for fixtures, with racecourses bidding for slots and revenues going towards overall prize money. In this respect, the OFT objections undoubtedly helped spur an emerging modernisation programme into action by leading to undertakings to abolish these unnecessary restrictions and to introduce rolling auctions for a subset of fixtures that had no great tradition (e.g. no auction of Derby Day which is traditionally run at Epsom).

Integrity and prize money

The third OFT objection was that BHB should not restrict prize money for particular races. The OFT implied that prize money should be used in an unrestricted way by individual racecourses to attract horses to run, regardless of the quality of the race. This would allow higher prizes for races run by lower-grade horses than those rated more highly and so create severe incentive problems, undermining the integrity of races (e.g. an owner would be tempted to hold back a high-quality horse in some races in order to move down the ratings and so qualify for a low-grade but higher prize money race against weak opposition). Meritocratic prizes are particularly important for the integrity of handicap races. Handicapping is a major element in the mix of creating exciting races with attractive betting opportunities. It is essential to the integrity of such races that horses have the incentive to be run true and so provide information for handicapping on merit.[44]

6. Outcome and conclusion

This was a case that set some racecourses against the sport's governing authority. It also set bookmakers against the rest in a classic fight over the allocation of the spoils derived from taking bets on British horseracing. Some very strong personalities and very old traditions were involved, using a very new weapon of competition law.[45] Modernisation was overdue but a careful path needed treading if it was not to trample on what underpinned its success.

In June 2004, four years after original notification, BHB reached agreement with the OFT.[46] The OFT was ultimately persuaded to withdraw its preliminary view that it should fragment British horseracing. It withdrew its challenge to those Orders and Rules 'monopolising' the sale of pre-race data and allowing the governing body to coordinate key elements of the overall shape of fixtures and race planning across the season. It also accepted the need for

---

[44] In fact, the modernisation programme proposed a more, not less, rigorous approach to linking prizes to race quality. Furthermore, unrestricted relative prize money would be impractical as a way of balancing race sizes (which was the supposed justification in the hypothesised 'market for British racing opportunities') because the supply of horses is very inelastic over the days or even hours necessary to fill a race, so the swings in prize money would have to be seriously large.

[45] The UK Competition Act (1998) became operational from 1 March 2000 and introduced almost identical prohibitions on anticompetitive agreements (Chapter 1) and abuse of dominance (Chapter 2) to those in EC Articles 81 and 82 respectively.

[46] OFT Case CP/1058/00 Notification of Governance Agreements 28 June 2004.

regulation of prize money in relation to race ratings. Two commitments were agreed in relation to the sale of pre-race data. First, licensing arrangements must be 'on an open, non-discriminatory and non-exclusive basis, at a fair market price'. Second, in the event of pricing disputes, an independent 'arbitrator will be required to resolve the dispute having regard to the needs of racing, the value of British horseracing to the bookmakers' business and, importantly, competition law'. BHB also proposed to link the allocation of funding to the racecourses generating most betting revenue and to give them more discretion to set race programmes (i.e. incentivising courses to provide racing most attractive to punters). BHB further undertook to relax a number of other Orders that could not be justified, for example, competition between racecourses was enhanced by the abolition of the fifty-mile rule, the introduction of a set of new fixtures that BHB proposed to auction to racecourses on three-year 'leases'.[47] Minimum prize money for the lowest-grade races was also adjusted to facilitate more racing for less able racehorses. After a quarter of a millennium of institutional evolution, it is not surprising that reform was needed, and these agreed changes sat naturally as part of a much wider modernisation programme started earlier by BHB chairman Peter Savill.

The wider economic lessons of this case include the need for a competition authority to address the efficiency motives for apparently anticompetitive agreements, the abolition of which may have severely negative side effects. There should be serious consideration of the counterfactual. It is also important to get the product definition right before rushing into multiple partial 'market definitions'. Where different groups of consumers buy into the same product and this creates externalities, great care is needed to make sure these externalities are appropriately addressed. This has been a common theme of much recent economic research on what have become known as 'two-sided markets'. Competition authorities should also beware of getting drawn inappropriately into commercial disputes. With huge sums of money at stake, businesses will work through every available court using every available law to try to gain a larger slice of the cake, even when this reduces the size of the cake. The best way to limit the consequent inefficiencies is to focus clearly on economic effects and for economists to make the economic arguments understood by the competition agencies and courts.

---

[47] This is an example of how bidding *for* the market can provide an alternative to more standard competition. This approach is familiar in the presence of natural monopoly (e.g. TV or rail franchises) where there are well-known dangers of ex-post compliance and renegotiation (Williamson, 1976). In the case of fixture auctions, such dangers are minimised by the presence of alternative racecourses which could credibly take over a fixture if the leaseholder tried to renegotiate.

Unfortunately, the legal issues in this case have been much harder to sort out. This case has links with a number of others which together touch on an enormous range of competition laws related to restrictive agreements, database rights, exploitative pricing, media rights and state aid. The courts have found the sale of pre-race data particularly confusing: is it excessive to negotiate a price of £100 million for something that costs only £5 million to compile? Or is £100 million a 'fair price' for something that provides access to a product costing many times that to create and which generates the buyer £1 billion in gross profits? Early court decisions and statements supported the BHB position (High Court, 2001; Advocate General of ECJ, July 2004). Later ones went against (ECJ, November 2004; UK Court of Appeal, July 2005), in particular undermining the rights over pre-race data. The last of these forced the UK Minister for Sport to agree that the HBLB must continue the Levy system until an alternative commercial mechanism can be found (though there appears to be no practical alternative to the sale of pre-race data). In a related case on the sale of pre-race data to Attheraces, a proposed television channel, the case was set up as an abuse of dominance by BHB, which lost on excessive pricing in the High Court (December 2005) before winning in the Court of Appeal (February 2007).[48] All this has created huge uncertainty and delayed the modernisation programme. Non-specialist courts clearly find these issues very difficult, thus providing an object lesson in the value of the economic approach to competition analysis.

Acknowledgements

I am grateful to David Elliott and Steve Davies for detailed comments on this chapter. I acted as an expert witness on behalf of the BHB during the period of its response to the Rule 14 Notice (2003–4). I learned an enormous amount about the organisation of horseracing from Greg Nichols, then Chief Executive of BHB, with additional detail from other BHB executives and representatives of various horseracing bodies. Guy Leigh led the legal team. I worked closely with David Elliott with Eric Morrison at PwC. Much of the economic analysis in this chapter was jointly developed with David and Eric, to whom I am most grateful, though I am sure they will agree that any errors remain mine.

---

[48] See Elliott (2007).

B.3

Vertical agreements

9 Efficiency enhancing or anticompetitive vertical restraints? Selective and exclusive car distribution in Europe

Frank Verboven

1. Introduction

Vertical agreements between the European car manufacturers and their dealers have existed since the emergence of the industry. They have been claimed to be necessary for an efficient distribution, though they also raise concerns about enhancing market power. One main vertical restraint has been selective distribution. This enables manufacturers to impose various criteria on their dealers, such as tying of sales and after-sales services, and to prohibit sales to independent resellers. A second main restraint has been exclusive distribution, through which manufacturers can assign an exclusive territory to their dealers. A third main restraint has been exclusive dealing (or the non-compete obligation), allowing manufacturers to prohibit dealers from selling multiple competing brands.

These restraints were initially allowed as individual exemptions under Article 81 of the EC Treaty. From 1985 they became institutionalised as a block exemption, applicable to the whole car sector. The exemption was very formalistic on which types of agreements were acceptable, so that in practice a standardised distribution system emerged, with all manufacturers adopting essentially the same selective and exclusive distribution agreements. After minor revisions in 1995, more drastic reforms took place in 2002. The European Commission aimed to adopt a more economic approach and give the manufacturers more freedom of choice between alternative distribution forms (hence avoiding the 'straitjacket effect'). At the same time, the Commission wanted to be stricter towards the manufacturers, because of a fear of 'cumulative anticompetitive effects' if all manufacturers adopt the same or similar vertical restraints. As a result, the new block exemption in 2002 no longer allowed manufacturers to impose both selective and exclusive distribution to their dealers, but rather made them choose to adopt one or the other. Furthermore, the conditions for exclusive dealing arrangements (or non-compete obligations) became stricter to the manufacturers.

This chapter documents the recent history of the car distribution system in Europe to show the European Commission's evolving attitude towards vertical restraints. Vertical restraints have become increasingly based on competition economics. During the mid-1980s, when the first block exemption was installed, the Commission had mainly been pre-occupied with restrictions to cross-border trade, to fulfil its goal of European integration. In more recent years, the Commission appears to have shifted its emphasis more towards the core competition policy concerns with vertical agreements, mainly the promotion of intrabrand competition (between dealers of the same brand) and to some extent also interbrand competition (between different manufacturers). We will argue that the Commission is finally focusing on the more relevant issues from a competition policy perspective, yet further improvements in economic analysis are strongly desirable. First, the policy objectives should become more transparent. Second, a deeper economic analysis is required regarding the recently adopted market share thresholds and regarding the various channels through which the vertical restraints may create efficiencies or anticompetitive effects. Recent empirical evidence suggests that the anticompetitive effects that were emphasised in the 2002 reforms (limited cross-border trade and domestic intrabrand competition) appear to be of less concern, suggesting that the stricter policy towards car producers may not have been warranted. However, before concluding that efficiency arguments in favour of the vertical restraints dominate, other possible anticompetitive effects (e.g. foreclosure of entry) need more careful empirical analysis in future work. Third, a stronger basis should be provided for the stricter policy towards distribution agreements in the car sector than towards distribution agreements in general, for which a parallel block exemption exists.

The outline of this chapter is as follows. In section 2 we describe the distribution system, how it has evolved and how it has been enforced. In section 3 we provide an economic analysis. We begin with a discussion of the various efficiencies that can be achieved by such agreements. We then turn to the possible anticompetitive effects, including the effects on cross-border trade, on intrabrand and interbrand competition given market structure, and on foreclosing new entry (e.g. by other foreign car manufacturers or spare-parts producers).

2. Distribution agreements in the car market

2.1 From individual to block exemptions

The vertical agreements between the European car manufacturers and their dealers were first subject to the national and subsequently to the European competition laws. Article 81(1) of the EC Treaty prohibits agreements that may affect trade between Member States and which may prevent, restrict or distort competition. Article 81(3) allows for exemptions, if there are benefits that outweigh the anticompetitive effects and if consumers receive a fair share of these benefits. In the early years, car manufacturers often submitted notifications to obtain individual exemptions for their own specific types of agreements. In 1965, to reduce the administrative burden in assessing similar agreements, the European Commission became authorised to grant block or group exemptions for certain categories of agreements falling under Article 81. Block exemption regulations essentially define a set of agreements and possibly market share thresholds for which there is a safe harbour, i.e. a presumption that the benefits from the agreement outweigh the anticompetitive effects. If the firm proposing the agreement has a market share above the threshold, the agreement is not necessarily illegal but an individual exemption needs to be obtained.[1] In addition, block exemption regulations define a set of hard-core restrictions or black clauses, with the presumption that the benefits do not outweigh the costs regardless of the firm's market share.

A key individual exemption was the European Commission's 1974 BMW decision, granting BMW the possibility of combining both selective and exclusive distribution.[2] As discussed by Wijckmans, Tuytschaever and Vanderelst (2006), this was a landmark case, as it laid the foundation for the future block exemptions for cars.[3] The European Commission hoped that other manufacturers would adapt their distribution systems accordingly. In 1985, after a long process of consultations with interested parties, the first block exemption for agreements in the car sector was eventually introduced,

---

[1] Since 1 May 2004, the exemption no longer needs to be requested and obtained. It applies automatically as long as the conditions in Article 81(3) are fulfilled. This implies the parties may need to show proof ex post if the question arises (e.g. because of a procedure).

[2] Bayerische Motoren Werke AG (1975) OJ L29/1.

[3] Wijckmans *et al.*'s contribution provides a very interesting analysis of the implications of the new regulation, complementary to this section.

Regulation 123/1985.[4] This regulation applied to agreements covering both sales and after-sales services; agreements covering only one of both aspects did not fall under the exemption. It effectively installed a system that combined both selective and exclusive distribution, as well as the possibility to engage in exclusive dealing agreements. It also included some black clauses, such as resale price maintenance. The regulation was renewed for another seven years in 1995, as Regulation 1475/1995, with only minor modifications to the previous system.

In 2002, a more drastic reform of the car distribution system was introduced, Regulation 1400/2002, with a one-year transition period for existing agreements and expiring in 2010. This block exemption followed a similar philosophy as the recently installed block exemption for distribution agreements in general, Regulation 2790/1999.[5] Nevertheless, it was considerably stricter because of a concern with the 'cumulative anticompetitive effects' of restrictive practices when almost all firms in the car market choose to adopt the same agreements. In essence, the new block exemption no longer allows the car manufacturers to combine both selective and exclusive distribution, and it forces exclusive dealing agreements to become less restrictive.

We now discuss the key properties of the distribution system in more detail. We begin with the period 1985–2002, then the period since 2002. Finally, we discuss enforcement of the competition laws.

2.2 The car distribution system between 1985 and 2002

The first block exemption, Regulation 123/1985, offered the possibility of both selective and exclusive distribution agreements, as well as exclusive dealing (non-compete obligation). Selective and exclusive distribution agreements have in common that they limit the number of authorised dealers and restrict their possibilities of resale. Table 9.1 compares how these restrictions work under both contractual forms. Under selective distribution, the manufacturer can impose quantitative and qualitative criteria on its dealers. Quantitative criteria are criteria that directly limit the potential number of dealers in a network. Examples are the direct fixing of the number of dealers. But also sales targets, minimum purchase obligations or minimum capacity requirements

---

[4] At the national level block exemptions already existed in some countries. For example, in the United Kingdom, the 1976 Restrictive Trade Practices Act provided a number of restrictions that were automatically exempt and did therefore not require registration. See the UK Competition Commission (2000a).

[5] Verouden (2004) provides a comprehensive discussion of the emergence of this block exemption regulation, against the background of the historic enforcement of Article 81 in general, and the increased role of economic analysis.

Table 9.1 Selective versus exclusive distribution

Distribution	Restrictions imposed on authorised distributors	Possibilities of resale
Selectivity	Quantitative and qualitative criteria	No sales to independent resellers
Exclusivity	Geographic territory	No active selling policies in other territories

may act as quantitative criteria as they affect the number of dealers that can be profitable in a geographic area. Qualitative criteria are, for example, minimum standards of staff training, advertising and marketing investments requirements, showrooms, demonstration cars, stock levels, performance of warranty works. Qualitative criteria also include the possibility to tie new car sales and after-sales repair and maintenance services, and to use the spare parts supplied by the manufacturer.[6] To protect the selective nature of the agreement, dealers are prohibited from selling to independent resellers. Hence, dealers are allowed to sell only to end consumers, to intermediaries with a written authorisation, or to other dealers within the manufacturer's distribution network.

Under exclusive distribution, the manufacturer can appoint a single dealer in a designated territory (e.g. a city or a municipality). To enforce exclusivity, the manufacturer can prohibit its dealers from engaging in active selling policies outside their territories, thus forcing them to concentrate their marketing and sales efforts within their own territory. This includes the location clause, i.e. the prohibition to set up secondary dealerships in other territories or abroad. It also includes the prohibition to advertise outside their own territory.

The block exemption regulation also allowed exclusive dealing agreements, or non-compete obligations, meaning that dealers could be prohibited from selling cars of competing brands. At that time, these restrictions (selective distribution, exclusive distribution and exclusive dealing) were acceptable as block exemptions to Article 81 without further investigation, regardless of the manufacturer's market share.

But the block exemption regulation also specified some black clauses, which are never acceptable (regardless of the market share). An important one is resale price maintenance (RPM) or vertical price fixing (though recommended retail prices or maximum prices fall under the block exemption). Another important black clause is the prohibition of passive selling to

---

[6] The distinction between quantitative and qualitative selectivity is especially relevant for the most recent block exemption, since the market share thresholds apply only to quantitative criteria, as discussed below.

consumers outside the territory or outside the country (as long as these sales do not result from active selling policies).[7]

The block exemption was renewed in 1995, Regulation 1475/1995. Despite a detailed investigation and consultation process, there were only some clarifications and minor relaxations of the restrictions to stimulate competition.[8] Regarding selectivity, the condition was made explicit that manufacturers should not prevent end consumers, or intermediaries with a written authorisation, to purchase from any dealer they want (e.g. a named consumer in the UK can use an intermediary to buy a car in Belgium). Dealers could also more easily purchase their spare parts from other sources than the car manufacturers (still provided that these were of matching quality and were not used in warrantee works). Regarding exclusivity, general advertising campaigns outside the territory became allowed, though personalised targeted advertising remained prohibited to consumers outside the territory. Finally, regarding exclusive dealing, dealers obtained the right to sell multiple brands, but only provided that these would operate under separate legal entities, separate showrooms and separate management. In practice, this meant that dealers could realise only limited cost savings in selling multiple brands.

2.3 The liberalisation in 2002

In 2002, the European Commission introduced a more drastic reform of agreements in the car sector, Regulation 1400/2002.[9] The new block exemption aimed to get rid of the rigid 'straitjacket model' for car distribution and to offer greater flexibility on acceptable agreements. It was much in the spirit of the block exemption for distribution agreements in general, Regulation 2790/1999, though it was considerably stricter on car manufacturers because of the fear of cumulative effects. The new block exemption still lists a number of black clauses that are not tolerated under any circumstances, notably RPM and the prohibition of passive selling outside the territory. There are several key differences that make the new system stricter on manufacturers than the system during 1985–2002.

First, manufacturers can no longer combine both selective and exclusive distribution. Hence, they have to opt for one or the other. In practice, most

---

[7] Dealers have the right not to sell to end consumers, as long as this is not forced by the manufacturers in an agreement.

[8] For more detailed comparisons between the 1985 and 1995 block exemption regulations, see the European Commission (2000) or the UK Competition Commission (2000a).

[9] These reforms were based partly on the Commission's own investigation and partly on commissioned studies of independent analysts and on a new round of consultations with the interested parties.

manufacturers (except Suzuki) have chosen to abandon exclusive distribution and adopt selective distribution. This means that they can impose certain objective qualitative or quantitative criteria on their dealers, including sales targets with some relaxations[10] and a maximum total number of authorised dealers selling new cars. Selectivity also implies that authorised dealers are prohibited from selling cars to independent resellers.[11] But because of the abandonment of exclusive distribution manufacturers can no longer prohibit their dealers from engaging in active selling policies outside their territory (whether through opening secondary outlets in other territories or abroad, or through personalised advertising campaigns outside their own territory).[12]

Second, the qualitative criteria in selective distribution have become stricter to manufacturers. They can still impose minimum training standards and standards on showrooms to their dealers, thereby effectively precluding pure internet companies as authorised dealers.[13] They can also still control the location of the dealers' primary sales outlets and may provide more favourable conditions to dealers in objectively defined areas: this gives manufacturers an instrument to ensure geographic coverage in the absence of exclusive territories.

However, manufacturers can no longer force their dealers to provide both sales and after-sales services; hence current dealers may decide to subcontract repair and maintenance to other authorised dealers. The reverse is also true, i.e. authorised repairers cannot be forced to sell new cars. This makes it easier for the previous independent repairers to become authorised repairers, provided that the objective quality criteria are met. Such a change can be significant given that the authorised dealers currently have a market share of 50 per cent of all repair and 80 per cent of repair of cars younger than four years.

Additional efforts are also made to make both the authorised and the remaining independent repairers more independent relative to their car manufacturers. It is stressed that the authorised repairers have the right to buy both original spare parts and spare parts of matching quality from other sources than the manufacturers, except under warrantee works, free servicing contracts or

[10] Manufacturers can terminate contracts if sales targets are not met, but only provided that the manufacturers have not limited supply. Bonuses associated with the sales targets should be based on sales including the sales to other authorised dealers within the manufacturer's network.

[11] As before, authorised dealers can sell to intermediaries with a written authorisation of end consumers. However, the intermediaries obtain more possibilities since dealers can no longer be restricted to sell at most 10 per cent of their sales to one intermediary. This facilitates the operations of intermediaries selling through the internet such as Virgin or OneSwoop in the UK.

[12] Since the block exemption allowed the location clause for a transition period until 2005, the manufacturers which opted for selective distribution could still partly benefit from exclusivity until then.

[13] However, authorised dealers can still sell through the internet if they satisfy the other standards. Furthermore, intermediaries acting on behalf of end consumers can sell through the internet.

recall operations.[14] The independent repairers, who do not satisfy the objective quality criteria, should be given access to all technical information, tools and equipment. Furthermore, they have the right to purchase original spare parts or parts of matching quality from the authorised repairers. Once again, the increased independence of authorised and independent repairers can be significant since the spare-part producers produce 80 per cent of all components. Although car manufacturers produced only 20 per cent of components themselves, they had control over most of the sales through their authorised networks.

A third difference with the former legal framework during 1985–2002 relates to the exclusive dealing or non-compete obligations. A manufacturer can no longer force its dealers to operate multiple brands under separate legal entities and separate management (though it can require that its cars be displayed within brand-specific areas in the showroom).[15] The manufacturer has the right to impose minimum purchasing requirements and to require that the dealers buy up to 30 per cent of its own brand (though the dealers should not necessarily buy these from the manufacturer and they may buy these from other dealers in the network). However, it does not have the right to require that the dealers buy a minimum percentage larger than 30 per cent (say, require at least 32 per cent). In practice, this means that dealers are guaranteed to be able to sell at least three different brands (but if all manufacturers impose a 30 per cent purchase requirement a dealer would effectively be able to sell only three brands). The authorised repairers who are not active in selling new cars have the right to service and repair cars from any other brand.[16]

The increased possibilities for multi-brand dealerships, together with the abandonment of the requirement to provide both sales and after sales, makes it possible, at least in principle, for supermarkets to enter into the business of selling new cars, of course provided that they satisfy the objective criteria. Supermarkets have frequently shown an interest in entering the car

---

[14] And even if the spare parts are distributed through the manufacturers, the original spare-part suppliers can now put their logo next to that of the car manufacturers without losing the characterisation of original spare part.

[15] 'Brands' are defined more narrowly than 'manufacturers'. For example, Volkswagen and Audi are two different brands, owned by the same manufacturer, VW Group.

[16] Manufacturers with market shares under 5 per cent may resort to the *de minimis* Notice on agreements of minor importance OJ C 371, 9.12.1997 to argue there is no cumulative foreclosure effect for vertical agreements (except hard-core restrictions). Porsche resorted to this Notice to obtain the possibility of exclusive dealing under the former rules (require separate showrooms and separate sales personnel for competing brands). However, this raises the issue of market definition. As discussed below, Brenkers and Verboven (2006) find that the relevant market should be defined at the segment level or even lower. This makes it questionable that Porsche indeed has a market share of 5 per cent or lower within the sports segment and therefore satisfies the conditions of the *de minimis* Notice.

distribution business (even with a limited number of brands). In practice, however, car manufacturers have used the possibilities of quantitative selectivity to avoid distribution through supermarkets. According to a study by Lademann (2001), consumers also show only limited interest in buying cars in supermarkets. Yet this study is based on survey questionnaire data and not on an empirical analysis of what consumers actually would do if distribution through supermarkets became available.[17]

A fourth difference with the former distribution systems is the introduction of market share thresholds above which the block exemption does not apply (so that manufacturers would need to request individual exemptions). These thresholds are close to those in the general block exemption regulation for distribution agreements. Exclusive distribution and exclusive dealing or non-compete obligations (meeting the conditions of the regulation) are safe harbours for manufacturers with market shares below 30 per cent. Quantitative selective distribution is a safe harbour if market shares are below 40 per cent (except for spare parts and maintenance where the threshold is 30 per cent). Qualitative selective distribution is not subject to market share thresholds.

In sum, the new system is stricter on manufacturers for the following reasons: (1) they can no longer apply both selective and exclusive distribution, (2) fewer qualitative criteria are allowed in selective distribution (no forced tying of sales and after-sales services), (3) the conditions for exclusive dealing (no-compete obligations) are stricter, and (4) the block exemptions apply only for market shares below certain thresholds (30–40 per cent).

2.4 Adoption and enforcement of the block exemptions

We first discuss the adoption of the block exemptions, showing that they had a 'straitjacket effect' with all car manufacturers adopting similar vertical restraints. We then discuss enforcement, first of the black clauses and then of the market share thresholds in the most recent 2002 block exemption.

Adoption of the block exemptions

All car manufacturers have used the benefits from the block exemption to make vertical agreements, though the empirical evidence is limited. Before the new block exemption regulation of 2002, all dealers active in new car sales were both selective and exclusive. After the reforms in 2002, the manufacturers had to

---

[17] Some independent supermarkets already exist, e.g. Cardoen in Belgium. These companies obtain most of their car supplies from excess volumes of the car manufacturers, or from imports from non-EEA countries (e.g. Turkey).

make a choice. However, most manufacturers (except Suzuki) actually adopted selective rather than exclusive distribution. Furthermore, the majority of the authorised dealers (67 per cent) still provide both sales and after-sales service, compared with 29 per cent providing after-sales services only and 4 per cent providing sales only. Finally, exclusive dealing has been and continues to be quite common practice in many countries, with a brand exclusive dealing rate of 70 per cent, compared with only 57 per cent in the US. It has been less popular in the Scandinavian countries where population density is low, with adoption rates below 50 per cent.[18] In sum, one can conclude that the block exemptions had a straitjacket effect, inducing most car manufacturers to adopt the same or similar vertical restraints, especially on the most important ones. This remains the case even after the 2002 reforms, despite the Commission's claimed attempts to get rid of the rigidity and stimulate innovative distribution systems.

Enforcement of black clauses

To appreciate the European Commission's most important concerns, it is instructive to consider the infringement cases to the black clauses, i.e. agreements that are not exempted regardless of the market share. Table 9.2 provides an overview of the cases since the first block exemption in 1985. Interestingly, the first case occurred only in 1998, the Volkswagen case. Among other things, the Commission found Volkswagen guilty of the following practices to its Italian dealers: threatening fifty dealers to terminate contracts if they continued to sell to foreigners, with twelve actual terminations; giving lower margins and bonuses to dealers selling to foreign customers; limiting supplies to some of the dealers. The Commission imposed a fine of €102 million, at that time the largest fine ever for a single firm. There were several subsequent cases, concerning different car manufacturers in several countries of the European Union. All cases relate to either to RPM, which the Commission refers to as 'serious' infringements, or to export restrictions, which the Commission refers to as 'very serious'. This overview shows the Commission's preoccupation with competition issues relating to the realisation of the European common market, rather than with more standard competition policy issues.

Enforcement issues regarding the 2002 market share thresholds

According to the most recent 2002 block exemption, the manufacturers are allowed to make vertical agreements, other than the black clauses, only if their

---

[18] The numbers in this paragraph come from Harbour Wade Brown, HWBI Management Briefing 3/06/7 and 5/05/2, available on the web.

Table 9.2 Infringement cases since the first block exemption in 1985

Date	Nature of infringement	Country	Company	Duration	Fine
1998	export restrictions	Italy	Volkswagen	1988–1998	€102 million*
2000	export restrictions	Netherlands	Opel	1996–2000	€43 million**
2001	RPM (restrict discounts)	Germany	Volkswagen	1996–1997	€31 million***
2001	export restrictions	Germany	DaimlerChrysler	1985–2001	€72 million
	restrictions on leasers	Germany, Spain		1997–2001	
	RPM (restrict discounts)	Belgium		1996–1999	
2005	export restrictions	Netherlands	Peugeot	1997–2003	€50 million

Notes:
* Reduced by Court of First Instance to €90 million in 2000.
** Reduced by Court of First Instance to €35 million in 2003.
*** Annulled by Court of First Instance in 2003. After appeal the annulment was reconfirmed in 2006 on the grounds that the Commission had not proved any actual acquiescence by the dealers.

market shares do not exceed a certain threshold level. If they have a larger market share, they are not protected by the block exemption and are therefore vulnerable to being sued for breach of Article 81. As discussed, the market share threshold level is 30 per cent for most vertical agreements. The only exceptions are quantitative selective distribution (new car sales) for which the market share threshold is 40 per cent, and qualitative selective distribution for which there are no thresholds. To apply these thresholds it therefore becomes critical to define the relevant car market on a sound basis. Should the market be, say, all car sales in the EU? Or should the geographic market be narrower, say at the national level? And should the product market be narrower such that an Opel Corsa is not seen as a close substitute for a BMW? The appropriate way to define an economically sound antitrust market is to conduct the well-known SSNIP-test or 'hypothetical monopolist' test. This test takes a group of products as the candidate relevant market, and asks whether a small but significant and non-transitory increase in price (in the range of 5–10 per cent) would be profitable. If the answer is yes, a relevant market is found. If the answer is no, this means that the hypothetical price increase caused too much substitution to other products, so that additional products need to be included in the market and the test should be applied again.

In a recent study, Brenkers and Verboven (2006) apply the economic logic of the SSNIP-test to define the relevant market, and subsequently ask whether the threshold market share conditions are satisfied. They consider five countries (Belgium, France, Germany, Italy and the UK) and assume that the geographic markets are the national markets (based on the limited observed cross-border sales despite the large international price differences). They then estimate an empirical demand model with differentiated products. This enables them to measure the extent of substitution between different car models and apply the SSNIP-test. They find that the relevant product markets can usually be defined at the level of the segment (e.g. compact cars), or often even narrower at the level of the origin within the segment (e.g. domestically produced compact cars).

Given these market definitions they then obtain the following findings on the applications of the market share threshold. Most mass producers violate the 40 per cent market share thresholds in their home countries and one mass producer (Volkswagen) even violates the market share thresholds in some foreign countries. In contrast, the niche players or Asian manufacturers almost never violate the 40 per cent threshold conditions. Violations of the 30 per cent threshold conditions are observed in more cases: by several additional mass producers in foreign countries and by several niche players. To our knowledge, these violations have not prompted the Commission to prohibit vertical agreements with dealers selling new cars.[19] The reasons for this are unclear to us, but it illustrates that many car manufacturers operate at the limits of the block exemption regulation and may not necessarily remain automatically eligible in the future.

While the market share criteria do not appear to have been strictly enforced, two recent cases show the Commission's commitment to enforce other aspects of the new block exemption regulation of 2002.[20] In 2006, after complaints from the dealer association, BMW and GM have explicitly recognised the principle of genuine multi-brand dealerships. They also accept the principle of qualitative selective distribution, implying that all repair shops who fulfil the qualitative criteria may become members of the manufacturer's authorised network.

3. Economic analysis

To prepare its block exemption regulations, the European Commission conducted various external economic studies. These provide an indication of what

---

[19] Market share violations have, however, affected contracts with repairers, since in most cases the manufacturers have a market share in repair over 30 per cent. This implies that typically only qualitative selective distribution is possible and no restrictions on the total number of repairers are allowed.

[20] See BMW IP/06/302 and GM IP/06/303.

was motivating the Commission in its various revisions of the block exemption. Most of these studies looked at the effects of the regulation on cross-border trade (including studies on international price differences), further illustrating the Commission preoccupation with the common market goal. More recently, the Commission showed a stronger interest in economic analyses of other issues as well (e.g. commissioned studies on intrabrand competition and on the link between sales and after-sales services).

The economic effects of vertical agreements are far less clear-cut than for most horizontal agreements. In the following sections, we provide an overview of the various competition issues emerging from the vertical agreements at issue. After a brief review of possible efficiency benefits we discuss the possible anticompetitive effects. Consistent with the European Commission's emphasis, we first discuss how the distribution system may have limited the possibilities for cross-border trade, thereby creating the possibility of international price discrimination. Next, we discuss how the distribution system may have limited domestic trade or intrabrand competition (between dealers of the same brand), thereby creating a mechanism to soften interbrand competition (between different manufacturers). Finally, we discuss how the distribution system may lie at the basis of foreclosure, of new entrants as well as spare-part manufacturers. We spend particular emphasis on the available empirical evidence regarding the possible anticompetitive incentives of the vertical restraints.[21]

We focus our discussion on the effects of the system as it was in place during the period 1985–2002 (and another few years of transition). There is most empirical evidence on that period, and it allows one to evaluate the significance of the reforms after 2002. We hope that our review of economic principles will stimulate a deeper economic analysis of the competition issues in the forthcoming review of the block exemption (to expire in 2010), with a more explicit treatment of both the efficiencies and the various channels through which anticompetitive effects may arise.

3.1 Efficiencies from distribution agreements

Mitigating double marginalisation problems

Since car manufacturers do not charge fixed franchise fees to their dealers, their primary profit source comes from setting wholesale prices above

---

[21] To put this evidence in a broader perspective, we refer to Lafontaine and Slade's (2005) review of the empirical evidence in relation to vertical agreements in general.

marginal costs (whether for the sales of new cars or for spare parts). Furthermore, the dealers have some geographic market power, because of quantitative selectivity and/or territorial exclusivity. This enables them to add a retail markup to the wholesale price, thereby creating the well-known double marginalisation problem: the retail price will be too high from a joint-profit maximising perspective.

Given that manufacturers do not impose fixed franchise fees and do have some market power because of selectivity and exclusivity, the problem may be overcome through the imposition of several accompanying vertical restraints. RPM may be used since this forces the dealers to set the price desired by the manufacturer, but this is a black clause. Instead, manufacturers may impose the weaker form of a price ceiling as an appropriate response to avoid double marginalisation. But if anything, car manufacturers appear to have attempted to impose black clause price floors (through maximum allowed discounts to the recommended retail prices), as illustrated by the above discussed infringement cases. This suggests that the vertical price policies were not motivated by attempts to remove double marginalisation. Nevertheless, quantity fixing or, less restrictively, minimum sales requirements may also resolve the double marginalisation problem. This may provide an efficiency rationale for the observed sales targets, promoted through the bonuses or threats to withdraw licences, which has been common across many car manufacturers.

Dealer services incentives and freeriding

Car manufacturers and their dealers provide both sales and after-sales services, the costs of which can be very high.[22] Both services include potentially significant costs in investing in infrastructure (showrooms, inventories, technical equipment), training of personnel, and time and quality of service. The empirical evidence on the importance of services is mixed. Marketing research studies by Mittal *et al.* (1999) and Verhoef and Langerak (2003) suggest that services indeed contribute to brand reputation and brand loyalty. But another study by Punj and Brookes (2002) finds that only a small fraction of the consumers finds the dealer an important factor in the purchase of a new car.

Regardless of their quantitative importance, car manufacturers would like to achieve the optimal level of dealer services. This is not guaranteed because of several opposing externalities. First, dealers do not take into account the beneficial impact of their services on the manufacturers' profits. This vertical

---

[22] According to the OECD (1997), a typical volume manufacturer was expected to invest up to €6.5 billion in its distribution network over the coming decade.

externality implies too little incentives to provide services. Second, dealers do not take into account the detrimental business-stealing effect of their services on competing dealers' profits. This horizontal externality may create too strong incentives to provide services; see Caillaud and Rey (1986) and Iyer (1998).

Third, the dealer services may contain public good aspects, from which the competing dealers may also benefit. This is especially the case for sales services that involve the provision of information (e.g. through well-established show-rooms, demonstration cars, test drives, or personalised communication). Competing dealers may freeride on these services, which reduces their own incentives to invest in services.

Vertical contracts can serve to better align the dealers' incentives to provide services with the car manufacturers' goals. Selective distribution forms a direct way to accomplish this. It enables the manufacturer to impose qualitative service criteria to its dealers, such as the size of the showroom, minimum requirements on equipment and personnel, etc. However, in practice it may be difficult to stipulate everything in a selective distribution contract.[23] As an alternative solution, manufacturers may aim to coordinate the sales services efforts either directly or through their national importers. Several importers indeed provide national advertising campaigns or regional distribution centres with showrooms and the possibility for test drives and other information.

Territorial exclusivity may be a third solution to achieve more optimal sales levels. Similar to RPM, territorial exclusivity creates dealer market power. This removes price competition and induces the dealers to compete more through services; see Telser (1960). It also increases travel costs and therefore increases the probability that consumers buy directly from the servicing dealer instead of going to a competing freeriding dealer. Finally, territorial exclusivity enables the manufacturers to take away the dealers' rents by terminating the agreement in case the service level has not been reached; see Klein and Murphy (1988). A side effect of exclusivity is the creation of double margin-alisation problems. As we discussed above, in the absence of franchise fees and RPM, this may be resolved through the sales targets and the accompany-ing bonuses.

According to an influential study of Lexecon (1985) freeriding between dealers may especially be a severe problem in an international context. The

---

[23] Arrunada et al. (2005) consistently take an incomplete contracting perspective as a way to resolve double-sided moral hazard between car manufacturers and dealers. They apply it to the contracts of twenty-three Spanish dealerships. They find that contracts typically restrict the dealers' decision rights and give manufacturers most monitoring and enforcement power. Abuse of this power is prevented by the mechanism of the manufacturers' reputational capital.

investments in distribution may differ considerably across countries. Parallel importers then have an incentive to purchase products in the countries where prices are low due low distribution costs, and sell them elsewhere. Arbitrage then takes place on differences in distribution costs rather than profits. According to Lexecon (1985) this motivates selective and exclusive distribution in pharmaceuticals as a way to prevent freeriding on services across countries. It may also provide an efficiency explanation for the car manufacturers to limit cross-border trade and prevent parallel imports through selective and exclusive distribution.

Manufacturer investment incentives and freeriding

The sales and after-sales services may not only be a cause of freeriding between dealers, but also between the manufacturers. For example, the investments in training of sales and technical personnel (whether paid by the dealer or the manufacturer) may not benefit only the own brand but also that of competing brands. To maintain sufficient incentives to invest, an exclusive dealing or non-compete agreement could provide a solution; see Besanko and Perry (1991, 1993).

3.2 Limited cross-border trade and international price differences

Obstacles to cross-border trade

The combination of selective and exclusive distribution makes it more difficult to engage in cross-border trade (or parallel imports) to take advantage of international price differences. Selectivity eliminates the role of independent resellers, whereas exclusivity makes it impossible for the authorised dealers themselves to actively sell their cars to consumers in other countries. Hence, cross-border trade can take place only if the local authorised dealers sell to one of the following three possible foreign agents: directly to the end consumers, to intermediaries with a written authorisation from end consumers, or to foreign authorised dealers within the manufacturer's network. Already during the preparations of the first block exemption in 1985, the European Commission had been preoccupied with the concern that the distribution system should form an obstacle to cross-border trade and should therefore be responsible for the large international price differences.[24] Consequently, it issued a Notice accompanying the block

---

[24] The Commission has shown a more general interest in promoting cross-border trade in the car market. In addition to its efforts to ensure the distribution system does not limit cross-border trade, it has also taken other measures to ensure that the technical requirements of cars were harmonised. See Goldberg and Verboven (2005) for a more detailed discussion on the Commission's other efforts to promote integration in the car market.

exemption regulation, which deals with cross-border movements and relative price differences between Member States.[25] One may distinguish between supply-side and demand-side measures.

To guarantee a sufficient supply to foreign agents, the Notice required that the authorised dealers should have access to all cars with similar specifications for sale in other countries at a reasonable surcharge (e.g. right-hand-drive cars for UK customers). This requirement became known as the 'availability clause' and was formally included in the next block exemption regulation of 1995. In practice, however, the manufacturers could limit their supply to their dealers through the system of sales targets. This gave the dealers stronger incentives to sell to local consumers, who may come back for after-sales services. Possibly as a result of this, foreign customers often faced long delivery lags or excessive surcharges.[26]

To protect the demand side, the Notice explicitly stated that end consumers, as well as their intermediaries, must not face excessive delivery lags, refusals to carry out warrantee works, or lack of cooperation in registering the cars at the border. The Notice also stated that international price differentials should not exceed 12 per cent for more than one year, or 18 per cent for a shorter period (after taking into account exchange rate fluctuations and cross-country tax differences). Although the European Commission subsequently began to monitor international price differences, it has never actually enforced the 12–18 per cent rule: international price differences have varied widely and persistently so, even after controlling for specification differences and even between countries with similar taxes and stable exchange rates. Furthermore, a new Notice in 1991 formally restricted the rights of the intermediaries to ensure that they would not behave like independent resellers.[27] Finally, as discussed by the UK Competition Commission (2000a), the foreign authorised dealers also had little incentive to buy cars from the local authorised dealers and sell them to their local consumers: since the manufacturers would typically not count such sales when determining whether the sales targets are met, they would face the risk of not earning bonuses.

---

[25] See EC Commission Notice, OJ 1985 C 17/3 of 18.1.1985.

[26] For example, an anonymous dealer survey by BEUC in 1986 revealed a refusal to sell to foreign consumers in 20 per cent of the cases; excessive delivery lags for right-hand-drive cars for the UK and lower discounts to foreign consumers. These costs obviously add to the high transportation and information costs for consumers seeking to purchase a car abroad.

[27] See EC Commission Notice, OJ 1991 C 329 of 18.12.1991. It formally clarified that intermediaries must not behave like independent resellers through various stipulations: they must avoid carrying a common name; they must not use supermarkets as outlets; and they must quote their prices only as 'best estimates'. Furthermore, intermediaries and dealers may not establish privileged relationships with each other in form of favourable conditions or sales amounts exceeding 10 per cent of the dealers' sales.

In sum, the selective and exclusive distribution system as it has been in place up to 2002 has provided only limited incentives to local dealers to sell their cars to foreign agents. At the same time, the role of intermediaries or foreign authorised dealers was restricted so that arbitrage activities had to come directly from end consumers, most of whom perceive high transaction costs. This conclusion is supported by the evidence: international price differences have been large and persistent, while at the same time the level of parallel imports has been small (at most 2 per cent and often less); see for example BEUC (1992) and Goldberg and Verboven (2005).

International price differences

While the selective and exclusive distribution system may have severely limited cross-border trade, one should not infer that the car manufacturers have deliberately set up the selective and exclusive distribution system to be able to maintain the large and persistent international price differences. It is first necessary to understand the sources of the international price differences. Verboven (1996) and Goldberg and Verboven (2001) address this question. A main conclusion is that differences in local distribution costs are an important explanation for the observed international price differences.[28] The remaining part is due to differences in markups, i.e. international price discrimination. Markup differences may follow from cross-country differences in conduct (e.g. collusion in the UK). They may also follow from intrinsic differences in tastes (e.g. national champions in France and Italy) or from markup adjustment in response to local cost differences. The latter may happen because of exchange rate fluctuations or because of differences in taxes which have to be paid in the country of use. For example, car taxes are very high for consumers in Denmark, and manufacturers have partly absorbed these by lowering their markups.[29]

Given that the distribution system enables firms to engage in international price discrimination, are they better off than in a system where they are constrained to charge uniform prices? Under monopoly, the question is generally affirmative, since more options are always better. Under imperfect competition, however, the possibility to price discriminate may reduce profits

---

[28] Local costs explain two-thirds of observed incomplete exchange rate pass-through, the phenomenon that exporters only partly lower their local prices when the foreign currency appreciates (and vice versa). Markup adjustment explains the remaining part.

[29] Intrinsic taste differences and markup adjustment in response to local cost differences are both examples of differences in price elasticities: the first is exogenous and the second is endogenous due to price elasticities being increased in price.

relative to uniform pricing since they have more instruments to compete; see for example Corts (1998). Brenkers and Verboven (2006) approach the problem empirically. They find that profits would not significantly decrease, and under some conditions may even slightly increase, if the firms would become constrained to charge more uniform prices. This finding needs some qualification, however, since their analysis is limited to a set of countries with similar tax regimes. The profit incentive may become more important when very high-tax countries such as Denmark are included.[30] Subject to this qualification, Brenkers and Verboven's analysis strongly indicates that the possibility to internationally price discriminate is not a main profit motive for the selective and exclusive distribution system but is only an unintended side effect.

Brenkers and Verboven also ask whether the possibility to price discriminate has affected consumer surplus and total welfare. They find that there may have been large distributional effects, from UK consumers to consumers elsewhere in Europe. However, total European consumer surplus is hardly affected. Given the negligible profit effects this implies that the possibility to price discriminate has had no important overall welfare effects. Put differently, the obstacles to cross-border trade may on balance be beneficial if they involve any convincing efficiency benefits (such as resolving the freeriding problems in servicing discussed above).

3.3 Limited domestic trade and softening interbrand competition

The distribution system may not only have restricted cross-border but also domestic trade. In principle, territorial exclusivity makes it less likely that consumers buy cars from distant dealers since active selling policies such as targeted advertising are not allowed. Furthermore, selectivity makes it impossible for independent resellers to sell cars elsewhere in the country. To the extent that these vertical restraints restrict domestic trade, there is limited domestic intrabrand competition, i.e. limited competition between dealers of the same brand. According to consumer organisations and policy makers, the available evidence indicates that intrabrand competition has been limited in the car market. The UK Competition Commission (2000a, 2.117 and 2.322) reports that the extent of out-of-territory sales is 39 per cent

---

[30] In various speeches, the Commissioner for Competition Policy Monti, who was in power at the time of the reforms in 2002, has stressed the need for harmonising taxes. Differing taxes may give manufacturers strong incentives to erect cross-border trade restrictions and charge lower markups in high-tax countries. This follows from Friberg's (2001) analysis on related issues on currency fluctuations.

of dealer sales, and interprets this as a low number since there are many commuting consumers in the UK. A long report of the European Commission (2000) has also expressed concerns with limited domestic intrabrand competition. The industry, in contrast, has argued that the distribution system creates sufficient domestic trade opportunities, for example because dealers have been allowed to do non-personalised advertising campaigns outside their territory since 1995. The industry has also interpreted the 39 per cent out-of-territory sales number to be sufficiently high.

Suppose the consumer organisations and policy makers are right, and that selectivity and exclusivity has not just restricted cross-border trade but also domestic intrabrand competition. As has been shown by Rey and Stiglitz (1995), under some circumstances limited intrabrand competition between dealers may also soften interbrand competition between the car manufacturers. The reasoning goes as follows. Limited intrabrand competition creates market power for the dealers. If the car manufacturer is a monopolist, this gives rise to Spengler's (1950) well-known double marginalisation problem, i.e. both the manufacturer and the dealer can charge a monopoly markup, giving rise to too high prices, too low demand and hence too low profits to the manufacturer. In contrast, if car manufacturers compete sufficiently intensively with each other, the limited intrabrand competition and the resulting dealer market power may serve as a way to reduce interbrand competition, i.e. soften competition between the car manufacturers and raise their profits.

It is ultimately an empirical question whether the mechanism of reducing intrabrand competition through selective and exclusive distribution to soften interbrand competition is indeed at work. Put differently, would competition between manufacturers intrinsically be sufficiently intense to make the mechanism profitable? Based on an empirical oligopoly model Brenkers and Verboven (2006) compute the manufacturers' profits under the assumption that the pre-2002 selective and exclusive distribution system indeed eliminated intrabrand competition so that the softening competition mechanism may apply. They then compare this with the profits under the assumption that the distribution system did not successfully eliminate intrabrand competition. They find that profits would actually be higher in the latter case, i.e. when the softening competition mechanism does not apply. Hence, Rey and Stiglitz's conditions that there should be sufficiently strong interbrand competition between manufacturers for the mechanism to work appear not to be satisfied in the European car market. The overall conclusion is that the mechanism of softening interbrand competition through limiting intrabrand competition presumably does not form a profit motive for the selective and exclusive distribution system. It should at most be seen as an unintended side effect that lowers the manufacturers' profits relative to a less restrictive distribution system. The rationale for the selective and exclusive distribution system should therefore be sought elsewhere, for example in efficiencies, or in foreclosure to which we turn in section 3.4.

This discussion assessed whether selective and exclusive distribution indirectly affect interbrand competition through their effects on intrabrand competition. However, other vertical restraints may have a direct effect on interbrand competition. In particular, this may be the case for exclusive dealing or non-compete obligations, which force dealers not to sell competing brands. This raises the search and other information costs to consumers, since they have to visit multiple dealers to learn about the price and quality of competing brands. Hence, exclusive dealing may directly reduce interbrand competition, in contrast with selective and exclusive distribution which may only do so indirectly through the channel of reduced intrabrand competition.

3.4 Foreclosure

The vertical agreements in the car market may not only have an impact on competition given the market structure. They may also affect market structure itself, by making the entry conditions of competing manufacturers and of the spare-parts manufacturers more difficult. We now discuss to what extent such foreclosure may be a source of concern in the car market.

Foreclosure of competing manufacturers

Under exclusive dealing firms force their dealers not to sell competing brands. Such a vertical restraint may create incumbency or first-mover advantages as it increases the costs of new firms trying to enter the market.[31] Historic evidence suggests that first-mover advantages have indeed been important in the car market. All major current European car manufacturers owe their success to their strength in their home markets: Volkswagen and Opel (taken over by GM) in Germany; Renault, Peugeot and Citroën in France; Fiat, Alfa Romeo and Lancia in Italy; Seat in Spain; Ford, Rover and Vauxhall (also taken over by GM) in the UK. With the elimination of tariff barriers in 1968 the opportunities to enter in foreign markets improved. However, because of the practice of exclusive dealing these firms had to set

---

[31] Exclusive dealing may also reduce interbrand competition, given market structure.

up their own distribution networks, a costly and slow process. Even today most manufacturers have considerably stronger positions in their home markets. Similar entry problems have been faced in more recent years by the Asian companies, first by the Japanese and more recently by South Korean car manufacturers.

According to the Chicago School a dealer would not find it in its own interests to make an exclusive dealing contract with a manufacturer, since this would prevent it from new contracts when potentially more efficient firms would enter the market; see e.g. Bork (1978). However, more recent theories suggest this argument is incomplete; see e.g. Rasmusen *et al.* (1991) and Segal and Whinston (2000a). The starting point of the argument is that there are many potential dealers who cannot coordinate when making contracts with an incumbent car manufacturer. The manufacturer can exploit this lack of coordination and make an exclusive dealing contract with each dealer. Each individual dealer has no incentive to refuse the incumbent's contract and go to a new entrant: this would not affect the entry decision of a new firm which would need to sign contracts with a large group of dealers to be able to profitably enter the market. In sum, while it may not be in the joint interests of a group of dealers to make exclusive dealing contracts, this is the best thing to do from the perspective of each individual dealer given that other dealers are doing the same.

The historic evidence on the car manufacturers' market shares suggests that first-mover advantages have been important. The strong correlations between market shares and dealer networks provide further support. However, there is currently no direct evidence on the role of exclusive dealing in foreclosing new entrants.[32] At the same time, evidence presented by the European Commission (2000) shows that exclusive dealing contracts have been considerably less popular in the rural areas, such as the Scandinavian countries. This is more consistent with an efficiency explanation: consumers prefer diversity whereas dealers need a minimum scale to be profitable. One may infer that the possible foreclosure incentives of exclusive dealing do not always outweigh their costs (in terms of forgone scale economies).

Foreclosure of spare-part manufacturers

Until 2002 selective distribution allowed manufacturers to force their dealers to provide both sales and after-sales services. There has been little evidence on

---

[32] Asker (2004) studies exclusive dealing agreements in the beer market of a US metropolitan area and finds no evidence on foreclosure.

the efficiency reasons for tying both services. Cost-side complementarities appear to be limited. The required technical knowledge for after-sales repair and maintenance services is much more specialised than the knowledge for sales services. Conversely, sales services require specific communication skills that are not needed to the same extent for repair and maintenance. The limited complementarity is evident from the specialised personnel for both tasks at most dealers. Demand-side complementarities between sales and after-sales services also seem limited, according to a market research study of Autopolis (2000) commissioned by the European Commission in preparation for the 2002 reforms.

An alternative explanation for the tying of sales and after-sales activities is foreclosure of the spare-parts manufacturers. Since the car manufacturers currently purchase about 80 per cent of their spare parts externally, their core business is building and selling a brand name. By tying sales and after-sales services, the manufacturers may be able to leverage their brand-based market power in the new car market to the after-sales market, where spare parts are needed for both repair and maintenance. This control over the after-sales market is the strongest for repair and maintenance works during the warrantee period, but it extends beyond that if the manufacturers can force the dealers to purchase spare parts from them. In principle, the spare-parts manufacturers can invest in a network of independent repairers to capture profits during the post-warrantee period, but this requires equal access to the car manufacturers' technical information, which is often not the case in practice. In sum, by tying sales and after-sales services, the car manufacturers control a dealer network with a strategic advantage over the spare-part manufacturers who want to sell to independent repairers. This allows them to obtain a significant fraction of the lucrative after-sales market, which according to some studies amounts to up to 50 per cent of the car manufacturers' profits.

While the foreclosure of spare-part manufacturers reduces the degree of competition in the repair and maintenance market, it may also have beneficial effects. Just as the owner of an essential facility in a network industry, the car manufacturers need to have sufficient incentives to invest in their brand name. When other firms can capture a significant fraction of these benefits, the investment incentives may correspondingly be reduced. We are not aware of solid empirical evidence on the effects of foreclosure of the spare-part manufacturers (whether by reducing competition or promoting sufficient investment in brands). This would clearly be important in further investigations.

4. Concluding remarks

The recent history of the car distribution system in Europe shows how the European Commission is gradually changing its interpretation of Article 81. The block exemption regulations during the 1980s and 1990s were preoccupied with the common market concerns, i.e. that the vertical agreements in the car market would create obstacles to cross-border trade and cause large international price differences. While the European car markets are still not fully integrated, progress has been made, not only through the policy regarding the distribution system but also through other measures, such as the harmonisation of technical standards in the mid-1990s. This progress towards a more integrated European car market may partly explain the Commission's shift in emphasis in the most recent 2002 block exemption. While the Commission still aimed to minimise obstacles to cross-border trade caused by the vertical restraints, it now shows a stronger concern with the core competition policy issues, in particular the promotion of intrabrand competition, i.e. competition between dealers of the same brand.

This shift in emphasis away from the common market concern is a welcome development. Recent research by Brenkers and Verboven (2006) indicated that the European welfare gains from reduced international price differences in an integrated market are limited at best (although there are potentially important distributional effects in favour of the current high price countries). Furthermore, the international price differences should only be interpreted as an unintended side effect and not as a main profit motive for the industry's desire to maintain the vertical restraints.

Nevertheless, considerable progress in economic analysis and policy remains desirable. The 2002 block exemption negotiations stressed the promotion of intrabrand competition and an increased dealer independence from their manufacturers. Yet the economic underpinnings of this new emphasis were rather limited and vague. As noted by Wijckmans, Tuytschaever and Vanderelst (2006), the Commission spent little emphasis on the promotion of interbrand competition, arguing in its Evaluation Report that 'there is currently reason to believe that effective interbrand competition exists in the European Union'. One interpretation of the Commission's attitude may be that it attempted to promote the consumers' interests (by encouraging intrabrand competition) without affecting too much the manufacturers' interests (by de-emphasising interbrand competition). Under this interpretation, the (small) dealers' interests may have been hurt most.

In the light of the expiration of the current block exemption regulation in 2010, further progress in economic policy towards the car distribution system may be realised on several fronts. First, the policy objectives should become more transparent, i.e. the importance that is given to the interests of final consumers, the dealers and the car manufacturers, and the relationship with the common market objective. Second, a deeper economic analysis is required regarding the various channels through which the vertical restraints may affect the various parties. Our own economic framework in section 3 stressed that there should be an explicit analysis of both the efficiencies and the anticompetitive effects of the alternative distributional arrangements. Recent empirical evidence suggests that the anticompetitive effects that were emphasised in the European Commission's 2002 reforms (limited cross-border trade and domestic intrabrand competition) appear to be of less concern. This suggests that the stricter policy towards car manufacturers may not have been warranted. However, before concluding that efficiency arguments in favour of vertical restraints dominate, other possible anticompetitive effects of the vertical restraints (e.g. foreclosure of new entry) need more careful empirical analysis. A deeper economic analysis also requires a better motivation of the market threshold criteria and additional transparency on whether and how they are being enforced. Third, a stronger basis should be provided for the stricter policy towards distribution agreements in the car sector than towards distribution agreements in general, for which a parallel block exemption exists. Since the current block exemption regulation for cars will expire simultaneously with the general block exemption in 2010, there is a unique opportunity to consider the possibility of letting car distribution agreements fall under this general block exemption. The argument for a special treatment of car distribution was the fear of the cumulative anticompetitive effects, when all manufacturers in the industry adopt the same or very similar agreements. However, such cumulative effects may also exist in other industries. Furthermore, the current uniformity in distributional agreements (where almost all producers ended up adopting quantitative selectivity) may be partly a consequence of the highly regulatory approach of the 2002 block exemption itself. To make progress on these issues, we hope that our overview will stimulate further economic analysis of car distribution agreements and a careful collection of additional empirical evidence, both by policy makers and academic researchers.

Acknowledgements

The author would like to thank, without implicating, Bruce Lyons and Frank Wijckmans for very helpful comments. The author has written two independent policy reports for the European Commission, in preparation of the block exemption reform in 2002 (Regulation 1400/2002): one on documenting and interpreting international price differentials (with Hans Degryse) and one on defining the relevant product markets for cars. These and other reports are available for download at: http://ec.europa.eu/comm/competition/car_sector/distribution/

10 Beer – the ties that bind

Michael Waterson

'You're walkin' tough baby, but you're walkin' blind to the ties that bind'

Bruce Springsteen

Introduction

It started with the Beer Orders (1989). A watershed decision was made by the Law Lords in July 2006. For one man, Bernie Crehan, this was the culmination of a fifteen-year episode in the pub trade, in which he has made legal history as the first UK case of damages for breach of competition law being awarded by a court. Possibly hundreds of other cases hung on their Lordships' decision and Nomura, the Japanese bank that took over the chain called Inntrepreneur, had a total potential liability of £100 million. And it all concerns Article 81, vertical agreements and the price of a pint of beer.

In 1989, the UK Monopolies and Mergers Commission (MMC) published its lengthy and long-awaited report on beer. The Commission '... recommended measures that eventually led brewers to divest themselves of 14,000 public houses. The MMC claimed that their recommendations would lower retail prices and increase consumer choice. There is considerable doubt, however, that their objectives were achieved' (Slade, 1998, 565). In its report, the MMC noted rising real prices of beer and seized upon the power of the then big six brewers exercised through their considerable tied estates as being a prime motor. Consequently, it recommended that the ties be substantially cut. At that stage, the MMC (unlike the present-day Competition Commission) did not determine remedies and it was left to the Department of Trade and Industry (DTI) to formulate the remedies (the Beer Orders) and the Office of Fair Trading (OFT) to supervise their implementation. Thus the OFT found itself implementing the Beer Orders in the face of a brewing industry determined to fight back.

In the partial move to unbundled retailing from brewing of beer, some former brewers decided to get out of brewing or retailing altogether. One development was the formation of pubcos, intervening between brewers and individual licensees. These pubcos, of which the largest was Grand Metropolitan, took over the ownership of pub chains from brewers but then either managed the pubs directly, or alternatively installed tenants under contracts similar to those tenants formerly had with the brewers. That is, the tenant was an individual entrepreneur, on a relatively short lease, purchasing fixtures and fittings, making pricing decisions and purchasing stock from the pubco or his nominated supplier. Pubcos typically negotiated agreements with brewers for exclusive supply of a particular brand of alcoholic drinks for some long period, then where relevant 'negotiated' agreements with their tenants for their exclusive orders of drink. One issue with these latter vertical agreements was whether they contravened (what is now) Article 81.

For example, a tenant subject to an exclusive supply contract has no option to switch if the brewer raises the wholesale price of beer. This was the matter considered in *Crehan*. Underlying it, and numerous similar cases, are several economic issues arising from a fundamental change in the business model of the beer industry, as well as a change in drinking habits in the UK. One remarkable thing is how a case relating to one individual has occupied so much court time, including a significant period in the European Court of Justice, the UK High Court, the Court of Appeal and several days in the House of Lords (June 2006).[1] The reason of course is that larger issues are at stake. Indeed, this case is but one of many similar cases brought by tenants, involving Inntrepreneur and Courage (its nominated supplier), Whitbread, Bass and Scottish & Newcastle, amongst other brewers.

To illustrate the difference between the various business arrangements under discussion, consider Figure 10.1. Brewer 1 manages pub 1 – it sets prices there directly. In pub 2, it has a tenant; that tenant is free to set retail price but is prevented from buying its beer from any but Brewer 1. Pub 3 is owned by a pubco, which has signed an exclusive arrangement with Brewer 1; pub 5 is similar but relates to Brewer 2. Finally, pub 4 is a so-called free house, able to buy from either brewer.

In this chapter, I set out the relevant facts relating to the general issue, discuss the main features of the economics involved, plus some of the legal arguments, examine this in the light of key cases and cover some implications.

---

[1] Indeed, according to press reports, Inntrepreneur's representatives paid £1.4 million of Crehan's costs into an account in order that the Lords' hearing went ahead!

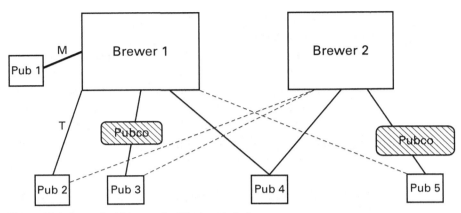

Figure 10.1 Conceptual framework of the beer industry

The economic framework

It is well known that in a vertical linkage relationship with some monopoly power at one or more stages, the interests of players at one stage will not coincide with those at another. For example, if I supply a good to someone, the price they set is probably not the price I would prefer they set to maximise my profits. In fact, if both of us have significant market power, once my margin plus my customer's margin is added to marginal cost, the final price may be above the monopoly level and demand cut back so much that profits could be increased by lowering price. Double or successive marginalisation, as this is called, is usually non-optimal. This clash of interests may be viewed as the result of various externalities in the relationship (Mathewson and Winter, 1984), although calling them externalities should not blind us to the possibility that devices to 'correct' them may be anticompetitive. For example, a brewer charging a tenant a premium over marginal cost for beer faces the problem that the tenant may in turn charge a premium over invoice price, thereby curtailing sales of the product in favour of other drinks. Therefore the brewer may wish to impose an obligation that the tenant takes at least a certain number of barrels of beer. This should encourage a lower retail price in order to meet the sales target. More controversially, the brewer may specify that the tenant does not do certain things, like buy soft drinks from other than a brewer-nominated supplier. In practice, arrangements between brewers and tenants have included many restrictions, some of which are pro-competitive (in the sense that they keep final prices down or spread risk) and some anticompetitive. A balance needs to be struck between the parties and between the parties and consumers.[2]

In order to provide a full economic analysis that reflects the essential features of the market, a model needs to incorporate some competition at the supply stage as well as competition at the final stage. The essential economic modelling of the situation is set out in Slade (1998) and derives from Rey and Stiglitz (1995). A version of this analysis is set out in Appendix 1 because, although straightforward, it is somewhat technical. A heuristic account appears below, building up from a simpler framework which begins by assuming a monopoly brewer.

Consider three alternative scenarios. For simplicity, each focuses entirely on (a single) beer as the product. Consider initially that there is a monopoly supplier of beer – the brewer. In the first scenario, the brewer is vertically integrated with its pub chain. The second has the brewer selling entirely to the many individual pub owners. In the third, the brewer sells to a pubco, which sells on to pubs.

It is well established that the optimal arrangement in the first case is for the brewer to price the input, beer, between divisions at marginal cost and to make its monopoly profit at the final level.[3] In scenario 2, the brewer alternatively takes its monopoly profit at the upstream production level and sells beer expensively to the pub owners. Hence, under reasonable assumptions, there is no difference between the outcomes in these cases. Specifically, one has a marginal cost transfer at the upstream stage, followed by monopoly pricing downstream (with a markup enforced on its managers by the brewer's price list), the other has a monopoly transfer at the upstream stage, followed by marginal cost pricing. If there is no possibility of substituting cheaper drinks at the downstream stage, the monopoly profit is taken in each case, and it is a matter of accounting within the brewer how this is allocated. This is optimal both in the sense that it improves the brewer's profit and that it is best for consumers, given that the brewer has a certain market power. If in the second scenario there is a possibility of substitution downstream, the brewer would be likely to impose arrangements that minimise this, for example requiring the pub owner to take a minimum quantity of beer, or requiring the pub owner to purchase other items such as wines and soft drinks from itself also.

---

[2] See e.g. Dobson and Waterson (1996) for further discussion on the general issue.

[3] This conclusion does rely very much on the assumption that the supplier does not face much competition. If competition is intense, it may be optimal from the firm's viewpoint to raise price above marginal cost, see e.g. Bonanno and Vickers (1988).

The third scenario is somewhat different. Here there is a clear danger of successive marginalisation. The brewer raises its price to the pubco above marginal cost. The pubco in turn adds on a margin, so setting a higher price to the pub owner than under either of the previous situations. The pubco's tenant, if there is one, may then add a third margin. This leads to lower total profits for the brewer and pubco taken together, with the added problem of higher consumer prices, unless the brewer and pubco bargain in a more sophisticated manner, recognising their mutual as well as opposing interests.

Of course, individual breweries do not exist in a vacuum. The model analysed in the appendix takes account of this by adopting a framework where there are two brewers, either selling into the free market (i.e. independently owned pubs) or selling to managed pubs of their own, or selling to tenants, or selling to pubcos under exclusive contracts. It must be admitted that in order to solve the model in a straightforward manner, a good deal of symmetry between the firms is assumed. The outcome is as follows. The free trade and managed house (vertically integrated) scenarios lead to essentially the same result as each other, with a relatively low price. This is driven by downstream competition.

In the case where the brewer sells to tenants a price somewhat above this results. Recall that a tenant sets her own retail price whereas a manager has little pricing discretion. Here, a new force comes in, not present in the monopoly situation considered earlier. The tenant will add a margin on to wholesale price. The brewer raises wholesale price above marginal cost in such a way that the tenant sets a final price which is optimal from the brewer's point of view, given the competition faced by the tenant. The brewer recognises that it faces a trade-off between making a big margin on the beer it sells but selling less beer given the competition between its tenanted pubs and the other brewer's pubs, and setting a lower margin but selling more beer.

Finally, consider the case of a pubco chain. Here there could be two successive contracts, between brewer and pubco and then between pubco and tenant. Therefore conceptually we could analyse the pubco–tenant relationship along the lines used analysing the brewer–tenant relationship, but then incorporate the margin added on by the brewer in selling to the pubco. Note that the brewer cannot capture profit from the pubco via a fixed fee, so that double marginalisation is likely in any case. This scenario leads to the highest prices amongst the various possibilities because of successive marginalisation, without the brewer being able to optimise the retail price.

Slade (1998) extends this model to show that

$$p^{chain} \approx p^{leased} \succ p^{tenanted} \succ p^{free} ? p^{managed} \succ c \qquad (1)$$

We may now see that there is a problem for a competition authority wishing to intervene in the market to get prices down. Reducing the number of tenanted houses will lead to a lowering of final prices in the market if the formerly tenanted pubs become free of tie. However, if the pubs are instead bought up by pubco chains, the clear danger is that the situation is worsened – prices rise on average rather than falling.

One of the implicit assumptions underlying all this analysis is that there is a paucity of competition in the brewing market. In addition, in order for pubcos to exist, they must not face too much competition with other channels of supply that would plausibly lead to lower beer prices for consumers.

The modelling here, as Slade explains, assumes in each case that the equilibrium involves a single contract type. Manifestly, this is untrue in the context of beer. Nevertheless, by modelling the simplest situation within the final sector, we can postulate likely outcomes in mixed situations.

Consider then a final market differentiated duopoly (e.g. two nearby pubs). Demand is symmetric, but one of them faces higher marginal cost of its input (beer). Marginal cost is constant in each case. Equilibrium is reached through price-setting behaviour. Straightforward algebra (sketched in Appendix 2) shows that the firm that charged the higher input price charges a higher final price, sells less than the other firm and obtains lower gross profit. Intuitively, the higher input price puts the firm at a disadvantage – it faces a trade-off between raising price thereby cutting its own demand and reducing its margin. Therefore, profits accordingly are lower.

Nevertheless, two (or more) players can easily co-exist in the market, so long as there is differentiation between them. Moreover, if the one facing higher variable costs also faces lower fixed costs (e.g. rent), its net profit need not be lower. Hence, a potential publican choosing between contracts, one of which implies a higher beer price but a subsidised rent, the other the possibility of discounted beer but a full rent, might choose either one depending on the precise contracts offered. Indeed, the former probably exposes the publican to less risk and may be preferred even if the earnings stream has a lower mean (an argument made by Yarrow in MMC *Beer*). Thus, someone with limited business experience might be drawn to a contract that promises a smoothed return. In this case, a lower rent is an example of what is later referred to as an 'offsetting benefit'.

On the other hand, a tenant facing both a higher beer price and a rent appropriate to a pub free of any tie would naturally earn a lower net profit than an otherwise equivalent pub either being charged a lower price for beer, or being charged a lower rent.

In respect of calculations of damages discussed later on, note that if particular premises has a pub licence, the value is likely to be higher as a public house than as a dwelling because licences are in limited supply. A plausible way to value the pub would be the discounted stream of earnings net of the labour costs etc. involved in generating those earnings. However, the earnings themselves will depend on the prices charged for key inputs. Thus the value of a pub 'in the open market' is not in theory determined unless the contract under which key inputs to the pub are supplied is specified. Value as a free house is likely to be higher than value under a supply tie. This conclusion appears to be accepted by experienced valuers of public houses (for example it becomes evident in Justice Park's thinking in the High Court in *Crehan*).

Legal analysis

The legal analysis of cases of this type (specifically, contracts between brewers and publicans or pubcos and publicans) takes on a particular form, but is clearly informed by economic considerations. The essential question is whether the arrangements struck between brewers/pubcos and tenants fell within the law. If an agreement is found to contravene competition law, it is invalid. Moreover, although the (English) High Court ruled at one stage that a party to an agreement could not claim damages as a result of the agreement being unlawful under Article 81, the European Court of Justice determined that a party to an agreement could obtain relief. Thus, in principle the way is clear for a private action for damages.

A large number of cases have been through at least some stages towards a claim for damages as a result of infringement of Article 81. A particular structure has built up, based upon a key EU case, *Delimitis*, relating to a German pub. This was decided by the ECJ, which is the highest European court that hears competition cases, and so it sets an important precedent. This case in turn followed an earlier EU judgment in *Brasserie de Haecht*, a Belgian bar. A key point established in these and similar cases is that, although a particular agreement between a brewer and a pub is of trivial significance for the European Community as a whole, the consequences of that agreement are nevertheless non-trivial. Any such agreement cannot be viewed in isolation, because it is likely to be just one example amongst a large number of similar agreements imposed by one party, which have a consequential impact upon competition in the market. For example, if there are 100 feasible outlets for a particular product, and one producer of that product has signed up exclusive deals with 98 of them, then it can be fairly concluded that the market is foreclosed to new entrants and that the established producer is maintaining a monopoly as a result of the agreements, although any particular instance of this agreement has a very small contributing influence to the overall effect. Similarly, if there are three producers, who have signed up respectively say fifty, thirty and eighteen outlets, the market would be foreclosed to entry, although dependent upon the nature of the distribution of outlets, competition between the three players would differ in its impact.[4]

The *Delimitis* precedent requires the competition authority to jump over a series of hurdles, set out diagrammatically in Figure 10.2, before an agreement is considered illegal. The first is whether the market can be considered foreclosed by the contracts, or entry significantly impeded by other factors. At the time of the relevant cases in the UK, the early 1990s, the on-trade channel constituted 81 per cent of total beer sales, with price movements distinctly different from the off-trade, therefore arguably constituting a separate market. Brewers were in control of over 90 per cent of the distribution and wholesaling of beer in the UK and to a significant extent operated through exclusivity agreements. Pub licences were limited by local magistrates and were a significant barrier to the entry of new pubs. Of course, a number of these things have now changed, in part as a result of the MMC report on Beer in 1988, but at the stage of the actions we are considering, brewers were arguably trying to hold on to their market power through variations in the original restrictive agreements that the competition authorities might be prepared to allow. Specifically, although the major brewers were forced to divest large numbers of pubs, they negotiated long-term exclusive agreements with the pub chains that resulted (Slade, 1998). In any event, the European Commission (DG4) determined in a number of decisions that the market was foreclosed at that time. This entry barrier test is known as the 'Delimitis 1' test.

Assuming the market is foreclosed, attention passes to whether the set of agreements of which the agreement in question is part contributes to the foreclosing effect. Essentially, this is seen as dependent on the significance of the set of agreements. A small brewer with a handful of pubs would be most unlikely to be seen as contributing, whilst a large market player with many thousands of pubs would likely be deemed as contributing. This significant effect test is known as the 'Delimitis 2' test.

[4] For example, if the fifty are in England, the thirty in Scotland and the eighteen in Wales, in effect a monopoly still exists assuming people do not travel far for the product.

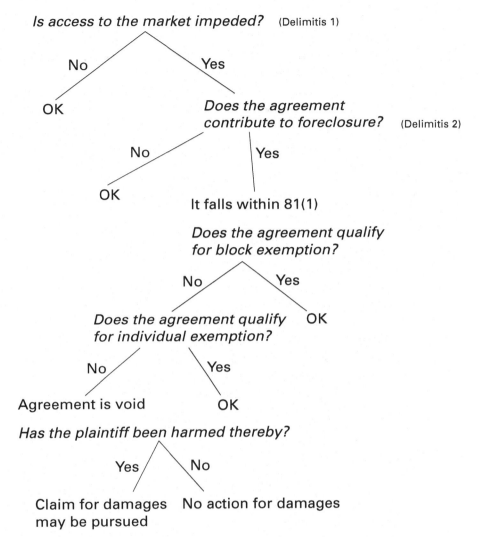

Figure 10.2 The *Delimitis* 'decision tree'

Nevertheless, vertical agreements may qualify for a block exemption under Article 81(3). Here, the law has changed somewhat, but at the time of the cases under discussion there was a specific block exemption for vertical agreements in the beer industry. If agreements were in a particular form, then they would satisfy the block exemption and would be allowed.

In practice, the agreements drawn up by brewers commonly did not satisfy the block exemption because they were too broad (not specifying the products or including products apart from beer), too long (e.g. for an indefinite period) or too unspecific. Nevertheless, a brewer could still apply for individual exemption under Article 81(3), if the agreement was viewed as providing benefits offsetting the restrictions applied by the agreement.

If the agreement does not escape under any of the above possible routes, then it contravenes Article 81 and is therefore void. Matters then turn on whether and how the tenant has been harmed by the agreement and the potential for damages to be claimed by the tenant.

Specific cases

A number of cases have been through this process. For example, in *Greene King*, the tenant fell foul of Delimitis 2. Greene King is a regional but not a national player (it was designated as regional in the MMC report), so its agreements were not viewed as significant enough to contribute to foreclosure. Three national brewers, Whitbread, Bass and Scottish & Newcastle, were each involved in very similar cases before the Commission. In each case, the tenant's arguments were accepted, to the extent that they passed the Delimitis 1 and 2 tests and none of the agreements qualified for block exemption. However, in each case, the brewer applied retrospectively for individual exemption, using the argument that they had provided sufficient offsetting benefits. In each case, this was accepted, so the cases fell at this hurdle.

Offsetting benefits in Bass

It is interesting to examine the arguments underpinning the 'offsetting benefits' analysis from an economist's viewpoint. We take the case of Bass, because it is well documented.

The Commission granted individual exemption to Bass from the provisions of Article 81 in respect of its agreements with tenants (retrospectively) from March 1991 to December 2002. Individual exemption is allowed if there are significant benefits in distributing the product. The Commission view beer supply agreements as having the potential to lead to such improvements in distribution (para. 168; subsequent bracketed numbers also refer to paragraphs in this judgment) and indeed it is easy to see that there are some potential benefits. (This is not to say that a beer supply agreement is the only, or even the most efficient, means of securing such benefits.) Logically, however, the benefits will not materialise if the typical tenant is forced into unfavourable terms of

Table 10.1 Assessing offsetting benefits

£/ barrel	1990/1	1991/2	1992/3	1993/4	1994/5	1995/6	1996/7
Price differential	19	22	26	35	41	45	48
Rent subsidy	16	15	19	23	22	22	24
Value added services	2	2	2	3	7	7	11
Support	2	2	3	3	9	9	9
Promotions	0	1	2	2	3	4	5
(Others not listed)							
Conclusion	3	1	1	− 2	3	3	2

Source: European Commission: *Bass*, Table 3.

business so as to be placed at a competitive disadvantage. It is clear that tenants pay more than free market prices for their beer, which does place them at a disadvantage. However, they receive inducements as a result of signing a tenancy agreement. Thus the question turned on whether the inducements sufficed to place the tenant on a 'level playing field' (176). The Commission concluded that on average 'the price differential is more than compensated by quantifiable countervailing benefits' (186) and hence that the leases qualify for individual exemption under 81(3).

Let us examine this proposition.[5] The Commission acknowledges that 'A brewer might … decide to "cash in" on his leverage vis-à-vis his tied customers' (174), e.g. by raising wholesale beer prices without increasing off-setting benefits. On the face of it, this is exactly what Bass did. In the Commission's Table 3 (extracted in Table 10.1) we see the price differential between tied and free trade going from £19 to £48 per barrel in regularly increasing intervals over the period from 1990/1 to 1996/7. Thus in order to justify an exemption, it is necessary to argue at least that the quantifiable benefits to tenants have increased regularly over the period. The major means by which this is demonstrated are that (i) rent subsidy has increased over the period, (ii) value added services have increased in value, (iii) a support franchise scheme has been instituted and (iv) promotions have increased in value. If none of these had occurred, on the figures in the table, a conclusion of a positive benefit in 1990/1 of £3 would have moved to a negative benefit (i.e. disbenefit) of £24 by 1996/7 and it is extremely unlikely that individual exemption would have been granted. We therefore need to look more closely at the value of the offsets.

---

[5] The Commission did not accept the arguments that follow, or at least the implication drawn from them.

Consider first the question of rent. It is difficult to establish what is the subsidy to rent afforded the tenant compared with the free market rental of the pub if 'free-of-tie', since this requires establishing a counterfactual. What is the 'un-tied' rent? The Commission uses a figure of 15 per cent as the average free-of-tie rental to income ratio and 11.36 per cent as the average rent paid for a pub in the tenanted estate (64, 65).[6] Pubs differ in their attractiveness and costs, so any average figure disguises some necessary variation. It would be impossible to take account of all sources of such variation, but one significant issue suggests itself. Essentially, the Commission is making the implicit assumption that the tenanted houses are in effect a random sample of the premises the brewer owns. If they are not, if for example they are on average smaller or less well situated, we might envisage that a lower ratio of rental to turnover might be what the market would command on account of a lower profit margin. There is a second point. The figures of 11.36 per cent and 15 per cent, giving a subsidy of 3.64 per cent of turnover, presumably must be applied to each year, i.e. the subsidy as a percentage of turnover is assumed constant. However, when converted into a subsidy per barrel equivalent, for Table 10.1, this results in an increasing figure which has a significant impact on the final figures. If, with nothing else changed, the rent subsidy were held constant in per-barrel terms over the period, the conclusion would be a negative figure for rent subsidy from 1992/3 onwards.

Second, consider value added services. There is a significant difference of viewpoint between Bass and many of its tenants regarding the value of the services gathered under this head. Again, two points. First, in its judgment, the Commission reduced by 25 per cent the value as perceived by Bass of these benefits. However, the overall calculation is rather sensitive to this percentage. If the reduction were to be 50 per cent not 25 per cent, then in 1996/7, the overall balance of beneficial effects to the tenant in Table 10.1 would be negative and the balance over the last seven years would be negative on average. This would lead to a very different view being taken on the balance of advantage in the tenancies and so also on the individual exemption afforded to Bass. Second, the figures are very sensitive to particular assumptions which may be erroneous. One may accept that the terms negotiated by Bass with suppliers of products such as glassware and insurance for their tenants' use can be regarded as a base point for price discussions elsewhere. Yet, is this a benefit which might be equated with a continuing, indeed rising, offsetting effect on

---

[6] Here we see a very curious coincidence – the figure of 11.36 per cent obtained 'from internal Bass documents' is *precisely* the same as the figure quoted as arising from a 'sample of S&N tied houses selected by the Commission ...' (*S&N* Decision, at (65)). This suggests either that an industry norm has been established by some means or that there is some confusion concerning the source of this 11.36 per cent.

beer prices? Many of the activities described under this head might be best thought of as providing knowledge. Once knowledge has been gained, it can be used freely without limit. Thus, to equate this benefit with an *increasing* offsetting benefit per barrel seems most peculiar, even if the range of information provided over time does increase.

Third, consider promotions: here we have a classic problem in a vertical relationship. One party wishes to promote products and both parties benefit. It is clearly misleading to say that 'these promotions are intended to increase the turnover of the individual lessee' (104). They are intended to benefit both parties, irrespective of whether they are exclusive to lessees or not. If we, somewhat arbitrarily, assigned the benefit half to tenants, half to Bass, this by itself would be enough to make the net conclusion over the last six years in Table 10.1 negative. Again, the outcome is seen to be extremely sensitive to the precise assumption made.

Finally, the agreements relate to beer and the Commission focus on the effect on beer. However, when examining offsetting benefits, another, perhaps crucial, side to the coin must be examined and another range of issues opened up. Are there other costs imposed on tenants as a result of their relationship with Bass which have not been taken into the equation? For example, does Bass impose restrictions or purchasing requirements on other drinks, crisps and the like which may be at above market prices? If offsetting benefits are to be brought into the equation, clearly offsetting costs must also be, in order to examine the complete picture.

Does *Crehan* jump the hurdles?

The Inntrepreneur–Crehan case (hereafter, *Crehan*) is by far the best known amongst the cases under review and has some significant differences from the brewer cases discussed above. Bernie Crehan was a tenant of Inntrepreneur, a pub company, which in turn had an exclusivity arrangement with Courage, the brewer, regarding supplies of beer to its pubs. The case relates essentially to Crehan's relationship with the pub chain, not the brewer, although there was a preliminary judgment concerning the link with the brewer. Inntrepreneur pioneered a novel type of lease, which appeared initially to find interest amongst prospective tenants through being assignable, but later led to widespread complaints, such that *Crehan* was being treated as a test case for possibly hundreds more similar ones. Crehan himself had been persuaded by Inntrepreneur to take on the leases of two adjacent pubs, The Phoenix and The Cock Inn, in July 1991. He went bust in 1993, claimed this was due to the high wholesale price of beer he was forced to take, preventing him from competing with other local pubs. He sued Courage (then a parent of Inntrepreneur) for damages in the English High Court, which dismissed his complaint. Following a period in the ECJ relating to an important technical legal point, the case was referred back to the High Court where Justice Park rejected his case, he appealed and his case was accepted by the Court of Appeal. It then went to the highest court in the land, the House of Lords, for final judgment.

The clearest brief summary of the hurdles through which the case needed to pass is provided by the Court of Appeal in its judgment. To use his words, the issues before Justice Park in the High Court were the following:

(1) Is Delimitis condition 1 satisfied?
(2) Is Delimitis condition 2 satisfied?
(3) Does the block exemption apply?
(4) Is it an abuse of process for Inntrepreneur to contend that there was no infringement of Article 81 and that the block exemption applies?
(5) Does Mr Crehan share responsibility with Inntrepreneur to such an extent that Mr Crehan's claim could not succeed?
(6) Are the damages claimed by Mr Crehan in respect of a type of loss against which he is protected by Article 81?
(7) Did the beer ties cause Mr Crehan's business failure at The Phoenix and The Cock Inn?
(8) What is the appropriate quantum of damages, and at what date should the damages be measured?

Some of these points need further explanation in order to appreciate their significance.

First, was the market foreclosed? Justice Park (High Court) said not (and was dubious about (2), the contribution of Inntrepreneur to any foreclosure), but on earlier occasions, the European Commission (in *Whitbread*, *Bass* and *Scottish & Newcastle*, 1999) had said yes to (1) and, for those firms, (2). For example in *Whitbread*:

[The] tying agreements ... have ... the cumulative effect of considerably hindering independent access to that market, for new national and foreign competitors.

Whitbread's tied sales, of which the notified agreements are a part, contribute significantly to the foreclosure of the UK on-trade market.

Park's decision left the Court of Appeal 'profoundly uneasy'. It followed the precedent set by the Commission, citing the 'principle of sincere cooperation'. Note that the Commission had declined to rule on whether Inntrepreneur itself contributed to the foreclosure effect it had observed, because by the time it came to consider it, the matter was of only historic interest. But it is important to note that at the relevant time Inntrepreneur had not managed to satisfy 81(3), nor

Table 10.2 Operation of retail outlets

Owner	Number of pubs		Source of beer
	1988	end 1992	
National brewers			
Allied	6678	4339 (tied)	
Bass	7190	4595 (tied	
Courage	5002	0 (tied)	
Whitbread	6483	4241 (tied)	
Scottish & Newcastle	2287	1850	
Regional brewers			
Greene King	766	851	
Vaux	577	769	
Former brewers			
Grand Met	6419	1650 (managed, free after 1991)	Courage
Inntrepreneur		4350 (tied)	Courage
Boddingtons	518	475	
New pubcos			
Pubmaster	466	2026 (including 734 leased from Allied)	
Greenall Whitley	1626	1500	Carlsberg-Tetley

Note: Several other regional brewers, smaller pubcos and the free trade have been omitted.
Source: House of Commons Agriculture Committee, fourth report, HCP 402, Session 1992–3, Table 6, pages 168–169.

individual exemption, although it did so later. For later reference, Table 10.2 extracts some of the relevant details concerning the sizes of the various pub estates.

Justice Park had considered the nature of the leases caused Crehan's business to fail. So *if* Crehan had passed (1) and (2), he would have been awarded damages.

Justice Park determined, after evidence, that Delimitis 1 was not in fact satisfied in the UK in 1991 and shortly thereafter. This might seem directly contrary to the decisions of the Commission in *Whitbread et al.* that the relevant United Kingdom market was foreclosed to the extent that it would have had to be for Delimitis condition 1 to be satisfied. As the Court of Appeal says (para. 74):

We are left profoundly uneasy by the judge's approach to the evidence. It is apparent from what the ECJ said in *Delimitis* that a comprehensive investigation and evaluation of a complex economic situation needs to be conducted before it can be determined whether or not *Delimitis* condition 1 is or is not satisfied. The judge rightly acknowledged (in para. 159) that he could not possibly embark on a detailed research investigation himself and that to do so would be inconsistent with the role of a judge in civil litigation in this jurisdiction. That is why such investigations have been entrusted to bodies such as the Commission, the MMC or Competition Commission and the OFT.

For this and other reasons, it concluded that the judge erred in law and that he should have held that Delimitis 1 was satisfied. The English court owed a duty of 'sincere cooperation' to the European Commission.

Despite being of the opinion that the case should have fallen at the first hurdle, Justice Park usefully argued each of the other points more or less fully in his judgment. He spent relatively little time on Delimitis 2, but suggested the case would have fallen at this hurdle also. The Court of Appeal disagreed:

> Again, in our judgment, the judge did not give due deference to Commission decisions. In the Whitbread, Bass and Scottish & Newcastle decisions the Commission had found that smaller tied estates had made a significant contribution to the foreclosure. A fortiori the Inntrepreneur tied estate must have satisfied that test (para. 116).

It was fairly apparent that the agreement did not qualify for block exemption and that individual exemption would not have been granted (at that time), because there was little in the way of offsetting advantages in exchange for the tie, by comparison with the Whitbread or Bass examples. Nor was it the case that Crehan bore significant shared responsibility, since he was offered a standard form lease as opposed to one purpose negotiated for his own situation.[7] Point (4) is a technical issue that need not detain us. Point (5) is in effect covered below.

Point (6) is a matter of more substance, both from an economic and a legal perspective. Crehan's problem was that the conditions of his lease and tie meant he could not compete on an equal footing with competitor pubs in the locality and that this was what caused his venture to fail. But Article 81(1) applies to distortions at the distribution stage, not at the retail stage. If he had been a prospective entrant into beer distribution, it would have harmed him. So is it valid to argue that he was harmed at the retail stage by a vertical agreement that was illegal under Article 81(1)? Clearly, the economic effect of the agreement was to make his offering uncompetitive with free-of-tie pubs' offerings. Moreover, the ECJ had previously expressed its view in a part of the case remitted there that Crehan's claim was valid in this respect. Therefore, although English law might well not allow the claim, Community law takes precedence.[8]

Whether the beer ties are what caused or what substantially contributed to Crehan's business failure cannot ever be known with certainty. However, had

---

[7] Apparently, this is a novel legal point, where the ECJ had made a ruling that conflicted with a previous Court of Appeal decision – see Whish (2003, 291–292).

[8] This is sometimes called the Principle of the Effectiveness of Remedies: a difference between English law and Community law here means that if English law were applied, no remedy would be available, which would be contrary to the spirit of the Community law allowing damages, which means that English law has to be dis-applied.

he run a manifestly badly managed operation, that would have been evidence against him. As it happens, although he was clearly a somewhat inexperienced businessman, the pubs appear to have generated plenty of witnesses to speak up for him, and his wife's cooking! So, to a reasonable degree of certainty, this aspect can be treated as demonstrated as accepted.

How much was Crehan damaged?

Finally, then, there is the question of damages.[9] It must have been somewhat galling for Bernie Crehan to learn that, had Justice Park accepted his representatives' arguments on Delimitis 1 and 2, he would have made Crehan a millionaire (£1.3 million, actually). The Court of Appeal awarded a more modest sum, around one tenth of that, but at least it did award something. How is it that two courts come to such a different view on what lawyers call 'quantum'?

The Court of Appeal's starting point is

that sum of money which will put the party who has been injured, or has suffered, in the same position as he would have been in if he had not sustained the wrong for which he is now getting his compensation or reparation. (*Livingstone* v *Raywards Coal* (1880))

This approach seems to commend itself in terms of both law and economics.

However, there is a fundamental difficulty in calculating damages in a case such as this. They relate to the 'hypothetical profits of a hypothetical business', in the words of the Court of Appeal. If someone sustains an injury at work, it might be reasonable to assume they would otherwise have continued to work normally on the set salary or wage. So it is the hypothetical earnings of a real activity. In the *Crehan* case, the appropriate assumption is that the hypothetical business consists of Crehan running the two pubs free of beer tie. So then if his beer costs were lower, he would set lower prices and gain more custom. Despite the difficulties fraught with evaluating how much exactly this would amount to, the two sides eventually agreed not to challenge the argued presumption that the lost profits between the dates the premises were tenanted and the dates of surrender (two years later) would be £57,121, no doubt a figure which looks spuriously accurate.

The second question regarding the business is, how long would he have run it for? Here the High Court took the view that it would have continued until 2003, the date of the action in that court. The Court of Appeal cited previous

---

[9] See Chapter 6 by Peter Møllgaard for a discussion of damages in relation to a cartel.

authority to the effect that it should be presumed in operation until the date the leases were given up, 1993. Beyond that point, it becomes even more questionable what is being valued – would he have given up the leases had he not been subject to the tie? It is essentially impossible to judge. But this is the main source of difference in the two alternative approaches to quantum. The normal legal view is that damages are those suffered at date of loss, i.e. in 1993.

The other main element in the calculation is the consideration he would have obtained from reassignment of the leases. Industry experts considered that a figure of 2.5 times the 'maintainable net profit [per year] after rent to include the value of the trade inventories', calculated as £25,186 per year across both pubs. Including 'marriage value' (£4,500 per year, again multiplied by 2.5) of the two pubs, this amounts to £74,215, to be added to the £57 k noted earlier. It is unclear whether all expenses of employees (for example, managers) have been deducted to render this true economic profit, but the 2.5 multiple presumably takes some assumption about this into account. The sums would bear interest.

Hopes dashed

However, celebrations following the Court of Appeal decision were short-lived (short-lived, that is, by comparison with the glacial pace of the case generally). Inntrepreneur appealed to the House of Lords, which heard the case in June 2006. There seems to have been some genuine uncertainty about the issues on which the Lords would focus. For example, some surprise was expressed that they had not wished to hear arguments on quantum. There was also a distinct possibility that they would have remitted aspects of the decision to the European courts, possibly the point that was determined by the Court of Appeal 'without perfect EU authority', point (6) above.

Nevertheless, in a scene reminiscent of Puccini's *Tosca*, the House of Lords crushed the case at the final stage. Operatics aside, it is worth dwelling on the reason. Essentially, they took the view that Justice Park had not been in error in putting relatively little weight on the EC decisions in *Whitbread et al.* that the market was foreclosed and relatively greater weight on the witnesses (including economists) he heard explaining the points.[10] This was because

---

[10] Note that although both systems are adversarial, this is very different from the US system whereby the DoJ takes a competition case to court. The witnesses arguing Crehan's case were not those who had carried out the investigation – they were merely interpreting the results of that investigation and may even have differed on details. Hence they might well be seen as at a disadvantage compared with those experts for Inntrepreneur putting forward their own views.

the EU decisions did not relate to Inntrepreneur itself, only to that set of brewers, starting with Whitbread, whose cases were considered. Thus the Lords took the view that the Court of Appeal should not have taken the Commission's decision on the Whitbread case as precedent but rather that Justice Park's decision on Delimitis 1 should stand.

To my clearly non-expert eye this seems a curious decision. The 'principle of sincere cooperation' would seem to me to suggest that if in the other cases the *industry* is viewed as foreclosed, then the UK courts should follow that judgment.[11] It was a judgment, made at a relevant time period, by an expert investigative team. Therefore, in my view, it appears at odds with this principle for *Crehan* to fall at Delimitis 1. What might be more arguable is whether *Crehan* should fall at Delimitis 2, because this is the element to which the principle need not apply. Although Inntrepreneur had more pubs under its control than, say, S&N (see again Table 10.2), it is a pubco not a brewer and its arrangements with a particular brewer, although several years long, are not perpetual. This issue has not been examined fully in any of the *Crehan* cases cited.

Final comments

Crehan was the first case in which an English court awarded damages concerning a claim relating to a breach in competition law. Thus, although damages were not eventually paid, the case is of historic interest. The law relating to beer supply arrangements has now changed, so is the case of relevance still or is it, as some say disparagingly, only of academic interest?

I would argue the case is important. As the law now stands, no tenant has received damages in court through this series of actions. One might view the *Crehan* case as a victory of English law over European law, or a victory of law over economics – the legal process of cross-examination of witnesses over the Commission's approach of evidence gathering and summary. But it is a defeat for those contemplating private action in competition claims.

---

[11] For example, in *Bass* we read 'Conclusion on the first Delimitis test … an examination of all tying arrangements, included but not limited to beer-supply agreements entered into, and the other factors relevant to the economic and legal context of the UK on-trade market shows that the brewers' tying arrangements had in 1990, and still have today … the cumulative effect of considerably hindering independent access to that market, for new national and foreign competitors' (3.3 at para. 144).

At a more personal level, the people involved as tenants in this series of actions against owners have suffered through an extremely slow, drawn-out and desperate process. Maybe some were foolish, but several have found that they fought one form of tie, to a particular brewer's beer, only to be bound by another, to a legal process which, in Crehan's case, lasted thirteen years.

Appendix 1 The Rey and Stiglitz (1995) vertical arrangements framework

Notation: upper-case letters refer to upstream values, lower-case refer to downstream. The letter p (P) is used for prices, c for marginal cost, D for the demand function, π (Π) for profit and ε for elasticity of demand. Superscripts are used to distinguish between the two producers' products, 1 and 2, with subscripts used for partial derivatives. Superscripts are also used to distinguish different scenarios.

There are two products, one from each producer, with final demand being $D^i(p^1, p^2)$; complete symmetry is assumed (e.g. $D_2^1 = D_1^2$).

The benchmark case:

Direct producer competition: Firms will choose prices to maximise

$$\Pi^1 = (p^1 - c).D^1(p^1, p^2)$$

Two-stage games:

1. No vertical arrangements – we superscript this case as c. Intrabrand price competition leads to zero markups in the second (retail) stage, so that $P^c = p^c$. Thus there is simply competition between the brewers. We may derive:

$$\frac{p^c - c}{p^c} = 1/\varepsilon^1(p^c, p^c)$$

2. Exclusive contracts, superscripted E. This is the case where each brewer sells its beer exclusively to a particular pubco, so these are somewhat distinctive. Each pubco by assumption has monopolistic power over some fraction, say θ, of the final demand for each product. As a result, it can charge a markup over input price. This will lead to second-stage retail prices p^{iE} (P^1, P^2)

$$\frac{p^{1E} - P^{1E}}{p^{1E}} = \frac{1}{\varepsilon^1}$$

where at the first stage, price P^1 is chosen to maximise:

$$\Pi^1 = (P^1 - c).D^1(p^{1E}(P^1, P^2), p^{2E}(P^1, P^2))$$

and similarly for 2. Thus:

$$D^1 + (P^1 - c)\left[D_1^1 . \frac{dp^{1E}}{dP^1} + D_2^1 . \frac{dp^{2E}}{dP^1}\right] = 0$$

Hence, after simplification and symmetry:

$$\frac{(P^E - c)}{P^E} = 1/[\varepsilon^1(p^E, p^E).\rho^1(p^E, p^E) + \varepsilon^2(p^E, p^E).\rho^2(p^E, p^E)]$$

Here, ρ^1 and ρ^2 are the elasticities of a given retailer's price to its producer's and the other producer's wholesale prices. We may expect that

$$1 > \rho^1 > \rho^2 > 0$$

3. Tenancy arrangement with fee transfer, superscripted T. This is the situation where the brewer has a tenant in place in the pub, again with exclusive dealing.

$$\Pi^1 = (p^1 - c).D^1(p^1(P^1, P^2), p^2(P^1, P^2))$$

Now the brewer wants to set the optimal final price, so maximises:

$$D^1 \frac{dp^1}{dP^1} + (p^1 - c)\left[D_1^1 \frac{dp^1}{dP^1} + D_2^1 \frac{dp^2}{dP^1}\right] = 0$$

Therefore:

$$\frac{p^T - c}{p^T} = 1/[\varepsilon^1 + \varepsilon^2.\rho^2/\rho^1]$$

Hence, by comparison with earlier expressions for the markup,

$$p^E \succ p^T \succ p^c$$

We can see that double marginalisation raises price above p^T.

Slade extends this framework to show that:

$$p^{chain} \approx p^{leased} \succ p^{tenanted} \succ p^{free} ? p^{managed} \succ c$$

which is equation (1) in the text.

Appendix 2 Modelling a duopoly with dissimilar costs

Using a notation essentially the same as in Appendix 1, suppose demand for product i is given by:

$$D^i = D^i(p^i, p^j) \quad \text{where } D^i_i < 0, \left| D^i_i \right| > D^i_j > 0 \ i, j = 1, 2; i \neq j$$

and further that the demand functions are symmetric.

Suppose marginal cost is c^i, c^j respectively; $c^i > c^j$, without further loss of generality. Profit is defined as

$$\pi_i = (p^i - c^i)D^i - F^i$$

where F refers to fixed costs, which were earlier ignored, and similarly for firm j. We might expect that $F^j > F^i$.

Straightforward maximisation with respect to price, treating the other player's price as given, yields

$$p^{i*} = c^i / (1/\varepsilon^i - 1)$$

where ε^i is the own price elasticity of demand, written as a positive number. Hence, if $\varepsilon^i = \varepsilon^j$ (>1) then $p^{i*} > p^{j*}$. Moreover, from the form of the demand function, $q^{i*} < q^{j*}$. Maximised profits can be written as

$$\pi^{i*} = p^{i*}q^{i*}/\varepsilon^i - F^i.$$

Since demand facing i is by definition elastic, revenue declines as price rises, so that if $\varepsilon^i = \varepsilon^j$ then profits gross of fixed costs and sales are larger for low-cost j than for i, and price is lower.

These expressions lead directly to the statements made in the text regarding relative magnitudes of price, quantity and gross profit.

Acknowledgements

I was involved in providing economic advice to a Birmingham firm of solicitors and barristers, Ferdinand-Kelly, which was retained on several cases brought by pub tenants against brewers, including the Bass and S&N cases. However, my arguments were not necessarily accepted by the Commission or the courts and this chapter should be considered to be solely my own opinion. I was not involved at all in the *Crehan* case. I would like to thank Morten Hviid and Margaret Slade for helpful discussions and Bruce Lyons for helpful comments and editing. None of these should be assumed to share my taste in music.

11 Parallel trade of prescription medicines: the Glaxo *Dual Pricing* case

Patrick Rey and James S. Venit[1]

1. Background

The prices of prescription medicines in the European Union are for the most part determined by measures adopted by the national health authorities of the various Member States and tend to differ substantially from country to country as a result of the different budgetary policies and priorities of the Member States concerned.[2] These price differences inevitably give rise to significant arbitrage opportunities and have been the source of a flourishing parallel trade in prescription pharmaceuticals from low- to high-priced countries.[3]

The Glaxo *Dual Pricing* case relates to a practice under which Glaxo sold its medicines to Spanish wholesalers at prices differentiated according to where the medicine would be consumed. Thus, the price for a medicine to be sold in Spain was set at the level mandated by the relevant Spanish pricing legislation. Products for export were sold at a price freely determined by Glaxo as permitted under Spanish law. In this way, Glaxo was able to sell in Spain at the government-required low price for domestic consumption but at a higher price if the product was to be re-exported to countries willing to pay more,

---

[1] We advised GlaxoSmithKline in the case under review. The views expressed are however those of the authors and do not necessarily reflect the views of GlaxoSmithKline.

[2] National price measures vary in the twenty-five member European Union and include measures that set the maximum sales price that can be charged or the reimbursement price, which in effect normally determines the maximum price charged. Although some Member States such as the United Kingdom do not regulate prices (the United Kingdom regulates profits instead), price regulation, often extending to intermediate levels of trade, is the rule in the majority of the Member States. Moreover, although national fiscal and other measures influence prices in other industries such as automobiles, the pharmaceutical sector is unique in that the payer is the party effectively determining the price, and price determination takes place prior to the marketing of the product.

[3] Parallel trade arises when a product is re-exported from the low-price country to one with a higher price. With other products, this arbitrage tends to equalise prices, but this need not happen when prices are regulated as in prescription pharmaceuticals. See Danzon (1998), Jenny (2002) and Nazzini (2003).

notably the UK. Thus, while not explicitly prohibiting parallel trade, the practice had the effect of reducing the incentives for wholesalers to re-export.

The EU goal of market integration as an overriding policy consideration has led the European Commission to treat the prevention or limitation of parallel trade as a hard-core restriction which has frequently attracted heavy fines, irrespective of the products and the regulatory environment in question. Until recently, this approach has been generally supported by the Community Courts.[4] Moreover, until recently, neither the Commission nor the Community Courts appear to have been willing to consider the specific economic issues raised by parallel trade in industries such as the pharmaceutical sector. As a result parallel trade in prescription medicines has been protected and, indeed, encouraged under the Commission's administrative practice and the European Courts' jurisprudence relating to both the free movement of goods[5] and the competition rules.[6]

Prior to the Glaxo *Dual Pricing* case,[7] some cracks had already begun to appear – in the form of *dicta* in the *Bayer Adalat* case,[8] which questioned both the efficacy and the legitimacy of the Commission's use of parallel trade to achieve a single market for pharmaceutical products and more pronouncedly

---

[4] The goal of market integration has a uniquely high profile in EC competition policy. The EC Treaty, in its first substantive clause (Article 2), sets out the goal of a 'common market' and Article 3 sets out the activities necessary to attain this, including 'the free movement of goods, persons, services and capital'. Article 4 incorporates 'the principle of an open market economy with free competition'. The Community Courts normally interpret all other articles in the Treaty, including Article 81 and Article 82, in a teleological way, which is to say in the context of the overall goals of the Treaty.

[5] See, most recently, C 267–268/95 *Merck* v *Primecrown* [1996] E.C.R. I-6285; [1997] 1 C.M.L.R. 83. In *Primecrown* the Court did acknowledge that the imposition of price controls was a factor that may in certain conditions distort trade between Member States but then went on to observe that 'it is well settled that distortions caused by different price legislations in a Member State must be remedied by measures taken by the Community authorities and not the adoption by another Member State of measures incompatible with the rules on free movement'. See para. 47.

[6] See, for example, *NV IAZ International Belgium* v *Commission*, Joined Cases 96–102, 104–105, 108, 110/82 [1983] ECR 3369, at paras. 24, 25 and 27, and *Sandoz* v *Commission* Case 277/87 [1990] ECR I-45, where the Court of First Instance upheld the Commission's decision (Decision 87/409/EEC in Case IV/31.741 [1987] O.J. L 222 10.8, p. 28) prohibiting a company's practice that displayed the words 'export prohibited' on its sales invoices. More recently, in *Volkswagen* v *Commission*, Case T-62/98 [2000] ECR II-2707 (see paras. 89 and 178), the Court of First Instance upheld the Commission's decision which had classified various measures making parallel imports more difficult (without excluding them altogether) as restrictions 'by object'.

[7] Case IV/36.957/F3 *GlaxoWellcome* (notification), IV/ 36.997/F3 *Aseprofar and Fedifar* (complaint), IV/37.121/F3 *Spain Pharma* (complaint), IV/37.138/F3 *BAI* (complaint), IV/37.380/F3 *EAEPC* (complaint) [2001] O.J. L302/1.

[8] Case T 41/96 *Bayer* v *Commission* [2000] ECR II-3383 and C 2–3/01 P *Bundesverband der Arzneimittel-Importeure eV* v *Commission* [2004] O.J. C 59/02. 'Dicta' refers to parts of a judicial opinion that either extend beyond the facts of the case in hand or are not necessary to resolve the legal issue before the court and therefore carry less authority in terms of precedent.

in the Advocate General's opinion in the *Sifait* case, which went further in arguing both that pharmaceutical companies had a legitimate interest in impeding parallel trade and that parallel trade might not be welfare enhancing.[9]

Section 2 sets out the essential details of the case. Section 3 provides a legal and economic analysis of the issues it raises and section 4 concludes.

2. The Glaxo *Dual Pricing* case

2.1 Glaxo-Wellcome's Spanish pricing agreement

On 6 March 1998, prior to the *Adalat* judgment, GlaxoSmithKline Beecham's (GSK) predecessor, Glaxo Wellcome plc (GW), notified its general sales conditions for Spain to the European Commission, in a request for a negative clearance declaring Article 81(1) inapplicable and, in the alternative, an exemption under Article 81(3).[10] These conditions, which applied to eighty-two medicines intended for sale to Spanish wholesalers, established two different price lists: Clause 4a prices applied to medicines to be resold for consumption in Spain pursuant to the Spanish reimbursement scheme and at the prices set by the Spanish government under Spanish law[11] in Spain, whereas Clause 4b prices were to apply for products that were sold outside of Spain and which, therefore, were not covered by the relevant Spanish price legislation. The Clause 4b products were priced at the prices that GW had requested in its original application for marketing authorisation in Spain (but which the Spanish authorities had determined should be reduced).

The GW notification was conceived of and brought as a test case designed to contest the economic analysis (or lack thereof) underlying the Commission's long-standing commitment to protecting parallel trade in prescription medicines as a means of furthering the single market. GW argued

---

[9] Case C-53/03 *SIFAIT v GlaxoSmithKline AEBE and GlaxoSmithKline plc* [2003] O.J. C 101/18. An Advocate General's report provides an influential independent opinion for ECJ judges but is not binding on them.

[10] Negative clearance would be a statement by the Commission that, having examined the facts, it found no grounds to take action; and exemption would be a finding that the practice was good for consumers, for example because it results in more rapid technical progress and such benefits are expected to outweigh any negative effect of higher price.

[11] The maximum wholesale price of medicines reimbursed by the Spanish sickness insurance scheme is determined by the Spanish Ministry of Health and Consumption and the *Comisión Interministerial de Precios de los Medicamentos* (Interministerial Commission on the Prices of Medicines). See Spanish Law 25/1990 and Royal Decree 271/1990.

in its notification that Article 81(1) did not apply because, *inter alia*, the pricing system was intended only to eliminate a distortion caused by inconsistent Member State price regulation. In its request for exemption under Article 81(3), GW furthermore argued that the Commission's policy of encouraging parallel trade in prescription medicines harmed rather than protected consumer welfare, thus challenging on economic grounds the foundations of the Commission's approach to parallel trade and market integration. In support of its arguments, GW introduced two economic studies, one on the need for a new approach to parallel imports and the other on the adverse effects of parallel imports on consumer welfare. An additional study refining these two initial studies was introduced during the course of the Commission's proceeding.[12]

2.2 The Commission's decision

Not surprisingly, the Commission did not evidence any willingness to abandon its traditional approach condemning interference with parallel trade as inconsistent with the single market. Thus in its Decision issued dated 8 May 2001, the Commission found that Article 81 applied to the notified sales conditions and held that they did not merit exemption.

The Commission's analysis under Article 81(1) was largely based on its determination, supported by its prior administrative practice and Court case law, that the notified sales conditions constituted a prohibited restriction 'by object'.[13] Because Clause 4 had much the same effect as an export ban or a prohibited dual pricing system, the Commission stated that there was no need to examine its anticompetitive effects nor, in principle, could it qualify for exemption.[14] The Decision did, however, summarily conclude in an analysis limited to a single paragraph that the Clause 4b prices also had the effect of restricting competition because they made parallel trade 'economically uninteresting' for a significant number of products covered by the notified agreement.

In refusing the exemption under Article 81(3), the Commission applied a rather summary analysis based in part on its doubts that a system that was

---

[12]   'Pharmaceutical Pricing in the EU – A Note in Response to the European Commission's Statement of Objections concerning Glaxo-Wellcome's Spanish Pricing Agreements' by Frontier Economics; 'The Effects of Parallel Imports on Social Welfare I: Critique' by Frontier Economics; 'The Effects of Parallel Imports on Social Welfare II: Critique' by P. Rey.

[13]   In other words it was the direct intention of the agreement (and not just its incidental effect) that parallel trade should be impaired.

[14]   Decision at paras. 118, 119, 124 and 125.

designed to and did in fact restrict parallel trade could ever qualify for exemption.[15] Thus it disputed that there was a direct link between parallel trade and any negative effect on R&D[16] and disputed the magnitude of whatever indirect effect there was.[17] It also rejected GW's argument that parallel trade has a disruptive effect on distribution[18] and that Clause 4 thus benefited consumers.[19] The Commission argued instead that no direct link had been established between parallel trade and a decrease in R&D,[20] that parallel trade benefited consumers by ensuring a second source of supply[21] and that consumers benefited from parallel trade under the various national reimbursement systems,[22] some of which were structured to encourage parallel trade.[23]

Again unsurprisingly, GSK appealed the Commission's decision on 23 July 2001 to the Court of First Instance, which issued its judgment on 27 September 2006.[24]

2.3 The judgment of the Court of First Instance

The Court's judgment annulled the decision insofar as the latter had (i) found that notified agreement restricted Article 81(1) by object and (ii) rejected the application for exemption under Article 81(3). However, the Court did uphold the Commission's finding that the notified agreement had had a restrictive effect within the meaning of Article 81(1). The Court further ordered the Commission to reconsider the application for exemption if GSK so desired.

The Court's judgment is groundbreaking for several reasons.[25] First, the Court established that it was necessary to consider the actual impact of parallel trade on consumer welfare and rejected the view that interference with parallel trade could be summarily condemned solely on the doctrinal grounds that it was incompatible with the single market. The Court moreover did so by placing consumer welfare at the heart of its analysis under Articles 81(1) and 81(3), making it the operative and decisive element for both assessments.

---

[15] Decision at para. 124; yet in para. 153 the Commission acknowledged that 'there is in principle no restriction which cannot be exempted under Article 81(3)'.
[16] Decision at paras. 155–161.   [17] Decision at paras. 162–169.   [18] Decision at paras. 170–176.
[19] Decision at paras. 177–186.   [20] Decision at para. 179.   [21] Decision at para. 183.
[22] Decision at para. 184.   [23] Decision at para. 185.
[24] Case T 168/01, *GlaxoSmithKline Services Unlimited* v *Commission* 27 September 2006. The CFI's judgment has been appealed by the Commission, GSK and the intervenors in Case T 168/01, EAEPC, *Bundesverband der Arzneimittel-Importeure eV* and *Aseprofar.*
[25] This may not be the end of the story as the CFI's judgment has been appealed by the Commission, GSK and the intervenors in Case T 168/01, EAEPC, *Bundesverband der Arzneimittel-Importeure eV* and *Aseprofar (Association of Spanish Exporters of Pharmaceuticals).*

Second, the Court emphasised the relevance of the regulatory framework applicable to the pharmaceutical industry in its analysis of the impact of parallel trade on consumer welfare under both Articles 81(1) and 81(3). In essence, it asserted that traditional market analyses could not be merely transposed to heavily regulated markets such as those of prescription medicines, which required instead a specific assessment of their functioning. Whilst this was thoroughly consistent with prior decisional practice,[26] the Court's application had far-reaching effects in its appreciation of a variety of issues, including its approach to whether the notified agreements amounted to illegal price discrimination.

Third, the Court asked the Commission to take into proper consideration the economic facts and arguments put forward by the parties, even when presented against a long-standing *per se* approach such as the Commission's uninterrupted support of parallel trade.

Incidentally, the Court also appeared to suggest that the relevant market for a case involving parallel trade in pharmaceutical products was comprised of the totality of such products that could be subject to arbitrage, thus clearly departing from prior approaches to market definition in cases involving pharmaceutical products under which markets had been defined on the basis of therapeutic application as defined in the ATC system of classification.[27]

These points, and the Court's annulment of that part of the Commission's decision refusing an exemption, are considered in greater detail below.

3. Analysis

3.1 The position of the Court

Consumer welfare

The Court refused to give any special status to parallel trade as an agent of supposed market integration. Rather, it asserted that, although 'parallel trade must be given a certain protection', this is the case only insofar as 'it gives final consumers the advantages of effective competition in terms of supply or price'.[28] The Court then added:

---

[26] For example, the *Night Services* case.

[27] The Anatomical Therapeutic Chemical classification system allocates drugs into different groups according to the organ or system on which they act and their chemical, pharmacological and therapeutic properties. Drugs are classified at five different levels, with level 3 most commonly used for competition analysis.

[28] Judgment at para. 121.

Consequently, while it is accepted that an agreement intended to limit parallel trade must in principle be considered to have as its object the restriction of competition, that applies only in so far as the agreement may be presumed to deprive final consumers of those advantages.

The Court therefore rejected the Commission's traditional, doctrinal stance that any measures restricting parallel trade must be automatically condemned as inimical to the single market. In effect, the Court replaced this *per se* approach with *a rule of reason* designed to examine the actual effects of parallel trade on *consumer welfare* in the relevant economic context.[29] Applying this rule of reason thus requires taking into consideration the environment in which the market operates; in the case of prescription medicines, this calls in particular for an analysis of the regulatory framework that contributes to shape the industry and determine the roles of the various actors.

Article 81(1)

In its notification and during the administrative procedure before the Commission, GSK stressed the importance of the fact that pharmaceutical prices were regulated by the state and that the state was ultimately the 'payer'.[30] The Court agreed with the relevance of the regulatory framework and noted: 'At no point does the Commission examine the specific and essential characteristic of the sector which relates to the fact that the prices of the products in question, which are subject to control by the Member States, which fix them directly or indirectly at what they deem to be the appropriate level, are determined at structurally different levels in the Community and, unlike the prices of other consumer goods, are in any event to a significant degree shielded from the free play of supply and demand.'[31] According to the Court, the existence of the regulatory framework means that 'it cannot be presumed that a parallel trade has an impact on the prices charged to the final consumers of medicines reimbursed by the national sickness insurance scheme and this confers on them an appreciable advantage analogous to that which it would confer if those prices were determined by the play of supply and demand'.

---

[29] The Court again expressly referred to a consumer welfare standard when it further noted at para. 122 that, given the legal and economic context in which the notified agreement operated, it was possible that wholesalers 'may keep the advantage in terms of price which parallel trade may entail, in which case the advantage will not be passed on to final consumers'.

[30] In the sense that it is the taxpayer, rather than the patient, that pays for most of the price of prescription medicines.

[31] Judgment at para. 133.

The Court's insistence on the need to take the regulatory framework into account does not introduce any new principle into Community law, which has long recognised that the application of competition rules must take into account the specifics of the sector concerned. However, this insistence had here significant novel consequences for assessing whether a notified agreement constitutes a restriction by object. While the Commission's finding that Clause 4b restricted competition by object was consistent with the approach adopted by both the Commission and the Court in cases involving such products as automobiles and tennis balls, in this case the Court found that the Commission's analyses could not be upheld since, prices being regulated anyway, it could not be presumed that parallel trade necessarily translates into lower prices.[32] Thus, the Court rejected an automatic *per se*, 'black-list' approach for determining whether Clause 4 constituted a restriction by object and asked instead to assess the effects of the provision, given the specific regulatory environment shaping the market for prescription medicines.

When assessing these effects, the Court however agreed with the Commission that the notified pricing measures did have the effect of restricting competition and of reducing 'the welfare of final consumers by preventing them from taking advantage, in the form of a reduction in prices and costs, of the participation by Spanish wholesalers in intrabrand competition on the markets of destination of the parallel trade originating in Spain'.[33]

Incidentally, the Court departed from the Commission's analysis in two dimensions. First, it considered that the relevant market might possibly be broader than argued by the Commission. Noting that parallel traders are primarily driven by the arbitrage possibilities arising out of the difference between prices in countries of origin and destination, rather than by the therapeutic indication of the medicines, the Court concluded that 'it was not manifestly incorrect to accept that all the medicines reimbursed by the Spanish sickness insurance scheme which are capable of being sold at a profit owing to the price differential between Spain and the Member State of

---

[32] See Judgment at para. 147: 'As the prices of the medicines concerned are to a large extent shielded from the free play of supply and demand owing to the applicable regulations and are controlled by the public authorities, it cannot be taken for granted at the outset that parallel trade tends to reduce those prices and thus to increase the welfare of final consumers. An analysis of the terms of Clause 4 of the General Sales Conditions does not permit the presumption that that provision, which seeks to limit parallel trade, thus tends to diminish the welfare of final consumers. In this largely unprecedented situation, it cannot be inferred merely from a reasoning of the terms of that agreement, in its context, that the agreement is restrictive of competition, and it is therefore necessary to consider the effects of the agreement if only to ascertain what the regulatory authority was able to apprehend on the basis of such a reading.'

[33] Judgment at para. 182.

destination constitute a product market'.[34] Second, the Court determined that whilst it was incontestable that GSK imposed 'unequal conditions' on Spanish wholesalers depending on where they resold the products in question, it had not been established that sales in Spain and sales outside of Spain constituted 'equivalent transactions' as would be required for the prohibition on discrimination set forth in Article 81(1)(d) to apply.[35]

Article 81(3)

In its request for exemption GSK had in essence argued that parallel trade harmed consumers by (i) interfering with efficient distribution by causing product shortages in source countries, in addition to delaying the initial introduction of innovative products in such countries, and (ii) interfering with governmental policy decisions as to the appropriate degree to which R&D should be encouraged, thereby ultimately reducing prices and the level of R&D in high-priced countries to the detriment of consumers in both high- and low-priced countries. This last argument was supported by an empirical submission on how and why pharmaceutical R&D is financed out of the revenues and profits of pharmaceutical companies and a more theoretical analysis explaining why the dynamic pricing effects of parallel trade would reduce overall consumer welfare (see below).[36]

In annulling the Commission's refusal to grant an exemption, the Court noted that it was applying the appropriate standard of judicial review in cases involving a complex economic assessment. Consistent with this approach, the Court stated that it would not substitute its own economic assessment for that of the Commission but, rather, would limit its analysis to assessing 'whether the facts have been accurately stated, whether there has been any manifest error of appraisal and whether the legal consequences deduced from those facts were accurate'.[37]

Applying this test the Court nevertheless came to the view that the factual arguments and evidence submitted by GSK in support of its claim for an

---

[34] See Judgment at para. 159.

[35] See Judgment at paras. 176–179. In particular, the Court recalled that Community law does not prevent even a dominant firm from charging different prices in different Member States when this is justified by variations in conditions of marketing and the intensity of the competition in the different Member States and concluded that it could not rule out that 'GSK applies different prices because different markets exist and not so that different markets will exist'.

[36] See P. Rey, 'Addendum to the note on 'The Adverse Effects of Parallel Imports on Consumer Welfare'', which builds on the previous note and on a more formal analysis, 'The Impact of Parallel Imports on Prescription Medicines', mimeo (2003), University of Toulouse.

[37] Judgment at para. 241.

exemption appeared 'to be relevant and credible, having regard to their content ... which is itself corroborated on a number of significant aspects by documents originating with the Commission'.[38] In particular, the Court cites the Commission in its own Communication on parallel trade in the pharmaceutical industry[39] and notes that in this Communication the Commission had itself concluded *inter alia* that:

- the pharmaceutical industry is characterised by intense competition in R&D;
- the pharmaceutical industry mainly relies on its own profits to finance its investments in R&D;
- the European pharmaceutical industry has been declining in competitiveness as a result of higher profitability in the US;
- Member States differ significantly as to per capita income and wealth and health care systems, with a positive link between healthcare expenditure and income;
- important differences in Member State prices are traceable to governmental price controls;
- it would be extremely difficult to establish a single price for the Community as low prices which might benefit immediate healthcare budgetary objectives would provoke a steady diminution of R&D investment, whereas high prices would reduce access to consumers and payers in those countries where high prices could not be afforded; and
- pharmaceutical companies charge different prices to take account of the different ability to pay.[40]

Given the credibility of these arguments and evidence that in the pharmaceutical sector the transfer of wealth from producers to intermediaries as a result of parallel trade 'does not bring any significant added value to the final consumer', the Court concluded that the Commission's decision rejecting the request for exemption was

viitated by a failure to carry out a proper examination ... *because* ... it did not validly take into account all the factual arguments and the evidence pertinently submitted by GSK, did not refute certain of those arguments even though they were sufficiently relevant and substantiated to require a response, and did not substantiate to the requisite legal standard its conclusions ... *that GSK had failed to prove that* ... parallel

---

[38] Judgment at para. 263.   [39] See COM (1998) 588 final.

[40] See Judgment at para. 264. To be sure, the Court warned that it did not mean that GSK's factual arguments were therefore 'necessarily well founded' or provided a complete and definitive picture of the Commission's position, but it did note that the Communication corroborated part of GSK's arguments and the economic analyses it had submitted, thus attesting to their reliability and credibility (see para. 265).

trade was apt to lead to a loss of efficiency by appreciably altering GSK's capacity for innovation, and second that Clause 4 of the General Sales Conditions was apt to enable a gain in efficiency to be achieved by improving innovation.[41]

It should be noted that the Court's judgment does not establish that GSK had succeeded in proving that the conditions for an exemption under Article 81(3) had been satisfied. Rather, the Court held that, in light of credible arguments to that effect, the Commission's rejection of those arguments was not sufficiently well grounded to sustain the conclusion that an exemption was not warranted.

In the end, the Court's judgment on the insufficiency of the Commission's analysis under Article 81(3) appears to be based, first, on its rejection of the 'peremptory' nature of the Commission's rejection of GSK's arguments, many of which it had itself accepted in other contexts,[42] and second, its refusal to accept the Commission's long-standing dogmatic presumption that 'an agreement providing that patented medicines reimbursed by the national sickness insurance schemes will be sold at different prices on different geographic markets, according the preferences of the final consumer who bears the cost, cannot be granted an exemption in any circumstances'.[43]

3.2 An economic perspective

Price discrimination and welfare

The economic literature has long recognised that parallel trade tends to impose uniform prices across countries, which in turn has a mixed impact on consumer welfare. In a context where different market conditions would lead to the emergence of different prices, imposing uniform prices across countries is likely to lead to some intermediate price. As a result, consumers who would have been confronted with the highest prices benefit from the imposition of price uniformity, but those consumers who would have enjoyed low prices instead suffer from the imposition of uniform prices.

Imposing uniform pricing conditions thus appears to have an ambiguous impact on consumers and total welfare (i.e. consumer surplus plus profits). A standard result for (third-degree) price discrimination is that if demand in each market is linear and costs are constant, then a sufficient condition for uniform pricing to enhance total welfare is that output does not rise. However, this base case should not be generalised to presume that price discrimination

---

[41] Judgment at para. 303.   [42] See Judgment at paras. 301 and 265.   [43] Judgment at para. 266.

is always harmful. Many works have confirmed this ambiguity.[44] For example, Varian (1985) has shown that, when returns to scale are constant,[45] imposing uniform prices results in a loss of total welfare, defined as the sum of consumer surplus and profits; it leads to a reduction in aggregate sales, weighted by the margins realised in each market. Examples where those sufficient conditions are satisfied have also been provided, confirming the ambiguity, from a welfare standpoint, of imposing price uniformity. While no general conclusion is possible without studying market characteristics more closely, some guidelines can, however, be provided. For example, Malueg and Schwartz (1994) have shown that the price uniformity imposed by parallel imports reduces total welfare when demand dispersion across markets is large.

The ambiguity remains when we consider consumer surplus alone: since some customers may gain while others may lose from the imposition of uniform prices, the overall consumer surplus may go either way. However, some guidelines can again be mentioned. For example, imposing price uniformity is likely to hurt more consumers when, in response, firms withdraw from high-elasticity markets. To see this, consider the extreme case of a monopolist serving two countries where market conditions would lead to different prices. If the firm must adopt a uniform price, it can in fact choose between two strategies: supplying both countries at some intermediate price or withdrawing from the low-price country[46] and supplying consumers from the other country at the same high price as before. Adopting the latter policy is particularly likely when the price differential is large, since supplying both markets would then involve a substantial loss of profitability in the high-price country. Whenever the firm chooses to withdraw from the low-price market, no consumer benefits from the imposition of uniform prices: consumers from the high-price country are offered the same price as before, while in the other country consumers have less choice than before and thus again incur a loss of surplus. Interpreting the lack of access to a product as a 'prohibitive' price for that product, imposing 'price uniformity' then leads in fact to even wider price dispersion, since prices that were previously set at affordable levels jump to unreasonable ones. Malueg and Schwartz generalise this argument to the case

---

[44] See Tirole (1988) (and more specifically section 3.2 on multi-market price discrimination) for an introduction to the literature, and Phlips (1983) and Varian (1989) for more detailed reviews. See Varian (1985).

[45] Hausman and Mackie-Mason (1988) provide general conditions under which price uniformity is welfare-reducing when there are increasing returns to scale. See Malueg and Schwartz (1994).

[46] 'Withdrawing' may take several forms in practice. It may, for example, consist in delaying the introduction of a new product.

of numerous markets and show that under price uniformity the firm has indeed an incentive to withdraw from many markets when demand varies substantially across them.

Even when some customers benefit from the imposition of uniform prices, assessing the value of price uniformity for 'consumers' is not a straightforward exercise and requires the assessment of trade-offs between the losses for some customers and the benefits to others. Two difficulties arise here. First, one has to define the principles used to achieve this trade-off. Second, one has to evaluate the trade-off in each particular instance, since otherwise ambiguity prevails: for example, focusing on total consumer surplus, there is no general prediction as to whether this aggregate surplus increases or decreases with uniform prices, so that a specific investigation is required.

Furthermore, merely adding up consumer surplus across countries ignores distributional concerns. For example, an equity concern might lead us to place a higher weight on the poorest countries, which are likely to be the ones where prices would be lowest in the absence of non-discriminatory rules. Thus, equity concerns would lead to a greater weight being placed on precisely those consumers who, being poorer, benefit most from non-uniform prices. As a result, equity concerns would make price diversity more desirable. This is particularly true when imposing uniform prices would lead firms to withdraw precisely from the poorest countries.

Non-price factors including R&D incentives

The foregoing analysis focused on prices, but consumers are often interested in other aspects such as quality, services, innovation and so forth, and different consumers may have different preferences over these other factors. For example, some consumers may be willing to pay more in exchange for higher quality, while other consumers may prefer a low-price, low-quality product. Similarly, some consumers may be willing to trade off higher prices against higher levels of R&D and the corresponding promise of better products for the future. If firms can charge different prices for different qualities, the previous price analysis still applies. However, if some dimensions of quality or services related to the product are difficult to identify in practice, then an additional concern arises, since imposing uniformity on prices may de facto impose some uniformity on other dimensions (such as quality) as well. For pharmaceutical products, for example, R&D is a key factor and some governments appear willing to accept higher prices in order to give higher incentives for R&D, so as to improve the development of new drugs. To the extent that the governments cannot directly compensate pharmaceutical companies for the additional R&D efforts that they may require (and indeed such compensations are subject to serious limitations), imposing uniform prices also imposes a uniformity of incentives to R&D and may thus generate inefficiencies and adverse effects on consumer surplus.

Indeed, in each country, national health authorities face a trade-off between budget concerns, which calls for setting low reimbursement prices, and the development of new treatments that will contribute to improve health conditions in the future, which calls for accepting higher prices. When analysing this trade-off, each government takes into consideration the specific economic and political environments it faces, as well as its own policy priorities; as a result, different countries are likely to adopt different solutions to this trade-off. In this context, parallel trade amounts de facto to imposing the policy choices of the most price-oriented countries on the other countries, more prone to contribute to R&D. This therefore imposes a restraint on the latter countries, which tends to reduce overall (present and future) consumer welfare in these countries, but it also harms the former countries, which do not benefit as much as before from the other countries' willingness to contribute to R&D. Therefore, the impact of parallel trade in this particular context differs significantly from the standard analysis for traditional marketed goods and services recalled above. In standard contexts, some consumers or consumer groups may lose while others may gain, since parallel trade would induce firms to adopt more uniform prices at some intermediate level in the range that would otherwise prevail, thus resulting in lower prices in some countries but higher prices in other countries. Here in contrast, parallel trade adversely affects all countries, by restricting the policy choices of those that would be most willing to contribute to R&D. Thus, the specificity of the regulatory environment in which the market for prescription medicines operates may call for a significant departure from the traditional attitude towards parallel trade.

This argument was presented by GSK in the proceedings but did not receive much attention by the Commission, which disputed any significant link between prices and R&D efforts. The Court of First Instance was, however, more receptive and while it noted that the empirical relevance remained to be assessed, it considered that the Commission had the duty to review carefully the economic evidence produced to sustain the argument. One may wonder whether these considerations are not also relevant for the application of Article 81(1) as well as Article 81(3) at least to the extent that it can be argued that an inherently pro-competitive agreement should not be deemed to be restrictive in the first place. However, at the very least, the Court made clear that the Commission could not ignore, for the sake of overriding principles, the economic facts and reasoning presented before it. Instead, it must assess the impact of pricing practices in the light of the economic reality of the markets concerned.

4. Concluding remarks

This case is interesting for several reasons. The Commission and the European Courts have a long history of protecting if not promoting parallel trade as a tool for market integration. This led to a *per se* approach, with the result that any restriction on parallel imports was automatically blacklisted as a restriction by object, unlikely ever to be exempted from legal prohibition under Article 81(3).[47] The Commission stuck to that approach in this particular instance, and its decision provides only a rather cursory review of the economic context at case. In contrast, the Court of First Instance departed from the *per se* approach. It placed consumers, rather than any other overriding principle, at the centre of the objectives of competition rules; thus, any application of these competition rules must be driven by the impact on consumers of the practices under review. Given the specificity of the markets for prescription medicines, where the 'customers', i.e. the national governments, directly or indirectly regulate the prices they are willing to pay, the Court then considered that it could not be *presumed* that restricting parallel imports impeded competition in a way that would harm consumers. In legal terms, it did not constitute a restriction *by object*, since prices were anyway regulated. And while the CFI followed the Commission's decision in deciding that GSK's provisions had a restrictive *effect* on competition, it also criticised the Commission's lack of analysis of the economic reality of the markets, as well as the lack of attention paid to the economic facts and reasoning presented by the parties. Although the Court emphasised that its judgment was not to be interpreted as a general openness towards restrictions on parallel trade, it did challenge the automatic approach that was prevailing until then. It pushed instead for a consideration of the actual economic effects of the provisions on consumers. We now await the position of the Court of Justice.

---

[47] In particular, parallel imports restrictions is one of the two provisions (together with resale price maintenance) that remained blacklisted in the guidelines on vertical restraints that the Commission adopted, following the review of its application of Article 81 to vertical agreements.

C

Mergers

Introduction

Firms propose mergers for many different reasons. For horizontal mergers they may be buying technology or customers in anticipation of synergies or economies of scale. For vertical mergers they may see advantages in coordinating activities and reducing transaction costs. For conglomerate mergers, they may expect economies of scope, perhaps in marketing a product range. Where technologies are evolving fast and in difficult-to-anticipate directions, they may even view mergers as an insurance policy or a way to experiment with new ideas. All these can be claimed as efficiency motives. Mergers are also a way to change corporate control. The threat of takeover is a discipline against an ineffective management team. The threat does not always work and some mergers are proposed by managers seeking personal aggrandisement at the expense of shareholders. Other mergers are a way for a family firm to capitalise on its wealth creation when there is no natural successor. A further motive, of course, is the pursuit of market power. Competition policy is important even if this is not the object of the merger – efficiency or corporate control motives may still result in mergers that have the effect of impeding competition.[1]

The EC Merger Regulation (ECMR) was first implemented in 1990.[2] The original test for a merger was that it would not be allowed if it created or strengthened a dominant position. Notice that it is not the current level of competition that needs to be assessed, but the change in competition that

---

[1] Empirically, we find that many mergers turn out to disappoint shareholders. This is not a concern for competition policy. Systematically poor selection of mergers by senior managers would suggest that corporate governance needs reform. It is not the role of a competition authority to act as a management consultancy. More relevant for competition policy is that firms often have no clear idea of specific efficiencies they are hoping to achieve and are rarely able to provide reasonable evidence that they will be achieved.

[2] See Lyons (2008) for an economic assessment of EC merger control.

would result from the merger. This requires the formation of an expectation of future competition to be compared with a counterfactual of what would happen in the absence of the merger. Merger appraisal is therefore subtly different from Article 81 and 82 investigations which appraise observed competition.[3] The wording of the test was reformed in 2004, replacing the original dominance test with the prohibition of mergers which would be a significant impediment to effective competition. It is not necessary to go into the nuances. Suffice it to say that this was not a huge change in merger appraisal but was a definite nudge towards more explicit analysis of economic effects.[4] Each of the mergers in this book pre-dates 2004 and some undoubtedly contributed to the climate for reform. It is sometimes argued that merger regulation need not be strict because firms that ex post exploit their market position can be investigated under Article 82. However, this is a dangerous assumption because Article 82 is almost never used to address exploitative pricing and is cumbersome to apply.

The economic analysis of mergers depends fundamentally on the range of businesses operated by each firm. Horizontal mergers between firms operating similar businesses raise most direct concern because they eliminate a direct competitor. This can affect two alternative types of pricing behaviour. First, the merger may enhance a firm's ability unilaterally to raise price. Second, it may enhance the ability for firms across the market to coordinate their pricing even without directly agreeing prices or exchanging information. Vertical and conglomerate aspects of a merger raise quite different concerns, in particular the ability to impede the effectiveness of rivals to compete. The six mergers considered in this part of the book are grouped in pairs according to these three categories of potential economic effect.

The first two chapters provide direct estimates of unilateral effects for horizontal mergers between firms with overlapping ranges of differentiated products. In such cases, market shares can be misleading. For example, the combination of two 20 per cent market shares may be either competitively innocuous (e.g. if consumers do not see the overlapping product ranges of the merging firms as effective substitutes) or competitively harmful (e.g. if remaining independent products are seen by customers as ineffective substitutes). It is therefore important to understand the pattern of substitutability between products (i.e. cross-elasticities of demand). Econometric methods use hard evidence

---

[3] Nevertheless, proper appraisal of harm and remedy in Articles 81 (other than cartels) and 82 does require an understanding of the counterfactual of competition in the absence of a business agreement or practice.
[4] As already discussed in the introductory chapter, 2004 saw a considerable number of other reforms, including horizontal merger guidelines. The non-horizontal merger guidelines followed in 2007.

to achieve this. The first step is to specify a demand model that captures the way people choose between alternative products (e.g. logit demand system). Statistical techniques can be applied to estimate this system from data on past prices and consumer purchases and so calculate cross-elasticities. An advantage of this approach is that it does not require a black-and-white market definition to rule some products into the market and others out. Instead, it estimates the shades of grey (i.e. cross-elasticities). The estimates can then be used in conjunction with a model of pricing behaviour to simulate (i.e. predict) the impact of a proposed merger.[5] The same techniques can be applied to apparently very different markets such as insurance or beer.

A logit model of consumer choice between non-life insurance companies is estimated by Gollier and Ivaldi to understand how consumers respond to price differences between different firms. Their work was used to advise a national competition authority about a proposed merger. Identities have been suppressed to preserve commercial confidentiality. The authors were working under severe pressure of time in a real merger situation, so this case illustrates what can be achieved in practice. Having used the limited amount of available data to estimate own-price elasticities, cross-elasticities and cost functions, the authors fed these parameters into a merger simulation. Assuming firms adopt unilateral pricing, they were able to estimate expected post-merger price changes. They predict small and statistically insignificant long-run price rises. Since consumers need to recognise and act on price changes, the authors conclude that the merger should be allowed subject to a remedy of better information for customers about price offers.

Slade is much less sanguine about the ability of simulation techniques to estimate unilateral effects. She compares a range of available techniques. Relatively simple demand models (e.g. logit) are attractive because they can be implemented in a short period of time and can be understood by non-experts. However, she argues that their predictions are often misleading. Complex models are more reliable but they require more time to implement and are less transparent (e.g. the econometrician has to make some subtle judgements). She illustrates the use of merger simulations and the sensitivity of predictions to modelling choices with an application to mergers in the UK brewing industry. Slade's estimates were not done under the pressure of an investigation and they include work that would have been too time-consuming to achieve during a live

---

[5] With much less econometric sophistication Davies and Lyons (2007) apply a much simplified form of merger simulation to be used as an indicator of possible effects (rather than as potentially decisive evidence). They provide estimates for six paper and pharmaceuticals mergers previously investigated by the EC.

case. She assesses the merger between S&N and Courage, which was allowed by the UK authorities without horizontal remedy, and the proposed merger between Bass and Carlsberg–Tetley, which was eventually blocked. She finds substantial differences in the estimated effects of each depending on the specification of the econometric demand model. She concludes that merger simulations should not be decisive but they should be used to focus analysis away from crude market shares and towards the degree of brand substitutability.

The next two chapters address a different type of price concern. This is that the merger might facilitate the coordination of prices. For our purposes, we can consider tacit collusion, collective dominance and coordinated effects as equivalent terms for when firms observe each other's behaviour and eschew profitable price cuts in the short run with a view to maintaining long-term high prices.[6] In addition to legal considerations, coordinated effects differ from an explicit cartel because it is much more difficult to reach an implicit agreement over price, let alone monitor it, without explicit communication. Although unilateral effects is the main line of argument in most European merger cases, confidence in arguing a collective dominance theory of harm rose through the 1990s until the 2002 Airtours appeal, which is the subject of one of our case studies. There are important differences in the analysis of coordinated compared with unilateral effects. In particular, it places a greater burden on understanding the behaviour of all major firms in the market, not just the merging parties. Coordination is more likely when market shares are fairly symmetric because this balances the incentives to undercut and to respond to rivals undercutting. It appears to be very difficult if there are more than two or three major firms in the market. The presence of a competitive 'maverick' with an aggressive business strategy can also disrupt coordination.

In 1999, the EC prohibited the merger of two package holiday operators, Airtours and First Choice, on the grounds of collective dominance. The merger would have reduced the number of major competitors from four to three. This decision turned out to be a landmark case for the application of economics in competition cases. The EC decision was appealed and the appeal upheld. In rejecting the EC reasoning, the CFI made explicit reference to the game theoretic underpinnings of the theory of tacit collusion to provide what have become known as the Airtours Criteria. These set out three conditions necessary for coordinated effects to be feasible: sufficient price transparency for rivals to know

---

[6] Tacit collusion is the traditional term used by economists. Collective dominance was the term used by the EC prior to the 2004 ECMR revision, since when 'coordinated effects' has been used. The reasons behind the different terminology are legal more than economic.

when one is cutting price, a credible response ('punishment') by other firms to exert a discipline on those who deviate from the collusion and the absence of 'external' constraints in the form of new or smaller firms expanding output in response to higher prices by the market leaders or of consumers switching to other products. Garces-Tolon, Neven and Seabright (two of whom advised on opposite sides in the appeal) take the opportunity to review the academic literature in order to clarify how the conditions favouring tacit collusion and the realistic expectation of collusive behaviour can each be established. They go on to assess the impact of the CFI decision and the extent to which the Court's criteria provide a reliable guide for the analysis of other markets.

A sequence of mergers in the newsprint and magazine paper industry had increased market concentration in the 1990s. There were also allegations of cartel activity. It is, perhaps, not surprising that the EC was highly suspicious of the proposed UPM Kymmene/Norske Skog/Haindl merger. Combined market shares for these relatively homogeneous products were insufficient to suggest that the merger would result in significant unilateral effects, but the merger would eliminate a potentially disruptive maverick in Haindl and the EC concern was for coordinated effects. However, the EC theory of harm was not conventional. The lack of price transparency in individually negotiated contracts meant price coordination was not very plausible. Instead, the EC considered the likelihood that firms would jointly limit capacity expansion in order to keep prices high. Kühn and Van Reenen argue that the irreversibility of investment makes capacity coordination highly unlikely. They go on to show that their theory of competitive behaviour was more consistent with the empirical evidence than was the EC hypothesis. After a thorough Phase II investigation, the EC agreed and cleared the merger without need for remedy.

Most mergers with vertical or conglomerate dimensions also have an element of horizontal overlap and the multiplicity of effects often makes them complex to analyse. The last two cases fall into this category, though one focuses on vertical effects and the other on conglomerate effects. The latter has become another important test case. Like for agreements, vertical and conglomerate effects in mergers should start from a different presumption to horizontal mergers because they are more likely to be benign. Such cases can also put a competition authority under different pressures because the main theory of harm is that rivals will be foreclosed. This can lead to fierce lobbying against the merger by rivals who may be motivated by either genuine fear of anticompetitive foreclosure or commercial concern about facing a more competitive rival. The role of economics is to identify which should be the true concern.

The merger of Neste Oy and IVO brought together the national monopoly in gas distribution with the largest supplier of electricity in Finland. Both firms were largely owned by the Finnish state and the merger was encouraged by the Finnish Ministry of Trade and Industry to create a 'national champion' in anticipation of the opening of the international electricity market. The merger had horizontal, vertical and conglomerate dimensions. Although gas and electricity are substitutes for some purposes, the main concern in this case was in vertical issues because gas is a significant element in the fuel mix for electricity generation. Neste owned the pipelines and all Finland's natural gas was imported from Russia in a joint venture owned 75 per cent by Neste and 25 per cent by Gazprom. Much hinged on the expected future evolution of the market. At the time, 1998, the form of electricity regulation was still being decided and there was only light regulation of gas. Increasing transmission capacity was planned for electricity between the Nordic countries and this was expected to remove IVO's dominance in Finland. Swedish generators were expected to invest in gas-powered plant in Finland near the Russian border in order to diversify their fuel sources. However, Stenbacka argues that the merged entity would be well placed to create entry barriers through its investment and pricing policies. He also argues that there would be no synergies that could not be reaped by appropriate contracts short of joint ownership. The EC decided the merger would impede competition but that a satisfactory remedy was to reduce state ownership of the joint venture with Gazprom to below 50 per cent so the electricity generator would not control the gas supply of its potential rivals.

GE/Honeywell was a merger proposal between two major American firms and it was destined to create substantial transatlantic tension and debate. Because of the global reach of their sales, the merger was investigated by both US and European authorities: it passed US scrutiny subject only to a small divestment; it was prohibited on a number of grounds by the EC; and the prohibition was upheld by the CFI only on narrow grounds and with considerable criticism of other aspects of the EC decision. GE was a huge conglomerate with activities including large global market shares in a wide range of aircraft engines and power systems. It also had enormous financial strength including a business called GECAS, which bought and leased aircraft to airlines and accounted for 10 per cent of new aircraft sales. Honeywell was the global leader in avionics, engine controls and power systems, and made a limited range of aircraft engines. This was a very complex merger with horizontal, vertical and conglomerate issues in an array of markets. The horizontal effects were relatively straightforward, though the case raised tricky issues about how to measure market share (e.g. when there is a joint venture) and how meaningful is market share when airlines find maintenance easier if all their engines come from one supplier and when there is bidding for engine sales. There were also interesting vertical issues, particularly relating to engine starters and to the GECAS policy of buying only GE engines with the possibility of extending that policy to Honeywell avionics and non-avionics. However, the most controversial element of the EC decision related to conglomerate effects. In particular, the EC argued that GE engines would be bundled with Honeywell products and this would foreclose rival suppliers who did not have the product range to offer bundled discounts. Vives and Staffiero provide an economic critique of all aspects of the EC decision, with particular detail on the bundling arguments. They also observe a significant transatlantic difference, not so much in the underlying economic analysis, as in the willingness of the EU authorities to consider possible long-term consequences while the US focuses on more certain short-term effects.

C.1

Measurement of unilateral effects

12   A merger in the insurance industry: much easier to measure unilateral effects than expected

Christian Gollier and Marc Ivaldi

1. Introduction[1]

This chapter reports an econometric analysis conducted for a real case, but the identities of the firms have been suppressed for confidentiality reasons. The merger was eventually approved by the relevant national authority. The study is aimed at providing a measure of unilateral effects of the proposed acquisition of A by B on an insurance market in a national market in Europe by means of an econometric model. In other words, it provides a measure of the impact of this notified merger on the insurance price and the consumer surplus. It is expected that the preservation of competition on insurance markets makes insurance premia closer to the actuarial values of the risk transfers, therefore improving the insurability of individual risks and their diversification through mutualisation. This yields a direct welfare gain due to the risk aversion of consumers. But insurability is also favourable to economic growth by disentangling investment decisions from risk aversion. The aim of this study is to determine whether the planned merger could jeopardise those collective benefits. This requires us to examine the recent evidence on prices, costs and market shares in order to estimate how much competition would be taken out by the merger and how competition would remain from continuing rivals.

The econometric model describing the functioning of the non-life insurance markets is based on several facts which are drawn from a descriptive analysis. First, for most segments of the market, mainly those concerning the individual consumer, it is observed that market shares are correlated among different lines of insurance. Consequently, what really matters is the strategy of each insurance firm taken as a whole, rather than in narrowly defined

---

[1] The authors acted as advisers to the competition authority.

markets. Second, with respect to potential antitrust concerns, what matters is the decision of consumers to choose among insurers based on their average commercial offering; inasmuch as insurers are applying second-order price discrimination should affect the analysis marginally. Third, differentiation in this market is significant, in particular the risk level, as measured by the loss ratio, i.e. the ratio of the number of claims to the number of policies varies among insurance firms. Fourth, after having experienced a wave of mergers before 2000, this insurance industry has since experienced a more stable situation.

The model is built to account for these facts. It is based on the recent literature on the econometrics of differentiated-products markets. It comprises a logit model to represent consumer choice and to explain market shares measured in terms of the number of policies, a Bertrand–Nash pricing equation to explain the average premium and a cost function that serves to obtain a measure of marginal costs from the observation of total claims and administrative costs. The model is estimated on an annual data set over the period 2000–3. The number of policies for each firm includes all insurance contracts on personal accidents and travel, fire and other damage to property, motor vehicle liability and general liability, because these insurance segments represent 90 per cent of the market and because data associated with these segments are more reliable. Thirteen insurance groups (firms) are represented in the data set on the period of estimation.

The model serves as a tool to simulate the merger. If all customers of A and B stay with their insurers after the merger and if competitors do not react, then one predicts a very high price. It is not a sustainable situation. One reasonably expects that some customers of B and A could move to other insurance companies and that they might change their pricing strategy. Hence it is required to simulate the new equilibrium after merger, as if all customers re-compute the optimal choice of insurance. This can be achieved using our estimated own- and cross-price elasticities and marginal costs.

Section 2 provides a descriptive analysis of the industry and section 3 sets out the model and its estimation. Section 4 simulates the merger and section 5 concludes.

2. Descriptive analysis

Annual panel data are available for the period 1990–2003. They concern all insurance companies present on the market and all segments of the market. For each year, firm and segment, data is available on the following variables:

total amount of claims, administrative costs, total amount of premia and number of policies. The amount of missing data is relatively small. In addition, for some segments (employer's liability, fire and other damage to property, motor vehicle liability and general liability) the number of accidents is available.

A descriptive analysis allows us to stylise five important facts that are useful to understand the working of the insurance market.

2.1 Correlation among insurance segments and their relative weights

First we can report on the market shares of insurance groups computed in terms of number of policies for the whole market and for different segments of the market over the period 2000–3. The merger concerns the first two groups, each representing slightly more than 20 per cent of the whole market.[2] It would provide to the combined entity a much larger market share than the other groups present on the market since the largest followers have market shares around 10 per cent of the whole market.

The descriptive analysis mainly shows that the market shares of each group in the different market segments are similar. We do not observe a group having a strong position in one segment and having no activity in another segment. The ranking among groups is almost identical from one segment to another. There is clearly a strong correlation between the market shares in each segment and the overall market shares. It is confirmed by Figure 12.1, where the market shares of groups in the fire and motor insurance segments are displayed together with their overall market shares.

Figure 12.2 shows that the shares of different insurance market segments are stable over time and four segments – personal and travel, fire, motor, general liability – together represent almost 80 per cent of the total number of policies. Given that the demand for insurance by business customers is more complex to estimate, setting aside the other segments – in particular employer's liability – should not involve a large distortion in the statistical results. For this reason, the econometric model below bears on the total number of policies for these four types of insurance. This solution avoids treating the question of policies for business groups. The analysis will therefore be made as if insurers offer an 'umbrella policy' covering these four insurance lines at the same time. The economic theory of insurance provides some arguments for why providing this bundling of contracts is optimal for policy holders.

---

[2] For confidentiality reasons, the ordering of firms is changed from one graph (or table) to the other. What it is important here is to compare firms.

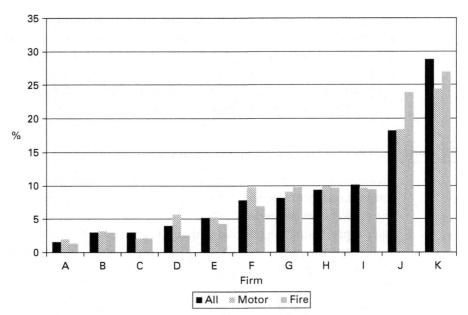

Figure 12.1 Market shares: motor and fire insurance segments versus overall insurance market

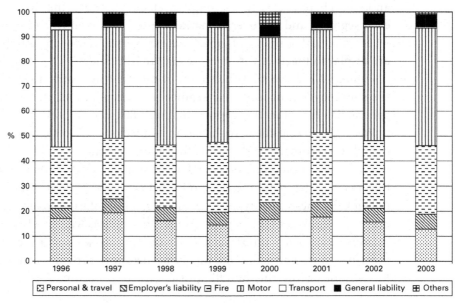

Figure 12.2 Distribution of insurance segments (by number of policies)

Without asymmetric information, an umbrella policy is an optimal risk-sharing arrangement. (See Arrow, 1971; Gollier and Schlesinger, 1995.) Under asymmetric information, bundling risks can alleviate the adverse selection problem when the various individual risks are correlated.

2.2 Correlation between number of policies and amount of premia

A standard problem in the measurement of market shares in insurance is related to the definition of the unit of service. Two methods can be used that are based respectively on the number of policies sold, or on the aggregate premium. Neither of them is completely satisfactory. However, Figure 12.3 shows that there is a strong correlation of market shares of insurance groups whether they are computed with respect to the number of policies or with respect to the total amounts of premia collected. Figure 12.4 also shows that the distribution among segments is not modified when this distribution is based on the amounts of premia instead of the numbers of policies as in Figure 12.2.

Together with the facts described in section 2.1, it appears that what really matters is the strategy of each insurance firm taken as a whole. With respect to potential antitrust concerns, what matters is the decision of consumers to

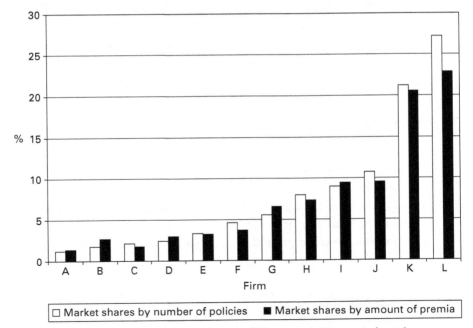

Figure 12.3 Market shares in terms of number of policies versus total amount of premia

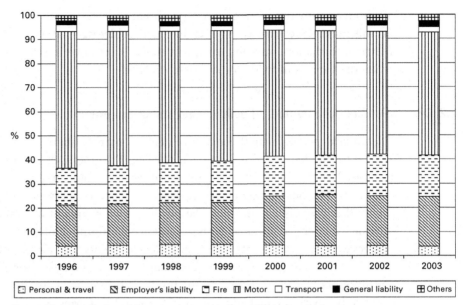

Figure 12.4 Distribution of insurance segments (by amount of premia)

choose among insurers based on their global commercial offering, averaged across the different lines of insurance; that insurers are applying second-order price discrimination should not affect the analysis.[3] In other words, what matters is the decision to enter in a relationship with an insurer based on the average price of its bundle of insurance contracts, i.e. the premium of its virtual 'umbrella policy'.[4]

2.3 Average prices are not rising and margins are fair

Figure 12.5 exhibits the temporal pattern of average premia for some insurance groups and for the insurance industry as a whole. Note that the average premium of B is below the industry average although B's premium rises while A's decreases. Note that the temporal pattern of the average premium for each firm is relatively unstable, which is also a sign of a very active market. The industry average premium has a slight negative trend in this period which could be interpreted as a sign of competition in the industry.

---

[3] In this context, second-order price discrimination refers to cases where a firm does not have precise information about the preferences of individual customers but it can use menus of contracts in order to extract the relevant information from its customers.

[4] Often customers buy all their insurance contracts from the same firm.

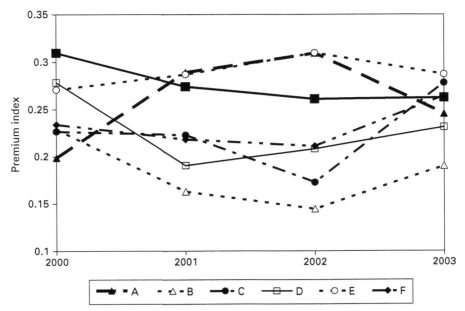

Figure 12.5 Average insurance premium (personal, motor, fire, general liability)

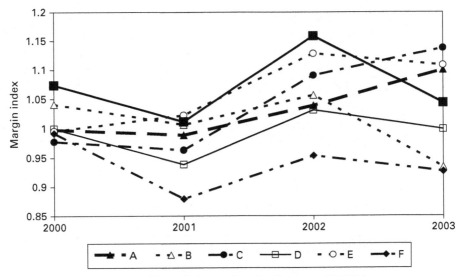

Figure 12.6 Average commercial margin (personal, motor, fire, general liability)

However, a change in the aggregate premium collected can originate from a reduction of the insured risks rather than from more effective competition between insurers. Therefore, it is better to examine commercial margins (see Figure 12.6). The commercial margin is computed as the ratio of total premia to total costs (i.e. the sum of total claims, administrative and acquisition costs) so the break-even reference point is one. Note that B is about to break even, in the sense that its average premium paid by its customers just covers the cost of their accidents. This ratio is an indicator of profitability of the sector. This profitability takes into account two important components of the balance sheet of insurance companies. First, selling insurance generates administrative and acquisition costs (including selection costs, monitoring costs and auditing costs) that are usually estimated to equal between 20 per cent and 30 per cent of the insurance premium in the non-life sector. Second, because of the inversion of the production cycle in this sector (i.e. premiums come in before claims go out), insurers can invest insurance premia on financial markets before paying indemnities to policy holders who have incurred an insured loss. This activity yields a return that must be taken into account to measure the overall efficiency of insurance companies. In the absence of information about the return of the financial reserves of the various insurance companies, it is not easy to infer whether the evolution of the technical results observed on Figure 12.6 comes from increased competition or from other factors, such as changes in anticipated returns on insurance reserves.

This ratio is also a good indicator of the insurability of risks in the economy. When it is close to unity, insurance premia are actuarially fair. This induces risk-averse households to purchase full insurance. This complete transfer of individual risks to insurers is efficient from the viewpoint of risk diversification. Insurance companies and mutuals wash away uncorrelated individual risks either by pooling in a mutual or by the transfer to financial markets in a shareholding insurance company. A loss ratio around unity is also useful for the growth of the economy, because the efficient risk transfer that it yields allows for disentangling investment decisions from risk aversion, both at the individual level and at the level of firms. Figure 12.6 reveals that this objective is approximately fulfilled by the insurance markets.

2.4 Insurance firms are differentiated in terms of risk level

Firms attempt to diversify their commercial strategies. There is an objective reason for this behaviour. In Figure 12.7, it is noticeable that the firms are differentiated in terms of their average risk level, measured by the frequency of accidents, as measured itself by the ratio of the number of claims divided by the number of policies. Note that B and A are among the firms having the lowest risk level. It is fair to say that the reason for their relatively low risk level should be related to the combined effects of their seniority and their large presence on the insurance market.

12. A merger in the insurance industry

Table 12.1 Statistics on the industry structure

	All firms			Firms having a market share higher than 1%	
	Maximum	Mean	# firms	Mean	# firms
1996	15%	4%	27	4%	15
1997	16%	4%	25	4%	16
1998	14%	4%	28	4%	16
1999	15%	4%	27	4%	16
2000	26%	5%	22	5%	12
2001	28%	5%	21	5%	13
2002	27%	5%	20	5%	14
2003	28%	6%	18	6%	12

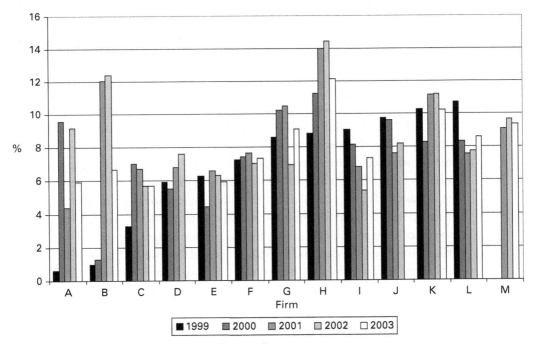

Figure 12.7 Annual claim frequency per firm

2.5 The structure of the insurance sector is stable since 2000

Finally Table 12.1 shows that, after having experienced a wave of mergers and consolidation before and during 1999, the industry remains relatively stable both in terms of average market share and number of active firms. The stability of the industry structure since 2000 invites us to fit the model only on the data covering the period 2000–3.

3. Empirical analysis

An econometric model of the insurance market is specified and estimated on the basis of available data and facts derived in the preceding section. This model is a particular case of a wider class of models that are used in econometrics of differentiated product markets to evaluate the impact of mergers.

3.1 Specification of the econometric model

The model comprises three main ingredients: a demand model to describe the choice of insurance by individual consumers, a cost model to approximate how claims are affected by the activity level of firms and a pricing behaviour model that describes the conduct of firms in Bertrand–Nash competition.

Demand

The theory of insurance demand has been developed by Mossin (1968). Its main result is that full insurance is optimal only if insurance premia are actuarially fair. However, because insurers must cover their administrative costs, insurance premia entail a positive loading factor. This induces households to optimally retain some of their risks. This can be done either by some coinsurance clauses (deductibles, caps on indemnities) or by leaving some of their risks uninsured. Under some weak assumptions on preferences, the insurance demand is decreasing in the premium rate, i.e. in the insurance price. Moreover, the demand for insurance is decreasing with wealth. Because of the cost incurred by switching insurer, it may be optimal for policy holders to stay with an inefficient insurer, as long as the inefficiency index does not exceed some small threshold. These switching costs may have a positive effect on the efficiency of insurance markets. Indeed, they imply some degree of loyalty of the policy holders to their insurer, which is beneficial for long-term risk sharing. These switching costs imply also that the demand addressed to each individual company is not completely elastic and that competition is imperfect. An important goal of this study is to examine these cross-price elasticities of insurance demand.

These ingredients are introduced in our econometric model in the following way. The preference structure of a representative consumer is represented

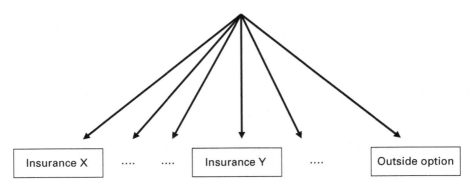

Figure 12.8 Consumer choice

by means of a logit model. (See Werden, Froeb and Tardiff, 1996, or Motta, 2004.) Here the consumer chooses between I different insurance groups. There is an additional choice, called the *outside option*, which is referred by index 0 in the sequel. This choice consists in buying insurance from a set of very small firms representing less than 3 per cent of the market all together or in buying no insurance at all. So there are $I+1$ choices (see Figure 12.8). Each choice, indexed by i, is described by a utility index which itself depends on three components: the price, p_i, a quality index, δ_i, and a random term u_i. First, the price is measured by the average premium. The sensitivity of the quality index to prices is driven by a parameter that we call the *marginal utility of income*, denoted by α. This parameter is assumed to be a function of gross domestic product (GDP) to account for the increase in wealth from one year to the other. Second, the quality index depends on a set of factors, x_i, namely the accessibility to the insurer (measured by the number of offices[5]), the reputation of this insurer (measured by its risk level observed by the consumer one period in advance) and a fixed effect which, among many possible effects, measures the loyalty of consumers to their insurer. Third, the random component combines all variables that are not observable by the analyst and play a role in the consumer choices.

In this context, the choice probabilities are measured in terms of market shares. Indeed, the market share of a product is the observed value of the probability that a representative consumer chooses this particular product. The market share of the insurance firm i, s_i, is obtained as the ratio of the number of policies held by the insurance firm i, namely y_i, over the market size, Y, that is to say:

---

[5] The number of offices is not necessarily the best proxy for accessibility. The number of agents or brokers was not available for all insurance companies on a systematic basis.

$$S_i = \frac{y_i}{Y} = \frac{y_i}{\sum\limits_{i=0}^{I} y_i}. \tag{1}$$

The number of policies associated with the outside alternative, y_0, is approximated by the number of policies held by the set of small firms. It can be enlarged arbitrarily if one believes that the market size is larger and should take into account all potential customers having no coverage.[6]

Mathematically, by using the logit model, one can write the logarithm of the market share s_i for insurance firm i as:

$$\ln(s_i) - \ln(s_0) = \delta_i - \alpha p_i + u_i, \tag{2}$$

where s_0 is the market share of the outside alternative. Moreover, we specify that

$$\alpha = \alpha_0 + \alpha_1 GDP, \tag{3}$$

and

$$\delta_i = \beta x_i, \tag{4}$$

where α_0, α_1 and the βs are parameters to be estimated. We refer to δ_i as the 'quality index' for each firm. For the sake of completeness, we apply the usual normalisation that the mean utility of the outside alternative, $i = 0$, is zero.

Cost

The insurance activity entails many sources of costs linked to the fight against adverse selection and moral hazard. Because individual risks are heterogeneous, it is essential for insurers to establish an efficient marketing mechanism to select the individual risks that they will accept to insure. The complexity of evaluating these risks on the basis of their observable characteristics may explain the large acquisition costs in the non-life insurance sector. Different companies have developed different marketing strategies, either with independent brokers, with local branches or offices, with bancassurance, or using new information technologies (internet, call centres). In addition to these acquisition and selection costs, the existence of an ex-ante moral hazard problem in insurance requires that insurers monitor the efforts of the policy holders to prevent risks to occur, generating monitoring costs (see Arrow,

---

[6] The consequence of enlarging the market share of the outside good is to increase the competitive pressure on the inside firms.

1971). Finally, because insured losses may be difficult to observe, there is an ex-post moral hazard problem (insurance fraud). This implies that insurers must invest in sophisticated technologies to audit claims. Selection costs, monitoring costs and auditing costs are estimated to be as large as 20–30 per cent of the insurance premium paid by the policy holder.

In this type of model, it is usual to assume constant marginal costs, i.e. the cost of selling one more policy is assumed to be independent of the size of the company. Here we propose to approximate marginal costs by means of a cost function. First, the assumption of constant marginal costs is unrealistic given what we just explained. Second, this assumption involves the estimation of one parameter – the marginal cost – for each firm. This is not ideal when the number of degrees of freedom remains limited as here. Third, estimating a cost function allows us to internalise the question of potential efficiency gains due to a merger within the equilibrium model of the industry.

We assume that, over the estimation period (2000–3), most input factors are fixed and are a function of the number of offices that corresponds to the size of the network. If C_i is the total cost of insurance firm i as measured by the sum of total claims and administration costs, if k_i is the number of offices held by this firm, then we assume that

$$C_i = \gamma_0 + \gamma_1 y_i + \gamma_2 y_i k_i + w_i, \tag{5}$$

where w_i is a random term representing measurement errors and γ_0, γ_1 and γ_2 are parameters to be estimated. The expectation is that the marginal cost of an additional policy is lower if the group has a larger network of offices, so $\gamma_2 < 0$. This simple linear model for the cost provides an excellent fit and permits to approximate the marginal cost, c_i, as

$$c_i = \gamma_1 + \gamma_2 k_i + \omega_i, \tag{6}$$

where ω_i is a random term representing unobserved shocks to marginal costs.

Pricing

Firms adopt Nash behaviour: they choose the prices of their products to maximise profits, given the prices set by the other firms. In maximising its profit π_i defined as

$$\pi_i = p_i y_i - C_i, \tag{7}$$

each firm trades off two effects when considering an increase in price by one unit: (i) it increases profits proportional to the current sales level of the firm,

Table 12.2 Estimation results

	Variable name	Parameter	Parameter estimate	t-value	1st stage R^2
Cost equation	Constant	γ_0	−160.3250	−0.02	1.00
	Number of policies	γ_1	0.2450	16.14	0.95
	No. policies * No. offices	γ_2	−0.0003	−2.34	0.97
Demand equation	Constant	β_0	6.1397	5.87	1.00
	Number of offices	β_1	−0.0028	−0.77	1.00
	Risk level lagged	β_2	−2.6449	−1.18	1.00
Marginal utility	Constant	α_0	38.1296	5.33	0.66
of income	GDP	α_1	−0.1728	−5.12	0.74

(ii) it reduces sales, which lowers profits proportional to the current markup. When the demand is specified as above, this trade-off is summarised by the pricing equation:

$$\frac{p_i - c_i}{p_i} = \frac{1}{\alpha p_i(1 - s_i)} \tag{8}$$

This equation states that the price–cost margin (i.e. the Lerner index) of firm i must be set equal to the inverse of the absolute value of the own price elasticity, that is here equal to $\alpha\, p_i\,(1 - s_i)$.

Equations (2)–(5)–(8) constitute the econometric model to be estimated.

3.2 Estimation

The model, which contains twenty parameters, is estimated by means of non-linear three-stage least squares implemented with the procedure MODEL of the SAS software.[7] It is fitted on a data set covering the period 2000–3 for reasons explained in section 2.5. Given that there are thirteen significant firms and four years of data, this provides fifty-two observations. As we use the risk level lagged once in the list of exogenous variables we use the year 1999 for defining the initial conditions. The procedure requires the use of instrumental variables. The set of instruments we have selected contains all exogenous variables as well as the market share and the price lagged once.

Estimation results are gathered in Table 12.2. We report only the most relevant parameters that impact on the simulations. Most parameters are

---

[7] 3SLS is an instrumental variables technique that simultaneously estimates all three equations.

Table 12.3a Estimated characteristics of insurance groups

Firm	Own-price Elasticity	Cross-price Elasticity	Marginal Cost	Average Cost	Return to Scale	Quality Index
A	−3.43	0.31	0.16	0.21	1.39	5.58
B	−3.24	0.06	0.13	0.19	1.45	3.42
C	−3.85	0.39	0.19	0.24	1.33	6.06
D	−3.68	0.68	0.18	0.24	1.47	6.49
E	−2.78	0.12	0.11	0.16	1.49	4.05
F	−3.54	0.39	0.16	0.24	1.47	5.78
G	−2.51	0.85	0.12	0.20	1.66	6.30
H	−3.64	0.05	0.15	0.23	1.51	3.48
I	−3.29	0.12	0.14	0.21	1.55	4.31
J	−4.41	0.10	0.20	0.24	1.19	4.90
K	−3.52	0.09	0.15	0.18	1.23	4.07
L	−4.54	0.06	0.23	0.24	1.23	4.02
M	−4.39	0.25	0.21	0.26	1.22	5.88

significant. The relatively high level of the first-stage coefficient of determination for the parameters of interest α_0 and α_1 indicates that they are relatively
well identified by our set of instruments. Note that the effect of the number of
offices is not significant on the quality index but it is strongly significant on the
marginal cost. Although statistically insignificant, the estimate for the parameter associated with the lagged risk level and the estimated value for the
marginal utility of income (parameter α) have the expected sign which should
be viewed as the signal of an economically meaningful model.

3.3 Discussion

Table 12.3a gathers estimates for different characteristics of insurance firms.
First, the own- and cross-price elasticities are relatively high. These numbers
suggest that the market is competitive and that insurance firms are perceived
as substitutes by their customers. Second, the cost function of insurance firms
exhibits increasing returns to scale. The average cost function is much flatter
than the marginal cost function and the ratio of average to marginal costs (a
standard measure of returns to scale) is substantially above one. Note that the
estimated marginal costs range from 0.11 to 0.23, that is to say, almost double
among firms, while the range of average costs spreads over the interval
between 0.16 and 0.26. A 1 per cent increase in the number of policies
(which corresponds to 7,750 policies on average) decreases the average cost

Table 12.3b Estimated versus observed markups

Firm	Estimated markup	Accounting markup
A	29.97	31.16
B	31.40	49.05
C	26.54	33.32
D	30.89	25.54
E	36.80	32.98
F	28.57	27.44
G	40.08	26.84
H	27.54	42.23
I	31.47	42.83
J	22.79	51.98
K	28.51	43.51
L	22.39	50.33
M	22.87	29.18

by only 0.001 per cent. However, a 1 per cent increase in the number of offices brings a 0.2 per cent fall in the marginal cost. This result shows that, although economies of scale are not negligible, economies of density due to a network effect are much more powerful.

Table 12.3a also shows that B has the third lowest marginal costs among insurance companies and both B and A have a relatively high quality index, indicating a high level of loyalty and trust of their customers.

Table 12.3b compares the estimated markups of some firms (i.e. substituting our estimated parameters into equation 8) to the actual ratios of premia to claims. These ratios could be considered as accounting markups. Note that the econometric model underestimates the markups, although the differences are relatively small for the largest companies.

4. Merger analysis

The model serves as a tool to simulate the notified merger between B and A. If all customers of A and B stay with their insurers after the merger, then one can predict a very high price if competitors do not react, i.e. keep the same prices. It is not a sustainable situation. One reasonably expects that some customers of B and A would switch to other insurance companies and that the latter would change their prices following the merger. Hence it is required to simulate the new Bertrand–Nash equilibrium after merger, as if all customers

Table 12.4a Simulated effects of the notified merger (with efficiency gains)

	Quality Index	Marginal Cost	Pre-merger Price	Post-merger Price	Change in Price	Pre-merger Margin	Post-merger Margin
A	6.30	0.21	0.28	0.28	0.86%	26%	26%
B	4.17	0.14	0.21	0.21	0.39%	33%	33%
C	5.99	0.17	0.25	0.25	1.19%	30%	30%
D	6.44	0.14	0.22	0.23	5.21%	37%	40%
E	4.48	0.12	0.19	0.19	0.76%	36%	37%
F	6.17	0.19	0.26	0.27	0.99%	27%	28%
G	6.84	0.14	0.23	0.23	1.61%	39%	40%
H	4.48	0.14	0.21	0.21	0.54%	33%	33%
I	5.17	0.21	0.28	0.28	0.28%	25%	25%
J	5.79	0.29	0.36	0.36	0.12%	19%	19%
K	6.38	0.22	0.29	0.29	0.78%	25%	25%

re-compute their optimal choice of insurance. We also need to consider what happens to costs. The first simulation (Table 12.4a) assumes efficiency gains in the sense that B, by acquiring all offices of A while maintaining the structure of its marginal cost function, can decrease the level of marginal costs. On the basis of the estimated model, it turns out the average premium of B's policies would increase by 1.6 per cent and the average premium of A's policies would increase by 5.2 per cent. Table 12.4a provides the results of the simulated equilibrium after merger. Note that, because of the endogeneity of marginal costs, these are different before and after merger. Using a bootstrap method, we show that neither of these price rises is significantly different from zero because the bootstrapped confidence interval always contains zero.

If there were no merger specific efficiency gains, the price increases would be much higher (see Table 12.4b). The new entity would then lose substantial market share. However, unlike many potential sources of efficiency gain that might be claimed, our assumed source is an existing network so the source of the efficiency is tangible, not speculative. Also, it could not be achieved in the absence of the merger.[8] Thus, the Table 12.4a results are more appropriate.

Consider again the results with efficiency gains in Table 12.4a. Note that each firm increases its price after merger by a non-negligible percentage. It is the sign that, at the present time, the insurance industry is far from the equilibrium. One

---

[8] In other words, we do not include merger specific efficiency gains. The efficiency gains are just the normal gains due to the cost structure we have estimated for this industry.

Table 12.4b Simulated effects of the notified merger (without efficiency gains)

	Quality Index	Marginal Cost	Pre-merger Price	Post-merger Price	Change in Price	Pre-merger Margin	Post-merger Margin
A	6.30	0.21	0.28	0.28	1%	26%	27%
B	4.17	0.14	0.21	0.21	1%	33%	33%
C	5.99	0.17	0.25	0.25	2%	30%	31%
D	6.44	0.14	0.22	0.28	26%	37%	29%
E	4.48	0.12	0.19	0.19	1%	36%	37%
F	6.17	0.19	0.26	0.27	2%	27%	28%
G	6.84	0.14	0.23	0.28	22%	39%	29%
H	4.48	0.14	0.21	0.21	1%	33%	34%
I	5.17	0.21	0.28	0.28	0%	25%	25%
J	5.79	0.29	0.36	0.36	0%	19%	19%
K	6.38	0.22	0.29	0.29	1%	25%	26%

should expect more consolidations and/or more adjustment in terms of pricing and marketing strategies. Meanwhile, the relatively high market share of the merged entity B/A raises legitimate concerns.

5. Conclusions

The econometric modelling of the insurance market pre-merger provides a quantification of some of the key issues in merger analysis. In the present case, we can highlight four such issues. First, B and A have the highest levels of attractiveness as measured by our quality index, but other firms are not lagging far behind. We interpret these results as showing the combined effect of reputation or aggressiveness of firms and/or loyalty of customers. Second, own-price elasticities are high, with an overall level of 3.6 per cent. Cross-price elasticities are smaller, with an overall level of 0.3 per cent. These numbers suggest that the market is competitive and that possibilities of substitution among firms are high. Third, when ranking marginal costs by increasing order, B arrives the second, while A is among the last firms. The estimated marginal costs double between the lowest and highest values. Fourth, the cost function exhibits increasing returns to scale. There is not much saving on cost due to an increase in the number of contracts administered by a single firm. Indeed the average cost is roughly flat as an increase of 1 per cent in the number of policies. However, there is a non-negligible network effect.

Using these findings to examine the effects of the proposed merger once consumers and firms have had time to adjust, it turns out the average premium of B's policies would increase by 1.6 per cent and the average premium of A's policies would increase by 5.2 per cent. Neither of these price rises is significantly different from zero. These results favour an approval of the merger

However, in the very short run, the relatively high market share of the entity B/A raises legitimate concerns because it takes time before customers are able to adapt their decisions, even if the transaction costs incurred when changing from an insurer to another are not so high. In order to facilitate the convergence of the industry to a new equilibrium, several actions could be applied. First, transparency of the merger should be enforced. In particular B's and A's customers should be informed of the operation, the business model chosen by the stakeholders and the consequences in terms of prices and offers. This situation calls for an involvement of the regulator of this industry which is able to monitor and to enforce the transparency of the operation. Second, given that B is cost-efficient, B might be forced to sell some of A's local area offices, in particular where competitors are weakly represented. Although this would involve some costs, it might be compensated by the increased degree of competition. However, a proper appraisal of this type of remedy would require further investigation and additional data.

Finally, in the longer term, the possibility of an investigation for abuse of dominant position if needed constitutes the Sword of Damocles above the merging entity.

Acknowledgement

We thank Adriana Azevedo Hernandez Perez for her efficient and valuable assistantship.

13 Merger simulations of unilateral effects: what can we learn from the UK brewing industry?

Margaret E. Slade[1]

1. Introduction

Unlike most of the chapters in this book, this one is not concerned with a specific case. Instead it is methodological. In particular, I discuss the use of simulation techniques to evaluate unilateral effects of horizontal mergers, bearing in mind the trade-off that exists between simple and complex models. On the one hand, a simple model can be implemented in a short period of time and it can be understood by non-experts. On the other hand, the conclusions concerning merger effects that can be drawn from a simple model can be very misleading. One is therefore often faced with the choice between implement-ability and accuracy. In this chapter, I assess the implications of that choice.

Due to the trade-off between simplicity and accuracy, it is unlikely that merger simulations will ever replace more traditional analysis, such as an examination of the extent and structure of the market and the merging firms' shares of that market. Instead, the two sorts of analysis should be complemen-tary and, if the limitations of simulation techniques are understood, they can be useful supplements. It is a mistake, however, to oversell their potential or their precision.

The use of simulations is illustrated with an application to mergers in the UK brewing industry, which is an important market that has received much atten-tion from competition authorities. In particular, there have been a number of mergers that have changed the structure of the market, as well as proposed but unconsummated mergers that would have had even more profound effects. Moreover, the positions taken by UK competition authorities towards brewery mergers have undergone fundamental changes in recent years.

---

[1] This research was supported by a grant from the UK ESRC.

The organisation of the chapter is as follows. I begin with a presentation of the general method that is used to solve horizontal merger simulations. That presentation is followed by more in-depth analyses of the building blocks that underlie the simulations – demand and costs. Section 4 discusses the UK beer market, the mergers and public policy towards those mergers, whereas section 5 presents the data, which is a panel of brands of beer. Section 6 looks at implementation. In particular, the sensitivity of predicted prices, costs, margins and merger effects to modelling choices is assessed. The chapter concludes with a more optimistic discussion of how quantitative techniques can be used to organise our thoughts concerning mergers, even if they are unreliable methods of obtaining point estimates of merger effects.

2. Simulation of unilateral effects

In North America, merger policy tends to be based on the notion of *unilateral effects*.[2] In other words, authorities usually attempt to determine whether firms in an industry have market power and how a merger will affect that power, assuming that the firms act in an uncoordinated fashion. In practice, this change is often evaluated as a move from one static Nash equilibrium to a second equilibrium with fewer players.[3]

European authorities, in contrast, tend to base their policy on the notion of dominance. In other words, they seek to determine whether a single firm or group of firms occupies a dominant position and whether the merger will strengthen that position.[4] Traditionally, single-firm dominance was emphasised. However, the notion of joint dominance has assumed increasing importance due to high-profile merger cases such as Nestle/Perrier, Gencor/Lonrho and Airtours. Joint dominance is usually taken to mean tacit collusion or *coordinated effects*.[5]

---

[2] US antitrust authorities, however, often use the notion of coordinated effects to analyse mergers in industries that produce homogeneous products (see, e.g., Sibley and Heyer, 2003).

[3] See, e.g., Hausman, Leonard and Zona (1994), Werden and Froeb (1994), Jayaratne and Shapiro (2000), Nevo (2000), Pinkse and Slade (2004) and Ivaldi and Verboven (2005).

[4] This is roughly equivalent to unilateral effects, though with stronger emphasis on the merging parties becoming the largest firm and with an expectation of stronger competition if there are other firms with similar market shares.

[5] See, e.g., Lexicon (1999), Kühn (2000), Compte, Jenny and Rey (2002) and Kühn (2005). Since 2004, the formal dominance test has been modified to emphasise that a merger should be prohibited if it results in a significant impediment to effective competition. This takes it closer to the formal wording used in North America.

UK competition authorities operated under a formal 'public interest' test at the time of the beer cases discussed in this chapter. In principle, this could be interpreted quite widely, but since the 1980s it had been interpreted as predominantly a competition test.[6] In spite of differences across regions, merger policy is converging towards a single standard.

In this chapter, I assess quantitative techniques that are based on the notion of *unilateral effects* and can be used to evaluate the competitive effects of horizontal mergers. In particular, I consider mergers in a market for a differentiated product with many brands. Under those circumstances, it is difficult for firms to collude tacitly and uncoordinated decision making seems more plausible.[7]

The goal of a merger simulation is to predict the equilibrium prices that will be charged and the quantities of each brand that will be sold under the new, post-merger market structure, using only information that is available pre merger. The advantage of such an approach is that, if the simulation can forecast accurately, it is much more efficient to perform an ex-ante evaluation than to wait for an ex-post assessment. In particular, competition authorities are reluctant to impose costly divestitures once a merger has been approved and it is anyway much more difficult to impose an ex-post remedy under the legislation.

An understanding of the method that is used to solve horizontal merger simulations is facilitated by an example. Consider the case of K firms that produce n brands of a differentiated product with $K \leq n$. The brands are assumed to be substitutes, but the strength of substitutability can vary by brand pair. It is standard to assume that the firms are engaged in a static pricing game. A market structure in that game consists of a partition of the brand space into K subsets, where each subset is controlled by one firm or decision maker. Specifically, each firm can choose the prices of the brands that are in its subset. A merger then involves combining two or more of the subsets and allowing one player to choose the prices that were formerly chosen by two or more players.

Consider a typical player's choice. When the price of brand i increases, the demand for brand j shifts out. If both brands are owned by the same firm, that firm will capture the pricing externality. If they are owned by different firms, in contrast, the externality will be ignored. After a merger involving substitutes, therefore, prices should increase, or at least not fall. The question that

---

[6] This has now been formalised in revised legislation so that the formal test took on the same wording as in the US, with mergers being prohibited if they would bring about a 'substantial lessening of competition'.

[7] Nevo (2000) and Slade (2004a) test and fail to reject the Bertrand assumption for breakfast cereals and beer respectively.

horizontal merger simulations aim to answer is by how much. Clearly the answer depends on the matrix of cross-price elasticities. Merger simulations have therefore focused on modelling and estimating demand. Nevertheless, it is also necessary to have estimates of costs, ideally marginal costs. A demand equation and a cost function are thus the basic building blocks upon which a merger simulation is based.

The purpose of this chapter is to consider the sensitivity of estimates of demand elasticities and marginal cost to alternative specifications, particularly of demand systems. How much does it matter if a short cut or simplified specification is used? Does it make a difference to the estimated competitive effects of a merger? The answers are important because consultants and agencies are making increasing use of sophisticated techniques and may be unaware of some of the dangers.

3. The building blocks

There are many ways to obtain estimates of demand and costs and, in what follows, I discuss some of them. When choosing a specification, one must keep in mind the important trade-off that must be made between simplicity and accuracy. In particular, time is of the essence, since the competition authority has only a limited period in which to decide whether a merger will be challenged. This means that simple models are preferred. If a model is constructed too hastily, however, it is apt to be simplistic and conclusions that are based on it are apt to be misleading. I therefore discuss specifications that range from extremely inflexible to moderately flexible.

3.1 Demand

Firms can possess market power because they have few competitors and thus operate in concentrated markets. Even when there are many producers of similar items, however, they can possess market power if their products have unique features that cause rival products to be poor substitutes. To evaluate power in markets where products are differentiated, it is therefore important to have good estimates of substitutability.

A number of demand specifications have been developed to deal with differentiated products. In this chapter I look at three functional forms – the logit, the nested logit and the distance metric – that range from extremely simple to more flexible. With all three, there are n brands of a differentiated product with output vector $q = (q_1, \ldots, q_n)^T$ and with the first two there is an outside good q_0 that is an aggregate of other products.[8] For expository purposes, I assume that there is only one market with exogenous size M.[9]

The logit

There are many specifications of demand that are based on a random-utility model in which an individual consumes one unit of the brand that yields the highest utility. The logit, which is the simplest of those specifications, results in the demand equation

$$ln(s_i) - ln(s_0) = \beta^T x_i - \alpha p_i + \xi_i, \tag{1}$$

where $s_i = q_i/M$ is brand i's market share, s_0 is the share of the outside good, x_i is a vector of observed characteristics of brand i, p_i is that brand's price and ξ_i is an unobserved (by the econometrician) characteristic.

The popularity of this equation is due to its simplicity and the fact that it can be easily estimated by instrumental-variables techniques. Its drawback is that it is highly restrictive. To illustrate, let ε_{ij} denote the price elasticity of demand $(\partial q_i/\partial p_j)(p_j/q_i)$.[10] With the logit-demand equation, those elasticities take the form

$$\varepsilon_{ii} = \alpha p_i(s_i - 1) \quad \text{and} \quad \varepsilon_{ij} = \alpha p_i s_j, \quad j \neq i. \tag{2}$$

The substitution patterns that are implied by (2) are unappealing. For example, all elasticities increase linearly with price and with market share[11] and all off-diagonal elements in a column of the elasticity matrix are equal (i.e. every product $i \neq j$ has the same cross-price elasticity with j). Furthermore, since s_i is i's share of the total market, which includes the outside good, estimated elasticities are very sensitive to the choice of the outside good. In particular, by defining the market, M, more generously, one can cause own-price elasticities to rise in magnitude and predicted markups to fall (see Appendix A). In this sense, simulations based on logit demand equations have much in common with more traditional analyses, which involve defining the market and calculating concentration indices based on firms' shares of

---

[8] The symbol ^{T} indicates the transpose of a vector. Thus, q represents a column of quantities for the n products and q^T represents a row with the same quantities.

[9] The single-market assumption can easily be relaxed, and it almost always is in practice.

[10] Note that $\varepsilon_{ii} < 0$ and $\varepsilon_{ij} > 0$.

[11] A second very simple demand model that has been used for merger simulations, the PCAIDS, also relies on the proportionality assumption and thus has similar problems. Specifically, it assumes that, when the price of one brand rises, the probability that a customer who stops purchasing that brand will switch to a particular substitute is proportional to the substitute's market share (see Epstein and Rubinfeld, 2002).

that market. In that situation, the merging parties often claim that the market is broad so that their shares and expected impact on competition will be small.

The nested logit

The nested logit (NL) is distinguished from the ordinary logit by the fact that the n brands or products are partitioned into G groups, indexed by $g = 1, \ldots, G$, and the outside good is placed in group 0. The partition is chosen so that like products are in the same group. For example, when the differentiated product is beer, the groups might be lager, ale and stout.

The NL estimating equation is

$$ln(s_i) - ln(s_0) = \beta^T x_i - \alpha p_i + \sigma ln(\bar{s}_{i/g}) + \xi_i \tag{3}$$

where $\bar{s}_{i/g}$ is brand i's share of the group g to which it belongs.[12] The parameter σ ($0 \leq \sigma \leq 1$) measures the within-group correlation of tastes, and the ordinary logit is obtained by setting σ equal to zero.

With the NL demand equation, the own- and cross-price elasticities take the form

$$\varepsilon_{ii} = \alpha p_i [s_i - 1/(1 - \sigma) + \sigma/(1 - \sigma)\bar{s}_{i/g}], \tag{4}$$

$$\varepsilon_{ij} = \begin{cases} \alpha p_j [s_j + \sigma/(1 - \sigma)\bar{s}_{i/g}], & j \neq i, \quad j \in g \\ \alpha p_j s_j, & j \neq i, \quad j \notin g. \end{cases}$$

The substitution patterns that are implied by (4) are only slightly more general than those implied by the logit. In particular, the off-diagonal elements in a column of the elasticity matrix (i.e. the cross-price elasticities with product j) take on at most two values, depending on whether the rival product is in the same or a different group. Also, it is not always clear what groups should be defined and into which one each product should be placed.

Extensions to the nested logit

There are at least two ways in which the NL can be extended. First, the price coefficient, α, can be a function of product characteristics, $\alpha_i = \alpha(x_i)$.[13] When the product is beer, for example, the characteristics might be the brand's alcohol content, product type (e.g. lager, ale or stout) and brewer identity, and the modification allows elasticities to vary with those characteristics.

---

[12] See McFadden (1974).   [13] This extension is used in Slade (2004a).

Second, the within-group correlation of tastes can vary by group, σ_g, $g = 1, \ldots, G$.[14] This modification allows cross-price elasticities to be systematically larger in some groups than in others. For example, stout drinkers might be less willing to switch than lager drinkers.

The distance metric

Brands of a differentiated product can compete along many dimensions in product-characteristic space. For empirical tractability, however, one must limit attention to a small subset of those dimensions. Nevertheless, it is not desirable to exclude possibilities *a priori*. The distance-metric (DM) demand model, which is based on a normalised-quadratic utility function, is somewhat more flexible than the NL. In particular, it allows the researcher to experiment with and determine the strength of competition along many dimensions.[15] Indeed, virtually any hypothesis concerning the way in which products compete (any distance measure) can be assessed in the DM framework. However, only the most important measures are typically used in the final specification.

A feature that distinguishes the DM from the NL is that, with the former, cross-price elasticities depend on attributes of both brands – i and j – whereas with the latter, they depend only on the characteristics of j. To achieve this dependence, however, one must interact prices with distance in characteristic or geographic space. Unfortunately, with a large number of brands it is impractical to include all rival prices on the right-hand side of the estimating equation and even less practical to interact those prices with own and rival characteristics. In what follows, I describe how one can formulate a tractable model that condenses this information.

With the DM specification, demands for the differentiated product are[16]

$$q_i = a_i + \sum_j b_{ij} p_j + \gamma_i y + \xi_i, \tag{5}$$

where y is aggregate income. Although the functional form is very simple, equation (5) is empirically intractable for most applications.[17] It is therefore necessary to impose some structure on the elasticities and the insight behind

---

[14] This extension is used in Slade (2004a) Brenkers and Verboven (2006).

[15] See Pinkse, Slade and Brett (2002) and Pinkse and Slade (2004).

[16] Equation (5) should be divided by a price index, $p_0(\delta_0 + \delta^T p)$. However, that index can be set equal to one in a cross-section or very short time series.

[17] The matrix $B = [b_{ij}]$ has $n(n+1)/2$ distinct parameters. For example, if there are sixty-three brands (as in our estimation in section 4), there would be around 2,000 elasticity parameters to estimate, and only sixty-three observations.

the DM is that they are determined by distances in a limited number of measurable product characteristics.

To simplify, assume that a_i and b_{ii}, $i = 1, \ldots n$, are functions of the characteristics of brand i, $a_i = a(x_i)$ and $b_{ii} = b(x_i)$. This assumption, which is similar to one of the extensions to the NL, allows own-price elasticities to depend on, for example, the quality of the product. In addition, the off-diagonal elements of B are assumed to be functions of a vector of measures of the distance, d_{ij}, between brands in some set of metrics, $b_{ij} = g(d_{ij})$. For example, when the product is beer, the measures of distance, or its inverse closeness, might be alcoholic-content proximity and dummy variables that indicate whether the brands belong to the same product type (e.g. whether both are stouts) and whether they are brewed by the same firm. The closer are two products i and j in these dimensions, the higher will be their cross-price elasticities. The function $g(\cdot)$ can be estimated by parametric or semiparametric methods. Finally, the random variable ξ, which captures the influence of unobserved product characteristics, can be heteroscedastic and spatially correlated.

The own- and cross-price elasticities that are implied by equation (5) are

$$\varepsilon_{ii} = \frac{p_i b(x_i)}{q_i} \quad \text{and} \quad \varepsilon_{ij} = \frac{p_i g(d_{ij})}{q_i}. \tag{6}$$

As with the NL, DM elasticities depend on prices and market shares. However, they can be modelled very flexibly. In particular, by choosing appropriate distance measures, one can obtain models in which substitution patterns depend on *a priori* product groupings, as with the NL. There are, however, many other possibilities. For example, one can also obtain models in which cross-price elasticities depend on continuous distance measures, such as differences in alcohol contents.

Discussion

In the application I assess whether the functional form chosen for the demand equation is an important determinant of predicted prices and markups. Due to the need to restrict attention to simple models, a simple parametric version of the DM equation with two distance measures is used. All four demand specifications are estimated from the same panel data set.

Alternatively, those equations could be calibrated, where by calibration I mean finding an exact solution for their parameters. To illustrate, consider the logit demand equation (1) with two product characteristics, x_1 and x_2. There are four parameters in that equation, $\beta_0, \beta_1, \beta_2$ and α. Calibration requires only as many observations as parameters; one simply solves the system of four equations for the four unknown parameters. Estimation, in contrast, is a statistical process that requires more observations than parameters. In what follows, I do not consider calibration. However, we know *a priori* that, although it is simpler, calibration is less accurate than estimation.

3.2 Marginal costs

A demand equation is one of the building blocks that is used to assess merger effects. In addition, one must have estimates of marginal costs, c_i, $i = 1, ..., n$. There are at least three methods that can be used to obtain those estimates.

Exogenous costs

With the first method, researchers obtain independent information (e.g. engineering or accounting data) on unit costs. Alternatively, industry experts might be able to suggest orders of magnitude based on their experience. This might be the only alternative in the absence of sufficient data for estimation. The exogenous information is then substituted into the first-order conditions, which are solved to obtain equilibrium prices and markups. The advantage of this method is its simplicity. The disadvantage is that, unless the cost data are very accurate, it is difficult to distinguish between average-variable and marginal costs. Exogenous estimates of marginal costs are denoted $\check{c}_i$, $i = 1, ..., n$.

Implicit costs

With the second method, which involves estimating marginal costs implicitly, researchers assume that firms are engaged in a particular game (e.g. Bertrand) and write down the first-order conditions for that game. Those conditions typically include marginal costs as well as demand parameters. One can therefore substitute the estimated demand parameters into the first-order conditions and solve those conditions for implicit costs. In other words, implicit costs are the estimates that rationalise the observed prices and the equilibrium assumption.

To illustrate, consider a simple pricing game where each firm produces one brand and sets its price so that $(p_i - c_i)/p_i = -1/\varepsilon_{ii}$. There are n first-order conditions of this form that can be solved for the n unknowns, c_i. With the example, given estimates of demand elasticities and observed prices, an implicit estimate of marginal cost is $p_i(1 + 1/\hat{\varepsilon}_{ii})$. This method is valid if the firms are indeed playing the assumed game. If they are playing a different game, however, the estimates of marginal costs so obtained are biased. The implicit estimates are denoted $\tilde{c}_i$, $i = 1, ..., n$.

Estimated costs

The third method involves estimating marginal costs econometrically from first-order conditions. In particular, one can replace c_i with a function of standard cost variables such as factor prices, v, and product attributes, x_i, $c_i = c(v, x_i)$, and estimate that function. To illustrate, with the example above, one could estimate the equation $p_i = c(v, x_i)\left[\frac{\varepsilon_{ii}}{1+\varepsilon_{ii}}\right]$. This procedure is subject to the criticisms of method 2. Furthermore, since demand and cost are estimated jointly, if the equilibrium assumption is incorrect, the misspecification contaminates the estimates of demand. A two-step procedure, with demand estimated in stage one and first-order conditions in stage two, is therefore recommended. Econometric estimates of marginal costs are denoted $\hat{c}_i$, $i = 1, \ldots, n$.

In the application, I also assess whether the method that is chosen to estimate marginal costs is an important determinant of predicted prices and markups.

3.3 The game

When products are differentiated, it is common to assume that the firms in the market are engaged in a static pricing game. This is, however, by no means the only reasonable assumption. For example, it is possible that firms choose some other variable, such as quantity, or a vector of variables, such as price and quality. In addition, if the firms collude tacitly or overtly, prices and markups will be higher than those predicted by Bertrand competition.[18] If, in contrast, competition is destructive or cutthroat, they will be lower. Indeed, the famous folk theorem of repeated games tells us that, if players are sufficiently patient, any outcome between competitive and joint-profit maximising can be supported as a subgame-perfect equilibrium of the repeated game.

Bertrand competition is an obvious focal point for the estimation of unilateral effects in markets where products are differentiated. However, it is also interesting to obtain bounds on possible outcomes, which can be done by examining predicted competitive and perfectly collusive prices and margins. The general method of solution is the same as that discussed in section 2. Indeed, given any equilibrium solution concept, one can obtain n first-order conditions that can be solved for the prices that correspond to that concept.[19] Bounds on prices and markups can be used to assess whether simulation predictions are sensitive to assumptions concerning the game that players are engaged in.

---

[18] In this case, one is no longer considering unilateral effects.
[19] If firms choose j variables, there will be $j \times n$ first-order conditions.

4. The UK beer market

4.1 International comparisons

Although beer markets have certain features in common across countries, cross-country differences are also striking. It is therefore useful to begin with a few international comparisons. Table 13.1 summarises some of the differences between the UK, US, Canada, France and Germany. This table shows that, when it comes to beer consumption per head and the fraction of beer sales that originate abroad, the UK lies between France and Germany, with Germany having higher per-capita consumption and France relying more heavily on imports. Consumers in the US and Canada, who are similar to each other, drink less beer per capita and tend to consume fewer imports than their counterparts in the UK. Finally, over time, per-capita beer consumption has fallen in most countries, whereas imports have risen.

Table 13.1 Selected international comparisons

Consumption/Head (Litres)	Country	1975	1985	1995	2003
	UK	118.5	109.2	100.9	101.3
	US	81.8	89.7	83.5	81.6
	Canada	87.0	82.2	66.5	68.4
	France	41.3	40.1	39.1	35.5
	Germany	147.8	145.4	137.7	117.7
Imports (%)	Country	1975	1985	1995	2003
	UK	4.4	6.0	8.8	10.7
	US	1.1	4.3	6.0	11.6
	Canada	0.6	4.4	3.3	9.7
	France	8.6	11.1	15.4	24.0
	Germany	0.8	1.2	2.3	2.8
Draught sales (%)	Country		1991	1996	2003
	UK		71	66	57
	US		11	10	9
	Canada		10	12	10
	France		25	23	23
	Germany		23	20	20

Source: The Brewers and Licensed Retailers Association and the British Beer and Pub Association.

Table 13.2 Three-firm concentration ratios in 1985

UK	US	Canada	France	West Germany (CR$_5$)
47	74	96	81	28

Source: The Monopolies and Mergers Commission (1989).

Table 13.3 Selected UK beer statistics

Year	1970	1980	1990	2000
% lager	7	31	51	63
Real ale/total ale (%)	NA	30	37	30
% on-premise sales	90	88	80	67
Number of brewers	96	81	65	57

Source: The Brewers and Licensed Retailers Association and the British Beer and Pub Association.

Whereas the UK is not an outlier with respect to the statistics contained in the first two parts of Table 13.1, it is clearly different from the other countries with respect to the ratio of draught to total beer sales, as can be seen in the last part. Indeed, draught sales in the UK accounted for almost three times the comparable percentages in France and Germany and about six times the percentages in North America. In all countries, however, draught's fraction has fallen, as more beer has been consumed at home.

Turning to production, Table 13.2 compares one important aspect of the industry – its concentration, or lack thereof, into the hands of a small number of brewers. The table shows concentration ratios that were calculated in 1985, before the UK mergers that are discussed below occurred.[20] The UK industry was clearly less concentrated than its counterparts in the US, Canada and France, where beer tends to be mass produced. Production in Germany, in contrast, where speciality beers predominate, was much less concentrated. It thus seems that brand heterogeneity and an unconcentrated brewing sector go hand in hand.

4.2 The UK industry

The UK beer industry has undergone substantial changes in both production and consumption in the last few decades, some of which are summarised in Table 13.3. Beers can be divided into three broad categories: ales, stouts and

---

[20] With the exception of Germany, the table shows three-firm concentration ratios. Any other concentration measure, however, would tell the same story.

lagers. Although UK consumers have traditionally preferred ales to lagers, the consumption of lager has increased at a steady pace. Indeed, from less than 1 per cent of the market in 1960, lager became the most popular drink in 1990, with sales exceeding the sum of ale and stout, and its popularity continues to grow. Most UK lagers bear the names of familiar non-British beers such as Budweiser, Fosters and Kronenbourg. Almost all, however, are brewed under licence in the UK and are therefore not considered to be imports.

A second important aspect of beer consumption is the popularity of 'real' or cask-conditioned ale. Real products are alive and undergo a second fermentation in the cask, whereas keg and tank products are sterilised. The statistics in Table 13.3, however, which show that real ale's market share has remained relatively constant, must be interpreted with caution, since they show percentages of the ale market. As a percentage of the total beer market, which includes lager, real products have lost ground.

The final trend in consumption is the decline in on-premise sales. On-premise consumption includes sales in bars, hotels and clubs, whereas off-premise consumption refers to beer that is purchased in a store and consumed at home, out of doors or in non-licensed establishments. Clearly, draught sales are a subset of on-premise consumption, since some packaged products are consumed in licensed establishments.

With respect to production, Table 13.3 shows that the number of brewers has declined steadily. Indeed, in 1900, there were nearly 1,500 brewery companies, but this number fell during the century and is currently below sixty. In addition to incorporated brewers, however, there are many microbreweries operating at very small scales. In fact, most brewers are small and few produce products that account for more than 1–2 per cent of local markets.

This snapshot of the UK beer industry shows significant changes in tastes and consumption habits as well as a decline in the number of companies that cater to those tastes. Nevertheless, as we have seen, compared with many other countries, the UK brewing sector was only moderately concentrated. Recent developments in the industry, however, have resulted in substantial changes in ownership patterns.

4.3 Public policy towards the UK beer industry

It is not unusual for the beer industry to attract the attention of politicians and civil servants. Government involvement in the industry stems from four concerns: the social consequences of alcohol consumption, the tax revenue obtained from alcohol sales, the level of concentration in the brewing

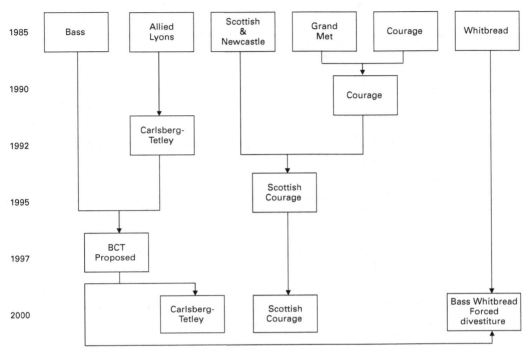

Figure 13.1 Developments in the UK brewing industry

sector and the extent of brewer control over retailing. In recent years, more-over, public scrutiny of the industry has accelerated. Indeed, there have been over thirty reviews by UK and European Union authorities since the 1960s. Many of those investigations were triggered by proposed mergers in the industry. Several, however, were more general assessments of prices, profits and tied sales.[21]

Figure 13.1 shows actual and proposed changes in the structure of the UK beer market. In particular, there were three consummated mergers: between Courage and Grand Metropolitan (Grand Met) in 1990, Allied Lyons and Carlsberg in 1992 and Courage and Scottish & Newcastle (S&N) in 1995. In addition, there were two proposed mergers that were denied: one in 1997 between Bass and Carlsberg-Tetley (CT) was prohibited and the second in 2000 between Bass and Whitbread eventually resulted in divestiture of Bass's brewing assets.

Each of the mergers is discussed below. However, it is difficult to understand the positions taken by the Monopolies and Mergers Commission (MMC) and

---

[21] For an analysis of tied sales in the UK brewing sector, see Slade (1998).

the Office of Fair Trading (OFT) with respect to the horizontal mergers without considering their views on the vertical links between brewers and their retail outlets. Vertical issues are therefore discussed first.

The Beer Orders

Prior to the late 1980s, a large fraction of UK public houses was owned by brewers and operated under exclusive-purchasing agreements (ties) that limited the pubs to selling brands that were produced by their affiliated brewer.[22] Competition authorities have long been concerned that those tying arrangements would somehow extend the market power that they perceived in the upstream or brewing sector to the downstream or retailing sector. Absent the system of ties, they believed that retailing would be competitive.

In the late 1980s, the OFT requested the MMC to undertake a major industry review. The product of that investigation was the 500-page MMC report entitled 'The Supply of Beer', which appeared in February 1989. The MMC recommended measures that eventually led brewers to divest themselves of 14,000 public houses. The Commission claimed that its recommendations would lower retail prices and increase consumer choice. There has been considerable doubt, however, that these objectives were achieved. Indeed, after divestiture, retail beer prices rose (Slade, 1998).

The MMC report is unclear about the economic reasoning that led to the decision to force divestiture.[23] Nevertheless, the MMC alleged that, due to high concentration, the brewers possessed market power and their involvement in retailing protected that power.

The Beer Orders were rescinded in 2002.

The mergers

After the Beer Orders, the brewing industry became more concentrated. Increases in brewing-market concentration were due to mergers, which the MMC allowed, as well as to the fact that some firms (e.g. Boddingtons) ceased brewing, whereas others (e.g. Courage) ceased retailing. Nevertheless, as we illustrate below, for some time the MMC favoured recommendations that focused on the retail sector and the vertical linkages between brewers and public houses in spite of their claim that the source of monopoly power lay in brewing.

---

[22] Such tying arrangements are illegal in the US. See Slade (2000) for a discussion of the legal differences.
[23] See Lafontaine and Slade (2007) for a summary of theories of anticompetitive foreclosure, exclusion and extension of horizontal market power through vertical integration, as well as the empirical evidence on the subject. They find that the evidence of anticompetitive effects is weak.

The Courage/Grand Met merger. The merger between Courage and Grand Met that occurred in 1990, just after the Beer Orders were passed, reduced the number of national brewers from six to five. At the time of the merger, Grand Met controlled 11 per cent of the beer market, whereas Courage controlled 9 per cent. The merger transformed Courage into the second largest producer, just behind Bass, which had a market share of 22 per cent. Nevertheless, three of the four MMC recommendations involved the tied estate rather than increases in brewing concentration *per se.*

The Allied Lyons/Carlsberg joint venture. In 1992, Allied Lyons, a British food company that owned breweries, formed a joint venture with Carlsberg, a Danish brewer. Their combined UK brewing assets were renamed Carlsberg-Tetley. At the time of the joint venture, Allied Lyons controlled 12 per cent of the beer market, whereas Carlsberg controlled 4 per cent. Their shares of the lager market, however, were higher, with 8 and 13 per cent, respectively. The joint venture became the third largest brewer, behind Bass and Courage. The number of national brewers, however, was unchanged, since Carlsberg was not one of them. The MMC was principally concerned with the fact that Carlsberg was one of a very few brewers without a tied estate.[24]

The Courage/S&N merger. In 1995, the merged firm Courage merged again with Scottish & Newcastle. This event, which reduced the number of national brewers from five to four, created the largest brewer in the UK. The combined firm, with a market share of 28 per cent, was substantially larger than Bass, which had a market share of 23 per cent and thus dropped from number one to two. In spite of the fact that the majority of the groups that were asked to comment on the merger favoured a full investigation by the MMC, the OFT did not refer the matter to the MMC. Instead, it allowed the merger to proceed subject to a number of undertakings, all of which involved the tied estate. The OFT rejected the idea of divestiture of breweries or brands but instead favoured 'the alternative remedy that has generally been adopted following previous references ... to weaken the extent of vertical links with the merged company' (DGFT, 1995).

The Bass/CT merger. The fourth and largest merger was proposed in 1997 but not consummated. This involved the number two and three brewers, Bass and Carlsberg-Tetley, and would have created a new firm, BCT, with an overall market share of 37 per cent. Moreover, it would have further reduced the number of national brewers from four to three. At the time, Bass controlled

---

[24] Brewers without tied estates are not vertically integrated into retailing and have no exclusive-purchasing agreements.

23 per cent of the beer market, CT controlled 14 per cent and Scottish Courage, which would have become the second largest firm, had a market share of 28 per cent. The MMC estimated that, after the merger, the Herfindahl/Hirschman index of concentration (HHI) would rise from 1,678 to 2,332. Furthermore, it noted that the US Department of Justice's 1992 Merger Guidelines specify that a merger should raise concerns about competition if the post-merger HHI is over 1,800 and the change in the HHI is at least fifty points. Nevertheless, the MMC recommended that the merger be allowed to go forward.[25] In spite of the MMC's favourable recommendation, the merger was not consummated because the President of the Board of Trade did not accept the MMC's advice.

The Bass/Whitbread merger. More recently, in May 2000, the world's largest brewer, the Belgian firm Interbrew, acquired Whitbread, the UK's fourth national brewer. That acquisition did not change the number of brewers in the UK, but it transferred the ownership of some brands. More importantly, in August of the same year, Interbrew also acquired Bass, which gave it a UK market share of approximately 36 per cent. This time the MMC did not approve the merger. Instead, it recommended that Interbrew be required to divest the UK brewing assets of Bass to a buyer approved by the Director General of Fair Trading. Interbrew appealed the MMC decision to the High Court, however, and won on a legal technicality.[26] Nevertheless, although Interbrew kept the Bass brand name, the majority of Bass Brewing's assets were sold to Coors in 2002.

The MMC's attitude towards earlier mergers in the brewing industry is puzzling. It seems that either it concluded that brewers had little market power or that large increases in concentration would not change that power. However, its own calculations estimated that brewing margins were approximately 30 per cent, which is moderately high. For example, margins of approximately 20 per cent are more common in the food sector.

The MMC's views, however, changed over the 1990s. In particular, early on the Commission was almost exclusively concerned with vertical relationships in the industry, whereas by the end of the decade a concern with horizontal concentration assumed prominence.

Was increased concern with horizontal market power justified? As a first cut to answering that question one can examine the market shares of the firms before and after each merger. Those shares are shown in Table 13.4, which

---

[25] The one economist on the Commission group investigating the merger, David Newbery, wrote a dissenting opinion.

[26] Specifically, it was decided that Interbrew had not been allowed sufficient time to consider alternative remedies.

Table 13.4 National brewer market shares, draught and packaged

Brewer	1985	1991	1996
Allied Lyons	13	12	14
Carlsberg	NA	4	
Bass	22	22	23
Courage	9	19	
Grand Metropolitan	11		28
Scottish & Newcastle	10	11	
Whitbread	11	12	13
Total	76	80	78

Source: The Monopolies and Mergers Commission (1989).

reveals that, with all three consummated mergers, a few years afterwards the merged firm's market share was less than the sum of the pre-merger shares. This is consistent with higher prices being set by the merging firms which then saw their combined market shares erode. It therefore suggests that increased efficiency, which one hopes would feed through into lower prices, did not overwhelm increased market power. However, although one might arrive at this conclusion with hindsight, it is more relevant to see whether one could have reached the same conclusion ex ante. In other words, could this reasonably have been predicted by an appropriate merger simulation analysis?

5. The data

5.1 Demand data

The data is a panel of brands of draught beers sold in different markets, where a market is a time-period/geographic-region pair. The panel also includes two types of establishments, multiples and independents. Brands that are sold in different markets are assumed not to compete, whereas brands that are sold in the same market but in different types of establishments are allowed to compete. A complete description of the data, which is summarised here, can be found in Appendix B.

For each observation, there is a price, PRICE, sales volume, VOL, and coverage, COV, where coverage is the percentage of outlets that stocked the brand. Each brand has an alcohol content, ALC. Moreover, brands whose alcohol contents are greater than 4.2 per cent are called premium, whereas those with lower alcohol contents are called regular beers. This distinction is captured by a dummy variable, PREM. Finally, brands are classified into four product types, lagers, stouts, keg ales and real ales, using dichotomous variables, $PROD_i$, $i = 1, \ldots, 4$. Those types form the basis of the groups for the nested logit.

A number of interaction variables are also used. Interactions with price are denoted PRVVV, where VVV is a characteristic. To illustrate, $PRALC_i$ denotes price times alcohol content, $PRICE_i \times ALC_i$.

5.2 Measurement of distance between brands

Using the same data, Pinkse and Slade (2004) experimented with a number of metrics or measures of similarity of beer brands. These included several discrete measures: same product type, same brewer and various measures of being nearest neighbours or sharing a market boundary in product-characteristic space. Two continuous measures of closeness, one in alcohol content and the other in coverage space, were also used.

They found that one metric stands out in the sense that it has the greatest explanatory power, both by itself and in equations that include several measures. That metric, WPROD, is the same-product-type measure that is set equal to one if both brands are, for example, real ales, and zero otherwise.[27] This is conceptually similar to creating logit nests in the same categories. A second measure, a similar-alcohol-content measure, is also included in their final specification. That metric is calculated as $WALC_{ij} = 1/(1 + 2 \mid ALC_i - ALC_j \mid)$.[28] I use the same metrics here.

To create average rival prices, the vector, PRICE, is pre-multiplied by each distance matrix, W, and the product is denoted RPW. For example, RPPROD is WPROD × PRICE, which has as ith element the average of the prices of the other brands that are of the same product type as i.

5.3 Cost data

The Monopolies and Mergers Commission performed a detailed study of brewing and wholesaling costs by brand and company. In addition, it assessed

---

[27] This measure was normalised so that the entries in a row sum to one.
[28] 1 is added to the denominator to avoid dividing by zero.

retailing costs in managed public houses.[29] A summary of the results of that study is published in MMC (1989). Although the assessment of costs was conducted on a brand and company basis, only aggregate costs by product type are publicly available. Those data, which are discussed in Appendix B, are used for the exogenous costs, $\check{c}$.

5.4 Estimation

Not only are own prices endogenous in a typical demand equation but, in a strategic setting, rival prices suffer from the same problem. This is true here because, unlike in a competitive industry, players are interdependent and choices are made simultaneously. The typical solution to the endogeneity problem is to use instruments, which are variables that are not correlated with the error (and thus are not correlated with the left-hand side variable) but explain prices. The use of an instrumental-variables technique overcomes the endogeneity problem but it raises problems of its own. In particular, it is necessary to obtain valid instruments. A number of possibilities were tried. Fortunately the qualitative nature of the results was not sensitive to that choice.[30]

6. Results

6.1 Demand

The four alternative demand equations are summarised in Table 13.5. Consider first the logit and its variants. With all three specifications, the market is sales of alcoholic beverages.[31] The outside good is therefore on- and off-premise sales of beer in bottles and cans as well as other alcoholic beverages. The table shows that the price coefficient, $-\alpha$, increases in magnitude and significance as one moves from the logit to the nested logit to the extension of the nested logit,[32] which is an indication that the estimated elasticities will be progressively larger. Furthermore, the parameter σ is large (recall that it is bounded by one) and highly significant, which indicates that

[29] Managed public houses are owned and operated by a brewer.
[30] See Pinkse and Slade (2004) for details.
[31] As discussed earlier, this is not an innocuous choice. In particular, more comprehensive choices (larger markets and smaller shares) yield higher own-price elasticities. Choosing the market to be beer, as seems more realistic, would thus result in worse fits to the data.
[32] Only one extension of the nested logit is shown – variation in σ by product type. When α was modelled as a function of product characteristics, there was little change in estimated elasticities.

Table 13.5 IV demand equations

Functional form	$-\alpha$	σ	σ_1	σ_2	σ_3	σ_4
Logit[a]	−0.0007					
	(−0.1)					
Nested logit[a]	−0.0026	0.830				
	(−1.0)	(12.3)				
Extended NL[a]	−0.0050		0.762	0.668	0.944	0.739
	(−1.7)		(12.4)	(9.6)	(12.9)	(9.3)
	PRICE	PRCOVR	PRPREM	PRNCB	RPPROD	RPALC
Distance metric[b]	−1.125	0.165	−0.030	−0.117	0.712	0.215
	(−2.9)	(7.8)	(−0.1)	(−2.7)	(2.6)	(1.6)

[a] Contains ALC, LCOV (the logarithm of coverage), product, time period and regional fixed effects. α is the coefficient of price, and σ measures within group correlation of utilities.
[b] Contains ALC, LCOV (the logarithm of coverage), time period, establishment type and regional fixed effects. A prefix of PR implies that price is interacted with that variable. A prefix of RP means that that distance measure is used to create an average rival price. Standard errors corrected for heteroscedasticity and spatial correlation of an unknown form. Asymptotic t statistics in parentheses.

the nested logit or its extension is preferred. Finally, when σ is allowed to vary by product type, there is substantial variation in the estimates of that parameter, indicating that, for example, products in nest 3 (i.e. keg ales) are more substitutable with each other than are products in nest 2 (stouts). This pattern seems intuitively reasonable.

Now consider the distance-metric demand estimates. Due to differences in dependent variables and functional forms, one cannot compare magnitudes of price coefficients directly. However, the price coefficients are clearly more significant than with the logit variants.[33] The estimates show that demand is more elastic for popular national brands with high coverage and for brands that have many neighbours in product-characteristic space.[34]

The estimated average own- and cross-price elasticities that are shown in Table 13.6 are easier to interpret, since they are comparable across demand specifications. That table shows that, using the logit, one would conclude that demand at the brand level is inelastic, which is clearly unrealistic. As one moves

---

[33] Recall that the price coefficients begin with PR.
[34] COVR is the reciprocal of coverage, LCOV is the logarithm of coverage and NCB measures the number of common-boundary neighbours in alcohol/coverage space (see Appendix B.)

Table 13.6 Estimated elasticities: brand averages

Functional form	Own-price elasticity	Cross-price elasticity
Logit	-0.97	0.0005
Nested logit	-2.4	0.0344
Extended NL	-3.4	0.0517
Distance metric	-4.6	0.0632
AIDS Hausman, Leonard and Zona (1995)	-5.0	0.121

from logit to nested logit to extended NL to distance metric, however, average own-price elasticities increase in magnitude.

All estimates are lower than the elasticities that were found by Hausman, Leonard and Zona (HLZ, 1994) for US brands.[35] However, since US brands are more homogeneous, they could be more substitutable and there is no *a priori* reason to expect that UK-brand elasticities will be as large as those found for the US.

The estimated cross-price elasticities display similar patterns – increasing as one goes down the table – and all are substantially below the HLZ cross-price estimates. However, HLZ consider fewer brands which, all else equal, will result in higher cross-price elasticities.

Inelastic demand at the brand level, as implied by the logit, leads to an unrealistic model. In particular, predicted prices will be negative on average.[36] For this reason, the logit is not discussed in the remainder of this chapter.

6.2 Costs

Table 13.7 shows exogenous costs, $\check{c}$, implicit costs, $\tilde{c}$, that were obtained under three demand specifications, and estimated costs, $\hat{c}$, that were obtained by estimating a marginal-cost function jointly with the distance-metric demand equation.

The exogenous costs show very little variation, which is due to the aggregate nature of the cost data that were released by the MMC. As noted earlier, those numbers are average variable costs and equal marginal costs only if marginal costs are constant.

---

[35] Hausman, Leonard and Zona use an AIDS demand system, which would not work here. In particular, such a system cannot incorporate many brands in each nest.

[36] For single-product firms, recall that the optimal Lerner index L_i is determined by the formula, $L_i = \frac{p_i - c_i}{p_i} = \frac{-1}{\varepsilon_{ii}}$. When $|\varepsilon_{ii}| < 1$, this relationship can hold if and only if $p_i < 0$.

Table 13.7 Summary of cost estimates

Method		Mean	Standard dev.	Minimum	Maximum
Exogenous, $\check{c}$		129.1	5.2	124.0	147.0
Implicit, $\tilde{c}^a$					
	Nested logit	79.0	14.6	51.6	132.3
	Extended NL	98.6	23.0	46.1	158.4
	Distance metric	128.0	35.7	35.1	205.5
Estimated, $\hat{c}^{a,b}$		133.5	40.6	30.9	211.7

[a] Static Nash equilibrium in price.
[b] Using the distance metric demand equation.

Table 13.8 Sensitivity of implicit costs to equilibrium assumptions

Assumption	Mean	Standard dev.	Minimum	Maximum
MC pricing	167.8	20.2	117.0	204.5
Bertrand	128.0	35.7	35.1	205.5
Joint-profit max	99.1	41.3	15.1	201.7

Using the distance metric demand equation.

The implicit costs were obtained from first-order conditions for a static pricing game (Bertrand) under three demand specifications. The table shows that those estimates increase as one moves from nested logit to extended NL to distance metric, which must be true. Indeed, when the estimated elasticities increase in magnitude, the implied markups fall. Holding prices constant, this can happen only if costs rise. On average, implicit distance-metric costs are closest to exogenous costs. However, there is substantially greater variation in the implicit-cost estimates.

Table 13.8 assesses the sensitivity of implicit costs to the assumption that is made concerning equilibrium behaviour. That table shows estimates that correspond to marginal-cost pricing, a static pricing game and joint-profit-maximising behaviour. The two extremes bound the possibilities that one might expect to observe. The table shows that implicit costs fall as one moves from competitive to imperfectly competitive to monopoly pricing. This pattern is also expected. Indeed, since prices are the same in all three scenarios, the only way for markups to increase is for costs to fall. Most of the variation across specifications, however, comes from variation at the low end. The maximum implicit cost is relatively constant.

It is important to notice that the numbers in Table 13.8 are bounds for the possible cost estimates only under the distance-metric specification. Indeed,

Table 13.9 Two-step GMM estimates of marginal-cost functions

EQN	VOL	PREM	ALC	PUBM	PROD$_1$	PROD$_2$	PROD$_3$	CONST	J statistic d.f.=8
1	0.0008	0.221		0.256	0.429	0.190	−0.011	4.519	12.1
	(2.5)	(3.4)		(3.2)	(5.1)	(4.4)	(−0.2)	(51.6)	
2	0.0012		0.178	0.257	0.359	0.239	−0.012	3.877	12.3
	(2.3)		(3.1)	(3.0)	(4.9)	(4.2)	(−0.2)	(2.9)	

Using the distance metric demand equation.
Asymptotic t statistics in parentheses.
Corrected for heteroscedasticity and spatial correlation of an unknown form.

Table 13.7 shows that the implicit costs obtained from solving a static pricing game using the nested-logit demand equation (79.0 and 98.6) are lower on average than the lowest possible estimates using the distance-metric specification (99.1 from Table 13.8). Cost estimates are thus very sensitive to both demand and equilibrium assumptions.

Finally, econometrically estimated costs were obtained using a two-step GMM procedure (demand estimated first and first-order conditions second) with a marginal-cost function that depends on volume, q_i, as well as product characteristics, x_i.[37] The estimated cost functions, which are shown in Table 13.9, indicate that marginal costs rise with output (VOL). In addition, marginal costs are higher for premium (high alcohol) beers and in managed public houses. Finally, it is more costly to produce lagers and stouts than ales.

Mean estimated costs are shown in the last row of Table 13.7.[38] On average, they are somewhat higher but not far from exogenous costs and more variable than both exogenous and implicit costs.

6.3 Predicted prices and margins

Table 13.10 shows predicted prices and margins under the three demand specifications. Those numbers were obtained by solving the first-order conditions for a static pricing game using the indicated demand function and the exogenous cost estimates, č. This exercise is in some sense the opposite of the one that was performed to obtain the implicit costs shown in Table 13.7. In that table, prices are held constant and the cost estimates are those that

---

[37] GMM is a very flexible instrumental-variable technique. A two-step procedure was chosen so that any misspecification in the nature of equilibrium would not contaminate the demand equation.

[38] The numbers shown in the table were evaluated at the means of the explanatory variables.

Table 13.10 Predicted equilibrium prices and margins

Demand model	Mean price	Standard dev.	Mean margin
Nested logit	244.7	44.2	89.5
Extended NL	211.0	38.1	45.1
Distance metric	168.4	29.5	30.4
Observed prices	167.8	20.2	29.9

From a static pricing game using the exogenous cost estimates, $\check{c}$.

rationalise the observed prices, given the estimated elasticities. In Table 13.10, costs are held constant and the predicted prices are those that rationalise the observed costs, given the estimated elasticities. It is therefore not surprising that, whereas implicit costs rise as one moves down Table 13.7, predicted prices and margins fall as one moves down Table 13.10. As in earlier tables, the prices that are obtained using the distance-metric demand equation are closest to the observed prices.

6.4 Merger simulations

The final exercise involves using the three demand equations with the exogenous costs to simulate changes in industry market structure. All simulations are performed using the procedure that is described in section 2. In particular, suppose that there are K firms or decision makers in the industry before an event and $K - J$ firms afterwards. If $J > 0$, the event is a merger, whereas if $J < 0$, it is a divestiture. In other words, a merger (divestiture) results in fewer (more) decision makers.

The data were collected in 1995, after the Scottish/Courage (SC) merger occurred and before the Bass/Carlsberg-Tetley (BCT) merger was proposed. The *status quo* is thus an industry with four national brewers and a number of smaller firms. Two events are considered. The first, which is a divestiture, involves undoing the Scottish/Courage merger. It is thus a move from four to five national brewers. The second, which is a merger, involves allowing Bass and Carlsberg-Tetley to combine. It is thus a move from four to three national brewers.

Table 13.11 summarises the results of those exercises. The first set of numbers (marked Status quo in the table), which merely duplicates the information that is contained in Table 13.10, is included for comparison purposes. The second and third portions of the table summarise the results of simulations of the two events. For each simulation, the table shows mean

Table 13.11 Merger simulations

Market structure	Demand model	Predicted price average	% change from status quo
Status quo (actual structure)			
	Nested logit	244.7	0
	Extended NL	211.0	0
	Distance metric	168.4	0
Scottish/Courage (divestiture)			
	Nested logit	198.2	− 19
	Extended NL	185.7	− 12
	Distance metric	167.4	− 0.6
Bass/Carlsberg-Tetley (merger)			
	Nested logit	413.0	69
	Extended NL	302.1	43
	Distance metric	173.5	3

Static pricing game using the exogenous cost estimates, *č*.

predicted prices and percentage changes from the status quo.[39] Predicted post-event prices are always compared to predicted status quo prices rather than to observed prices, since that comparison gives each demand model the benefit of the doubt. In particular, since the NL models over predicted prices in the *status quo*, comparisons with observed prices would predict unreasonably large changes (in absolute value) for most specifications.

First consider differences in predictions across events. With the simple logit, brand-level demand was estimated to be inelastic on average. For that reason, the table does not show logit simulations. However, we know *a priori* that the logit model would predict price changes that are not very different in magnitude across mergers. This is true because the sums of the pre-merger market shares of the merging firms, as well as the changes in the HHI, would have been roughly equal for the two events.[40]

The simulations that are shown in Table 13.11, in contrast, predict smaller changes for the Scottish/Courage merger than for BCT. This is partly due to the fact that the similarity of the merging firms' brands was less for SC. In particular, whereas Courage had two best-selling lagers, Fosters and Kronenbourg, S&N had little presence in the lager market. In contrast, both Bass and Carlsberg-Tetley had best-selling lagers, Carling and Carlsberg, respectively. Unlike the

---

[39] Note that the merging firms raise prices more than the non-merging firms.
[40] Although the sum of the pre-merger national-market shares was 30 per cent for SC and 37 per cent for BCT, the SC sum was 37 per cent of the pre-merger markets in the data.

logit, the other specifications are capable of capturing these differences in brand fit across mergers.

Now consider differences in predictions across specifications, which are substantial. In particular, predicted price changes are greatest for the nested logit, second for the extended NL and smallest for the distance metric. This pattern is due to the fact that the estimated cross-price elasticities increase as one moves from the first demand model to the third. In other words, the brands become more substitutable.

The price changes that are predicted by both NL models seem unrealistically large, especially when one notes that, although each event involves only two firms, the averages that are shown in the table reflect the prices of all brands in the market. Clearly, changes in the prices of the affected brands are larger than average changes.

Finally, note that I have not mentioned merger-related economies, an issue that is potentially important.[41] A complete merger-simulation model requires a cost function that is capable of capturing economies of scale and scope. Unfortunately, it is not obvious how one should embed long-run cost functions in merger-simulation exercises, which are by assumption short run. In addition, there are important merger-related dynamic issues, such as entry, exit and brand repositioning. Those issues only make the problems that I have been discussing more complex.

7. Conclusions

What conclusions can we draw concerning the effects of the mergers? That is a difficult question, since the conclusions that one draws depend on the model that one uses and the parameter values that one chooses for that model. Personally, I think that the decisions that were taken were not misguided. However, I would not want to justify this stance in a court of law on the basis of the econometric evidence.

We can, however, draw more general conclusions from the analysis. First, the predictions about markups and merger effects that can be obtained from simple models are often very misleading. Unfortunately, however, a number of economists have attempted to convince competition authorities that user-

---

[41] My personal opinion on this subject is that, in the horizontal context, merger-related economies are often exaggerated. In particular, in manufacturing, most economies of scale and scope occur at the plant level. Moreover, although there are often substantial economies in distribution, distributional costs are often not a high fraction of total costs.

friendly canned programs can provide reasonable predictions. In particular, in addition to per-merger market shares, those programs often require only one or two numbers as inputs.[42] This can be true, however, only if all elasticities are functionally related to one another in ways that are preset by the program. Put another way, this means that answers are determined by functional form and only back-of-the-envelope calculations are required.

Second, merger models that rely heavily on market shares and a choice of the outside good are not very different from traditional analyses that involve market definition and calculation of share-based indices of concentration. Moreover, in some sense they are worse, since they are less transparent and they offer point predictions of merger effects that give spurious impressions of accuracy.

The first two points can be illustrated using the simple logit demand model. Suppose that 100 brands of a differentiated product are produced in an industry. There are then 10,000 different own- and cross-price elasticities. However, as we have seen, all off-diagonal entries in a column of the logit elasticity matrix are identical. Nevertheless, one might be tempted to conclude that that fact is unimportant, since there are still 100 different cross-price elasticities, one for each brand. Whereas this is true, it is not very interesting, since relative magnitudes are determined entirely by market shares. Furthermore, absolute magnitudes can be manipulated by a strategic choice of the outside good, with larger markets implying lower markups. Clearly, this is also true of traditional merger analysis. However, most non-economists who work in the area understand the role that market definition plays. Unfortunately, they are less apt to realise that the choice of the outside good plays a similar role. Nevertheless, the logit model has been used extensively by competition authorities.[43]

Third, models that are capable of predicting with some accuracy are often difficult to construct and estimate. Moreover, there are many modelling choices that must be made that require experience and judgement. Unfortunately, when such models are used, other economists can criticise those modelling choices on technical grounds that serve to confuse lawyers, tribunal members and jurors.[44] When this occurs, the econometric evidence is apt to be disregarded, since the 'experts' do not agree and no one else can understand what they are saying.

---

[42] To illustrate, the abstract of a recent working paper states that a particular simulation program 'can be implemented using market shares and two price elasticities'.

[43] See, e.g., Werden and Froeb (2002).   [44] See, e.g., Hausman and Leonard (2005).

Does this mean that we, as antitrust economists, are caught in a Prisoner's Dilemma? Would we all be better off if simulation models did not exist? Not necessarily. I think that there is a role for quantitative techniques to play, but we must be careful not to oversell them.

An understanding of the strengths and weaknesses of different merger models can serve to organise our thoughts concerning mergers. In particular, we should stop thinking about market definition and market shares and think about brand fit instead.[45] For example, a merger between two firms that produce lagers can have very different consequences from one between a producer of lager and a producer of stout, even though the HHI changes by the same amount after the two mergers. Clearly, this is due to the fact that cross-price elasticities differ in the two cases. One might therefore counter that it is merely necessary to define smaller submarkets (e.g. lagers and stouts) and calculate shares of those submarkets. Whereas this is partly true, it begs the question, since there can be other important dimensions along which brands compete. Furthermore, since those dimensions can be continuous (e.g. alcohol content), the 0/1 classification under which brands are in the same or in different markets is frequently not helpful.

There is a second way in which merger simulations can help us think sensibly about merger effects in circumstances where mergers might be challenged. Specifically, academic evidence on brand elasticities and merger effects is beginning to accumulate and much of that work was not undertaken in a consulting environment. Presumably, the authors of many of those studies were interested in learning about the industry and were not motivated by considerations of winning a case. Furthermore, since published articles have been subjected to the refereeing process, their credibility is increased. One should be able to draw on that literature to obtain a better understanding of the forces that determine substitution patterns in particular industries. This will usually mean drawing qualitative conclusions from quantitative evidence rather than focusing on point estimates. Moreover, back-of-the-envelope calculations can be based on such studies and as long as everyone understands the assumptions that underlie those calculations and no spurious claims of accuracy are made, they can be useful. However, we should eschew generic, one-size-fits-all merger models and numbers that come out of black boxes.

---

[45] This discussion applies to industries that produce differentiated products. The traditional analysis is much better suited to handling mergers among firms that produce homogeneous products (see Slade, 2004b).

Appendix A: The role of the outside good

Consider the logit demand equation (1), which is equivalent to

$$ln(q_i) - ln(M) = ln(q_0) - ln(M) + \beta^T x_i - \alpha p_i + \xi_i. \tag{7}$$

or

$$ln(q_i) = ln(q_0) + \beta^T x_i - \alpha p_i + \xi_i. \tag{8}$$

It is obvious from (8) that the choice of q_0 affects only the estimate of the constant term. In particular the estimate of α is unaffected.

On the other hand, own- and cross-price elasticities, which are given by

$$\varepsilon_{ii} = \alpha p_i(s_i - 1) \quad \text{and} \quad \varepsilon_{ij} = \alpha p_i s_j, \quad j \neq i, \tag{9}$$

are sensitive to the choice of q_0. Specifically, since s_i falls when the market is defined more broadly, the elasticities increase.

To understand the implications of this fact, consider the following example. There are two 'inside' goods that are symmetric and one outside good to be chosen. We wish to compare the situations in which one firm owns the two inside goods (monopoly) to separate ownership (duopoly).

Under monopoly, it is straightforward to show that the price/cost margins or Lerner indices will be set so that

$$L_i^M = \frac{-1}{\varepsilon_{ii} + \varepsilon_{ij}}. \tag{10}$$

Under duopoly, in contrast, the cross-price effects will be ignored and each firm will set a margin according to

$$L_i^D = \frac{-1}{\varepsilon_{ii}}. \tag{11}$$

Let the estimate of α be $\hat{\alpha}$,[46] the average price be $\bar{p}$, and suppose that $\hat{\alpha}\bar{p} = 20$. Figure 13.2, which is based on those parameter values, contains graphs of predicted markups, $\hat{L}^M$ and $\hat{L}^D$, as functions of the share of the outside good, s_0. It shows that, as one moves from larger to smaller markets, duopoly markups double. Monopoly markups, in contrast, increase much more rapidly.

[46] Since there are only two brands of the differentiated product, for estimation purposes one must use data from a number of markets.

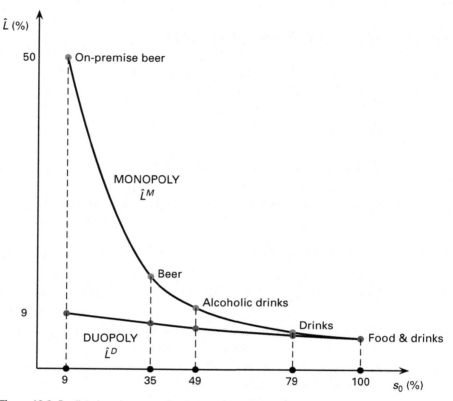

Figure 13.2 Predicted markups as a function of the share of the outside good

The figure also highlights several plausible choices of q_0. The inside good is draught beer. The smallest market is on-premise beer sales, which means that the outside good is on-premise consumption of beer in bottles and cans. The next market candidate is beer sales, which includes off-premise sales, the third is alcoholic beverages, which includes wine and spirits, the fourth is drinks, which includes soft drinks, juices and bottled water, and the broadest market is food and beverages.

One can imagine a case where the two parties present evidence obtained from the same merger-simulation model. The defence, however, claims that the outside good should be food and beverages and notes that markups are small (5 per cent) and that they will not change after the merger.[47] The

---

[47] The qualitative conclusions do not depend on the fact that merger to monopoly is considered. Indeed, if there are three inside goods and the producers of two of them want to merge, the defence would still claim that markups will not change after the merger, whereas the plaintiff would claim that they will increase by 75 per cent.

plaintiff, in contrast, claims that the market is on-premise beer sales, that markups are substantial and that they will increase five-fold after the merger. Moreover, each party demonstrates that the simulation program produces tight confidence intervals around his or her preferred estimates.

Appendix B: The data

B1: Demand data

Most of the demand data were collected by StatsMR, a subsidiary of A. C. Nielsen Company. An observation is a brand of beer sold in a type of establishment, a region of the country and a time period. Brands are included in the sample if they accounted for at least one half of 1 per cent of one of the markets. There are sixty-three brands. Two types of establishments are considered, multiples and independents, two regions of the country, London and Anglia, and two bi-monthly time periods, Aug./Sept. and Oct./Nov. 1995. There are therefore potentially 504 observations. Not all variables were available for all observations, however. When data for an observation were incomplete, the corresponding observation was also dropped in the other region.[48] This procedure reduced the sample to 378 observations.

Establishments are divided into two types. Multiples are public houses that either belong to an organisation (a brewer or a chain) that operates fifty or more public houses or to estates with less than fifty houses that are operated by a brewer. Most of these houses operated under exclusive-purchasing agreements (ties) that limited sales to the brands of their affiliated brewer. Independents, in contrast, can be public houses, clubs, or bars in hotels, theatres, cinemas or restaurants.

For each observation, there is a price, sales volume and coverage. Each is an average for a particular brand, type of establishment, region and time period. Price, which is measured in pence per pint, is denoted PRICE. Volume, which is measured in 100 barrels, is denoted VOL, and coverage, which is the percentage of outlets that stocked the brand, is denoted COV.

VOL is the dependent variable in the distance-metric demand equation. With the nested logit specifications, in contrast, the dependent variable is LSHARE – the natural logarithm of the brand's overall market share – where

---

[48] Observations were dropped in both regions because prices in one region are used as instruments for prices in the other.

the market includes the outside good. The outside good here consists of all other alcoholic beverages. Beer's share of the alcoholic-beverage market averaged 55 per cent.[49]

In addition, there are data that vary only by brand. These variables are product type, brewer identity and alcohol content.

Brands are classified into four product types: lagers, stouts, keg ales and real ales. Unfortunately, three brands – Tetley, Boddingtons and John Smiths – have both real and keg-delivered variants. Since it is not possible to obtain separate data on the two variants, the classification that is used by StatsMR was adopted. Dummy variables that distinguish the four product types are denoted $PROD_i$, $i = 1, ..., 4$. The product types also form the basis of the groups for the nested logit specifications and those specifications include an explanatory variable LGSH, the natural logarithm of the brand's share of the group to which it belongs.

There are ten brewers in the sample, the four nationals, Bass, Carlsberg-Tetley, Scottish Courage and Whitbread, two brewers without tied estate,[50] Guinness and Anheuser Busch, and four regional brewers, Charles Wells, Greene King, Ruddles and Youngs. Brewers are distinguished by dummy variables, $BREW_i$, $i = 1, ..., 10$.

Each brand has an alcohol content that is measured in percentage. This continuous variable is denoted ALC. Moreover, brands whose alcohol contents are greater than 4.2 per cent are called premium, whereas those with lower alcohol contents are called regular beers. A dichotomous alcohol-content variable, PREM, that equals one for premium brands and zero otherwise, was therefore created.

Dummy variables that distinguish establishment types, MULT = 1 for multiples, regions of the country, LONDON = 1 for London, national brewers, NAT = 1 for nationals, and time periods, PER1 = 1 for the first period, were also created.

Finally, a variable, NCB or number of common-boundary neighbours, was created as follows. First, each brand was assigned a spatial market, where brand i's market consists of the set of consumers whose most preferred brand is closer to i in taste space than to any other brand. Euclidean distance in alcohol/coverage space was used in this calculation. Specifically, i's market consists of all points in alcohol/coverage space that are closer to i's location in

---

[49] When the logits are estimated, the log of the share of the outside good is moved to the right-hand side of the equation, where it is captured by market fixed effects.
[50] Brewers without tied estate are not vertically integrated into retailing.

that space than to any other brand's location. NCB_i is then the number of brands that share a market boundary (in the above sense) with i, where boundaries consist of indifferent consumers (i.e. loci of points that are equidistant from the two brands). This variable is designed to capture the number of products that are close substitutes for a given brand.[51]

B2: Cost data

Brewing and wholesaling costs include material, delivery, excise and advertising expenses per unit sold. Retailing costs include labour and wastage. Finally, combined costs include VAT. Two changes to the MMC figures were made. First, their figures include overhead, which is excluded here because it is a fixed cost. Second, their figures do not include advertising and marketing costs. Nevertheless, several of the companies report advertising expenditures per unit sold and the numbers in the table are averages of those figures.

Costs were updated to transform them into 1995 pence per pint. To do this, the closest available price index for each category of expense was collected and expenditures in each category were multiplied by the ratio of the appropriate price index in 1995 to the corresponding index in 1985.

If average variable costs (AVC) in brewing are constant, these numbers are marginal costs, but if AVC vary with output, they either over or underestimate marginal costs. However, it is difficult to predict the direction of the bias. Indeed, due to the presence of fixed costs, AVC can increase with output even when there are increasing returns.

---

[51] The details of this construction can be found in Pinkse and Slade (2004).

C.2

Coordinated effects

14 The ups and downs of the doctrine of collective dominance: using game theory for merger policy[1]

Eliana Garces-Tolon, Damien Neven and Paul Seabright

1. Introduction

Merger control has been an explicit responsibility of the European Union since 1990. During that time there has been a significant evolution in the way mergers are analysed, as well as in the institutional setting within which merger control is implemented. This chapter looks at just one aspect of this complex evolution – the development of a doctrine of collective dominance making use of game theory. The economic phenomenon of market power had to be cast until recently under the notion of a dominant firm.[2] In ordinary English language there can be only one 'dominant' individual in any group, so only one dominant firm in any market. But there can be market power when several firms are powerful even if none of them is dominant. Accordingly, European competition law had to stretch the concept of dominance to accommodate the concept of market power, by the ingenious invention of the idea that firms can be dominant collectively. This may sound a bit like the notions of group monogamy, or democratic centralism, but it has a logic that we shall examine in more detail below.

Until *Airtours*, collective dominance was not associated with any particular type of oligopolistic interaction that might lead to the exercise of market

---

[1] The first two authors currently work for the European Commission. Damien Neven was consultant to Airtours at the time of the Commission investigation and the subsequent appeal to the Court of First Instance. Paul Seabright was consultant to the Commission during the appeal to the Court, though not during the initial investigation. One aim in writing the current paper is to demonstrate that economists who have been consultants to parties on opposite sides of a case may nevertheless be able to agree on the relevant economic framework for analysing the case. All three authors are writing here in their personal capacity, and the views expressed in their paper should not be taken as indicative of the views of the European Commission or of any other organisations with which they have been associated. All three would like to express their gratitude to Paloma Repullo-Conde for excellent research assistance.
[2] Since 2004 the criterion has changed: all proposed mergers notified to the Commission are examined to see if they would 'significantly impede effective competition' in the EU rather than according to whether they 'create or strengthen a dominant position' as was the case before 2004. However, the Airtours case we consider below was examined under the former criterion.

power when none of the firms can be seen as individually dominant. Yet strategic interactions among the few are a pervasive phenomenon in modern economies, which most of the time has no anticompetitive implications at all. Anticipating, reacting to and seeking to influence the behaviour of competitors is an entirely normal part of business behaviour and is how most businesses carry out their activities, to the great benefit of their customers, shareholders and employees. It is, in short, how competition works. When do strategic interactions become a matter of legitimate public concern? This question was at the core of the *Airtours* decision.

The Commission asserted (para. 54) that:

It is sufficient that the merger makes it rational for the oligopolists, in adapting themselves to market conditions, to act – individually – in ways which will substantially reduce competition between them, and as a result of which they may act, to an appreciable extent, independently of competitors, customers and consumers.

Even if earlier case law (in particular *Gencor/Lonrho*[3]) had made loose reference to a mechanism of coordination in which the threat of enhanced rivalry triggered by short-term competition would support the collective exercise of market power, the Commission also indicated (para. 55) that:

Nor does it regard a strict retaliation mechanism, such as that proposed by Airtours in its reply to the Statement of Objections, as a necessary condition for collective dominance in this case; where, as here, there are strong incentives to reduce competitive action, coercion may be unnecessary.

This approach led to a conspicuous clash between the Commission and the Court over the Commission's allegedly unwarranted extension of its grounds for intervention.

The subsequent Court procedure clarified the doctrine that collective dominance should refer to a situation in which firms may coordinate their behaviour so as to act as though they were a monopoly or something close to it, even though they are apparently independent firms. Economists would call this tacit collusion and formulate it in terms of an equilibrium outcome in a repeated game. The Court chose to make explicit reference to this game theoretic framework and faced the challenge of bridging the gap between game theory and appropriate evidentiary standards. This challenge is different in merger control from that in ordinary antitrust investigations. In an antitrust investigation the authorities need to establish whether it is likely that

---

[3] Commission Decision 97/26/EC, Case No. IV/M.619 – *Gencor/Lonrho*, OJ L 11, 14.1. 1997, p. 30; judgment of the Court of First Instance of 25 March 1999 in Case T-102/96 *Gencor v Commission*.

collusion, explicit or tacit, has in fact taken place, and a range of types of evidence may be appropriate (including reports of the expectations of managers and so on). In merger control they need to establish whether the merger creates conditions under which tacit collusion is more likely than it was before, since the merger could be blocked (under the standard prevailing at the time) only if it 'creates or strengthens a dominant position'; evidence that collusion has taken place may be relevant to establish the existence of a collective dominant position. But evidence on the creation of such a position or its strengthening when it is has been established can only rely on general characteristics of the industry, plus general theoretical and empirical arguments linking those characteristics to probable future behaviour. So analysing collective dominance in a merger control setting focuses the investigation on the question: what are the economic conditions under which tacit collusion is likely?

Game theory is the prime source of inspiration to answer this question. So analysing tacit collusion in merger control is interesting for reasons that go far beyond the (so far relatively limited) number of cases in which it has played a decisive role. Game theory has often been criticised as a tool for economists on the grounds (roughly) that since it can explain anything it explains nothing; in some quarters it is considered to be like the chorus in a Greek tragedy, giving a melancholy interpretation of events as they unfold but doing nothing to help the actors in the drama master their fate. Since the theory of tacit collusion is the bridgehead for the use of game theory within public policy, its usefulness or otherwise is a fascinating test of its potential. Whether game theory yields satisfactory and useful insights here is an important indicator of its potential in other fields of public policy.

This chapter focuses on the theory of tacit collusion and what it tells us about how both the conditions favouring tacit collusion and the existence of collusive behaviour itself can be diagnosed. It goes on to assess the impact of the Court of First Instance decision in the *Airtours* case, which set out for the first time with the authority of legal precedent the criteria to be used to establish the likelihood of a merger creating the conditions for tacit collusion. We ask to what extent the Court's criteria provide a reliable guide to future policy in a range of different markets.

One should not be left under the impression that coordination is the only respect in which firms may exercise market power together even when none of them has enough market power to count as individually dominant. They may each exercise some market power independently (without any form of tacit coordination) and the sum of the effects of their individual exercise of market power may add up to something important. The most common manifestation of this is discussed in the US DoJ Horizontal Merger Guidelines under the heading of 'unilateral' effects. The revision of the merger regulation in 2004 has made it clear that such effects would be also captured by EU authorities (under the heading of 'non-coordinated effects').

2. The theory of tacit collusion

2.1 What is tacit collusion?

Tacit collusion is a market situation in which firms, without any explicit understanding, coordinate to gain higher-than-competitive profits in the market. The resulting conduct might look like a cartel agreement but is in fact a tacit understanding that all firms are individually better off by acting in a way that acknowledges and exploits their interdependence. European competition authorities refer to such a phenomenon as 'collective dominance' because tacitly colluding firms act at least in some dimensions of their decision space as a single dominant firm and can thereby exert market power collectively. Collective dominance normally has negative effects for consumers in terms of higher prices, lower quantities, lower quality or lower innovation.

What exactly does 'acknowledging their interdependence' mean in this context? The notion has two component parts. First, firms that acknowledge their independence know that by their behaviour they can influence the behaviour of their competitors. For instance, a firm that lowers its prices may believe that it is likely to provoke a retaliation in the form of lower prices by its competitors. Whereas the notion of Nash equilibrium in one-shot games, on which the idea of non-collusive interaction in imperfectly competitive markets is founded, implies that each firm takes its competitors' behaviour as given and responds passively to it, collusion – which is analysed as a Nash equilibrium of a more complex dynamic or at least repeated game – means that firms adopt strategies that are contingent on what their competitors do. The behaviour of competitors is thereby influenced and this interdependence can be used to induce all firms to behave more like a single dominant firm than it would otherwise be in their interests to do. This second component is important: a firm with some individual market power may realise that if it increases its output this will have a dampening effect on prices in the market – other firms will also be obliged to lower their prices to sell the output they have produced. But if the anticipated response of other firms is just a passive accommodation of the first firm's output increase, it is not interdependence in the sense we need for tacit collusion. Indeed, it is just the perception of a downward-sloping demand curve! For it to become tacit collusion the firms involved must each be setting higher prices, and lower outputs, than they would if they anticipated that other firms would just respond passively to their behaviour – they must believe that high prices prompt high prices and any behaviour that lowers prices provokes an active and conscious retaliatory response.

What kind of evidence might lead us to conclude that firms were acknowledging their interdependence in this way? The difference between 'responding passively' and 'responding actively and consciously' does not sound very precise. We even know that in theory it cannot be made precise: Klemperer and Meyer showed in 1989 that firms competing in supply functions rather than just in prices or in capacities could sustain any outcome from the competitive to the monopoly outcomes as a Nash equilibrium of a one-shot game.[4] What this means is that, provided their strategies of passive accommodation to each other's behaviour are sufficiently sophisticated (that is, are represented as supply functions rather than just as fixed quantities or fixed prices), it needs no conscious reaction to maintain outcomes close to those of a monopoly. Still, nobody claims that the supply functions described by Klemperer and Meyer describe the actual decision making of most businesses: in practice there is indeed a common-sense distinction between expecting that a rival's price or output will be affected by one's own behaviour and expecting the rival actively to respond. What evidence could tell us whether this is indeed happening?

The first thing to note is that the evidence relevant to determining whether firms are *capable* of acknowledging their interdependence is not at all the same as the evidence relevant to determining whether they are *actually* doing so. *Actually* acknowledging their independence will leave traces within the decision-making hierarchy of each firm. This is not the same as evidence of explicit collusion, which requires (at least) proof of communication between firms. Tacit collusion, by contrast, would involve firms in a calculation that their current strategy makes sense only because it would be impossible to deviate from this without provoking a reaction by rivals – such a calculation will usually leave traces in the form of memoranda or other documents available to key decision makers. Note that if the tacit collusion is working well no actual deviations may be observed – so paradoxically it may be easier to find evidence

---

[4] Klemperer and Meyer (1989). Stigler (1964).

of tacit collusion when it operates imperfectly than when it operates without a hitch. We discuss below what evidence might help to show that certain behaviour could best be interpreted as a deviation from tacit collusion.

By contrast, evidence that firms are *capable* of acknowledging their behaviour is not necessarily behavioural evidence at all – it is more typically evidence about the characteristics of products and conditions of their supply, factors independent of the behaviour of any one firm even if past behaviour may indicate that the firms in question were acting interdependently at the time.

Using the theory of tacit collusion in merger control therefore requires looking for quite different evidence from that required in the setting of anti-cartel policy. The latter requires evidence of actual behaviour. The former may also include evidence about capability and incentive to use that capability. To see this we first set out the theory of tacit collusion in simple formal terms.

2.2 Models of tacit collusion

The necessary elements for explicit collusion in a market were first described by Stigler (1964) and still form the basis for the analysis of tacit coordination. These are the identification of the terms of the agreement, the possibility of detecting deviations and the existence of a punishment mechanism. The terms of coordination must clearly identify the commonly agreed behaviour. In order to coordinate, firms must have some idea of what is expected from them and in particular what kinds of competitive behaviour will be met by a retaliatory response. They must know which dimension of competition is subject to coordination (e.g. price, output, innovation) and they must know what values of those variables that will elicit retaliation from their competitors. The more diverse or uncertain are the firms and the market conditions under which transactions take place, the more difficult it will be for firms to agree on the terms of coordination. Similarly, the more opaque the outcome of the transactions and the more varied the types and circumstances of the transactions, the more difficult the monitoring of the coordination will be and the more likely that deviations will occur. Stigler also pointed to the potentially destabilising reactions of potential entrants and large customers.

More recently, modern economic theory has accepted that some market conditions can be conducive to coordination without the need for an explicit agreement on the terms of coordination and the rules of retaliation.[5] Most business strategies have the property that two or more firms choosing their

---

[5] For a discussion of the implications of modern theory see Baker (1993).

strategies taking as given the strategy of their rivals will do less well by their own objectives than if they could collectively agree on an enforceable joint decision. (Game theorists refer to this as the generic inefficiency of Nash equilibrium.[6]) This is illustrated by the Prisoner's Dilemma game, in which two prisoners can each reduce their jail time if they cooperate not to confess but once a prisoner stays silent the other can break free and harm his partner if he does confess. Cooperation in this game is the efficient outcome, but it is not a Nash equilibrium because silence by any one prisoner is not the best response to the silence of the other inmate. Similarly, in a market characterised by price competition in which firms agree to raise prices, the best response to the existing high prices by any given firm is to undercut the agreed price and increase sales at the relatively high margins. For collusion of any type, explicit or tacit, to be possible some way must be found to transcend the logic of the Prisoner's Dilemma.

The analysis is very different when approached with an intertemporal perspective and firms are allowed to interact repeatedly. Repeated interaction may allow firms to react to deviations from the collusive outcome in ways that hurt the deviator.[7] Predicting such retaliation may eliminate the incentives to deviate and adopting the collusive strategy may indeed be the best strategy for all firms. In a dynamic framework, a stable and self-enforcing tacit collusion may therefore be a Nash equilibrium.

Formal underpinnings[8]

To illustrate the importance of repeated interaction formally, let a strategy s_i be the set of responses a_i of a firm i to all the possible observed market behaviours of competitors. The strategy includes all the responses a_i that are a best response to the current and expected actions of other firms – that is to say, they are the set of strategies that maximises the expected payoff of the firm to each possible strategy of its competitors, given its probability distribution over the parameters of the game. In a dynamic game, every response a_i is composed of a sequence of actions over time. In a Nash equilibrium, all firms' responses at every period are optimal responses to the observed actions of the remaining firms. The Nash equilibrium of an infinitely repeated game, or an oligopoly supergame as it is sometimes called, is the set of equilibrium responses over time for each of the firms. It represents a path over time of optimal actions by all firms. These actions

---

[6] Except in the special case of those supply functions that sustain a monopoly price in the model of Klemperer and Meyer.

[7] For a discussion on dynamic oligopoly games see Shapiro (1989).

[8] In this technical subsection, the key results are highlighted in italics for readers without a formal economics training.

may not be perfectly predictable since they may involve what are known as 'mixed' strategies – namely strategies that involve randomisation between particular actions (much as a footballer taking a penalty kick may choose at random between shooting left and shooting right so as to prevent the goalkeeper from guessing his intentions).

Nash equilibria assume that the structure of the game is common knowledge among the participants. This does not mean that there is full information about the parameters, but rather that there is a set of probability distributions over those parameters, representing each player's uncertainty about events in the game, and the parameters of that set of probability distributions are known to all the participants (who all know that the others know them, and so on). But even with this assumption, determining the likely outcome of a market interaction is in fact not so simple. *It is well known that dynamic games can have multiple equilibria, some of which may be a sequence of stable outcomes, some of which may not, some of which may involve different degrees of cooperation and some of which may involve no cooperation. It is therefore unrealistic to approach tacit collusion as an equilibrium that we can predict with certainty in some markets where certain conditions exist. But in a dynamic environment, tacit collusion can indeed be a possible equilibrium as firms weigh the loss of the extra profits of coordination against the short-run gain of a deviation.* For tacit collusion to be a best response for all firms, the future losses caused by retaliation must outweigh the short-term profits of deviating. This requires that deviation would threaten future coordination, in the sense that the best response of the remaining firms to the deviation, *after the deviation has occurred*, would be to suspend coordination at least temporarily. In other words the punishment threat must be credible. Technically, this imposes the requirement that punishment strategies must be subgame perfect equilibria (that is to say, they must remain rational for all players in every subgame of the game, whether the subgame is actually reached or not). The requirement for credible punishments renders explicit enforcement of agreements unnecessary and is the main contribution of modern game theory to the analysis of tacit collusion.

However, although explicit enforcement of agreements is not necessary for tacit coordination, this does not mean that whether or not collusive agreements are reached explicitly is irrelevant to market outcomes. Under a cartel, firms can communicate before they interact on the market and can therefore potentially choose the equilibrium outcome that maximises the total industry profit and provides the maximum possible benefits for all players. Under tacit collusion, the collusive outcome may not be Pareto optimal in the sense that, even though there is nothing to be gained with an individual deviation, firms could still increase their profits if they could collectively decide to move to a new equilibrium. *The implication is that tacit collusion does not necessarily produce an outcome that is close to monopoly outcomes; indeed, tacit collusion is likely to be less profitable than explicit cartels.* In cases of multiple possible equilibria, it may happen that one equilibrium is a 'focal point'. This means that a particular choice of equilibrium becomes obvious to the firms even though it may not be the preferred one for the joint industry. Published list prices, public announcements or pre-existing practices may signal to the firms which is the obvious choice or the focal point. The existence of focal points reduces the complexity of defining the terms of coordination though it may make it harder to reach the joint profit-maximising outcome. Additionally, tacit collusion may not be perfect or completely stable. Collusion might be on one aspect of competition and not on others or may involve only a fraction of the competitors in a market. Coordination may alternate with period of instability where firms temporarily deviate or strongly react to perceived actions by competitors. Such coordination may still potentially inflict serious harm on consumers.

The main principle in the analysis of tacit collusion is that coordination will appear when each firm expects a higher profit stream if it coordinates rather than if it chooses to deviate. Each firm compares the profit stream under both scenarios and decides which is the more profitable. Only when coordination is the most profitable option *for all firms* will tacit collusion arise as an equilibrium. *Given the existing strategies of competitors, two factors determine the relative profitability of deviation for each firm: the potential gains of a deviation and the relative valuation of present profits relative to future profits. The potential gains of a deviation will be themselves determined by two factors: how much can be gained during the period of deviation and how much forgone future profit will there be due to the reaction and retaliation of competitors. Credible punishments will produce sufficiently high losses to tip the balance towards favouring coordination.* Formally, the stream of profits of a firm can be expressed as follows:

$$\pi_i = \pi_{i0} + \sum_{t=1}^{\infty} \delta^t \pi_{it}$$

If the firm chooses to stick to the coordinated outcome, the stream of profits will be

$$\pi_i = \frac{1}{1-\delta} \pi_i^C$$

where π_i^C are the profits under collusion in each period. If the firm chooses to deviate, the profit stream will be the profits of deviation today π_i^D plus the discounted value of the profits determined by the retaliation strategy. For simplicity, we assume that after a deviation, firms revert to a static stage game equilibrium that produces profits π_i^{NC} in each period. The firm will choose to coordinate in all periods as long as in each period the profit stream from coordination is larger than could be obtained by deviating:

$$\frac{1}{1-\delta}\pi_i^C > \pi_i^D + \frac{\delta}{1-\delta}\pi_i^{NC}.$$

Friedman (1971a) proved that when the discount factor δ is close to 1 and detection is fast, tacit collusion can be the optimal response of firms in infinitely repeated games. *High discount factors imply a higher preference for future versus current profits (a low rate of discounting of the future) and render coordination more likely by decreasing the relative value of the gains of deviation. Rapid detection also limits the profits of the deviation since it limits the time during which those profits can be obtained. More generally, any factor that limits the gains of deviation or increases the speed of detection will increase the likelihood of a coordinated outcome.* This result showed that, given certain conditions about the profitability of deviating from tacit coordination and the firm's discount factor, tacit collusion is a possible market outcome. There is nonetheless the requirement that the deviation inevitably disrupts the coordination in a way that lowers the firm's profit in the future. Abreu (1986) showed that there are credible punishment designs that are more effective than a pure reversion to the static stage game in symmetric environments and which allow sustainable collusion equilibrium even with lower discount factors. The punishment he describes consists of all the firms adopting the worst outcome possible for the deviating firm, a price war for instance, and then reverting to the collusive outcome in the following period. This retaliation strategy imposes all the cost of deviation in the near period and the credibility of the punishment is supported by the fact that firms can then revert to the profitable coordinated outcome. In Abreu's terms the 'grim present' is made possible by the 'credible rosy future'.

It is straightforward to see that the temptation to cheat will be greater when there are more firms in a market, since the market share, and therefore profits, that await the cheating firm are larger compared to what they can expect from their share of a collusive outcome. It follows that asymmetries in market share will increase the likelihood that at least one of the colluding firms will be tempted to cheat. We return to these points below.

Price versus quantity competition: what difference does it make?

The simplest version of the theory of tacit coordination is set in a model of competition with homogeneous products and quantity setting by firms. It is a natural framework to the extent that quantity decisions, unlike price decisions, automatically translate into a particular market share outcome that may be more easily monitored and observed. More importantly, price competition models of fairly homogeneous markets with fixed costs or increasing returns lead to problems in the determinacy of equilibria which can make theoretical analysis difficult. But it is important to note that the results presented above do not presuppose any particular mode of competition and show instead that, given enough capacity for detection and reaction by competitors, tacit coordination can definitely arise in any competitive setting.

Nevertheless, one important difference between price and quantity competition should be noted here since it affects the answer to the question what kinds of evidence may be relevant to establishing whether tacit coordination is taking place. Under ordinary, non-collusive oligopolistic competition, prices are strategic complements, meaning that each firm's unilateral best response to the increase of prices by its rivals (without any consideration of retaliation) is to increase its own prices. This makes pricing behaviour a difficult tool for diagnosing collusive behaviour, since different firms' prices will tend to move together (even after controlling for common shocks) whether they are colluding or not. The difference between collusive and non-collusive price correlations is therefore a matter of degree and not of kind. However, quantities are strategic substitutes, meaning that each firm's unilateral best response to an increase in the capacities of its rivals is to *reduce* its own capacity. Quantity (or capacity) behaviour is therefore rather better suited to diagnosing collusive behaviour, since different firms' capacities will not tend to move together unless they are colluding (provided, that is, one can control adequately for common shocks, which is not always a straightforward thing to do). The difference between collusive and non-collusive capacity correlations *is* therefore a matter of kind and not just of degree.

2.3 The conditions facilitating tacit collusion

A whole body of literature is dedicated to determining the conditions that increase or decrease the likelihood of a (sufficiently) stable coordination. The results of this literature, which are discussed below, centre on the factors that permit the existence of a credible punishment, allow sustainable terms of coordination, facilitate detection and more generally reduce the gains from a deviation.

Credible punishment is the cornerstone of the theory of tacit collusion and it is what makes possible the theoretical possibility of a tacit collusion that survives over time. There are two important elements of a credible punishment: it must be severe enough to impose losses that at least cancel the gains of deviation and it must remain the optimal response of competitors after the deviation has actually occurred. Coordinated outcomes that are able to produce large gains will require the existence of very drastic reactions following the detection of deviations. Conversely, the more severe the punishment, the more effective the coordination can be. Also, in order to be credible, punishments that impose costs on retaliating firms that go beyond the sole loss of the benefits of coordination must be accompanied by a future compensation that gives them more than just the returns of the competitive outcome.

Because price-setting games in fairly homogeneous products can produce a very competitive outcome with prices close to marginal cost, a simple reversion to competition can be close to an optimal punishment under price competition even when the discount factor is not very close to one. Similarly, when there is a stronger preference for current income, an industry in which price wars can be particularly damaging will be further able to sustain coordination compared to quantity-setting environments. This must be balanced against the fact that deviation can be very profitable in a price-setting environment, particularly where there are no capacity constraints and there are many other firms the sales of which the deviator can easily capture with a small price decrease. Tacit collusion will not be sustainable when there is a very substantial proportion of the market than can be very quickly captured by any single firm. However, this requires firms to be able greatly to expand capacity in a short period of time, which is often an unrealistic assumption.

For this reason, tacit collusion in price-setting environments is commonly discussed in a two-stage competition framework in which firms first make capacity, sunk cost or investment decisions and then compete on price with the limitations imposed by the first-stage choice. Both the possibility to determine capacity or investment and the consequent constraint that this decision imposes on future behaviour have consequences for the existence of a credible punishment and therefore for the likelihood of tacit collusion in the industry.

The starting point is a classic paper by Kreps and Scheinkman (1983), which analyses firms producing homogeneous products, which invest unilaterally in capacity and then compete unilaterally in prices. They show that the result is the same outcome as if they had directly competed in quantities (provided certain technical conditions are met, notably governing the allocation of output among buyers when prices are identical). A series of later papers considers how such competition can produce tacit collusion in the repeated game. Brock and Scheinkman (1985) examine the case of exogenous capacities and show that in price competition between symmetric firms with capacity constraints, the optimal punishment is the reversion to the mixed strategy Bertrand equilibrium which produces the profits obtained when all rivals produce at capacity and the firm prices optimally with respect to the residual demand. They go on to show that a larger number of firms with unused capacity in the market will increase the effectiveness of the punishment and therefore enhance the stability of tacit coordination. The presence of unused capacity in the market, approximated in their model by the number of symmetric firms with excess capacity, is an essential element for a credible punishment to exist. Brock and Scheinkman argue that the number of firms can increase to the point that the gains from coordination are small enough to destabilise the collusive equilibrium.

In their analysis of two-stage games of competition, Benoit and Krishna (1987) establish that excess capacity occurs in all equilibria that support prices above the competitive Cournot equilibrium level, making it an indispensable feature of tacit collusion. Davidson and Deneckere (1990) go on to examine the investment decisions of firms in two-stage games where coordination happens only in the price-setting second stage. They find that investment in capacity, and particularly investment in excess capacity, will be positively correlated with the likelihood of collusion in the second stage. It will also be positively correlated with the level of collusion sustainable in the price-setting stage. High discount rates, approximated by low interest rates, and low capital investment costs will tend to raise capacity investments and therefore will increase the likelihood and efficacy of collusion.

The results obtained above apply to models with symmetric firms. Most results of models introducing asymmetric capacities have tended to indicate that asymmetry in firm capacity makes collusion more difficult. Lambson (1994) shows that collusion can exist with asymmetric capacities but it will involve adjusting capacity utilisation in such a way as to decrease incentives to cheat and allow effective punishment. Lambson shows that if no retaliating firm can supply the whole market, the existence of a credible punishment will result in smaller firms exhibiting lower capacity utilisation. On the contrary, if one large firm can supply the whole market, credible punishment can imply that the large firm exhibits lower capacity utilisation. Compte, Jenny and Rey (2002) conclude that if the total capacity of rival firms is not enough to supply the market, asymmetric capacity will destabilise tacit collusion since the largest firm will have an incentive to cheat and the remaining firms will not be able to effectively retaliate. However, if the degree of asymmetry is such that one firm is large enough that it can supply the whole market, tacit collusion may be secured by this asymmetry. Dechenaux and Kovenock (2003) describe a model in which prices and quantities are simultaneous decisions. In such a model, small firms can undercut the price of large firms and put a cap on their sales, just enough to prevent retaliation by larger firms. Asymmetric capacities and prices will entail asymmetric punishments which can sustain tacit collusion.

The elements that make tacit collusion possible can be mostly related to the possibility and credibility of retaliation when a firm deviates from collusive behaviour. This generally implies the ability to increase output and sales to an extent that will damage the business of the deviator. It also implies knowing when deviation occurs and retaliation is called for. Before examining the details of the *Airtours* case and how it resulted in an attempt to put these principles into practice, we review the literature analysing not the conditions under which tacit coordination can take place but the nature of the resulting equilibrium and how it might differ from competitive environments. We also briefly discuss the impact of collusion on welfare.

2.4 The nature of competition with tacit collusion

Colluding firms are aiming to produce a market outcome close to the one we would see under a monopoly. But tacit collusion rarely allows for the level of coordination and efficiency of a single monopoly firm. Diverging interests, issues of communication and overall information uncertainty will decrease to some degree the ability to collude efficiently. A relevant question is to ask whether economic theory sheds light on the predicted behaviour of collusive industries under different market circumstances. Ideally, we would want to be able to get some behavioural patterns that would be indicative of the presence of collusion. We discuss below some of the most important findings regarding the effect of various market conditions on collusive equilibria.

Shocks and cycles

Optimal prices under any type of competition will react to changes in market demand conditions, and firms engaging in tacit collusion must be able to do so if they are effectively to exploit monopoly power. However, there are several reasons why a collusive industry might not react in the same way a monopolist would in the face of changing demand conditions and why an industry engaging in tacit collusion might react differently from one engaged in an explicit cartel. First, if communication is difficult, it may be hard to signal a new coordinated outcome in the face of frequently changing market conditions. Even if fast and effective signalling were possible, firms may have different optimal responses to the fluctuations in demand. And even in the face of symmetry, there are reasons to believe that demand shocks can threaten the stability of tacit collusion and will have consequences for the extent to which prices can be raised through coordination. There has been an unresolved debate about whether prices in a collusive industry move with or against the business cycle. Rotemberg and Saloner (1986) argue that in industries with cyclical demand, tacit collusion is likely to be less effective during booms when demand is high. This is because benefits from deviating by lowering prices are larger since there is a larger market to gain. Yet the losses inflicted by retaliation will be smaller since retaliation occurs in the next period when the level of demand is lower (assuming high demand today does not imply high demand tomorrow). Increased incentives to cheat and weaker retaliation can therefore destabilise tacit collusion during periods of high demand, particularly so if firms are impatient and value current profits more than future profits. Rotemberg and Saloner argue that deviations and price wars are more likely during booms and that those collusive outcomes that survive will do so at lower levels of price in order to limit the gains from potential deviation. In the presence of capacity constraints, collusive prices will exhibit less of this countercyclical characteristic since the limited ability to increase output will limit the incentives to deviate. This idea is further developed by Staiger and Wolak (1992), who include capacity constraints and endogenous capacity decisions in their model. One may see 'price wars during booms' as long as firms have enough excess capacity to serve substantial additional demand, but as the cost of investment rises and capacity constraints kick in, incentives to deviate diminish. During slumps, falling capacity utilisation will trigger a softening of collusion, which can degenerate into short price wars. Varying market shares in an industry with some remaining capacity constraints can, in this context, be interpreted as a sign that the industry is not able to sustain a collusive outcome. When capacity constraints disappear due to very low demand, price wars are replaced by a lower stable uniform price. With endogenous capacity, it will be the cost of adding capacity which will determine whether the industry will exhibit price wars during booms or price wars during moderate demand falls. A less effective collusion during booms will happen when the cost of capacity is cheap while unstable collusion during demand slumps will occur when adding capacity is costly and there is little excess capacity in the industry.

Haltiwanger and Harrington (1991) use other arguments to rebut the idea that collusion may be more stable during periods of low demand. They claim that the important factor in determining the stability of collusion, *ceteris paribus*, is the expected evolution of demand, not its current level. In Rotemberg and Saloner, states of demand are independent across periods. Haltiwanger and Harrington claim that a more realistic model is to assume that an observed high demand today creates expectations of a high demand tomorrow and a low demand today generates expectations for future falls in demand. Business cycles exhibit serial correlation and there are successive periods of increasing or falling demand. With this observation in mind, and applying a similar reasoning to that of Rotemberg and Saloner, they show that deviation is less likely in periods of increasing demand and that, on the contrary, collusive outcomes are less stable in periods of falling demand. Collusive prices are then procyclical.

Bagwell and Staiger (1997) use a more sophisticated characterisation of the business cycle to study collusive behaviour. They assume positively correlated demand conditions but add the possibility of downturns or upturns. They also allow for short-lived unexpected shocks during any phase of the cycle. They find that during a boom or recession phase, prices may be procyclical. Collusive prices may tend to rise with demand when demand is growing and fall with falling demand. This phenomenon will be more accentuated the longer the recessions are expected to be. Before downturns prices may fall, and before upturns prices may increase, indicating that with negative correlation of demand growth rates, collusive prices will be countercyclical. Within the broader demand cycles, unexpected transitory demand surges may trigger lower prices both during booms and recessions. The results of Rotemberg and Saloner are then to be understood as applying only to unexpected transitory shocks in demand rather than to business cycles. The question of whether collusive prices move with or counter to demand business cycles is ultimately an empirical question. Unfortunately, available studies do not resolve the issue, with some evidence of cartels collapsing during periods of high demand and some collapsing during recessions.

Imperfect monitoring

Changing demand conditions will affect the stability of collusion even when those changes are fully observed and even predicted. What happens when firms are not immediately aware of market demand conditions, and particularly when they do not know the demand conditions that their competitors are facing?

Green and Porter (1984) showed that collusion is still possible with imperfect information about prices and demand, but it will be somewhat unstable and characterised by periods of price wars. A situation of demand uncertainty implies that when the sales of firms turn out to be lower than expected, a firm cannot know whether the fall in sales is due to lower prices by the competitor or to a decrease in demand. This is because, although some monitoring is feasible, the outcome which is monitored (price or market share) is an imperfect predictor of the rival firm's conduct. Green and Porter argue that firms in a colluding industry with imperfect monitoring will react by behaving as if the rival had cheated when the price falls under some predetermined 'trigger price'. Below this price, firms will revert to the Cournot non-collusive oligopoly outcome for some period of time, after which they will revert to the collusive outcome. The lower the trigger price, the longer the reversion to the non-collusive outcome will need to be, to ensure that the rarity of retaliation is compensated by its severity. The 'trigger-price strategy', as this optimal strategy has been named, supports durable although imperfect collusion. A conclusion of the Green and Porter paper is that evidence of periods where prices and profit sharply decrease in an industry should not automatically be interpreted as evidence that collusion is unlikely or collapsing. It might instead be evidence of optimal behaviour in a collusive industry with imperfect information on rivals' behaviour.

Abreu, Pearce and Stacchetti (1986) relax Green and Porter's assumptions on the possible behaviour of firms and more generally characterise optimal collusive equilibria for industries with imperfect monitoring. The only constraint they impose is firm symmetry. They do not impose a trigger-price strategy or a reversion to Cournot as the only alternative to the collusive outcome, and they allow for past outcomes to determine current decisions. Still, they find that the optimal collusive path involves only two states, a 'high' and a 'low' production level, and that the firm needs only to look at the price and output in the previous period to know which one to choose. The optimal 'trigger' price will not be dependent on previous outcomes. The general idea of Green and Porter therefore survives generalisation, although it still applies only in situations in which punishment cannot be targeted to one specific firm. When such punishments are available and there is a public signal indicating possible deviation, it might be possible to maintain the overall efficiency of the collusion through a system of transfers that penalises only the potential cheater.[9] In such cases, price wars or sub-optimal behaviour will not necessarily be observed as part of the optimal collusive path.

---

[9] See Fudenberg *et al.* (1994) and Matsushima (1989).

Private information and communication

Imperfect monitoring is aggravated when firms get different signals from the market. In the previous discussion shocks to the market outcome being monitored are similarly perceived and interpreted by all firms. This may not necessarily be an accurate description of real markets. Product differentiation, for example, may result in one firm experiencing a surge in demand while its main competitor is experiencing a demand fall. While the latter firm would think that some firm might be undercutting prices, the former will not have such an impression. Kandori and Matsushima (1998) find that in markets with private and imperfect signals, collusion is still feasible if firms establish the incentives to communicate voluntarily among themselves and that the behaviour of any given firm can be inferred from the communication outcomes perceived by its rivals. They show that delays in communication can enhance the efficiency of the collusive outcome when firms' actions are affected by their private information. This has obvious implications for the stability of tacit collusion by comparison with explicit cartels, since communication in such cases has often to be carried out indirectly (for example via industry associations) or by inference from public announcements made ostensibly with other aims in mind. Compte (1998) similarly concludes that a system of voluntary communication may help coordination even when firms do not have an incentive to tell the truth, provided that not everyone's information is necessary to detect deviation. He also argues that private signalling and the ability to delay the timing of the communication can increase the efficiency of the collusion.[10] Both papers underline the facilitating role of communication in situations where information on the market outcome is private and imperfect. However, this does not imply that communication is strictly necessary for a collusive equilibrium in repeated games with imperfect monitoring and private information.

Private information may originate because a particular firm experiences a shock in its production costs, making it either more or less efficient than its rivals. Efficient coordination requires that low-cost firms are assigned a higher market share, but this will be possible only if the high-cost firm is somehow compensated with transfers or promises of future higher market shares.[11] Side payments and express communication are generally illegal and are therefore assumed not to exist under tacit collusion. Their occurrence would turn the

---

[10] Delaying the release of information is also found to increase the efficiency of collusion in markets with public information. See Abreu et al. (1991).

[11] See Schmalensee (1987).

tacitly collusive industry into an explicit cartel. Athey and Bagwell (2001) show that price-setting tacit collusion can be achieved in the presence of privately known random shocks to costs, but firms must grant 'market share favours' to some firms as rewards for cutting production in high-cost circumstances.[12] Although the requirement to compensate the firm by granting higher marker shares in the future may involve productive inefficiencies, this becomes less likely when firms are very patient. Therefore a firm's private information on its production conditions need not preclude efficient coordination. Athey and Bagwell also demonstrate that, as in the full information model, communication is not necessary with patient firms. With more impatient firms the role of communication becomes ambiguous as it can either destabilise or facilitate coordination. Restricting communication will have no effect on the ability to collude of patient firms but will still tend to lower the efficacy of coordination with sufficiently impatient firms. More importantly, and contrary to common belief, fluctuations in market shares will be pervasive under such types of coordination. Yet in the case where asymmetric punishment is impossible and punishment must be borne by all firms equally, there is an equilibrium coordination path which involves price rigidity.[13] This equilibrium will result in inefficient collusion, with prices not responding to individual firm shocks. The inefficiency will be compensated by the elimination of the risk of reacting sub-optimally to misinterpreted signals. Such types of coordination will never exhibit price wars and will produce inefficient price rigidity.

Investment, innovation and entry

Free entry is generally thought to prevent coordinated equilibria because positive profits will induce profit-eroding entry.[14] But when there are large sunk costs that need to be incurred prior to production, these investments may be subject to tacit collusion in turn. A two-stage game in which firms first choose their capacity level and then compete on prices produces market outcomes similar to the Cournot outcome, as we discussed above. With an infinite repetition of this sequential decision, we are faced again with the existence of multiple equilibria involving production levels anywhere between the competitive and the monopoly outcomes.

---

[12] The model crucially assumes that past history information is public.

[13] See Athey *et al.* (2004).

[14] Friedman and Thisse (1994) nevertheless show that collusion can exist with free entry as long as firms enter and increase size gradually and the number of potential entrants is bounded.

It is generally possible to describe within an industry how capacity adjusts to changing market conditions. But it is much more difficult to explain the investment decisions and to identify the nature of the game leading to particular patterns of capacity investments. Gilbert and Lieberman (1987) examine evidence of the chemical product industry and conclude that investment patterns show indicia of both coordination and pre-emption. Large firms generally invest to maintain their market share in the market over the long run but use pre-emptive investment to impose the sequencing of capacity expansion. In markets with large upfront investments and sunk costs, it is not uncommon to see firms announce investment plans well in advance to signal future actions to competitors. Farrell (1987) argues that cheap talk, where firms announce their entry or investment plans without any need to commit to them or any cost to not following up, can produce a coordinated outcome. The condition is that the announcement must represent a Nash equilibrium action by the firm, that rivals expect the firm to follow up and that the firm actually does follow up. If this is so, the announcement can induce coordination with asymmetric outcomes. This model applies only when firms produce somewhat complementary products and entry by anyone is preferred to no entry, normally because the new market provides a complementary good or service to another market in which the firms are also active.

Christensen and Cave (1997) examine the evidence in the pulp and paper industry, where this condition is less likely to hold, and find evidence of frequent announcements of capacity expansion projects which are subsequently abandoned. Their conclusion is that cheap talk is not always effective and the level of credibility of the investment announcements matters. The quality of information and the level of experience of a firm also determine the likelihood that it will abandon a project. Both Gilbert and Lieberman (1987) and Christensen and Cave (1997) are unable to truly identify the underlying model of investment decision. They produce regularities that seem to be consistent with elements of Cournot-style competition but that fall short of excluding coordinated strategies.

Product differentiation and semi-collusion

In industries that exhibit some element of product differentiation, firms compete not only on price but on quality, brand name and innovation. It is possible that in such industries firms coordinate prices but aggressively compete on innovation, advertising and product quality. Fershtman and Gandal (1993) argue that semi-collusion in the second stage only of a two-stage game is not generally profitable as firms will over-invest in first-stage capacity or R&D and this will tend to at least offset the benefits brought by higher collusive prices. The conclusion is that firms are better off fully competing. Fully colluding or colluding only in the first investment stage is an even more profitable alternative. Consumers are also generally worse off under second-stage semi-collusion because first-stage decisions do not compensate for the higher level of prices. Brod and Shivakumar (1999) argue that collusion can benefit both firms and consumers when there are spillovers to innovation and the level of differentiation is not too large. On the other hand, if products are only moderately substitutable and there are no spillovers to R&D, both consumers and firms would be hurt by semi-collusion, as predicted by Fershtman and Gandal (1993). Product differentiation therefore seems to decrease the benefits and incentives for colluding only at the production level. But Ross (1992) argues that product differentiation can also increase the stability of collusion. Differentiated products reduce the magnitude of possible retaliation but also decrease the incentives to deviate. Under certain market conditions, differentiation will help stabilise collusion. Product differentiation could even play the role of market allocation in a collusive industry.

Fershtman and Pakes (2000) suggest that the scope for product differentiation in a very concentrated industry will make collusion in the second stage of an investment-pricing game beneficial for consumers. They find that collusion at the pricing stage can result in a less concentrated market, with more product variety and higher quality. These benefits can more than offset the negative effect of the higher prices on consumer welfare, although this is not necessarily the case. Their results are valid for a very concentrated industry in which the competitive world generates a 'winning' firm that becomes dominant upon successful innovation. But if there is scope for collusion, the successful firm will accommodate other innovative firms and a higher level of innovation and quality will ensue. The possibility of collusion thus generates dynamic incentives to enter and innovate so there will be more entry and product variety than under the competitive scenario. In this model, the benefits of collusion are guaranteed by the limited entry that would exist even under competition.

The literature on tacit collusion in repeated games has grown rapidly and there is a large number of different models drawing a plethora of conclusions. The brief literature review presented above is enough to illustrate the variety of possible settings under which tacit collusion can in principle occur and the different manifestations that it may take in a market. In the next section, we discuss practical conclusions that could be derived from the theoretical analysis.

2.5 Practical implications for determining the likelihood of tacit collusion

The basic theory of tacit collusion does provide some necessary conditions for tacit collusion to be a possibility. A collusive equilibrium requires optimal strategies that involve credible retaliation in the face of deviation. It also requires that firms have access and respond to some type of information indicating that a deviation has taken place. A tacitly collusive industry requires that collusion is the preferred outcome for all significant suppliers and potential suppliers in the market. Finally, collusion is sustainable if and only if firms put sufficient weight on future profits.

As can be seen from this selective review, the various models of tacit collusion show that under certain market circumstances the necessary conditions for successful coordination are more (or less) likely to be met. Nevertheless, Ivaldi *et al.* (2003) summarise some general conclusions about the factors that affect the likelihood of collusion. These conclusions provide neither sufficient nor necessary conditions for tacit collusion but they can be considered to apply in a wide range of circumstances.

1) Collusion is more difficult when there are more competitors.
2) Market share symmetry is not in itself a facilitating factor, but market share *asymmetry* may be the result of more profound and relevant asymmetries (in cost or capacities, for instance) that tend to make collusion more difficult to sustain.
3) Entry barriers facilitate collusion.
4) Frequent interaction and frequent price adjustments facilitate collusion.
5) Market transparency facilitates collusion.
6) For a fixed number of market participants, collusion is easier to sustain in growing markets, where today's profits are small compared with tomorrow's ones. However, market growth may be associated with market characteristics detrimental to collusion, for instance because they increase the likelihood of future entry.
7) Business cycles and demand fluctuations hinder collusion.
8) Collusion is more difficult in innovative markets.
9) Cost asymmetries hinder collusion; indeed, cost asymmetries are the best way to interpret the phenomenon of the 'maverick' firm.
10) When firms are differentiated in quality, collusion is more difficult, the larger the competitive advantage of the high-quality firm. However,

the impact of horizontal differentiation appears quite ambiguous. Product differentiation may exacerbate informational problems in non-transparent markets.

11) Multi-market contact may make collusion easier.

12) Buyer power makes collusion more difficult.

13) Structural links and information exchanges between firms make collusion easier.

14) Club and network effects hinder collusion.

On the face of it, this list is impressive, since it appears to indicate that we know quite a lot about the conditions under which tacit collusion is likely to occur. However, a long list of conditions is not much help unless we know something about the relative weight to be attached to each condition – how can we evaluate a market where half the conditions appear to be favourable and half of them unfavourable, for instance? And how can the various conditions be measured?

As for the evidence to be drawn from observed market outcome, it is equally difficult to find a perfectly identifying conduct that would establish collusion. Still, sporadic price wars, excess price rigidity in the face of market or private shocks, or evidence of signalling by firms could be interpreted as indicia of imperfect (but working) tacit collusion. But these manifestations are certainly not sufficient evidence of coordination. Also, unstable market shares or a high degree of product differentiation, normally associated with competitive outcomes, can also be consistent with collusive equilibria.

It becomes immediately apparent that assessing the likelihood of tacit collusion is a balancing exercise. What evidence to consider and how to weight it? These difficulties were exposed in a stark form by the *Airtours* case, which jolted the European Commission out if its previous optimism that intuitive judgement plus some general principles would be enough to place its decisions beyond judicial reproach, and which we consider in more detail in section 3 below.

Before we go on to discuss how to handle the evidence, let us first summarise from our previous discussion what the evidence will actually be. Table 14.1 shows the nature of the evidence that is pertinent to answering the different questions competition authorities might ask about tacit collusion.

Having summarised what the theory can teach us about assessing the likelihood of tacit collusion, we now proceed to consider the *Airtours* case and examine to what extent economic theory has been able to guide policy in this area.

Table 14.1 Evidence of collusion

Setting	Question	Evidence type	Evidence of communication that increases likelihood of collusion	Evidence generally supportive of collusion over competition	Evidence not distinguishing collusion from competition
Cartel policy	Are firms explicitly colluding?	Firm behaviour	Directly between competitors	Capacity co-movements	Price co-movements
Cartel policy/ merger policy	Are firms tacitly colluding?	Firm behaviour	Within firm Indirectly to competitors	Capacity co-movements Sporadic price wars Price rigidity	Price co-movements
Merger policy	Would merger increase the capability and incentive for tacit collusion?	Expected behaviour	Within firm Indirectly to competitors	Few firms Frequent interaction Entry barriers Transparency Predictability – Market stability Symmetry	

3. The *Airtours* case

3.1 The facts

Airtours and First Choice were, and still are, two UK tour operator companies (though Airtours has been part of the Thomas Cook group since 2007). The former operated across seventeen European countries, while the latter operated mainly in the UK and Ireland. As their joint worldwide turnover exceeded €5 billion and they did not achieve more than two-thirds of this turnover within one Member State, when Airtours decided to acquire First Choice on 29 April 1999, the decision had a Community dimension.

On 3 June the Commission undertook a Stage II investigation as it had concerns about the compatibility of the merger with the common market. A month later, on 9 July, the Commission sent the applicant a statement of objections with the reasons it had to believe the merger would lead to a collectively dominant position in the UK. On 7 September the Commission received a set of undertakings from the applicant. A final decision was made on 22 September 1999, when the Commission declared the merger incompatible with the common market. Two months later the applicant appealed to the Court of First Instance but did not obtain judgment until 6 June 2002, when the Commission's decision was overturned.

3.2 Relevant market analysis and market structure

In previous decisions concerning this market, as well as in the *Airtours/First Choice* case, the Commission accepted that the relevant geographical market was on a national basis: in particular, Ireland and the UK would have two separate relevant markets. The basic reason for this definition was due to their differences of structure of the industries and their evolution. However, there were other reasons, such as the fact that the brochures were prepared for the 'home state', which meant that a consumer travelling with a foreign tour operator would have to deal with a different brochure (possibly in a foreign language), with arranging separately the flight to the departure airport chosen by the company and with redressing possible complaints as the law that would apply would be the one from the foreign country.

Airtours and First Choice were two vertically integrated companies, both downstream, with the travel agencies, and upstream, with the airline operations, and their operations overlapped in the UK and Ireland. These tour operators supplied mainly package holidays. At the time this was considered to be a different market from the holidays in which consumers organised travel by themselves, using internet booking and low-cost airlines for example. These independent holidays are undoubtedly more of a competitive constraint now than they were at the time of the decision.

The product market was divided into long-haul[15] and short-haul destinations in foreign packages as the aircraft were not considered interchangeable, the prices were very different, as were the type of consumers, and because of large differences in the length of flights. Since both parties were far more important in the short-haul sector, and since neither the independent travel agencies nor the suppliers of airline seats nor the supply of travel services on the internet were considered to provide close enough substitutes for the services of the parties to exert an appreciable competitive discipline upon them, the relevant product market was finally defined as the market for short-haul foreign package holidays.

---

[15] The long-haul destinations include all those whose time of flight from the UK substantially exceeds three hours.

The relevant product market structure in the UK market, at the time of the notification, included four large tour operators,[16] which were all vertically integrated, and a 'fringe' of small tour operators,[17] which were not integrated and operated on a 'niche' basis. The Commission argued that the effective competition that the 'fringe' could offer to the majors was quite restricted[18] as the small ones did not benefit from economies of scale or scope and therefore had higher costs of operation. However, in the Court's later analysis of the market it was shown that small tour operators could indeed compete effectively.[19] In fact, the 'fringe' firms were able to obtain similar hotel prices, had no real problem in terms of airline seats,[20] and were capable of responding to opportunities created by undersupply.[21]

One of the reasons why the small firms were able to react to possible undersupply of the majors was the fact that the 'fringe' tour operators normally set their capacities after the majors and this provided them with some time for reaction even though the packages were 'produced' 12–18 months in advance of the following season (this involved booking hotel rooms, leasing aircraft, printing brochures and so on). This reduced the risks for the smaller firms.

3.3 Collective dominance

The Commission argued that the concentration would lead to the creation of a collective dominant position with the two other leading groups left after the merger in short-haul package holidays in the UK.[22] There were considered to be no significant problems created by the merger in the Irish market.[23] The reasons for this were, first, that the number of large remaining firms would be

---

[16] Each of those major firms had a market share of more than 10 per cent of the market. According to the Commission's numbers Thompson had 27 per cent of the market share, followed by Airtours with 21 per cent, Thomas Cook with 20 per cent and First Choice with 11 per cent. The figures differ if we take into account Airtours numbers. In this case Thompson had 30.7 per cent of the market share, followed by Thomas Cook with 20.4 per cent, Airtours with 19.4 per cent and First Choice with 15 per cent. See para. 72 in Commission Decision of 22 September 1999, Case No. IV/M.1524 – Airtours/First Choice.

[17] None of the 'fringe' firms had a market share which exceeded 5 per cent. Court of First Instance Decision of 6 June 2002, Case T-342/99 – Airtours/Commission of the European Communities, para. 66.

[18] Commission Decision of 22 September 1999, Case No. IV/M.1524 – Airtours/First Choice, para. 78.

[19] Court of First Instance Decision of 6 June 2002, Case No. T-342/99 – Airtours/Commission of the European Communities, para. 251.

[20] Court of First Instance Decision of 6 June 2002, Case No. T-342/99 – Airtours/Commission of the European Communities, para. 232.

[21] Court of First Instance Decision of 6 June 2002, Case No. T-342/99 – Airtours/Commission of the European Communities, para. 218.

[22] Commission Decision of 22 September 1999, Case No. IV/M.1524 – Airtours/First Choice, para. 58.

[23] The merger would result in a duopoly in a relatively undeveloped market that was just starting to grow and, therefore, had great incentives for future entry and competition.

reduced to three. Second, the merger would increase transparency,[24] thereby favouring collusion between the large tour operators. Third, given that there was already a tendency towards actual tacit collusion, the merger would enhance it.[25] Fourth, there existed several mechanisms for retaliation.[26] Finally, the 'fringe' firms[27] would be even less capable of competing in the market[28] than before the merger.

The Court in its judgment focused on three main questions in assessing the claim of collective dominance.[29] First, each oligopoly firm needed to be able to monitor the rest so as to check that they did not deviate from the common policy, and in case of deviation they should have been able to punish the deviating firm. Second, there needed to exist great incentives so as not to deviate from that policy over time – that is to say, there would have to be a lot to lose from deviating while a small gain from doing so. Third and last, the reaction of both actual and future competitors and consumers had to be taken into account, as their reaction in the hypothetical situation of undersupply would determine whether the colluding firms could expect to make significant profits.

Both the Commission and the Court therefore spent much time examining the characteristics of the market with a view to assessing the extent to which these would facilitate tacit collusion.

3.4 Market characteristics

The Commission argued that certain characteristics of the market favoured collusion between the largest tour operators.[30] The first characteristic was that the products offered in this market (the different short-haul foreign destinations) were relatively homogeneous, as all packages included both travel and hotel accommodation. Even though Airtours argued that the quality of the packages varied, around 85 per cent of customers were mainly influenced by the price and most of them chose intermediate three-star/self-catering types of accommodation.[31]

---

[24] Commission Decision of 22 September 1999, Case No. IV/M.1524 – Airtours/First Choice, para. 147.
[25] Commission Decision of 22 September 1999, Case No. IV/M.1524 – Airtours/First Choice, para. 138.
[26] Commission Decision of 22 September 1999, Case No. IV/M.1524 – Airtours/First Choice, para. 151.
[27] The 'fringe' firms are the small tour operators which are not vertically integrated.
[28] Commission Decision of 22 September 1999, Case No. IV/M.1524 – Airtours/First Choice, para. 86.
[29] Court of First Instance Decision of 6 June 2002, Case T-342/99 – Airtours/Commission of the European Communities, para. 62.
[30] Commission Decision of 22 September 1999, Case No. IV/M.1524 – Airtours/First Choice, para. 86.
[31] Commission Decision of 22 September 1999, Case No. IV/M.1524 – Airtours/First Choice, para. 88.

The second characteristic, according to the Commission, was low demand growth,[32] especially given that most of it was due to acquisitions of existing firms and not to organic growth. However, this assertion was severely criticised by the Court because whatever the source of growth, there had been continuous growth in the last decade in the demand for short-haul foreign packages.[33] There was also a dispute between the Commission and Airtours in terms of the volatility of this demand,[34] as the former stated that the volatility was due largely to the predictable influence of the business cycle, while Airtours argued that it was due mainly to unpredictable exogenous shocks. With respect to market shares, once again Airtours and the Commission did not agree,[35] with Airtours arguing that the market was competitive since market shares had been fluctuating, dynamic and volatile, while the Commission argued that these fluctuations were due mainly to acquisitions and were thus uninformative about the competitive state of the market.

The third characteristic was the transparency of the market.[36] Here the main issue was the extent to which firms could infer from market data the extent to which their rivals might be adhering to, or deviating from, a tacitly collusive outcome. Airtours claimed that it was nearly impossible to monitor rivals' behaviour given that there were thousands of individual prices for package holidays, so it would have been impossible to agree upon a collusive price and to monitor deviations from that price.[37] In addition, because the output is perishable and there is uncertainty about the distribution of demand, prices change very fast and unpredictably in the later part of the season, reflecting discounting of unsold holidays. Although the Commission was of the view that systems such as the 'yield management systems'[38] or 'VIEWDATA'[39] that favoured the exchange of information might make for price transparency even so the investigation quickly converged on the hypothesis that the real object of the hypothetical tacit collusion

---

[32] Commission Decision of 22 September 1999, Case No. IV/M.1524 – Airtours/First Choice, para. 92.

[33] Court of First Instance Decision of 6 June 2002, Case T-342/99 – Airtours/Commission of the European Communities, para. 123.

[34] Commission Decision of 22 September 1999, Case No. IV/M.1524 – Airtours/First Choice, paras. 94 and 95.

[35] Court of First Instance Decision of 6 June 2002, Case No. T-342/99 – Airtours/Commission of the European Communities, paras. 109 and 110.

[36] Commission Decision of 22 September 1999, Case No. IV/M.1524 – Airtours/First Choice, para. 102.

[37] Commission Decision of 22 September 1999, Case No. IV/M.1524 – Airtours/First Choice, para. 108.

[38] 'These systems are designed to enable yields (profit margin) to be optimised at varying levels of sales across the different selling periods (and in particular the "lates" period).' Commission Decision of 22 September 1999, Case No. IV/M.1524 – Airtours/First Choice, para. 106.

[39] VIEWDATA is 'a computerised booking system which displays in real time the availability and prices of holidays supplied by participating tour operators, which includes all the large ones and some of the "fringe" '. Commission Decision of 22 September 1999, Case No. IV/M.1524 – Airtours/First Choice, para. 107.

would not be prices but capacities, which are set between a year and eighteen months in advance of the selling season and are relatively difficult to change thereafter. In addition capacities (known in this industry as 'bed nights') could be considered a relatively homogeneous dimension along which to aggregate holidays, giving a good picture of the overall competitive stance of a firm independently of uncertainties about quality and other characteristics. The Commission stated that 'in this industry there is, therefore, no need to coordinate on price' (para. 91). The Commission believed that capacities did not change much from one year to the next and that any such changes would be relatively easy to detect from market data. The Court disagreed, claiming that tour operators did not just renovate their old capacities but regularly introduced modifications depending on their forecasts,[40] so that the information obtained in the previous year would not be enough to make the market transparent.

The fourth characteristic was the presence of important barriers to entry.[41] Airtours argued that these were very low, given that there had been entrance and exit, that there were no regulatory constraints and that the financial requirements to enter this market were not overwhelming. However, in the Commission's opinion the market was much more concentrated than when the UK Monopolies and Mergers Commission had carried out a report on this very market in 1997 and inferred from this the presence of higher barriers to entry than had previously existed, due to the extent of vertical integration in the market. However, the Court found that even if the merger proceeded this would not imply great alterations of the market structure and upheld the main conclusions of the MMC Report.

The fifth and final characteristic was the presence of buyer power.[42] Once again Airtours and the Commission completely disagreed as the former believed that the buyers could shop around and so they had a certain degree of power, while the latter claimed that this was not feasible given the fact that there was 'directional selling' in the agencies which belonged to integrated tour operators and that the information on the brochures was limited.

3.5 The Court judgment and the 'Airtours criteria'

The Court of First Instance gave its judgment on 6 June 2002, nearly three years after the Commission's decision. It found the decision to be 'vitiated by a series of errors of assessment as to factors fundamental to any assessment of

---

[40] Court of First Instance Decision of 6 June 2002, Case No. T-342/99 – Airtours/Commission of the European Communities, para. 164.
[41] Commission Decision of 22 September 1999, Case No. IV/M.1524 – Airtours/First Choice, para. 115.
[42] Commission Decision of 22 September 1999, Case No. IV/M.1524 – Airtours/First Choice, para. 124.

whether a collective dominant position might be created'. It also for the first time specified what these factors were, in terms that have come to be known as the 'Airtours criteria':

- The market must be sufficiently transparent to enable each member of the oligopoly to monitor whether other members of the oligopoly are 'cheating' (i.e. acting independently of the oligopoly and deviating from the coordinated behaviour).
- The oligopolists' coordination must be sustainable over time, meaning that there must be a credible threat of punishment that will deter companies from 'cheating'.
- The common policy of the oligopolists must be able to resist external constraints, such as new entrants, the ability of smaller operators to compete and the ability of customers to switch products in response to price increases.

The judgment was a major shock to the Commission and contributed to a significant overhaul of internal procedures, including eventually the appointment of a chief economist. On the face of it, the judgment also helped to clarify the way in which the Commission needed to analyse tacit collusion, along much more explicitly and rigorously economic lines than before. However, recent developments have raised some new and difficult questions.

3.6 An economic assessment

It is evident from the theory as we have set it out in section 2 that the three 'Airtours criteria' are in some sense necessary before one could reasonably judge that any market was likely to be characterised by tacit collusion. If any of these three fail to be satisfied, attempts by the parties to price in a tacitly collusive way would always be vulnerable to undercutting by members of the group.

The difficulty, of course, lies in determining how to apply the criteria in any given case. In the particular case of the UK package holiday market, competition can be understood in terms of the model of Kreps and Scheinkman (1983), cited in section 2 above and extended to a context of repeated interaction between the firms.[43] In such a model, the prior choice of capacities constrains the prices that will prevail in the subsequent period, even when

---

[43] See also Staiger and Wolak (1992) which explicitly incorporates repeated interaction into a Kreps–Scheinkman set-up. However, Staiger and Wolak have collusion over prices as well as over capacities, which was not part of the Commission's case. Thus, despite the very considerable economics literature, this precise model of tacit collusion, proposed by the Commission, had not previously been rigorously explored.

these are determined by a process of Bertrand competition. As the Commission expressed it, 'constraining the overall amount of capacity put on to the market ensures that the market will be kept tight. If capacity is constrained, prices and profits will be higher than otherwise, whatever competition takes place during the selling season' (para. 56). Furthermore, capacity can be measured in one unambiguous dimension (the number of bed nights available in any given season), so the transparency issue concerned only how the potential collusive behaviour could be observed by the parties, not how to define it in the first place. The Court did not dispute these features.

What the Court took exception to was the Commission's view as to how the parties could monitor each other's capacity decisions in time to retaliate against any capacity increases large enough to be considered 'deviations'. In the Court's words:

The Commission alleges at paragraph 105 of the Decision that each of the four integrated operators is thus well able to monitor the total amount of holidays offered by each of the others [during the planning period] and that changes made by each individual operator at that stage may be identified by the other major tour operators as a result of their dealings with hotels or their discussions about seat requirements and availability, the purpose of which is to obtain or supply capacity or to negotiate swaps of seats and slots ... However, the Commission fails to prove those allegations (paras. 171–172).

This was the clinching weakness of the Commission's case. Had the Commission been able, for example, to cite internal documents showing that the identification of the capacity choices of rivals was a common industry practice, the Court might have been persuaded that some of its other doubts (for instance, over whether retaliation against a deviation in capacity setting would be sufficiently rapid and massive to act as an adequate deterrent) did not justify striking down the decision. Indeed, its doubts about the deterrent effect of retaliation against a deviation were expressed in the context of its general scepticism about the ability of rivals to detect a deviation in the first place (paras. 198–199).

Reflecting on these criticisms, in the light of the game theoretic analysis developed earlier, suggests to us that a practical procedure for establishing whether the 'Airtours criteria' apply in any given case could be set out in the following five steps:

- First, determine the focus of tacit collusion – the price of a main product, the total capacity put in place – the level of which can be constrained by the parties independently of other strategies they may undertake.
- Next, show that constraining the level of this variable beyond what the parties would choose if they were competing independently (call this the non-cooperative level) would significantly increase the joint profits of

the parties, taking account of any reactions that could be anticipated from firms outside the collusive group.

- Next, show that deviations of this variable from the collusive level could be detected with a high degree of confidence.
- Next, show that firms detecting deviations by their rivals would have an interest in reverting to the non-cooperative level; by this we mean not a precise calculation of profitability but rather an assessment of the broad plausibility, given the quantities involved, that returns would be high enough to compensate them for doing so in the face of a deviation.
- Finally, show that this would impose losses on the deviating firm that, taking into account any delays and uncertainties in the retaliation, would more than offset any gains from its original deviation.

Furthermore, the judgment appeared to have established that each of the steps in the procedure needed to be independently established before collective dominance was shown to be a significant danger. From this it would seem to follow that if it cannot clearly establish each of these steps in the argument it should allow a merger to proceed.

Given that the merger regulation imposes the same standard of proof on the Commission for authorisations and prohibitions, the Court judgment could be understood as resting on very strong presumption that coordination is difficult so that compelling evidence would be required to meet the standard of proof for a finding of collective dominance. In the absence of such evidence, the Commission would also naturally be considered to have met its standard of proof for a finding that collective dominance would not prevail.

3.7 Postscript on Sony–BMG

However, significant doubt has been cast on this by the judgment of the Court in a more recent case, that of Sony–BMG. In a judgment of 13 July 2006, the Court annulled the Commission's decision approving the creation of a joint venture combining the recorded music businesses of Sony and Bertelsmann Music Group (BMG). The Commission had considered the risk of collective dominance in this market but had decided to approve the joint venture on the grounds that:

- there was little price transparency in the market, as substantial effort was required to identify the level of discounts offered on albums, making tacit collusion more difficult. Moreover, the heterogeneity in the content of

albums, which had implications for the prices charged, reduced price transparency;[44]
- while there existed possible methods of retaliation against any member of the oligopoly that deviated from the situation of tacit collusion on prices between the allegedly dominant companies (such as excluding the deviator from the conclusion of new joint ventures, refusing to license songs from the deviator's compilations or terminating existing joint ventures), there was no evidence of any such retaliatory action having been taken in the past.

The CFI further stated that the three 'Airtours criteria' may in some cases be established on the basis of what may be a 'very mixed series of indicia and items of evidence relating to the signs, manifestations and phenomena inhered in the presence of a collective dominant position'. For example, close alignment of prices above a competitive level might, in the absence of a reasonable alternative explanation, be sufficient to establish the existence of collective dominance, even in the absence of firm direct evidence of market transparency.

The CFI judgment is surely a reminder that the same standard of proof applies to prohibitions and clearances under the merger regulation. But more fundamentally, the judgment calls for a re-examination of the Commission's approach in assessing collective dominance that is at least as profound as that following the *Airtours* judgment, since it involves considering not just what should be the investigative and decision procedures of the Commission but how to deal with ambiguity and uncertainty in the evidence. The luxury of considering that, in case of doubt, a case should be cleared is no longer an option. Following the judgment, there is no longer an initial prior belief that coordination is so difficult to achieve that in the absence of converging evidence from a set of indicia that coordination is likely, it can safely be presumed that it is unlikely to take place. In the presence of mixed evidence with respect to relevant factors, a specific analysis needs to be undertaken to support the conclusion that coordination would not take place. As indicated above, economic theory provides limited guidance for the conduct of this exercise.

Following the annulment by the CFI, the Commission examined the merger a second time and has confirmed its finding. In its decision, the Commission examined in great detail whether firms' behaviour could be interpreted as the outcome of coordination. The structure of prices across

---

[44] It is worth noting that in one respect this market appears somewhat *less* immediately adapted to tacit collusion than the package holiday market since, unlike in the latter where capacity (numbers of bed nights) is the obvious focus of any collusion that might take place, it is much less clear in the case of recorded music what would be the appropriate dimension of collusion.

different types of albums, the evolution of prices over time, the structure of rebates were scrutinised to assess whether net prices could be seen as a focal point of coordination. The Commission also analysed in detail whether retail prices could be used in order to infer net prices. The evidence appears to be consistent in pointing to the absence of coordination. This case is however unusual in terms of the amount of the information and quantitative evidence that has been available. How to deal with cases in which evidence is more limited and conflicting thus remains to be seen.

15

Capacity constraints and irreversible investments: defending against collective dominance in *UPM Kymmene/Norske Skog/Haindl*

Kai-Uwe Kühn and John Van Reenen

1. Introduction

Scrutiny of potential mergers by the European Commission typically focuses on unilateral effects or single-firm dominance. But in a series of important cases starting with *Kali and Salz*, *Nestlé-Perrier* and most importantly *Airtours*, the Commission has showed itself concerned over the issue of 'joint dominance'. However, until the judgment on *Airtours* there had been controversial debate whether 'joint dominance' was equivalent to the idea of coordinated effects as used in the US: the concern that the merger could increase the likelihood of consumer harm by making tacit collusion easier. But although the Court effectively established that a joint dominance finding required a 'coordinated effects' analysis, the practical implementation of such an approach has remained difficult. A particular challenge is how to bring empirical evidence to bear on finding or rejecting the existence of coordinated effects of a merger.

In this chapter we examine a case in newsprint and magazine paper – *UPM Kymmene/Norske Skog/Haindl*. The case involves two separate transactions in which Haindl sold all of its business to UPM Kymmene and the latter sold some of Haindl's major assets on to Norske Skog. The case arose because the Haindl family, which had run the business, wanted to withdraw from management activities. Haindl was an attractive target for UPM Kymmene because of its modern plant and low production costs. However, an outright takeover was likely to cause serious competition concerns, especially in magazine paper. The purchase was therefore combined with a deal to sell significant Haindl capacity, primarily in magazine paper, on to Norske Skog. The latter had at the time become a major player in newsprint. This deal allowed Norske Skog also to become a significant player in magazine paper. Effectively splitting Haindl assets between UPM Kymmene and Norske Skog thus addressed some competition concerns and allowed Norske Skog to achieve a strategic goal in its expansion plans.

The case is of particular interest because coordinated effects were the primary focus of the Commission's analysis. Indeed, the Commission very quickly developed serious concerns in phase 1 of the proceedings about the scope for tacit collusion in the industry, which were expressed in a statement of objections in phase 2. We discuss how collusion theory combined with empirical evidence was used to convince the Commission that the merger was unlikely to have coordinated effects and to clear the merger without remedies despite its strong initial objections.

The Commission's worries were easily understandable given the industry context at that time. In 2001 the Commission was faced with the third major merger proposal in the European publication paper industry since 1995. In addition, the industry had come under close scrutiny because of a Commission investigation of alleged collusive behaviour in the newsprint market that had run for several years. Furthermore, the company that was about to be purchased, Haindl, was considered at the time a pioneer in the investment into new equipment and the use of recycled paper as an input for paper production. The Commission clearly felt that a particularly disruptive 'maverick' competitor would be taken from the market.

Despite the previous consolidation, concentration in the industry was not high enough for a credible unilateral effects case to be made. But the history of the industry had all the ingredients to raise potential concerns about coordinated effects (i.e. tacit collusion). However, such a case was not straightforward. Individual contracting combined with capacity constraints made it highly unlikely that coordination in prices was easy to achieve. The Commission therefore went for an alternative route, claiming that firms were able to jointly limit capacity expansion in order to keep prices high.

We describe the arguments and counter-arguments over the Commission's claim of coordinated effects. In particular, we show how a defence was built by carefully constructing theoretical arguments on the basis of specific industry characteristics. A variety of evidence was used to support an alternative competitive story of industry behaviour over time. We then show that irreversible investments make coordination highly unlikely and demonstrate how evidence for irreversibility and the implied pre-emption effects can be used to support the claims of the theory. Our discussion also sheds some light on the use of evidence from market announcements and information-sharing institutions in the context of a coordinated effects case. We regard this paper as a case study of how, through a careful presentation of alternative theories and their empirical implications, a coordinated effects analysis can be focused on empirical evidence that can resolve the case in favour of the firm.[1] The Commission conceded in its decision that the irreversibility argument and the supporting evidence undermined any coordinated effects claim.

In section 2 we give a brief introduction to the markets for newsprint and magazine paper. Section 3 illustrates the evolution of the industry in the 1990s and explains why the Commission had concerns about the price patterns observed. In section 4 we then describe the case made by the Commission. We continue in section 5 with a discussion of the theoretical arguments that coordinated conduct in markets with irreversibility is highly unlikely and present the type of evidence that would support a conclusion that the market satisfies the conditions under which one should find a low likelihood of collusion. Finally, we take up the issue of short-run coordination on 'down-time' after negative demand shocks in section 6 and discuss the use of market-transparency arguments in the case in section 7.

2. The markets for newsprint and magazine paper

Paper production covers a fairly large range of products, which all have in common that some kind of wood pulp is converted to paper. Some companies active in paper production like UPM Kymmene are broad conglomerate firms active in most of these production areas. Other companies like Haindl and Norske Skog specialise in the production of 'publication paper', which this merger was concerned with. Publication paper includes the broad categories of 'newsprint' and 'magazine paper'.

Newsprint is primarily used for the publication of newspapers. The manufacturing of newsprint requires either mechanical pulp (derived from wood) or recycled pulp (derived from recycled paper). Besides labour, energy is a very important input for newsprint production. Newsprint comes in a variety of grades depending on weight, type of finishing and brightness. Despite such gradations the Commission and the parties agreed to treat all of these varieties as a single market.

---

[1] We are less confident that it is possible generally to build a satisfactory case that a merger should be blocked on the basis of coordinated effects. This means competition authorities will generally be in a relatively weak position in such cases. This paper attempts to show that a fairly rigorous and convincing defence can be built by relying on a combination of theoretical arguments and simple empirical evidence.

Magazine paper is primarily used for consumer magazines, catalogues and advertising materials. The quality requirements for these three areas of usage can be quite different. The basic ingredient for magazine paper is again pulp. In addition to mechanical and recycled pulp, chemical pulp is used. In contrast to newsprint there is typically heavy use of coating chemicals and chemical fillers. The Commission decided for the purposes of the investigation to define two different markets for magazine paper. Based on a price-correlation analysis, the highest-quality paper (wood-free coated reels), which is heavier and brighter than other types of magazine paper, was found to be in a separate market. This market definition issue was unimportant for the actual case.

In the geographical dimension, UPM Kymmene suggested that the market should be treated as worldwide. However, in newsprint the three largest North American producers were participating in the European market only with very small amounts. In magazine paper this participation was even lower. For this reason the Commission concluded that the geographic market was only European-wide.

The proposed merger occurred at the end of an important consolidation wave in the publishing paper industry in the 1990s. In 1995 UPM and Kymmene merged to become the largest firm in terms of capacity in magazine paper. In 1998 a merger between Stora and Enso created the largest newsprint producer in terms of capacity share. The top five firms in the newsprint market (Stora Enso, UPM Kymmene, Norske Skog, Holmen and Haindl) at the time of the merger had between 70 per cent and 80 per cent capacity share and between 60 per cent and 70 per cent share in sales.[2] Given that Haindl held 10–15 per cent capacity share and 5–10 per cent share in sales, the merger brought about a significant increase in concentration. It was not obvious to what extent asymmetries would be significantly affected by the merger. The leading firm in the market, Stora Enso, held about 20–25 per cent market share in sales and capacities. The transaction moved UPM Kymmene from a group of three firms (including Haindl) with 10–15 per cent market share in capacities into the number two position in the same range and just behind Stora Enso, but ahead of Norske Skog at 15–20 per cent.

In the magazine market the three leading firms were UPM Kymmene (25–30 per cent capacity), Stora Enso (20–25 per cent capacity) and M-Real/Myllykoski (10–15 per cent capacity), followed by a group of firms in the 5–10 per cent range: Haindl, Norske Skog, Burgo and SCA. The total capacity and sales shares of the

---

[2] Market share figures are taken from the non-confidential version of the Commission's decision. All numbers reported here come from publicly accessible data, i.e. the Commission's decision or data from the industry association CEPIPRINT.

three largest firms together with Norske Skog and Haindl were between 75 per cent and 85 per cent, so that the magazine market was somewhat more concentrated than the newsprint market. Without the sale of magazine paper assets to Norske Skog, UPM Kymmene would have achieved close to 40 per cent capacity share (and close to 35 per cent share in sales). The deal with Norske Skog brought the capacity share in the range of 30–35 per cent and moved Norske Skog into a more significant market position with 10–15 per cent capacity share. Note that strong asymmetries in capacity holdings remained in this market after the transactions despite the fairly concentrated overall structure of the market.

A number of important structural features characterise both markets. First, there are substantial scale economies for given production capacity. Plant costs have a fixed cost element in the order of 45 per cent for a machine operating at full capacity. The average cost of production steeply decreases with volumes for any given plant.

The second fact of great importance for the operation of the industry is that capacity decisions are lumpy and irreversible. Newsprint and magazine paper are produced on large paper machines. At the time of the merger a new efficient newsprint machine had a capacity of up to 400,000 tonnes a year. Such a machine would have covered about 3–4 per cent of total EEA consumption of newsprint at that time. The cost for such a modern machine was in the order of €500 million. New machines take about two years to build and are highly durable. Most importantly, capacity decisions are difficult to reverse because much of the investment is sunk. It has to be mentioned that there are alternative ways to expand capacity, for example through the rebuild or upgrade of an existing machine. However, these opportunities are limited because of technical considerations. Even rebuilds are lumpy and costly and generate the additional cost of a machine not being available over the time of the rebuild. Rebuilds and upgrades therefore do not make it possible to smoothly adjust capacity to short-run fluctuations in demand.

Third, demand is highly volatile and very inelastic. The demand for newsprint and magazine paper is a derived demand. It inherits its volatility from the volatility of demand by advertisers for space in newspapers and magazines. Industry demand is therefore extremely vulnerable to aggregate shocks in economic activity, which is the variable driving advertising demand. According to all the evidence the demand for newsprint and magazine paper is also fairly price inelastic. Estimates used by the Commission range between −0.15 and −0.3 for newsprint and between −0.3 and −0.6 for magazine paper. In the short run demand is even less elastic since production quantities of downstream users of paper tend to be committed for some period of time. There is only limited scope for 'production smoothing' through the building and depletion of stocks, because newsprint is perishable. Storage beyond three months is usually not possible. A second factor that limits production smoothing is technological. In general it is extremely inefficient to use machines at anything else but optimal capacity utilisation. In times of low demand it is therefore best to adjust by switching off whole machines.

Finally, the contracting practices of the industry are central for understanding market behaviour. Contracting is on an individual basis with each buyer for periods of, typically, one year.[3] These contracts in principle commit both sides to a given price for a given expected quantity. In practice there is, however, an important asymmetry. Paper producers are generally committed to the price of the contract even when a high demand realisation occurs and producers hit capacity constraints. However, when demand is low customers will often seek to renegotiate the price downwards. In fact, some of the larger buyers will even specify such asymmetric commitments in the purchase contract. The partial downward flexibility of prices arises in all likelihood because the actual quantity delivered cannot be fully controlled through the contract. Buyers do not take one delivery for the year but call up deliveries on the contract in irregular intervals and at varying quantities throughout the year. This means they do not have to take delivery if their need of paper turns out to be low. It is harder to explain why prices do not adjust upwards when demand is unexpectedly high. It appears that the parties believe that delivery can be enforced as long as the paper company is not fully capacity constrained.

3. The evolution of the industry in the 1990s

As a background for the case we begin by describing the behaviour of the industry during the 1990s. First, we describe the price movements that created the initial impression on the side of the European Commission that coordinated conduct might already be a problem pre-merger. We then show that the price dynamics observed in the 1990s are consistent with a non-collusive explanation based on the major characteristics of the industry that we highlighted in the previous section. To simplify the exposition we analyse only the price and capacity dynamics in the newsprint market. A similar analysis can be conducted for different categories of magazine paper.

---

[3] Contracting can be longer in newsprint or shorter in magazine paper, but yearly contracting is the typical form contracts take.

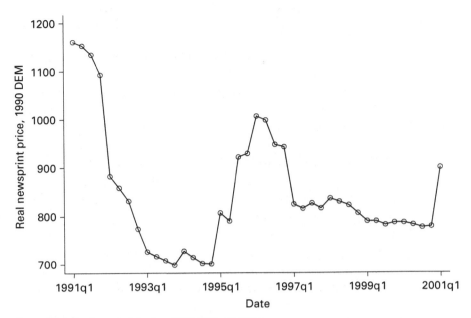

Figure 15.1 Real newsprint price, 1990 DEM per tonne
Source: Pulp & Paper International (PPI) (www.paperloop.com)

In Figure 15.1 we plot the quarterly average real prices per tonne of newsprint in 1990 DEM (Deutsche Mark). The graph illustrates the trend towards sharply lower prices in the publication paper industry during the 1990s. Fourth-quarter prices for newsprint in 2000 are about 30 per cent lower in real terms than in the first quarter of 1990. This trend reflects the efforts in the industry to reduce costs. Gaining cost advantage is a major competitive factor in the industry and the graph shows how this is translated into falling prices over time.

The Commission's concerns about coordinated effects of mergers were raised by the behaviour of prices in the period between the beginning of 1997 and the end of 2000. In this period prices seem remarkably stable over time. In addition, there is a sharp upward spike in prices at the beginning of 2001. Given the contrast with the much more volatile prices before this period, the Commission conjectured that firms might be artificially stabilising prices by coordinating policies on capacity expansion.

The merger occurred on the background of a European cartel investigation into the newsprint market. This investigation covered the period 1989 through 1995. The case was closed only in September 2002, after the Haindl transaction had been approved by the Commission. It should be noted that the steeply declining prices in the period up to 1995 do not contradict a charge of collusion. Possibly the prices could have fallen much faster. However, the concerns about coordinated conduct in the merger case clearly did not arise from the price pattern in the period of the alleged cartel but from the price stability at the end of the 1990s.

We now show that the steeply declining pricing pattern between 1991 and 1995 as well as the stable pricing pattern between 1997 and 2000 can be explained as the result of an uncoordinated (competitive) outcome generated by the specific demand, capacity and contracting conditions in the industry. Suppose that there is no collusion in a market. Then prices in a world with capacity constraints are determined by the current realisation of demand relative to existing capacity. However, in markets with long-term contracts prices typically are set for a whole year and will be determined by expected demand and not realised demand. If firms suffer an unexpected negative demand shock during the contracting period, capacity utilisation will be low and prices will adjust downwards only with a lag. We can verify whether the data is consistent with these market characteristics being the main drivers of prices by using data on demand forecasts and capacities in addition to the price data presented in Figure 15.1.

Figure 15.1 suggests that the history of price changes in this industry over the last ten years can be divided into four periods. In the early 1990s (period 1) prices for newsprint and magazine paper fell very sharply and then increased rapidly in 1995 (period 2). Prices then, again, fell sharply in 1996 and early 1997 (period 3). After late 1997 (period 4), prices were fairly stable until the increase in the first quarter of 2001, which is the part of the price path that raised the Commission's suspicions.

In interpreting this price history, the capacity utilisation figures reported in Figure 15.2 are particularly helpful. The early 1990s were characterised by a global recession. As can be seen from Figure 15.2, capacity utilisation dropped well below 95 per cent and prices fell sharply by 30 per cent.[4] Low prices and low capacity utilisation in this period are consistent with a reduction in demand due to the recession combined with a considerable expansion in capacity that firms had committed to before the downturn. Reflecting low demand and capacity utilisation in 1993 and industry expectations that continued low demand would remain,[5] contract prices were still low in

---

[4] We understand that given accounting conventions used by CEPIPRINT at the time a 95 per cent capacity utilisation figure would correspond – at least approximately – to full capacity utilisation in an economic sense.

[5] The sharp rebound of demand in this year surprised the industry: CEPIPRINT's Demand-Supply Report of February 1995 records that the size of the rebound took the industry by surprise: 'Recent changes in direction of the world economic pendulum have witnessed the paper markets of Europe rebounding from recession with astounding strength.' The CEPIPRINT forecast made at the start of 1993 underpredicted 1994 Western European newsprint demand by 8.7 per cent and the 1994 forecast underpredicted 1995 demand by 5.7 per cent.

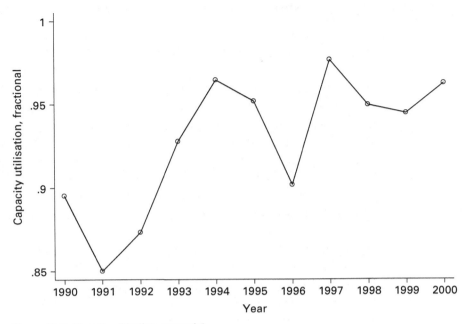

Figure 15.2 Capacity utilisation, newsprint
Source: Calculated from delivery and capacity data reported in CEPIPRINT Demand and Supply
Report: Newsprint and Magazine Paper Grades (various years)

1994. Given such low prices, capacity utilisation in newsprint jumped to over
96 per cent in 1994. There was no sharp price increase in the course of 1994
because of the rigidities imposed by the annual contracts. However, prices
increased sharply at the end-of-year negotiations for 1995, from DEM 825 to
DEM 964 per tonne.[6]

Possibly cautioned by the surprise of 1994, paper firms signed an unusually
large number of six-month contracts (instead of the standard yearly ones),
which would allow faster adjustment to rising demand. This change in contract length combined with higher-than-predicted demand growth in 1995
(see footnote 7) explains the large price jump between the second and third
quarters of 1995. The demand situation fed through fully to the market at the
end of that year when the contract price for yearly contracts was adjusted and
the newsprint price rose to DEM 1,236.[7]

[6] The prices quoted in the text are nominal DEM; prices displayed in Figure 15.1 are real, 1990 DEM.
[7] Note that the response to increased uncertainty makes sense given the pattern of downward price
flexibility and upward price rigidity in the contracts. If uncertainty increases it becomes more likely
that prices cannot rise as a response to unexpectedly high demand. This means that the paper company
would ask for higher prices to cover this risk. When full adjustment to the demand shock increases
efficiency, both buyer and seller can increase joint benefits by agreeing to have the price adjust more
frequently. The buyer realises part of the gains through lower initial prices.

The year 1996 (period 3) illustrates the opposite phenomenon: a large unanticipated negative demand shock hits the industry. Given the high prices that had been negotiated at the end of 1995, an unexpected decline in demand drove capacity utilisation down to 90 per cent. CEPIPRINT's Demand–Supply Report of February 1996 had forecast newsprint deliveries of 9,300 for 1996, but its report of June 1997 records a realisation of only 8,715 – 7 per cent below forecast. As we have discussed, there is more of a possibility of renegotiating contractual prices downward after a negative demand shock. This led to a gradual decline of the price from DEM 1,236 in the first quarter to DEM 1,176 in the fourth quarter. When all long-term contracts adjusted at the beginning of 1997, the price fell back further to DEM 1,034.

From 1997 to the second quarter of 2000 (period 4), demand recovered and remained strong. However, considerable new capacity was introduced in Europe so that the effects of any growth in demand were offset by large capacity increases. There was also a slump in overseas demand from Asia. These factors had a moderating effect on price increases, and concerns about the longer run (e.g. the impact of electronic media) contributed to a climate of greater uncertainty. In these circumstances we see paper producers conclude a greater number of longer-term contracts exceeding the standard one-year term. As a result prices looked very stable over the period. Only at the 2000 end-of-year negotiations do we finally see sharp price increases getting through.

We can therefore explain the price dynamics in the market by competitive forces taking into account capacity constraints, demand volatility and the desire of market participants to hedge increased demand risk through longer-term contracts. We see that demand is very volatile and prices reflect demand forecasts and to a much smaller extent realised demand due to contracting induced lags in price adjustments. Both the steep price declines at the beginning of the period and the smoother prices at the end of the period can be explained by the same underlying set of market forces.

4. The Commission's coordinated effects case

The Commission never considered a theory of unilateral effects in this case but always focused exclusively on the possibility of coordinated effects. It seemed to acknowledge that based, on the price movements and capacity utilisation figures observed, there appeared to be little evidence for any price coordination. In addition, and consistent with the strong emphasis on issues of transparency in the decision, the Commission leaned heavily on the argument that transaction prices were not observable in order to dismiss the possibility of coordination in long-run contract prices.

Instead, the Commission focused on two issues. First, it was concerned that newsprint producers could coordinate investment decisions, reducing the rate of capacity expansion in order to increase transaction prices. Second, it claimed that firms could coordinate on the use of downtime in order to support short-run prices when short-run demand reductions occurred.

In the remaining sections of this chapter we systematically analyse these possibilities in the light of economic theory and the available empirical data. In particular, we emphasise what kind of data were of importance to support the theories that were used in the defence against coordinated effects.

Here we first sketch the Commission's approach. At first glance the approach closely resembles a traditional checklist approach. The Commission lists a number of criteria that are commonly considered to favour coordinated conduct. If they are present this weighs in negatively for the merger, if they are not, this weighs in positively for the merger. The Commission claimed that the product was homogeneous, that demand was very inelastic, and mentioned the existence of multi-market contact, limited buyer market power and high entry barriers as criteria that pointed towards a danger of coordinated effects. The Commission also claimed that the removal of a player would make the market more transparent and less uncertain, which would facilitate coordination.[8] On the other hand the Commission listed the limited stability of market shares, lack of transparency on capacity expansion projects and prices, as well as the lack of symmetry in cost structures as elements not conducive to collusion. According to the Commission, simply weighing these observations would be a sufficient basis for a decision. The decision discusses the possible coordination mechanism only 'for the sake of completeness' (para. 126 of the decision).

But, at a closer look, the Commission's analysis is more sophisticated than traditional checklist approaches. Its greater emphasis on issues of asymmetry between competitors and the role of market transparency is closer to modern economic theory and empirics (see Dick 2002 and Kühn 2008). The Commission has also stuck closely to the common wisdom that the disappearance of a competitor will facilitate collusion directly. The conceptual approach to coordinated effects analysis in Dick (2002) is along these lines. He describes an asymmetry increasing merger as leading to a trade-off between a firm disappearing making collusion easier and the asymmetry making collusion harder.

---

[8] See Kühn (2008) for a discussion why such traditional criteria are not meaningful indicators of the danger of collusion.

However, the theoretical analysis of such models by Compte, Jenny and Rey (2002) and Kühn (2004) shows that selling assets to other firms in the market is not the same as exiting the market with the assets.[9] What matters in these models is the asymmetry between the largest and smallest firms in the industry, not the reduction of the number of firms in the market. This suggests that arguments based on the 'elimination of a competitor' may be very misleading in an analysis of coordinated effects. The discussion in the Commission decision also appears to appeal to a variant of the disappearing firm argument: the elimination of a 'maverick'. Haindl was a very innovative firm. It was the first to heavily invest in production facilities that could use recycled pulp. This process significantly reduces marginal cost. It was therefore considered a pioneer in investment, innovation and cost reduction. The Commission was concerned about such a dynamic firm disappearing from the market.[10] The problem of the Commission's approach in general is that there is currently no satisfactory method to weigh the different criteria against each other.

We suggest an approach to the problem that focuses the analysis much more on the theoretical implications of the specific characteristics of the industry and a systematic use of industry evidence. For that purpose we can first do a backward-looking empirical analysis to see whether earlier mergers in the industry show any sign of the presence of significant coordinated effects. If previous mergers had a significant impact on prices and capacity expansion there would be *prima facie* evidence for significant merger effects. Second, to do a prospective analysis one will want to focus the analysis directly on the incentives to collude under the particular circumstances of the industry. For example, we can ask: how difficult is it to collude in capacity if investments are irreversible? If the answer is 'very difficult', other aspects of the market do not even need analysis. If collusion is difficult even when markets are completely transparent and symmetric, the criteria of transparency and symmetry do not matter any more because coordinated effects are already unlikely in the worst-case scenario. A negative test for coordinated effects can therefore focus on the elements of the market that are most important for undermining collusion incentives. This illustrates how a simple weighting of a list of criteria for the ease of collusion will not necessarily lead to an appropriate analysis.

---

[9] Essentially, the incentives for deviating from a given collusive agreement do not change for non-merging firms, while they do change when the assets of an exiting firm are removed from the market. See Kühn (2008) for a careful explanation of this effect.

[10] In retrospect the whole industry has invested in this technology and it may be that part of the impression created was a result of the lumpiness in investment.

5. Is there evidence for significant effects from previous mergers?

The first approach to assessing the likelihood of coordinated effects is to see whether previous large mergers have had any discernible effect on behaviour in the market. This is, of course, difficult to gauge. To generate a rough picture we can look for a structural break in the behaviour before and after a previous large merger event.

An example is the Enso/Stora merger in 1998. The Commission initially believed that it provided evidence for significant merger effects. As evidence for this view the Commission points out that capacity utilisation in the newsprint market had remained high after this merger (close to 96 per cent for the leading five suppliers) and prices had been 'extremely stable'. The Commission claims that this points to a structural break since it contrasts dramatically with the pattern observed in the first half of the 1990s, when there were periods of excess capacity and declining prices. The Commission suggests that the post-1998 stability 'could be seen as an indication that capacity is being adjusted to keep prices stable'.

We have already explained that the pattern of prices and capacity utilisation can be rationalised without any appeal to coordinated behaviour. However, there is still the possibility that investment behaviour changed after the Enso/Stora merger.

In order for a claim of anticompetitive merger effects to be supported by evidence we would want to see a structural break in which the investment rate in the industry was significantly reduced or significantly fell behind the rate of growth in expected demand. Such a conclusion is not consistent with the facts as shown in Table 15.1. Over the period 1998 through 2000, newsprint capacity grew at an average annual rate of 2.1 per cent compared with only 1.6 per cent between 1990 and 1997. Hence investment in newsprint has been *higher* since the Enso/Stora merger, not lower.[11]

Can the recent increase in the rate of capacity expansion be explained by an increase in the rate of the expected growth of demand? Table 15.1 compares the growth of capacity to the growth of demand over the same period using two-year-ahead forecasts from CEPIPRINT. This is the appropriate variable if there is approximately a two-year lag[12] between the decision to build and

---

[11] The magazine paper capacity data show similar trends.

[12] Similar results obtain if one uses the one-year-ahead delivery forecasts or the three-year-ahead delivery forecasts from CEPIPRINT.

Table 15.1 Comparing capacities and *forecast* deliveries before and after the Enso/Stora merger: average percentage growth rates per annum in newsprint, 1994–2000

1. Growth in capacity 1994–7	2. Growth in capacity 1998–2000	3. Two-year-ahead forecast growth in deliveries 1994–7	4. Two-year-ahead forecast growth in deliveries 1998–2000
1.29	2.06	4.69	−0.28

Source: CEPIPRINT Demand–Supply Report, Newsprint and Magazine Paper Grades (various years). The 'two-year-ahead forecast' is based on (for example) the forecast growth of deliveries for the February 1999–January 2000 period made in February 1998. These forecasts were available only from 1992 which is why the first available observation is for 1994.

when the capacity comes on-stream. Here the picture is even starker. There is a much larger acceleration in investment relative to expected demand post-merger than pre-merger.

On the basis of this first-cut analysis, the facts do not support the view that there has been a restriction of capacity expansion in the period since Stora and Enso merged.

However, the data analysis above might not reflect the real change in incentives because the period between 1998 and 2000 was relatively short and the merger effect could have occurred after 2000. To assess the plausibility of such an argument we can also look at planned capacity extensions as documented in the CEPIPRINT demand and supply reports. The CEPIPRINT Demand–Supply Report for March 2001 forecasts an increase in Western European deliveries (i.e. from Western European suppliers to Western European consumers) of 571,000 tonnes over the three-year period 2001–3 (an average annual growth rate of 2.0 per cent using 2000 as the base year). But the report also forecasts that *exports* of newsprint from Western European suppliers will fall by 413,000 tonnes. This is mainly because of increasing capacity in local production in Far Eastern markets. As a result, total demand from Western European producers is expected to grow over the three years by only 158,000 tonnes (an annual rate of 0.5 per cent). At the same time, the report also forecasts that capacity will increase over the three years by 206,000 tonnes (or an annual rate of 0.7 per cent). So there is a surplus of forecasted capacity increases over forecasted demand increases of 48,000 tonnes. It is also worth noting that even if we had seen some kind of capacity slowdown, this could have been for many other reasons completely unrelated to the Enso/Stora merger. With greater uncertainty (e.g. the increasing uncertainty over the importance of alternative non-paper advertising such as internet-based advertising) 'real options' effects should be expected to cause a delay in investment (see Bond, Bloom and Van Reenen (2007), for econometric evidence of the importance of real options for investment). Indeed, there has been widespread speculation about the impact of electronic media on paper producers.[13]

6. Can there be coordinated effects in capacity expansion decisions?

The conventional wisdom

Coordination on capacities is generally believed to be one of the most difficult problems for firms to resolve. In homogeneous goods industries with large capacity investments, like the paper and pulp industry, there are recurring episodes of persistent overcapacities that firms find very difficult to eliminate for both strategic and competitive reasons. This is particularly apparent in the history of legalised, explicit cartels. Examples include the Norwegian cement industry from 1927 to 1968[14] and the German cartel in the coal and steel industries in the 1920s and 1930s.[15] Even in these cases of sanctioned cartels firms were still unable to coordinate capacity choices. These apparent diffi- culties of coordinating capacity decisions are reflected in the economic litera- ture, which often directly assumes that firms can collude in prices but not in capacities. In the literature this assumption is justified either with an appeal to the stylised facts we cite above or with an intuitive argument about the role of irreversible, long-term decisions like capacity investments. For example:[16]

... in the absence of perfect enforcement, agreement on a capacity-reduction may be much less likely than agreement on a price-hike: if a firm cheats on the former, its opponent is in a weak position, while any change in price is easily reversible.[17]

The theory

The central problem for collusion on capacities identified by the conventional wisdom is the irreversibility of capacity expansions.[18] Once new capacity has

---

[13] A report produced in September 1999 by the BCG group suggested that newspapers and in particular classified advertising could be threatened by the online formats (Boston Consulting Group: Paper and the Electronic Media: Creating Value from Uncertainty. September 1999).

[14] See Steen and Sorgard (1999).   [15] See Bloch (1932).

[16] See also Davidson and Deneckere (1990), 523; and Fershtman and Muller (1986), 214.

[17] Osborne and Pitchik (1987) at 414–415.

[18] Under the term irreversibility we include cases in which the option value of waiting to withdraw a unit from the market is very high.

been brought on-stream, its effects are persistent. However, at the time of the case, the precise effects of irreversible capacity investments on collusion had not been modelled formally in the theoretical literature. The problem with irreversible capacity is that the game is no longer a repeated game for which we know how to fully characterise the set of equilibria.[19] Investments in capacity have persistent effects for the rest of the game. In this case standard ways of characterising optimal punishment equilibria cannot be applied. Both the price-setting incentives and the incentives for further investments will depend on the capacity installed and its distribution across firms. However, the most basic feature of all collusive models will be preserved. The scope for collusion will depend on the short-run gains from deviation and the potential long-run losses from switching to a low-profit equilibrium. Existing theory can then give some guidance as to the effects of irreversibility on firms' incentives to collude.

Irreversibility changes the structure of incentives because any capacity expansion is a commitment device for the future. This means that any deviation from restricted capacity levels also commits a deviating firm to higher capacity in the future. The effect is well known from the pre-emption literature.[20] Essentially, a deviator can put a lot of capacity on the market. This *commits* him to be a large producer in all future periods. The competing firms now have a choice. They can either greatly expand their capacity as a punishment response – and destroy the profitability of the industry for the deviator and themselves alike – or they can accommodate in their capacity investments and lose market share but remain profitable. Clearly they will decide to remain profitable. But this means that the incentives of a deviator are very considerably increased relative to the standard repeated game model. In the standard model the deviator gets a benefit for only one period of deviation, but afterwards an unfavourable equilibrium will be played. With irreversibility, the deviation does *not* lead to only one period of benefits: rather it also changes the playing field for the whole future, shifting benefits from other firms to the deviator *over the whole time horizon of the industry*.

To get a clearer intuition about the effect consider a simple Cournot model with irreversible output expansions. Irreversibility then means that output can only be increased from the previous period but not decreased. Suppose that the punishment equilibrium involves a return to the worst Markov perfect equilibrium for the deviator starting from the output distribution generated

---

[19] See Abreu, Pearce and Stacchetti (1990).

[20] This has recently been fully worked out for capacity investment models with subsequent price competition by Allen, Deneckere, Faith and Kovenock (2000).

from the deviation. A deviator then accomplishes two things at the same time. He moves market share to himself in the first period, as in any other collusion model. But then he also acts as a first mover (Stackelberg leader) in quantity setting for future periods. When a Markov perfect continuation equilibrium is played, the deviator can never do worse than a Stackelberg leader. But this guarantees the deviator vastly higher profits than a return to a one-shot Nash equilibrium in a traditional supergame model. Hence, the deviator benefits from the ability to pre-empt its rivals in all future periods in precisely the same fashion as in the entry deterrence literature.[21] Kühn (2001b) formalised this intuition in the Cournot model with linear demand and showed that *collusion cannot be sustained at any discount factor*.[22]

The combination of the basic economic arguments of collusion theory combined with the insights of the theory of pre-emption in capital investments will necessarily lead to the conclusion that the incentives for collusion in capacity will be vastly reduced under irreversibility. The result may not be quite as extreme as the impossibility result of Kühn (2001b) when demand grows over time or when there is depreciation.[23] However, the basic argument shows that irreversibility undermines collusion in a *qualitatively* much more dramatic way than other market features that limit collusion. Hence, there is a tight economic argument linked to irreversibility and pre-emption incentives that suggests that coordinated effects are highly unlikely when irreversible capacity decisions are involved.

Empirical evidence on the assumptions of the theory

To support the applicability of this theory to the specific case empirically, three pieces of evidence can help. First, we want convincing evidence that investments are irreversible. Second, there should be some evidence that pre-emption is a concern for the investment decisions of the firms. And third,

---

[21] See Dixit (1980) or Allen *et al.* (2000).

[22] There is some relatively simple intuition for this surprising result: with irreversibility and quantity setting it is always possible for the deviator to expand output so much that in any continuation equilibrium the rivals will not increase their output at all after a deviation. In Kühn's (2001b) particular specification with linear demands the deviator can obtain exactly the same profits from such a strategy as he can obtain by sticking to the collusive output. However, by only slightly reducing his output below this critical output he can strictly increase his profits in the deviation period and only induce a second-order effect on future profits, which are discounted, slightly. Since this argument holds for any discount factor, we have shown that collusive output reductions can never be sustained.

[23] In a model in which firms set irreversible capacities first and then set prices, similar effects are at work since (from the results of Allen *et al.*) a sufficient capacity expansion does lead to a best response of limiting capacity by competitors.

investments should be credibly communicated to the market as soon as they become irreversible.

One feature that causes considerable irreversibility is the combination of large sunk costs with a high degree of uncertainty about market demand. Most of the costs of having a plant available in the paper industry are the initial costs of building the plant. Since such plants are highly industry-specific, these costs cannot be recovered by simply selling the plant on to the second-hand market. This means that disinvestments can occur only by scrapping a plant. But scrapping a plant also involves some cost and there is no recovery of benefits, so that decommissioning is very unattractive. In addition, the industry is subject to substantial demand and cost shocks. In the presence of strong sunk cost effects, disinvestments get delayed because firms want to avoid the investment costs they may have to incur when times get better. Even relatively small sunk costs can generate large irreversibility effects,[24] because of this option value of maintaining capital investments. This is often called a 'real option' effect. In industries such as the paper and pulp industry in which investments are lumpy and involve massive sunk costs, this effect would make us expect that investments are (to a first approximation) irreversible.

The irreversibility assumption seems to agree well with the basic feature of the industry that paper machines tend to be in operation for time periods of fifty years and longer. However, we can generate a more convincing test for irreversibility from a very simple observation. If investments are not irreversible then variations in demand in an overall growing market should lead to countercyclical disinvestment decisions (i.e. substantially more old plant should be scrapped during a slump than during a boom). But if irreversibility is very important, a machine should get scrapped only when it is completely depreciated – at least to a first approximation.

The market evidence appears to confirm this feature. Figure 15.3 shows the total quarterly amounts of disinvestments, over the ten-year horizon considered in the case, as reported in the Paperinfo data set. The data set gives details of the projects undertaken in the pulp and paper industry in the EEA between 1990 and 2000. Three facts stand out. First, there is no evidence of large-scale capital scrapping in the early 1990s. Second, there are several quarters where

---

[24] Analytical approximations indicate that the effects of irreversibility are substantial. Suppose that the sunk entry cost is 10 per cent of the variable cost of production and there are no exit costs. Assume also that the annual standard deviation of project returns is 20 per cent and the risk-free interest rate is 5 per cent. In Dixit (1991), the critical revenue level that triggers entry is approximately 33 per cent higher than the critical revenue level at which exit occurs. The Marshallian approach, which ignores irreversibility, would give a corresponding figure of 0.5 per cent.

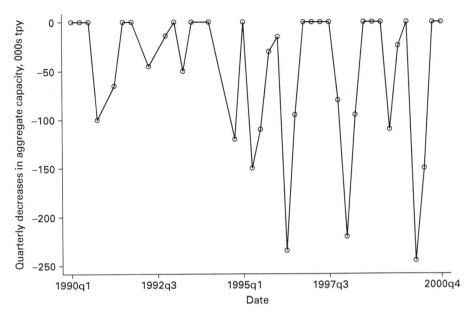

Figure 15.3 Disinvestments in pulp and paper
Source: Paperinfo Global Capacity Projects Database (paperinfo.fi). Includes all disinvestment projects undertaken by Western European paper suppliers between 1990 and 2000. Data are unavailable for quarters not indicated by a circle.

disinvestment is literally zero. This is consistent with the notion that there are large sunk costs associated with investment, so it may often be worth 'doing nothing'. Similar 'zones of inaction' are observed amongst industries where there are irreversibilities associated with large sunk investment costs.[25]

Third, if capacity was reversible then we should expect to see a counter-cyclical pattern in the data: more scrapping during bad times (1991–3 and 1996) than in good times. In fact there is no cyclical pattern in the data. In contrast, capacity expansion appears to be procyclical, increasing at times when demand is expected to increase. Figure 15.4 shows that *positive* capacity expansions are correlated with CEPIPRINT demand indicators (newsprint delivery growth) in the newsprint industry.[26]

The natural conclusion is that irreversibilities are large and that disinvestment is very difficult in the industry.

[25] For example Caballero, Engle and Haltiwanger (1995). Another point is that if there was collusion one would expect to see coordinated scrapping – this has not occurred.

[26] The aggregate CEPIPRINT net capacity data and the aggregated Paperinfo investment and disinvestment data match up well when adjusted for timing. The magazine paper aggregates do not match up well, suggesting an under-recording problem. The near random pattern of disinvestments is also present in magazine paper.

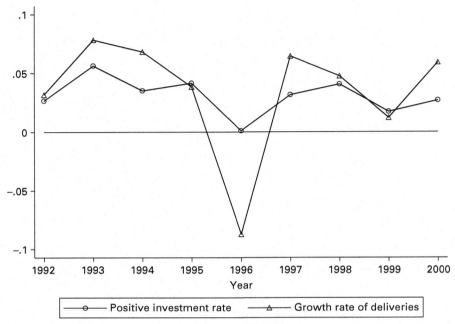

Figure 15.4 Annual positive newsprint investment and growth rate of demand
Notes: The annual positive investment rate is defined as the ratio of positive annual investment in newsprint capacity from the Paperinfo data set to lagged total CEPIPRINT newsprint capacity. The purpose of dividing investment by lagged capacity is to normalise the data. The growth rate of demand is defined as the first difference in the natural logarithm of newsprint deliveries.
Source: Calculated from CEPIPRINT Demand–Supply Report: Newsprint and Magazine Paper Grades (various years) and Paperinfo Global Capacity Projects Database (paperinfo.fi) (various years).

Capacity forecasts and announcements as coordination devices

In order to make a pre-emption story credible it must become known to the market when irreversible investments have been committed to. This feature is also present in the industry. Major investment decisions become known through public announcements that are partly made credible by obligations of the firm vis-à-vis the financial markets. It seems clear that if a firm has made an irreversible commitment to an investment, this will be known by the competitors. Furthermore, at least one of the parties in the proceedings documented that pre-emption concerns played a role in the timing of investments, so that the theoretical story appeared to be confirmed by what became known to the Commission about actual investment processes. The theoretical framework therefore seemed to closely match the central features of the market in question.

Despite this evidence that pre-emption opportunities in the industry undermine incentives to comply with collusive agreements, the Commission nevertheless focused its analysis in the decision on the existence of potential coordination mechanisms. From a theoretical perspective this may appear strange because any form of communication can have an effect only if substantial collusion is in principle possible. But the Commission had clear doubts whether it should interpret the announcements in the market as evidence for a commitment mechanism for pre-emptive irreversible investments or in a more traditional way as instruments for the coordination of investments.

The Commission's investigation especially focused on whether announcements of investment plans were reversible or not. The idea was that an announcement of capacity expansion by a firm that was not reversible allowed others to react and retaliate before a commitment to an irreversible investment occurred and hence make the theoretical mechanism described inoperable. This argument overlooked the fact that a firm would have an incentive to keep its investment plans secret until commitment was achieved and announce its plans only then.

Although the argument of the Commission was essentially beside the point, evidence about investment announcements is not irrelevant for the credibility of the theoretical argument proposed in this section. If the theory is true we should find evidence that firms are very secretive about investment plans and that announcements almost always occur when there is effective commitment to the investment (i.e. construction contracts etc. have been written). A fairly complete source of such initial announcements can be found on the PPI website (www.paperloop.com). We examined fifty-one recent announcements under 'Week in Review', 'Printing News'/'Expansions and Modernisations' and 'Converting News'/'News and Information'/'Expansions and Modernisation', classifying them into (i) announcement of plans, (ii) committed announcement, (iii) realisation. We found twenty-nine announcements of completions or realisations, twenty-four of commitments and only three announcements of plans (some releases contained more than one type of announcement). Hence the evidence from the PPI site suggests that the announcement of plans is not common, lending further support to the theory of the case proposed in this section.

7. Coordinated effects on short-run prices or 'downtime'

Although most contracting takes place in yearly contracts, there is also some short-run contracting during the year, even in the newsprint market. The Commission initially raised concerns that firms could coordinate conduct to raise prices in the short run. There seems to have been agreement in the case that coordination on prices would have been difficult since prices and discounts are individually negotiated and can hardly be considered observable.

However, the Commission argued that for a given level of capacity firms could raise prices in the short run by coordinating on taking downtime for the machines. This issue can be addressed in two ways. First, we can consider whether the characteristics of the market make such coordination credible. Second, we can investigate whether the observed periods of downtime can be well explained in a competitive context.

We first investigate whether collusion on downtime can ever be credible. In this discussion we abstract from possible issues of market transparency that are discussed in the next section. One way of interpreting downtime is to consider the possibility of firms coordinating the use of downtime to raise (unobserved) prices. Note that in industries with capacity constraints this type of collusive agreement is difficult to sustain. First, when the industry operates at the capacity constraint there is no issue of collusion. Collusive periods can therefore occur only in periods of excess capacity. However, in the presence of capacity constraints the ability to punish deviations in the future will typically be constrained. Sustaining collusion requires the punishment of deviations in the long run. Given capacity constraints, harsh punishments can typically not be given in a single period, but have to be spread over time. However, if the industry quickly returns to full capacity utilisation, severe punishments are impossible. These conditions seem to be the ones prevailing in the paper industry. Although there are periods of excess capacities, there was expected long-run growth in demand during this period that was expected to push sales towards full capacity utilisation even after a negative shock. This would have been different in a declining industry. In such an industry there is a trend to greater and greater excess capacities so that firms become less and less capacity constrained over time. This means that the future ability to punish is greater. The specific circumstances of the industry considered are therefore very important when assessing the ability to collude.[27]

Given the significant asymmetries between firms in costs and capacities and serious doubts about the transparency of downtime decisions, there is little evidence that this collusive mechanism could work in practice.

---

[27] A second way the Commission suggested that downtime could have collusive effects was through a commitment to reduce the incentives to compete in prices in the short run. However, we understand that the start-up and shut-down costs for machines are not particularly high and that downtime periods are fairly short. Given these facts it appears highly implausible that capacity downtime could be used as a credible commitment device to raise prices in short-run negotiations. Indeed, no evidence was presented in the case that would suggest otherwise.

To further support the notion that downtime is not used for collusive purposes it helps to analyse why downtime may be taken in a competitive environment. If we can show that there are strong unilateral incentives for taking downtime, a collusive explanation is even less plausible. For such an analysis the characteristics of the industry are again crucial. First, competition in this industry is to a large extent in long-term contracts, most of which are concluded at the beginning of the year. Under these contracts buyers in practice remain free to purchase less at given contractual prices than initially contracted for. Sellers then face a shortage of sales relative to their capacities. They can then decide whether to sell additional paper by lowering prices or saving on the costs of keeping a machine running.

Frequently, it may be much more efficient to shut down machines temporarily because the additional sales will not justify the costs of keeping machines running. The reason for this is directly related to the low elasticity of demand. Significant additional sales can be achieved only through very large price cuts because paper demand by newspapers is extremely inelastic in the short run. Such large price cuts would not be profitable for a producer relative to the costs saved from shutting down a machine. An innocent explanation for market-related downtime will therefore be more plausible if the market-related downtime is short relative to the planning horizon of paper users. This appears to be the case in the data since downtime is taken for short periods up to two weeks. The observation that there is more downtime in periods of low demand realisations is therefore clearly not evidence of collusion over downtime.

8. Assessing market transparency

While the Commission appears to have accepted the characterisation of the incentive structure arising from irreversible investments, it still focused its discussions in the decision on the question of market transparency and the observability of decisions. We discuss this issue in this section because it illustrates an overemphasis on the market transparency question.

Market transparency matters for the issue of coordinated effects only insofar as it facilitates the monitoring of rivals' decisions in an uncertain environment and reveals to competitors when deviations occur.[28] When theoretical considerations suggest that coordinated effects are highly unlikely even in the presence of perfect market transparency, there is no reason even to

---

[28] The issue of market transparency has been carefully discussed in a report to the European Commission by Kühn and Vives (1995) and in Kühn (2001a).

consider this issue. However, for completeness, we use this section to discuss some of the ways market transparency has been analysed in this case.

Theoretically, firms could try to use announcements to coordinate on a collusive equilibrium. We know that cheap talk can achieve coordination in games with multiple equilibria. For example in *US* v *Airline Tariff Publishing* there were a huge number of announcements, counter announcements and withdrawals which arguably could have been used to establish a collusive agreement.

The Commission suggested during the proceedings that capacity forecasts distributed by the industry association CEPIPRINT could be used to coordinate investment decisions. The Commission suggested that a pattern existed in which capacity forecasts were monotonically adjusted downward over time. This view was apparently influenced by empirical results of Christensen and Caves (1997) about the US pulp and paper industry. They found that in smaller markets subsequent project announcements of rivals would trigger the abandonment of projects previously announced.

We have already seen that announcements seem to lead to pre-commitments in the European context. This contradicts a view in which announcements are used as cheap talk for coordination purposes. This result is further strengthened by an analysis of the three-year, two-year and one-year-ahead forecasts as well as realised outcome for the five years 1996–2000. *Monotonically declining forecasts never occur for newsprint.*[29]

For the period 1996–2000, we have calculated the differences between two adjacent forecasts. For each grade of paper, there are three differences: three-year ahead minus two-year ahead, two-year ahead minus one-year ahead and one-year ahead minus actual. For each grade difference there are five observations. The difference between two adjacent forecasts can be regarded as a forecast error. The usual hypothesis is that the expected forecast error is zero. The Statement of Objections claimed that the expected forecast errors are positive. Table 15.2 gives summary statistics by grade and difference. Three of the mean differences are negative. The sample standard deviations are so high compared with the means that none of the estimated means is significantly different from zero at the 5 per cent level.

The data in the analysis are consistent with the hypothesis that the expected forecast errors are zero.

[29] They occur once over the ten-year time horizon for each magazine paper category considered in the case. Overall, the pattern occurs twice out of fifteen occurrences. The Commission had initially cited the example from one magazine paper category as evidence for its view.

Table 15.2 Summary statistics for differenced forecasts

Grade	Variable	Mean	Sample standard deviation	Standard deviation of estimate of mean	T-statistic
News	F3 – F2	6.8	256.2	114.6	0.1
News	F2 – F1	144.8	295.2	132.0	1.1
News	F1 – Actual	−99.6	133.4	59.7	−1.7

Note: F3 is the three-year-ahead, F2 the two-year-ahead and F1 the one-year-ahead forecast.
Source: CEPIPRINT's Demand–Supply Report, Newsprint and Magazine Grades (various years).

Even if the pattern described by the Commission would have been found in the data it is not clear whether such evidence would have constituted good evidence for coordination. Christensen and Caves (1997) and Doyle and Snyder (1999) (for the car industry) interpret such patterns as evidence for efficient information sharing about demand conditions.

Information sharing should not be seen as inevitably a bad thing. Evidence for communication channels on aggregate forecasts of demand and public statements like investment announcements have many plausible efficiency enhancing explanations. They can arise from efficient information sharing or the desire to properly inform financial markets. Such information can also help the customer side in planning their decisions. For these reasons Kühn and Vives (1995) have argued that information exchanges that are on aggregate data or that are announcements to the public should not be subject to antitrust scrutiny. Unfortunately, it is apparently seen as legitimate to consider them as negative factors in assessing coordinated effects in mergers.

9. Conclusion

In this chapter we have reviewed the analysis of the merger involving the split of Haindl and its sale to the competitors Norske Skog and UPM Kymmene. We have shown how coordinated effects analysis has to be adapted to the specific market features. Concentrating on features that make collusion very difficult one can find strong arguments against the existence of coordinated effects. We have shown how the basic theoretical insights can be supported by the qualitative features of empirical data – even where a rigorous test would not be possible.

The merger was cleared without remedies in phase 2 of the merger proceedings. Although the Commission stuck to its emphasis on market transparency issues and arguments about the commitment effects of announcements, it in the end agreed with the argument that with irreversible investments collusion is extremely hard.

Shortly afterwards, the pending collusion case was closed in the autumn of 2002. However, this was not the end of suspicions about conduct in the markets for publishing paper. After UPM Kymmene was involved in a US collusion case in an unrelated market, new management conducted a wide internal review to detect any potential anticompetitive activities. In an attempt to obtain a general clean slate for the company, they reported to the US Department of Justice suspicious activities in several markets in the paper industry. We are unaware of the exact claims the new management of UPM Kymmene made. But it is important to note that under the US system anything that could serve as evidence for collusion in some market that is withheld by the firm could jeopardise any antitrust immunity achieved in markets where it matters. UPM Kymmene therefore had strong incentives to disclose even fairly ambiguous evidence on collusion. The allegations of UPM Kymmene led to the European Commission opening another investigation into the newsprint and magazine paper markets in 2004. The Commission raided the company headquarters of the major European players in the publishing paper business. However, it appears that little evidence for collusion was found, so that the Commission closed the case in November 2006.

Whether or not one believes that there were attempts to collude in this industry after the year 2001, market performance appears to support the economic analysis of a limited scope for collusion in this industry: since 2001 price cost margins in the industry have been at a record low and competitive pressure has led to major reorganisation efforts by some of the firms. It appears almost impossible to predict in merger proceedings whether firms might attempt to collude at some point in the future. However, our analysis shows that a careful analysis of the structural features of the industry, as distinct from a simple checklist approach, can help in making reasonable predictions for the likely success of any hypothetical coordination attempts.

Acknowledgements

We are grateful to Jim Adams, Bill Bishop, Cristina Caffarra, Bruce Lyons and Hugh Wills as well as participants at the CCP seminar 'Cases in European Competition Policy: The Economic Analysis' at the University of East Anglia for helpful comments and discussions. Both authors were involved as consultants in the case for Norske Skog. The views expressed in this paper are our own and do not reflect those of anyone else save the authors. The authors are grateful to the Economic and Social Research Council for financially supporting this work through the Centre for Economic Performance.

C.3

Vertical and conglomerate effects

16

Vertical effects between natural gas and electricity production: the Neste–IVO merger in Finland

Rune Stenbacka

1. Background and introduction

In early 1998 the Finnish firms Neste Oy and Imatran Voima Oy (IVO) merged. It brought together a national monopoly in gas distribution with the largest supplier of electricity in Finland. The merger was evaluated by the European Commission, which reached its decision in June 1998.[1] This chapter offers an evaluation of this merger in light of an analysis of the markets for natural gas and electricity production in Finland. The analysis is conducted with the perspective taken prior to the merger, in particular prior to the introduction of Nord Pool, i.e. the common power exchange between Sweden, Norway and Finland. For that reason we describe market conditions in terms of data available prior to the merger. Typically this refers to data on a yearly basis from 1996.

Neste focused on oil, energy (natural gas, liquefied petroleum and heat supply) and the chemical business. The Finnish state was the dominant shareholder, owning 83 per cent of the shares in Neste, which had a turnover of ECU 9,018 million. IVO was the largest Finnish energy company with business activities consisting of power and heat generation, power trading and electricity distribution and supply, operation and maintenance of power plants, energy measurement and grid services. The Finnish state owned almost 96 per cent of the shares in IVO, which had a worldwide turnover of ECU 2,342 million. The merger, which was prepared in late 1997 and proposed in early 1998, is one of the largest mergers in the industrial history of Finland. The firms had a combined worldwide turnover exceeding ECU 10,000 million and a Community-wide turnover exceeding ECU 8,000 million, but they did not achieve more than two-thirds of the aggregate Community-wide turnover

---

[1] Case No. IV/M.931 – Neste/IVO (02/06/1998). Office for Official Publications of the European Communities, Luxembourg.

within one and the same Member State. Thus, the proposed merger clearly had a Community dimension, meaning the European Commission had the mandate of evaluating the merger. The main purpose of this chapter is to evaluate the merger between Neste and IVO from the point of view of the performance of the markets for natural gas and electricity primarily in Finland.

As the dominant owner of both firms the Finnish government and the Ministry of Trade and Industry actively promoted the merger as an action of industrial policy with the intention of creating a domestic champion, which would have the financial strength required to compete more successfully in the emerging international energy markets in northern Europe. Neste strongly supported the merger, whereas the management of IVO was much more reserved. However, the proponents of the merger never presented any public calculation or detailed characterisation whatsoever of possible implied synergy gains.

The academic literature and competition authorities typically classify mergers into three general categories: horizontal, vertical and conglomerate mergers. The proposed merger between Neste and IVO included elements of all of these three forms of merger, but in the present analysis we will emphasise primarily the vertical and horizontal dimensions.

In general, mergers, in particular horizontal ones, tend to soften competition in the industry, thereby promoting profits of the merged firm. Second, if the merger involves synergies with relationship to the use of capital, assets or other fixed factors of production, the merger would generate a more efficient unit of production, thereby generating benefits not only to the merged firm but potentially also to consumers. Third, as an outcome of rational behaviour a takeover occurs when there is a disparity of valuation between a buyer and a seller in the sense that the buyer has more optimistic expectations regarding the future prospects of the firm it takes over or that the buyer expects that it can run the acquired entity more efficiently than the seller could do by remaining independent. Finally, it is far from uncommon that the management in control of the acquiring entity does not pay attention to whether a merger adds to the profits, but that it rather acts with motives based on prestige, power and individual monetary rewards associated with managing a large and expanding corporate empire. In this analysis we do not distinguish between these possible explanations for this particular merger. We simply present an industry-level analysis of the markets for natural gas and electricity production in Finland with the main purpose of evaluating the consequences of a merger between Neste and IVO from the point of view of the performance of the markets for natural gas and electricity in Finland as well as the Nordic countries more generally. Considerations of energy policy or industrial policy are essentially outside the scope of this analysis.

Our analysis starts with a brief description of the markets for natural gas and electricity production, after which the relevant nature of competition in these industries is characterised. Section 4 offers an evaluation of the consequences of a merger between Neste and IVO. This evaluation pays particular attention to the implications of vertical integration between the natural gas market and the industry for generation of electricity as well as to the aspects of horizontal integration in the market for private household heating. Section 5 offers a discussion of alternative forms of cooperation between Neste and IVO. The analysis is summarised in a final section.

2. The natural gas industry and its economic characteristics

2.1 Basic description of the natural gas industry

All the natural gas used in Finland was imported from Russia, where it was extracted by the Russian gas supplier Gazprom. Gasum Oy, owned 75 per cent by Neste and 25 per cent by Gazprom, had a monopoly position as importer of natural gas. Gasum owned and operated the transmission system of natural gas and the market for sales of natural gas was characterised by Gasum's monopoly position. Furthermore, through its other activities in the energy sector Neste had strategic gas interests also apart from the profitable Gasum operations as such.

Total natural gas imports amounted to 34.7 TWh in 1996. In total, the Finnish industry accounted for 48 per cent of the consumption of natural gas, of which the paper and pulp industry alone consumed 30 per cent. Combined district heat and power generation by energy companies stood for 38 per cent of the natural gas consumption, whereas other power production made up 7 per cent and district heat production 5 per cent of the consumption.

2.2 Natural gas in electricity generation

From the point of view of the present evaluation a crucial aspect of natural gas lies in its use as a source for electricity generation. As illustrated in Table 16.1, natural gas had a 10.4 per cent market share as raw material for electricity generation in 1996.

Table 16.1 The share of various energy sources in the generation of electricity in 1996 in Finland

Hydro power	16.7%	
Nuclear power	26.6%	
Coal	20.9%	
Oil	2.1%	
Natural gas	10.4%	
Peat	8.2%	
Other indigenous energy sources	9.8%	
Net imports	5.3%	
Total	100%	70.0 TWh

Table 16.2 The share of natural gas in electricity generation 1992–6

1992	7.7%
1993	7.9%
1994	8.8%
1995	9.7%
1996	10.4%

As Table 16.2 makes clear, the market share of natural gas in electricity generation had increased quite substantially during the years prior to the merger.

At the time of the merger natural gas was expected to become an increasingly important energy source in Finland as well as in the Nordic countries more generally, even though natural gas was not necessarily very competitive relative to certain other fuels for electricity generation. In particular, in Neste's marketing natural gas was extensively presented an alternative fuel to nuclear power. We will return to the reasons for this later on. Natural gas was expected to increase its market share as fuel for electricity generation and the speed of this development depended on how the uncertainty regarding the future of Finnish nuclear power was resolved, on the extent to which coal-fired power was phased out as well as on the evolution of general environmental and energy policies. Potential investments to increase pipeline capacity in Finland were highly dependent on decisions regarding the direction of future energy policy in Sweden. But estimations within the energy industry seemed to agree that planned pipeline extensions to Sweden (and, perhaps, even further) could be operational no earlier than 2010. We will return to a discussion of the relative costs of electricity generation from different fuels in section 3.

2.3 Switching costs and potential competition in the natural gas market

In order to generally assess the performance of the market for natural gas, and the extent to which this market was disciplined by potential competition from other forms of fuel, it is first of all justified to clarify the magnitude of the switching costs by which gas customers were locked in by their relationship with the gas supplier. In principle, such switching costs could have technical reasons associated with sunk investments which were needed for the customer to make use of the natural gas. Switching costs could also be created through the use of long-term supply contracts. We proceed by reviewing each of these aspects separately.

In principle, and at least in the long run, gas faced competition from alternative fuels. However, it seems reasonable that the cross-elasticities of demand were very low in the short run in markets where consumers had made sunk investments such as central heating systems. The cross-elasticities were potentially higher for industrial firms if these were able to switch to alternative fuels quicker and at lower relative costs. However, from the point of view of electricity generation it seemed to be a stylised fact that it was extremely expensive to turn a gas-based unit into a generator producing electricity based on some alternative fuel. At the time of the merger, in some existing power plants light fuel oil could partly and only very temporarily substitute for natural gas, for instance during an interruption in the supply of natural gas, but, as was well known, oil was extremely expensive as a fuel for electricity generation. Replacing natural gas with another fuel which was competitive for use in CHP-plants (plants for combined heat and power production) typically required several years of planning and reconstruction. Thus, it seemed to be a good approximation of reality to consider the production technology of electricity generation to be *completely inflexible* with respect to the fuel when evaluated *at the level of a gas-based generator*. In this sense the technology of electricity generation implied that the generating units faced extremely high switching costs if they were to consider an alternative fuel.

Gasum's supply of natural gas to the electricity-generating firms was based on long-term contracts. The delivery contracts on natural gas typically specified that resale was forbidden without the permission of Gasum. Typically, these contracts were signed for periods of an order of magnitude of ten years and the prices were indexed to appropriate energy-cost indices. Long-term contracts clearly represented an efficient form of contracting which minimised transaction costs as evaluated from the point of view of joint surplus for the seller and the buyer, both of which faced a technology characterised by highly irreversible and sunk investments.

The supply of natural gas to electricity generators involved highly asset-specific investments of an irreversible character from the perspective of both the seller and the buyer. Unless there were competing suppliers available for a gas-based generator of electricity, such a producer would be highly vulnerable to a holdup by the fuel supplier in the form of a hike in the price of natural gas once the generator capacity was installed. Conversely, the pipeline for supply of natural gas could be considered to be a completely sunk investment and once that capacity was installed an electricity generating firm with a fuel-flexible production capacity would have a very strong bargaining position in its relationship with the supplier of natural gas. Within the framework of such a technology long-term contracts which minimised the probability for holdups to occur were efficient. Vertical integration was another mechanism which could eliminate the possibilities of holdups. We will return to an evaluation of vertical integration between a monopoly supplier of natural gas and a leading player in the electricity market in section 4.

When making an assessment concerning the nature of the relevant form of competition in the market for natural gas it has to be remembered that long-term contracts form an essential aspect of efficiency in the natural gas market. Therefore it seemed highly justified to view the relevant form of competition to be competition with respect to delivery contracts valid for very long periods. In practice, different forms of fuel for electricity generation could compete in a relevant way only when the electricity-generating firm decided which fuel to use for a particular generator based on offers from different fuel sources in the form of long-term delivery contracts.

Formally, at the time of the merger Gasum was under the surveillance of the Finnish antitrust authorities (the Office of Free Competition) as a consequence of its dominant position in the Finnish natural gas market. The antitrust authorities required the pricing of natural gas to be transparent and non-discriminatory. Further, Gasum was formally prohibited from tying the conditions of natural gas supply to the delivery of other fuels. The regulatory framework for the natural gas market nevertheless exhibited a clear inconsistency relative to the foreseeable reforms in the regulation of the electricity market as far as the same firm (Gasum) was allowed to maintain a monopoly position with respect to production, transmission and distribution of gas. Namely, at the time of the merger the suggested, and subsequently approved, regulation of the electricity market separated the production, transmission and distribution of electricity and placed an upper limit (20 per cent) for the extent to which electricity producers were allowed to own the network of electricity transmission. At the time of the merger final decisions concerning the details of the regulatory framework applying to the electricity market were, however, still pending, as was a significant reform of the general Finnish legislation concerning merger control.[2] It should also be emphasised that the supplier of natural gas faced no regulation whatsoever regarding the conditions (access fee, etc.) by which potential customers of natural gas were connected to the pipeline. We will return to the crucial evaluation of how a vertical integration of large players in the markets for natural gas and electricity generation might affect the efficiency and power of available regulatory policies.

3. The electricity supply industry and its economic characteristics

As was made clear in section 2.2, Finnish electricity was, at the time of the proposed merger, predominantly generated from five sources: hydro power, natural gas, coal, nuclear power and peat.[3] Each of these sources had a fuel-specific relationship between the fixed costs and the marginal costs for electricity generation. Furthermore, and importantly, as inputs of electricity generation each of these fuels exhibited a source-specific risk from the point of view of the electricity producer. Such input-specific risks were associated with, for example, fluctuations in world market prices, changes in political attitudes and environmental policies, fuel delivery disturbances and natural resource constraints and disturbances/accidents in the operation of nuclear power plants.

The electricity-generating industry was characterised by substantial economic risks associated with the fuels as production inputs and, in addition, the industry faced strong fluctuations in demand. For firms operating under such circumstances flexibility constituted a particularly valuable asset, which formed the basis for competitiveness in the long run. In the previous section we characterised how the technology of electricity generation exhibited extremely high switching costs for the generating units if these were to consider an alternative fuel. Because of this technological feature a firm in the electricity market could establish production flexibility only by creating a *fuel-diversified portfolio of electricity-generating units*. In other words, a well-diversified portfolio of fuel-specific power plants constituted an essential strategic instrument based on which electricity-generating firms established competitive

---

[2] Soon after the merger the outlined regulation of the electricity industry as well as the general legislation for merger control were approved.

[3] In addition, a non-negligible share of electricity is generated in association with the processes for the production of paper and pulp.

advantage in the long run. In fact, production flexibility based on access to a well-balanced network of channels for fuel provision together with the possibility to adjust the capacity utilisation between power-generating units was a central feature when determining the nature of long-run competition in the electricity market.

The investigation of the merger by the European Commission[4] estimated that IVO had a market share of about 40 per cent at the level of electricity production in Finland. The other main electricity producer, Pohjolan Voima, which was owned mainly by a number of large industrial companies, held a market share of about 23 per cent. Furthermore, it was estimated that 19 per cent of the electricity production was generated in association with industrial processes and that the remaining supply came from other producers, mainly municipal power companies. Furthermore, the investigation by the European Commission suggested that IVO's share of the 'free' wholesale market was considerably higher than 40 per cent. Based on the wholesale to distributors and industry, IVO's market share of electricity was claimed to be close to 60–70 per cent [exact market share is a trade secret]' (para. 39 in Case No. IV/M.931 – Neste/IVO). The difference between this estimate of IVO's share of the 'free' wholesale market and IVO's ordinary market share was explained by the very high proportion of captive production on behalf of IVO's rivals. In this respect the investigation of the European Commission raised the issue of whether the electricity generation by industrial producers or by the so-called 'Mankala' – companies with industrial producers as shareholders – should have been included in the definition of the relevant market or not. Clearly, industrial producers did affect the performance of the market for production and wholesale of electricity. Of course, if industrial producers could buy electricity at a price below their own marginal production costs they would have made use of such an opportunity and not fully utilised their own capacity. Conversely, if the available market price exceeded the marginal production costs of the industrial producers these would have switched to a higher degree of self-generated electricity. Thus, by switching between self-supply and market purchases the industrial producers had a significant influence on the market price, and the effects of this type of market players should certainly be included when defining the relevant market.

The investigation undertaken by the European Commission did not explicitly declare whether IVO had a dominant market position in the national Finnish market for production and wholesale of electricity. We here evaluate

---

[4] Case No. IV/M.931 – Neste/IVO, Office for Official Publications of the European Communities, Luxembourg.

IVO's market dominance in light of the dominance test developed by Melnik, Shy and Stenbacka (2008). According to this test the dominance threshold, denoted S^D (S_2), is determined by the market share of the second largest firm (S_2) as well as by a parameter (γ), which captures an assessment of the relative importance of potential competition according to

$$S^D(S_2) = \frac{\sqrt{\gamma^2(S_2)^2 + \gamma + 1} - 1}{\gamma}.$$

If we insert $S_2 = 0.23$ as the market share for the second largest firm and if we explore the sensitivity to the assessment of potential competition by letting the parameter of potential competition γ vary over the very extensive interval from 0.25 to 5 we find that the dominance threshold would belong to the interval [0.34, 0.48]. The high-end threshold (48 per cent) captures the case with $\gamma = 0.25$ and corresponds to a scenario where potential competition imposes a very strong threat on the firm with the largest market share, whereas the opposite holds true for the low-end threshold (34 per cent). Clearly, the parameter γ capturing the relative importance of potential competition plays a major role for the determination of the threshold of dominance. Admittedly this parameter is exogenous and introduced ad hoc. However, Nord Pool, the common power exchange between Sweden, Norway and Finland, started its operation in Finland in the beginning of 1997. Essentially Nord Pool was known to define an integrated market design for the countries involved and it was accompanied by credible investment plans for increasing the capacity of transmission between the Nordic countries. Essentially, this was the start of a development towards a Nordic electricity market.[5] In light of such a development potential competition from Sweden and Norway would constitute severe potential competition, thus justifying a high dominance threshold implied by a low value of γ. In light of such a predictable development it would have been hard to convincingly classify IVO as a firm with a dominant market position. Interestingly, the Finnish Competition Authority (FCA) initiated in 1993 a case where it required IVO to cancel certain types of long-term contracts. In its legal evaluation of this requirement the Finnish Competition Council (the national court for competition issues) reached the conclusion that the FCA had not been able to present evidence that IVO had a dominant market position in the Finnish

---

[5] The Sector Inquiry dated 10 January 2007 on the gas and electricity industries conducted by the European Commission presents evidence and arguments in support of the general view that the relevant geographical electricity market is currently larger than national for Finland and Sweden.

market for wholesale of electricity. The FCA was required to present a more complete market analysis as a basis for an evaluation of market dominance, but it never presented such an analysis.

At the time of the proposed merger IVO had the most diversified fuel mix by a far margin among the significant Nordic electricity producers. The fuel mix of the leading Swedish electricity producers included no natural gas at all or at most access to natural gas only to a marginal extent. Also, in other respects, according to industry analysts, the fuel mix of IVO's Swedish competitors fell clearly below the diversification exhibited in IVO's fuel portfolio. Consequently, in a Nordic perspective IVO had a superior production flexibility. Although the Swedish electricity producers had access to a larger average supply of competitive hydro and nuclear power, IVO had a greater flexibility to substitute lower-cost fuel than the Swedish rivals in periods of low rainfall or, even more importantly from a long-run perspective, when the share of nuclear power as fuel for electricity generation most probably would be substantially reduced in Sweden within the near future.[6] For this reason entry by Swedish producers into the Finnish electricity market in order to achieve access to Russian natural gas was very important from the point of view of the performance of the Finnish as well as the Nordic electricity market. Figure 16.1 illustrates the role of natural gas in order to create a diversified fuel mix in Finland for electricity generation in the long run. A similarly constructed figure for Sweden would very clearly reveal the strategic importance for Swedish producers of access to Russian gas.

Estimations of fuel-specific variable costs of electricity generation have always represented a valuable business secret for the firms in the industry. In Figure 16.1 we show a common view among industry analysts regarding the relative variable costs of generating electricity with different fuels. It should be emphasised that this figure serves illustrative purposes only and no attention should be paid to the absolute increases in variable costs when moving from one fuel to a more expensive one. For that reason we do not report the units on the axis measuring the variable costs of producing one MWh on the left side of Figure 16.1. On the horizontal axis we have indicated an approximation of the fuel-specific production capacities in Finland in 1996. It should be remembered, as shown in Table 16.1, that the electricity demand in 1996 was 70.0 TWh. Figure 16.1 also illustrates that the demand fluctuations were most likely captured by fluctuations in electricity production associated with the least efficient fuels: condensing power and imports taking place based on spot market

---

[6] At the time Swedish politicians had committed themselves to no future expansion of nuclear power in accordance with the outcome of a referendum.

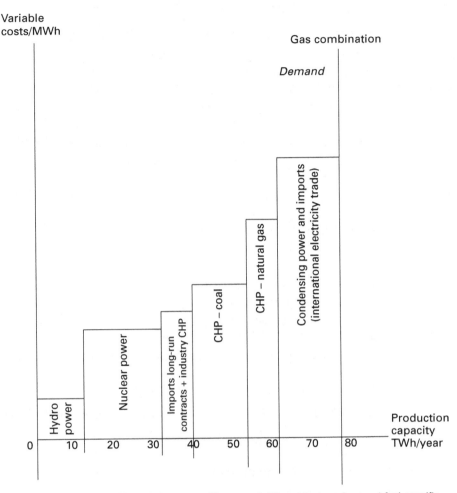

Figure 16.1 Illustration of the relative competitiveness of different fuels and present fuel-specific production capacities in Finland with implications for the creation of a diversified fuel portfolio in the long run

trade in electricity. It should be emphasised that Figure 16.1 is an overly simplified illustration in several respects. It is almost impossible to estimate variable costs of electricity production based on industry CHP and it is also difficult to characterise an average variable cost for imports based on long-run contracts. These categories of electricity production are located in Figure 16.1 in a way intended to illustrate the general point that they represented rather competitive forms of electricity generation.

During the years prior to the merger the Finnish electricity market had been largely deregulated and many regulatory obstacles to free competition had been removed. But long-term contracts still represented a mechanism for reducing the distortions and inefficiencies created by holdup problems exactly as was argued to be the case for natural gas. It was justified to view competition with respect to long-term delivery contracts to represent the relevant perspective when evaluating the nature of competition in electricity markets. It should be emphasised that this perspective refers to the time when the frequency of customers switching from one supplier to another was low. The subsequent introduction of Nord Pool and the significant trade in financial contracts – such as standardised Nord Pool futures contracts – has significantly changed the nature of competition.

4. An evaluation of the consequences of a merger between Neste and IVO

In this section I will make use of the essential economic characteristics of the markets for natural gas as well as electricity in order to evaluate the consequences of a merger between Neste and IVO for the performance of the energy markets more generally. In particular, I will pay attention to whether the merger was likely to create or strengthen such a dominant market position that this market dominance could be expected to significantly impede competition in the relevant market(s). Throughout the discussion in this section I will repeatedly pay attention to the impact of a merger on the ability of the authorities to fulfil regulatory tasks and commitments.

4.1 Vertical integration: the natural gas market and the generation of electricity

From an antitrust perspective long-term delivery contracts formed the relevant concept of competition in both the markets for natural gas and electricity. As the supply of natural gas, including all the stages of import, transmission and sales, was persistently monopolised by Gasum, it seems particularly important to assess the impact of a Neste–IVO merger on potential competition or entry.

When contemplating full-scale entry into the Finnish electricity market a potential entrant knew that it could achieve the flexibility which was necessary for competitiveness in the long run only by having access to a diversified portfolio of fuels from which to produce electricity based on all the main fuels. At the time of the merger Swedish electricity producers were in the process of planning new and extended entry into the Finnish market. For example, Vattenfall was known to have plans for investing in a gas-based power plant near the border between Finland and Russia. At the same time, natural gas represented the source of less than 1 per cent of Vattenfall's electricity generation, while at the same time it was known that the Swedish energy policy commitments dictated that the share of nuclear power as fuel for electricity generation was going to be reduced substantially in Sweden within the near future. Thus, from the point of view of Vattenfall as well as other Swedish electricity producers, access to natural gas from Russia via a gas-based generator in Finland seemed crucial in order to secure competitiveness in the long run. As the Finnish and Swedish networks for electricity transmission were connected with a cross-border transmission capacity which was expected to increase substantially, the direct access to natural gas from Russia had substantial long-run implications for competition, and thereby for the performance of the electricity markets, in both countries. In particular, the issue of access to natural gas from Russia also substantially affected trade in electricity between Finland and Sweden.

One could argue that Swedish electricity producers might have had access to natural gas from sources different from Gasum as well. Even though such an argument is perfectly correct, access to several competing suppliers of natural gas would have importantly affected the conditions incorporated in long-run supply contracts. More favourable supply contracts would, in turn, have increased the competitiveness of the electricity producer. Consequently, direct access for Swedish electricity producers to natural gas from Russia would under all circumstances have had profound implications for the performance in the long run of the electricity markets in both Finland and Sweden.

The issue of Swedish investments designed to create gas-based production capacity in Finland had implications in both countries for the degree of competition in the electricity markets as evaluated from a long-run perspective. For that reason the conclusions regarding the competition effects of the vertical integration between Neste's natural gas monopoly and IVO's electricity production/supply were not sensitive to whether we consider the relevant geographic market to be restricted to the Finnish national market alone or whether it is considered to be Nordic in a more general sense. Indeed, at the time of the merger the European Commission as well as the parties involved seemed to agree that the relevant market was national in a geographical sense (paras. 22 and 24 in Case No. IV/M.931 – Neste/IVO).[7]

---

[7] The subsequent development of the electricity market justifies the view, apparently supported also by the Sector Inquiry 2007 on the gas and electricity industries conducted by the European Commission, that the relevant market today most likely includes at least both Finland and Sweden, and that under all circumstances the relevant market is significantly larger than the national Finnish market.

A merged Neste–IVO would have had access to a substantially extended set of entry-preventing measures with respect to foreign entry into the Finnish electricity market when compared with the situation without such a merger. For example, a merged firm would operate with drastically changed incentives to make use of, for example, access pricing and pipeline location as strategic instruments in order to influence existing rivals as well as potential entrants in the electricity market. In particular, it would have been in the profit-maximising interest of such a merged company to create strategic entry barriers in the presence of a potential entry threat. For example, a vertically integrated Neste–IVO would have had incentives to exploit its first-mover advantage by coordinating pipeline location and the location of its own plants for generation of electricity and distance heat in such a way so as to eliminate the profitability of rival entry. At the time of the merger the existing regulatory policy regarding the markets for natural gas and electricity left the competition authorities with very limited instruments for the detection of such forms of strategic entry prevention, which could have qualified as abuse of a dominant market position.

As the pricing of natural gas was required to be transparent and non-discriminatory while the pricing of access to the pipeline was not regulated at the time of the merger, a vertically integrated firm would have had an incentive to make strategic use of a two-part tariff for the purpose of entry prevention. In addition, a vertically integrated firm would have had an incentive to distort its revelation of information to antitrust authorities in order to support an entry-preventing two-part tariff. Further, a vertical integration would have made it possible for a merged Neste–IVO to engage in cross-subsidisation between its natural gas and electricity businesses and it would have been extremely hard for outside observers, like the competition authorities, to detect such cross-subsidisation. Facing such a vertically integrated firm the effective implementation of competition laws would have meant an enormous challenge to the ability of antitrust authorities for information processing and industry analysis.

As the arguments above have made clear, the vertical integration of the natural gas monopoly of Neste (Gasum) with IVO's electricity production/supply would have created an integrated firm with powerful strategic instruments which such a firm could have made use of in order to abuse its potentially dominant market position. And, of course, such an integrated firm would have had strong incentives to exploit the strategic opportunities which a merger would offer. There are strong reasons to assume that it would have been far too optimistic to have faith in the ability of competition authorities to exercise behavioural control relative to potential abuse of the strategically determined dominant market position. Therefore it seems justified that the competition authorities would specify structural and irreversible restrictions regarding aspects of ownership and organisation of the vertically integrated firm as a precondition for approval of a merger.

4.2 Vertical integration: the power generation of industrial customers

Natural gas was used not only by firms, like IVO, producing electricity to be traded. Industrial customers using natural gas for heat as well as generation of electricity for their own energy needs constituted approximately 45 per cent of the overall consumption of natural gas. In situations of disturbances in the delivery of natural gas such industrial customers typically had to turn to traded electricity in order to guarantee that their industrial processes were not disrupted. From the point of view of such industrial customers potential disturbances in the delivery of natural gas were expensive. As long as the supply of natural gas came from a firm which was separated from the electricity-producing industry, such a gas supplier had an incentive to mini-mise disturbances in the gas delivery. However, if the supplier of natural gas were to be merged with a big producer in the market for traded electricity, disturbances in the delivery of natural gas might actually turn out to be very profitable. In the presence of such a disturbance these industrial customers were then forced to shift to electricity consumption, which would increase the profitability of the vertically integrated supplier of energy. As IVO had the most flexible basis for electricity generation as well as excess capacity, it was very likely that these industrial customers in Finland would have had to turn to IVO to cover for such disturbances. At the time of the proposed merger, IVO's market share for traded electricity was estimated to be approximately 60–70 per cent in Finland according to the investigation undertaken by the European Commission, while it was about 25 per cent in the Nordic countries. This scenario represented a perfect example of classical price squeezing and, of course, it would have been in accordance with profit maximisation on behalf of a merged Neste–IVO to exploit such a mechanism of price squeezing.[8] More precisely, the merged Neste–IVO would have controlled the supply of natural gas (upstream) as an input for electricity generation (downstream). Under such circumstances it could have increased the price for natural gas offered to rival electricity generators, while keeping the electricity price unchanged. The effect would have been to reduce or eliminate, i.e. squeeze,

---

[8] The same argument could probably also be extended to apply for some local gas-dependent public producers of heat and electricity.

the profits or margins of downstream competitors. Of course, it was a matter of engineering to find out to which extent the reasons for potential disturbances in gas delivery can be technically verified ex post. It is unlikely that the vertically integrated Neste–IVO would have deliberately disturbed supply of natural gas. Structurally a merged Neste–IVO would nevertheless have had lower incentives to invest in a reliable delivery system and it seemed highly questionable whether this incentive for price squeezing could be eliminated by regulation.

4.3 Horizontal integration: the market for private household heating

A merger between Neste and IVO did not represent only a vertical integration. In the market for residential heating the implications would be those of a straightforward horizontal merger, because oil-based and electricity-based heating systems were substitutes. The residential heating was a significant industry associated with substantial market size. It was estimated that electricity supply for residential heating constituted approximately 20 per cent of IVO's sales. The distribution of market shares in 1996 across heating systems based on different fuels is reported in Table 16.3.

Generally IVO was considered to deliver 50 per cent of electricity used for the heating of private households, while Neste was estimated to have approximately a 75 per cent market share of oil deliveries for the same purpose. Taking into account the role of the potentially merging partners in the generation of district heating it would hardly have created any upper bias to consider a merged Neste–IVO firm to have had at least a 50 per cent market share in the Finnish residential heating market.

Academic research in the field of industrial economics has quite extensively explored the implications for industry profits, consumer surplus and total welfare of horizontal mergers in oligopolistic markets. A merger might generally

Table 16.3 The choice of heating system in the residential heating market (one-family houses) in Finland in 1996

Fuel type	%
Electricity	64
Oil	16
District heating	9
Wood	10

be profitable because the merged firm, without being more efficient than parent firms, has greater market power. If the merger does not generate efficiency gains it is most likely to reduce total welfare from the point of view of society. A merger might also be profitable because the formed firm is more efficient than the parent firms. Even if such a merger increases industry concentration and market power, the associated cost savings create the possibility that the overall effect of the merger on market performance could be positive. In general, the structure of cost savings from mergers could be of a static nature, based on economies of scale or scope, or they could be of a dynamic nature, based on learning or changed incentives for investments in R&D.

In the long run and with the perspective taken at the time when the type of heating system was selected, oil-based and electricity-based systems were substitutes in the market for private household heating. However, from a technological point of view it seemed impossible, or at least very hard, to identify any complementarities between Neste's business of refining and marketing of oil and IVO's electricity generation. As a matter of merger control it would actually have seemed reasonable to place the burden of proof for the identification of such complementarities and synergies on those promoting the merger. Consequently, with one's attention restricted to this market it seemed to be a reasonable approximation of reality to classify a merger between Neste and IVO as a horizontal merger increasing market power without generating any associated efficiency gains. For that reason such a horizontal merger would most likely have undesirable welfare consequences in a long-run perspective.

Strategic price competition actually incorporates a mechanism re-emphasising the undesirable welfare consequences in the long run of a merger in this market. Clearly, if two oligopolists supplying two differentiated products merge, the surviving firm finds it optimal to charge higher prices for these products than two separate firms would. Such a conclusion holds, because, when pricing a product, the merged firm internalises the reduction of demand on the other product associated with a price decrease. Now, if there is a rival firm producing a third, differentiated product, this rival finds it optimal to charge a higher price for its own product in response to the price increases generated by the merger. This conclusion by which a merger will induce a price increase as a best response on behalf of a rival firm is a consequence of price decisions serving as strategic complements according to the terminology of the modern theory of strategic competition analysis.

The selection of heating system had strong lock-in effects, and there would typically be extremely high costs associated with switching from a heating system based on one fuel to a system based on another fuel. Essentially, a switch from one heating method to another would typically have required a major renovation. Thus, in a short-run perspective there was very limited substitutability between electricity and oil in space heating. For that reason one could argue that space heating with different fuels represented separate markets in the short run.[9]

5. Alternative forms of cooperation between Neste and IVO

A full-scale merger might not have been the only way to achieve the potential benefits of coordination between the activities of Neste and IVO. A variety of alternative organisational arrangements seemed conceivable. In general, all forms of cooperation falling short of a complete merger, however, tend to at least partly replicate the welfare implications and antitrust concerns of a complete merger. Nevertheless it appears justified to comment on some of the most likely candidates of organisational form for cooperation falling short of a full merger.

A reasonable form of cooperation could have been a gas-centred joint venture whereby Neste's supply of natural gas would be united with IVO's gas-powered electricity production. Such a joint venture would probably have been sufficient in order to internalise potential synergy effects by eliminating distortions associated with underinvestment created through possible holdup problems. Also such a gas-centred joint venture could have avoided some antitrust concerns which were associated with the vertical integration of natural gas supply to IVO's non-gas-powered electricity production. Further, in comparison with a complete merger such a gas-centred joint venture would, of course, altogether have avoided concerns of horizontal merger in the residential heating market.

Nevertheless it is hard to see how a gas-centred joint venture could have avoided the general antitrust concerns associated with the vertical integration of natural gas supply and electricity production/supply even though these would have occurred to a lower extent. In addition, the arguments for substantial reforms of the regulatory framework facing the natural gas market would have remained basically unchanged.

In the previous sections it has been argued that diversification with respect to the fuel mix constituted a central determinant of competitiveness in the

---

[9] At the time multi-fuel technologies with heating systems making it possible to switch between oil and electricity were more largely adopted in some other countries.

long run. A gas-centred joint venture would not have been well diversified and therefore its competitiveness in the long run could have been questioned. If, however, the decisions of this joint venture would have been coordinated with those of IVO's non-gas-powered electricity-production facilities, this joint venture would not at all have reduced the potential competition problems generated by a complete Neste–IVO merger.

In addition to gas-centred joint ventures, alternative organisational forms of cooperation between Neste and IVO seemed possible. In order to make sure that a joint venture between Neste and IVO would not have simply replicated the market performance of a complete Neste–IVO merger, the organisational form for the cooperation had to satisfy a central condition. The organisational structure forming the basis for the cooperation had to constitute a credible commitment that the decision making of the joint venture would be sufficiently independent from that of the partners. Such a credible commitment could be based on an extended ownership structure for the joint venture in combination with structural measures to guarantee that the operational decisions of the joint venture were delegated to its management in a way which would have prevented coordination relative to operational decisions of the partners.[10]

6. The decision of the European Commission

Prior to the decision of the European Commission on the Neste–IVO merger, Neste–IVO and its major shareholder, the Finnish government, submitted the following commitments. Prior to the merger Neste owned 75 per cent of the shares in Gasum with the remaining 25 per cent held by Russian Gazprom. Conditional on an approval of the merger, Neste–IVO undertook to sell 50 per cent of the shares in Gasum, thereby reducing its ownership share in Gasum to 25 per cent within a specified time horizon. The Finnish state was offered 24 per cent of the shares and the remaining 26 per cent were sold to Finnish or European corporations independent of Neste–IVO and subject to approval from the Commission. Consequently, the Finnish government, directly through its shareholdings as well as indirectly through its control of Neste–IVO, held an effective shareholding of 49 per cent in Gasum. Overall the required change of

---

[10] In light of general competition policy at the EU level the creation of joint ventures does not raise antitrust concerns in cases where they 'contribute to improving the production or distribution of goods or to promoting technical or economic progress' without imposing unnecessary restrictions on competition.

shareholding and board membership ultimately guaranteed the structural independence of Gasum from the merged Neste–IVO and in that respect it was an effective remedy of the vertical competition issue.

Furthermore, the supervisory board of Gasum had eight members. The structure of the board essentially meant that the chairman and three members would always form a winning coalition. To fulfil the general requirement that Neste–IVO would not be in a controlling position in Gasum, Neste–IVO committed that none of its representatives on the supervisory board would act as chairman. Also, the government of Finland committed to ensure that Neste–IVO would not have a controlling position in Gasum. These were structural undertakings intended to make sure that Neste–IVO's position in Gasum changed from one of sole control into one of a minority owner. Furthermore, the undertakings also implied that Neste–IVO would not be able to block decisions regarding Gasum together with either Gazprom or the Finnish state.

In its decision dated 2 June 1998 and subject to full compliance with the commitments made by Neste–IVO and the state of Finland, the Commission decided not to oppose the merger and to declare it compatible with the common market. The Commission declared that the relevant markets were those of natural gas and electricity, with the geographical dimension restricted to Finland in both cases. Furthermore, the Commission took the view that there were separate markets for each type of fuel used for space heating. For that reason the Commission considered the merger to have no anticompetitive effects on the markets for space heating.

7. Concluding evaluation

The present analysis is founded on the essential economic characteristics of the markets for natural gas as well as electricity in order to evaluate the consequences of a merger between Neste and IVO for the performance of the energy markets in Finland as well as in the Nordic countries more generally. We summarise the main findings of the analysis as a concluding evaluation below.

A merger would represent a vertical integration between a monopolist in the natural gas market and the major player in the market for electricity production/supply. Based on the nature of competition in these markets the analysis demonstrates that the merger created an integrated firm with powerful strategic instruments which the merged firm had an incentive to exploit in ways such that the merger was likely to significantly impede competition in the relevant market(s). These anticompetitive effects were not restricted to Finland, but they had a substantial impact on trade in electricity between EU countries. In particular, the trade between Finland and Sweden was directly affected.

There were strong reasons to consider behavioural merger control exercised by competition and regulatory authorities to be insufficient in order to prevent the merged firm from getting access to strategic instruments which could have facilitated abusive behaviour. This risk could be eliminated (or reduced) only by making approval of the merger subject to significant structural restrictions.

In the residential heating market the implications of a merger between Neste and IVO were those of a straightforward horizontal merger. With attention restricted to this market the analysis found reasons to classify a merger between Neste and IVO as a horizontal merger increasing market power without generating any associated efficiency gains in the long run. Thus, in the long run such a merger would undoubtedly induce price increases and it would therefore most likely have undesirable welfare consequences. However, precisely as the Commission argues, in a short-run perspective there is very limited substitutability between electricity and oil in space heating. For that reason one could consider space heating with different fuels to represent separate markets in the short run.

Immediately after the approval of the merger the Permanent Secretary of the Ministry of Trade and Industry, Matti Vuoria, was appointed as new chairman of the board for the merged Neste–IVO. The merged Neste–IVO was quickly formed into the Fortum Corporation. Fortum's shares were quoted on the Helsinki Stock Exchange for the first time on 18 December 1998. Over the years Fortum has steadily strengthened its market position in the electricity market by acquiring other electricity producers to some extent in Finland, but mostly in other northern European countries. In September 2003 Fortum published its plan for spinning off its oil business into an independent company to be listed on the Helsinki Stock Exchange. This was realised in 2005 when the Neste Oil Corporation was separated from the Fortum Corporation. The shares of the Neste Oil Corporation were first quoted on the Helsinki Stock Exchange on 8 April 2005.

Acknowledgements

The author was an adviser for IVO in this merger case. The author wants to thank Harri Pynnä, Joacim Tåg and Lennart Hjalmarsson for comments. Of course, the author bears full responsibility for potentially remaining mistakes.

17

Horizontal, vertical and conglomerate effects: the GE–Honeywell merger in the EU

Xavier Vives and Gianandrea Staffiero

1. Introduction

The European Commission (EC) declared in July 2001 the merger between General Electric (GE) and Honeywell 'incompatible with the common market' according to the Merger Regulation established in the Council Regulation (EEC) No. 4064/89.[1] Article 2(3) of such regulation states that 'a concentration which creates or strengthens a dominant position as a result of which effective competition would be significantly impeded in the common market or in a substantial part of it shall be declared incompatible with the common market'.

The EC formally based its decision to block the merger on two pillars:

- the strengthening of GE's dominant position in the markets for large commercial aircraft engines and for large regional aircraft engines, and the creation of a dominant position on the markets for corporate jet engines;
- the creation of a dominant position in the market for avionics and non-avionics aerospace components, where Honeywell enjoyed a leading position, and in the market for small marine gas turbines.

The main channels by which the merger would create and strengthen dominant positions consisted in horizontal overlaps and vertical and conglomerate integration. The combined market share of the merging parties, the influence and leverage of the financial arms of GE, GECAS and GE Capital, and the ability and incentive to bundle products are behind the conclusions of the EC. The end result would be monopolisation of some markets (like

---

[1] The Regulation was later replaced by the Council Regulation (EC) No. 193/2004, where the meaning of the Article mentioned here was preserved via a slightly different wording of Article 2(3): 'A concentration which would significantly impede effective competition [...], in particular as a result of the creation or strengthening of dominant position, shall be declared incompatible with the common market.' The spirit of this change consists in allowing for the consideration of anticompetitive effects even when the merger does not result in dominance in the strict meaning of the term.

engines for large regional jet aircraft), vertical foreclosure in engine starters, and foreclosure and eventual exit of rivals of the merger entity.

The decision was appealed by GE and Honeywell to the Court of First Instance (CFI), which in December 2005 (with the merger long 'dead') decided to uphold it.[2] The CFI, however, supported only the parts of the reasoning behind the decision related to horizontal overlap between the merging parties. Other parts were instead found to be 'vitiated by manifest errors'; this was the case for vertical effects and, most notably, for conglomerate effects.

The decision of the EC spurred a lively debate in economic and policy circles, not least because the merger had previously passed the scrutiny of the US Department of Justice (DoJ), subject only to the divestiture of the military helicopter engine business and other minor requirements.

Section 2 describes the markets involved in the merger. Sections 3 to 5 present the lines of arguments by the EC, along with the CFI responses, on the alleged dominance of GE and horizontal overlaps with Honeywell, vertical effects and conglomerate effects. Section 6 presents the US DoJ position. In Section 7 we provide an economic assessment of each of the disputed effects the merger would have had on competition. Section 8 concludes.

2. The markets involved

The EC considered two main markets (jet engines and aircraft components and systems) and an auxiliary market for engine controls as input in the production of engines. The market for power systems was also analysed.

2.1 Jet engines

The EC stressed that 'engines compete in order to be certified on a given platform' first, then they also compete 'when airlines buying the aircraft platform select one of the available certified engines or when airlines decide on the acquisition of aircraft with different engines (whether or not the aircraft offers an engine choice)' (para. 9). In the market for jet engines, three distinct sectors were defined: large commercial aircraft (more than 100 seats, range greater than 2,000 nautical miles, cost over US$35 million), regional jet aircraft (30–90+ seats, less than 2,000 nautical miles range, cost

---

[2] *General Electric v Commission* (CFI case T-210/01). Honeywell's application was dismissed by the CFI 'mainly on technical grounds related to the scope of the action' (CFI, Press Release No. 109/05).

up to US$30 million) and corporate jet aircraft (designed for corporate activities, cost varying between US$3–35 million).

Large commercial aircraft. GE, Rolls-Royce (RR) and Pratt & Whitney (P&W) were the three main independent suppliers of engines for large commercial aircraft, which were divided in the EC's scheme into wide-bodies and narrow-bodies according to seats and distances typically covered. Both types are manufactured by Boeing and Airbus. The engine suppliers also operate via joint ventures, the most notable being CFMI (50–50 between GE and French SNECMA) and International Aero-Engines (IAE), controlled by P&W and RR.

Regional jet aircraft. Regional jets were produced by Embraer, Fairchild Doner, Bombardier and BAe Systems. The EC distinguished between small regional jets (30–50 passengers) and large regional jets (70–90+), arguing that substitutability was not feasible among the two categories. For small regional jets, GE (alone and through CFMI), P&W and RR were active in the market, while engines for the 'large' regional jets were supplied only by GE and Honeywell, the two parties in the attempted merger.

The engines for large commercial aircraft and for regional aircraft may be sold to airframe manufacturers or directly to the airlines.[3] In the latter case the airframe manufacturers leave the choice of engine (among a certified list) to the airlines. Those may have preferences for engines because of commonality effects related to the standardisation of an airline's fleet or part of it, leading to economies of scale (for example, in maintenance of engines).

Corporate jet aircraft, manufactured by Bombardier, Cessna, Dassault and Raytheon, was subdivided in heavy, medium and light. GE, Honeywell, RR and P&W were present in the market and, following the EC's assessment, a horizontal overlap between GE and Honeywell existed in the medium segment. The engines for corporate jets are typically chosen by the airframe manufacturers.

Maintenance, repair and overhaul (MRO) activities, part of the 'after-markets', are important due to the intense wear of jet engines. Services and spare parts are provided by engine manufacturers, besides independent shops and airlines' maintenance departments, and are a source of large streams of revenues.

2.2 Aerospace components: avionics and non-avionics

Honeywell manufactured a range of aviation products, besides engines, over which it enjoyed a leading position which allegedly would be converted into outright dominance were the merger to go ahead.

---

[3] Engines can also be sold to leasing companies. We will refer to this possibility later.

Avionics products relate to equipment used to control navigation and communication of the aircraft as well as flying controls. For large commercial aircraft, customers were aircraft manufacturers and airlines. For regional and corporate aircraft, manufacturers were the only customers and typically bought avionics as part of an integrated cockpit. Standard avionics products, which are not part of integrated systems, are 'Buyer-Furnished-Equipment' (BFE), i.e. can be chosen by airlines. Non-avionics products include a variety of systems such as auxiliary power units, environmental control systems, electric power, wheels, brakes and others. With the exception of highly consumable parts such as wheels and brakes, non-avionics products are 'Supplier-Furnished-Equipment' (SFE) selected by the airframe manufacturers.

The EC maintained that Honeywell was a leading supplier of avionics, enjoying a market share around 50–60 per cent, while its main competitors were Rockwell Collins (20–30 per cent), Thales (10–20 per cent) and Smiths Industries (0–10 per cent), and also in non-avionics, rivalled by United Technologies Corporation (UTC), through its subsidiary Hamilton Sundstrand, and to a lesser extent by BF Goodrich, SNECMA and Liebherr (no market shares indicated in this case).

2.3 Engine controls

Engine controls are necessary inputs for the production of engines. Honeywell was active in this market, in particular as a producer of engine starters, where it enjoyed a 50 per cent market share, while its main competitor, Hamilton Sundstrand, had more than 40 per cent according to the EC (and sold to the associated company P&W).

2.4 Power systems

The market for small marine gas turbines, defined to include turbines up to 10 MW, was composed by P&W Canada, RR/Allison, Honeywell and GE. Lumpy and cyclical demand rendered the estimation of market shares difficult. However, the EC established that for turbines below 5 MW, where the bulk of the demand is concentrated, Honeywell and GE had market shares around 70–80 per cent and 10–20 per cent, respectively. These shares moved to 40–50 per cent and 25–30 per cent, respectively, when considering the whole 0.5–10 MW range. GE and Honeywell argued against the existence of a horizontal overlap with technical substitutability issues and the lack of geographical overlap in the market activities of the two firms in this sector.

3. GE dominance and horizontal overlap with Honeywell

In the market for engines of large commercial aircraft, the definition of market shares was based on the installed base and orders backlog for aircraft still in production and excluded those which were no longer manufactured as no orders could be placed.

Taking account of joint ventures (CFMI, between GE and French SNECMA, was allocated 100 per cent to GE and IAE, between P&W and RR, was allocated equally between them), the resulting market shares of the installed base of aircraft still in production were:

- GE/CFMI: 52.5 per cent;
- P&W/IAE: 26.5 per cent;
- RR/IAE: 21 per cent.

Looking forward, the order book of aircraft still in production reinforced the position of GE/CFMI:

- GE/CFMI: 65 per cent;
- P&W/IAE: 16 per cent;
- RR/IAE: 19 per cent.

Objections by the parties focused on the failure to take into account the revenues still accruing from engines used in out-of-production aircraft and the overall dynamics of the market over the previous decades. The EC argued that market shares affect competitive conditions for future orders via incumbency effects, due to lower costs for airlines from fleet and engine commonality. Since airlines could only buy aircraft still in production, and revenues (especially from after-market services) mainly accrued from engines for aircraft still in production, the objections were dismissed. Furthermore, the EC noted that 'on 10 of the last 12 platforms for which airframe manufacturers offered exclusive positions, GE managed to place its products' (para. 164). The EC highlighted the case of the whole range of Boeing 777 aircraft, sold as a package including aircraft and engines, against normal practice by which airlines buy them separately (para. 167).

In the market for engines of large regional jet aircraft, the merged entity would enjoy 100 per cent control of the jet engine supply of platforms not yet in service (Honeywell's 10 per cent would be added to GE's 90 per cent) and 90–100 per cent of the overall engine installed base on the existing platforms, so that any form of price competition would be prevented and the incumbency advantage would be enhanced. The only engines by Honeywell in this market were those used to power Avro jets.

In the market for corporate jet aircraft engines, the horizontal overlap would lead to a dominant position, with 50–60 per cent market share overall and 80–90 per cent in the medium segment (building on GE's 10–20 per cent). Bundling and vertical integration effects would reinforce foreclosure of competitors.

In power systems the EC argued that there existed significant horizontal overlap among the parties, resulting in a market share between 65 per cent and 90 per cent of the market for small marine gas turbines, against the parties' contention that they focus on turbines of different dimensions and therefore do not compete with each other. The dominant position of the merged entity would also be reinforced by high development costs acting as barriers to entry.

MRO activities are an important source of revenues for engine manufacturers. The EC underlined that both the 'spare parts' and the MRO service markets had seen the GE's foothold becoming stronger in the past years vis-à-vis competitors. Commonality effects were claimed to reinforce GE's position.

Conclusions on GE's dominance and horizontal overlaps

The EC concluded that GE enjoyed a position of dominance, on the basis of high current and prospective market shares, in the market for engines for large commercial aircraft, which, as shown in the following sections, would be extended to Honeywell products.

Horizontal overlaps existed for engines of large regional jet aircraft, engines of corporate jet aircraft and power systems. In those markets, positions of dominance would be created or strengthened by the merger.

The CFI found in its 2005 decision that the EC analysis of horizontal overlaps – unlike the other parts of the EC analysis – was not vitiated by manifest error of assessment. This was the basis for upholding the decision to block the merger.

4. Vertical effects

The EC identified potential vertical foreclosure dangers with the leasing company of GE, GE Capital Aviation Services (GECAS), and with Honeywell's engine starters.

4.1 GECAS

GECAS bought planes in order to lease them to airlines, often engaging in 'speculative' purchases that were not linked to any requests by its customers. Besides the obviously different type of risk involved in leasing instead of buying, the value added by this activity consisted in providing airlines with readily available aircraft, something which is not usually possible when buying directly from manufacturers. GECAS's contribution to GE's sales consisted in its 'GE-only' policy, by which almost all the aircraft it purchased were powered by GE or CFMI engines. As a consequence, when manufacturers selected engines as part of their aircraft on sole-source platforms (i.e. when the choice is not given to the airlines), they would prefer, *ceteris paribus*, to buy GE or CFMI engines, as one of the potential buyers of their aircraft displays this strong 'preference'. The EC argued that GECAS's policy of buying only aircraft with GE engines allowed it to 'seed' smaller airlines by creating and enhancing fleet commonality effects. GECAS's 10 per cent market share, in a highly fragmented market, would suffice to foster its role as 'launch customer', tilting the market towards GE and, after the merger, Honeywell's products.

The CFI upheld the view that GECAS did foster GE's dominance, but also found that there was not sufficient evidence that the merged entity would have an incentive to extend those 'GE-only' practices to Honeywell's SFE and BFE products, as there existed a huge difference in prices between engines for large commercial aircraft and large regional aircraft, on the one hand, and each of the avionics and non-avionics products, on the other. Imposing the condition to have Honeywell's components may not be profitable if it jeopardises profits on engines. Furthermore, the assertion that such practices would necessarily result in dominance was deemed questionable since there was a distinct market for each of the avionics and non-avionics products, and the EC's arguments lacked a thorough analysis of the effects on those different markets.

4.2 Honeywell's engine starters

Honeywell was a 'key supplier of engine controls to engine manufacturers' and 'the leading, if not the only, independent supplier of engine starters'. The fear was that the merged entity 'would have an incentive to delay or disrupt the supply of Honeywell engine starters to competing engine manu-facturers … Likewise, the merged entity could increase the prices of engine starters or their spares, thereby increasing rival engine manufacturers' costs and reducing even further their ability to compete against the merged entity' (para. 420). The EC's arguments seem to point to RR as the main loser. P&W was manufacturing engine starters mainly for its own use and another supplier, Hamilton Sundstrand, belonged to the same group as P&W. The EC argued that those suppliers, as well as Honeywell, would not find it profitable to sell engine starters to RR in light of profit considerations regarding the whole group to which they belonged or would belong after the merger. Other independent suppliers (Urenco, Microturbo, Parker and Sumitomo) would not be a feasible alternative.

The parties' proposal to divest Honeywell's engine starters was rejected by the EC mainly on technical grounds, related to the failure to include air starter valves in the divestiture.

The CFI did recognise that GE–Honeywell could disrupt the supply of engine starters to competitors and that the sacrifice of profits in starters might be amply compensated by even a tiny percentage increase in the market share for large commercial aircraft at the expense of P&W and RR. However, the CFI stated that the EC committed a manifest error of assessment as it failed to take into account the deterrent effect of Article 82 of the Treaty: the disruption of supply of engine starters of the merged entity would be a clear abuse of dominant position.

5. Conglomerate effects

The EC identified two main potentially anticompetitive conglomerate effects relating to the financial arm of GE, GE Capital, and to the practice of bundling.

5.1 GE Capital

GE's financial strength through GE Capital and the overall GE stance as the world's largest company in terms of market capitalisation 'clearly represent a significant competitive advantage over P&W and RR' (para. 32), in particular in terms of GE's ability to engage in risky R&D projects and to absorb potential failure. Furthermore, GE could also afford aggressive pricing strategies with heavy discounts on the catalogue prices for engines. Those discounts were seen as resulting in the 'weakening of engine competitors and ultimately in foreclosing them from current and future platforms and airline competitions' (para. 112) and not in lower costs for customers, as the latter had to spend more in later phases on maintenance and spare parts manufactured by the original supplier, so that the 'total average cost of an engine has actually increased between 10 per cent and 30 per cent in real terms' (para. 113). GE's strength was also employed to provide significant financial support to airframe manufacturers to obtain engine exclusivity and to airlines in order to gear their purchasing behaviour towards GE engines and to vertically integrate in repair shops in the after-markets (e.g. servicing, repair, replacement parts).

The CFI provided arguments that substantially mirror those related to GECAS: GE Capital did probably affect GE's ability to reach dominance, but this would not imply that dominance in Honeywell's components would arise from the merger.

5.2 Bundling

Most controversially, the EC argued that the combination of GE and Honeywell across a range of products would reinforce existing dominance and create further dominant positions by foreclosing rivals. The main concern was the ability of the merged company to bundle, for example engines and avionics, to the disadvantage of specialist producers in either field and ultimately to the disadvantage of consumers.

The EC claimed that 'the merged entity will be able to offer a package of products that has never been put together on the market prior to the merger and that cannot be challenged by any other competitor on its own' (para. 350), so that the new entity may promote the selection of Honeywell's BFE- and SFE-option products by selling them as part of a broader package comprising engines and GE's ancillary services such as maintenance, leasing, finance, training and so forth.

'Packaged offers' could take the form of mixed bundling, where complementary products are sold in a package priced at a discount with respect to the sum of the prices of individual components, or pure bundling, where components cannot be purchased separately. The latter can take the form of technical bundling, so that components are rendered incompatible with the complementary ones provided by competitors.

Bundling would reduce the profits of competitors up to causing their eventual exit from the market.[4] The EC decision did not present a detailed reasoning about *how* bundling may lead, in the markets concerned, to foreclosure of competition: 'the various economic analyses have been subject to

---

[4] 'The ability of the merged entity to cross-subsidise its various complementary activities and to engage in profitable forms of packaged sales will have an adverse effect on the profitability of competing producers of avionics and non-avionics products, as a result of market share erosion. This is likely to lead to market exit of existing competitors and market foreclosure ...' (para. 398).

theoretical controversy, in particular as far as the economic model of mixed bundling, prepared by one of the third parties,[5] is concerned', but 'the Commission does not consider the reliance on one or the other model necessary for the conclusion that the packaged deals that the merged entity will be in a position to offer will foreclose competitors from the engines and avionics/non-avionics markets' (para. 352). The EC argued that, even if one were to accept that the overall demand for aircraft equipment is relatively inelastic, the demand for the products of individual firms would still be elastic enough so that bundling with discount would 'lead to a re-allocation and therefore to a shift of market shares in favour of the merged entity' (para. 376).

In the aerospace component (avionics and non-avionics) market the EC identified Honeywell as the unique competitor in a position to offer a 'complete range of avionics equipment', enjoying a competitive advantage both for SFE and for BFE products. Packaged deals including components and engines, that competitors would be unable to match,[6] would result in a change from Honeywell's leading position to downright dominance and effective foreclosure of competitors' presence in the market.

In the market for engines for large commercial aircraft, GE's dominant and Honeywell's leading positions in their respective markets would allow them to engage in packaged offers of complementary products such as engines, avionics and non-avionics products and related services. As a consequence, the merger would strengthen GE's existing dominance and also contribute to dominance in the other segments: the engines for large regional jet aircraft and for corporate jet aircraft.

The relevance of countervailing power of customers was downplayed by the EC on the grounds that customers would not refuse lower prices resulting from packaged deals. On the possibility that the two large airframe manufacturers, Boeing and Airbus, would aim at preserving competition, the EC stressed that none of them would be willing to place itself at a disadvantage by selecting a more expensive combination of products than the packaged deals offered by the strongest competitor on the other side of the market.

The undertakings submitted by the parties included a 'no-bundling' behavioural commitment. The EC replied stating a preference for ex-ante structural to ex-post behavioural solutions, where the latter would involve 'endless litigation' in the phase of controlling for effective compliance.

---

[5] The Commission is referring here to the model presented by Frontier Economics and Professor Choi on behalf of RR that we are going to discuss later.
[6] The possibility of teaming arrangements by rivals was not seen as a credible alternative by the EC.

The EC's bundling analysis resulted in some of the greatest controversy, both amongst economists and with the antitrust authority across the Atlantic. The CFI stated that the EC had not provided convincing arguments showing that the merged entity would have engaged in bundling former GE's engines with former Honeywell's avionics and non-avionics products.

The CFI maintained that only 'in the sector for large commercial aircraft, for which the Commission has defined distinct markets both for jet engines and for each avionics product, that the Commission's case on bundling could conceivably be sustained' (para. 404).[7] Moreover, the fact that the final customer in that segment would not always be the same imposed additional restraint to the potential scope of bundling. Namely, bundling would be possible, 'in case of airframe manufacturers, only between GE engines and Honeywell SFE-standard products on sole-source platforms and, in case of airlines, only between GE engines and Honeywell BFE/SFE option products on multi-source platforms'. The timeline of purchasing, whereby engines tended to be selected earlier than avionics and non-avionics, would not *per se* preclude bundling practices, but would impose extra commercial effort to enforce bundling offers as opposed to pricing individual components.

In the CFI's view, the EC failed to recognise the potential harmful effect on profits of *pure* bundling practices, whereby purchasers would be compelled to buy the whole package. For instance, a buyer with only a marginal preference for GE engines may be put off by the request to buy also Honeywell products; the costs of losing some demand for engines could well offset the benefit of fostering demand for avionics and non-avionics. Also, the EC should have taken into account the deterrent effect of Article 82. Therefore, the EC had not established that the merged entity would engage in *pure* bundling.

The likelihood of *mixed* bundling practices, on the other hand, was reinforced, in the EC's view, by the existence of previous practices by Honeywell. Such evidence was deemed 'of little relevance' by the CFI, on the grounds that engine prices were markedly higher than avionics and non-avionics products and hence the commercial dynamics of all encompassing bundling by the merged entity would be substantially different.

The supporting economic analysis was deemed insufficient by the CFI. After pointing out that the EC neither adopted nor rejected the model defined by Professor Choi,[8] which had previously been used in the EC's Statement of

---

[7] In the market for engines for corporate jet aircraft, GE presence was quite limited and hence the bundling possibilities mainly involved Honeywell's engines and components and were not significantly affected by the merger (para. 402). Market definition and related technical issues exclude the remaining possibilities.

[8] This is discussed in section 6 below.

Objections, the CFI states that 'no evidence or analysis is put forward which is such that it might establish that there was a real likelihood of such an incentive [for mixed bundling] existing after the merger' (para. 449). The bulk of the limited EC analysis consisted in rejecting the parties' contention that the demand for their products was relatively inelastic, on the ground that there would still be, in any case, elasticity in terms of demand for individual products: offering discounted bundles would result in higher market shares. Elasticity would reinforce the 'Cournot effect', whereby a firm that sells a wide range of complementary products derives advantages from offering discounts which, although reducing profit margins on a discounted item, results in selling a larger quantity of all the products in the range. The CFI maintained that a proper evaluation of Cournot effects should rely on detailed empirical analysis regarding the size of price cuts, the consequent shifts in sales and the variation in profit margins of the participants. The lack of such analysis undermined the EC's conclusions and incentives to bundle cannot be seen as 'direct and automatic consequence of the economic theory of Cournot effect' (para. 456).

The CFI also maintained that the EC had provided insufficient evidence and the reasoning to support the view that the merged entity would use discounted bundles as a strategic device to maximise long-term profits via exclusion of rivals. For example, GE's joint venture partner, SNECMA, would have little interest in participating in a discount scheme for CFMI engines in order to boost sales of GE–Honeywell's avionics. Finally, the EC had once again failed to recognise the deterrent effect of Article 82 on anticompetitive practices.

6. The US view

In the US Department of Justice view, the only antitrust issue related to horizontal overlap in the US helicopter engines, and repair and overhaul services for certain Honeywell engines. As a consequence, divestiture remedies (agreed by the parties) affected only those areas and the merger was approved. The thrust of the US analysis of the merger is strikingly different from the European one.[9] Competition in the market for jet engines for large commercial aircraft was seen to be fierce and to result in deeply discounted

[9] See the remarks of the Deputy Assistant Attorney General of the Antitrust Division Deborah Platt Majoras (2001).

engine prices. GE's position might be seen as 'leading' but 'nowhere near dominance' (Platt Majoras, 2001) given that P&W and RR were enjoying growing revenues and profits and investing heavily in the development of next generation engines, and also in light of the latest 2001 contract awards. Even assuming the assignment of all CFMI sales to GE, the consideration of the special case of GE's sole-source contract for the Boeing 737 should drive towards a more balanced assessment of market positions; namely, excluding those sales, GE's share would be 44 per cent, instead of 65 per cent, in the share of outstanding orders for engines for large commercial aircraft. With regard to engines for large regional aircraft, the US contemplated thrust and aircraft characteristics that made GE and Honeywell's engines part of different markets. The EC referred to seats and this made Honeywell's engines used by Avro part of the same market as GE's engines.

The harshest criticism on the US side hits the 'range effects' theory, i.e. the possibility that the merged entity would engage in mixed bundling and offer discounted packages including Honeywell's products. Platt Majoras observes that 'entrenchment', an alleged anticompetitive consequence of conglomerate mergers via higher efficiency and stronger financial position of already dominant firms, was eliminated as a basis for challenging non-horizontal mergers in 1982 with the DoJ new Merger Guidelines and the Federal Trade Commission Statement on Horizontal Mergers. It was recognised that 'efficiency and aggressive competition benefit consumers, even if rivals that fail to offer an equally "good deal" suffer loss of sales or market share'. In this case, the Cournot effect from bundling complementary products enhances consumer welfare: as the merged firm internalises the negative externality on demands for complements caused by high prices, the new prices decrease, moving closer to marginal costs and hence increasing allocative efficiency.[10] GE's ability to provide cheaper finance results in a source of efficiency as any other valuable asset, and if cheaper capital leads to more investment and discounted prices, this eventually benefits consumers. The impact of GECAS on GE's success is downplayed by the DoJ on the basis of the small GECAS purchasing share, of a lower relevance of commonality for airlines, and of the empirical analysis of the factors behind GE's contracts as sole suppliers for airframe manufacturers. As in GE's case, Honeywell's competitors are seen also as much stronger than in the EC's representation, and the possibility of teaming arrangements is deemed viable.

---

[10] See Kolasky (2001).

Platt Majoras (2001) stresses the general policy pursued by US authorities which mainly consists in fostering competition as a means to efficiency and not as an end in itself, so that conglomerate mergers are not to be blocked, as a general rule, insofar as they enhance efficiency even if they place less efficient firms at risk of exiting the market. The trade-off, in terms of consumer welfare, between the positive effect of short-term efficiency brought about by the market and the possible long-term negative effect of enhancing market power of the merged entity, if some competitors are forced out of the market, is intrinsically hard to assess. It involves many steps, including the quantification of the efficiency, of the time it takes for exit of rivals to happen and of the likelihood that the latter will not be able to develop counter-strategies, of the assessment of the future price increase stemming from market power, and of the possibility of new entrants in the market.

Overall, the US authorities conclude that while horizontal and vertical mergers should raise the attention of regulators, as they may eliminate competitors and suppliers or customers, respectively, and therefore reduce or distort competition and undermine market efficiency, 'antitrust should rarely, if ever, interfere with any conglomerate merger', as this type is found to have the potential to generate efficiency via infusion of capital, diversification of risk, meshing of R&D, improving management and fostering entrepreneurship.

7. The pillars of the EC decision: an economic assessment

We have set out the three different views of the EC, CFI and US DoJ. What light can careful economic analysis cast on who was right on what? As we have seen, the case of the EC is founded on the dominance of GE in the market for large commercial aircraft, reinforced with vertical and conglomerate effects with their financial arms GE Capital and GECAS, which, via bundling, would extend to Honeywell's avionics and non-avionics products. Added reasons to block the merger are a vertical foreclosure argument related to engine starters and horizontal overlaps between GE and Honeywell in the large regional jet engines market. We deal with these issues in turn.

7.1 Horizontal issues

Was GE dominant even without Honeywell?

The pre-merger dominance of GE stands at the basis of arguments related to the strengthening and extension effects of the merger. The EC analysis of the market for large commercial aircraft engines raises the issue of market share as an indicator of market power. The term 'bidding market' has been used by critics of the EC decision to suggest that current shares say little about future success in markets characterised by periodic very large contracts. Each contract should be won on a technical and commercial basis, that is, on the quality of the product and on price competition, so capable and efficient competitors should be able to gain contracts irrespective of what market share has arisen from previous experience. The 'bidding market' description of the engines market is shared, among others, by the DoJ, Patterson and Shapiro[11] (2001) and Grant and Neven (2005). Patterson and Shapiro underline that credible competitors in the market continuously bid for contracts and that the EC acknowledges in its decision that GE won contracts via 'heavy discounting practices'. Engaging in heavy discounting was seen by the EC as evidence of dominance based on superior financial strength but it was viewed as evidence of competitive pressure by the US DoJ.[12]

Second, even if one agrees with the EC and the CFI that market shares are a relevant indicator of market power, the very definition of shares is contentious. The EC calculation for GE's market share is done using only the installed base and orders for currently manufactured aircraft, and it adds the engines produced by CFMI, its joint venture with French SNECMA. The latter is a big proportion of GE's share, and a driver of the reversal of previous market leadership by P&W comes from CFMI's contract as sole supplier for the Boeing 737, the most successful aeroplane in history. The rationale for looking at installed base stems from switching costs and learning effects associated with engines that provide inertia in the orders of airlines. The exclusion of engines for out-of-production planes is justified because there is nothing to compete for. With regard to the share of CFMI, the EC's rationale was to assign the share solely to the firms acting as independent suppliers as the other firms could not act as a competitive constraint to GE.[13]

Nalebuff (2003) argues that assigning to GE the whole CFMI quota, removing engines on planes out of production and other relevant choices

[11] Carl Shapiro acted as an economic expert for GE–Honeywell in its presentation to the EU Merger Task Force, along with Barry Nalebuff, Patrick Rey, Shihua Lu and Gerg Vistnes.
[12] Grant and Neven (2005) point out that evidence suggests that 'the nature of competition is such that emphasis is on future competitions, not on ones that have already been decided', so that in its market share-based approach, the EC 'would appear to have ignored the dynamics of the market'.
[13] Kolasky (2001) points out that SNECMA competes with Honeywell in the market for landing gears, so that the EC should explain why the French firm would not object to the policy extension of dominance in favour of Honeywell products.

should be justified according to the goal of market share assessment. If the revenue stream is the object of interest, then engines on the whole installed base, instead of only engines on planes in production, should be considered; this would reduce GE's share to 41 per cent. Furthermore, GE should be assigned only half of CFMI's share (because this is what GE gets in terms of revenues), which reduces GE's market share to 36 per cent. Combining both corrections, GE's share would be only 28 per cent. When market power is the main issue, Nalebuff's conclusions become more radical. Most of CFMI's share comes from the exclusivity contract for the Boeing 737, whose terms were pre-negotiated between the parties (Boeing and GE/SNECMA) so that CFMI does not have the ability to control engine prices on orders from airlines. Excluding its exclusive contract sales GE's share drops to 10 per cent or 20 per cent depending on whether out-of-production planes are considered.[14] Similar results are obtained when the objective is to understand the potential for bundling. As engines offered to Boeing by CFMI are offered at a predetermined deal, the only way to propose a discounted bundle would be via future discounts on Honeywell's components subject to having bought the CFMI powered plane. This would make sense only as long as it determines an increase in plane sales. An obvious issue arises in relation to the small price of Honeywell's components with respect to the cost of the engine and plane: there is little scope for the 'tail to wag the dog'.

Indeed, the market share calculations of the EC do not seem to succeed in proving the inclination of the merged entity to use bundling strategies and eventually foreclose the competitors of Honeywell. With regards to their relevance for the assessment of extant market power and horizontal effects, the main issues relate to the very nature of market interactions. The infrequency of bidding contests and their big impact on the evolution of market shares suggest the importance of understanding what has driven GE's success in recent bids, most notably on CFMI's contract with Boeing, and whether those same conditions are likely to continue into the future or, rather, whether it is likely that current or future competitors will enjoy a level playing field. Ultimately, the question revolves around incumbency effects which the EC links to commonality.

We do consider that the EC was right in not taking at face value the claims that in a 'bidding market' existing shares do not indicate market power. The reason is that the assumptions needed for the claim to be true are very

---

[14] Kolasky (2001) states that excluding the contract with Boeing 737, even if we assign 100 per cent of remaining sales by CFMI to GE we get a more balanced market share picture: GE 44 per cent, P&W 23 per cent, RR 27 per cent.

stringent and boil down to the adequacy of the Bertrand model with homogeneous product (and constant known marginal cost with no capacity constraints) as a description of the market.[15]

However, the relevance of commonality was probably overstated by the EC, as aggressive bidding was the main factor of GE's success in the market for engines. In any case a more detailed empirical study on the bidding dynamics and the market share inertia due to commonality should have been undertaken.

All in all, we conclude that the case for GE's dominance in the market for large commercial aircraft engines was not sufficiently grounded on empirical analysis.

Horizontal overlaps with Honeywell

At the time of the EC decision the horizontal overlap issue attracted relatively little attention as it was perceived that relatively limited divestiture could settle those concerns. On the US side, Kolasky (2001) and Platt Majoras (2001) pointed out the remarkable *lack* of overlap among GE and Honeywell, two big players in the aerospace industry. The CFI, however, stressed the growing importance of the large regional aircraft sector while arguing that the merger would strengthen GE's dominant position in the market for engines in that sector, and that the feasibility of proceeding with the merger with divestiture remedies would be questionable (e.g. it would be difficult to find a credible buyer for the business). In the large regional aircraft engine market, the merger would have created a 100 per cent market share, by adding to GE's 90 per cent the remainder of the market as defined by the EC.

Although it makes sense to consider the switch from a very large market share to 100 per cent as a strengthening of dominance, this 'monopoly' is highly sensitive to market definition. While the definition of the EC is based on seats and cost consideration, the DoJ relied on engine power. Furthermore, Kolasky (2006) remarks that the hypothetical monopoly test was not employed to see whether one could see the engines in question as part of the same market.

Be that as it may, the parties did offer the divestiture of the relevant Honeywell's engines as a remedy for antitrust concerns in the sector of the engines for large regional aircraft. It remains unclear whether the practical issues related to finding a buyer or to the uncertain environment that Avro producers would have faced really meant that the remedy was not feasible.

---

[15] See Chapter 5 in Vives (1999) for the assumptions and analysis of the Bertrand model and Klemperer (2007) for a more explicit analysis of competition issues in 'bidding markets'.

However, it seems hard to believe that the prohibition of such a wide-ranging merger should hinge on an apparently modest difficulty with implementing this divestiture.

7.2 Vertical foreclosure

Engine starters

The fear was that the merged GE–Honeywell would disrupt the supply of starters to engine producers like RR. However, for a vertical merger to lead to foreclosure of rivals, several conditions need to be fulfilled. The vertically integrated firm must have the ability and the incentive to raise rivals' costs in a significant way and the consequence must be that prices downstream increase. If one neglects the possible penalties for breach of existing commitments, whenever there is the *ability* to raise rivals' costs (and this is the case with imperfect competition upstream and with the upstream division of the vertically integrated firm being a relevant supplier) there tends to be the *incentive* to do so. This is so because sales to rivals increase their production and hurt the vertically integrated firm. Given that the revenues on starters are relatively low, such a foreclosure strategy may indeed be profitable.[16] Furthermore, whenever pre-merger the upstream division sets price above cost, the downstream division of the vertically integrated firm sustains lower costs (because of the elimination of the double margin), sells more, while rivals sell less and have a reduced derived demand for the input. The impact on the downstream final prices of engines is ambiguous. They may go down because the direct effect of the elimination of the double margin often dominates the potential indirect effect of raising rivals' costs. The possibility of entry (for example, of RR producing its own starters) should also be considered.

Given these uncertainties, we think that the standard to show vertical foreclosure up to blocking the merger was not satisfied by the EC analysis. In this sense we do find the CFI view, based on the deterrent effect of Article 82, quite reasonable.

---

[16] However, rivals' costs need not increase in equilibrium. In particular, other upstream producers may replace the vertically integrated firm. Here the merging parties and the EC disagree. The EC does not see any viable alternative supplier of starters to RR to replace Honeywell (Hamilton Sundstrand because it belongs to the same group as P&W, Microturbo because it is in the same group as SNECMA, and others for different reasons).

The role of GECAS

The most immediate objection involving GECAS's role consists in its limited market share. The EC sets it at around 10 per cent, others (see e.g. Nalebuff, 2003) at 5–7 per cent according to different criteria, so that even the position as market leader (with respect to another leasing company, ILFC) may be questioned. The relevance of GECAS's behaviour even when its share is relatively small is at the core of the Archimedean or pivotal leveraging theory proposed by Reynolds and Ordover (2002).[17] Their main point is that if a group of customers prefers a given characteristic of a good and all the others are indifferent, then the profit-maximising firm is going to include it (if not too costly). In this case, the reasoning would especially apply to aircraft manufacturers selecting GE engines for sole-source platform and, if the merger had been allowed, Honeywell's products for SFE equipment. For the Archimedean theory to work, a number of assumptions are needed. First, a firm (in this case GE–Honeywell) must be present both as supplier of components to intermediate manufacturers of aircraft (Airbus, Boeing, Bombardier) and as a buyer (GECAS) which leases the product to final consumers (airlines). Those final users can also buy directly the planes. The intermediate manufacturers make exclusive choices with respect to which system (aerospace components) will be incorporated into their products. End users and intermediate manufacturers are indifferent about the choice made by the manufacturer. Finally, product price exceeds incremental cost both for producers of the intermediate products and for system suppliers.

Suppose also that prior to the merger, the downstream purchaser GECAS had no internal preference, either with respect to the systems or with respect to the intermediate product. Then, after the merger, the downstream purchaser GECAS implements the policy of purchasing only those intermediate products (aircraft) in which the components of the upstream systems affiliate are embedded. Knowing that, the intermediate producers choose to embed those systems (Honeywell's components) in order to be able to supply to GECAS. This situation can be seen as an equilibrium if rival suppliers do not react. Reynolds and Ordover argue that the history of the impact of GECAS towards GE's dominance in the engines markets strongly suggests the inability of competitors to counteract the strategy that the merged entity would carry out. Furthermore, they maintain that the empirical evidence contradicts the idea that GECAS's rivals shift away from GE's powered aircraft. Eventually,

---

[17] The authors worked on behalf of UTC, a competitor of GE in several markets: the P&W division manufactures jet engines and the Hamilton Sundstrand division produces aircraft systems.

GE–Honeywell would be able to impose higher prices for its product even in the short run, while in the long run this effect would be stronger following the likely exit by existing Honeywell rivals.

The theoretical argument is supported with evidence based on the increase in market shares enjoyed by GE in the period in which GECAS started to purchase new planes, 1996–2000. Reynolds and Ordover (2002) show that the share for competitive-engine large commercial aircraft ordered with GE engines by speculative leasing companies (including GECAS) rose from 40 per cent to 60 per cent approximately, while in the same period the corresponding share declined by 5 per cent (from 50 per cent to 45 per cent, approximately) when considering demand from airlines. Nalebuff (2003) contradicts this evidence and shows that correct market share assignment in the competitive engine choice market results in a lower increase in the sales to leasing companies and in a slight *decrease* of GE's (including CFMI) overall share, from 52.3 per cent to 50.6 per cent.[18] Two main effects are behind these results: GECAS's rivals (most notably ILFC) did shift away from GE's powered aircraft and leasing companies' demand simply replaced direct demand from airlines. Similarly, the US DoJ also disagrees with Reynolds and Ordover's market share assignments (see Emch, 2003).[19] Other critical remarks by Nalebuff concern the real role of GECAS: as its business consists in leasing to airlines, it is conceivable that GE would have enjoyed benefits from increments in demand for GE-powered aircraft directly from airlines or from other leasing companies.

The effect of GECAS in relation to the merger hinges on its supposed change in demand behaviour, applying a 'GE-only' policy also to Honeywell components. For this strategy to be successful, the assumption on the pre-merger indifference between components should hold tight, so that expectations of the increase in the quantity demanded by GECAS are enough to tilt choices in favour of Honeywell despite the small magnitude of GECAS's market share. But this assumption implies basically no product differentiation

---

[18] Among the flaws alleged to exist in Reynolds and Ordover (2002) there is the inclusion of aircraft for which no choice is available and other technical issues.

[19] This was not the only instance of disagreement on factual analysis. While for large commercial aircraft the engines are typically not embedded and can be selected by airlines or leasing companies, large regional jets entail the choice of a sole engine supplier, i.e. they are selected by the aircraft manufacturers and not by airlines and leasing companies. This makes the comparison with SFE aerospace components more immediate. During the late 1990s, GE was selected by the three main manufacturers (Fairchild Dornier, Embraer and Bombardier) for their new jets over alternatives from P&W and RR. Here the disagreement lies on the real availability of alternatives, as GE's engines for large regional jets were more developed at the time, but especially on the real role of GECAS as, according to Nalebuff (2003), the decision to engage in speculative purchasing of new planes happened *after* GE engines were selected for those jets.

and does not seem to fit well with the market for aerospace components. Whether the Archimedean leverage theory can work in the presence of differentiated components is essentially an empirical question.

Overall, the uncertainty on whether GECAS had significantly affected the behaviour of manufacturers in favour of GE's engines becomes much stronger when we move towards the hypothesis that its role would have resulted in market foreclosure for Honeywell's competitors. The case for GECAS causing dominance in the avionics and non-avionics markets is weak. The position of the CFI accepting the potential contribution of GECAS to GE's dominance but denying the extension to Honeywell's markets looks therefore reasonable.

7.3 Conglomerate effects: consolidating and extending dominance

The CFI accepted that the EC's argument for GE's pre-merger dominance was 'not vitiated by manifest error'. The CFI saw manifest errors in a later stage, where the EC maintained that GE's dominance would be extended into Honeywell's markets as a result of GE's financial strength and the practice of bundling. Let us examine those issues in turn.

Financial leverage through GE Capital

The financial strength of GE was seen by the EC as part of GE's toolkit for dominance. However, no explicit deep-pocket predation theory of harm was proposed. In the presence of imperfect capital markets there are several potential theories of effects on competition. For example, Bolton and Scharfstein (1990), in a model where financial contracts are observable, argue that a deep-pocket firm may have an incentive to undermine the performance of rivals causing their exit. The key issue here is whether GE's deep pocket, coupled with other conglomerate effects, could actually induce the exit of rivals in the engine or aerospace components markets.

Internal funds are crucial in the face of imperfect capital markets (in particular for high-risk R&D projects like engine development and other aerospace equipment). The financial muscle could be used to foster R&D in those segments facing more competition with the potential outcome of discouraging rivals' innovation activity.

The profitability of cross-subsidies is a debated issue in the academic literature. A conglomerate has to decide how to allocate its financial resources among its subsidiaries. Stein (1997) argues that 'winner-picking', i.e. shifting resources towards the most profitable subsidiaries, tends to be preferred to cross-subsidisation. In other words, group affiliation may even reduce, *ceteris paribus*, the availability of funds to a firm facing tough competitive conditions, as opposed to others operating in conditions of dominance. However, Cestone and Fumagalli (2003) point out that cross-subsidisation may be a profit-maximising strategy when it is used to sustain presence in the most competitive market, which would otherwise be abandoned. The channel by which large resources result in the entrenchment in the competitive market consists in ameliorating the 'agency problem': a cash-poor firm would have difficulties in raising funds to stay in a market where the profits to be pledged are limited. Furthermore, Cestone and Fumagalli develop a product market model based on a 'winner-takes-all' hypothesis, related to R&D competition, and find that, conditional on entering the market, group-affiliated firms tend to compete more aggressively than 'stand-alone' ones, due to higher flexibility in the available resources. The R&D effort strategy tends to exhibit a relatively flat reaction function, so that high R&D effort by rivals has a limited effect in discouraging its own effort.[20] Overall, their analysis suggests that subsidiaries in a financially powerful group tend to be more resilient to rivals' aggressive strategies and, in turn, are potentially tougher competitors. This may have a pro-competitive effect but may also result in the exclusion of rivals.

Whether this theoretical possibility could entail the exit of rivals of GE (like RR) or of Honeywell is another matter that requires very careful assessment based on empirical analysis.[21] The EC seemed to be saying that the financial strength of GE gives the company an advantage in R&D and a deep pocket to make life difficult for rivals, and at the same time increase overall prices (by raising prices in the after-markets). However, if airlines are rational customers, they should not be misled into buying engines that have a relatively low purchase price but high maintenance costs.

The financial capabilities of rivals such as P&W or RR and the countervailing power of buyers should also be carefully analysed. P&W is a division of the large UTC and both were active also in the military sector with the external (technological and financial) effects that this implies. The strength of both firms appears to be confirmed by the evolution of their stock. Indeed, the stock market reaction in the period when it seemed that the deal would be cleared by the EC shows the aerospace competitors of GE and Honeywell overperforming the market benchmark (this is the case for UTC and RR, as well as

---

[20] The 'winner-takes-all' framework implies that R&D effort levels of the different competitors are strategic substitutes, i.e. a non-conglomerate invests less in R&D if the rival conglomerate has an incentive to invest more.

[21] For example, empirical evidence cited by the DoJ (Kolasky, 2001) suggests that GE's rivals did in fact succeed in securing the financing they needed.

Rockwell and Smiths, for example). GE in fact was underperforming, which suggests that perhaps Honeywell's shareholders were obtaining the better part of the deal. The market scepticism about the profitability of the deal for GE and the overperformance of competitors does not fit well with foreclosure prospects for rivals (although it would be consistent with the deal having anticompetitive horizontal effects).[22] In relation to the power of buyers it seems sensible to think that large airlines, the second largest leasing company (ILFC) and aircraft manufacturers such as Boeing and Airbus all have substantial clout in the market and would be interested in keeping alive viable competitors to GE and Honeywell.

Bundling

As we have seen above, the EC did not deem necessary to rely on any specific economic model in order to show that the merged entity would be able to offer packages of products that competitors would be unable to challenge. It asserted that bundling would result in a shift in market shares in favour of the new entity and foreclosure of rivals (supported by some third-party evidence).

Let us explore first the model presented by Professor Choi on behalf of RR, which constituted the basis of bundling arguments in the Statement of Objections, but was not included in the EC's final decision. Choi (2001, see also 2007) built up a model of product differentiation based on a linear demand system specification for the complementary components produced by firms. Consumers, whose tastes are uniformly distributed, must buy one engine and one set of avionics/non-avionics. Firms are assumed to be price setters. One further underlying assumption is that the same price (for a given product or for a bundle) is charged to all consumers. In this framework, Choi analyses the impact of the GE–Honeywell merger assuming that there are two engine suppliers (GE and RR) and two avionics/non-avionics suppliers (Honeywell and a competitor). The merged entity is assumed to be able to engage in *mixed bundling* only, i.e. to offer a package of the two products at a discount from the sum of the two prices when the goods are bought separately. Pure bundling, whereby goods are not offered on a stand-alone basis, could reinforce foreclosure effects on future generations of aircraft products.

Choi simulates, with parameters argued to match the industry's configuration, the effects against an initial symmetric situation, where each consumer buys one engine and one aerospace component according to the 'distance'

---

[22] See Grant and Neven (2005).

from their ideal product (no price differences initially exist between the two engines, nor between the two components). Choi finds that mixed bundling by the merged entity results in higher prices for stand-alone components and a lower price of the bundled set by the new firm, which gains market share. The main route by which this happens with complementary goods can be explained as a 'Cournot effect' (Cournot, 1838): before the merger, each firm does not take into account the positive externality of its sales on the demand for complementary goods. The merged firm, instead, internalises such effects and hence lowers prices. If mixed bundling is possible it can furthermore limit this positive effect to the demand for its own products. Stand-alone prices are set higher in order to undermine the demand for the rivals' products. Competitors will respond by cutting prices but not to the point of countering completely the reduction in their market shares, as they do not benefit from the 'internalisation' of complementarities. Their profits decrease, while the profits of the merged firm may increase (it expands market share and the decrease in prices may expand the total market).

The Cournot effect implies that the merger would enhance consumer welfare if goods were eventually offered by a monopolist. As instead there are competitors in the market, the effects of merger and bundling strategies becomes less straightforward. It remains true that if the merger and bundling occur, the price of the bundle will in general be lower than the sum of the prices when goods are sold on an individual basis. This stems from the externality effect. However, the strategic response by competitors will in general consist in decreasing their own prices, so that overall the bundling strategy may have a positive or negative effect on the profits of the merged entity, with respect to the sum of the pre-merger profits of the two entities.

In Choi's analysis, bundling gives a competitive advantage to the merged entity: to use mixed bundling is optimal *given* the prices of competitors (but still profits may decrease with respect to the situation in which the merged entity commits not to bundle). For some parameter constellations the merger is not profitable (neither with nor without mixed bundling).[23] What we do know is that if mixed bundling happens then rivals' profits tend to decrease.[24] The impact on consumers' welfare is potentially ambiguous with

---

[23] Nalebuff (2000) finds in a model with inelastic demand that the profits of a pure bundling strategy are negative as a consequence of the strategic response of competitors, although the latter suffer from a much more pronounced profit reduction. In his model, and by construction given the optimality of initial choices with symmetry and inelastic demand, bundling can only reduce welfare.

[24] However, Nalebuff and Lu (2001) find that when asymmetry in importance exists among goods (e.g. due to the much higher cost of engines vis-à-vis avionics/non-avionics), then the incentive to bundle and the impact on competitors tend to vanish.

heterogeneous consumer preferences since some consumers may gain and others lose (those that before the merger purchased a 'mix-and-match' system); however, the impact becomes negative if the reduction in the profits of the rivals leads to their exit.

Nalebuff (2003) casts doubts on the results of Choi's simulations and on the overall validity of his approach. He argues that prices in aerospace are typically negotiated for jet engines and avionics, rather than being proposed in a list valid for all buyers. In those markets there is no unique price for a given product towards all clients. The latter, in fact, receive different conditions depending on the strategic impact for the producer of securing the contract (with an eye on the ensuing stream of profits), on the perceived bargaining power of the two parties in the negotiation (which also depends on the assumed valuation of the customer of the product involved and feasible alternatives) and on other relevant features. Nalebuff points out evidence that, in fact, prices charged to different customers for the same products (engines and aerospace components) vary considerably. With a simple modelling exercise based on two product types and cost symmetry among producers, he shows that if prices are negotiated and customers' valuations are known by firms, then bundling cannot be profitable. This means that firms can price discriminate perfectly and that there is localised Bertrand competition for every customer. In those circumstances the outcome is known to be very competitive.[25] In this case it does not pay to use bundling strategies (as bundling complementary products does not pay with perfect competition).[26] However, this model is extreme in assuming perfect knowledge of customers' valuations and is difficult to square with an industry with large R&D expenses that have to be recovered with margins over costs. The single price model of Choi can be interpreted as the case where firms have no knowledge about customers while the perfect knowledge model of Nalebuff is the other extreme.

---

[25] See Thisse and Vives (1988).

[26] The intuition is straightforward: if the producer bundles the two goods and both are the most preferred by a customer, he will be able to extract precisely the same margin he could get without bundling. In other words, the margin will correspond to the sum of the two margins if goods were sold on an individual basis. If neither good is the most preferred by the customer, then the goods are not sold whether they are bundled or not (as he would need to sell below-cost). When only one of the two goods is preferred by the customer, bundling may result in lower profits. Assume, for instance, that without bundling the producer would sell good A, as it is the most preferred by the customer, but not good B, as a competitor with the same cost structure (e.g. with constant marginal cost c) produces a good that the customer finds to have a greater value than B, and denote with x the difference in value. Then, in order to convince the customer to buy the bundle, the margin which could be achieved by selling only good A has to be reduced by the quantity x (as the competitor is willing to lower the price of his good down to c) in order to sell the bundle that includes good B.

The reality of the aerospace market is certainly in between and only a careful empirical analysis could shed some light over this issue.

A further argument was raised about the practicality of bundling engines with avionics and non-avionics components on the basis that they are typically sold in different moments in time. Contractual arrangements may ameliorate the timing problems, but if prices are negotiated the offering of discounts for bundles may be trickier to achieve. According to Nalebuff (2003) there would be no basis on which to offer a discount on future components conditional on having bought an engine, or vice versa (i.e. on the engine conditional on buying components in the future). However, it is possible that if the interaction is repeated the merged entity may try to develop a reputation on offering better conditions for those who buy both the engines and the avionics and non-avionics components. A much more clear-cut issue relates to the main fact behind GE's position in the market for engines for large commercial jets: prices of the engines for the Boeing 737 are pre-negotiated with Boeing, which renders unfeasible the implementation of a bundling strategy. If the 'bundle' were proposed the price of aerospace components could easily be inferred simply by subtracting the previously established engine price.

The results of Choi and Nalebuff's models suggest an impact of mixed bundling on the profits of GE–Honeywell rivals which ranges from moderate to significant. The indicators also point to a pro-competitive effect of the merger in terms of lowering prices. It is a robust fact that for given prices of competitors GE and Honeywell would have an incentive to use mixed bundling. However, mixed bundling may or may not be profitable from the point of view of a merged GE–Honeywell in equilibrium.[27]

A hotly debated issue was whether the potential decrease in profits of a rival to a merged GE and Honeywell would induce exit in order to save fixed avoidable operation costs. This could happen as an outcome of 'innocent' bundling by GE and Honeywell, that is, in a situation in which the merged entity does not try strategically to force exit of rivals. However, the exit scenarios remain speculative because of the sensitivity of the profit impact of bundling to the variations of the model. Furthermore, the rivals of GE–Honeywell could try to fight back the reduced bundle price of the merged entity by coordinating bundled offers, reducing costs, improving service or product quality.

---

[27] Bundling may be used also as a price-discrimination device (see, e.g., McAfee *et al.*, 1989). This happens when consumers also derive utility from buying one good individually. For example, in comparison to selling two products under monopoly conditions, bundling can enhance profits but often favour consumers too. In the aircraft industry consumers buy systems (jets, avionics and non-avionics) and therefore the price-discrimination aspect of bundling is not so relevant (and it did not play any role in the case).

It is even harder to support a theory that the merged entity would engage in *strategic* bundling to induce exit and enjoy subsequent price increases. A predation story needs to justify why the merged firm would sacrifice current profits. A decrease in short-run profits would represent the cost of predation and then the pattern of recoupment should be established (at least as a cross-check to the theory of harm). The EC hinted at predatory behaviour[28] but made no effort to sustain a coherent predation story and argued instead that it was sufficient to rely on the short-term profitability of bundling.

If pure bundling, when the goods involved cannot be bought individually, were to become feasible for the merged entity relatively soon, a foreclosure case could be made on the basis of the Whinston (1990) model, provided that the merged firms can credibly commit to the bundling strategy and there is a sunk cost of entry.[29] This is a modern version of the leverage theory of a firm with substantial market power in one market extending it to another independent market. Chicago School arguments (see e.g. Posner, 1976) have largely succeeded in the rebuttal of the traditional story according to which a firm would be able to leverage its market power by tying its monopolised product 'A' to another product 'B' it supplies in a *competitive* market (with constant returns to scale).[30] The firm finds it profitable to compete aggressively against any new entrant in one of the markets, as losing sales for one good implies losing them on the other as well: its willingness to lower prices as a competitive response is therefore augmented by the bundling strategy. Commitment is paramount in this strategy as the firm would, ex post, optimally react by unbundling products so as to maintain maximum rents in one of the markets. When complementary goods are involved, however, it does not pay to tie and foreclose except in the special cases where there is an unrelated use of component B (this could be a replacement parts market) or there is an inferior competitively supplied component alternative to A. These special circumstances were not examined in the GE–Honeywell case (for example, taking A as the engine market and B as the avionics and non-avionics components market).

Commitment to bundling can also make a difference when R&D incentives are considered. Tying can be profitable even without inducing exit because it

---

[28] See Giotakos *et al.* (2001).

[29] The possibility of technical bundling by GE and Honeywell was mentioned in the EC decision but not adequately established according to the CFI.

[30] The argument is that monopoly profits can be reaped only once; that is, in order to sell B at a price above the competitive level it would have to forgo a part of its monopoly rents on good A.

increases the tying firm's R&D incentives in the tied good market (since it can spread out the cost of R&D over a larger number of units) while the R&D incentives of the rival firm diminish. If this R&D effect dominates the decrease in profitability due to the increased price competition, tying is beneficial (Choi, 2004). Furthermore, in complementary markets tying makes successful entry prospects more uncertain and discourages investment by entrants because they have to succeed in both markets (Choi and Stefanidis, 2001). In the case of the merger of GE and Honeywell it could have been argued that tying closed system engines and avionics would force competitors to be successful simultaneously in both and this would reduce their incentives to innovate. The outcome would have been that GE–Honeywell would over-invest and the competitors under-invest in innovation (and this would be bad for welfare when there is a low probability of success since then there would be too little diversification).

The US approach to bundling was very different. The DoJ was not willing to consider the potential harm done in the long term by the merger given that the estimated effect on prices would be to reduce them in the short term. In contrast, the EC started (particularly in the Statement of Objections) with the idea that the ability and the incentive to bundle by the merged entity would lead naturally to foreclosure of rivals but then, as we have seen, the bundling model was dismissed in the final decision.

Concerns in terms of increased difficulty by existing competitors to stay in the market and by new ones to enter could potentially arise as a result of the possibility of bundling products, provided bundling were a feasible strategy. The question is whether the EC had a coherent theory of harm and whether it was tested to the requisite standard. For this it is necessary to show: (i) that there is a robust incentive to bundle for the merged entity, and that either the bundling practice is established in the industry or the merger will make it possible; (ii) that bundling will decrease profits of rivals for a substantial period so as to induce exit; and (iii) that the exit of rivals will end up damaging consumers. Given that the merger would most likely produce a short-run competitive impact the expected discounted potential medium- and long-run harm should be weighted against this short-run benefit.

The EC analysis did not measure up to this standard. Indeed, it is difficult to disagree with the CFI on the fact that the EC did not prove that bundling would emerge, nor that eventually it would have led rivals to exit the market and that a position of dominance would be strengthened. *A fortiori*, it is far from clear that overall long-term consumer welfare would diminish, when the positive effect of more aggressive competition and internalisation of pricing effects among complements are balanced against the negative effect of the potential (and yet unproved) exit of rivals.

Among the remedies proposed by the parties, there was the commitment not to bundle GE products with Honeywell products. This was found to be insufficient as it would be intrinsically a remedy to be policed ex post, and the 'lack of formality' of bundling makes the monitoring difficult and costly. However, the remedy seems far more attractive than the outright prohibition of the merger, given the uncertainties arising from the analysis of bundling and the deterrent effect of Article 82 against abuse of dominance.

8. Conclusions

This is a very complex merger case which involves horizontal, vertical and conglomerate issues in an array of markets. The EC's initial challenge to the merger, as set out in the Statement of Objections, presented a theory of foreclosure based on bundling of GE and Honeywell products. The early analysis, originating in a model commissioned by Rolls-Royce, was quietly dropped and the EC moved to a more encompassing dynamic foreclosure and possible predation story based on the alleged dominance of GE strengthened by its financial arm and bundling capacity. The end result was that the merger was blocked.

The CFI upheld the EC's decision on the basis of horizontal overlap issues, which had attracted relatively little attention before the appeal. This is somewhat surprising since it seems that the existing overlap could have been resolved by relatively minor divestiture remedies, as had been the case in the decision by the US DoJ. The CFI dismissed the conglomerate effects arguments, bundling in particular, because of 'manifest errors of assessment'. With regard to the analysis of vertical integration between engine starters and engines, the EC failed according to the CFI to take account of the deterrent effect of Article 82.

Does the outcome of the case mean that bundling arguments should be disregarded for merger analysis in the future? This would be too hasty a conclusion. Bundling may, in general, raise antitrust concerns in terms of the possibility to reinforce market power. Furthermore, the competition authority should try to look at the long-term consequences of mergers and not only at the short-run ones. This presents a challenge because long-term effects have to be discounted for time and probability of occurrence. In the words of Platt Majoras (2001), US authorities are 'humble about our ability to make those judgements, which necessarily involves predictions far out in the future' and have 'more confidence in the self-correcting nature of markets'. The US approach moves one step further than the CFI correction of the decision of the EC, putting the emphasis on potential, pro-competitive short-run effects of the merger. This seems to indicate that a major difference between the US and EU approaches is that in the EU authorities are willing to venture into looking at the long-term consequences of a merger while in the US more long-term possibilities are discounted more heavily.

Competition authorities should present a concrete economic theory of harm, check it for internal consistency with economic models and contrast it with the empirical evidence available, history of the industry and, if possible, documentation on the strategies of the firms. The analysis should be carried out taking into account the potential efficiencies of the practice, e.g. bundling, from the beginning. In the GE–Honeywell case this could have been a predatory or dynamic foreclosure theory. The EC had a legitimate case to look at such a possibility, but the bar on the standard of proof to block a merger on such grounds is indeed very high and, on this occasion, the EC's arguments fell short of the mark. In this case, the potentially anticompetitive impact of bundling, as well as financial leverage, could have been dealt with ex post, on the basis of Article 82.

The GE–Honeywell case, together with other cases in which the CFI has amended the decisions of the EC, has contributed to push for the enhancement of the economic analysis capabilities of DG Competition at the EC (with the creation of the position of Chief Competition Economist responsible for a team) and to its internal restructuring to further the independent scrutiny of merger investigations. In terms of the transatlantic debate, perhaps the most enduring legacy of the GE–Honeywell case will be in making apparent the tension in regard to merger analysis between the more 'practical' short-term US approach versus the more 'ambitious' long-term view of EU authorities. A basic underlying issue is whether merger policy should deal with conditions that make exclusionary/predatory behaviour more likely and what is the standard which this analysis must be subjected to. The challenge for economic analysis is to provide operational tools to assess the trade-offs involved.

Acknowledgements

We are grateful to Bruce Lyons for helpful comments. Vives was retained by the European Commission to advise on some specific economic aspects of the merger and he is grateful to the Abertis Chair of Regulation, Competition and Public Policy at IESE Business School for support. The views expressed in the paper are only those of the authors.

Bibliography

Abreu, Dilip (1986), 'Extremal Equilibria of Oligopolistic Supergames', *Journal of Economic Theory*, 39: 191–225

Abreu, Dilip, Paul Milgrom and David Pearce (1991), 'Information and Timing in Repeated Partnerships', *Econometrica*, 59: 1713–1733

Abreu, Dilip, David Pearce and Ennio Stacchetti (1986), 'Optimal Cartel Equilibria with Imperfect Monitoring', *Journal of Economic Theory*, 39: 251–269

(1990), 'Towards a Theory of Discounted Repeated Games with Imperfect Monitoring', *Econometrica*, 58: 1041–1064

Adilov, Peter and Peter J. Alexander (2006), 'Horizontal Merger – Pivotal Buyers and Bargaining Power', *Economics Letters*, 91(3): 307–311

Aghion, Philippe, Richard Blundell, Rachel Griffith, Peter Howitt and Susanne Prantl (2004), 'Entry and Productivity Growth: Evidence from Microlevel Panel Data', *Journal of the European Economic Association*, 2(2–3): 265–276

Ahn, Sanghoon (2002), 'Competition, Innovation and Productivity Growth: A Review of Theory and Evidence', *OECD Economics Department Working Paper* No. 317

Allen, Beth, Raymond Deneckere, Tom Faith and Dan Kovenock (2000), 'Capacity Precommitment as a Barrier to Entry: A Bertrand-Edgeworth Approach', *Economic Theory*, 15: 501–530

American Bar Association, Section of Antitrust Law (1996), *Proving Antitrust Damages – Legal and Economic Issues*, Chicago: American Bar Association

Armstrong, Mark (2002), 'The Theory of Access Pricing and Interconnection' in Martin E. Cave, Sumit Kumar Majumdar and Ingo Vogelsang (eds.), *Handbook of Telecommunications Economics*, Volume 1, Amsterdam: North-Holland

(2006), 'Competition in Two-Sided Markets', *RAND Journal of Economics*, Special Issue on Two-Sided Markets, 37(3): 668–691

Armstrong, Mark and Robert Porter (2007), *Handbook of Industrial Organization*, Volume 3, Amsterdam: North-Holland

Armstrong, Mark and David Sappington (2007), 'Recent Developments in the Theory of Regulation' in Armstrong and Porter (eds.), *Handbook of Industrial Organization*, Volume 3, Amsterdam: North-Holland

Armstrong, Mark and Julian Wright (2007a), 'Mobile Call Termination', SSRN Working Paper, September

(2007b), 'Two-Sided Markets, Competitive Bottlenecks and Exclusive Contracts', *Economic Theory*, 32(2): 353–380

(2009), 'Mobile Call Termination', *The Economic Journal*, June

Arrow, Kenneth J. (1971), *Essays in the Theory of Risk Bearing*, Chicago: Markham Publishing Co.

Arrunada, Benito, Luis Garicano and Luis Vazquez (2005), 'Completing Contracts Ex Post: How Car Manufacturers Manage Car Dealers', *Review of Law and Economics*, 1(1): 1–22

Asker, John (2004), 'Diagnosing Foreclosure due to Exclusive Dealing', mimeo, Stern School of Business

Athey, Susan and Kyle Bagwell (2001), 'Optimal Collusion with Private Information', *RAND Journal of Economics*, 32: 428–465

Athey, Susan, Kyle Bagwell and Chris Sanchirico (2004), 'Collusion and Price Rigidity', *Review of Economic Studies*, 71: 317–349

Autopolis (2000), 'The Natural Link between Sales and Service: An Investigation for the Competition Directorate General of the European Commission', available at: www.europa.eu.int/comm/competition/car_sector

Bagwell, Kyle and Robert Staiger (1997), 'Collusion over the Business Cycle', *RAND Journal of Economics*, 28: 82–106

Baker, Jonathan B. (1993), 'Two Sherman Act Section 1 Dilemmas: Parallel Pricing, the Oligopoly Problem, and Contemporary Theory', *Antitrust Bulletin*, Spring: 143–219

Banks, David (2001), *Breaking Windows*, New York: Macmillan Free Press

Baxter, William F. (1983), 'Bank Interchange of Transactional Paper: Legal Perspectives', *Journal of Law and Economics*, 26: 541–588

Becker, Gary S. (1968), 'Crime and Punishment: An Economic Approach', *Journal of Political Economy*, 76(2): 169–217

Benoit, Jean-Pierre and Vijay Krishna (1987), 'Dynamic Duopoly: Prices and Quantities', *Review of Economic Studies*, 54: 23–36

Bernheim, B. Douglas and Michael D. Whinston (1998), 'Exclusive Dealing', *Journal of Political Economy*, 106(1): 64–103

Berry, Steven and Peter Reiss (2007), 'Empirical Models of Entry and Market Structure' in Armstrong and Porter (eds.), *Handbook of Industrial Organization*, Volume 3, Amsterdam: North-Holland

Besanko, David and Martin K. Perry (1993), 'Equilibrium Incentives for Exclusive Dealing in a Differentiated Goods Oligopoly', *RAND Journal of Economics*, 24(4): 646–668

BEUC (1992), 'Parallel Market for Cars in the EC', European Bureau of Consumer Unions, 229/92

BHA (2007), 'Determination of the 47th Horserace Betting Levy Scheme': Submission of British Horseracing Authority, available at: www.britishhorseracing.com/inside_horseracing/

Bishop, Simon and Mike Walker (2002), *The Economics of EC Competition Law*, London: Sweet & Maxwell

Bloch, Kurt (1932), 'On German Cartels', *Journal of Business*, 5(3): 213–222

Bloom, Nicholas, Stephen R. Bond and John Van Reenen (2007), 'Uncertainty and Company Investment Dynamics: Empirical Evidence for UK Firms', *Review of Economic Studies*, 74: 391–415

Bolton, Patrick and David S. Scharfstein (1990), 'A Theory of Predation Based on Agency Problems in Financial Contracting', *American Economic Review*, 80(1): 93–106

Bolton, Ruth N. and Venkatesh Shankar (2003), 'An Empirically Derived Taxonomy of Retailer Pricing and Promotion Strategies', *Journal of Retailing*, 79(4): 213–224

Bonanno, Giacomo and John Vickers (1988), 'Vertical Separation', *Journal of Industrial Economics*, 36(3): 257–265

Bork, Robert (1978), *The Antitrust Paradox*, New York: Macmillan Free Press

Brenkers, Randy and Frank Verboven (2006a), 'Liberalizing a Distribution System: The European Car Market', *Journal of the European Economic Association*, 4(1): 216–251

(2006b), 'Market Definition with Differentiated Products: Lessons from the Car Market' in Jay Pil Choi (ed.), *Recent Developments in Antitrust: Theory and Evidence*, Cambridge, Mass.: MIT Press

Bresnahan, Timothy and Shane Greenstein (1996), 'Technical Progress and Co-invention in Computing and in the Uses of Computers', *Brooking Papers on Economic Activity: Microeconomics*, 1–78

Bresnahan, Timothy and Peter Reiss (1991), 'Entry and Competition in Concentrated Markets', *Journal of Political Economy*, 99(5): 977–1009

Brewers and Licensed Retailers Association (various years), *Statistical Handbook*, London

British Beer and Pub Association (2005), *Statistical Handbook*, London

Brock, William A. and José A. Scheinkman (1985), 'Price Setting Supergames with Capacity Constraints', *Review of Economic Studies*, 52(3): 371–382

Brod, Andrew and Ram Shivakumar (1999), 'Advantageous Semicollusion', *Journal of Industrial Economics*, 47: 221–230

Bryant, Peter G. and E. Woodrow Eckard (1991), 'Price Fixing: The Probability of Getting Caught', *Review of Economics and Statistics*, 73(3): 531–536

Cabellero, Ricardo J., Eduardo M. R. A. Engel and John C. Haltiwanger (1995), 'Plant Level Adjustment and Aggregate Investment Dynamics', *Brookings Papers on Economic Activity*, 2: 1–39

Cabral, Luis M. B. (2000), *Introduction to Industrial Organization*, Cambridge, Mass.: MIT Press

Caillaud, Bernard and Bruno Jullien (2003), 'Chicken and Egg: Competition Among Intermediation Service Providers', *RAND Journal of Economics*, 34(2): 309–328

Caillaud, Bernard and Patrick Rey (1986), 'A Note on Vertical Restraints with the Provision of Distribution Services', mimeo, Paris: INSEE and Cambridge, Mass.: MIT

Calzada, Joan and Tommaso Valletti (2008), 'Network Competition and Entry Deterrence', *Economic Journal*, 118: 1223–1244

Camilli, Enrico L. (2006), 'Optimal Fines in Cartel Cases and the Actual EC Fining Policy', *World Competition: Law & Economics Review*, 29(4): 575–605

Carlton, Dennis W. and Alan S. Frankel (1995), 'Antitrust and Payment Technologies', *Review*, Federal Reserve Bank of St Louis, November: 41–54

Carlton, Dennis W. and Jeffrey M. Perloff (2000), *Modern Industrial Organisation*, 3rd edition, London: HarperCollins

Carlton, Dennis W. and Michael Waldman (2002), 'The Strategic Use of Tying to Preserve and Create Market Power in Evolving Industries', *RAND Journal of Economics*, 33(2): 194–220

Cestone, Giacinta and Chiara Fumagalli (2003), 'The Strategic Impact of Resource Flexibility in Business Groups', *RAND Journal of Economics*, 36: 193–214

Chang, Howard, David S. Evans and Daniel D. Garcia Swartz (2005), 'The Effect of Regulatory Intervention in Two-Sided Markets: An Assessment of Interchange-Fee Capping in Australia', joint Center AEI-Brookings and Center for Regulatory Studies related publication 05–29

Chen, Zhijun and Patrick Rey (2007), 'On the Design of Leniency Programs', IDEI Working Paper, No. 452

Choi, Jay Pil (2001), 'A Theory of Mixed Bundling Applied to the GE/Honeywell Merger', *Antitrust*, 16: 32–33

(2004), 'Tying and Innovation: A Dynamic Analysis of Tying Arrangements', *Economic Journal*, 114: 83–101

(2007), 'Antitrust Analysis of Tying Arrangements', in Jay Pil Choi (ed.), *Recent Developments in Antitrust: Theory and Evidence*, CESifo seminar series, Cambridge, Mass.: MIT Press

Choi, Jay Pil and Chrisodoulos Stefanidis (2001), 'Tying, Investment, and the Dynamic Leverage Theory', *RAND Journal of Economics*, 32(1): 52–71

Christensen, Laurits Rolf and Richard E. Caves (1997), 'Cheap Talk and Investment Rivalry in the Pulp and Paper Industry', *Journal of Industrial Economics*, 45(1): 47–53

Church, Jeffrey R. and Roger Ware (2000), *Industrial Organization: A Strategic Approach*, Boston: Irwin McGraw-Hill

Clarke, Roger, Steve Davies, Paul Dobson and Michael Waterson (2002), *Buyer Power and Competition in European Food Retailing*, Cheltenham: Edward Elgar

Coase, Ronald H. (1960), 'The Problem of Social Cost', *Journal of Law and Economics*, 3(1): 1–44

Competition Commission (2000a), 'New Cars: A Report on the Supply of New Motor Cars within the UK', London: HMSO

(2000b), 'Supermarkets: A Report on the Supply of Groceries from Multiple Stores in the United Kingdom', Cm. 4842, London: TSO

(2003a), 'Safeway plc and Asda Group Limited (owned by Wal-Mart Stores Inc); Wm Morrison Supermarkets plc; J. Sainsbury plc; and Tesco plc: A Report on the Mergers in Contemplation', Cm 5950, London: TSO

(2003b), 'Vodafone, O2, Orange and T-Mobile: Reports on References Under Section 13 of Telecommunications Act 1984 on Charges Made by Vodafone, Orange, O2 and T-Mobile for Terminating Calls Made by Fixed and Mobile Networks', London: HMSO

Compte, Oliver (1998), 'Communication in Repeated Games with Imperfect Private Monitoring', *Econometrica*, 66: 597–626

Compte, Olivier, Frédéric Jenny and Patrick Rey (2002), 'Capacity Constraints, Mergers and Collusion', *European Economic Review*, 46(1): 1–29

Connor, John M. (1997), 'The Global Lysine Price-Fixing Conspiracy of 1992–1995', *Review of Agricultural Economics*, 19(2): 412–427

(2001), '"Our Customers are Our Enemies": The Lysine Cartel of 1992–1995', *Review of Industrial Organization*, 18(1): 5–21

(2004a), 'Global Cartels Redux: The Amino Acid Lysine Antitrust Litigation (1996)' in John E. Kwoka, Jr and Lawrence White (eds.), *The Antitrust Revolution: Economics, Competition, and Policy*, 4th edition, Oxford University Press: 252–276.

(2004b), 'Price-Fixing Overcharges: Legal and Economic Evidence', American Antitrust Institute Working Paper 04–05

(2005), 'Optimal Deterrence and Private International Cartels', Draft Paper, Purdue University, Ind., May

Connor, John M. and Yulija Bolotova (2006), 'Cartel Overcharges: Survey and Meta-analysis', *International Journal of Industrial Organization*, 24: 1109–1137

Corts, Kenneth S. (1998), 'Third-Degree Price Discrimination in Oligopoly: All-Out Competition and Strategic Commitment', *RAND Journal of Economics*, 29(2): 306–323

Cournot, Antoine (1838), *Recherches sur les principes mathématiques de la théorie des richesses*, Paris: Hachette

Court of First Instance (CFI) Decisions see European Court Decisions

Danzon, Patricia M. (1998), 'The Economics of Parallel Trade', *Pharmaeconomics*, 13(3): 293–304

Davidson, Carl and Raymond Deneckere (1990), 'Excess Capacity and Collusion', *International Economic Review*, 31(3): 521–541

Davies, Stephen, Heather Coles, Matt Olczak, Chris Pike and Chris Wilson (2004), 'The Benefits of Competition: Some Illustrative UK Case Studies', *DTI Economics Paper* No. 9, available at: www.berr.gov.uk/files/file13299.pdf

Davies, Stephen and Bruce Lyons (1989), 'Introduction' in Stephen, Davies, Bruce, Lyons, Huw, Dixon and Paul, Geroski (eds.), *Economics of Industrial Organisation*, London: Longman

(2007), *Mergers and Merger Remedies in the EU: Assessing the Consequences for Competition*, London: Edward Elgar

Davies, Stephen and Adrian Majumdar (2002), *The Development of Targets for Consumer Savings Arising from Competition Policy*, Chapter 4, Office of Fair Trading Economic Discussion Paper 4

Dechenaux, Emmanuel and Dan Kovenock (2003), 'Endogenous Rationing, Price Dispersion and Collusion in Capacity Constrained Supergames', Krannert Working Paper No. 1164, Ind.: Purdue University

Deloitte (2006), 'Economic Impact Review of British Racing', commissioned by BHB and available at: www.britishhorseracing.com/inside_horseracing/

(2007), 'The Deterrent Effect of Competition Enforcement by the OFT', OFT962, London: Office of Fair Trading

Demsetz, Harold (1973), 'Industry Structure, Market Rivalry and Public Policy', *Journal of Law and Economics*, 16(1): 1–10

Dick, Andrew R. (2002), 'Coordinated Interaction: Pre-Merger Constraints and Post-Merger Effects', mimeo, US Department of Justice, available at: www.crai.com/Agenda/Dick.pdf

Director General of Fair Trading (DGFT) (1995), Memo to the Secretary of State for Trade and Industry

Dixit, Avinash (1980), 'The Role of Investment in Entry-deterrence', *Economic Journal*, 90: 95–106

(1991), 'Analytical Approximations in Models of Hysteresis', *Review of Economic Studies*, 58: 141–151

Dobson Consulting (1999), *Buyer Power and its Impact on Competition in the Food Retail Distribution Sector of the European Union*, Brussels: European Commission DG Competition, available at: www.europa.eu.int/comm/competition/publications/studies/bpifrs/

Dobson, Paul W. (2002), *The Economic Effects of Constant Below-Cost Selling Practices by Grocery Retailers*, London: UK Federation of Bakers

(2005), 'Exploiting Buyer Power: Lessons from the British Grocery Trade', *Antitrust Law Journal*, 72(2): 529–562

(2007), *Micro-marketing and Discriminatory Practices in UK Grocery Retailing*, report submitted to the Competition Commission, available at: www.competition-commission.org.uk

Dobson, Paul W., Michael Waterson and Alex Chu (1998), 'The Welfare Consequences of the Exercise of Buyer Power', Research Paper No. 16, London: Office of Fair Trading

Dobson, Paul W., Roger Clarke, Steve Davies and Michael Waterson (2001), 'Buyer Power and its Impact on Competition in the Food Distribution Sector of the European Union', *Journal of Industry, Competition and Trade*, 1(3): 247–281

Dobson, Paul W. and Roman Inderst (2007), 'Differential Buyer Power and the Waterbed Effect: Do Strong Buyers Benefit or Harm Consumers?', *European Competition Law Review*, 28(7): 393–400

Dobson, Paul W., Ken Starkey and John Richards (2004), *Strategic Management: Issues and Cases*, Oxford: Blackwell Publishing

Dobson, Paul W. and Michael Waterson (1996), 'Vertical Restraints and Competition Policy', Research Paper No. 12, London: Office of Fair Trading

(2005), 'Chain-Store Pricing across Local Markets', *Journal of Economics and Management Strategy*, 14(1): 93–119

(2006), 'Micro-marketing and Chain-Store Competition: Customized vs. Uniform Store-Level Pricing', University of Loughborough, mimeo

Doyle, Maura P. and Christopher M. Snyder (1999), 'Information Sharing and Competition in the Motor Vehicle Industry', *Journal of Political Economy*, 107(6): 1326–1364

EAGCP (2005), 'An Economic Approach to Article 82', Report for the European Commission (DG Competition), available at: http://llec.europa.eu/dgs/competition/economist/eagcp.html

European Court (including CFI) Decisions cases

Airtours v *Commission*, 6 June 2002, Case T-342/99

Bayer v *Commission* Case T 41/96 [2000] ECR II-3383 C 2–3/01 P

Bundesverband der Arzneimittel-Importeure eV v *Commission* [2004] OJ C 59/02

EAEPC *Bundesverband der Arzneimittel Importeure eV and Aseprofar* Case T 168/01

EAEPC Case IV/37.380/F3 [2001] OJ L302/1

General Electric v *Commission*, 14 December 2005, Case T-210/01

GlaxoSmithKline Services Unlimited v *Commission* Case T 168/01, 27 September

Honeywell v *Commission*, 14 December 2005, Case T-209/01

Merck v *Primecrown* C 267–268/95 [1996] ECR I-6285

NV IAZ International Belgium v *Commission*, Joined Cases 96–102, 104–105, 108, 110/82 [1983] ECR 3369, at paras. 24, 25 and 27

Sandoz v *Commission* Case 277/87 [1990] ECR I-45

Scottish & Newcastle (OJ 1999 L186/28) Case IV/35.992/F3

SIFAIT v *GlaxoSmithKline AEBE and GlaxoSmithKline plc* Case C-53/03

Stergios Delimitis v *Henninger Brau* Case C-234/89 [1991] ECR, AG 1–935

Volkswagen v *Commission*, Case T-62/98 [2000] ECR II-2707 (see paras. 89 and 178)

Whitbread (OJ 1999 L88/26) Case IV/35.079/F3

Ellickson, Paul B. and Sanjog Misra (2006), 'Supermarket Pricing Strategies', Working Paper 06–02, Department of Economics, Durham, N.C.: Duke University

Elliott, David (2007), 'What is an Excessive Price? The View of the UK Courts', *Competition Law Insight*, 31 July

Emch, Eric R. (2003), 'GECAS and the GE/Honeywell Merger: A Response to Reynolds and Ordover', Department of Justice Economic Analysis Group Discussion Paper, EAG 03–13

Epstein, Roy J. and Daniel L. Rubinfeld (2002), 'Merger Simulation: A Simplified Approach with New Applications', *Antitrust Law Journal*, 69: 883–906

European Commission (2000), 'Report on the Evaluation of Regulation (EC) No 1475/95 on the Application of Article 85(3) of the Treaty to Certain Categories of Motor Vehicle Distribution and Servicing Agreements',

European Commission Decisions
  Airtours v *First Choice* 22 September 1999, Case No. IV/M.1524
  Aseprofar and Fedifar Case IV/36.997/F3
  BAI Case IV/37.138/F3
  Bass OJ L 186/1 Case IV/36.081/F3
  General Electric/ Honeywell, 2001 – Case No. COMP/M.2220, downloadable at: ec.europa.eu/comm/competition/mergers/cases/decisions/m2220_en.pdf
  GlaxoWellcome Case IV/36.957/F3
  Microsoft Decision 23.04.04 Case COMP/C-3/37.792
  Neste/IVO (1998), Case No. IV/M.931 (Luxembourg)
  Roberts v *Greene King* 1998, Case No. IV/36.511
  Scottish and Newcastle, OJ L186/28 1999, Case No. IV/35.992/F3
  Spain Pharma Case IV/37.121/F3
  Whitbread, OJ L88/26 1999, Case No. IV/35.079/F3

Evans, David, Albert Nichols, Bernard Reddy and Richard Schmalensee (2001), 'A Monopolist Would Still Charge More for Windows: A Comment on Werden', *Review of Industrial Organization*, 18: 263–268

Evans, David S. and Richard Schmalensee (2005), *Paying with Plastic*, 2nd edition, Cambridge, Mass.: MIT Press

Farrell, Joseph (1987), 'Cheap Talk, Coordination and Entry', *RAND Journal of Economics*, 18: 34–39

Farrell, Joseph and Michael L. Katz (2006), 'The Economics of Welfare Standards in Antitrust', *Competition Policy International*, 2(2): 3–28

Fershtman, Chaim and Neil Gandal (1993), 'Disadvantageous Semicollusion', *International Journal of Industrial Organization*, 12: 141–154

Fershtman, Chaim and Eitan Muller (1986), 'Capital Investments and Price Agreements in Semi-collusive Markets', *RAND Journal of Economics*, 17: 214–226

Fershtman, Chaim and Ariel Pakes (2000), 'A Dynamic Oligopoly with Collusion and Price Wars', *RAND Journal of Economics*, 31: 207–236

Finkelstein, Michael O. and Hans Levenbach (1983), 'Regression Estimates of Damages in Price-Fixing Cases', *Law and Contemporary Problems*, 46(4): 145–169

Frankel, Alan S. (1998), 'Monopoly and Competition in the Supply and Exchange of Money', *Antitrust Law Journal*, 66(2): 313–361

Friberg, Richard (2001), 'Two Monies, Two Markets? Variability and the Option to Segment', *Journal of International Economics*, 55: 317–327

Friedman, James (1971a), 'A Non-cooperative Equilibrium for Supergames', *Review of Economic Studies*, 38(113): 1–12
  (1971b), 'A Non-cooperative View of Oligopoly', *International Economic Review*, 12(1): 106–122
  (1983), 'Advertising and Oligopolistic Equilibrium', *Bell Journal of Economics*, 14: 464–473

Friedman, James and Jacques-François Thisse (1994), 'Sustainable Collusion in Oligopoly with Free Entry', *European Economic Review*, 38: 271–283

Fudenberg, Drew, David Levine and Eric Maskin (1994), 'The Folk Theorem with Imperfect Public Information', *Econometrica*, 62: 997–1039

Fumagalli, Chiara and Massimo Motta (2006), 'Exclusive Dealing and Entry: When Buyers Compete', *American Economic Review*, 96(3): 785–795

Furse, Mark (2006), *Competition Law of the EC and UK*, 5th edition, Oxford University Press

Gans, Joshua S. and Stephen P. King (2000), 'Mobile Network Competition, Customer Ignorance and Fixed-to-Mobile Call Prices', *Information Economics and Policy*, 12(4): 301–328

(2001), 'Using "Bill and Keep" Interconnect Agreements to Soften Network Competition', *Economics Letters*, 71(3): 413–420

Gans, Joshua S., Stephen P. King and Julian Wright (2005), 'Wireless Communications' in Sumit Kumar Majumdar, Ingo Vogelsang and Martin E. Cave (eds.), *Handbook of Telecommunications*, Volume 2, Amsterdam: North-Holland

Genakos, Christos, Kai-Uwe Kühn and John Van Reenen (2006), 'The Incentives of a Monopolist to Degrade Interoperability: Theory and Evidence from the PC and Server Market', mimeo

Genakos, Christos and Tommaso Valletti (2007), 'Testing the "Waterbed" Effect in Mobile Telephony', mimeo

Gerber, David J. (1998), *Law and Competition in Twentieth Century Europe: Protecting Prometheus*, Oxford: Clarendon Press

Geroski, Paul (2004), 'Is Competition Policy Worth It?', speech on the opening of the Centre for Competition Policy at the University of East Anglia, available at: www.competition-commission.org.uk/our_role/speeches/index.htm

Gilbert, Richard and Martin Lieberman (1987), 'Investment and Coordination in Oligopolistic Industries', *RAND Journal of Economics*, 18: 17–33

Giotakos, Dimitri, Laurent Petit, Gaelle Garnier and Peter Luyck (2001), 'General Electric/ Honeywell – An Insight into the Commission Investigation and Decision', *EC Competition Policy Newsletter*, 3: 5–13

Goldberg, Pinelopi K. and Frank Verboven (2001), 'The Evolution of Price Dispersion in the European Car Market', *Review of Economic Studies*, 68(4): 811–848

(2005), 'Market Integration and Convergence to the Law of One Price: Evidence from the European Car Market', *Journal of International Economics*, 65(1): 49–73

Gollier, Christian and Harris Schlesinger (1995), 'Second-Best Insurance Contract Design in an Incomplete Market', *Scandinavian Journal of Economics*, 97(1): 123–135

Grant, Jeremy and Damien Neven (2005), 'The Attempted Merger between General Electric and Honeywell: A Case of Transatlantic Conflict', *Journal of Competition Law and Economics*, 1: 595–633

Green, Edward and Robert Porter (1984), 'Non Cooperative Collusion Under Imperfect Price Information', *Econometrica*, 52: 87–100.

Griffin, Joseph P. (1998), 'Foreign Governmental Reaction to US Assertion of Extraterritorial Jurisdiction', *European Competition Law Review*, 19: 64–73

Gual, Jordi, Martin Hellwig, Anne Perrot, Michele Polo, Patrick Rey, Klaus Schmidt and Rune Stenbacka (2006), 'An Economic Approach to Article 82', *Competition Policy International*, 2(1): 111–154

Haltiwanger, John and Joseph Harrington (1991), 'The Impact of Cyclical Demand Movements in Collusive Behavior', *RAND Journal of Economics*, 22: 89–106

Harrington, Joseph E. (2004), 'Post-cartel Pricing during Litigation', *Journal of Industrial Economics*, 52(4): 517–533

Hart, Oliver (1983), 'The Market Mechanism as an Incentive Scheme', *Bell Journal of Economics*, 14(2): 366–382

Hatton, Catriona, Christoph Wagner and Hector Armengod (2007), 'Fair Play: How Competition Authorities Have Regulated the Sale of Football Media Rights in Europe', *European Competition Law Review*, 28(6): 346–354

Hausman, Jerry, Gregory Leonard and J. Douglas Zona (1994), 'Competitive Analysis with Differentiated Products', *Annales d'Economie et de Statistique*, 34: 159–180

Hausman, Jerry and Gregory Leonard (2005), 'Using Merger Simulation Models: Testing the Underlying Assumptions', *International Journal of Industrial Organization*, 23: 693–698

Hausman, Jerry and Jeffrey Mackie-Mason (1988), 'Price Discrimination and Patent Policy', *RAND Journal of Economics*, 19: 253–265

Hayek, Friedrich A. (1949), 'The Meaning of Competition' in Friedrich A. Hayek (ed.), *Individualism and Economic Order*, London: Routledge

(1960), *The Constitution of Liberty*, University of Chicago Press

Hendricks, Ken and Rob Porter (2007), 'An Empirical Perspective on Auctions', in Armstrong and Porter (eds.), *Handbook of Industrial Organization*, Volume 3, Amsterdam: North-Holland

Hicks, John R. (1935), 'Annual Survey of Economic Theory: The Theory of Monopoly', *Econometrica*, 3(1): 1–20

Hoernig, Steffen (2007), 'On-net and Off-net Pricing on Asymmetric Telecommunications Networks', *Information Economics and Policy*, 19(2): 171–188

Holt, Charles A. (1995), 'Industrial Organization: A Survey of Laboratory Research' in John Henry Kagel and Alvin E. Roth (eds.), *The Handbook of Experimental Economics*, Princeton University Press, 349–443

House of Lords (UK) (2006), *Inntrepreneur v Crehan*, UKHL 38; key earlier stages of this case can be found at (2003) EWHC 1510 (Ch) (Park J's High Court judgment), (2003) EuLR 663, (2004) EWCA Civ 637 (the Court of Appeal's judgment) and EuLR 693, also *Courage Ltd v Crehan* (Case C-453/99), (2002) QB 507

Ivaldi, Marc, Bruno Jullien, Patrick Rey, Paul Seabright and Jean Tirole (2003), 'The Economics of Tacit Collusion', Report for DG Competition, European Commission, available at: http://ec.europa.eu/competition/mergers/studies_reports/studies_reports.html

Ivaldi, Marc and Szabeles Lorinscz (2004), 'A Full Equilibrium Relevant Market Test: Application to Computer Servers', mimeo, University of Toulouse

Ivaldi, Marc and Frank Verboven (2005), 'Quantifying the Effects from Horizontal Mergers: The European Heavy Trucks Market', *International Journal of Industrial Organization*, 23: 669–692

Iyer, Ganesh (1998), 'Coordinating Channels under Price and Nonprice Competition', *Marketing Science*, 17(4): 338–355

Jayaratne, Jith and Carl Shapiro (2000), 'Simulating Partial Asset Divestitures to "Fix" Mergers', *International Journal of the Economics of Business*, 7(2): 179–200

Jenny, Frédéric (2002), 'Pharmaceuticals, Competition and Free Movement of Goods', *EU Competition Law & Policy, Developments & Priorities*, Helenic Competition Commission, Athens Conference, 19 April: 77–87

Jones, Alison and Brenda Sufrin (2007), *EC Competition Law: Text, Cases and Materials*, 3rd edition, Oxford University Press

Kandori, Michihiro and Hitoshi Matsushima (1998), 'Private Observation, Communication and Collusion', *Econometrica*, 66: 627–652

Karlinger, Liliane and Massimo Motta (2006), 'Exclusionary Pricing and Rebates in a Network Industry', mimeo, EUI

Kirzner, Israel M. (1978), *Entrepreneurship and Competition*, University of Chicago Press

Klein, Benjamin and Andres Lerner (eds.) (2008), *Economics of Antitrust Law*, Cheltenham: Edward Elgar

Klein, Benjamin and Kevin Murphy (1988), 'Vertical Restraints as Contract Enforcement Mechanisms', *Journal of Law and Economics*, 31(2): 265–297

Klemperer, Paul (2007), 'Bidding Markets', *Journal of Competition Law and Economics*, 3: 1–47

Klemperer, Paul D. and Margaret A. Meyer (1989), 'Supply Function Equilibrium in Oligopoly', *Econometrica*, 57(6): 1243–1277

Kobayashi, Bruce H. (2001), 'Antitrust, Agency and Amnesty: An Economic Analysis of the Criminal Enforcement of the Antitrust Laws against Corporations', *George Washington Law Review*, 69(5–6): 715–744

    (2005), 'The Economics of Loyalty Discounts and Antitrust Law in the United States', *Competition Policy International*, 1(2): 115–148

Kolasky, William J. (2001), 'Conglomerate Mergers and Range Effects: It's a Long Way From Chicago to Brussels', speech made before the George Mason Symposium, Washington DC, 9 November

    (2006), 'GE/Honeywell: Narrowing, but Not Closing, the Gap', *Antitrust*, 20(Spring): 69–76

Kovacic, William and Carl Shapiro (2000), 'Antitrust Policy: A Century of Economic and Legal Thinking', *Journal of Economic Perspectives*, 14(1): 43–60

KPMG (2003), 'Aalborg, Århus, Odense og Københavns Kommuner: (in Danish) Report on Calculation of Damages in Connection with the Trade Between [ABB] and the Municipalities During the Period 1991–1998', Copenhagen

Kreps, David M. and José A. Scheinkman (1983), 'Quantity Precommitment and Bertrand Competition Yield Cournot Outcomes', *Bell Journal of Economics*, 14(2): 326–337

Kroes, Neelie (2005), 'The First Hundred Days', 40th Anniversary of the Studienvereinigung Kartellrecht 1965–2005, International Forum on European Competition Law, Brussels, 7 April

Kühn, Kai-Uwe (2000), 'An Economist's Guide through the Joint Dominance Jungle', mimeo

    (2001a), 'Fighting Collusion by Regulating Communication between Firms', *Economic Policy*, 32: 169–204

    (2001b), 'A Model of Collusion and Irreversible Investment', mimeo, University of Michigan

    (2004), 'The Coordinated Effects of Mergers in Differentiated Goods Markets', CEPR Discussion Paper

(2005), 'The Coordinated Effects of Mergers in Differentiated Products Markets', CEPR Discussion Paper

(2008), 'The Coordinated Effects of Mergers' in Paolo Buccirossi (ed.), *Handbook of Antitrust Economics*, Cambridge, Mass.: MIT Press

Kühn, Kai-Uwe, Robert Stillman and Cristina Caffara (2005), 'Economic Theories of Bundling and their Policy Implications in Abuse Cases: An Assessment in Light of the Microsoft Case', *European Competition Journal*, 1: 85–122

Kühn, Kai-Uwe and Xavier Vives (1995), 'Information Exchanges among Firms and their Impact on Competition', Office for Official Publications of the European Community, Luxembourg

Kwoka, John and Larry White (1989), *The Antitrust Revolution: Economics, Competition and Policy*, 1st Edition (now in its 5th Edition), New York: Oxford University Press

Lademann, Rainer P. (2001), 'Customer Preferences for Existing and Potential Sales and Servicing Alternatives in Automotive Distribution', study prepared for the European Commission

Laffont, Jean-Jacques, Patrick Rey and Jean Tirole (1998), 'Network Competition: II. Price Discrimination', *RAND Journal of Economics*, 29(1): 38–56

Lafontaine, Francine and Margaret E. Slade (2008), 'Exclusive Contracts and Vertical Restraints: Empirical Evidence and Public Policy', in Paolo Bucciross (ed.) *Handbook of Antitrust Economics*, Cambridge, Mass.: MIT Press, 391–414

(2007), 'Vertical Integration and Firm Boundaries: The Evidence', *Journal of Economic Literature*, 45: 631–687

Lal, Rajiv and Ram Rao (1997), 'Supermarket Competition: The Case of Every Day Low Pricing', *Marketing Science*, 16(1): 60–80

Lambson, Val E. (1994), 'Some Results on Optimal Penal Codes in Asymmetric Bertrand Supergames', *Journal of Economic Theory*, 62(2): 444–468

Landes, William M. (1983), 'Optimal Sanctions for Antitrust Violations', *University of Chicago Law Review*, 50(2): 652–678

Leibenstein, Harvey (1966), 'Allocative Efficiency vs. "X-Efficiency"', *American Economic Review*, 56(3): 392–415

(1973), 'Competition and X-Efficiency: Reply', *Journal of Political Economy*, 81(3): 765–777

Levenstein, Margaret and Valerie Y. Suslow (2003), 'Contemporary International Cartels and Developing Countries: Economic Effects and Implications for Competition Policy', *Antitrust Law Journal*, 71(3): 801–852

Lexecon (1985), *The Economics of Gray-Markets Imports*, Chicago

(1999), 'Joint Dominance', Competition memo, London

London Economics (1997), 'Competition in Retailing', Research Paper No. 13, London: Office of Fair Trading

Lowe, Philip (2006), 'The Evolution and Regulation of the Payments System', address to the Payments System Conference at Melbourne Business School, March

Lyons, Bruce (2007), 'The Paradox of the Exclusion of Exploitative Abuse', Chapter 3 in *The Pros and Cons of High Prices*, Swedish Competition Authority, 32–46

(2009), 'An Economic Assessment of EC Merger Control: 1958-2007', CCP Working Paper 08–17, in Xavier Vives (ed.) (2009), *Competition Policy in the EU: Fifty Years on from the Treaty of Rome*, Oxford University Press, Ch. 6, 135–175

Macieira, João (2006), 'Extending the Frontier: A Structural Model of Investment and Technological Competition in the Supercomputer Industry', mimeo, Northwestern University

Malueg, David A. and Marius Schwartz (1994), 'Parallel Imports, Demand Dispersion and International Price Discrimination', *Journal of International Economics*, 37(3–4): 167–195

Martin, Stephen (2001), *Advanced Industrial Economics*, 2nd edition, Oxford: Blackwell

Mathewson, Frank and Ralph Winter (1984), 'An Economic Theory of Vertical Restraints', *RAND Journal of Economics*, 15(1): 27–38

Matsushima, Hitoshi (1989), 'Efficiency in Repeated Games with Imperfect Monitoring', *Journal of Economic Theory*, 48: 428–442

McAfee, R. Preston, John McMillan and Michael D. Whinston (1989), 'Multiproduct Monopoly, Commodity Bundling, and Correlation of Values', *Quarterly Journal of Economics*, 104(2): 371–384

McFadden, Daniel (1974), 'Conditional Logit Analysis of Qualitative Choice Behavior' in Paul Zarembka (ed.), *Frontiers in Econometrics*, New York: Academic Press, 105–142

McGuire, Timothy W. and Richard Staelin (1983), 'An Industry Equilibrium Analysis of Downstream Vertical Integration', *Marketing Science*, 2(2): 161–192

Megginson, William L. and Jeffrey M. Netter (2001), 'From State to Market: A Survey of Empirical Studies on Privatization', *Journal of Economic Literature*, 39(2): 321–389

Melnik, Arie, Oz Shy and Rune Stenbacka (2008), 'Assessing Market Dominance', *Journal of Economic Behavior & Organization*, 68(1): 63–72

Mittal, Vittas, Pankaj Kumar and Michael Tsiros (1999), 'Attribute-Level Performance, Satisfaction and Behavioural Intentions over Time: a Consumption-System Decision Approach', *Journal of Marketing*, 63: 88–101

Monopolies and Mergers Commission (1981), 'Discounts to Retailers', HC 311, London: HMSO

(1989), 'The Supply of Beer', London: HMSO

(1997), 'Bass PLC, Carlsberg A/S, and Carlsberg–Tetley PLC: A Report on the Merger Situation', London: HMSO

(1999a), 'British Telecommunications plc: A Report on a Reference Under Section 13 of Telecommunications Act 1984 for Calls Made from its Subscribers to Phones Connected to the Networks of Cellnet and Vodafone', London: HMSO

(1999b), 'Cellnet and Vodafone: A Report on a Reference Under Section 13 of Telecommunications Act 1984 on the Charges Made by Cellnet and Vodafone for Terminating Calls from Fixed-Line Networks', London: HMSO

Mossin, Jan (1968), 'Aspects of Rational Insurance Purchasing', *Journal of Political Economy*, 76: 533–568

Motta, Massimo (2004), *Competition Policy: Theory and Practice*, Cambridge University Press

Motta, Massimo and Thomas Rønde (2006), 'Exclusive Contracts: Between Foreclosure and Protection of Investments', mimeo, EUI

Nalebuff, Barry J. (2000), 'Competing Against Bundles' in Peter Hammond and Gareth D. Myles (eds.), *Incentives, Organisation, Public Economics*, London: Oxford University Press, 323–336

(2003), 'Bundling, Tying and Portfolio Effects: Part 2 – Case Studies', DTI Economic Paper 1, London

Nalebuff, Barry J. and Shihua Lu (2001), 'A Bundle of Trouble', Yale School of Management Working Paper

Nazzini, Renato (2003), 'Parallel Trade in the Pharmaceutical Market, Current Trends and Future Solutions', *World Competition*, 26(1): 53–74

Neven, Damien J. (2006), 'Competition Economics and Antitrust in Europe', *Economic Policy*, 21(48): 741–791

Nevo, Aviv (2000), 'Mergers with Differentiated Products: The Case of the Ready-to-Eat Cereal Industry', *RAND Journal of Economics*, 31(3): 395–421

Nickell, Stephen (1996), 'Competition and Corporate Performance', *Journal of Political Economy*, 104: 724–746

Nickell, Stephen, Daphne Nicolitsas and Neil Dryden (1997), 'What Makes Firms Perform Well?', *European Economic Review*, 41: 783–796

North, Douglass C. (1991), 'Institutions', *Journal of Economic Perspectives*, 5(1): 97–112

Ofcom (2006), 'Mobile Call Termination: Market Review', London: Office of Communications

Office of Fair Trading (1989), 'Supply of Beer (Tied Estate) Order', SI 1989 No. 2390

(2003), 'The British Horseracing Board and the Jockey Club: A Summary of the OFT's Case', *OFT654*, April

(2006), 'The Grocery Market: The OFT's Reasons for Making a Reference to the Competition Commission', *OFT845*, May

Olley, Stephen and Ariel Pakes (1996), 'The Dynamics of Productivity in the Telecommunications Equipment Industry', *Econometrica*, 64(6): 1263–1297

Organisation for Economic Co-operation and Development (1997), 'Market Access Issues in the Automobile Sector', OECD proceedings

(2000), *Review of Regulatory Reform in Italy*, Chapter 1: 'The Role of Competition Policy'

(2003), *Review of Regulatory Reform in France*, Chapter 3: 'The Role of Competition Policy'

(2004), *Review of Regulatory Reform in Germany*, Chapter 3: 'The Role of Competition Policy'

(2005), *Competition Law and Policy in the EU*

Osborne, Martin J. and Carolyn Pitchik (1987), 'Cartels, Profits and Excess Capacity', *International Economic Review*, 28(2): 413–428

Patterson, Donna and Carl Shapiro (2001), 'Transatlantic Divergence in GE/Honeywell: Causes and Lessons', *Antitrust*, 16(Fall): 32–33

Pepall, Lynne, Dan Richards and George Norman (2008), *Industrial Organization: Contemporary Theory and Empirical Applications*, 4th edition, Oxford: Blackwell

Perry, Martin K. and David Besanko (1991), 'Resale Price Maintenance and Manufacturer Competition for Exclusive Dealerships', *Journal of Industrial Economics*, 39(5): 517–544

Phlips, Louis (1983), *The Economics of Price Discrimination*, Cambridge University Press

Pinkse, Joris and Margaret E. Slade (2004), 'Mergers, Brand Competition, and the Price of a Pint', *European Economic Review*, 48: 617–643

Pinkse, Joris, Margaret E. Slade and Craig Brett (2002), 'Spatial Price Competition: A Semiparametric Approach', *Econometrica*, 70(3): 1111–1155

Platt Majoras, Deborah (2001), 'GE-Honeywell: The US Decision', speech made before the Anti-Trust Section of the State Bar of Georgia, 29 November

Plott, Charles R. and Vernon L. Smith (2008), *Handbook of Results in Experimental Economics*, Volume 1, place: Elsevier

Polinsky, A. Mitchell and Steven Shavell (1994), 'Should Liability Be Based on the Harm to the Victim or the Gain to the Injurer?', *Journal of Law, Economics, and Organization*, 10(2): 427–437

Porter, Robert H. (1983a), 'Optimal Cartel Trigger Price Strategies', *Journal of Economic Theory*, 29: 313–338

(1983b), 'A Study of Cartel Stability: The Joint Executive Committee, 1880–1886', *Bell Journal of Economics*, 14(2): 301–314

(2005), 'Detecting Collusion', *Review of Industrial Organization*, 26(2): 147–167

Posner, Richard (1976), *Antitrust Law*, University of Chicago Press

PricewaterhouseCoopers (2002), ALSTOM PowerFlowSystems A/S (in Danish): 'Report A: Theoretical and Analytical Framework for Determination of Economic Effects of an Alleged Cartel Formation'; 'Report B: Description of Plaintiffs' Models for Calculating Damages'; 'Report C: Comments on the Plaintiffs' Models for Calculating Damages'; 'Report D: Alternative Calculation of Damages based on ALSTOM's Actual Transactions'; 'Report E: Alternative Calculation of Damages based on ALSTOM's Economic Profit', Hellerup, Copenhagen

Punj, Girish and Richard Brookes (2002), 'The Influence of Pre-Decisional Constraints on Information Search and Consideration Set Formation in New Automobile Purchases', *International Journal of Research in Marketing*, 19(4): 383–400

Raskovich, Alexander (2003), 'Pivotal Buyers and Bargaining Position', *Journal of Industrial Economics*, 51(4): 405–426

Rasmusen, Eric, J. Mark Ramseyer and John S. Wiley (1991), 'Naked Exclusion', *American Economic Review*, 81(5): 1137–1145

Rey, Patrick (2003), 'The Impact of Parallel Imports on Prescription Medicines', mimeo, University of Toulouse

Rey, Patrick and Joseph Stiglitz (1995), 'The Role of Exclusive Territories in Producers' Competition', *RAND Journal of Economics*, 26(3): 431–451

Rey, Patrick and Jean Tirole (2007), 'A Primer on Foreclosure', in Armstrong and Porter (eds.), *Handbook of Industrial Organization*, Volume 3, Amsterdam: North Holland

Reynolds, Robert J. and Janusz Ordover (2002), 'Archimedean Leveraging and the GE/ Honeywell Transaction', *Antitrust Law Journal*, 70: 171–198

Richardson, Russell (1999), 'Guidance without Guidance – A European Revolution in Fining Policy? The Commission's New Guidelines on Fines', *European Competition Law Review*, 20(7): 360–371

Rochet, Jean-Charles and Jean Tirole (2002), 'Cooperation among Competitors: Some Economics of Payment Card Associations', *RAND Journal of Economics*, 33(4): 549–570

(2003a), 'An Economic Analysis of the Determination of Interchange Fees in Payment Card Systems', *Review of Network Economics*, 2(2): 69–79

(2003b), 'Platform Competition in Two-Sided Markets', *Journal of the European Economics Association*, 1(4): 990–1209

(2006a), 'Tying in Two-Sided Markets and the Honour-All-Cards Rule', mimeo, IDEI, Toulouse University

(2006b), 'Must-Take Cards and the Tourist Test', mimeo, IDEI, Toulouse University

(2006c), 'Two-Sided Markets: A Progress Report', *RAND Journal of Economics*, Special Issue on Two-Sided Markets, 37(3): 645–663

Ross, Thomas (1992), 'Cartel Stability and Product Differentiation', *International Journal of Industrial Organization*, 10: 1–13

Rotemberg, Julio and Gapth Saloner (1986), 'A Supergame Theoretic Model of Price Wars during Booms', *American Economic Review*, 76: 390–407

Rubinfeld, D. (2004), 'Maintenance of Monopoly: U.S. vs. Microsoft (2001)', Case 19 in John E. Kwoka and Lawrence J. White (eds.), *The Anti-Trust Revolution*, Oxford University Press

Sachs, Jeffrey (1993), *Poland's Jump to the Market Economy*, Lionel Robbins Lectures, Cambridge, Mass. and London: MIT Press

Scherer, Mike and David Ross (1990), *Industrial Market Structure and Economic Performance*, Boston, Mass.: Houghton Mifflin Company

Schmalensee, Richard (1987), 'Competitive Advantage and Collusive Optima', *International Journal of Industrial Economics*, 5: 351–367

Schumpeter, Joseph A. (1943), *Capitalism, Socialism and Democracy*, London: Routledge

Segal, Ilya R. and Michael D. Whinston (2000a), 'Naked Exclusion: Comment', *American Economic Review*, 90: 296–309

(2000b), 'Exclusive Contracts and Protection of Investment', *RAND Journal of Economics*, 31: 603–633

Sen, Amartya K. (1993), 'Markets and Freedoms: the Achievements and Limitations of the Market Mechanisms in Promoting Individual Freedoms', *Oxford Economic Papers*, 45(4): 519–541

Shapiro, Carl (1989), 'Theories of Oligopoly Behavior' in Richard Schmalensee and Robert D. Willig (eds.), *Handbook of Industrial Organization*, Volume 1, Amsterdam: North Holland/Elsevier Science Publishers, 329–414

Sibley, David S. and Ken Heyer (2003), 'Selected Economic Analysis at the Antitrust Division: The Year in Review', *Review of Industrial Organization*, 23(2): 95–119

Slade, Margaret E. (1998), 'Beer and the Tie: Did Divestiture of Brewer-owned Public Houses Lead to Higher Beer Prices?', *Economic Journal*, 108: 565–602

(2000), 'Regulating Manufacturers and Their Exclusive Retailers' in Morten Berg and Einar Hope (eds.), *Foundations of Competition Policy*, London: Routledge

(2004a), 'Market Power and Joint Dominance in the UK Brewing Industry', *Journal of Industrial Economics*, 52: 133–163

(2004b), 'Models of Firm Profitability', *International Journal of Industrial Organization*, 22: 289–308

Smith, Adam (1776), *An Inquiry into the Nature and Causes of the Wealth of Nations*

Smith, Howard (2004), 'Supermarket Choice and Supermarket Competition in Market Equilibrium', *Review of Economic Studies*, 71(1): 235–263

Spector, David (2005), 'Loyalty Rebates: An Assessment of Competition Concerns and a Proposed Structured Rule of Reason', *Competition Policy International*, 1(2): 89–114

Spengler, Joseph J. (1950), 'Vertical Integration and Anti-Trust Policy', *Journal of Political Economy*, 58(4): 347–352

Staatsanwaltschaft München (2005), *Anklageschrift*, Beglaubigte Abschrift, Munich, 18 March

Staiger, Robert W. and Frank A. Wolak (1992), 'Collusive Pricing with Capacity Constraints in the Presence of Demand Uncertainty', *RAND Journal of Economics*, 23(2): 203–220

Steen, Frode and Lars Sorgard (1999), 'Semicollusion in the Norwegian Cement Market', *European Economic Review*, 43(9): 1775–1796

Stein, Jeremy C. (1997), 'Internal Capital Markets and the Competition for Corporate Resources', *Journal of Finance*, 52(1): 111–133

Stephan, Andreas (2006), 'The Bankruptcy Wildcard in Cartel Cases', *Journal of Business Law*, August: 511–534

Stigler, George J. (1964), 'A Theory of Oligopoly', *The Journal of Political Economy*, 72(1): 44–61
  (1976), 'The Xistence of X-Efficiency', *American Economic Review*, 66(1): 213–216
  (1987), 'Competition' in S. N. Durlauf and L. E. Blume (eds.), *The New Palgrave Dictionary of Economics*, reprinted in 2008 edition, Palgrave Macmillan

Sutton, John (2007), 'Market Structure: Theory and Evidence', in Armstrong and Porter (eds.), *Handbook of Industrial Organization*, Volume 3, Amsterdam: North-Holland

Telser, Lester G. (1960), 'Why Should Manufacturers Want Fair Trade?', *Journal of Law and Economics*, 3: 86–105

Thisse, Jacques-François and Xavier Vives (1988), 'On the Strategic Choice of Spatial Price Policy', *American Economic Review*, 78(1): 122–137

Tirole, Jean (1988), *The Theory of Industrial Organization*, Cambridge, Mass.: MIT Press

US Department of Justice (2001), 'Range Effects: The United States Perspective', Antitrust Division Submission for OECD Roundtable on Portfolio Effects in Conglomerate Mergers, downloadable at http://www.usdoj.gov/atr/public/international/9550.htm

Van Reenen, John (2004), 'Is There a Market for Workgroup Servers?', Centre for Economic Performance Discussion Paper No. 650
  (2006), 'The Growth of Network Computing: Quality Adjusted Prices for Network Servers', *Economic Journal*, 116: 29–44

Varian, Hal (1985), 'Price Discrimination and Social Welfare', *American Economic Review*, 75: 870–875
  (1989), 'Price Discrimination' in Richard Schmalensee and Robert D. Willig (eds.), *Handbook of Industrial Organization*, Amsterdam: North-Holland

Veljanovski, Cento (2007), 'Cartel Fines in Europe – Law, Practice and Deterrence', *World Competition*, 30: 65–86

Verboven, Frank (1996), 'International Price Discrimination in the European Car Market', *RAND Journal of Economics*, 27(2): 240–268

Verhoef, Peter and Fred Langerak (2003), 'On the Role of Dealers in Brand Loyalty Decisions in the Automotive Industry', mimeo, Erasmus University, Rotterdam

Verouden, Vincent (2004), 'Vertical Agreements and Article 81(1) EC: The Evolving Role of Economic Analysis', *Antitrust Law Journal*, 71: 525–575

Vickers, John (1995), 'Concepts of Competition', *Oxford Economic Papers*, 47(1): 1–23
  (2005), 'Public Policy and the Invisible Price: Competition Law, Regulation, and the Interchange Fee', presented at the International Payments Policy Conference: 'Interchange Fees in Credit and Debit Card Industries: What Role for Public Authorities?' at the Federal Reserve Bank of Kansas City
  (2006), 'Discussion of Neven (2006)', *Economic Policy*, 21(48): 781–786

Vives, Xavier (1999), *Oligopoly Pricing: Old Ideas and New Tools*, Boston: MIT Press
  (2008), 'Innovation and Competitive Pressure', *Journal of Industrial Economics*, 56(3): 419–469

Vives, Xavier (ed.) (2009), *Competition Policy in the EU: Fifty Years on from the Treaty of Rome*, forthcoming, Oxford University Press

Waelbroeck, Denis (2005), '*Michelin II*: A per se Rule Against Rebates by Dominant Companies?', *Journal of Competition Law and Economics*, 1(1): 149–171

Werden, Gregory (2001), 'Microsoft's Pricing of Windows and the Economics of Derived Demand Monopoly', *Review of Industrial Organization*, 18: 357–362

Werden, Gregory J. and Luke M. Froeb (1994), 'The Effects of Mergers in Differentiated Products Industries: Logit Demand and Merger Policy', *Journal of Law, Economics, and Organization*, 10: 407–426

(2002), 'The Antitrust Logit Model for Predicting Unilateral Competitive Effects', *Antitrust Law Journal*, 70: 257

Werden, Gregory J., Luke M. Froeb and Timothy J. Tardiff (1996), 'The Use of the Logit Model in Applied Industrial Organization', *International Journal of the Economics of Business*, 3(1), 83–105

Whinston, Michael D. (1990), 'Tying, Foreclosure, and Exclusion', *American Economic Review*, 80(4): 837–859

(2001), 'Exclusivity and Tying in *US* v. *Microsoft*: What We Know, and Don't Know', *Journal of Economic Perspectives*, 15(2): 63–80

Whish, Richard (2003), *Competition Law*, 3rd edition, London: Butterworths

(2008), *Competition Law*, 6th edition, London: LexisNexis UK

Wijckmans, Frank, Filip Tuytschaever and Alain Vanderelst (2006), 'The Motor Vehicle Distribution Block Exemption' in Frank Wijckmans, Filip Tuytschaever and Alain Vanderelst (eds.), *Vertical Agreements in EC Competition Law*, Oxford University Press

Wilks, Stephen (1999), *In the Public Interest: Competition Policy and the Monopolies and Mergers Commission*, Manchester University Press

Williamson, Oliver E. (1976), 'Franchise Bidding for Natural Monopolies: In General and with Respect to CATV', *Bell Journal of Economics*, 7(1): 73–104

(1985), *The Economic Institutions of Capitalism*, New York: Macmillan Free Press

Wils, Wouter P. J. (1998), 'The Commission's New Method for Calculating Fines in Antitrust Cases', *European Law Review*, 23(3): 252–263

(2006), 'Optimal Antitrust Fines: Theory and Practice', *World Competition*, 29(2): 183–208

Wright, Julian (2002), 'Access Pricing under Competition: An Application to Cellular Networks', *Journal of Industrial Economics*, 50(3): 289–316

(2003), 'Optimal Card Payment Systems', *European Economic Review*, 47(4): 587–612

Index